CONTENTS ✧ W9-ARY-967

New
England

Fodor's 90

New England

FODOR'S TRAVEL PUBLICATIONS, INC.
New York & London

ISBN 0–679–01796–8

The Introduction in this volume is adapted from INSIDE NEW ENGLAND
by Judson Hale
Copyright © 1982 by Judson Hale
Reprinted by permission of Harper & Row, Publishers, Inc.

Fodor's New England

Editor: Vernon Nahrgang
Associate Editor: Chris Heath
Area Editors: Carolyn Cohen, Alma Eshenfelder, Kimberly Grant, Pamela Matz,
  Marilyn Stout, Jane Zarem
Contributors: Stephen Bennett, Helen Dalzell, Judson Hale, Christie Lowrance,
  Robert Murphy, William Scheller
Drawings: Sandra Lang, Michael Kaplan
Cartography: Jon Bauch Design, Pictograph
Cover Photograph: Peter Beck

Cover Design: Vignelli Associates

Special Sales

Fodor's Travel Publications are available at special discounts for bulk purchases
(100 copies or more) for sales promotions or premiums. Special editions,
including personalized covers, excerpts of existing guides, and corporate
imprints, can be created in large quantities for special needs. For more
information, write to Special Marketing, Fodor's Travel Publications, 201 East
50th Street, New York, NY 10022. Enquiries from the United Kingdom should
be sent to Fodor's Travel Publications, 30–32 Bedford Square, London WC1B
3SG.

MANUFACTURED IN THE UNITED STATES OF AMERICA
10 9 8 7 6 5 4 3 2 1

FOREWORD

New England lures the visitor with recreational opportunities, major cultural institutions and activities, gratifying scenic attractions, and a sense of place that gives many travelers a comfortable feeling of being at home. All these things are discussed in the pages of this guide.

As the U.S. bicentennial observances conclude—1989 saw the anniversaries of the sitting of the first Congress and the inauguration of the first President—visitors to New England will find frequent reminders of sites and events important in the early years of American history. These echoes of the past add dimension to New England travel and provide a rich learning experience that everyone, and families in particular, will enjoy.

While every care has been taken to assure the accuracy of the information in this guide, the passage of time will always bring change, and consequently the publisher cannot accept responsibility for errors that may occur.

All prices and opening times quoted here are based on information available to us at press time. Hours and admission fees may change, however, and the prudent traveler will avoid inconvenience by calling ahead.

Fodor's wants to hear about your travel experiences, both pleasant and unpleasant. When a hotel or restaurant fails to live up to its billing, let us know and we will investigate the complaint and revise our entries where the facts warrant it.

Send your letters to the editors of Fodor's Travel Publications, 201 E. 50th Street, New York, NY 10022.

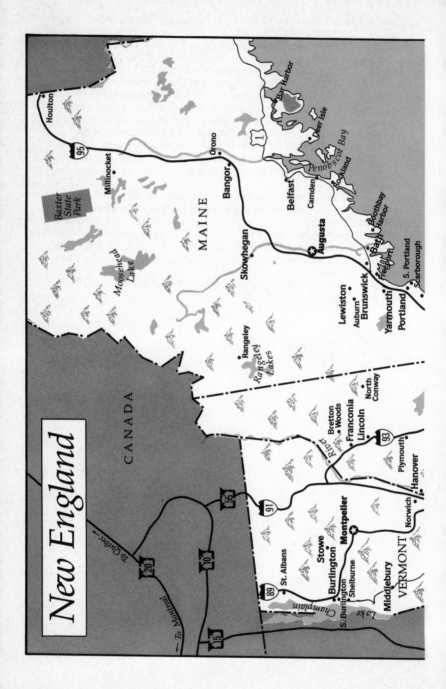

New England

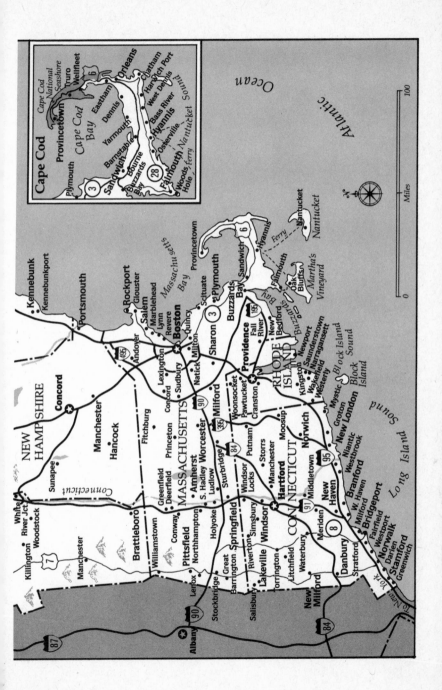

YANKEE COME HOME

By
JUDSON D. HALE, SR.

The following is adapted from Inside New England, *published in 1982 by Harper and Row.*

A "Yankee" has been variously defined as an American, a northern American, a New Englander, an old native of Vermont, Maine, or Cape Cod, and an old Vermont native who eats apple pie for breakfast—with a knife.

There is no real consensus on the word. Some define it by geography; others maintain it is more a state of mind.

The same is often said about New England. However, in actual fact, New England consists of everything within the geographical boundaries of Maine, New Hampshire, Vermont, Massachusetts, Rhode Island, and Connecticut. No more, no less. Six very proud, very independent, and very different entities, which, together, represent a formidable political, economic, and spiritual force in America. The American character, as it's generally perceived, is derived historically from the people who inhabited and migrated west from these six states.

Maine's Four Faces

Maine is beautiful and Maine is ugly. I remember driving from Sedgwick to Brooksville several summers ago and stopping at the top of Caterpillar Hill. There before me was Maine the beautiful—Walker Pond in the foreground, the ocean beyond dotted with dark, pine-covered islands

1

of all shapes and sizes, the bridge crossing Eggemoggin Reach, so familiar to yachtsmen, Deere Isle with its thin road winding down towards Stonington, and, in the far distance, the Camden hills. This is the Maine that lives in the hearts of all New Englanders as well as visitors—the Maine of artists, of poets, of the soul.

Then there is backcountry Maine, "the Maine that artists do not paint, writers do not usually describe, and visitors do not talk about," wrote Charles E. Clark in *Maine, A History*. It is "the Maine where scrubby woodlands alternate with bleak, unshaded villages marked by an old general store and a Baptist Church, but also by a laundromat, a couple of gas stations, and a Dairy Joy, and where the houses may have sheet metal roofs . . . " People in backcountry Maine say a house is a house, but a house with a shed is a village. This is the Maine that shows up near the bottom of annual United States per capita income listings.

A third Maine is the forested wilderness, the Maine of white-water canoeing, hunting, fishing, mosquitoes big enough to carry you away, old Maine guides, lumbering, and tall tales. In *The Jonesport Raffle*, author John Gould recalls a fishing story contest in Montana that a Maine backwoodsman decided to enter by mail. "The prize was to be a new fly rod, but he (the Mainer) said he never used a rod—he hid on the bank of the stream and clubbed the trout with a baseball bat when they came up to pick blueberries."

Still another Maine is potato Maine, hugging the New Brunswick border for over a hundred miles, an open, rolling area that everyone in the United States has heard about but fewer than several outsiders have ever been to! School starts in Aroostook County in mid-August, and that's bad news for kids. On the other hand, all the schools then close for three whole weeks in September to enable children to spend (legally) dawn-to-dusk days harvesting potatoes. Up there, that's known as a bad news—bad news story.

I once asked a little New Hampshire first grader touring the *Yankee* offices if she'd like to pick potatoes in Maine in September instead of going to school. She said, "Sure—it wouldn't last long, anyway. No one lives in Maine all year 'round. Maine's closed in the winter."

Although traditionally Down Easterners are noted for their plain and direct manner of communicating, I think Mainers are actually the most *indirect* of all New Englanders. To obtain a straight answer to a straight question in Maine is often next to impossible.

For example:

Visitor: "Can you tell me where the hotel is in this town?"

Mainer: "What hotel?" (Mainers like to answer a question *with* a question.)

Visitor: "Oh, is there more than one hotel here?"

Mainer: "Didn't know there was any."

Somewhere deep within the Maine psyche is a strong instinct to avoid being pinned down.

Frugality and Shrewdness in New Hampshire

New Hampshire and Vermont are often lumped together by outsiders, but residents of both states are aware how remarkably different each is from the other. New Hampshire is mentally oriented to small businesses and manufacturing. On the other hand, there's probably no other state in the union as rural in complexion as Vermont. New Hampshire is politically conservative. In recent years, Vermont has enacted some of the most liberal environmental legislation in the nation, including the banning of all billboards. I'm always conscious of the immediate difference one "feels" when crossing the Connecticut River from Vermont to New Hampshire or vice versa. Much of Vermont is open farmland. New Hampshire is almost completely forested. So many of Vermont's villages appear almost unreal—as if they had been created by Grandma Moses. New Hampshire's villages seem totally unconscious of whether or not they are picturesque. (Thus, many are not.)

In a cultural sense, the two states lean away from each other, too—Vermont in spite of itself, towards New York and New Yorkers; New Hampshire towards Massachusetts and southern New England.

Like Maine, New Hampshire has more than one personality. There's the prosperous, booming if somewhat faceless southern half of the state that has all but become a suburb of Boston. Then there's the northern half. Up there are towns like Pittsburg, the largest town east of the Mississippi River, with a 30-mile-long main street that rambles through a wilderness of lakes, mountains, and evergreen forests, inhabited by moose, bear, deer, loons, a few humans, and snowmobiles. Movie theaters, department stores, and hospitals are as far as twenty miles away. Many jobs are further.

"When people ask us how we like living up here in the northern New Hampshire woods," a Colebrook man told me recently, "it's like asking someone who has eaten porridge every single day of his entire life, 'How's the porridge?' "

Though frugality and shrewdness in business dealings are traits characteristic of New Englanders as a whole, I think New Hampshirites are the most frugal of all. Possibly it has something to do with the overall conservative and business orientation of the state.

A typical New Hampshire story, for instance, concerns two Berlin (remember—pronounced *Ber*lin) men discussing the hard financial times. One asks the other how in the world he has managed to feed his large family on such a low income.

"I'll tell you," is the reply, "I find out what they don't like and then I give 'em plenty of it."

Vermont's Responsibilities

Being a Vermonter carries with it some heavy responsibilities. To be precise, six of them.

1) First of all, a Vermonter must possess a great deal of common sense. Although 100,000 adults living in Vermont today never finished high school, ignorance is not a lack of education but rather a lack of common sense.

"That Hardwick road sign back there is pointing off in the wrong direction, isn't it?"

"Sure it is, but anyone with a little common sense knows how to get to Hardwick."

2) A Vermonter is expected to display a certain amount of dry humor. Senator George Aiken fulfilled this Vermont duty throughout his political career—as did Cal Coolidge—and the country appreciated the effort. It's somehow comforting to Americans when a Vermonter acts like "a Vermonter." We all smiled and felt good inside when Aiken advised President Lyndon Johnson to declare the Vietnam war won and pull out the troops. It would not have been as amusing or even as wise if someone from another state had said it.

3) A Vermonter must have integrity. Its state government does. Historian Neal Peirce ranks it as one of only five states in America—and the only state in New England—that is free of political corruption. (The oth-

ers: Minnesota, Wisconsin, Oregon, and Hawaii.) The old story is that
there are so few nickels in Vermont that every politician knows where each
one is located, making it impossible for anyone to steal one.

The closest thing to official "manipulating" of finances I've ever heard
about in Vermont—and the story is actually more an example of honesty—occurred at a small country church then located outside Rutland. Because the congregation had dwindled down to almost nothing, the members decided to disband. The question of the disposal of funds in the
church treasury came up during the final meeting, when the treasurer reported there was a sum of eighty dollars on hand. One of the members
suggested that forty dollars of this be given to Zeke Tuttle, a church member who was ill with tuberculosis at the time.

Several months later, a member who had not attended the final meeting
ran into the church treasurer in town and asked him whatever became
of the money in the treasury of the now-disbanded church.

"At our last meeting, we voted to give forty dollars of the eighty we
had to Zeke Tuttle because he was sick," the treasurer replied.

"What about the rest?"

"Well," said the treasurer without a hint of hesitation, "I wasn't feeling
any too good myself, so I kept the rest."

4) Vermonters, unlike Mainers, are expected to speak in a simple, direct, no-nonsense manner. Possibly it's all part of the Vermont version
of honesty and integrity.

Many, many Vermont stories, like those collected in Keith Jennison's
book, *"Yup . . . Nope" and Other Vermont Dialogues,* feature this sort of
direct approach in conversation:

Question: "What do you suppose they'll do when old man Appleby
dies?"

Answer: "Bury him."

Question: "Think it's ever going to stop snowing?"

Answer: "Always has."

Question: "Can you tell me when the next train leaves for Boston?"

Answer: "It left more'n ten years ago."

There must be a thousand more of these.

5) A Vermonter has the responsibility to be a free and independent
thinker. Independence and freedom are honored throughout New England
but in Vermont they are virtually a religion. An Ethan Allen statement
along that line is a popular quote: "I am as determined to preserve the
independence of Vermont as Congress is that of the Union, and rather
than fail I will retire with my hardy Green Mountain boys into the caverns
of the mountains and make war on all mankind."

6) Finally, some Vermonters are expected to be willing to put in a
full hard day's work for a meager day's pay. Throughout the state, but
particularly in the three northern counties known as the Northeast Kingdom, there is much poverty.

Charles Morrissey describes it with brutal clarity:

"Do the touring shutterbugs who snap pictures of scenic Vermont vistas
ever wonder who lives in all the trailers and all the shacky houses they
don't record on films? Do they notice the sad and ugly towns they drive
through to get to the pristine villages which outsiders have restored?"

Nonetheless, most residents of the Green Mountain State would agree
that Vermont is "an experience" as well as a geographic area of New England, but to outsiders, who own most of the state anyway, Vermont is
a place you feel homesick for even before you've left it.

Puritan Massachusetts

Massachusetts is called the Hub of the Universe. That's not a name given in jest. As a Massachusetts native, I can say that pride in the Bay State has always spilled over into what outsiders might consider to be arrogance. The Massachusetts image exported to the outside seems to consist of Harvard, Boston Brahmins, the Puritans, the Kennedys and their accent, liberalism, do-gooders, Concord/Lexington, and a sort of "we know best" attitude toward the rest of America. Not included in the exported image are the high taxes and cost of living, the interminable political corruption, racial antagonism, and the fact that besides lawyers the Massachusetts legislature is dominated by funeral directors.

The notion that a region's humor often is based on regional personality traits, much exaggerated, is borne out by Massachusetts. Its high self-esteem shines forth in all the old favorites, such as . . .

Two Massachusetts (or Boston) women went to San Francisco and ran into a particularly hot spell there. As they were stewing on Treasure Island, one said to the other, "My dear, I never expected to be so hot in San Francisco." To which her companion replied, "But, my dear, you must remember that we're 3,000 miles from the ocean."

Or, and there are many variations to this one . . .

A visitor in Boston sought to speak with A. Lawrence Lowell, then president of Harvard, who had been called to Washington by President William Howard Taft for a White House conference on education. The visitor was informed by the secretary in Lowell's outer office that "The president is in Washington seeing Mr. Taft." Tell that story to many Massachusetts residents, most Bostonians, or *any* Harvard graduate, and they won't understand why it's funny.

Massachusetts is still fueled by the Puritan ethic, probably more so than any other New England state. When the late Mary Peabody, mother of Governor Endicott Peabody and wife of the late Malcolm Peabody, Episcopal Bishop of central New York, went to St. Augustine, Florida, at age 72 to join in a civil rights demonstration and ended up in jail, she was considered by many people across America as simply a meddling, do-gooding, old coot looking for headlines. New Englanders knew better. While not everyone agreed with her actions, she was recognized as being sincere. The tradition she was exemplifying runs strong and deep in Massachusetts.

"Do your duty, do your part in life—that's what being a New Englander means to me," she later told my Dublin, New Hampshire neighbor, author Richard Meryman, when he talked with her in her Cambridge home fourteen years later. "Doing your duty, caring for things that are good and true, being a terrible prig, I suppose."

The fuel shortage had begun at the time of Meryman's *Yankee* interview. "I don't allow myself a fire if I don't have anybody here," said this frail, then-86-year-old widow lady, as she sat, covered by a shawl, the thermostat set at sixty, in her ancestral home surrounded by memorabilia of her distinguished, wealthy, and influential ancestors.

"In my mother-in-law's Bible, after she died, I found a little note she had written to herself. It said, 'Remember to be cheerful.' I think that's very important, not to complain, to say you're lonely all the time. All I say is, I'm cold all the time . . . I'm very frugal. Also, the thing to do is to save energy. So I put on layers like the Chinese. My layers of clothes."

After reading this I felt like calling John Winthrop, Cotton Mather, or any of the old-time Massachusetts Puritans and asking them to let poor old Mary Peabody off the hook. Tell her she can have a fire now. She can say she's lonely. Let her alone! But of course that wouldn't help. *She* would tell *them* how it ought to be. The Puritan tradition doesn't depend upon "permission" from anybody, past or present. For Mary Peabody, the only voice of authority was that which was deep within her—the voice of her New England Conscience.

West of the general Boston area is, naturally and logically, western Massachusetts. Because of its political isolation, growing educational institutions, and curious mixture of old-time natives and idealistic but maturing dreamers left over from the hippie generation, Ralph Nader once referred to western Massachusetts as "the most interesting part of the United States." In what's known as the Pioneer Valley, bankers are likely to grow organic vegetables, communes are running hard-nosed businesses for profit, the solar-heated Williamsburg General Store sells unsalted potato chips, and, as a food cooperative worker was heard to remark, "It's hard to find a good Swiss cheese that's politically acceptable."

Accuracy in Rhode Island

The State of Rhode Island and the Providence Plantations are the official names. Other names for it have been "The Plantation of the Otherwise-Minded" and "Rogues Island." At one time the greatest slave-trading colony in America, Rhode Island was the first civilized community anywhere that allowed freedom of religion. Of its Roger Williams psyche emphasizing freedom of conscience and action, Massachusetts Puritan Cotton Mather said, "If a man lost his religion, he might find it at this general muster of opinionists."

Little Rhody or The Ocean State is still a "general muster of opinionists" and, as such, has just naturally developed a reputation for tolerance. It has the only fishing cooperative in New England; it calmly abides various elements such as the Mafia in its little midst; of all today's native New Englanders, only Rhode Islanders will tolerate adding a can of tomato (ugh!) soup to the end of their clam chowder recipes; and probably due to its "sweatshop," nonunion costume jewelry factories, its average factory wage is almost 20% below the national average.

Of course, it's small. Only 47½ miles long and, at most, 40 miles wide. Yet it has more people than either Vermont or New Hampshire. If you live in the Rhode Island countryside you can, as they say, be in the city in seven minutes. But, like a person of small stature, Rhode Island absolutely refuses to be overlooked or ignored in any situation. Once a Rhode Islander gets started on the subject of Rhode Island, he or she can almost, but not quite, become downright belligerent.

"Do you realize Rhode Island was the *first* colony to disregard the British stamp act?" a museum curator suddenly sprung on me as we were sifting through some photographs of nineteenth-century Cranston (pronounced "Creeanston").

"We were also the *first* to officially renounce allegiance to Great Britain," the little bombardment continued, "among the *first* to adopt the Articles of Confederation, and *first* to fire a cannon at any British naval vessel."

"Really?" I responded, attempting to lift the appearance of my own interest to his earnest level. "Oh, sure," he continued, "and the *first* Baptist Church is in Providence, the *first* Jewish Synagogue in America is in Newport, the country's *first* cotton mill, started by Samuel Slater, was begun in Pawtucket in 1790, the *first* lighthouse on the American coast was built at Beavertail back in 1749 . . . " and on and on.

Concern for accuracy—particularly historical accuracy—is a trait shared by all New Englanders, but it seems most highly developed in Rhode Islanders. Their noted tolerance in other matters evidently does not extend to errors.

When we mentioned in an article that the distance from Rhode Island to New York was many miles, we heard not a word from our subscribers in New York, the second largest state for the number of *Yankee* subscriptions. From Rhode Island we received an avalanche of mail, each letter and postcard pointing out to us that the two states actually border one another—out in Long Island Sound. Many gave us a seagull analogy. "A seagull, should he choose to, might sit in the water at a certain point in Long Island Sound and have his tail in New York, his beak in Rhode Island, and his left wing in Connecticut."

In southern Massachusetts, near Webster, is a lake we once called in *Yankee* Lake Chargoggagoggmanchauggauggagoggchaubunagungamaugg. A few days after the issue was sent out, we heard from several Rhode Islanders who told us we had misspelled it. It should have been Lake Chargoggaggoggmanchaugagoggchaubunagungamaug. We noted and corrected the error in our next issue.

Connecticut Yankees

Historically, Connecticut is the most "Yankee" of all the New England states. If you are of the school that believes that the Dutch were responsible for the word "Yankee" (evolving from "John Cheese"), then it is logical to believe it was the Dutch in New York who began applying the term to their English neighbors in Connecticut.

Connecticut Yankees were principally responsible for establishing the smart, shrewd, clever, and, well, slippery reputation of Yankees everywhere. Early Connecticut peddlers, with their leaky calf weaners, wooden nutmegs, defective clocks, and cigars that would not draw, traveled from town to town around New England and eventually the entire country—always moving fast enough to be out of town before anyone realized they'd been had. It was often said, "You might as well try to hold a greased eel as a live Connecticut Yankee."

Now, when two Connecticut Yankees bargained together, that was the stuff of stories—hundreds of them. This one's typical:

While plowing his fields one spring, a Connecticut farmer's horse suddenly expired and fell lifeless in the field. The farmer left it lying there still hitched to the plow and walked several miles to the house of his neighbor who, it so happened, had tricked the farmer's wife into buying what turned out to be a fake nutmeg the year before. He found his neighbor whittling something out on his back doorstep. "Ben," he said after suitable exchanges on the weather, "I feel like swapping something today. You know that black and white horse of mine?"

"Yes," replied his neighbor as he continued to whittle, "I know him well."

"Well, then, you know he's younger than your big bay but he may not be as big and strong. How would you like to swap your bay horse for him?"

"Even?"

"Yes. Even."

"You've got a deal," said his neighbor, and they solemnly shook on it, whereupon the farmer, typically honest about his double-dealings and with a pleased smile on his face said, "Well, Ben, your brand-new horse is dead. He's lying out in the field. Keeled over while I was plowing with him this morning."

"All right, fine," replied his neighbor. "My big bay horse died last night before last, and his skin is hanging out in the back shed."

But there was a more positive side to the Connecticut Yankee. In time his ingenious approaches, clever ideas, original thinking, and skillful craftsmanship evolved into a virtue proudly claimed by *all* New Englanders today. In fact, it's claimed by all Americans. Usually preceded by the words "good" and "old," it's now known as Yankee Ingenuity, and it's credited with, among other things, winning World War II.

Connecticut has a valid point in claiming Yankee Ingenuity as its own. Since the United States Patent Office opened in 1790, Connecticut has averaged more patents each year per thousand of population than any other state in the Union or any other country in the world! Nutmeggers have invented everything from the submarine, anesthesia, radar speed detectors, sky hooks, and the grinder to the cotton gin, pistols with revolving cylinders, lattice-truss covered bridges, and the lollipop. And it was a Connecticut inventor, one Samuel Morey, who *steamed* down the Connecticut River in 1787, fourteen years before "Tricky Bob" Fulton did *his* steamboat thing.

Like New Hampshire, Connecticut has a split personality. There's Fairfield County with its "Gold Coast" New York bedroom towns of New Canaan, Darien, Westport, Stamford, Greenwich et al. And then there's the rest of Connecticut. From time to time, a movement begins to lop off Connecticut's Fairfield County from New England and either give it to New York or make it a state on its own. That will never happen, of course. One doesn't disown one's own brother simply because he has become, over the course of many years, rich, white, Protestant, successful, Republican, country-clubby, and in love with New York City and the train ride to and from.

The coast of Connecticut is divided, too. From New Haven on down to the New York line is general industrial ugliness occasionally relieved by fancy yacht sanctuaries. Yet many harbors from New Haven east have lobster boats and a "Down East" look. The towns in the general area around the mouths of the Connecticut and Thames Rivers—Groton, Stonington, Old Saybrook, Old Lyme, Essex—are among the most picturesque and well-to-do in all of New England. They're also *very* protective of their privacy. In Garson Kanin's *Tracy and Hepburn,* the late Spencer Tracy told a story about a Sunday dinner with Katharine Hepburn, a Connecticut native, and her family at their beach house in Old Saybrook. They were all debating the basic "rights of the common man" when the actress's father, in the middle of an impassioned speech on the subject, spotted a lone stranger walking along the beach in front of the house. In an instant, the whole family was out on the porch yelling, "Hey—this is private property! Get off the beach immediately!" When the intruder had been properly routed, Dr. Hepburn and family returned to the table and, a bit short of breath, took up the defense of the common man once again.

The very nature of the Connecticut Yankee is that of a survivor. So if the future can be called an everlasting extension of the past, Connecticut will always be Connecticut—Fairfield County and all, insurance companies and all, changes and all—forever and ever.

What other state in the Union can *ever* truthfully say that one of its existing daily newspapers reported the story of the Boston Tea Party as straight news? The *Hartford Courant* did, and shortly thereafter counted among its advertisers a Virginian named George Washington.

Coming Home to New England

Each New England state shares the characteristics of the other five to some degree. Mix Maine's tall stories and run-around manner of answering questions with New Hampshire's frugality and Vermont's common sense, integrity, and laconic, wise humor. Then add the Puritan ethic of Massachusetts with a generous dash of Rhode Island tolerance, pride, and concern for historical details. Top all that with a dose of Connecticut's shrewdness and Yankee Ingenuity and, behold, New England! For authentic additional flavoring, garnish with the ethnic influences of the French, Portuguese, Irish, Italians, Poles, and Armenians and, for good measure, throw in some fickle weather, five thousand or more legends, a ghost or two, exactly nine versions of the word ayuh (an outsider can learn the nine definitions and when to use each but can never, in a lifetime, learn the proper pronunciations), a good old-fashioned Rhode Island clambake and a smattering of clam chowder (*without tomatoes*), baked beans, codfish, lobsters, maple syrup, jonnycake, hulled corn, and apple pie.

And yet New England means something slightly different to each New Englander.

At a recent church supper in Springfield, Massachusetts, following a talk about New England I gave at an historical society there, we all started discussing what New England meant to each of us.

"New England is where neighbors help neighbors mend each other's fences, and New England is where they say what they *mean.*"

"New England is where it all began and where a feeling of continuity is still strong."

Several people chose to describe it in physical or visual terms.

"New England is the little village in the Christmas cards—and what many outsiders are surprised about is that the little village really exists!"

"New England is coming into Northeast Harbor under sail after a beautiful day in Frenchman's Bay—and picking up the buoy the first time around!"

"New England is eating homemade coffee ice cream and sitting on the cannon in front of the Old Sloop Church in Rockport, Massachusetts, watching some fife and drum corps march by in the Fourth of July parade."

A visitor from Cleveland, Ohio, at the table said, "New England—it all seems so *substantial.*"

Finally, an elderly, distinguished-looking gentleman at the head of the table said quietly, "To me, New England is coming home." We all nodded in agreement, but none of us wished to risk diminishing the statement by attempting further explanation.

However, I think we could all *feel* his meaning. "Coming home" constitutes, perhaps, an image that doesn't necessarily have anything to do with maple-shaded village greens, lobsters, Beacon Hill, Vermont's orange hills in autumn, or anything else commonly associated with our region. "Coming home" is a personal, very private image of New England.

At a certain time when I'm as old or older than the gentleman in Springfield, I know where I'll be, wherever I am. It will be very early on a calm, warm late-June morning on New Hampshire's Lake Winnipesaukee. I'll walk down to the water's edge below my camp on Sleepers Island, rest on the bench I built three years before, and sip from a mug of hot coffee. The sun will glisten through the tall pine trees behind me. In the distance, I'll hear the faint sound of an outboard motor, but the huge lake before me, lying there in its myriad of undulating reflections, will be otherwise free of human activity. Then, far down near The Witches and Forty Islands, I'll see a dark, faintly ominous-looking band of ruffled water creeping slowly toward me along the entire breadth of the lake from Meredith Bay to Moultonborough Neck. There'll be long-ago voices and laughter like distant music. A solitary leaf on the poplar tree leaning over the shore near me will flap lazily as if in preparation for the daily summertime wind—inevitably on its way as always. While I wait for it calmly in the temporary magical stillness of early morning, just as I have done a thousand times before, I'll look across the water to the hills that rise over the faraway shores and then on and on beyond for miles and miles of misty-blue mountains to the north.

FACTS AT YOUR FINGERTIPS

FACTS AND FIGURES. Of all the regions in the United States, New England is the smallest, most compact, and easiest to travel in. Its six states—Connecticut, Maine, Massachusetts, New Hampshire, Rhode Island, and Vermont—are among the best geared for every type of tourism, from the super deluxe package to backwoods camping. Covering an area of almost 67,000 square miles, with a population of approximately 12.3 million people, New England is a unique blend of natural and man-made wonders. It is an area equally blessed with spectacular scenery and cultural wealth. As the first part of the country to have been developed by European settlers, it boasts a sense of history that is unparalleled in the United States.

When considering the pertinent facts and figures for New England, it quickly becomes apparent that there is a difference in scale here compared to other parts of the country. For example, the region's largest city, Boston, has a population of less than 600,000—compared to New York's over 7 million (based on the 1980 census). Distances between major points of interest are much shorter. And the changes in terrain, customs, and folklore come quickly and drastically. The area is seemingly condensed—and yet the expanses of its White and Green Mountain ranges, the winding Appalachian and Heritage trails and an endless supply of rivers, lakes, and waterfalls give it a feeling of great expansiveness.

The coastline runs 473 miles, much of it rugged and rocky, yet there are stretches suitable for swimming. Inland, which is 75 percent forest, is largely mountainous, with New Hampshire's Mt. Washington capping the region at 6,288 ft. Given this setting, it is easy to understand that the first New England fortunes were made from fishing and shipping in the 17th and 18th centuries. In the 19th century this was one of the first areas in the nation to industrialize. Today, almost every type of modern industry is represented, with computers leading the technological way and such craft-based goods as shoes and furniture representing the region's more traditional bent.

PLANNING YOUR TRIP. To savor New England, get in a car, choose your destination, and take as much time as possible getting there. You're in Robert Frost country, where the road less traveled may lead to a cemetery dating back to the 1600s or a sugar house where you can learn how maple syrup is made. There will be many fascinating stops and side trips en route to your destination.

Once you get out of the cities (often a formidable task, particularly in Boston during rush hour), traffic thins considerably. Routes are generally well marked and roads are well maintained. State tourist offices have maps and brochures to help you plan. In the Boston area, be sure to get a copy of the Greater Boston Convention and Visitors Bureau Official Guide to Boston, Box 490, Boston 02149 (800–858–0200), which highlights several interesting day trips.

Because the New England states are so close together, a bus tour is another good way to see the sights. Those with limited time can see a great deal on a one-day tour. Brush Hill Tours, 109 Norfolk St., Boston, MA 02124 (800–343–1328 in the Boston area, 800–647–4776 out-of-state) offers 11 one-day sightseeing tours around Boston, to Cape Cod, and to

Newport, Rhode Island. The Gray Line, 275 Tremont St., Boston 02116 (617–426–8805) offers tours of Boston as well as one-day tours up the New England seacoast and, in season, to foliage country. Globus-Gateway, 69–15 Austin Street, Forest Hills, NY 11375 (718–268–7000 in New York, 800–221–0090 out-of-state) operates a nine-day tour through upstate New York and into New England during foliage season each year. Paragon Tours, 680 Purchase Street, New Bedford, MA 02741 (800–999–5050) runs three-day bus tours to Maine, Vermont, and Lake George, New York, each fall.

An extensive bus system operates throughout New England and is an excellent option for those wishing to plan their own itineraries. Peter Pan Bus Lines (and Trailways), 555 Atlantic Avenue, Boston, MA (617–426–7838) serves areas west of Boston, including western Massachusetts, Hartford and New Haven, Connecticut, upstate New York, and New York City.

Vermont Transit Lines and Bonanza Bus Lines, at the Greyhound Terminal, 10 St. James Avenue, Boston, MA (617–423–5810) service areas north and south of Boston, respectively.

AMTRAK also services New England and offers numerous tour packages which are explained in their extensive Travel Planner. For information and/or a copy of this guide call the Tour Department at 800–USA–RAIL.

Tour-planning companies like Innovatours, Inc., Box 1610, Framingham, MA 01701 (617–626–2222) specialize in planning motor coach tour packages for groups of 30 or more which last one or more days through New England. Uncommon Boston Ltd., 65 Commonwealth Avenue, Boston, MA 02116 (617–731–5854) custom designs tours for individuals with special interests. If you want to visit candy companies throughout the region, or visit high-tech companies, they'll set it up. They also provide interpreters and guides to ride in your car.

TOURIST INFORMATION. New England USA, 76 Summer St., Boston, MA 02110 (617–423–6967 or 800–847–4863 outside Massachusetts) will send you a free, comprehensive Travel Planner suggesting trips and destinations throughout New England.

New England Vacation Center, 630 Fifth Ave., Concourse Shop #2, New York, NY 10020 (212–307–5780) will also provide free information on the region.

For further information on each state:

Connecticut—Tourism Division, Department of Economic Development, 210 Washington St., Hartford, CT 06106 (203–566–3948).

Maine—Maine Publicity Bureau, 97 Winthrop St., Hallowell, ME 04347 (207–289–2423).

Massachusetts—Tourism Department, Department of Commerce, 100 Cambridge St., Boston, MA 02202 (617–727–3201).

New Hampshire—Office of Vacation Travel, Box 856, Concord, NH 03301 (603–271–2666).

Rhode Island—Tourism Division, Department of Economic Development, 7 Jackson Walkway, Providence, RI 02903 (401–277–2601 or 800–556–2484).

Vermont—Vermont Travel Division, 134 State St., Montpelier, VT 05602 (802–828–3236).

WHEN TO GO. Something is always in season in New England. Summers are the most culturally active, with major music festivals at Tanglewood in the Berkshire Mountains of Massachusetts and in the Bretton

Woods of New Hampshire. Freshwater and saltwater beaches abound, and fishing, swimming, and boating are popular activities.

Fall is unquestionably the most colorful season, and for many a "pilgrimage" to view the foliage is an annual event not to be missed. The season starts in early October in the more northern reaches of the area, moving southward as the month goes on.

Winter is given over to downhill and cross-country skiing, ice fishing, and snowmobiling.

Spring brings the flowering of apple blossoms, dogwood, rhododendrons, lilacs, and forsythia. The waterfalls are at their most dramatic, and the earth, thawing after the winter snows, is rich and hearty.

Except where there are ski resorts, the mountains are most popular in summer and fall, and coastal areas are most popular in the summer. Prices often reflect this, and many accommodations are booked well in advance.

Tourists are discovering that New England can be as enjoyable, far more economical, and less crowded off season. Bar Harbor, Maine, holds a special charm on a crisp winter's day, and motel rates are greatly reduced. Many of Newport, Rhode Island's fabled mansions are open from early April through October, and a visit other than during peak summer season can be most enjoyable.

Because city hotels are less crowded on weekends, many offer special packages which may even include theater tickets. The Greater Boston Convention and Visitors Bureau puts out a Weekend Package Guide, and other tourism departments will be glad to tell you about similar packages.

TIPS FOR BRITISH VISITORS. *Passports.* You will need a valid passport (cost £15) and a U.S. visa (which can only be put in a passport of the 10-year kind). You can obtain the visa either through your travel agent or directly from the *United States Embassy,* Visa and Immigration Department, 5 Upper Grosvenor St., London W1A 2JB (tel. 01–499–3443). Visas can be applied for only by post. No vaccinations are required for entry into the U.S.

Customs. If you are 21 or over you can take into the U.S. 200 cigarettes, 50 cigars or 3 lbs. of tobacco (combination of proportionate parts permitted); 1 U.S. liter of alcohol. Everyone is entitled to take in duty-free gifts to a value of $100. Be careful not to take in meat or meat products, seeds, plants, fruits, etc., and certainly no nonprescription narcotics.

Returning to Britain, you may bring home: (1) 200 cigarettes or 100 cigarillos or 50 cigars or 250 grams of tobacco; (2) two liters of table wine and, in addition, (a) one liter of alcohol over 22% by volume (most spirits), (b) two liters of alcohol under 22% by volume (fortified or sparkling wine), or (c) two more liters of table wine; (3) 50 grams of perfume and ¼ liter of toilet water; and (4) other goods up to a value of £32.

Insurance. We recommend that you insure yourself to cover health and motoring mishaps with *Europ Assistance,* 252 High St., Croydon CRO INF (01–680–1234). Their excellent service is all the more valuable when you consider the possible costs of health care in the U.S. Trip cancellation insurance and insurance to cover loss of luggage (if it isn't already covered in an existing homeowner policy) may be wise. The Association of British Insurers, Aldermary House, Queen St., London EC4N 1TT (01–248–4477) will give comprehensive advice on all aspects of vacation insurance.

Tour Operators. The price battle that has raged over trans-Atlantic fares has meant that most tour operators now offer excellent budget packages to the U.S., though most are likely to include only a few days in New

England. Among those offering fly-drive or more extensive tours through this region are:

Aer Lingus Holidays, Aer Lingus House, 83 Staines Rd., Hounslow, Middlesex TW3 3JB (tel. 01–569–4001).

Albany Travel (Manchester) Ltd., 190 Deansgate, Manchester M3 3WD (tel. 061–833–0202).

Cosmos America, Tourama House, 17 Homesdale Rd., Bromley, Kent BR2 9LX (tel. 01–464–3400).

Renown Holidays, 19 Connaught St., London W2 2AY (tel. 01–723–6689).

Speedbird, Alta House, 152 King St., London W6 0QU (tel. 01–741–8041).

Air Fares. Consult the small ads of the *Times,* the *Guardian,* the *Evening Standard,* and the travel sections of the Sunday newspapers for budget flight offers. Look for flights to Boston, in the heart of New England or to New York. Check the extras carefully; prices quoted may not include airport taxes and supplements. Virgin Atlantic Airways, 7th Floor, Sussex House, High St., Crawley, West Sussex RH10 1BZ (0293–38222), may have a bargain seat; the APEX offers of the major airlines are also worth investigating.

Hotels. For booking in advance, you can write or phone directly to smaller inns and bed and breakfasts. Some may require a deposit, which you can pay by credit card or international money order. Write well ahead, however, as inns in particular often fill up as much as six months in advance for weekends during fall foliage and summer music festival seasons. Reserve at major hotels through your travel agent. For further information on accommodations, write to the *New England Innkeepers Association,* Box 4977, Hampton, NH 03842, in the U.S.

WHAT IT WILL COST. Travel in New England tends to cost more than travel in many other parts of the country. Gasoline and accommodations are more expensive and, in isolated and tourist areas, a hamburger can set you back $5.

Prices in cities are higher than in the country and resort areas during tourist season. Boston is the most expensive city in New England to stay in and even to park your car. A double room at the Sheraton Boston, as of this writing, ranges from $160 to $215, plus $12 a day to park. A double at the Sheraton in Portland, Maine, ranges from $95 to $125, and parking is free.

A meal in a moderately priced restaurant in either place won't vary greatly, but in the cities there will be more to choose from. A deluxe dinner for two that cost $100 in Boston will cost considerably less in Providence, Rhode Island, or Augusta, Maine.

Gasoline prices increase the farther north you travel, partly because the tankers have to haul it a greater distance and partly because of supply and demand. Gasoline is one product that tends to be cheaper in the cities than in the country, and it is wise to fill up your tank before you hit the road.

Seasonal activities attract many, and prices reflect their popularity. Skiing, one of the north country's greatest attractions, has become an expensive proposition. A one-day weekend lift ticket at Vermont's Mt. Ascutney is $27. A family of four can easily spend $125 for a day's skiing at any but the smallest areas. Museums and historic homes in towns throughout New England generally charge a nominal admission fee.

Some tips for controlling costs. Accommodations. If you have a car, choose a motel outside city limits. A double room at the Howard

Johnson Lodge in Revere costs $87, has free parking, and is just a short drive from Boston.

Check into the lodgings available at local YMCAs and YWCAs (write or call YMCA of the USA, 101 N. Wacker Dr., Chicago, IL 60606 312–977–0031). Consider efficiency apartments and/or cabins, or camping in either public or private campgrounds. During the summer, investigate whether the colleges and universities in the area you will be in offer dormitory rooms to visitors. A directory of some 200 such opportunities all over the United States is *Mort's Guide to Low-Cost Vacations and Lodgings on College Campuses, USA–Canada* ($7.00) from Mort Barish Associates Inc., Research Park, 218 Wall St., Princeton, NJ 08540.

Take advantage of city hotel weekend packages.

If you're planning a holiday in the country, consider a bed-and-breakfast facility. During ski season, look for a place that offers weekday rates or dormitory arrangements.

Restaurants. Take advantage of early-bird specials—generally from 5:30 P.M. to 6:30 P.M. They're designed to get in an extra sitting and offer a smaller selection at reduced prices.

All-you-can-eat buffets and Sunday brunches are good ways to stoke the fires on limited funds.

On the coast look for "in-the-rough" places which serve up lobsters and clams on paper plates. You'll experience a New England dining tradition while you save money.

If you want to try one of the fancier places without going for a bundle, eat lunch there. The prices are lower and the food as good (though portions are generally smaller than at dinner).

Use of the word "Family" in a restaurant's name indicates that prices are moderate and that a children's menu is available.

Attractions. *Plan ahead!* This will enable you to take advantage of reduced rates. Boston's Museum of Fine Art has free admission every Saturday morning. Tanglewood Music Festival has open rehearsal, at greatly reduced admission, every Saturday morning in season. Many ski areas offer enticing midweek lift ticket rates.

Senior Citizen Discounts. Members of the AARP (American Association of Retired Persons), the NRTA (National Retired Teachers Association), the National Association of Retired Persons, the Catholic Golden Age of United Societies of the U.S.A., the Old Age Security Pensioners of Canada, and similar organizations benefit increasingly from a number of discounts, but the amounts, sources, and availability of these change, so it is best to check with either your organization or the hotel, motel, or restaurant chain you plan to use.

HINTS TO THE MOTORIST. New England is adequately supplied with interstates, parkways, freeways, thruways, and turnpikes. But plan to spend as much time as possible off them or you will miss the secondary and back roads that make a visit here memorable. They afford a real chance to take in the countryside, to stop at antique and craft shops, to appreciate the Georgian, Greek Revival, and Federalist architecture, or to visit some outstanding small museum.

The speed limit on highways in Connecticut, Massachusetts, and Rhode Island is 55 mph. The speed limit in New Hampshire is 65 mph; in Vermont it is 65 mph on most sections of I–89 and I–91; in Maine it is 65 mph on interstate highways in nonurban areas, and 55 mph on interstates in urban areas (Portland, Lewiston/Auburn, Bangor) and all other highways. Speed limits are strictly enforced. Also be careful to obey the speed

limit on secondary roads. It may drop immediately from 45 to 25 mph
as you enter towns and the police are often quick to fine unsuspecting of-
fenders.

The major highways have frequent rest stops and gas stations, and you
will only occasionally encounter a desolate stretch of highway, such as
those in central and upper Maine, where you will wonder where to find
the next service station. But it's wise, particularly when traveling on secondary roads away from city centers, to carry any spare parts that may
be unique to your vehicle. Foreign car repairs, particularly, can be a bit
spotty.

In cities a car can be a major headache. Parking, if available, can be
costly, and traffic, particularly during morning and evening rush hours,
horrendous. Why not leave your car in the hotel or motel parking lot and
use public transportation? It's efficient, economical, and a whole lot easier
on your nervous system.

WHAT TO TAKE. There is wisdom in the Yankee adage "If you don't
like the weather in New England, wait a minute." The gentle sea breeze
that makes the coast a refuge on hot, humid days can feel like an arctic
blast if a fog rolls in that evening. Temperatures can plummet 20 degrees
as you ascend Mt. Washington. A cold, gloomy November morning may
turn into a brilliant, 60-degree afternoon.

Therefore, dressing in layers is a good bet. You can cover up with a
warm sweater or jacket when a nor'easter suddenly blows in to ruin a perfect beach day, or remove it when your ski resort's wood stove starts working too hard.

With its many resorts and tourist attractions, New Englanders tend to
be informal when they travel. Dress is generally quite casual in restaurants, although a few city restaurants and hotel and resort dining rooms
may require men to wear jackets and ties (and will often provide them
upon request).

Boston is the most cosmopolitan of the New England cities, and dress
tends to be a bit more formal here, although it is not uncommon to see
tourists in jeans and sneakers. At the shore or in the country sports clothes
are the standard. Most restaurants and bars, however, will not let you in
without a shirt or shoes, or if you're in a bathing suit.

Generally speaking, it is always a good idea to make a checklist of what
you'll need. It will save time and reduce confusion. Except for backwoods
campers, you'll be able to stock up on anything you might forget or run
out of, so don't weigh down your baggage with excess film or other items
that are easily obtained on the road.

ACCOMMODATIONS. New England has accommodations to suit
every taste and budget. Most of the major hotel chains are well represented
in the larger cities, and small, independent motels still thrive—particularly
in the outskirts. There are numerous resort hotels in tourist areas such
as Hyannis on Cape Cod and New Hampshire's White Mountains.

The cost of accommodations tends to increase as you approach city centers, though a few venerable second-rate hotels still stand—particularly
in some of the smaller cities. Hotel chains offer many amenities like indoor
pools, room service, and restaurants. Motel accommodations are generally
fairly basic, although many have outdoor pools and most are now hooked
up to cable or satellite dishes and offer in-room movies.

Once you travel away from urban centers your options narrow. The
number of accommodations will be in direct proportion to an area's popularity—either with business people or tourists.

Coastal tourist areas like Bar Harbor, Maine, and Mystic, Connecticut, have many small motels to choose from, although in season they fill up fast. Many close for a few months in the winter, although towns like Ogunquit, Maine, and Newport, Rhode Island, are becoming increasingly popular in winter and more motels are now remaining open all year. Ski areas like Stowe, Vermont, and the White Mountains have also become popular year-round and offer an excellent range of accommodations.

In some of the more remote tourist areas such as Moosehead Lake, Maine, and the Connecticut Lakes in New Hampshire, housekeeping cabins offering comfortable but very basic accommodations are common.

Some of the hotel/motel chains which operate throughout New England include:

Holiday Inn (800–465–4329). At the upper end of the moderately priced scale, and offering amenities such as swimming pool (often indoor), color TV, restaurants, and entertainment.

Howard Johnson (800–654–2000). Similar in price and amenities to Holiday Inn.

Marriott Hotel (800–228–9290). Tend to be more expensive, often offering health spas, upscale dining, and sleek architecture.

Quality Inn (800–228–5151). Similar in price and amenities to Holiday Inn.

Sheraton (800–325–3535). Similar in price and amenities to Marriott Hotel.

Susse Chalet (800–258–1980). Economy priced, basic, clean, comfortable rooms.

Even moderately priced chains will cost more in cities, and, in general, the larger the city, the higher the price. Hotel chains will gladly send you their directories.

Bed and Breakfasts. The bed-and-breakfast industry evolved from the guest-house business and is booming. Throughout New England folks have hung chintz curtains in their spare bedrooms and hung out signs announcing they're open for business. You can stay in a remodeled farmhouse in rural Woodstock, Vermont, or a 150-year-old house in Wellfleet on Cape Cod once owned by a sea captain. Prices vary tremendously—from $28 to $120 per day—as do rules. Some don't accept pets; others refuse small children; some forbid smoking. But all serve breakfast.

Inns are also popular and tend to be more expensive than bed-and-breakfast facilities, but also often provide more services, like public rooms, bars, and restaurants. Meals range from communal homestyle to haute cuisine.

Guest houses, bed-and-breakfast facilities, and inns give tourists an opportunity to get a good taste of the region in less uniform surroundings than motels or hotels.

Reservation services are listed throughout this guide under the areas they serve; those that serve all New England include:

B & B Registry, Box 8174, St. Paul, MN 55108 (612–646–4238).

INNter Lodging, Box 7044, Tacoma, WA 98407, is a cooperative in which members must make their own homes available for bed and breakfast for a certain period during the year but are thereby entitled to service from other members.

Pineapple Hospitality, Inc., 384 Rodney French Blvd., New Bedford, MA 02744 (617–990–1696), has listings for more than 150 homes throughout the region.

Guidebooks on the subject include: *Bed and Breakfast in the Northeast* by Bernice Chessler (Globe-Pequot, Old Chester Rd., Chester, CT 06412);

Country Inns of New England by Patricia Brooks and Fran Jurga Garvan (101 Productions, 834 Mission St., San Francisco, CA 94103); *Country Inns of America* (separate volumes are available on lower and upper New England); published by Holt, Rinehart and Winston, 383 Madison Ave., New York, NY 10017; *Fodor's Bed & Breakfast Guide* (Fodor's Travel Publications, Inc., 201 East 50th St., New York, NY 10022).

Other Budget Accommodations. Accommodations at hostels are dormitory-style with common rooms and kitchen shared by all. No drugs or alcohol are allowed, lights-out is at 11 P.M., and you must be a member to take advantage of the low rates (approximately $4–$9 per person, per night). In season it is wise to reserve ahead; write or phone directly to the particular hostel you plan to stay in. Write to American Youth Hostel Association, Inc., Box 37613, Washington, D.C. 20013.

YMCAs and YWCAs often offer clean, simple accommodations. Write or call YMCA of the USA, 101 N. Wacker Dr., Chicago, IL 60606 (312–977–0031).

During the summer some colleges and universities offer dormitory rooms to visitors. Again, a directory of some 200 such opportunities all over the United States is *Mort's Guide to Low-Cost Vacations and Lodgings on College Campuses, USA–Canada* ($7.00) from Mort Barish Associates Inc., Research Park, 218 Wall St., Princeton, NJ 08540.

DINING OUT. Heavily forested, and with thin rocky soil, New England is hardly a rich agricultural area, yet even at the first Thanksgiving, in 1621, the earliest New Englanders managed to feast on corn and beans, venison, roast duck, roast goose, eels, clams, wheat bread, corn bread, leeks, watercress, wild plums, and home-made wine; and ever since, New England has enjoyed a culinary tradition that is both plain and solid on the one hand and richly satisfying on the other. The early settlers found strawberries, cranberries, blackberries, blueberries, melons, pumpkins, squash, four kinds of corn (white, blue, yellow, and red), turkeys, maple sugar, woods teeming with game, tidelands that yielded clams, oysters, and scallops, and fish "at our doorstep." New England's first fortunes were made from the sea, in fishing and shipping, and seafood is still an important part of this region's diet, but it is certainly not the only pleasure of dining out here. A few possibilities, among many:

For seafood there's lobster stew, baked stuffed haddock, and broiled Boston scrod; clams and oysters either steamed or fried; codfish balls; Block Island swordfish; crabs and scallops. And if you go in summer you may be lucky enough to enjoy a beach party where clams or lobsters will either be boiled over an open fire of driftwood or will be packed with corn in seaweed and baked over hot stones. New England clam chowder is a fine and special art form all its own and one in which everyone is his own artist. Clams, pork, spices, onions, milk, butter, and wine or cider are the ingredients, but the proportions and the seasoning are personal matters, and disputes over the use of tomatoes and the distinction between clams and quahogs can take on theological overtones.

To make a New England boiled dinner, some prefer saltpork as the center around which the vegetables are arranged, while others make it with corned beef, particularly around Boston. Baked beans is yet another area of controversy where every variation of bean, molasses, pork, and baking technique has its own defenders. There is, however, a delightful recipe for the rich brown bread that always goes with baked beans that is gratifyingly clearcut as well as lyrical: one cup of sweet milk, one cup of sour; one cup of corn meal, one cup of flour; teaspoon of soda, molasses one cup; steam for three hours, then eat it all up.

Cornbread, Indian pudding, apple pandowdy, mincemeat pie, deep dish apple or blueberry pie, and in Vermont, sharp cheeses and sweet maple syrup and sugar. Everywhere are apples and blueberries, poultry, dairy products, and potatoes. Cape Cod produces cranberries, and in southern New England cherries and peaches are grown. Although nowadays some of the finest old New England inns take pride in their sophisticated international cuisine, the region's typical cooking is still very much alive and well and still reflects that "plain style" beloved of its Puritan ancestors. But there is nothing gloomy, pinched, or austere about this plain style. It is, like New England craftsmanship, a kind of simple, direct respect for the materials native to the region. In their own distinctive way, New Englanders always have eaten well. They still do.

It's not unusual today to pass through a small town in Maine and find a Chinese restaurant next to a lobster shack across from a pizzeria. As the ethnic mix continues to expand in New England, so does the choice of cuisines. But outside the larger cities, which offer everything from Kosher to Korean food, small family restaurants and hamburger houses still predominate, and most serve good, simple, and economical Yankee fare.

Restaurant prices vary tremendously. On the high side, dinner for two with a good bottle of wine at a deluxe restaurant in one of the major cities can run upward of $100. Even a meal for two at some of the new, upscale pizza parlors can cost $30. Diners and luncheonettes are at the other end of the spectrum, where a homecooked meatloaf dinner can cost as little as $3.

New England cities are generally a composite of old and new, and so are their restaurants. It's still possible to find good, inexpensive places next door to the newest theme restaurants. Some of the best food and most reasonable prices are in ethnic neighborhoods like Boston's Chinatown and Providence's Portuguese section.

Smaller towns, which offer fewer choices, tend to have one expensive restaurant, one moderately priced, and one inexpensive. As you travel farther north, however, you may want to stop at the first diner you come to: it may be the only restaurant open for the next 50 miles.

Numerous chains operate throughout New England, and their fare is generally economical and predictable. McDonald's, Burger King, Arby's, and Wendy's are all present in abundance, and particularly visible at highway interchanges. Kentucky Fried Chicken, though not as popular as in some other parts of the country, is still the major chicken franchise. Pewter Pot Family Restaurants, Friendly's, and International House of Pancakes offer table service and a bit less hectic atmosphere. Papa Gino's and Pizza Hut are the major pizza chains. Howard Johnson and Holiday Inn offer reliable eating at reasonable prices.

Reservations are advisable at better restaurants, especially when there is a ski area or a music festival nearby, as well as ascertaining what the dining hours are (they tend to be fairly limited in this part of the country). Dress codes depend upon the establishment, but New Englanders generally lean toward the casual—without being unkempt. Only the more exclusive eateries and better city restaurants require men to wear jackets. Children's menus are frequently available, senior citizen discounts less common.

Always call ahead to check which credit cards are accepted.

DRINKING LAWS. All New England states have a minimum drinking age of 21, and all strictly enforce "drinking and driving" laws. Penalties range from strict fines to mandatory loss of license. The best advice in the six-state area is *do not drink and drive!* Following are local laws.

Connecticut: Beer, wine, and liquor are sold in package stores and some drugstores in nearly all cities and towns. Grocery stores are permitted to sell beer. No package liquor sold on Sun., Good Friday, and Christmas. Liquor served by the drink in licensed bars, restaurants, and hotels at local option, according to existing statutes.

Maine: Bottled liquor is sold only at state liquor stores and agencies; beer and wine are sold at grocery stores. Alcoholic beverages may be sold by the bottle Mon.–Sat. and on Sun. where approved. By local option, alcoholic drinks may be sold in hotels, restaurants, and bars Mon.–Sat. 6 A.M.–1 A.M.; Sun. and Memorial Day, noon–1 A.M.

A mandatory deposit on beer and soft drink bottles and cans is returned when empties are returned to stores or redemption centers.

Massachusetts: Drinks may be ordered until 1 A.M. (2 A.M. in some towns) daily; until midnight (1 A.M. in some towns) Sat. Serving hours Sun. are from 1 P.M. (11 A.M. in some towns) to 1 A.M. Package liquor sold until 11 P.M. in package stores; no sales Sun. There is a mandatory bottle return law. Some towns have chosen not to allow liquor sales.

New Hampshire: Liquor is sold in stores operated by the State Liquor Commission. These stores are generally open 10 A.M.–5:30 P.M. Mon.–Sat. (later on Fri.) except legal holidays, and Election Day. Some of their larger stores, however, remain open Sun. Beer, ale, and wine may be sold for off-premises consumption by grocers and druggists having proper permits; individual glass sale of liquor, beer, or wine is permitted at licensed restaurants, hotels, and clubs. Most golf club bars and cocktail lounges are closed until noon on Sun.

Rhode Island: Legal hours are 6 A.M.–1 A.M. daily, Sun. from noon. No sales Christmas Day. Package stores are closed Sun. and certain holidays. In some areas drinking is permitted until 2 A.M. from June until Sept., and weekends Oct. to May.

Vermont: Bars are illegal except in restaurants and hotels. Most are open until 2 A.M. weekdays and 1 A.M. Sat. No sale of alcoholic beverages is permitted Sun. 1 A.M.–noon. Consumption of alcoholic beverages allowed until 2:30 A.M. weeknights and until 1:30 A.M. Sat. Hours of operation are the same with or without entertainment. The minimum age of 21 does not apply to those who reached the age of 18 by June 30, 1986.

Bottled beer and light wine to take out are sold at stores with second-class licenses. Bottled liquor is sold at state liquor stores and agencies. Local option forbids the sale of liquor in some Vermont towns. However, it is all right to bring in your own liquor and buy setups.

TIPPING. Tipping is supposed to be a personal way of thanking someone who has given you attentive, efficient, and personal service. When you get genuinely good service, feel secure in rewarding it; but when you feel that the service you get is slovenly, indifferent, or surly don't hesitate to tip accordingly.

These days the going rate for tipping is 15%. In restaurants, that's before taxes. In better restaurants, with a bill of $60 or more, 20% is fair.

TIME, BUSINESS HOURS, AND HOLIDAYS. Eastern Daylight Time is in effect from the first Sun. in Apr. until the last Sun. in Oct.

Business hours are generally 8 or 9 A.M.–5 P.M., but some stores, especially in the many communities used to catering to vacationers, are likely to stay open later in the evening.

National holidays observed throughout New England include New Year's Day, Martin Luther King's Birthday, Washington's Birthday, Memorial Day, Fourth of July, Labor Day, Columbus Day, Veteran's Day, Thanksgiving, and Christmas.

Travelers should be aware that some states observe their own holidays (for example, Patriots Day in Massachusetts, which occurs on the Monday closest to April 18) and state offices may be closed even when federal offices are open; or local municipalities can have their own days of observation. Check with the Chambers of Commerce or tourist bureaus in the areas you will be traveling to find details on local observances.

Federal office buildings open at 8 A.M. and close at 6 P.M. and are not open on weekends. Offices are generally open from 8 or 9 A.M. until 4:30 or 5 P.M. Call the office you are planning to visit to get their exact hours.

SUMMER SPORTS. From the coastline to the ridgelines, from Newport, Rhode Island, to Newport, Vermont, just about every part of this six-state region is fertile ground for some kind of summer activity. It may be passive like riding a windjammer off the coast of Maine, or you may want to participate in the Berkshires' September Josh Billings RunAround which combines biking, canoeing, and running.

Following is a sampling of sports available in New England.

Biking: It has become one of *the* sports of the 80s because it is economical, can be done most anywhere there's a road (but not permitted on some highways), and is good for you. Some cities and towns maintain special bike trails, like the Dr. Paul Dudley White Charles River Bike Path, a 25-mi. circuit between Science Park in Boston and Watertown Sq. Contact the Metropolitan District Commission, 20 Somerset St., Boston, MA 02108 (617–727–5215). Vermont Country Cyclers, Box 145, Waterbury Center, VT 05677 (802–244–8751), has hundreds of hosted weekend (and longer) bicycle tours in Vermont and Maine. New Hampshire Publishing, Box 70, Somersworth, NH 03878 (603–692–7327), has bike tour guides to several states.

Boardsailing: Also known as windsurfing, its popularity is increasing rapidly, and the colorful sails can be spotted just about anywhere there is wind and water.

Canoeing/Kayaking: With all the lakes and rivers in this region, it's understandable that canoeists flock to the area. Whether it's paddling down the Saco River from New Hampshire into Maine or perhaps across Stockbridge Bowl in the Berkshires, New England has the quality and quantity for canoeists. Kayaking is less well-known but a kick of a sport, zipping across the water like an oversized waterbug. The Appalachian Mountain Club (5 Joy St., Boston, MA 02108) has a canoe chapter and a fine guide (*New England Whitewater River Guide*, $8.95).

Diving: Southern New England, especially the Rhode Island–Cape Cod area, is especially popular for scuba diving. Dive shops, in many cases, serve as unofficial clubs. For information: Ocean State Scuba in Jamestown (401–423–1662), Alpine Diver's World in Warwick (401–941–4000), Coastal Diving Services in Newport (401–847–6766).

Golf: Big and small. The men pros come to Pleasant Valley near Worcester, Massachusetts, and near Hartford, Connecticut; the women pros visit Danvers, Mass.; and there are all sorts of state and regional tourneys. Beyond that, though, there are many championship courses (Robert Trent Jones, for instance, did the courses at Woodstock and Warren, Vermont, and Carrabassett Valley, Maine). Two southern Vermont resorts, Stratton Mountain and Mount Snow, have golf schools.

Rafting: In Maine on the Penobscot, Kennebec, and Dead rivers. Contact: Maine Publicity Bureau, 97 Winthrop St., Hallowell 04347 (207–289–2423) for a directory of white-water-rafting outfitters.

Hiking: The Appalachian Trail terminates at Mount Katahdin in Maine and the route threads its way through New Hampshire, Vermont, Massachusetts, and Connecticut. The Appalachian Mountain Club (5 Joy St., Boston, MA 02108) does an admirable job of maintaining huts, marking trails and putting out guides. Possible backup for guides: New Hampshire Publishing, Box 70, Somersworth, NH 03878; or contact The Maine Appalachian Club, Box 283, Augusta, ME 04330.

Running: The Boston Marathon (held Patriot's Day in April) and Falmouth Road Race get the headlines, but there are road races throughout New England all summer. The Chamber of Commerce and tourism bureaus can give you specifics on competitions and/or special courses. The Boston Globe has extensive race information in its Sunday sports pages.

Swimming: Whether you choose a quick plunge at Maine's icy seashore, a leisurely dip at Ocean Beach in New London, Connecticut, or a freshwater splash in New Hampshire's Lake Winnipesaukee, you're never far from a place to swim. Many of New England's finest beaches are open to the public free of charge (although there is often a fee for parking). A word to the wise: Get there early on a hot day!

Tennis: Many resorts, hotels, and motels have one or more courts, as do a great number of cities and towns throughout the region. Major tournaments in the region include the U.S. Pro Championships at Longwood Cricket Club, near Boston, in mid-July; the Volvo International at its new site, Stratton Mountain, VT, in early August; the Stowe Grand Prix in mid-August; and the Hall of Fame Classic in July at the Casino in Newport, RI. The women pros hit Newport in mid-July, right after Wimbledon.

Windjammers: These tall-masted beauties ply the coast of Maine (Camden is the preeminent port but they also sail weekly from Rockport and Rockland) and Lake Champlain. A pleasant mix of sunning and sailing, weather permitting. The Lake Champlain jaunts, which go for three or six days, are the only known inland windjamming in the United States and perhaps the world.

For cruise information contact: Maine Windjammer Assoc., Box 317, Rockport, ME 04856 (800–624–6380) or Nicholson Yacht Charters, 1430 Massachusetts Ave., Cambridge, MA 02138 (617–661–8174) or Ocean Escapes Worldwide Charters, 9 Ferry Wharf, Newburyport 01950 (617–465–7116) or contact the Chamber of Commerce in the area you are planning to visit.

Yachting/Sailing: Just about every wrinkle of the coastline, from southwestern Connecticut to Down East in Eastport, Maine, has some kind of marina or dock for ocean sailors. Newport, RI, Marblehead, MA, and the central portion of Maine's coast—say, from Boothbay to Bar Harbor—are prime areas. Lake Winnipesaukee and Lake Champlain are the major inland spots, along with Lake Memphremagog in northern Vermont, New Hampshire's Lake Sunapee, and a handful of smaller lakes.

WINTER SPORTS. To many, New England has become almost synonymous with **skiing,** and with good reason: There are ski areas in every New England state, and some of them offer the finest skiing in the east. And cross-country ski-touring centers now proliferate the region. The most challenging downhill skiing areas are up north and include Cannon Mountain, Wildcat, and Waterville Valley in New Hampshire; Killington, Stowe, and Stratton in Vermont; and Sugarloaf and Sunday River in

Maine. Among the top cross-country ski centers: Stowe, Vermont; Acadia National Park, Maine; and Jackson, New Hampshire. Lance Tapley's *Ski Touring in New England and New York* (Stone Wall Press, Boston) provides excellent information.

Other winter sports popular in New England include:

Snowmobiling—Popular in state parks and forests that permit it. Many provide well-marked trails; the Interconnecting Trail System in northern and western Maine has more than 100 miles of groomed trails. (For information, contact individual state Fish and Wildlife Departments. See *Hunting*.)

Sled dog races—Held during the first three months of the year in the northern New England states.

Ice skating—In the Boston area, the Metropolitan District Commission, 20 Somerset St., Boston, MA 02108 operates 22 indoor and outdoor rinks. Many other cities and towns provide outdoor rinks. Be sure to check conditions before you test the ice.

Ice fishing—A fishing license is required for this sport which is rapidly gaining in popularity throughout New England.

HUNTING. In the late fall, hunting brings many people to New England, out after deer, bobcat, moose, and bear. There is bow-and-arrow hunting in some areas. For hunters who can take frigid, rough lake water, there are whistlers (goldeneye) and bluebills (scaup) for the taking from late Nov. to early Dec.; on Cape Cod, waterfowl, quail, pheasant, and rabbit lure many a sportsman from late Oct. through Nov.

All states have specific regulations and require a variety of licenses. Be sure to check before you set out.

Connecticut: Hunters not previously or currently licensed must complete 6 to 15 hours of safety instruction (no fee) before applying for a new license. Contact Franklin Management Area (203–642–7239), or Wildlife Bureau, Department of Environmental Protection, 165 Capitol Ave., Hartford, CT 06106 (203–566–4683).

Maine: Open for deer hunting in Oct. with bow and arrow only. Deer hunting with firearms usually opens for two weeks in Nov. Bear are in season from May 1 through the Sat. after Thanksgiving. Write to Department of Inland Fisheries and Wildlife, State House, Augusta, ME 04333 (203–289–2043) for information.

Massachusetts: Hunting for designated species permitted at certain times of the year by licensed hunters. Licenses can be purchased at city and town halls or from authorized sporting goods dealers, or by mail from Division of Fisheries and Wildlife, Saltonstall Building, 100 Cambridge St., Boston, MA 02202 (617–727–3151). Ask for a copy of the Abstracts of the Fish and Wildlife Laws.

New Hampshire: To obtain a license, hunters must have a hunter safety course or previous license. Licenses required for all game and are available at many sporting good stores and gas stations throughout the state. Contact New Hampshire Fish and Game Department, 34 Bridge St., Concord, NH 03301 (603–271–3421).

Rhode Island: To obtain a license, hunters must have a hunter safety course or previous license. Those between the ages of 12 and 15 need a youth license, and must be accompanied by a licensed hunter 21 years of age or older. Contact Rhode Island Department of Environmental Management, 9 Hayes St., Providence, RI 02903 (401–277–2771).

Vermont: Licenses required for all ages and available from town clerks or sporting goods dealers. State publishes a guide to hunting and a 60-page digest of fish and wildlife laws. Contact Vermont Fish and Game Department, Information and Education Division, Waterbury, VT 05676.

FISHING. Freshwater fish abound in many lakes, ponds, streams, and rivers throughout the region and favorite catches include trout, bass, perch, pike, pickerel, and land-locked salmon. Surf casting and deep-sea fishing for giant tuna, swordfish, white marlin, and blue marlin are popular along the coast.

All states require a license for freshwater fishing, and none require a license for saltwater sport fishing. Contact each state for specific regulations and license information. (See *Hunting,* above.)

Maine requires a special license for catching Atlantic salmon, for lobstering, and for ice fishing. New Hampshire's book of rules is available free of charge from the Fish and Game Department. Vermont publishes a free guide to fishing available from the Fish and Game Department, and requires all fishermen except those under 15 years to be licensed.

CAMPING AND HIKING. Connecticut: Many state parks and forests are open for camping Apr. 15–Sept. 30, and offer excellent hiking trails open throughout the year, weather permitting. For detailed information on fees and regulations contact: Department of Environmental Protection, 165 Capitol Ave., Hartford, CT 06103 (203–566–2304).

Maine: About half the state parks, as well as Acadia National Park, allow camping. For information write: Maine Forest Service, State House, Augusta, ME 04333 (207–289–2791). Facilities in privately owned campsites range from simple basics in the wilderness to deluxe cabins and cottages. The Maine Publicity Bureau, 97 Winthrop St., Hallowell, ME 04347 (207–289–2423) will provide a current listing of trailer parks and campsites.

Massachusetts: The Metropolitan District Commission supervises 14,700 acres in 10 reservations around Greater Boston. Many of them provide excellent hiking. Camping is permitted only on Lovell's Island in Boston Harbor, and a permit is required. For a copy of their MetroParks guide and/or more information write MetroParks, 20 Somerset St., Boston, MA 02108 (617–727–5215).

The Berkshires and the Appalachian Trail both offer excellent hiking. The Appalachian Mountain Club, 3 Joy St., Boston, MA 02108 (617–523–0636) can provide specific information. The Massachusetts Department of Tourism, 100 Cambridge St., Boston, MA 02202 (617–727–3201) publishes a free brochure listing public and private camping areas.

New Hampshire: Campsites are available in the state parks, the White Mountain National Forest, and in privately owned campgrounds. For a complete listing write to the New Hampshire Campground Owners Association, 30 Bonny St., Nashua, NH 03062 for the New Hampshire Camping Guide.

For novice and expert hikers there is a vast network of marked trails throughout the state. For information contact New Hampshire Office of Vacation Travel, Box 856, Concord, NH 03301 (603–271–2666).

Vermont: The Department of Forests, Parks and Recreation operates 35 campgrounds with 2,200 campsites. Contact the Department of Forests, Parks and Recreation, Montpelier, VT 05602. The state has about 90 private campgrounds. Write to the Vermont Association of Private Campground Owners and Operators, c/o Brattleboro North KOA, RD 2, Box 110, Putney, VT 05346, for a free brochure.

For information on hiking opportunities write the Vermont Travel Division, 134 State St., Montpelier, VT 05602 (802-828-3236).

Rhode Island: The Tourism Division, Rhode Island Department of Economic Development, 7 Jackson Walkway, Providence, RI 02903 (401-277-2771) can provide information on camping facilities and permits.

Hiking is excellent in the state's woodlands and beaches. Contact the Rhode Island Department of Economic Development, Tourist Promotion Division, 7 Jackson Walkway, Providence, RI 02903 (401-277-2601) for information.

TELEPHONES AND EMERGENCY NUMBERS. Connecticut: Area code is 203. A local call from a pay telephone costs 15 cents.
Maine: Area code 207. A local call from a pay telephone costs 20 cents.
Massachusetts: Area code for Boston and surrounding towns is 617. Area code for Cape Cod and the rest of eastern Massachusetts (roughly, east of the Connecticut River) is 508. Area code for western Massachusetts is 413. A local call from a pay telephone costs 10 cents.
New Hampshire: Area code 603. A local call from a pay telephone costs 10 cents.
Rhode Island: Area code 401. A local call from a pay telephone costs 15 cents.
Vermont: Area code 802. A local call from a pay telephone costs 10 cents.

Pay telephones can usually be found at shopping centers, in public buildings, at gas stations, and at highway interchanges.

In larger urban areas the universal emergency number for police, fire department, ambulances, and paramedics is 911. In many smaller municipalities and rural areas it will be necessary to dial the full telephone number of the department needed. Telephone directories contain crucial emergency numbers in their inside front covers, or you may dial 0 for the telephone operator, who will put you in contact with assistance.

SAFETY. A certain amount of caution should be exercised in any city, and a little more in the larger, more crowded ones. It is not advisable to walk in parks or on deserted streets after dark (although you may feel completely comfortable doing so in some smaller towns). Carrying traveler's checks rather than cash is a good idea any time; remember to keep a record of the checks' serial numbers. Always lock your car and don't leave valuables in sight in your car or even in your hotel room. Most hotels have safes where you can store valuables instead. Try to park your car in well-lit garages or parking lots and if you're nervous, ask the attendant to accompany you to your car. In crowded places like department stores or buses, keep a good hold on your purse or wallet. In public rest rooms, hold onto your purse rather than hang it on the hook provided.

If you're planning to hike overnight, report your intended route to police or park authorities. Be sure to carry a first-aid kit and suitable clothes and provisions. Weather in the mountains—particularly the Mt. Washington area—is extremely unpredictable and subject to drastic drops in temperature.

Hitchhiking is illegal on many highways, and the motorist who stops for a rider can be fined. Never stop for strangers.

INFORMATION FOR DISABLED TRAVELERS. The following agencies and publications can provide useful information for planning a barrier-free trip through New England:

Society for Advancement of Travel for the Handicapped, 26 Court St., Brooklyn, NY 11242, provides data on special tours for the handicapped and on who runs them.

Rehabilitation International, 1123 Broadway, New York, NY 10010, publishes a list of access guides for various countries.

International Air Transport Association (IATA), 2000 Teel St., Montreal, PQ H3A 2R4, Canada, publishes the *Incapacitated Passengers' Air Travel Guide,* which is available free.

Access Tours, a travel agency specializing in travel arrangements for the handicapped, can plan tours for groups of four or more with any disability. They can be reached at Suite 1801, 123–33 83d Ave., Kew Gardens, NY 11415 (718–263–3835).

LTD Travel, a newsletter packed with useful travel tips and helpful bibliographies for the disabled traveler, can be obtained from 116 Harbor Seal Court, San Mateo, CA 94404. The letter also provides thorough evaluations of travel destinations from the perspective of a handicapped traveler.

RECOMMENDED READING. Fiction: A superb evocation of the New England temperament is John P. Marquand's Pulitzer Prize novel, *The Late George Apley.* For the early history that is still so vividly present in New England, the historical novels of Maine's Kenneth Roberts, *Arundel, Oliver Wiswell, Rabble in Arms,* etc., are solidly researched and well written. Edith Wharton's famous *Ethan Frome* is a rather narrow view of an archetypal New England of her imagination that the visitor is highly unlikely to see.

Nonfiction: Although they were written in the late 1930s, the individual state volumes of the Federal Writers Project are still surprisingly useful. The background information—history, geography, geology, flora, fauna, etc.—has not changed. The political, social, and economic material is out of date but makes interesting comparisons with present conditions. The sightseeing material—specific sites, monuments, museums, natural beauty—is still very helpful, as are in particular the suggested walking itineraries. At your public library.

For a thorough, serious, and unvarnished look at this region as it is today, see *The New England States, People, Power, and Politics in the Six New England States,* by Neal R. Pierce (W.W. Norton, 1976). For an informative and amusing look at New England and New Englanders, read Judson Hale's *Inside New England* (Harper & Row, 1982).

For specific areas, try, among others: *The Proper Bostonians,* by Cleveland Amory (Parnassus, 1984); *The Old Post Road* (Boston to New York), by Stewart H. Holbrook (McGraw-Hill, 1962); *Connecticut: A New Guide,* by William Bixby (Scribners, 1974); *The Outermost House* (Cape Cod), by Henry Beston (Ballantine, 1976). If out of print, these books can probably be found at your local library.

Many of Henry David Thoreau's reflections in *Cape Cod* (available in various editions) are still relevant today. John Mitchell's *Ceremonial Times* (Doubleday, 1984) is a good introduction to the environmental history of a small part of Massachusetts, and by extension, much of New England. Randolph Langenbach and Tamara Hareven's *Amoskeag* (Pantheon, 1978) is an oral history, with photos, of the life of a Merrimack Valley mill town. Michael Hoel's *Land's Edge* (Little Publishing Co./Globe Pequot Press, 1986) tells about New England's coastal landforms.

The great photographer of New England was Samuel Chamberlain; any of his books will give you a beautiful evocation of the flavor of this region.

Guidebooks: Those with an interest in hiking the thousands of miles of trails throughout this region should obtain a copy of the Appalachian

Mountain Club trail book for the particular area in which they'll be staying. Lance Tapley's *Ski Touring in New England and New York* (Stone Wall Press, Boston) is excellent for cross-country skiers. And an outstanding guide to the local flora and fauna is *A Sierra Club Naturalist's Guide to Southern New England,* by Neil Jorgenson (San Francisco, 1978). Antique collectors will do well to follow the advice of *The Weekend Connoisseur,* by Joan Brasin (Dolphin, 1979), which covers New England extensively.

Regional Publications: *Vermont Life, New Hampshire Profiles, New England Monthly,* and *Yankee* offer picturesque accounts of the New England that most visitors seek. For a closer look at the daily life of New England, read the *Maine Times* and the *New Hampshire Times,* weekly newspapers specializing in feature articles, investigative journalism, and the long-range issues and problems that confront New England and often the nation. The livelier side of Boston can be found in the *Boston Phoenix,* a weekly tabloid, and the monthly magazine *Boston.*

TOURING NEW ENGLAND

By
WILLIAM G. SCHELLER

William G. Scheller, an adopted New Englander, has lived in Vermont and Massachusetts for more than 18 years. A frequent contributor to National Geographic Traveler, *the* Christian Science Monitor, *and numerous other regional and national publications, he has written five travel books, including* More Country Walks Near Boston *and* New York: Off the Beaten Path. *Mr. Scheller makes his home in Newbury, on Massachusetts's North Shore.*

Unquestionably the smallest homogenous region in the United States, New England at first seems to be the most easily approachable as well: There it is, appended like a crooked handle to the state of New York.

Well, it's only that simple if you want it to be. Once you start to think about New England, about how many approaches there really are and about how many different New Englands you find when you try them, you begin to wonder whether that word "homogenous" ought really to apply. Take the drive across the George Washington Bridge from New Jersey, for example; once you get past the Bronx and the suburbs of New York's Westchester County you still have a long way to go before you break the hold of Connecticut's "bedroom communities" and find a stretch of coast that might grace a calendar or a post card. Drive up the Hudson valley 50 or 100 miles before veering east into upland Connecticut or the Berkshire hills of Massachusetts, and you will find yet another New England—more like the picture books, perhaps, but nonetheless a nearly identical cousin to upstate New York.

What about New England the way a southbound Canadian might first encounter it? Take away the customs stations, and no one would know the difference. But when you come down out of the flatlands of the St. Lawrence Valley and cross the boundary into Vermont, it seems that for once nature has corroborated the political delineations: The broad plains give way to mountains, almost as abruptly as you can say, "I have nothing to declare." Much of Canada's border with Maine is quite another matter. Here you will find no difference at all between American pine trees and those which are subjects of Her Brittanic Majesty.

This leaves one more approach, and it is the oldest one of all. Very few modern travelers first reach New England by sea, but if we are to have any hope of understanding this place, of organizing a systematic approach to its many separate regions, we could do worse than to plot our explorations as the first white settlers did. We'll start where they did, as well. Boston is our choice, for Boston is the Hub of New England. Apologies to Plymouth, where English men and women were 10 years before they landed at Boston. But the Hub has spokes, and they make it convenient for us to branch out as we please, finding the different New Englands to which the highways lead.

Heading Down East

Let's start with a bit of confusion. When you leave Boston and head "Down East," you're not heading *south* along the New England coast (which, once you passed the Cape Cod Canal, would actually be west) but *north*. It all has something to do with sailing lingo and the direction of the winds. Just remember that when you leave Boston and set out for Maine—whether by sloop or station wagon—you're heading Down East.

Not that you get there right away. Although Massachusetts claimed Maine as a sort of colony's colony in the years before the Revolution, the two states are not contiguous, and you've a way to go from Boston before you even reach coastal New Hampshire, which separates the two states. To put yourself in the right frame of mind, try to build a little more time into your trip and take the side roads that meander along Massachusetts's North Shore. You'll be rewarded by the narrow streets and snug harbor of Marblehead, by the stately homes of Salem traders, and by the salt-sprayed, rocky coast of Cape Ann, where Gloucester and Rockport stand so far out to sea that they seem the very bowsprit of the state of Massachusetts.

Just past the mouth of the Merrimack River is the New Hampshire border. Newburyport, on the Massachusetts side of the border, and Portsmouth, 16 miles north on the New Hampshire side, are similar in many ways although Portsmouth is larger and, with its naval base, more cosmopolitan. Both cities were mercantile powerhouses in the heady days before the War of 1812; both are virtual museums of the elegantly chaste Federal architecture peculiar to this coast. Both, too, have used restoration and tourism to battle back from economic oblivion. If you're driving between Newburyport and Portsmouth, by the way, don't take I–95. Allow yourself the extra time to navigate the ocean-hugging curves of Route 1A, which are well worth the traffic you'll have to deal with (in summer) as you pass through the pleasantly tacky resorts of Salisbury and Hampton Beach.

Cross the Piscataqua at Portsmouth and you're in Maine. If you stay on Route 1, you'll know this is true because nowhere in the Western World, it seems, are there so many discount outlets. (They culminate north of Portland in the town of Freeport, once known primarily for L. L. Bean's

24-hour outdoor equipment emporium but now recognized as the outlet capital of the universe.) If you want the older Maine flavor, though, our advice is to stick to the coast, passing through York, Ogunquit, Kennebunkport, and the Rachel Carson National Wildlife Refuge. At Cape Elizabeth, just south of Portland, you can see the lighthouse at Two Lights made famous in the Edward Hopper painting. Next comes Casco Bay and the northernmost of the economic miracle cities of the New England coast.

Twenty years ago a lot of people thought Portland was going to give up and slide into the bay. A city of 70,000-plus is too big to be quaint, and the desolate Portland waterfront seemed almost beyond redemption. The downtown area held on, however, and with an influx of service and high-tech jobs came a healthy supply of the enthusiasm and money needed for rehabilitation. Waterfront buildings have been restored, retail businesses and restaurants have moved in, and it's no longer a joke to talk about buying a condo in Portland. It's a very attractive little city, with an excellent art museum and even—what greater indicator of urban-renewal success?—its very own Portland String Quartet.

Beyond Portland lies the real rockbound coast of Maine, and exploring it by car is largely a matter of making an innumerable series of right turns off Route 1. Each of these detours will take you to the end of a craggy little peninsula, often with even craggier islands beyond: This is a world of lonely lighthouses, towns made up of six white houses and a general store, and crooked little inlets where lobster boats and pleasure craft take refuge from the open Atlantic. The names are pure Maine: Boothbay Harbor, Wiscasset, and Damariscotta; Monhegan Island and tiny, remote Matinicus; Friendship, Camden, and Castine. Turn off Route 1 at Ellsworth to reach the most storied of Maine's coastal islands, Mt. Desert Island, site of the famous resort community of Bar Harbor and of lovely Acadia National Park (part of the park is on Isle au Haut, accessible by ferry from Stonington). A trip to Acadia should include a climb to the top of Cadillac Mountain, the first place in the United States to be touched by the rays of each morning's sun.

The Maine coast continues its tortuous, granite-ribbed way beyond Mt. Desert Island to Eastport and Lubec, where Quoddy Head stands as the easternmost point in the United States. Opposite Lubec is Campobello Island, beloved summer home of President Franklin D. Roosevelt. But that is another country, another time zone. If you've gotten this far, you've run out of Maine coast, and you've come even farther from Boston than mere distance would suggest.

Inland Maine

The interior of Maine is frequently disparaged, but while it is true that there are interminable piney stretches off I-95 or 201 or the back roads where trailer parks seem to be the prevailing mode of architectural expression and employment is seasonal at best, inland Maine is too varied simply to be written off as a northern Appalachia. Hard upon the New Hampshire border in the westernmost part of the state is the Rangeley Lakes country, with its rolling hills and splendid fishing. Farther north is enormous Moosehead Lake, 40 miles long, with its northern reaches extending into that part of Maine belonging largely to the paper companies that harvest the pines and issue visitors permits to drive gravel-surfaced logging roads to lakes and campsites as remote as anything the Northeast can offer. Yet not all of northern Maine is a private preserve set aside to feed the pulp mills. Baxter State Park, north of Millinocket, comprises 200,000 acres of virtual wilderness that includes Maine's highest peak, 5,268-foot Mt.

Katahdin. Beyond Baxter is the equally expansive Allagash Wilderness Waterway, extending from the very top of Maine and encompassing both shores of a river that canoeists throughout America dream of: the Allagash. Maine, to put it plainly, is an awfully big state, about as big as all the rest of New England. Driving the coast is a fine way to see some of its most dramatic scenery; but to skip the interior is to miss much of the state's substance—and its heart.

New Hampshire

We've already seen a tiny portion of New Hampshire in traversing its short coastline between Boston and Maine. But the seacoast is only one face of New Hampshire. To get to know the varied terrain and multifaceted character of the state, we turn inland from Portsmouth or, starting from Boston, take I–93 toward Manchester and branch out onto the byways.

We seldom think of the northern New England states in terms of industry—with the exception, perhaps, of the odiferous paper mills of the far north—but Manchester, New Hampshire, was once one of the industrial capitals of the United States and an international leader in the manufacture of textiles. The vast Amoskeag Mills, largely silent since the Great Depression and the migration of textile jobs to the South, still stand along the banks of the Merrimack River in downtown Manchester. And New Hampshire's largest city is far from idle: Along with Nashua and a growing belt of suburbs arrayed just north of the Massachusetts border, southern New Hampshire is gaining a reputation as "Route 128 north" because of its growing involvement in the field of high technology. This part of the Granite State has grown so quickly during the past fifteen years that many area residents are beginning to wonder if New Hampshire's traditional antipathy toward intensive zoning, strict environmental legislation, and state taxation can long survive the new population pressures. In any event, visitors wishing to experience the rural New Hampshire that inspired longtime resident Robert Frost will have to venture farther north and west, past the state capital of Concord and into the rolling hills of the Connecticut valley beyond Keene. There is lovely scenery in the southwest corner of the state, where 3,165-foot Mt. Monadnock (just off Route 124) offers a strenuous day's hike and magnificent summit views.

The central section of New Hampshire offers a variety of attractions for the traveler. A drive up the Connecticut valley will bring you to the pretty village of Cornish, where the artist Maxfield Parrish and the sculptor Augustus St. Gaudens lived and worked, and to Hanover, home of Dartmouth College and its Winter Carnival. Farther east, the towns of Laconia and Meredith are the gateways to Lake Winnipesaukee, the state's largest lake. There's a fine state beach near Glendale, and a cruise on the excursion boat *Mt. Washington* is still as much fun as it was back in the days of her steam-powered, paddle-wheeled predecessor.

When you have come this far north in New Hampshire, clear skies will have granted you glimpses of majestic Mt. Washington itself. New England's tallest (6,288 feet) mountain, the lord of the Presidential Range, towers over a wilderness fastness that has been attracting visitors since the first of the White Mountains resorts opened in the mid-1800s and steam trains from Boston carried frock-coated and corseted vacationers out to "take the air" for a month or more at a time. Few of us have that much leisure time to spare nowadays, but it would be a pity to limit a White Mountains experience to a day's drive along Route 302 (hideously overdeveloped between Conway and North Conway) or the beautiful but frequently traffic-jammed Kancamagus Highway. Anyone with the time and the constitution ought to get out and hike among these mountains. The Appalachian Mountain Club, headquartered at Pinkham Notch, maintains an inviting chain of huts a day's hike apart and sells detailed guides to the region's network of trails, some of them leading through federally designated wilderness areas. As for Mt. Washington itself—well, it is a formidable climb. You won't need ropes and carabiners, but you *will* need strong legs, a good lunch, and a healthy appreciation of the capriciousness of the weather. The strongest winds on earth, well over 200 miles per hour, have been recorded on the summit, and the local climate can quickly turn nasty even on the lower slopes. If you want the summit without the work, take the auto road—or better yet, the steam-powered Mt. Washington Cog Railway.

North of the White Mountains, New Hampshire grows narrow, hemmed in by the Connecticut River and the Maine border. This is beautiful country, forested and remote like northern Maine, and it's worthwhile to press ahead along Routes 16 and 3 toward the Canadian border. Some of New England's best fishing is found in this northernmost corner of the state, in the string of Connecticut lakes that make up the headwaters of the Connecticut River. This is the old north woods of fly rods and Adirondack chairs, dinner bells at rustic lodges, and poker games around the fire. And it's a long, long way from the mills of Manchester and the suburbs along the Massachusetts border.

Vermont

Ask someone who has never been to New England to picture the place, and it's a safe bet that if he doesn't conjure up the bricks of Boston or the rockbound coast of Maine, his image will be a village in Vermont. Few of our national icons since the days of Currier and Ives have changed as little as that village, and few are as accessible to us today. Of course, things may not be what they seem on the surface; the fellow sitting in that white house on the town common may be a consultant from New York working on a home computer, and the farmer down the road may milk his herd on behalf of an absentee owner. Yet appearances count for a great deal in this state, precisely because people have worked so hard to keep them what they are. Vermont is a state its residents believe in, even if they've just arrived last year or are here only for the summer.

You'll have to work a bit at getting to Vermont. The only quick overland route is I–91, which follows the Connecticut valley from Connecticut and Massachusetts; if you're setting out from our hypothetical starting point of Boston, you'll have to follow Route 2 or poke through the hill towns of southwestern New Hampshire. Vermont's Route 9 is the picturesque trail through the southernmost part of the state, where the Hoosac Range of the Berkshires rises into the Green Mountains; it begins at Brattleboro, on the Connecticut River, and extends westward to Bennington. Both are fine old towns, and both offer access to quick routes north if you can't wait to hit the slopes. But to collect a string of some of the prettiest Vermont villages, head to Wilmington, halfway between Brattleboro and Bennington, and begin winding your way north on Route 100.

Wardsboro, Jamaica, Londonderry, Weston—here are the white steeples, general stores, village greens, and cozy inns so familiar to the mind's eye. To the east lie a tangle of country roads and more pretty towns, while to the west ranges the worn, wooded spine of Vermont, the Green Mountains. By the time you get to Weston, you will also have passed roads leading to Mt. Snow, Stratton, Magic Mountain, Bromley, and some of the finest skiing in America. All this, and Killington, Sugarbush, and Stowe yet to come! Take the time, if you can, to ride one of the chairlifts or gondolas even when there's no snow on the ground. It's an especially fine way to see the fall foliage without being part of a 15-mile-per-hour "leaf-peeker" motorcade.

About a third of the way up the state Route 100 reaches Plymouth, sacred ground to old-school Vermonters who venerate the place as the hometown of Calvin Coolidge. In fact, Silent Cal made his name in Massachusetts, and some of us prefer our Green Mountain virtues as exemplified by the late Senator George Aiken.

Just beyond Plymouth you will reach Route 4 and face several choices. (In the best of all possible worlds, you would stay in Vermont an extra week and choose all of them.) You can continue north on 100 or Route 12, along the eastern slope of the Green Mountains, enjoying gorgeous upland scenery and a succession of small towns until you reach the state capital at Montpelier. Or you can head east, drive through spectacular Queechee Gorge near White River Junction, and set out through the gentle hills of the upper Connecticut valley. Last but not least, you can take Route 4 east through Rutland and explore the lush dairy country of the Champlain valley.

Lake Champlain forms a good two-thirds of the western border of Vermont. Narrow, almost riverlike for nearly half its length, the lake is nevertheless bridged at only one point—a reminder, perhaps, of Vermont's ancient distrust of the "Yorkers" against whose land claims Ethan Allen fought so furiously. Allen, incidentally, launched his famous raid on Fort Ticonderoga from the Vermont side of Lake Champlain. In our day, the Champlain valley of Vermont is the state's prime dairyland. There was a time, hardly twenty-five years ago, when it was said of Vermont that there were "more cows than people." Since then the smaller herds on the hill farms have proved less and less profitable, and the biggest dairy farms are now located on the fertile lowlands near the lake. This doesn't mean that you won't see gentle, black-and-white Holstein cattle along most Vermont roadsides.

The most scenic road through the Champlain valley is Route 22A, but if you'd like to mix rural sightseeing with a look at one of New England's more inviting college towns, leave 22A at Bridport and take Route 125 to Middlebury. The gracious buildings of Middlebury College lend character to the town without overwhelming it, and a stately red brick inn stands near the green. (Not far from here, in East Middlebury, is the Waybury Inn, the exterior of which is used to represent the inn on TV's *Newhart.*)

Just as New Hampshire gets narrower as you go farther north, Vermont gets wider. Once you find yourself north of Middlebury and Montpelier, it's a good idea to think in terms of east-west rather than north-south travel. A good place to use as a base of operations is Burlington, Vermont's largest city, built on a hillside overlooking Lake Champlain. Burlington is a college town—the home of the University of Vermont and its medical school—with a lively, pedestrian-oriented downtown bustling with shops and restaurants. Whatever else you do here, make sure you go to Battery Park to watch the sun set over the Adirondacks, with Lake Champlain in the foreground. William Dean Howells called it the most beautiful sunset in America.

If you head north and east out of Burlington, you can explore the Lake Champlain islands of North and South Hero, with their quiet villages and farms, and then swing back eastward to St. Albans, where a big maple sugar festival is held each spring. Hugging the Canadian border, you may continue east to Newport, at the southern end of 33-mile-long Lake Mephramagog (superb fishing here), and on into the loneliest part of Vermont, the Northeast Kingdom. In this realm of mountains, forests, and isolated farms, there are actually townships where no one lives; even in some places where there are people, there was no electricity until after 1960. Head back to civilization by way of St. Johnsbury, where there is a museum of the maple industry, and take Routes 2, 15, and 100 to Stowe, the quintessential ski resort in the shadow of Mt. Mansfield. Route 100? Yes, the very same. Now you can head south and catch the places you missed on the way up.

Massachusetts

Massachusetts is more than Boston. The whole state lies west of the Hub—but don't head straight for the Berkshires without making a few stops within an hour's drive of Boston. You might wish to begin your westward peregrinations by visiting the places where two American Revolutions began, in Lowell and at Lexington and Concord.

Lowell? Yes, the American Industrial Revolution began here when a group of smart Boston capitalists decided that the powerful flow of the Merrimack River could be put to work turning the machinery of textile mills. The racket of the power looms has all but ceased now, and the old mill buildings and indeed all of downtown Lowell have been reborn as components of an imaginative national historical park. As you tour Lowell, think of the soldiers in this revolution: the mill hands, men and women from up-country Yankee farms and Canadian villages and all the countries of Europe, who built this country as surely as did John Adams and Paul Revere.

We all know about the Revolution that began in earnest at Lexington and Concord after its fires had smoldered for many years in the streets and meeting halls of Boston. Here the Minuteman National Historical Park commemorates the events of April 19, 1775, when farmers and villagers fought British regulars at Lexington Green and by Concord's "rude bridge that arched the flood." Comfortable suburbs now, these towns once reeked of musket fire. Concord gained even greater fame in the following century, when it became identified with the work of such residents as Ralph Waldo Emerson, Henry David Thoreau, and Nathaniel Hawthorne.

Follow Route 2 westward along the northern tier of the state, through a skein of towns and small cities where Yankee craftsmen have made everything from combs (Leominster) to chairs (Gardner) to tools (Miller's Falls). South of Athol, about a half-century ago, they also made a reservoir, the vast Quabbin, by evacuating and flooding four towns. Dubbed by one author an "accidental wilderness," the considerable tract of land that makes up the Quabbin watershed is a naturalists's paradise that offers the sight of eagles on the wing.

At the point where Route 2 meets the Connecticut River you will reach the town of Greenfield, with Deerfield just to the south. The site of terrible, French-incited Indian raids at the close of the seventeenth and the beginning of the eighteenth centuries, Deerfield was abandoned throughout the remainder of the colonial period; today it contains not only a priceless collection of period homes but also the prestigious Deerfield Academy, a preparatory school. The valley of the Connecticut south of here is called the Pioneer Valley, in honor of the settlers who came here when it seemed as far from Boston as Idaho does today; the Deerfield attacks notwithstanding, they stayed and built the valley towns of Northampton, Holyoke, Amherst, and Springfield. You might opt to head south into the valley along Route 5, beginning at Greenfield, and continue west if you have

the time. Route 2 from Greenfield to Williamstown is the Mohawk Trail
(200 years ago it was a pathway to New York and Mohawk territory),
and it is a fine route to take into the approaching Berkshires.

Although some will call them mountains, the Berkshires are really hills
in physiognomy and disposition. This is a gentle landscape that has long
known the hand of man, although we are fortunate that the touch has been
light and, for the most part, respectful. Williamstown, at the very northwestern corner of Massachusetts, is the home of Williams College and a
town that seems to have been designed by a Hollywood prop department
for a 30s campus movie. But touch the bricks: they're real, and the art
museum and summer theater you'll find here are as good as any in New
England.

Although Route 7 is virtually the Main Street of the Berkshires and
can be used for a quick trip south to Pittsfield, Stockbridge, and Great
Barrington, this part of the state invites back-road meandering more than
any other. Just south of Williamstown is 3,491-foot Mt. Greylock, highest
point in Massachusetts, standing entirely within a forested state reservation. At Hancock, on the New York State line, an entire village is devoted
to the lives and artisanship of the Shakers, and just outside of Pittsfield
is a farmhouse called Arrowhead, where a different craft was practiced:
Here a 30-year-old New Yorker sat at his desk, looked out at the Berkshire
hills that reminded him of rolling waves, and wrote *Moby Dick*. Herman
Melville was but one of a number of writers who made their summer
homes in the Berkshires in the mid-nineteenth century; Oliver Wendell
Holmes, Sr., and Nathaniel Hawthorne also had lodgings hereabouts.

Today's Berkshires are known largely as a summer capital of music,
dance, and drama, and the greatest of all the seasonal festivals commences
each June when the Boston Symphony Orchestra takes up residence at
Tanglewood. Pack a picnic (the real show-offs bring silver candlesticks),
bring a blanket, and sit under the stars while Seiji Ozawa and company
provide the evening's entertainment. Next day, drive down to Stockbridge
and take in the Norman Rockwell Museum. Highbrow, middlebrow, it's
all in the Berkshires.

If you've held off on that Pioneer Valley visit so far, take Route 20 or
the Massachusetts Turnpike back east into Springfield. Here is an old industrial city—guns, machine tools, even Indian motorcycles—that is alive
and well, with a first-rate assemblage of museums at its core and even the
National Basketball Hall of Fame. On the way back to Boston visit Old
Sturbridge Village, a working re-creation of preindustrial New England,
and the city of Worcester with its fine museums of art and science and
the collections of the American Antiquarian Society. By the time the Boston skyline appears at the end of the Pike, it may seem as if "Hub of the
Universe" is an afterthought to the rest of Massachusetts.

Down to the Cape

There is a perennial rivalry in Massachusetts between the North and
South shores that simmers to the surface in the *Boston Globe* every few
years. Basically it involves North Shore types who boast of the ancient
maritime prowess of Salem and Newburyport, the Brahmin estates of Cape
Ann, and an altogether more important place in the world. South Shore
partisans, for their part, dismiss the North-of-Boston crowd as a bunch
of stuffed shirts who go fox hunting, and point to the quiet, irreproachable
traditions of the Quincy Adamses and the *Mayflower* lineage of Plymouth.
Having been to the North Shore on our way to Portsmouth and points

north, we'll just have to head in the other direction and make up our minds for ourselves—or at least come as close as we can without moving here.

The first thing a visitor notices when setting out from Boston on the Southeast Expressway on a weekday morning is that an awful lot of people commute into the city from the South Shore. Yet the place does have a history and a character and important points of interest that exist quite apart from the briefcase and carpool crowd.

The first thing is to get *off* that expressway—at least after you've gotten as far as Quincy and the Adams National Historical Site. Here is the birthplace and burial place of two American presidents and the family seat of a clan that has had more impact on American politics and intellectual life than any other. Adams furniture, books, and personal possessions are preserved at the site.

Now follow Route 3A down through the coastal towns from Hingham to Duxbury and take whatever side roads will lead you to Massachusetts Bay. Cohasset, Scituate, and especially Duxbury are charming seacoast towns with gracious, weathered-shingle homes and fine ocean views. The major stop along this seaside trail is Plymouth, which calls itself "America's Home Town." It is just that, even though a good many more of us came by way of Ellis Island than the *Mayflower*. The Pilgrims did indeed land here, perhaps even stepping onto Plymouth Rock. You can see the Rock at Plymouth, along with the Pilgrims' burial ground, a replica of the *Mayflower* that actually made the Atlantic crossing 30 years ago, and Plimoth Plantation, one of the best-researched and most fascinating period villages in the United States.

Once past Plymouth, you are on your way to the Cape. This is cranberry country, sandy, scrubby, and low. You might stop at South Carver to see how the berries are grown (by way of a ride on the narrow-gauge Edaville Railroad) or wander through the pine barrens of Myles Standish State Forest. But chances are that by now you've got the Cape on your mind—and there it is, just the other side of the Sagamore Bridge over the Cape Cod Canal.

Cape Cod has fascinated landsmen ever since Henry David Thoreau visited, found it to be a place of poor farmers and fishermen, and walked the great beach that bares itself to the Atlantic between Nauset and Provincetown. If Thoreau were to come back today, he would find the beach much the same (although, thanks to erosion, his actual route would be several hundred feet out to sea), and no doubt he would be awestruck at the extent to which the rest of the world has discovered this isolated bit of glacial moraine and barrier beach. For many of us, discovering or annually rediscovering the Cape has become a matter of finding those places that haven't become *too* built up, *too* well acquainted with the droves of summer (and, increasingly, off-season) visitors. As a general rule, assume that the heavier concentrations of resort development lie along the south (Nantucket Sound) shore of the Upper Cape—that is, the part closer to the mainland.

Some of the prettier, less modernized towns are Chatham, on the Atlantic at the very elbow; Brewster, near the elbow's inside crook; and Wellfleet, on the bay side at the bulge in the forearm. As for unspoiled beaches, the finest on the Cape—and perhaps the most beautiful in America—are along the ocean side of the Lower Cape, the part beyond the elbow. Here President Kennedy created the Cape Cod National Seashore; here development is mercifully forbidden. The dunes, sand cliffs, and beaches of Eastham, Wellfleet, Truro, and the Province Lands at Provincetown are as pristine and elementally gorgeous as they were in Thoreau's day.

Provincetown stands at the very tip of the Cape, its crafts boutiques clustered along Commercial Street more thickly than the fish-drying racks Thoreau remarked on when he passed this way. Among them are the motels and bed and breakfasts and gay bars and seafood restaurants that make a bicycle the only logical transportation here—and perhaps make some of the natives long for the first nor'easters of October. Yet underneath it all it is a pretty little village. Try to savor it in the off-season, as a quaint old fishing port.

South of the Upper Cape lie the islands of Martha's Vineyard and Nantucket. You can fly to them or reach them by ferry (make your car reservations well in advance, in summer); the Vineyard is a short trip, Nantucket is 30 miles out to sea. For a first visit travelers will most likely choose one island or the other, so it might help to know that they aren't exactly alike.

Martha's Vineyard is bigger, it has a more varied landscape, and there are more year-round residents. There are, consequently, more year-round settlements—the towns of Vineyard Haven, Oak Bluffs, Tisbury, and Edgartown. Edgartown is the posh spot on the island, with sea captains' great white mansions and docks lined with the "if-you-have-to-ask-you-can't-afford-one" class of boats. The back roads are delightful, especially by bicycle, and the colorful Gay Head cliffs at sunset are one of the most breathtaking sights in all New England. But just a few miles away the interior of the island has an up-country rather than a nautical feel to it; here there are farms, a working winery, and a dense, piney state forest.

You never feel far from the ocean on Nantucket, and you aren't. The beauty here is spare, never lush, but all the more intense for that. And there is only one town, only one settlement that doesn't close up after Labor Day. Nantucket town, once the greatest whaling port in the world (as you may have read in Melville) is one of the most complete case studies in historic preservation you are likely to find anywhere. One suspects that a proposed doghouse or toolshed would have to be shingled in the cedar that grows silvery with time. The style does blend nicely, though, with the serene beauty of the moors that make up much of the scenery on Nantucket. This is bicycling country too, with ocean vistas never more than a few miles in any direction. For the island's most spectacular day trip, though, you'll have to walk. Park at the end of Wauwinet Road and trudge through the sand to Great Point; at the lighthouse the ocean nearly surrounds you, and you come to understand Nantucket for what it is.

Rhode Island

Rhode Island has the same sort of image problem that New Jersey has: People think of it as a place that you pass through rather than visit on its own, and their recollections of that passage are often of an aging industrial zone followed by miles of nondescript suburbs and countryside.

This isn't really fair. Rhode Island actually packs a lot of variety into a very small area; it has history, miles of lovely seacoast, and, in Providence, an urban center that has come impressively back to life over the past 10 years. If you're really intent on seeing New England, don't skip Rhode Island, and don't just pass through.

When you drive from Boston, Worcester, or New Bedford, your introduction to Rhode Island will most likely be Providence. Don't be put off by the faded industrial neighborhoods you'll see from the interstate highway; the best approach to the city is to head right downtown, put your car in a garage, and set out on foot. Be sure to see the state capitol, with its magnificent unsupported marble dome (there are only four of these in the world); the campus of Brown University, off Prospect Street, with its many eighteenth-century structures; and the beautifully restored Georgian and Federal period houses of Benefit Street. Within a single square mile of downtown Providence it is possible to lose any impressions you may have had of the city as a drab, workaday place.

If any place in Rhode Island has wide name recognition throughout the rest of the country, that place must be Newport. Newport, which stands at the approach to Narragansett Bay from Rhode Island Sound, was a major colonial seaport. Impressive as some of the old sea captains' homes may be, however, it was a later building spree that put this place on the map. In the years just after the Civil War, new business opportunities made it possible for a handful of families to make more money than it had ever been thought possible to make in America, and a lot of that money was translated into brick and stone along Newport's Bellevue Avenue overlooking Rhode Island Sound. This is where the multimillionaires of America's Gilded Age built their summer "cottages"—The Breakers, The Elms, Château-sur-Mer, Marble House, and a host of other palaces. Since no one can afford to live this way today—if they can, they consider it imprudent to do it so conspicuously—the great houses are open to the public, who for the small price of admission are free to tour the halls and salons. Newport's other claim to fame is yacht racing. And from 1851 to 1983 the America's Cup races were all held in the waters off Newport.

If Newport seems a little busy but you'd still like the flavor of a small seaside town, head across the bridge to Jamestown. It's less crowded and developed, although no longer as pleasantly remote as it was before the bridge went up in the late 1960s. Many locals resent the fact that Conanicut Island, on which Jamestown is located, is now so easily accessible from Newport and mainland points.

It's not likely that they'll ever build a bridge to Block Island, which lies almost 10 miles out to sea off the south coast of Rhode Island and is accessible by ferry from several points within the state as well as from New London, Connecticut. Block Island is tiny—roughly three by five miles, though less than a mile across at the neck just north of town—and inhabited, after the last ferry leaves, by only as many people as can fit into a small collection of inns and guest houses. Block Island has been left purposely underdeveloped, and thus it will appeal to those who think that things have gotten a bit too landlubberish even on Martha's Vineyard and Nantucket.

Connecticut

New Englanders of a more curmudgeonly stamp occasionally talk about ceding Connecticut to the Middle Atlantic States, but the fact is that no good Yankee should want to give up a territory named for a bit of trading chicanery. The accepted derivation of Connecticut's sobriquet, the Nutmeg State, has to do with the practice of selling wooden nutmegs as the real thing. No one is impugning the state's present-day business ethics—after all, they make nuclear submarines for the navy in New London—but the wooden nutmeg story does have a certain devilish charm.

If you're coming down coast from Boston you'll probably enter Connecticut via Route I–95 at Westerly, Rhode Island (there's a charming resort just south of here at Watch Hill, Rhode Island). Get off the interstate and follow the signs for Mystic, at the Mystic River estuary on Long Island Sound. Here's where you'll find Mystic Seaport, which does for the seafaring life of the early nineteenth century what Massachusetts's Old Sturbridge Village does for the inland farming towns. The Seaport has a fine collection of old sailing vessels, chief among them the venerable whaler *Charles W. Morgan.* Dockside structures suggest the life of a shipbuilding town of 150 years ago, and the Seaport's galleries are filled with maritime art and artifacts.

Between New London and New Haven the shore roads are worth turning onto; near Madison, Hamonasset Beach State Park offers fine swimming in the temperate waters of Long Island Sound. Beyond New Haven the coast tends to get a bit more built up—but let's not get ahead of ourselves. New Haven itself should be our next major stop, involving as it does the attraction of one of America's oldest and most prestigious institutions of higher learning, Yale University. The best way to see Yale is to take a guided tour, offered without charge, and the art and natural history museums and those parts of the libraries open to the public can easily provide a day or two of diversion. Even if you have only a few hours at your disposal, by all means take a walk around the Yale campus. This is one of the nation's great troves of collegiate Gothic architecture, dating from a time early in this century when Oxford and Cambridge were taken for physical as well as spiritual models for American universities.

North from New Haven is the Connecticut capital of Hartford, a busy city on the Connecticut River that seems always to have been in the insurance business. It is the headquarters of a good many companies that write policies on our lives and property, yet another business that is still located here offered another form of "insurance" to the men who tamed the west a hundred years ago and more. The Colt Patent Arms Company, now a component of Colt Industries, made and still makes the famous Colt revolvers of which it was said, "God made all men, but Colonel Colt made them equal." You can see an impressive collection of Colt firearms at downtown's Baldwin Museum of Connecticut History, and then balance your Hartford experience within the more pacific confines of the Wadsworth Atheneum. The Atheneum, the nation's oldest public art museum, houses American and European works and an archaeological collection as well. Finally, don't leave Hartford without a visit to the Mark Twain House, an extravagant Victorian confection in which the author spent the happiest years of his life.

West of Hartford, toward the northwestern corner of Connecticut, the rising hills and small towns present prospects reminiscent of Massachusetts's Berkshires. And in the state's northeastern section (once again, stay off the monotonous track of the interstate highway, in this case I–84) you'll find the least-explored and perhaps least-developed part of Connecticut. Towns like Brooklyn, Eastford, and Windham are the very stuff of everyday New England, without the cachet (and the summer crowds) of the Berkshires, Massachusetts North Shore, or Vermont.

Boston: Past and Present

And so we return to Boston, the New England metropolis that has been inventing and re-inventing itself for almost 360 years. The past decade of that long span has served to make the task of discovering Boston more difficult than ever; ironically, what was once thought of as the most staid and "finished" of American cities has become increasingly tricky to pin down. The historical shrines along the Freedom Trail—the Old State House and Old South Meeting House, King's Chapel and Faneuil Hall—are surrounded today by forests of skyscrapers that many critics say represent the "Manhattanization" of Boston. The old Italian North End is slowly "going condo"; the Back Bay is becoming known more for its shopping and chic restaurants than for its quiet residential blocks and their superlative architecture.

For many travelers, it is this very dynamic newness that by now has come to express the essence of Boston. Those who look for something older may have to do a bit more work and exercise a little more imagination, but the traditional city remains if they want it. To these readers we suggest a walk through the city on a Sunday afternoon in the spring or fall, preferably when the weather isn't perfect—a walk that should begin on Beacon Hill and take in the littlest side streets; wind past Government Center to take in the back corners of the North End, where ancient monuments like Paul Revere's House and the Old North Church crop up at the turn of a step; and continue through the vacant downtown streets, through the Common and Public Garden and along a Beacon Street that still belongs to the ghost of Oliver Wendell Holmes. As afternoon shadows lengthen, walk along the Charles River toward Harvard Square as Archibald MacLeish did on the night he decided to become a poet rather than a lawyer. Cross the river into Cambridge and consider what possessed men to build a college in the wilderness. Boston and all New England were built that way, too, and we're lucky to have so much left of them.

CONNECTICUT

By
ALMA ESHENFELDER

A member of the Society of American Travel Writers and the New York Travel Writers Association, Alma Eshenfelder has had many travel articles published. Her radio program "Travel Time" has been broadcast weekly since 1971.

"The Constitution State" is the legend that appears on Connecticut license plates, a reminder that Connecticut's Fundamental Orders, adopted in 1639, were the basis for Connecticut's Constitution, a model for the other states, and an influence on the writing of the Constitution of the United States.

The original settlers of Connecticut emigrated from the Massachusetts Bay Colony in 1633–1634 in search of rich lands for farming. The northern and middle sections of the state provided the land, and the colony was established. Connecticut was one of the 13 original states, and it was the fifth to ratify the U.S. Constitution—on January 9, 1788.

From the beginning, commercial history records the first banks established in Hartford, New London, and New Haven in 1792, indicating the development of business interests and their requirements. Three years later the Mutual Assurance Company of the City of Norwich was incorporated, another first for the state.

At the turn of the century, in 1802, Waterbury's brass industry began, while other factories making muskets and textiles were opening up in other parts of the state. And vast numbers of other products followed.

Newspapers in Norwich (1796) and New Haven (1812) began publication and continue to this day, although with name changes. The *Hartford Courant* which started in 1764 has the oldest record for continuous publication.

Industry

Connecticut is a small state—in New England, only Rhode Island is smaller—but it is a rich state, ranking second in per capita income in 1983 according to the U.S. Census Bureau. Its prosperity is attributed to the steady growth of the state's economy.

In this century Connecticut has been known chiefly for its industrial development. The coastal areas were highly attractive to industry because water transportation was handily available for imports of raw materials and the shipment of exports abroad. During the past decade, Fairfield County, in Southwestern Connecticut, has boomed as major corporate headquarters relocated themselves here and gave Stamford's skyline the look of a large city. New hotel construction has added to the trend. New London County has also seen an influx of research and development work, much of it associated with Electric Boat, a division of General Dynamics in Groton, builders of the nation's nuclear-powered submarines, and United Technology Corporation in Hartford, predominant in providing the needs of the aerospace programs.

Pharmaceutical research and development is noteworthy at the ever-expanding Pfizer plant in Groton. Danbury, once noted for its hat factories, is better known today as headquarters for Union Carbide. Brass continues to be associated with Waterbury. Hartford rightfully lays claim to being the "insurance capital of the United States." Aetna, Travelers, and Prudential insurance companies have their headquarters here, and their landmark office buildings are architecturally acclaimed.

The Military Influx

Military bases have brought thousands of families to the New London and Groton communities. The U.S. Navy Submarine Base is on the east side of the Thames River north of Groton. The U.S. Naval Underwater Systems Center is in New London; the work here of marine scientists is in the pursuit of world peace through undersea research, investigations, and problem-solving.

The U.S. Coast Guard Academy's beautiful campus is in New London on the west side of the Thames River. It is one of four U.S. military academies; West Point, Annapolis, and the Air Force Academy are the others. The Coast Guard Academy has the distinction, however, of being the only one where admission is by competitive examination. This is a four-year coeducational institution with the degree of Bachelor of Science and the officer's rank of Ensign awarded at graduation. The U.S. Coast Guard's Research and Development Center is at Avery Point in Groton, near the mouth of the river.

Educational Institutions

Across the highway from the Coast Guard Academy is Connecticut College, a four-year coeducational liberal arts college that will reach its century mark in a couple of decades.

Colleges and universities throughout the state predate Connecticut College—some by centuries. Oldest is Yale, chartered in 1701 and located in

New Haven since 1717. Only two other universities in the United States are older than Yale.

Two of Connecticut's other well-known educational institutions with noble histories and notable alumni are Trinity College in Hartford, established in 1823, and Wesleyan University in Middletown, founded in 1831.

The state today has numerous other exceptional colleges, universities (most with excellent postgraduate advantages), and junior and community colleges, as well as technical schools and preparatory academies. They attract students from around the world, and in their wake come parents, friends, and contemporaries who become enamored of the scenery, climate, or the other advantages of southern New England.

Connecticut's development and growth has tremendously increased city and suburban populations. Municipal services and schools have had to expand to meet community needs. Real estate values have burgeoned and homes at any price are in short supply. Condominiums have mushroomed throughout the state.

Connecticut's Second Largest Industry

Tourism has far exceeded the $2.5 billion annual goal once eagerly sought by state officials. Employment in the tourist industry, although seasonal in some areas, is generally constant because this is a four-season state.

Winter sports at several ski areas bring in skiers from surrounding states and beyond. Night skiing at some areas provides evening exercise, and on weekends the slopes are extremely popular, especially with families.

Foliage tours in autumn have long attracted tour groups to New England, and Connecticut takes second place to no other state for the beauties of this season. The Connecticut River valley is especially beautiful, with the regal colors of the changing woodlands often reflected in the calm waters of the Connecticut River. Litchfield County and the hills in the northern half of the state vie for attention during autumn.

Southern Connecticut is generally associated with summer activities because of its 253 miles of shoreline which borders Long Island Sound. This is the season for yachtsmen, sports fishermen, swimmers, sun-worshippers, and anyone looking for boat trips. A few hours on the river, a day-long cruise out on the sound, an island-hopping cruise that might last a full week—all are available from ports along the coast.

Beaches in general are privately owned or reserved for town residents and their guests. New London, however, has a municipally owned public beach at Ocean Beach Park. (Nonresidents of the city pay a small fee.) And the state has three excellent public beaches on Long Island Sound: Rocky Neck in East Lyme, Hammonasset Beach in Madison, and Sherwood State Park in Westport.

Golf courses and public and private clubs are scattered from one end of the state to the other, and most of them welcome visiting players. Early reservations must be arranged, particularly in Fairfield and Hartford counties, where more and more golfers come from outside the immediate areas.

Other participant sports and many spectator sports have schedules throughout the year. Spectator sports—for which legal gambling is available—include jai alai, teletrack, and dog racing. Football, basketball, and hockey tournaments are held in Connecticut. Baseball, soccer, diving, and swimming competitions add to the Connecticut sports scene.

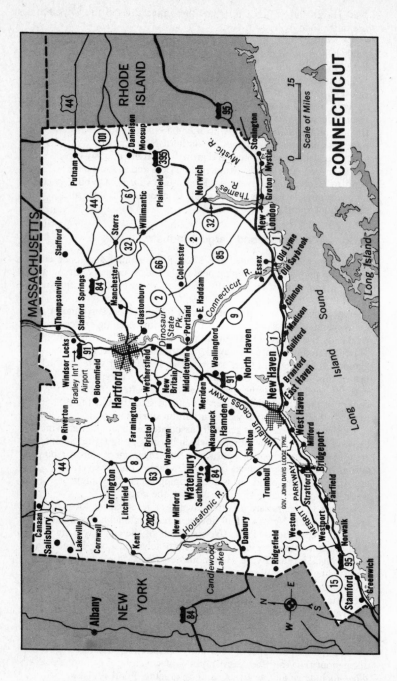

CONNECTICUT

Cultural Attractions

Museums, nature centers, and specialized attractions have been popular in Connecticut over the centuries. The Wadsworth Atheneum in Hartford is one of the oldest public art museums in the United States. Peabody Museum in New Haven is a natural history museum with a vast collection.

Theaters, theme parks, zoos, symphonies, ballet companies, specialized libraries, children's museums, planetariums, public gardens, and train and trolley museums are attractions of which Connecticut is proud.

In 1986, the Mashantucket Pequot Indian tribe introduced high-stakes bingo to Connecticut with the opening of a bingo hall with seats for more than 1,600 people in Ledyard, just north of Groton. It has thrived since its opening and is a mecca for players from throughout New England and the mid-Atlantic states. Package tours that include weekends of play have contributed to the economy through patronage at hotels and restaurants and side trips to the many tourist attractions in the vicinity. Profits from this enterprise are earmarked for a multimillion-dollar museum dedicated to the Indians of the Northeast and their culture. It will also be located on the Ledyard reservation.

Traveling through Connecticut

Although highways in Connecticut have been upgraded and major expressways extend east from New York State to Rhode Island and north from New Haven to Massachusetts, portions of the state are still served only by secondary roads. These roads encounter beautiful scenery as they traverse rural areas and pass through country towns and villages; they give a boost to sightseeing in Connecticut.

Transportation from city to town or town to metropolitan areas outside the state is not always simple when public transportation is required. However, Amtrak's routes along the shoreline between New York and Boston and from New Haven to Springfield, Massachusetts, have convenient schedules. Metro-North, a commuter line running between New Haven and New York, provides necessary transfers to the northern suburbs. On another route it serves the Litchfield Hills.

Bus or motor coach transportation is available to some destinations, but there is limited service in suburban areas. Going diagonally across the state would take time, patience, and considerable planning.

Bradley Airport in Windsor Locks is a newly enlarged facility with service of about 20 major airlines; using this airport is a pleasure, but getting there during commuter hours can be nerve-wracking because of the heavy traffic in and out of Hartford.

Ferry service across Long Island Sound continues, weather permitting, year-round to Fishers Island and Orient Point, New York, from New London. Block Island Service from New London is seasonal, as is service to Port Jefferson, New York, from Bridgeport.

Seasons determine touring patterns in Connecticut as each section of the state is noted for its own seasonal attractions. Although winter is winter and summer is summer, the temperature and amount of precipitation vary throughout the state. Northern Connecticut is several degrees cooler in winter, with snow and ice longer lasting; below-zero temperatures do occur in January and February but are seldom continuous for long periods of time.

Because of the proximity to Long Island Sound, foggy conditions are often prevalent in the coastal areas. Humidity in July and August can be annoying—especially during the day, when temperatures reach 90° F. and above.

Perhaps the ideal seasons to visit Connecticut are spring and autumn, when average temperatures are in the high 60s and low 70s. Rainy days are associated with the equinox; hurricanes that have passed through Connecticut occurred in late August and September.

If you wish, you can select your itinerary with an eye on the calendar. Connecticut's Division of Tourism in the Department of Economic Development (210 Washington St., Hartford 06106) has several "tour loops" in its *Vacation Guide,* which is sent on request and offers a wealth of information for visitors to the state. These prescribed routes have been carefully designed with points of interest along the way described, albeit briefly. A state map is available for the asking; it includes valuable supplementary material for a visitor.

Accommodations in Connecticut include deluxe hotels, a wide range of motels, country inns, guest houses, and bed-and-breakfast homes. The state offers excellent restaurants in metropolitan areas as well as in rural areas and along the coast in seaside towns.

Seasonal Attractions

In autumn country fairs and colorful displays at roadside stands combined with ideal weather and "leaf-looking" bring scores of out-of-state visitors to the rural areas. Antique shows and sales are a year-round attraction. Christmas season events are scheduled everywhere, and carol-singing accompanies the tree-lighting ceremonies. In spring the dogwood blooms and the mountain laurel, the state flower, gives the roadsides a blush of pink. Daffodils appear in meadows and rows of tulips in residential areas— forerunners of the June roses that are a sight to behold in public gardens such as Elizabeth Park in Hartford and Mohegan Park in Norwich.

Summer is a time for the seashore and picnics; the state highway department has established picnic areas along the highways for the convenience of travelers.

General information about Connecticut can be obtained from the Governor's State Information Bureau, 800–842–2220.

Exploring Connecticut

SOUTHWESTERN CONNECTICUT:
FAIRFIELD COUNTY

Southwestern Connecticut, with shoreline and rural towns, borders New York State and has long been a virtual suburb of New York City. Commuters have traveled via local trains between Grand Central Station in Manhattan and the shoreline and rural towns for decades. The Connecticut Turnpike (I–95), called the Governor John Davis Lodge Turnpike since October 1, 1986, and the Merritt Parkway (Rte. 15) carry steady commuter traffic to and from New York.

The Shoreline—Greenwich to Milford

Entry into Connecticut from the west is through Greenwich, perhaps the most affluent town in the state. Here real estate values have soared during the recent decade and the residential community abounds with stars of stage, screen, and television as well as corporate executives. Many of the latter have followed the move of their company headquarters to Fairfield County.

Stamford, with a population of just over 100,000 in its 39-square-mile area, has become a center for major international corporate headquarters. The arrival of so many offices has brought vast numbers of employees, and new resident families have meant new satellite commerce, increasing public services and enlarging schools.

The skyline of Stamford has developed rapidly; the old city (settled in 1641) is so diversified now that it has become the major trade center of Fairfield County.

Just east of Stamford and the small suburban town of Darien is Norwalk, a city of some 100,000 that has experienced a renaissance during the past five years. South Norwalk boasts excellent restaurants with ethnic and classic menus, ateliers, and shops.

Although there are New York commuters who live deeper into Connecticut, Westport, next along the shore, is about as far as most will go.

Along the coastal roads, access to the beaches along the sound is through state or municipal parks. Most beachfront property is privately owned, and shore towns close to New York City have closed their beaches to out-of-towners because of overcrowding. Sherwood Island State Park in Westport offers picnicking, fishing, and swimming in Long Island Sound.

Further along the shoreline is Fairfield, where, in the spring, this typical New England town enjoys the mass flowering of pink and white dogwood. The display of Connecticut dogwood is as breathtaking as the Japanese cherry trees in bloom in the Potomac River Basin.

Bridgeport, Connecticut's largest city, with a population just under 150,000, has long been called the Park City because there are over 1,300 acres of parks within its boundaries. It is also known as the industrial capital of Connecticut because of the diverse products—from electrical appliances to clothing and rifles—manufactured here and distributed throughout the world.

P. T. Barnum, the founder of the Barnum and Bailey Circus and a former mayor of Bridgeport, has long been remembered here. His elaborate mansion stands opposite Seaside Park, two and a half miles of shoreline and his gift to the city. He established The Barnum Museum (820 Main Street), which houses mementos of Jenny Lind (the Swedish nightingale), the clothes of Tom Thumb and his wife (the famous midget couple), and more than 5,000 other objects related to Barnum's life. The Barnum Museum, built in 1892, reopened in June 1989 following a two-year restoration and renovation that added a 7,000-square-foot art gallery where world-class traveling exhibits will be displayed.

Also in Bridgeport is Connecticut's largest zoo, the Beardsley Zoological Gardens, which includes a children's zoo and pony rides.

Continuing eastward on either I–95 or Route 1, signs approaching Stratford give directions to the Connecticut Center for the Performing Arts, which is on 12 acres in Stratford. It is now under the jurisdiction of the Office of Parks and Recreation of the State of Connecticut. The theater grounds, adjacent to the confluence of the Housatonic River and Long Island Sound, are open to the public.

North, along the west bank of the Housatonic River in Stratford, is the Sikorsky helicopter plant. The adjoining tarmac usually has several of the aircraft parked there, and often they may be seen lifting off or landing.

Milford, east of Stratford, has the distinction of being a crossover point from the Merritt Parkway east to I–95, or vice versa in a westerly direction. The Merritt continues on through Berlin toward Hartford with a change of name to Wilbur Cross Highway (the designation remains Route 15).

Milford is a shoreline town, a short drive midway between Bridgeport and New Haven. Milford Jai Alai, 311 Old Gate Road, is open evenings and matinees several days a week from May to October.

New Haven

While Hartford has its extensive collection of Colt revolvers, New Haven is proud of a gun made here that joined the six-shooter in winning the West, the famous Winchester repeating rifle. The development of the Winchester rifle, from 1866 to the present, is shown through models in the gun museum, which houses a massive collection of 5,000 pieces of war and hunting equipment ranging from guns of every variety to bullets, bayonets, and bandoliers.

Hardly a Connecticut town is without a wildlife sanctuary, refuge, formal garden, or nature trail. New Haven is no exception. On Wintergreen Avenue, the West Rock Nature Center has a zoo, ponds, picnic area, trails, and the Judges' Cave. The story is told on a plaque bolted to a boulder: "Here, May 15th, 1661, for some weeks thereafter, Edward Whalley and his son-in-law William Goffe, members of parliament, General Officers in the Army of the Commonwealth and signers of the death warrant of King Charles I, found shelter and concealment from the officers of the Crown after the Restoration." Then the final sentence: "Opposition to tyrants is Obedience to God!" The two men who had sent the king to his

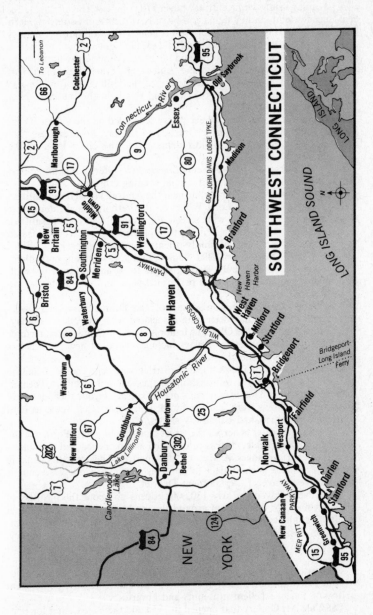

SOUTHWEST CONNECTICUT

death had fled England when their leader, Cromwell, was deposed and King Charles had mounted the throne. The cave is high up on West Rock.

A sweeping midtown facelift has taken place in New Haven during recent decades, eliminating slums and blighted streets and adding modern buildings. New Haven's redevelopment is near its historic Green, 16 acres of land laid out by founding fathers in 1638 and graced by churches, a library, the City Hall built in 1861, and the Federal Building, which houses the U.S. District Court, U.S. Attorney's office, and other offices of the federal government. Charles Dickens described the Hillhouse of his time as the "most beautiful street in America: and this is in the center of New Haven."

Throughout the year, special events are scheduled on the Green. There are free summer weekend jazz concerts, and in May, Powderhouse Day commemorates Benedict Arnold's demand for the city's keys to the Powderhouse.

In suitable weather, New Haven's *Liberty Belle* offers a lunchtime harbor cruise, weekend cruises, and special evening cruises.

Teletrack, a well-marked building near the Amtrak New Haven railroad station, in the vicinity of Long Wharf on the harbor, is a theater where horse races are shown on a wide screen. Pari-mutuel betting is permitted.

New Haven takes great pride in the turn-of-the-century carousel located at Lighthouse Point, a local family-oriented amusement park.

Long Wharf Theater, just off I–95 at well-marked exits in both directions, is one of Connecticut's leading stages for drama. Numerous well-known actors and actresses have performed here, and the theater has an enviable reputation.

Yale Repertory Theater is an adjunct of Yale Drama School. Its Director, Lloyd Richards, has been long associated with the National Playwrights Conference at the O'Neill Memorial Theater Center in Waterford. The Yale Rep annual series of plays includes works of new playwrights and new versions of the classics.

Downtown New Haven's theater district was rejuvenated with the handsome and expensive refurbishing of the venerable Shubert Theater, reopened in 1984. This was once a pre-Broadway tryout theater where many notable shows were first produced; today it is often home to road companies of established Broadway shows.

The Palace Theater is across the street from the Shubert. Formerly the Roger Sherman Theater, it was refurbished and reopened and now offers a variety of performances. A Museum of American Theatre with changing exhibits is housed in the Palace lobby. This section of College Avenue is now the New Haven Entertainment District.

While New Haven's nearly 130,000 citizens go about the business of making things for distribution around the world, near the Green several thousand students from around the world go about the business of learning. Yale, one of the finest institutions of higher learning in the country, has long been a center for medical research, among other scientific pursuits.

The visitor can have an overview of the university by taking a free guided tour (for information call 436–8330). Extra time might well be spent in any of Yale's excellent museums and libraries.

The Yale Art Gallery that opened in 1953 and the Yale Center for British Art and British Studies (1973) have priceless collections of masterworks. Particularly prized are the original John Trumbull paintings of the Revolution. Yale's Peabody Museum of Natural History ranks with the best in the country. Yale has a collection of musical instruments, and Beinecke Library, a rare book and manuscript library, is connected by an underground tunnel to Sterling Memorial Library, the main Yale University Library.

Albertus Magnus, a Catholic coeducational college, Southern Connecticut State College, and South Central Community College are all in New Haven. The University of New Haven is in West Haven, and Quinnipiac College is nearby in Hamden.

From New Haven, the Wilbur Cross Parkway (Rte. 15) and I–91 head north to Hartford, passing through Wallingford, home of the well-known Choate–Rosemary Hall School. Among its graduates were John F. Kennedy and Adlai Stevenson.

Meriden is where the Episcopalians in Connecticut first worshipped. And a side trip from Meriden leads to New Britain, the "hardware city," where small appliances and tools are manufactured.

PRACTICAL INFORMATION FOR SOUTHWESTERN CONNECTICUT

Note: The area code for all Connecticut is 203

HOW TO GET THERE AND AROUND. By plane: The Bridgeport Airport in Stratford and Tweed–New Haven Airport in New Haven serve this area. At Bridgeport: Delta Connection/Business Express, 800–345–3400; Piedmont/Jet Stream, 800–251–5720, U.S. Air, 800–428–4322; and Continental, 800–525–0280. At Tweed–New Haven: Delta Connection/Business Express, 800–345–3400; and Continental, 800–525–0280.

By train: Amtrak shoreline service between Washington and Boston includes stops in Stamford, Bridgeport, and New Haven. Metro-North has express service between Grand Central Station in Manhattan and Stamford with local service between New Haven and Stamford.

By bus: Greyhound Bus Lines has terminals in Bridgeport and New Haven for service to New York Port Authority Terminal as well as points north and east of these cities. For schedules, rates, and other information call 800–556–3815.

By ferry: The trip between Bridgeport and Port Jefferson, Long Island, is 90 min. Cars are permitted. Reservations are required. Pick it up at Union Sq. Dock in Bridgeport. Exit 27 of I–95 to State St. to Dock. In Connecticut, call 334–5993; in Port Jefferson, 516–473–0286.

By car: Greenwich, in Fairfield County, the first Connecticut town above the New York State line, is accessible via I–95 or the Merritt Pkwy. (Rte. 15). Both of these routes go through the shoreline towns of Fairfield County with exits along the way indicating Connecticut routes to the north as well as into local town centers.

Car rentals: Agencies for major car rental companies are located in most Connecticut towns and are listed in local telephone directories.

HOTELS AND MOTELS. Although it is impossible to list all accommodations in all towns, a representative group is included here. For others, consult the local Chamber of Commerce in the town in which accommodations are needed.

Accommodations that follow are listed by average price range for double occupancy as follows: *Deluxe,* $75 and up; *Expensive,* $50–$74; *Moderate,* $30–$49; *Inexpensive,* under $30.

Rates in Fairfield County during the year are generally consistent, although in urban areas weekend package rates may apply. Inquiries should be made directly to the hotel or motel for specific rate categories, including family and senior-citizen discounts.

Fairfield County is the most affluent area of Connecticut and nearer New York the accommodations tend to be in the *deluxe* and *expensive* categories.

Darien

Ramada Inn, 50 Ledge Rd., 06820; Exit 10, I–95 (655–8211). *Expensive.* Restaurant for lunch and dinner. No pets. Senior-citizen rates.

Howard Johnson Motor Lodge, 150 Ledge Rd., 06820; Exit 11, I–95 (655–3933). *Expensive.* Restaurant and coffee shop. Tennis, golf, and boating nearby.

Fairfield

Fairfield Motor Inn, 417 Post Rd., 06432; Exit 22, I–95 (255–0491). *Expensive.* Restaurant, cocktail lounge with entertainment. Nearby tennis and golf.

Greenwich

Howard Johnson Greenwich, 1114 Boston Post Rd., Riverside 06878; Exit 5, I–95 (637–3691). *Deluxe.* A restaurant and cocktail lounge; an outdoor pool, cable TV, and films.

Showboat Motor Inn, 500 Showboat Rd., 06830; Exit 3, I–95 (661–9800). *Deluxe.* Located on the riverfront with some rooms having balconies with a water view. Dockage available. Dining room open from 7 A.M.

Hyatt Regency Greenwich, 1800 East Putnam Ave., Old Greenwich 06870 (637–1234). *Expensive.* An English manor-style hotel, opened in 1986 with 353 rooms, two restaurants (one full-service cafe and another serving Continental cuisine); the Gazebo bar in the Atrium lobby. Lounge entertainment on Tues.–Sat. evenings. Gift shop, health club, and indoor pool.

Milford

Hampton Inn, 129 Plains Rd. 06460; Exit 36, I–95 (874–4400 or 800–HAMPTON). *Inexpensive.* Opened 1986. One of a motel chain particularly suited to traveling business people. Continental breakfasts.

Best Western, 1015 Boston Post Rd. 06460 (878–3575). *Inexpensive.* Accessible from I–95 via Exit 39A. One of a chain.

Howard Johnson Lodge, 1052 Boston Post Rd. 06460 (878–4611). *Inexpensive.* Health club, indoor and outdoor pools, game room. Restaurant and lounge.

New Haven

Park Plaza Hotel, 155 Temple St., 06510 (772–1700). *Moderate.* Central downtown hotel with restaurant, coffee shop, and lounge. Walk through to large shopping mall. Inside parking garage.

New Haven Inn and Conference Center, 100 Lily Pond Ave., 06525 (387–6651). *Moderate.* Serving Continental breakfast. Fitness center and indoor pool.

The Inn at Chapel West, near Yale campus (777–1201). Restored 19th-century mansion with unusual antique furnishings and bric-a-brac. Continental breakfast, high tea, Sunday brunch.

Norwalk

Courtyard by Marriott, 474 Main Ave., 06851 (849–9111). *Moderate.* Lounge and restaurant. Indoor pool.

Holiday Inn, 789 Connecticut Ave., 06854; Exit 13, I–95 (853–3477). *Expensive.* A large property with restaurant, coffee shop, and cocktail lounge. Indoor pool and sauna. Pets.

Stamford

The Inn at Mill River, 26 Mill River St., 06902 (325–9100 or 800–325–0345). *Deluxe.* Elegance here is found throughout, from the entrance lobby to guest suites and rooms. Award-winning Swan Court Restaurant.

Crown Plaza Hotel, 700 Main St. 06901; Exits 8 north or 7 south on I–95 (358–8400 or 800–HOLIDAY). *Deluxe.* A large midtown property with restaurant, cocktail lounge, evening entertainment, indoor pool, sauna and health center.

Stamford Marriott, 2 Stamford Forum 06901; Exit 8, I–95 (357–9555 or 800–228–9290). *Deluxe.* Strikingly modern, full-service hotel with restaurant, cocktail lounge with nightly entertainment. Indoor-outdoor pool. Sauna. Health center. Garage with valet service.

Westin Hotel–Stamford, 2701 Summer St. 06905; Exits 8 north or 7 south on I–95 (259–1300). *Deluxe.* A 500-room property with restaurant, cocktail lounge, health center, sauna. Indoor pool.

Stratford

Best Western Lord Stratford Hotel, 225 Lordship Blvd., 06497 (375–8866 or 800–528–1234). *Expensive.* Coffee shop, cocktail lounge entertainment. Health club. Beach and boating nearby.

Westport

Inn at Longshore, 260 S. Compo Rd., 06880 (226–3316). *Deluxe.* An all-seasons property on Long Island Sound where there is swimming, golf, tennis, and cross-country skiing. Continental breakfast. Restaurant.

Westport Inn, 1595 Post Rd. East, 06880; Exits 18 north, 19 south on I–95 (259–5236). *Expensive.* Restaurant and lounge. Near golf, tennis, beach, and boating.

INNS, GUEST HOUSES, BED AND BREAKFASTS. For *moderately* priced bed-and-breakfast rooms contact Nutmeg Bed & Breakfast, 222 Girard Ave., Hartford 06105 (236–6698) or Bed & Breakfast Ltd., Box 216, New Haven (469–3260 after 4 P.M.) Unlike other parts of Connecticut and New England, accommodations in inns tend to fall in the *expensive,* sometimes even *deluxe,* categories.

Greenwich

Homestead Inn, 420 Field Point Rd., 06830; Exit 3, I–95 (869–7500). Fine old 18th-century, colonial-style inn in residential area near Long Island Sound. Excellent restaurant and a small lounge.

New Canaan

The Maples Inn, 179 Oenoke Ridge, 06840 (966–2927). Late 19th-century building with appropriate antique furnishings. Continental breakfast.

Roger Sherman Inn, 195 Oenoke Ridge, 06840 (966–4541). A mid-18th-century structure furnished with antiques. Restaurant and lounge.

Norwalk

Silvermine Tavern, Silvermine and Perry Aves., 06850 (847–4558). A charming late 18th-century country inn beside a running stream and waterfall. Several dining rooms in the restaurant. Continental breakfast served.

Westport

Cotswold Inn, 76 Myrtle Ave., 06880; Exit 17, Rte. I–95 (226–3766). A charming, small, exclusive country inn. Serving a full breakfast, and in warm weather tables are in the garden for a pleasant beginning to the day.

RESTAURANTS. The menus in southwestern Connecticut restaurants are, by and large, as varied and extensive as those in moderately priced restaurants in New York City or other metropolitan areas. They are often in attractive country or seaside settings. Many old homes have been converted into "inns" which serve meals. For relaxed, cozy dining, with a cheery fireplace in winter, a green pasture view, or a window overlooking the sea, there are some picturesque locations listed here. Price ranges given are based on a full meal, exclusive of alcoholic beverages, tax, and tip: *Deluxe,* $30 and up; *Expensive,* $25–$29; *Moderate,* $15–$24; *Inexpensive,* $14 and under.

Bridgeport

Paris Bistro, 3546 Main St. (374–6093). *Deluxe.* French- and Italian-inspired cuisine. Reservations. Closed Sun.

Tumbleweed's, 4485 Main St. (374–0234). *Moderate.* Substantial lunch and dinner menus in an informal atmosphere suitable for families. Daily specials.

Ocean Sea Grill, 1328 Main St. (336–2133). *Moderate.* Operating since 1934. Lobster specialty heading menu of fresh seafood. Proprietor also owns large wholesale seafood market. Meat dishes available.

Fitzwilly's, 2536 East Main St. (334–1775). *Inexpensive.* Sandwiches, soups, salads as well as entrees. Open late.

Darien

Chuck's Steak House, 1340 Boston Post Rd. (655–2254). *Moderate.* One of a chain specializing in charbroiled steaks and lobster tails.

Fairfield

Anacapri, 238 Commerce Dr. (335–3999). *Deluxe.* Featuring Italian cuisine in attractively appointed dining room. Open daily for lunch and dinner.

Gregory's, 1599 Post Rd. (259–7417). Pleasant decor and seasonal American fare. Lunch, dinner, Sunday brunch.

Mayur, 52 Sanford St. (259–0763). *Moderate.* The menu here includes many Indian specialties with a special vegetarian section. Open daily.

Greenwich

Homestead Inn, 420 Field Point Rd. (869–7500). *Deluxe.* This lovely colonial inn dates back to 1759. Traditional French cuisine and unusual specialties daily. Small cocktail lounge and organist on Sat. evenings. Proper dress and reservations.

Tapestries, 554 Old Post Rd. (629–9204). *Deluxe.* Dining here in an elegant atmosphere. Menu is French-inspired with desserts made on the premises. Closed Sun. Reservations.

Boodles, 21 Field Point Rd. (661–3553). *Expensive.* Dine on the glassed-in sunporch or in the cozy dining room with a fireplace in this large Victorian house. Varied American menu with fresh seafood specials.

Jardine's, 3 River Rd. (661–0204). *Expensive.* Nouvelle cuisine served in a two-story restaurant overlooking the Mianus River.

Portofino, 18 W. Putnam Ave. (869–8383). *Expensive.* A small cozy Italian restaurant specializing in foods of Northern Italy.

Showboat Restaurant, 500 Steamboat Rd. (661–9800). *Expensive.* The showboat is the riverboat "Mark Twain." Lobster, seafood, and steak are featured. Music and dancing on weekends. Breakfast available.

New Canaan

Roger Sherman Inn, 195 Oenoke Rd. (966–4541). *Deluxe.* A country inn with five individually decorated dining rooms. Superb Continental cuisine. Cocktail lounge with pianist. Summer dining on the terrace.

Gates, 10 Forest St. (966–8666). *Expensive.* Named for the 19th-century Austrian gates so prominent here. Interesting specialties. A variety of live music during the week and weekends. Lunch, dinner, Sunday brunch.

Nantucket Cafe, 15 Elm St. (972–0831). *Expensive.* Seafood specialties and old New England seashore ambience. Lunch and dinner.

New Haven

Robert Henry's, 1032 Chapel St. (789–1010). *Deluxe.* A fine dining experience here in the former Sherman Tavern property. Innovative menus in a charming environment, with evidence of professionalism in every way.

Azteca, 14 Mechanic St. (624–2454). *Expensive.* Located in New Haven's historic district. Mexican and southwestern cuisine served in a dining room reflecting western schemes, replete with cacti.

Basel's, 993 State St. (624–9361). *Expensive.* Authentic Greek cuisine and wines. Live Greek music and dancing weekends.

Blessings, 45 Howe St. (624–3557). *Expensive.* Northern Chinese cuisine with over 100 dishes served generously. Exotically named cocktails.

Delmonaco's, 232 Wooster St. (865–1109). *Expensive.* Prepared to order Northern Italian food, expertly served. Located in restored Wooster Sq. area. Closed Tues.

Lou's Lunch, 263 Crown St. (562–5366). *Inexpensive.* Quick service. Reputedly the home of the original hamburger.

Pepe's, 157 Wooster St. (865–5762). *Inexpensive.* Noted for pizza. "The best in the U.S.A." some New Haveners report.

Picnic on the Green, 900 Chapel St. (777–6661). *Inexpensive.* 18 eateries at Chapel Sq. Ethnic, finger food, deli, natural and raw bars, desserts, ice cream, and so forth.

Norwalk

Apulia Italian Restaurant, 70 N. Main St., South Norwalk (852–1168). *Moderate.* Homemade pasta and Apulia's own recipes.

Portofino Clam House, 18 S. Main St., South Norwalk (838–8722). *Deluxe.* Excellent seafood.

Silvermine Tavern, Silvermine Ave. (847–4558). *Expensive.* 200-year-old inn, decorated with American antiques and primitive paintings. Patio dining in summer; cozy fireplaces in winter. Traditional American menu with fresh seafood featured.

Skippers Restaurant, Calf Pasture Beach Rd. (838–2211). *Moderate.* A dockside location that attracts pleasure boaters in summer.

Ridgefield

Le Coq Hardi, Big Shop Lane (431–3060). *Deluxe.* Unusual French-inspired cuisine served in an interestingly restored building. Jackets and reservations required.

Stamford

Le Coq Hardi, in the Westin Hotel, 2701 Summer St. (357–0098). *Deluxe.* Fine French cuisine served in a charming atmosphere. Jackets are required at dinner. Reservations are necessary.

Pellicci's, 98 Stillwater Ave. (323–2542). *Moderate.* Family-run Italian restaurant for over 30 years. Very popular for good reason. Homemade bread, excellent pastas and pizzas.

Stratford

Fagan's, 946 Ferry Blvd. (378–6560). *Moderate.* Overlooks Housatonic River. Near Shakespeare Theater. Fine seafood, steak, and other New England specialties.

Weston

Cobbs Mill Inn, Rte. 57 (227–7221). *Deluxe.* Pre-Revolutionary inn beside millpond and waterfall. Delightful place for cocktails and dinner and browsing in adjacent country store. Varied menu with venison and game in the autumn.

Westport

LeChambord, 1572 Post Rd. E. (255–2654). *Deluxe.* Distinguished French fare. Daily specials fresh from the market.

Chez Pierre, 146 Main St. (227–5295). *Expensive.* A charming, informal bistro centrally located among Westport's shops and boutiques. French provincial menu.

Ocean House, 1563 Post Rd. E. (259–4005). *Expensive.* Not fancy, but freshest seafood poached or broiled. Crisp vegetable salad and fresh fruit bowl for dessert.

The Three Bears, Rte. 33 (227–7219). *Expensive.* Westport's oldest eating establishment, originally a stagecoach stop. An outstanding Tiffany lamp collection. Seafood, steak, veal specialties. Children's portions.

TOURIST INFORMATION. Tourist information centers in Southwestern Connecticut are located in Greenwich, eastbound on the Merritt Parkway/Rte. 15 (seasonal); in Stamford on I–95, northbound; on Rte. 7 in Canaan (seasonal); and at all MacDonald restaurants on I–95 in Darien, Fairfield, and Milford.

Several regional district information centers offer a wealth of information on their member towns. These districts include: Bridgeport Convention and Visitors Bureau, 10 Middle St., Bridgeport 06604 (576–8494); Litchfield Hills Visitors Commission, Box 1776, Marbledale 06777 (868–2214); Yankee Heritage Tourism District, 297 West Ave., The Gate Lodge, Norwalk 06850 (854–7810). The Greater Stamford Convention & Visitors Bureau, 2 Landmark Sq., Suite 110, Stamford 06901–2410 (359–3305); Waterbury Convention and Visitors Commission (for Waterbury only), 156 W. Main St., Waterbury 06702 (597–9527).

For general Connecticut information, Tourism Division, Department of Economic Development, 210 Washington St., Hartford 06106 (566–3948) or Department of Environmental Protection, 165 Capitol Ave., Hartford 06106 (566–2304) or Commission on the Arts, 190 Trumbull St. Hartford 06103 (566–4770).

SEASONAL EVENTS. May: Dogwood Festival, Greenfield Hill in Fairfield (mid-May); Handcraft Fair, Westport (late May).

June: Victorian Fair at the Lockwood-Matthews Mansion in Norwalk (early June); West Haven's Annual Arts and Crafts Fair (mid-June); St. Andrew Annual Italian Festival, New Haven (late June); Barnum Festival, Bridgeport (late June–early July).

July: 4th of July Annual Fireworks displays in Norwalk and Bridgeport; jazz concerts on the Green in New Haven.

August: Shoreline communities unite for Long Island Sound American Festival—Norwalk to New Haven (to mid-Oct.); Oyster Festival, Milford (mid-Aug.).

September: Oyster Festival, Norwalk (early Sept.) In-water Boat Show, Norwalk (mid-Sept.). North Atlantic Sailboat Show, Stamford (mid-Sept.); annual fall Antique Show, New Haven (late Sept.). In New Haven, Yale University football schedule begins for the season.

October: Fall-foliage trolley trips at Shore Line Trolley Museum, East Haven.

Country fairs take place throughout this part of Connecticut as well as the rest of the state. For full schedules contact Association of Connecticut Fairs, 190 South Road, Box 363, Somers 06071.

TOURS. In New Haven, Yale University offers special tours for persons interested in art, architecture, engineering, science, or in a general tour of the university. Arrangements for special group tours may be made at the Yale University Information office (436–8330). Also in New Haven, the New Haven Convention and Visitors Bureau (787–8822) will arrange city tours. Information concerning boat rides is also available at this office.

Industrial tours available in this area include Pepperidge Farms (bakery) in Norwalk, on the Westport border (748–6095); Southern New England Telephone Company, 227 Church St., New Haven (786–3100). One month's advance notice is required.

The New Haven *Register,* 40 Sargent Dr. (772–3700), and the Waterbury *Republican-American,* 389 Meadow St. (574–3636), have tours through their daily and Sun. newspaper plants. Advance registration is required.

PARKS, FORESTS, NATURE CENTERS, AND ZOOS. Although there are no national parks or forests in Connecticut, state parks and forests are located throughout the state. For information concerning any of these, contact: Parks and Recreation Division, Department of Environmental Protection, 165 Capitol Ave, Hartford 06106 (566–2304).

State parks and other attractions in the area include:

Sherwood Island State Park in Westport. One of the state's three public beaches. About 2 mi. of sandy beach on Long Island Sound.

Bartlett Arboretum, a University of Connecticut supervised property, Rte. 137 in Stamford. Exit 35 from the Merritt Parkway. Woodland trails and gardens.

Connecticut Center for the Arts, 1850 Elm St., Stratford (738–8321). Theatrical productions seasonally; the grounds have picnic areas.

Beardsley Zoological Gardens, Noble Ave., Bridgeport (576–8082). A large zoo with a small section especially to interest children. Open year-round except major holidays.

Connecticut Audubon Society Fairfield Center, 2325 Burr St., Fairfield (359–6305), is an extensive nature center with trails especially designed for elderly and handicapped. Museum and Library. Closed Mon. and major holidays.

The Maritime Center, North Water St., South Norwalk (800–243–2280), on five acres of waterfront has exhibits, audiovisual presentations, and an aquarium that illustrate the history and maritime environment on Long Island Sound.

Stamford Museum and Nature Center, 39 Schofieldtown Rd., Stamford (322–1646). Over 100 acres plus a 19th-century farm. There are nature trails, museum exhibits, and planetarium shows. Open daily except major holidays.

East Rock Park, E. Rock Rd., New Haven (787–8142). City arboretum and rose garden. Nature trails.

Lighthouse Point Park, 2 Lighthouse Rd., New Haven (787–8005). Large park on Long Island Sound. Swimming, nature trails, antique carousel. Seasonal. Admission and parking fees.

West Rock Nature Center, Wintergreen Ave., New Haven (787–8016). Large nature center with native animals. Hiking trails. Free.

SPORTS. Golf: The State Tourism Division, Department of Economic Development, 210 Washington St., Hartford 06106 (566–3385) has a "Golf" brochure listing public and private golf courses throughout the state. For nonresidents, early reservations at any of the following 18-hole courses in this area would be necessary, especially on weekends: In Bridgeport, Fairchild Wheeler Golf Club, Eastern Tpke. (576–8083); in Danbury, Richter Park Golf Course, Aunt Hack Rd. (792–2550); in Fairfield, H. Smith Richardson Golf Course, Hoydens Lane (255–6094); in Norwalk, Oak Hills Park, Fillow St. (853–8400); in Stamford, Sterling Farms Golf Course, Newfield Ave. (329–8171).

Swimming: Sherwood Island State Park in Westport (226–6983) is on Long Island Sound where the sandy beach is about 2 mi. long and fine for swimming. Fishing, too, is possible here.

River expeditions: River trips, canoeing, as well as hiking and rock climbing expeditions, are available through White Creek Expeditions, 99 Myanos Rd., New Canaan 06840 (346–3308 or 345–8355).

Most of the major hotels and motels in this section of the state indicate access to nearby facilities for **tennis** and **boating** and will make the necessary arrangements for their guests. Others should consult the local Chamber of Commerce or visitors bureau.

SPECTATOR SPORTS. Hockey: New Haven Night Hawks, AHL, New Haven Coliseum. Seasonal. Ticket and schedule information (787–0101).

Football games are played at the Yale Bowl. There's **basketball** at the New Haven Coliseum.

Jai Alai: Bridgeport Jai Alai, 255 Kossuth St. (576–1976), seasonal; Milford Jai Alai, 311 Old Gate Lane (877–4242), seasonal.

Horse racing: Teletrack, 600 Long Wharf Dr. (789–1943). Simulcast of live horse racing.

HISTORIC SITES AND HOUSES. Most historic houses are owned and attended by local historical societies and are open usually only seasonally. The best source of information in each case would be the local public library.

Darien

Bates-Scofield Homestead 45 Old Kings Hwy., 06820 (655–9233). A mid-18th-century saltbox, authentic antique furniture, herb garden.

Greenwich

Bush-Holley House (c. 1685), 39 Strickland Rd., Cos Cob (869–6899). Late 17th-century saltbox, colonial furnishings. Also the site of the John Rogers statuary exhibit. Closed Sun. and Mon.

New Haven

New Haven Colony Historical Society Museum, 114 Whitney Ave. (562–4183). Historical and industrial museum, antique toys, library. Closed Mon.

Pardee-Morris House (1750), 325 Lighthouse Rd. (562–4183/467–0764). Restored and authentically furnished mid-18th-century home. Interesting gardens. Seasonal.

Norwalk

Lockwood-Mathews Mansion (1864), 295 West Ave. (838–1434). Mid-19th-century home, château-inspired design. A National Historic Landmark.

Stamford

Hoyt-Barnum House (1699), 713 Bedford St., is authentically furnished in early 18th-century style. Maintained by the Stamford Historical Society, 1508 High Ridge Rd., 06903 (329–1183 or 322–1565). Visits by appointment only.

Stratford

David Judson House and Museum, 967 Academy Hill (378–0630). Mid-18th-century farmhouse, well furnished. A National Historic Landmark. Seasonal.

MUSEUMS AND ART GALLERIES. There are several interesting museums as well as fine art collections in this area. Call ahead to check days, hours, admission fees.

Bridgeport

Bridgeport Museum of Art, Science and Industry and Planetarium, 4450 Park Ave. (372–3521). Art, industrial displays, some antiques. Planetarium shows. Closed Mon.

The Barnum Museum, 820 Main St. (331–1104). A scale model replica of The Greatest Show on Earth, with 3,000 hand-carved miniatures, is only one of more than 5,000 objects related to the life and career of P. T. Barnum, the greatest American showman. Closed Mon. and holidays.

East Haven

Shore Line Trolley Museum, 17 River St. (467–6927). A variety of street-cars. Rides on trolleys along 3-mi. track near the shore. Seasonal and off-season weekend schedules.

Greenwich

Bruce Museum, Museum Dr. (869–0376). A mixture of art, science, history, and anthropology here. Closed Mon. and holidays.

New Haven

New Haven Colony Historical Society, 114 Whitney Ave. (562–4183). Local antiques, including dolls and toys; research library. Closed Mon.

Peabody Museum of Natural History at Yale, 170 Whitney Ave. (432–5050 or 432–5799). A vast collection of exhibits, minerals, animal displays, and ecological exhibits. Closed major holidays.

Yale Center for British Art, 1080 Chapel St. (432–2800 or 432–2850). Paintings, prints, sculpture, rare books from Elizabethan times to 1800s. Closed Mon. and major holidays.

Yale University Art Gallery, 111 Chapel St. (432–0600). American, European, African, pre-Colombian, Near and Far East art collections. Seasonal.

Yale Collection of Musical Instruments, 15 Hillhouse Ave. (432–0822). Some instruments date to 16th century. Concert series. Closed Aug.

Stamford

Stamford Museum and Nature Center, 39 Schofieldtown Rd. (322–1646). Over 100 acres plus a 19th-century farm. There are nature trails, museum exhibits, and planetarium shows. Open daily except major holidays.

MUSIC AND STAGE. Bridgeport —**Downtown Cabaret Theatre,** 263 Golden Hill St. (576–1636). A year-round professional company. Weekend performances. Children's program Sat. afternoons. "Bring your own picnic" environment.

In New Haven—**Long Wharf Theatre,** Sargent Dr. (787–4282). A small-capacity theater but one with a fine reputation for excellent productions, both new and classic plays. Schedules on request. Series subscriptions available.

Yale Repertory Theatre, Chapel & York Sts. (432–1234). Plays scheduled during the university calendar year include productions of classics as well as new plays. Schedules and rates on request. Subscription series.

In Stamford—**Stamford Center for the Performing Arts, Hartman Theatre,** 61 Atlantic St. (323–2131). A variety of professional performances are held here during the year, including theater, opera, symphony concerts, ballet, and special events. Home of Pilobolus Dance Theater.

In Westport—**Westport Country Playhouse,** 25 Powers Court (227–4177). Some of the leading professional theater artists have performed here in new plays and revivals. Schedules on request.

Fairfield County as in most of Connecticut has concerts scheduled throughout the year and these range from symphonies to pop and jazz. In New Haven during July and Aug. there are jazz concerts on the Green. The New Haven Symphony has performances during the year and for a schedule or information call 776–1444. The Yale Information Office (432–4488) can supply information concerning concerts sponsored by the University or held on the campus.

Details concerning other schedules available on inquiry locally either at the public library or at the Chamber of Commerce.

SHOPPING. Stamford Town Center, Greyrock Pl. between Tresser Blvd. and Broad St., is one of the largest shopping centers in the state. The enclosed mall has more than 100 stores, several chain department stores, restaurants, and parking for 4,000 cars.

Also in Stamford, the **Ridgeway Shopping Center** at Summer and Sixth Sts. has two chain department stores and 60 other shops.

Westport downtown has numerous interesting boutiques, art and book shops, plus a miscellany of specialty shops. This shopping extends to Boston Post Rd. East and West.

Norwalk's redeveloped SONO district has encouraged small boutiques of special interest to visitors, as do the special restaurants in this area. A Factory Outlet group of stores located near I-95 is a mecca for bargain hunters.

Bridgeport and New Haven downtowns have large shopping malls as well as well-known department stores with chains in other major cities. Individual shops and boutiques are located throughout these cities, all offering interesting merchandise.

SOUTHEASTERN CONNECTICUT
AND THE COASTAL AREA

East of the Connecticut River

Along the southeastern shoreline east of the Connecticut River, over the Baldwin Bridge from Old Saybrook to Old Lyme, the shoreline route proceeds to the eastern boundary of the state as it joins Rhode Island—a distance of 35 miles.

Exit 72 from the Connecticut Turnpike leads to the beautiful, unspoiled town of Old Lyme. Its Congregational church has appeared in many architectural books and on calendars, and it has been a popular subject for the many artists who, over the years, have gathered in Old Lyme. The wide main street, with lush green trees, high privet and box hedges, and tall lilac trees surrounding historic old homes, give the appearance of that typical New England town everyone imagines.

The Florence Griswold House at 96 Lyme Street is an art museum, once a home to several nineteenth-century American painters. Also on Lyme Street, the Lyme Art Association Gallery has changing exhibits, and the Lyme Academy of Fine Arts nearby has a faculty of recognized professional artists.

On Route 156 in Old Lyme, heading east along the shore toward Niantic, is the Hall Mark Ice Cream Place, a landmark in this area. Sandwiches and snacks are available but the homemade ice cream is worth a stop (open May to October).

Waterford

Route 213, which intersects Route 156 in Jordan Village, Waterford, leads to two important points of interest. The Harkness Memorial State Park has a beautiful beach but, ironically, no swimming is allowed because the state does not provide lifeguards here. There are acres of grassy lawns for picnics or strolling and, during the summer, exquisite flower gardens. The mansion, once the summer home of the late philanthropist Edward Harkness and his wife, is not furnished, but on exhibit in the rooms are some of the 900 life-size bird paintings in watercolor bequeathed by the Brooklyn-born artist Rex Brasher. Outdoor concerts are scheduled for midsummer evenings, with seating on the wide lawn overlooking Long Island Sound.

Still farther along on Route 213 is the Eugene O'Neill Memorial Theater Center, one of the country's renowned experimental theaters. This is the home of the National Playwrights Conference, the National Drama Critics Institute, and the National Theatre Institute. Visitors are always welcome, and readings from the plays of new playwrights during the summer have become increasingly popular.

New London

Continuing along Route 213 to New London, a visit to the Monte Cristo Cottage is especially interesting to anyone concerned with theater. This was the summer home of the great American playwright Eugene O'Neill at the time set in his autobiographical play *Long Day's Journey Into Night*. The property was owned by his actor father James O'Neill, whose major role as the Count of Monte Cristo was the origin of the name of this house at 325 Pequot Avenue. Operated as an adjunct to the O'Neill Theater Center, the house is furnished in the style of the early twentieth century, when the O'Neills lived in it. It is a museum and an extensive library of theater publications and literary memorabilia, with emphasis on the life and works of Eugene O'Neill. Monte Cristo Cottage is open to the public at specified times and by appointment (203–443–0051).

A short distance away, Ocean Beach Park in New London, a municipally owned and operated park, has one of the most popular beaches on Long Island Sound. There is a picnic place, restaurant and cafeteria, and cocktail lounge as well as a broad boardwalk, beachside food, and recreational concessions. The feature here is the wide, white-sand beach. An Olympic-

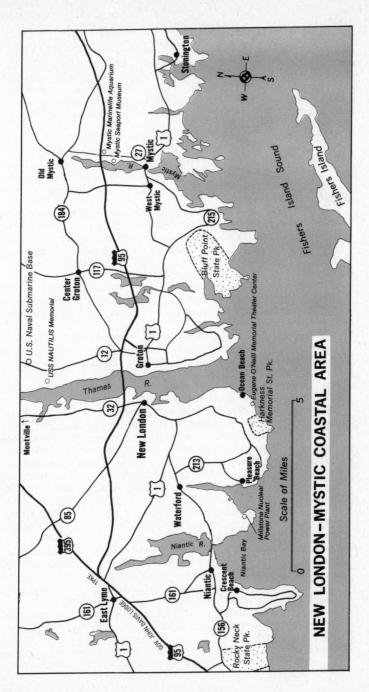

NEW LONDON–MYSTIC COASTAL AREA

Stonington

Mystic Marinelife Aquarium
Mystic Seaport Museum
Mystic
1
27
West Mystic
Old Mystic
184
95
117
Center Groton
U.S. Naval Submarine Base
USS NAUTILIS Memorial
215
Bluff Point State Pk.

Fishers Island Sound

Fishers Island

11
Groton
12
Ocean Beach
Eugene O'Neill Memorial Theater Center
Thames R.
32
Harkness Memorial St. Pk.
New London
Montville
213
Pleasure Beach
1
Waterford
Millstone Nuclear Power Plant
85
Niantic R.
395
Niantic Bay
TPKE
GOV. JOHN DAVIS LODGE
Niantic
161
Crescent Beach
East Lyme
161
156
Rocky Neck State Pk.
1
95

Scale of Miles
0   5

size swimming pool is an added attraction for swimmers. Visitors from out of town are welcome but are charged a modest entrance and parking fee.

New London is a small, seacoast city, merely six square miles and one of the earliest settlements in the state (1646). Located on the west side of the Thames River, the city has always been sustained by its proximity to the sea. Along with New Bedford and Nantucket, New London was home port for numerous whaling and sealing ships that sailed on expeditions around Cape Horn, into the south and north Pacific searching for the elusive sea creatures.

When sealing and whaling were prosperous, vast fortunes were made in New London. The Public Library of New London, which opened in 1892, was made possible through the bequest of a whaling man. The Lawrence and Memorial Associated Hospitals, today the area's primary medical center, began through the interest of Sebastian Lawrence, whose ships sailed from New London.

Some of the homes of these courageous seafarers, who may have gone to sea for years at a time, have been restored and are reminders of those nineteenth-century days when New London was in its glory.

Continuing this long maritime tradition, New London has been, since the early 1900s, the home for the U.S. Coast Guard Academy, one of the country's four military academies. Visitors may tour the grounds, visit some buildings including the library-museum and nonsectarian chapel, and—when in port—the training barque *Eagle*. This is the ship that leads the tall ships parades in various parts of the United States and is a training ship for the academy cadets.

Eagle was the German ship *Horst Wessel*. When she became a prize of World War II, she was renovated and renamed and brought over from Germany to the U.S. Coast Guard—always a beautiful sight with sails full as she sails downriver and out to sea.

Periodic parades of the cadet corps on review attract visitors to the academy drill grounds when weather permits.

The New London County Historical Society is located in the Shaw Mansion on Blinman Street. Built in 1756 for Captain Nathaniel Shaw, a wealthy shipowner and trader, many of the Society's collections relate to the son, Nathaniel, Jr., who at the outbreak of the Revolution was named naval agent for Connecticut. The naval office for Connecticut was established then at the Shaw Mansion, and it was here that the first naval expedition under the Second Continental Congress was outfitted in 1776.

The Hempsted Houses at 11 Hempstead Street are among the few remaining seventeenth-century houses in Connecticut. The Joshua Hempsted House (1678) survived Benedict Arnold's burning of New London, The Nathaniel Hempsted House (1759) is one of two surviving mid-eighteenth-century cut-stone houses in the state. The house stands on part of the original six-acre land grant received by Robert Hempsted in 1645. The property is owned and cared for by the Antiquarian and Landmarks Society, an organization that supports the restoration and maintenance of several historic buildings in towns throughout the state.

Nathan Hale Schoolhouse stands on Captain's Walk near the railroad station in downtown New London. The Sons of the American Revolution care for this historic site.

The Olde Towne Mill, built in 1650 by John Winthrop, Jr., as a gristmill, rebuilt in 1800 and restored more recently, is in its original location on Mill Street, under the Gold Star Memorial Bridge (I-95).

North from the Olde Towne Mill, and across from the U.S. Coast Guard Academy, on Mohegan Avenue, is the Lyman Allyn Museum, an art museum with collections of early American furniture, porcelains, silver, costumes, Greek and Roman artifacts, Oriental sculpture, and nineteenth-century dollhouses, dolls, and toys.

Connecticut College, also on Mohegan Avenue, a coeducational liberal arts college, is the cultural center of the city. It adjoins the museum property to the north. Dance, drama, music, and sports programs attract many people from within and outside the local community.

The 70-acre Connecticut College Arboretum is a stand of virgin forest where there are 400-year-old trees. The Thames Science Center nearby is a center for environmental interests, with nature trails, a lecture series, and a natural history museum.

Mitchell College on the Thames River waterfront, on Pequot Avenue, is a two-year community college attracting a student body from many parts of the United States and abroad. It contributes to the cultural scene in the city and offers day and evening classes of special interest to area residents.

A new museum (1986) of local history is the New London Maritime Society Museum in the New London Custom House on Bank Street. This granite building was built in 1833 and designed by Robert Mills, America's first Federal architect who was appointed by President Andrew Jackson.

Because the Society owns the original documents and building specifications, any renovations made to this oldest custom house building—which is in continuous use—will have authentic plans. A featured exhibit in this museum is a Fresnel lens that was used in the New London Ledge Lighthouse at the confluence of the Thames River and Long Island Sound.

Groton

The expansive U.S. Naval Submarine Base across the Thames River in Groton is the headquarters for the North Atlantic fleet. Regulations concerning visitors to the base should be checked in advance.

Just south of the main entrance to the Base are the USS *Nautilus* Memorial Park and Submarine Museum and Submarine Force Library. The museum memorializes the submarine service with exhibits dating back to the first submersible, the *American Turtle* (1775), invented by David Bushnell, a native of Old Saybrook. Other exhibits graphically depict U.S. naval undersea history through the years. The USS *Nautilus* is permanently berthed here, and visitors may go on board. Also on the property is the Submarine Force Library, available only to researchers by appointment. As this is a federally owned and operated property there is no admission fee.

The Electric Boat Division of General Dynamics Corporation is to the south, on Thames Street. Nuclear submarines, from the USS *Nautilus,* the first nuclear-powered submarine, to the more recent Tridents continue to be built and serviced at this location.

The 135-foot Groton Monument, offering a panoramic view of the harbor, marks the spot where, in 1781, American soldiers at Fort Griswold surrendered to traitor Benedict Arnold and his British cohorts, then were treacherously cut down to the last man.

The Pfizer Company's Research and Development Division shares the western shore of the Thames River with Electric Boat.

Mystic

The community of Mystic, half of which is in the Town of Groton and half in the Town of Stonington, is divided by the Mystic River. Route 1 crosses the river via an unusual bascule bridge, built in 1922 to replace an earlier drawbridge.

Local industry has revolved around the sea from the time the riverbanks were first settled. During the nineteenth century shipbuilding was concentrated among several shipyards along the riverbanks.

On the site of the Geo. Greenman & Bros. Shipyard (Greenmanville Avenue, Route 27) is the Mystic Seaport Museum, one of the major outdoor museums in this country. It has gallery exhibits of marine paintings, figureheads, scrimshaw, full-scale ship models and half models, and vast treasures from seagoing expeditions, but the main focus is on the *Charles W. Morgan.* The *Morgan,* last of the nineteenth-century wooden whaleships, built in 1842, has been here permanently since 1942, when brought from her home port of New Bedford.

A recreated mid-nineteenth-century New England coastal village has been developed to provide an authentic backdrop for the ship. Other period vessels and buildings, some of them moved from other parts of New England, some of them reproductions, make up the scene. A maritime library has extensive collections for research scholars.

A million-dollar Visitors Center was completed in 1987 for improved visitor reception and orientation. Located at the South Entrance, it is adjacent to the Mystic Seaport Museum Store, a veritable department store with stocks of nautical gifts, clothes, reproductions from the museum collections, books, prints, and foods indigenous to the area. A separate two-story section, the Mystic Maritime Gallery, deals in maritime art and is the largest dealer of this kind in this country.

There is an admission charge for entrance to the Seaport grounds, but not to the Mystic Seaport Store or to the Seamen's Inne, a full-service restaurant located at the north end of the complex.

At the intersection of I–95 (Exit 90) and Route 27 is Olde Mystic Village, a shopping center with more than 60 shops, each with a mid-eighteenth-century architectural design. There are numerous overnight accommodations and restaurants in the immediate vicinity to suit every taste.

Here, too, is the Mystic Marinelife Aquarium (education and research is its stated purpose) with over 6,000 marine specimens living in tank environments that reflect as closely as possible their natural habitats. There is an hourly demonstration of the training and abilities of several species of sea mammal in the 1,400-seat Marine Theater. Seals, sea lions, and shore birds have their own special outdoor complex, created to resemble their natural environment.

Stonington

The borough and town of Stonington have been carefully preserved to continue a way of life precious to residents. Early homes remain in pristine condition; the one-street "downtown" shopping area hasn't changed (other than occasional store occupants) over the years, and the people of Stonington intend to keep things just that way.

A walk through the village leads to the Old Lighthouse Museum, a granite structure built in 1843. This was Connecticut's first lighthouse operated by the government until 1889. Today, the building is a museum operated and maintained by its present owners, the Stonington Historical Society. Six small gallery rooms have displays of Stonington memorabilia, portraits, weapons, and whaling gear.

Ledyard

The small suburban town of Ledyard was land once occupied by the Pequot Indians and then settled in 1635. Driving through this mostly residential and farming area, one is very much aware that an Indian heritage still prevails in the names one sees in the community.

The Mashantucket Pequot Indians have a reservation here. At the intersection of Routes 2 and 214 they have developed a popular—though specialized—tourist attraction: This Indian tribe has built a Super Bingo Hall, seating more than 1,600. Players have been arriving from all New England states and beyond since its opening in the summer of 1986. This gaming hall is operated by the tribe, and income is designated for construction of a major museum on the reservation dedicated to Indian history, culture, and lore.

North of Ledyard, crossing the Thames River via the Preston-Montville bridge to Route 32, the history of the Mohegan Indians is recalled. Reminders of Uncas, chief of the Mohegans, include the name of Uncasville, a community contiguous to Montville.

The Tantaquidgeon Indian Museum on Route 32 houses a small collection of Indian relics. In the yard are the frames of both a longhouse and a roundhouse, dwellings common to the eastern Indians, who did not live in the kind of teepees favored by the western Indians.

PRACTICAL INFORMATION FOR SOUTHEASTERN CONNECTICUT

Note: The area code for all Connecticut is 203

HOW TO GET THERE AND AROUND. By plane: Trumbull Airport, Groton, serves the Groton–New London area, with several airlines offering schedules to major airports in New York, Boston, Newark, and Hartford for connecting flights.

By train: Amtrak on the Northeast Corridor Shoreline route makes stops at New Haven, Old Saybrook, New London, and Mystic as it travels from Washington D.C., and New York to Boston.

By bus: Several motorcoach lines traveling from New York to Boston and Cape Cod have major terminals in cities on the shoreline. South East Area Transit, SEAT, runs regular schedules throughout the area from its terminal site in downtown New London. Call 886-2631 for schedules.

By car: I–95 and Rte. 1 run almost parallel from New Haven to the state line in Rhode Island, although I–95 is a thruway and Rte. 1 goes through more heavily populated areas, through the shoreline towns and villages. At the Gold Star Memorial Bridge that connects Groton and New London, Rte. I–84 begins and runs through the countryside to the borderline at Westerly, Rhode Island.

By boat: Nautical-minded travelers arrive on yachts, and motor boat marinas dot 253 miles of Long Island shoreline.

There are ferries that run between Bridgeport and Port Jefferson, Long Island; New London and Fishers Island, New York; Block Island, Rhode Island, and Orient Point, Long Island. Car reservations are suggested with extra fare and deposit required. For Bridgeport–Port Jefferson, telephone in Connecticut, 367–3043 or in New York, 516–473–0286; for Block Island and Orient Point, 442–7891 or 442–9553; for Fishers Island, from City Pier, New London, 443–6851.

HOTELS AND MOTELS. There is just about every variety of accommodation in this southeastern Connecticut area, and because this is a summer-oriented vacation community the rates are higher during the warm weather seasons. Most rooms in hotels and motels have TV and air-conditioning, and pools are outdoor unless otherwise noted. Accommodations are listed by average price for double occupancy during the periods when rates are highest. At other times there would be an appreciable percentage decrease. Price ranges used are: *Deluxe,* $70 and up; *Expensive,* $50–$69; *Moderate,* $30–$49; *Inexpensive,* under $30. Always check for senior and family rates.

Branford

Branford Motor Inn and Conference Center, on U.S. Rte. 1, Exit 55, I–95, 06405 (488–8314). *Moderate.* Coffee shop, restaurant, and cocktail lounge. Sauna. Near New Haven.

MacDonald's Motel, on U.S. 1, Exit 55, I–95, 06405 (488–4381). *Inexpensive.* Some family units. Near Hammonassett State Park. Swimming and boating nearby. Near restaurants.

Clinton

Clinton Motel, 163 East Main St., Exit 63, I–95, 06413 (669–8850). *Inexpensive.* Small. Restaurants, water sports, tennis, and golf nearby.

East Lyme (Niantic)

Howard Johnson Motor Lodge, Exit 74, I–95, 06357 (739–6921). *Moderate.* 24-hour restaurant. Bar. Indoor pool. Saunas. Family rates.

TraveLodge, Exit 74, I–95, 06357 (739–5483). *Moderate.* Restaurant and cocktail lounge with entertainment. Golf and beaches nearby.

Morton House, Main St. (Rte. 156), Niantic 06357 (739–8564) *Inexpensive.* Large Victorian hotel facing Long Island Sound. Restaurant and bar.

Susse Chalet Motor Lodge, Exit 74, I–95, 06357 (800–258–1980). *Inexpensive.* Part of chain. Indoor pool. Adjoining restaurant. Golf and beaches nearby.

Groton

Gold Star Motel, 156 Kings Highway, off Rte. 184, 06340 (446–0660). *Moderate.* Indoor pool and sauna, exercise and game rooms. Restaurant and lounge.

Groton Motor Inn, jct. I–95 and 184, 06340 (445–9784). *Moderate.* Medium-sized motel with restaurant, bar, and room service. Spacious grounds overlooking Thames River. Near U.S. submarine base and historic sites.

Quality Inn, 404 Bridge St., 06340 (445–8141). *Moderate.* Restaurant and cocktail lounge with entertainment nightly. Near tourist attractions and shopping centers.

Sojourner Inn, 605 Gold Star Highway (Rte. 184), 06340 (445–1986). *Moderate.* A recently built small inn with guest rooms and suites. Restaurant and bar. Package rates on request.

Madison

Madison Beach Hotel, 94 W. Wharf Rd., 06443 (245–1404). *Expensive.* Restaurant, lounge, entertainment, beach swimming. Seasonal.

Mystic

The Inn at Mystic, jct. U.S. 1 and Rte. 27, 06355 (536–9604). *Deluxe.* A refurbished Victorian mansion overlooking coves and Mystic Harbor. On property of Mystic Motor Inn and the award-winning Flood Tide Restaurant.

Howard Johnson Motor Lodge, I–95, Exit 90, 06355 (536–2654). *Expensive.* Restaurant and bar, indoor pool and sauna. Some efficiencies. Golf and tourist attractions nearby.

The Mystic Hilton, Coogan Blvd., 06355 (572–0731; 800–826–8699). *Expensive.* Meeting and function rooms, guest rooms and suites. Dancing nightly; The Moorings restaurant and lounge. Indoor and outdoor pools and fitness center. Special package rates.

Ramada Inn, I–95, Exit 90, 06355 (536–4281). *Expensive.* Restaurant and bar. Playground. Indoor pool. Pets. Family rates.

Days Inn, Rte. 27, 06355 (572–0574). *Moderate.* A 122-room unit of the motel chain. Restaurant.

New London

Lighthouse Inn, Lower Blvd., 06320 (443–8411). *Deluxe.* Period furnishings in renovated mansion rooms, others in adjacent lodge. Restaurant and lounge. Across from Long Island Sound and white-sand beach. Near Ocean Beach Park.

Radisson New London, 35 Gov. Winthrop Blvd. 06320 (443–7000) *Expensive.* New London's only downtown hotel. Winthrop's Restaurant, cocktail lounge, and conference rooms. New in 1987.

Holiday Inn, Frontage Rd. 06320, I–95, Exits 82A north, 83 south (442–0631). *Expensive.* Restaurant. Lounge with entertainment most evenings. Near Connecticut College and U.S. Coast Guard Academy.

Norwich

Norwich Inn, on W. Thames St., Rte. 32 (886–2401). *Deluxe.* Elegance describes the public and guest rooms, and the spa which is in a separate building. Week-long and weekend spa programs are offered at all-inclusive rates. Excellent restaurant. Tea served daily. Property surrounded by a public golf course.

Sheraton-Norwich, Exit 80, Rte. 395, 06360 (889–5201). *Expensive.* A city hotel in a country setting. Restaurant and lounge with entertainment evenings. Indoor and outdoor pools. Sauna. Tennis courts nearby. Function and conference rooms.

Old Lyme

Bee & Thistle, 100 Lyme St., 06371 (434–1667). *Moderate.* Relaxed atmosphere in colonial rooms. Restaurant serving breakfast, luncheon, and dinner.

Old Lyme Inn, 85 Lyme St., 06371 (434–2600). *Moderate.* A most charming renovated Victorian house with antique furnishings and a fine French-inspired restaurant. Bar. Closed Mons.

Old Saybrook

Howard Johnson Motor Lodge, Ferry Point Rd. Exit 69, Rte I–95, 06475 (388–5716). *Moderate.* 24-hour restaurant, cocktail lounge, bar. Indoor pool, sauna.

Waterford

Blue Anchor Motel, 563 Boston Post Rd., 06385 (442–2072). *Moderate.* Rooms in main house, cottages, and motel. On Niantic River, convenient to boating and fishing. Beach privileges available.

Lamplighter Motel, Exit 81, I–95, 06385 (442–7227). *Moderate.* Some efficiencies. Miniature golf. Near historic sites, colleges, and U.S. Coast Guard Academy.

INNS, GUEST HOUSES, BED AND BREAKFASTS. Rooms in private homes or homes that have been refurbished for the purpose of bed-and-breakfast accommodations are becoming more and more popular in southeastern Connecticut. For the best arrangements, an area bed-and-breakfast registry should be consulted and reservations made in advance, especially during warm weather months. Try Nutmeg Bed & Breakfast, 222 Girard Ave., Hartford 06105 (236–6698) or Seacoast Landings B & B Registry, 133 Neptune Dr., Groton 06340 (442–1940). A sampling of inns follows. Inns in this area are generally *moderately* priced.

Groton

Shore Inne, 54 East Shore Ave., Groton Long Point 06340 (536–1180). A shorefront property. Family-style breakfast. Privileges for use of Long Island Sound beach nearby. Restaurants within driving distance.

Ledyard

Applewood Farms Inn, 528 Col. Ledyard Hwy., 06339 (536–2022). A rural setting within easy driving to Mystic, area beaches, and tourist attractions.

Mystic

The Adams House, 382 Cow Hill Rd., 06355 (572–9551). A restored late-18th-century colonial in a rural section of Mystic.

New London

Queen Anne Inne, 265 Williams St., Exits 83 north, 84 south, I–95 (447–2600). Central location. Full breakfast and afternoon tea. Beautifully restored Victorian house with period furnishings.

Noank

The Palmer Inn, 25 Church St., Noank 06340 (572–9000). A restored mansion by the sea. Near Mystic and area tourist attractions.

RESTAURANTS. Restaurants throughout the southeastern Connecticut shoreline area vary in many ways: ambience, cuisine, price, and service

CONNECTICUT

and are in locations ranging from shorefront to country. Prices ranges based on a full meal exclusive of beverages, tax, and tip are: *Deluxe,* $30 and up; *Expensive,* $25–$29; *Moderate,* $15–$24; *Inexpensive,* $14 and under.

Branford

Chez Bach, 1070 Main St. (488–8779). *Moderate.* Vietnamese cuisine. Reservations. Closed Mons.

Jonathon's, 225 Montowese St. (483–0073). *Moderate.* A menu of wide variety including pasta and seafood.

Groton

The Fisherman, on Groton Long Point Rd. in Noank (536–1717). *Expensive.* Seafood restaurant overlooking the water. Serving fresh local fish primarily. Cocktail lounge. Reservations on weekends.

Abbott's Lobster in the Rough, 117 Pearl St. in Noank (536–7719). *Moderate.* Seasonal, informal, well known for its fresh seafood. BYOB.

The Golden Cup, Rte. 184 (443–6228). *Moderate.* In Groton Motor Inn, overlooking Thames River. Traditional menu. Entertainment and dancing weekends.

Guilford

The Century House, 2455 Boston Post Rd., Exit 57, I–95 (453–2216). *Expensive.* Fine French cuisine served in a renovated foundry. Excellent service, linen, crystal, fresh flowers.

Sachem Country House, 111 Goose Lane (453–5261). *Expensive.* Convenient stop just off I–95 at Goose Lane exit. Country ambience. Seasonal specialties. Closed Mon.

The Little Stone House, 506 Whitfield St. (453–2566). *Moderate.* Enjoy fresh seafood and a view overlooking the docks where the fishermen unload their catches.

Madison

The Wharf, 94 W. Wharf Rd. (245–0005). *Expensive.* The restaurant at Madison Beach Hotel. New England seafood specialties as well as beef and poultry. Views of the sound add to the ambience. Reservations. Closed Mon.

Friends & Company, 11 Boston Post Rd. (245–0462). *Inexpensive.* Specializing in foods prepared to order.

Mystic

Flood Tide at the Inn at Mystic, Rtes. 1 and 27 (536–8140). *Expensive.* Overlooking Mystic Harbor. Serving throughout the day. Award-winning French-inspired menu.

J. P. Daniels, Rte. 184, Old Mystic (572–9564). *Expensive.* Provincial French cuisine. A restored barn with simple country decor.

Seamen's Inne, Greenmanville Ave., Rte. 27 (536–9649). *Expensive.* At Mystic Seaport on Mystic River. Typical New England menu for luncheon and dinner. Oyster bar. Sun. brunch.

The Mooring in the Mystic Hilton Hotel, Coogan Blvd. (572–0731). One of the better restaurants in the area, for both ambience and culinary expertise.

Margaritaville, 12 Water St. (536–4589). *Moderate.* Mexican foods are the specialties in this barnwood restaurant. Fireplaces and hanging plants. Salad bar. Located in historic downtown Mystic in renovated factory building.

New London

Lighthouse Inn, Lower Blvd. (443–8411). *Expensive.* A renovated Victorian mansion overlooking Long Island Sound. Traditional New England menu with beef and seafood specialties. Live music and dancing on Sat. nights.

Ye Olde Tavern, 345 Bank St. (442–0353). *Expensive.* Family-owned and operated, serving charbroiled steaks, chops, and freshly caught seafood. Bar.

Chuck's Steak House, 250 Pequot Ave. (443–1323). *Moderate.* Part of a chain of cozy, small steak houses serving charbroiled meats and fish. This dining room has windows on three sides overlooking the Thames River and adjacent marinas.

The Gondolier, 92 Huntington St. (447–1781). *Moderate.* On Whale Oil Row in downtown New London. Attracts tourists and local aficionados of Italian fare. Bar.

Paisano's, 655 Bank St. (443–3275). *Moderate.* Italian home cooking. Small, attractive bistro in downtown New London.

Norwich

Norwich Inn, Rte. 32, New London Road (886–2401). *Deluxe.* Elegance prevails throughout the inn, and the menu, changing daily, reflects the general ambience.

Huntington's Restaurant at Sheraton Norwich, Exit 80, Rte. 395 (889–5201). *Moderate.* Interesting menu with frequent buffets. Nightly entertainment in Benedict's Tavern.

Old Lyme

Bee & Thistle Inn, 100 Lyme St., Rte. 1; Exit 70, I–95 (434–1667). *Expensive.* An old, restored country inn serving three meals daily. Reservations suggested, especially for breakfast.

Old Lyme Inn, 85 Lyme St., Rte. 1; Exit 70, I–95 (434–2600). *Expensive.* A restored 1870 mansion with floor-to-ceiling windows overlooking Old Lyme's Main St. The decor is French-inspired, punctuated by white linen, crystal, and roses. The menu is in French and the limited selections change seasonally. Homemade soups, pastry, and desserts.

Old Saybrook

The Dock, at Saybrook Point, overlooking the mouth of Connecticut River (388–4665). *Moderate.* Seafood is the specialty, served in dining room with windows on three sides with ample view of river.

Stonington

Harbor View, 60 Water St. (535–2720). *Deluxe.* Overlooks Stonington Harbor and dragger docks. Typical New England waterfront scene. French influence on some seafood specialties. Bar.

TOURIST INFORMATION. The free Vacation Guide issued on request from the Connecticut Division of Tourism, 210 Washington St., Hartford 06106 (566–2496) is filled with information of value to the visitor to this area. It includes lists of lodgings, attractions, and recreational and camping facilities, as well as other incidental points of interest.

Information is readily available from the Greater Hartford Convention and Visitors Bureau, 1 Civic Center, Hartford 06103 (728–6789), and the New Haven Convention and Visitors Bureau, 155 Church St., New Haven 06510 (787–8822). A list of roadside areas, motorists' hints, information booth sites, and a Connecticut State map may be obtained from the Department of Transportation, 24 Wolcott Hill Rd., Wethersfield 06109 (566–5280).

Mystic Seaport's new Visitors' Center will offer orientation and information concerning the vicinity. A state-owned and -operated information center is on Rte. I–95 south in North Stonington. Another information center is The Southeastern Connecticut Tourism District, 27 Masonic St.; Box 89, New London 06320 (444–2206).

SEASONAL EVENTS. Although this is an area where summer activities predominate, there are concerts, antique shows, and other special events taking place here during the off-season. The colleges will supply information on events on the campuses and the local newspaper, the *New London Day,* publishes a weekend edition that lists the upcoming events.

Country fairs take place frequently in this area and schedules are available from the Association of Connecticut Fairs, 190 South Rd., Box 363, Somers 06071.

For information on art shows, crafts, theater, concerts, etc., contact the Connecticut Commission on the Arts, 190 Trumbull St., Hartford 06106 (566–4770).

April and May: Charter fishing usually begins in late Apr. or early May and Ocean Beach Park in New London is open Memorial Day weekend–Labor Day.

June: The Yale-Harvard Rowing Regatta in New London (mid-June) is a highlight of the summer; there are symphony and jazz concerts on the Green in New Haven.

July: The International Food and Sail Festival at City Pier in New London, and summer concerts at Harkness Memorial Park in Waterford; the Annual Ancient Muster, Fife and Drum Corps in Deep River. Handcrafts Exposition on the Green in Guilford.

August: U.S. Coast Guard Anniversary Celebration, New London (early Aug.); Clinton Bluefish Festival (mid-Aug.); Mystic Outdoor Arts Festival; Lyman Allyn Outdoor Antiques Show & Flea Market in New London; Ocean Beach Arts & Crafts Show also in New London.

September: Bluefish Tournament, Niantic (to mid-Oct.).

October: Dyer Dhow Derby at Mystic Seaport.

During the autumn there are numerous foliage tours throughout the region and information on these may be obtained from local tourist information centers.

December: Lantern-light tours and Carol Sing at Mystic Seaport Museum (advance tickets for this are usually sold out early in the season). Torchlight Parade, Muster and Carol Sing, Old Saybrook.

TOURS. Heritage Trail Tours, Box 138, Farmington 06034 (677–8867) has several tours through the area, stopping at historic sites, tourist attractions, and interesting restaurants for lunch or dinner. Reservations required.

Mystic Clipper and **Mystic Whaler** cruise Long Island Sound on 3- to 5-day summer cruises. Mystic Whaler, 7 Holmes St., Mystic 06355 (536–4218).

Voyager. Day sails on this 50-ft. schooner from Mystic on Long Island and Block Island sounds. Steamboat Wharf, Mystic 06355 (536–0416).

Thames River Cruises. Dinner and jazz cruises; boats are docked at Thames Boatel and Harbor Inn, 193 Thames St., Groton 06340 (445–8111).

Because sightseeing tours are being introduced each season and because the schedules and point of departure for each varies, it would be well to inquire at one of the local information centers.

PARKS AND NATURE CENTERS. Fort Griswold State Park; Monument St. in Groton (445–1729). Seasonal. No admission charged. A memorial obelisk dedicated to Revolutionary War heroes. Historical museum displays.

Hammonassett Beach State Park, Exit 62, I–95 in Madison (245–2785). Large campsite and 2 mi. of Long Island Sound beachfront. Picnicking facilities. Parking fees.

Connecticut College Arboretum, Williams St., New London (447–1911). Native trees and shrubs on over 400 acres. Pond and hiking trail. Free.

Ocean Beach Park, Ocean Ave., New London (447–3031). A recreation area with pool and white-sand beach for swimming. Amusement park and picnic area. Restaurant and lounge. Snack food concessions. Seasonal. Fee for parking.

Mohegan Park, Mohegan Park Rd., Norwich (886–2381, Ext. 210). A small zoo and a memorial rose garden. Seasonal.

Harkness Memorial State Park, Rte. 213, Waterford. Beautiful flower gardens. Ample picnic facilities. White-sand beach on Long Island Sound, but swimming is not allowed. Admission charged.

VINEYARDS AND WINERIES. Crosswoods Vineyard, 75 Chester Main Rd., North Stonington (535–2205). 30 acres, overlooking Long Island Sound. Free tours by appointment.

Stonington Vineyard, Taugwonk Rd., Stonington (535–1222).

SPORTS. In all seasons there are opportunities in southeastern Connecticut for participant sports, but during the summer the activities in, on, or near the water usually take precedence; this coastline, along Long Island Sound, is ideal for boating, fishing, swimming, or just lazing in the sun on a white-sand beach. Some of the possibilities for year-round activities include:

Golf: In Groton the Shennecosset Golf Club, Plant St. (445–0262), 18 holes; in Stonington, Pequot Golf Club, Wheeler Rd. (535–1898), 18 holes; in Norwich, Norwich Golf Course, W. Thames St. (889–6973), 18 holes.

Tennis: In Waterford, Waterford Health and Racquet Club, 6 Fargo Rd. (442–9466), five indoor tennis courts, fitness center, and professional instruction.

Racquetball: The New London Sports Complex, 145 State Pier Rd., New London (442–0588) has seven climate-controlled racquetball courts, and a fully equipped fitness center.

FISHING. Marinas along the shore in Groton, Noank, Mystic, New London, Waterford, and Niantic are home ports for sportfishing charter boats licensed to carry no more than six passengers. In Groton and Waterford there are party boats licensed to carry more than six, and these go out on regular half-day or full-day schedules Apr.–mid-Nov.

The State Board of Fisheries and Game, a division of the Department of Environmental Protection, 165 Capitol Ave., Hartford 06106 (566–2304) has information concerning freshwater fishing.

HUNTING. Small-animal hunting is regulated by the state. The Department of Environmental Protection, 165 Capitol Ave., Hartford 06106 (566–2304) will furnish information on seasons and licenses.

CAMPING. The Parks and Recreation Division of the Department of Environmental Protection, 165 Capitol Ave., Hartford 06106 (566–2304) provides a list of parks, forests, snowmobiling, campsites, and camping applications.

SPECTATOR SPORTS. Football games in the fall are played in college and university stadiums throughout the area, including the University of Connecticut at Storrs, the U.S. Coast Guard Academy in New London. Schedules are usually available at local Chambers of Commerce or at the school's information offices.

Stock car racing in Waterford is seasonal and in New London, the Yale-Harvard Rowing **regatta** in June attracts many.

HISTORIC SITES AND HOUSES. There are countless historic sites and restored homes in this area. Call ahead to check days, hours, and admission fees.

Clinton

Stanton House, 63 E. Main St. (669–2132). Late 18th-century house with some original furnishings. Early merchandise displays including antique dinnerware. Seasonal.

East Lyme (Niantic)

Thomas Lee House (1660) and **Little Boston School** (1734), Rte. 156 (739–6070). Original property had one room called "Judgment Hall" said to be the one-time courtroom of Judge Thomas Lee. 17th-century furnishings. Seasonal.

Groton

Groton Monument and Fort Griswold (Fort Griswold State Park), Monument St. and Park Ave. (445–1729). Memorial obelisk; museum of Revolutionary War memorabilia. Park open year-round. Monument seasonal.

Guilford

Hyland House. 84 Boston Post Rd. (453–9477). Mid-17th-century colonial saltbox with period furnishings and walk-in fireplaces built for cooking. Seasonal.

Thomas Griswold House, 171 Boston St. (453–5452). Late 18th-century saltbox. Seasonal.

Madison

Allis-Bushnell House and Museum, 853 Boston Post Rd. (245–4567). Late 18th-century house with exhibits of antique dolls, toys, and early household utensils. Seasonal.

New London

Joshua Hempsted House (1678), 11 Hempstead St. (443–7949). One of the oldest 17th-century houses in the state. Early American furnishings. Seasonal.

Monte Cristo Cottage, 325 Pequot Ave. (443–0051 or 443–5378). Turn-of-the-century summer home owned by the family of playwright Eugene O'Neill. Theater library. Mon.–Fri. afternoons and by appt.

Nathan Hale Schoolhouse (1774), Captain's Walk. Where Nathan Hale taught prior to enlisting for service in the Revolutionary War. Seasonal.

Nathaniel Hempsted House (1759), Hempstead and Truman Sts. (443–7949). A mid-18th-century cut-stone house often referred to as the Huguenot House. Seasonal.

Olde Towne Mill (1650), Mill St. (444–2206). Built originally for Gov. John Winthrop, Jr., and was later a gristmill. Restored several times over the years. Grounds open year-round. Building seasonal.

Shaw Mansion, 11 Blinman St. (443–1209). Mid-18th-century stone mansion, home of Nathaniel Shaw. Served as Connecticut naval office during the Revolution. Local historical records and local history library. Tues.–Sat. afternoons. Closed major holidays. Admission charged.

Norwich

Leffingwell Inn (1675), 348 Washington St. (889–9440). A historic, accurately restored and furnished home of Thomas Leffingwell. Seasonal, winter by appt.

Stonington

Denison Homestead (1717), Pequotsepos Rd. (536–9248). The history of a family representing several generations and furnished with their belongings. Seasonal and by appt.

Old Lighthouse Museum (1823), on the point (535–1440). One of the oldest lighthouses in the U.S. Miscellaneous historical exhibits.

MUSEUMS AND ART GALLERIES. This area has several specialized museums as well as some fine art collections. Call ahead to check days, hours, and admission fees.

New London

Lyman Allyn Art Museum, 625 Williams St. (443–2545). Connecticut silver and furniture. American, European, and Oriental art. Dollhouses and toys.

Thames Science Center, Gallows Lane, near Connecticut College campus (442–0391). Exhibits of chiefly environmental subjects. Films and lecture programs. Open daily.

Norwich

Slater Memorial Museum and Converse Art Gallery, 108 Crescent St. (887–2506). American, Oriental, Egyptian, African, and Indian paintings and sculpture.

Old Lyme

Florence Griswold House Museum, 96 Lyme St. (434–5542). Once the home of the Old Lyme Art Colony. Changing exhibits during the summer. Local history.
Lyme Academy of Fine Arts, 84 Lyme St. (434–5232). Early 19th-century building. On National Register of Historic Places. Changing exhibits and special programs.
Lyme Art Association Gallery, Lyme St. (434–7802). Summer gallery shows. Seasonal.

MUSIC, DANCE, AND STAGE. Musical events predominate among the area's performing arts productions. Concert series have been established over the years in New Haven, New London, at the University of Connecticut at Storrs, and in many of the smaller towns.

Yale at New Haven, Connecticut College, and the U.S. Coast Guard Academy at New London, as well as other independent sponsors, offer a wide variety of concerts. Performers in the area range from touring symphony orchestras, theater orchestras, bands, fife and drum corps, barbershop quartets, operettas and operas, to contemporary combos.

Dance concerts, although less frequent, are also presented often by internationally known troupes and others, including local groups.

In New London, the Garde Arts Center on Captain's Walk is a 1,545-seat theater where various drama, dance, and musical performances are held.

Area choral groups throughout southeastern Connecticut frequently present oratorio-type concerts, sometimes with symphony orchestra accompaniment.

Schedules for music, dance, or theater performances and the companies vary seasonally, and therefore current information concerning schedules and ticket prices should be sought from the local tourist information offices, college, or university public relations offices, or from a local library.

SHOPPING. Southeastern Connecticut offers a variety of shopping experiences in novel shopping centers that seem to have sources for just about anything anyone could desire. New Haven's downtown shopping mall right in the center of town is in contrast with **Olde Mistick Village** where there are individual buildings for each little boutique—all designed to reflect colonial architecture. **Crystal Mall** in Waterford offers still another kind of shopping experience with over 100 stores, numerous restaurants and food counters, attracting thousands of shoppers.

Antique shops are dotted throughout the area and are particularly found on country roads. Route 1 from New Haven to the Rhode Island line is a continuous shopping area with everything from furniture, seafood, linens, clothing of all kinds, automobile supplies, to boats and cars—to cite just a few types of merchandise available in the small shoreside towns and villages.

Some of the downtowns have been redeveloped in recent decades and, in direct competition with the malls, seem to be doing well.

NIGHTLIFE AND BARS. Most hotels and motels have cocktail lounges that provide live entertainment on weekends; some nightly. Other bars that are popular with locals and are truly "finds" for visitors to the area are opening up. Consult the local newspaper for location, hours, current music offered (this varies in some cases several times a week).

NORTHEASTERN CONNECTICUT

Northeastern Connecticut is the quiet corner of the state; several towns in this section date to settlements founded in the eighteenth century. The region has remained rural and there are no tall buildings, no heavy downtown traffic, few major highways. Here the major promotion directs a visitor to "serenity and beauty and tranquility." Country roads invite long walks and bicycling, and in autumn the changing colors of the foliage are the main attraction. Here are picturesque rivers and streams, lakes and ponds, and state forests. Overnight accommodations are in country inns or bed-and-breakfast facilities that are typically Connecticut.

This was Indian land, and it was with the acquisition from the Indians that the local history began. A fine compendium of historic points of interest has been issued jointly by several of the regional historical societies. This document presents, with illustrations, maps, and suggested walking and driving tours, a background study of the area. The Northeast Connecticut Visitors District, Box 9, Thompson 06377, will provide information for anyone wishing to obtain a copy or will provide the names and addresses of the several historical societies. This district office provides visitor information concerning the region and guides to overnight accommodations and restaurants.

In and Around Coventry

Among historic sites open to the publc in Coventry is the Nathan Hale Homestead. Hale was hanged by the British in Manhattan and buried in an unmarked grave, and his brother, Richard, is in a grave in the Dutch West Indies; their father, Deacon Hale, expressed his love for his sons on a cenotaph he erected in a burial ground in Coventry, now known as the Nathan Hale Cemetery. The Revolutionary War collection in the Hale house is of historic significance.

Lebanon, another village with a classic green, is southeast of Coventry via Route 87. Jonathan Trumbull's home was on the green. He was a towering figure in the Revolution who won praise from Washington: "But for Jonathan Trumbull, the war could not have been carried to a successful conclusion."

Trumbull was governor of the Connecticut Colony when war broke out. His sympathies were with the revolutionaries, and he lent his prestige, his money, and his efforts to further the war effort. From a building near his home, the "war office" of the Revolution, Trumbull marshalled supplies and men to keep the army fighting. So efficient and effective was this man that Washington was often heard to say, "Let us consult Brother Jonathan." Trumbull's house and the "war office" may be visited. He was the first governor of the State of Connecticut.

Nearby is his son's home, the artist known for his paintings of early American statesmen and his famous *The Signing of the Declaration of Independence.*

In Woodstock,"Roseland Cottage" (on Route 169, on the Common) is distinguished by its exterior color. It is an example of a Gothic Revival cottage surrounded by handsome gardens and landscaping and appropriately designed outbuildings, including a bowling alley. This house is striking among the traditional colonial homes of this country town. It is maintained and operated by the Society for the Preservation of New England Antiquities.

The Prudence Crandall School, named for its founder, was the first school in New England exclusively for black girls. Founded in 1833, it is now a museum operated by the state.

Famous worldwide is Adelma Simmons' Capriland Herb Farm on Silver Street, in Coventry, where thirty-one different gardens of herbs and scented geraniums are the main attraction. The gardens surround an eighteenth-century dwelling which is always decorated according to the season and where herb luncheons are featured daily, except Sundays. These luncheons are by advance reservation from April 1 until December only; they include a guided tour and lecture through the herb gardens, preceding the meal. Herbs and herb products are for sale along with herb-associated items in one of several outbuildings on the property. A bookshop stocked with volumes on gardening and herbs features books written and published by Adelma Simmons; it provides ample souvenirs for the visitor to take home.

Wineries have been on the increase in Connecticut in recent years and several are in this area: Hamlet Hill Winery on Route 101 in Pomfret and St. Hillary's Winery on Webster Road in North Grosvenordale, the latter noted for wines made of several locally grown fruits. The Nutmeg Vineyard and Winery on Bunker Hill Road in Coventry uses what they call a "classic European" process of winemaking. Tours of the vineyards and wine tasting have lured many visitors here; hours are seasonal, so it's a good idea to make an appointment before visiting.

Antique auctions and shops vie with artists' ateliers and art galleries for those visitors whose interests lie in these areas. Treasures may be found in this section of the state.

Old cemeteries may not be for everyone; however, for people interested in "rubbings" there are ancient slate and granite monuments in the local cemeteries.

Factory outlets are reminiscent of the time when there were prosperous spinning and weaving mills in this part of Connecticut. The old factories and mills not only brought prosperity but were the foundations for the communities in which they were established. The factories had mill houses for their workers and their families, and a company store stocked clothing and groceries. Some mill owners had a company farm for raising poultry and vegetables, and the factory owners' homes were among the largest and most elegant in the towns.

Stonewall Stables in Lebanon, "a nonprofit, educational corporation, dedicated to the preservation of all aspects of the horse and horse-drawn vehicles," attracts visitors interested in horses and the collection of carriages. Tour guides here dress in 1900-period costumes and enlighten visitors on horsemanship and the lifestyle of the turn of the century. There are guided tours on Sundays; driving instruction and carriage and sleigh rides are included in the Stables' annual program.

The main campus of the University of Connecticut is in Storrs, near Mansfield, where the first silk mill in America was located (1829). "UConn" is a bustling, ever-growing institution. The campus buildings are set on rolling hills with ponds and streams between them. The university began as an agricultural school and is one of the oldest and most respected in the country. Several branches of the university in cities throughout the state include a medical center and dental and law schools.

Norwich

Norwich, settled in 1660, has been an industrial city since its earliest years. It is at the head of the Thames River, where water power from the Shetucket and Yantic rivers, flowing into the Thames, provided the power for manufacturing plants. Textiles were particularly important, along with paper (an early paper mill began in 1766) and tool and die fabrication plants. Thermos bottles were for years a leading product here.

Visitors to Norwich should see the town's most important historic house, the Leffingwell Inn (1675), 348 Washington Street at the junction of Routes 2 and 169. The home of Norwich industrialist Christopher Leffingwell, it has been authentically restored and furnished with fine antiques. Continental officers met here to plot war plans, and George Washington visited frequently.

The Slater Memorial Museum, dedicated in 1888 and located on the grounds of Norwich Free Academy, is noted for its Greek, Roman, and Renaissance plaster casts, American art, furniture from the seventeenth to the twentieth centuries, American Indian artifacts, and Oriental, African, and European art and textiles. In 1906, as an adjunct to the Slater, the Converse Memorial building was built; it provides six spacious exhibition galleries and facilities for the Norwich Art School.

Near the Yantic River Falls in the northern part of the city is Indian Leap, so named because the Mohegan Indians drove the Narragansetts over the cliff in 1643 during their Battle at Great Plain.

Mohegan Park and Memorial Rose Garden on Mohegan Road have a small zoo, picnic area, and a profusion of roses in bloom in June. The Rose Arts Festival, an annual event in Norwich, was inspired by this array.

When traveling north from Norwich via routes I–395 and 138, visitors to the Voluntown area should include Pachaug State Forest in their itinerary. This is one of the largest preserves in the state (23,115 acres) and includes a 22,000-acre lake, a popular place among freshwater fishermen.

Willimantic, Storrs, Putnam

Willimantic, northwest of Norwich, was chartered in 1893. Known as "the thread city" because of the thread-making mills here, it has more recently become known as the location of Eastern Connecticut State University. This is a rural, largely residential area.

Storrs is a community or village in the town of Mansfield, a settlement on land formerly owned by the Mohegan Indians dating back to 1692. This is almost entirely farming country. Connecticut's Agricultural College had its origins here in 1881; this institution developed into what is now the sprawling main campus of the University of Connecticut.

Once a mill town, Putnam, settled in 1693, was named for Israel Putnam, a military man and a local hero. Throughout the area, Major General Israel Putnam's name is memorialized in a variety of ways, and legends of his war years are prolific.

This "quiet corner" of Connecticut can provide a vacation of relaxation without the hurly-burly of urban ambience. It is country. It is woods and forests and lakes and ponds. It is farmland with rolling hills and green meadows. And the people who live here are doing everything possible to keep it just that way.

PRACTICAL INFORMATION FOR
NORTHEASTERN CONNECTICUT

Note: The area code for all Connecticut is 203

HOW TO GET THERE AND AROUND. This part of Connecticut is most accessible by car. The nearest airport is Hartford's Bradley International (where there are major car rental companies). Bonanza buses (800–556–3815) make stops in Putnam, Willimantic, and Danielson.

The main highway running through northeastern Connecticut is I–395. It runs north from Norwich through Danielson and Putnam to the Massachusetts border. Rte. 32 also from Norwich heads north through Willimantic, Coventry, and Willington where it joins I–84.

A network of secondary roads in this area not only gives the tourist a wide choice of scenery but affords opportunities to visit towns and villages that are reminiscent of early Connecticut.

HOTELS AND MOTELS. This is rural Connecticut, the "quiet corner," and there are not the urban accommodations here that one finds in cities. Country inns and bed and breakfasts predominate although an occasional small motel may be found along the highway. Price ranges for the following listings are: *Expensive,* $55 and up; *Moderate,* $35–$55; *Inexpensive,* under $35. A sales tax of 7½% is added.

Ashford

Ashford Motel, 15 Snow Hill Rd, Ashford 06278 (684–2221). *Inexpensive.* A medium-sized motel with coffee shop in a woodland setting of 140 acres. Pets.

Chaplin

Pleasant View Lodge Motel, Rte. 6, 06235 (455–9588). *Inexpensive.* Lounge and restaurant. Golf, tennis, and boating nearby.

Dayville

Bon Aire Motel, R.R. 10, Box 78, Dayville 06241 (774–4515). *Moderate.*

Mansfield

Willimantic Motor Inn, Rte. 195, Box 258, 06250 (423–8451). *Moderate.* Golf and boating nearby.

Plainfield

Plainfield Motor Inn, Lathrop Rd., 06374 (564–4021). *Moderate.* Lounge and restaurant. Nearby golf and tennis. Near Greyhound Race Track.

INNS, GUEST HOUSES, BED AND BREAKFASTS. For rooms in a bed-and-breakfast guest home, contact a bed-and-breakfast registry such as Nutmeg Bed & Breakfast, 222 Girard Ave., Hartford 06105 (236–6698).

A list of bed-and-breakfast inns follows. These generally fall in the *Moderate–Expensive* categories.

Brooklyn

Tannerbrook, Rte. 169, 06234 (774–4822). Interesting, restored colonial home in rural area. Swimming, private lake. Some rooms with fireplace. Restricted smoking. No pets. Children over five years. Full breakfast.

Pomfret

Cobbscroft, Rtes. 44 and 169, 06258 (928–5560). A restored, late 18th-century property. Watercolor gallery. Continental breakfast. No smoking or pets.

Col. Angell House, Wright's Corner, Pomfret Center 06259 (928–3531). No smoking and children over six only. Closed holidays.

Selah Farm, Rtes. 44 and 169, Pomfret Center 06259 (928–7051). Full breakfast. Property on 25 sprawling acres across from Pomfret and Rectory schools.

Putnam

Felshaw Tavern, Five Mile River Rd., 06260 (928–3467). A restored mid-18th-century tavern. Full breakfast. Private baths.

King's Inn, Grove St., 06260; Exit 96, Rte. 395 (928–7961). Continental breakfast. Nearby golf and tennis.

Storrs

Farmhouse on the Hill above Gurleyville, 418 Gurleyville Rd., 06268 (429–1400). This is a working farm near University of Connecticut. Full breakfast served.

Thompson

The Samuel Watson House, Rte. 193, 07277 (923–2491). A 1767 Colonial house with several fireplaces and an art gallery. Smoking restricted.

Woodstock

The Inn at Woodstock Hill, Plaine Hill Rd. 06281 (928–0528). Restored country home. Continental breakfast and tea served afternoons. Some rooms with fireplaces. Lunch and dinner served in the dining room.

RESTAURANTS. Country restaurants tend to be less formal than those in urban communities. The local kitchens are known for area specialties, generally using products fresh from local farms so menus tend to be seasonal and recipes are indigenous to the area. The following price ranges are based on a full meal, exclusive of beverages, tax, and tip: *Expensive,* $25–$30; *Moderate,* $15–$25.

Brooklyn

The Golden Lamb Buttery, Hillandale Farm, Rte. 169 (774–4423). *Expensive.* Luncheon Tues.–Sat.; dinners Fri. and Sat. only, by reservation. June–Dec. Numerous farm-fresh vegetables and an imaginative gourmet menu uniquely served.

Coventry

Caprilands Herb Farm, Silver St. (742–7244). *Moderate.* Herb lecture-luncheons by reservation daily except Sun. Seasonal. An 18th-century farmhouse and outbuildings surrounded by 31 different herb gardens.

Thompson

Vernon Stiles Inn Restaurant, Rte. 193 (923–9571) *Expensive.* A charming country inn built around an 18th-century home. Handsome antique furnishings. Tap room, lounge, and dining rooms.

Willimantic

The Clark's, Corner Meadow and North Sts. (423–1631). *Expensive.* Small family restaurant since 1949. Imaginative American cooking. Cocktail lounge.

TOURIST INFORMATION. The best source of information about Connecticut's "quiet corner" is from the Northeast Connecticut Visitors District, Box 9, Thompson 06277 (923–2998) or Tourism Division, Economic Development Commission, 210 Washington St., Hartford 06106 (566–3948).

SEASONAL EVENTS. The University of Connecticut provides the area with diverse events throughout the year and calendars of events are provided by the area visitors district office, address above. These events range from dramatics to football to concerts, sing-alongs, and even "fun-runs." Often professional ensembles are scheduled at the Jorgenson Theater at the university. The public information office, University of Connecticut, Storrs 06268 (486–2000) would provide schedules and ticket information.

PARKS AND FORESTS. This is an area where state forests cover large areas of the land and are popular destinations for family vacations or outdoor recreation. Two of the large state forests are the following:
Pachaug State Forest, 23,115 acres, is northeast of Norwich on Rte. 49 near Voluntown. It is a popular location for families seeking a good place to fish, swim, or enjoy their boats on Hopeville Pond. There are family campsites and hiking and cross-country ski trails.
Natchaug State Forest, 12,935 acres, is off Rte. 198 in Eastford, north of Willimantic. There are camping facilities for backpackers as well as family campsites. Added features are the hiking and horse trails as well as the good fishing in the Natchaug River.
For further information concerning state parks and forests call 566–2304, Parks Department and Recreation Division, of Environmental Protection.

SPORTS. Golf, tennis, fishing, and hunting as well as camping, lake swimming, skiing, and other participant sports have special appeal throughout the region.
For **golf** there are courses in Coventry, Skungamaug River Golf Course (18 holes), Folly Lane (742–9348) and Twin Hills Country Club (18 holes), Rte. 31 (742–9705). In Norwich, Norwich Golf Course, W. Thames St., Norwich (889–6973).

Tennis courts available to the public are at private campgrounds, or nearby. These include Strawberry Park, Box 830, Pierce Rd., Norwich 06360 (886–1944) and Circle "C" Campground, RFD No. 1, Box 23A, Voluntown 06354 (564–4534).

Freshwater **swimming** in lakes would be best found at the state forests such as Pachaug.

Skiing: There are **cross-country ski** trails as well as **snowmobile** trails at Pachaug State Forest.

HUNTING AND FISHING. State regulations designate allowable hunting and fishing seasons. Information and licenses may be obtained at local town halls; or additionally available for fishing in some bait and tackle shops near lakes, ponds, or streams. Information can be requested from Parks and Recreation Division, Department of Environmental Protection, 165 Capitol Ave., Hartford 06106 (566–2304).

CAMPING. For a complete list of campsites and their facilities, an inquiry to the State Parks and Recreation Office, Department of Environmental Protection, 165 Capitol Ave., Hartford 06106 (566–2304) would bring a complete list. The *Vacation Guide,* published by the Tourism Division, Department of Economic Development, 210 Washington St., Hartford 06106 (566–3385) also has a list of state campsites as well as private campgrounds.

SPECTATOR SPORTS. Spectator sports in Northeastern Connecticut feature the football, basketball, and other varsity games at the University of Connecticut. Schedules from the University Athletic Department Information Office, Storrs, 06268, for mail requests.

The Greyhound Race Track (dog racing) in Plainfield is a major attraction in Connecticut, where there are pari-mutuel betting facilities. For information, contact Division of Special Revenue, Box 11424, Russell Rd., Newington 06111 (566–2755).

HISTORIC SITES AND HOUSES. Because of the long history of the Northeastern Connecticut settlements and the cooperative efforts of the historical societies (the Association of Northeastern Connecticut Historical Societies), the area offers the history buff a gold mine of interesting historic sites and houses. The document produced by the Windham County historical societies would be of great value as a guide to visitors with this specific interest. Write to Northeast Visitor District, Box 9, Thompson 06277 or call 923–2998.

Sites range from the statue and grave of General Israel Putnam, famous Revolutionary War commander to the Brooklyn Fair Grounds—the oldest continuously operating country fair in America, to early spinning and weaving mills and mill villages, to birthplaces, homes, and family dwellings of statesmen and patriots as well as typical homes of generations of area residents.

Because of the wealth of these properties, even the most concise listing could not do the area justice, but the following is a sampling. Call ahead to check days, hours, and admission fees.

Canterbury

Prudence Crandall School, on the Canterbury Green (546–9916 or 506–3005). New England's first school for black girls (1833). Closed Mon., Tues., and national holidays.

Coventry

Nathan Hale Homestead, South St. (742–6917). Built in 1776 by Deacon Hale, Nathan Hale's father. Open May 15–Oct. 15. Closed Mon.

Lebanon

Jonathan Trumbull House, on the Green, Rte. 87 (642–7558). This house, dating from 1735, was the home of Connecticut's colonial governor (1769–1784). Open May–Oct. Closed Mon.

Jonathan Trumbull, Jr. House, on the Green, Rte. 87 (642–6040). This is the home once occupied by Governor Trumbull's son. There are interesting 18th-century antiques among the furnishings.

Mansfield

Gurleyville Grist Mill, near I–95 in Mansfield (429–6526). Connecticut's only remaining stone gristmill, built in 1830. A miller's house nearby is a small museum.

Woodstock

Roseland Cottage, Rte. 169 (928–4074). Distinguished for its pink color, this home, with some of the original furnishings, has been noted as an example of Gothic Revival architecture. Open to the public June–Sept. 15.

MUSEUMS. Historical societies in some towns have museums of local history, but probably the most outstanding museum in the district is the **William Benton Museum of Art** at the University of Connecticut at Storrs, which is open to visitors daily, Mon.–Sat. 10 A.M.–4 P.M. and Sunday 1–5 P.M. Permanent and traveling exhibits are of special interest. For schedules of events here as well as those of the Schools of Music and Drama and the university film schedule, call the 24-hour Infoline, 486–2106, or send an inquiry to the University of Connecticut School of Fine Arts, U–128, Room 202, 875 Coventry Rd., Storrs 06268. The **State Museum of Natural History,** at the University in Storrs (486–4460), has collections dealing with archaeology and wildlife; a mounted Great White Shark caught in area waters is a highlight of the collections.

In Brooklyn, the **New England Center for Contemporary Art** on Rte. 169 is a museum of 20th-century art on several floors in a restored 18th-century barn. Traveling exhibits supplement permanent displays and artists are in residence here during the summer. Seasonal. Weekdays 1–4 P.M. and weekends 1–5 P.M. Free.

MUSIC AND STAGE. Most of the concerts and stage shows in this area center around those offered by the University of Connecticut either at Jorgenson Nutmeg Theater or Jorgenson Auditorium, in Storrs.

Jorgenson Nutmeg Theater, University of Connecticut, Storrs 06268 (486–2106). Home of the Nutmeg Theater Company and a stage for visiting theatrical road companies. Schedules and ticket information on request.

Jorgenson Auditorium, University of Connecticut, Storrs 06268 (486–4226). Annual concert series by subscription as well as available individual tickets. Well-known symphony and chamber music concerts are held here as well as dance concerts and recitals.

Data General Cultural Center, Rte. 169, Woodstock 06281. For information concerning programs (928–2946). For tickets and reservations, contact The Pomfret Spirit Shop, Rte. 169, Pomfret 06259 (928–2946). Professional theater road companies perform here and a subscription series of concerts is also available. Some semiprofessional local programming is also presented here.

Bradley Playhouse, 30 Front St., Putnam 06260 (928–7887). Concerts and classic films are presented here.

SHOPPING. The northeastern Connecticut area is not particularly known as a shopping center. There are the usual small shops in the towns, but probably the outstanding merchandise to be found are the treasures for sale in the numerous antique shops scattered through this part of the country. Running a close second would be the factory stores which usually dispose of "seconds" from the local mills. Items vary from time to time, and fabrics would lead any list.

In season, the farm markets and roadside stands offer produce raised and sold by the local farmers. Some add preserves and bakery to their daily offerings with fruit pies, in season, popular among buyers. Autumn's harvest is most colorful at these stands and markets, and the variety of garden flowers give extra color to the displays.

THE HARTFORD AREA

Hartford, Connecticut's second largest city after Bridgeport, has been the state capital since 1875. The Old State House (1796) on Constitution Plaza in downtown Hartford was the site of the Legislature until the new Capitol was completed. Today the Old State House is a museum, and the Senate Chamber and unsupported spiral staircase with a unique architectural design are of special significance. The only Gilbert Stuart full-length portrait of George Washington hangs here in its original setting.

This is a red brick Federal building with a white dome (the new Capitol's dome is gold), designed by the Boston architect Charles Bulfinch, whose designs for public buildings are recognized throughout New England.

The present Capitol is at the highest point in Bushnell Park in the heart of the city. The Governor and top state officials have offices in this building, but most employees work in the State Office Building on Washington Street, across the Park.

On Capitol Avenue, across another street from the Capitol, is the Raymond E. Baldwin Museum of Connecticut, named for the former Governor (1939–1945) who later became a U.S. Senator (1946–1949) and a Connecticut Supreme Court Justice (1959–1963). Historical exhibits include the original Connecticut charter (1662), industrial displays, paintings by renowned colonial artists, and even a duplicate of the Connecticut Charter. On the night of October 31, 1687, in the famous Charter Oak incident, the original charter was stolen and hidden.

Also in the Capitol complex are the State Armory and Bushnell Memorial. The Armory is the headquarters for the Connecticut National Guard. Across from the Armory is the *Hartford Courant* building, home of the oldest daily newspaper in continuous publication in the United States.

Bushnell Memorial is a handsome auditorium that serves the community as a cultural center. Symphonies, opera, and ballet companies, Broadway productions, lecture series, and films are scheduled here, usually attracting capacity audiences.

With the completion of the Hartford Civic Center, New England's largest convention and entertainment center, downtown Hartford experienced a renaissance that continues. The Civic Center includes a vast shopping mall with restaurants, shops, and boutiques. The parking garage accommodates 4,000 vehicles. The Civic Center is home to Connecticut's National Hockey League Hartford Whalers, and professional hockey has become one of Connecticut's leading spectator sports.

Trinity College and the University of Hartford bring students from distant states and abroad to join those with Connecticut addresses.

West on Farmington Avenue and set in a parklike landscape is the largest Federal-style structure in the United States, the home office for Aetna Life & Casualty Co. Two other major insurance companies, Travelers and Prudential, have their headquarters in Hartford in spectacular modern structures. They and other insurance companies have earned the city a reputation as "insurance capital of the United States."

Farther out on Farmington Avenue, at 351, is Nook Farm with the old Victorian home of Mark Twain and the neighboring house in which Harriet Beecher Stowe lived and worked. A very active Mark Twain Memorial Commission brought back some of the original furniture, furnishings, and belongings of the author and his family to make this a museum (open to the public).

The Mark Twain House is perhaps Hartford's most publicized tourist attraction. The Stowe house, too, has been furnished with original pieces, including some of Mrs. Stowe's floral paintings. This house–museum is operated in conjunction with the Mark Twain House.

Hartford has several attractive parks: Keney and Goodwin Parks have public golf courses, and Goodwin has playgrounds and picnicking and swimming facilities.

West Hartford and the Suburbs

West Hartford out to Avon and Farmington are suburbs of the capital, prosperous, well-kept residential communities with miles of tree-shaded streets, attractive homes, and landscaped properties. Some sections are remote and exclusive.

The University of Hartford's parklike campus is actually locatedin West Hartford. It is a diverse university founded in 1957, the result of a merger of three long-established institutions: the Hartford Art School (1877), Hillyer College (1879), and Hartt School of Music (1920). Situated on 200 suburban acres four miles from downtown Hartford, the University has more than 4,000 full-time students.

The Children's Museum of Hartford fascinates children with exhibits ranging from colonial artifacts to natural history displays and planetarium shows.

From West Hartford, Route 44 goes over Avon Mountain and down into the town of Avon. Greater Hartford's growing population seems to be pushing up the mountain, where the most fashionable and expensive estates, situated on the mountainside, have magnificent views of the city in the distance below.

In Avon, the Avon Old Farms School for Boys resembles a small English school in the Cotswolds. Visitors are welcome to arrange for guided tours at the alumni office.

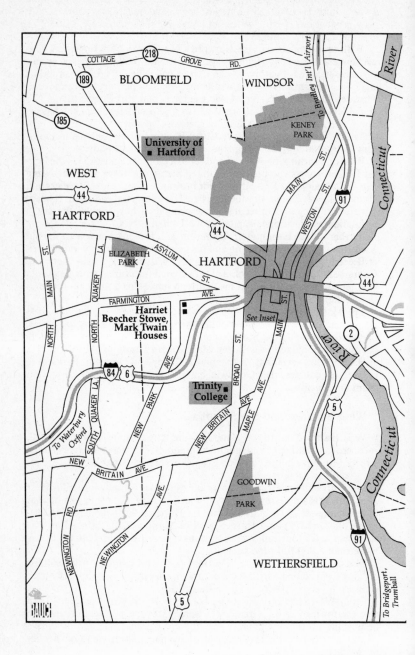

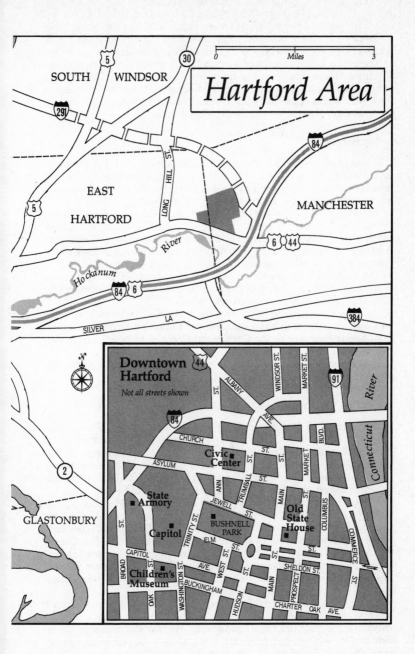

Hartford Area

SOUTH WINDSOR

EAST HARTFORD

MANCHESTER

Hockanum River

GLASTONBURY

Downtown Hartford
Not all streets shown

Civic Center

State Armory

Capitol

BUSHNELL PARK

Old State House

Children's Museum

Connecticut River

In the adjoining community of Farmington, another residential area, is the prestigious Miss Porter's School for Girls and the University of Connecticut's Medical School and Center. The most important horse show in the east takes place early each May at the Polo Grounds in Farmington, sponsored by the Children and Family Services organization.

There are two interesting museums in Farmington: The Stanley-Whitman House (1660), one of the oldest frame houses in Connecticut, is open to the public. The Hill-Stead Museum (1901) is an art museum filled with works of Monet, Manet, Whistler, and others, all collected by the mansion's former owners during their travels.

Wethersfield

Wethersfield was the first settlement in Connecticut (1634). A great deal of the town's history has been preserved in three handsomely restored homes of the seventeenth and eighteenth centuries. These houses are within the largest authentic historic district in the state.

The Joseph Webb House (1752), located near the Wethersfield Green, reflects the way of life of a wealthy Connecticut family during the American Revolution. Accounts from the diary of General George Washington note that this house was an important meeting place for American Revolutionary War generals, who discussed battle plans.

The Buttolph-Williams House (1692) is an example of the more severe conditions that prevailed in its day; the large kitchen has numerous artifacts that reflect a more arduous way of life.

The Silas Deane House (1776) was the home of a Wethersfield attorney and state legislator who was a special envoy to Europe during the Revolution, having been sent by the Continental Congress to raise funds to support the war.

In addition to these properties, the visitor to Wethersfield can see some 150 homes that were built prior to 1850.

East of Hartford

One of the state's largest employers, United Technologies Corporation, maintains headquarters in East Hartford across the Connecticut River from the capital. The Pratt & Whitney Division of UTC, makers of airplane engines, is also located here. Other divisions of the company are Hamilton Standard in Windsor, engaged in aircraft and aerospace life-support projects, and Sikorsky Helicopters in Stratford.

North of East Hartford are the towns of Ellington, Manchester, Tolland, Vernon, and South Windsor. Most of this area is rural except for the city of Manchester, which has a history of textile mills that date back to the cotton looms brought here in the eighteenth century. The Cheney Silk mills made the city famous in the nineteenth and early twentieth centuries. This heritage is maintained through the Cheney Brothers National Historic District—200 acres that include the Cheney Homestead, birthplace of the brothers who started the mills.

To the north of Hartford is East Granby, where the Old Newgate Prison and first chartered copper mine (1707) are now open to the public. Visitors may enter the main mine shaft and see the site that was once a prison for British sympathizers and prisoners of war during the American Revolution. This was Connecticut's State Prison until 1827.

Surrounding the city of Hartford are country suburbs with historic and legendary backgrounds. Most are typical small towns and villages with their central village greens and well-kept and restored houses, many with white picket fences. Around these small towns are the farms, forests, and country landscape for which Connecticut has always been famous.

PRACTICAL INFORMATION FOR THE HARTFORD AREA

Note: The area code for all Connecticut is 203

HOW TO GET THERE. By plane: The city is served by major U.S. airlines at Bradley International Airport located at Windsor Locks, a suburb in Metropolitan Hartford.

Commuter air service is available between Bradley International Airport (Windsor Locks), Tweed–New Haven (New Haven), Bridgeport (Stratford), Waterbury–Oxford and Trumbull (Groton–New London). Commuter airlines using Bradley International Airport include Business Express (the Delta Connection), Eastern (Continental), and USAir.

Connecticut Limousine Service is available from New Haven south and west to Bradley and between Hartford and New York airports—Kennedy and LaGuardia. For fares and schedules, call 800–922–6161.

By rail: Amtrak operates between Penn Station in New York City and Springfield, Massachusetts, with stops in Hartford. Call 800–872–7245 for details.

By bus: From the Greyhound Terminal, 409 Church St., there is intercity bus service furnished by Greyhound, Arrow, and Bonanza lines. For information call 547–1500. There is a TTY telephone line for persons handicapped in hearing or speech: 800–345–3109.

By car: Hartford is in the heart of Connecticut and major highways converge here, including Rtes. 84, 91, 44, 2, 4, 44A, and 15 via 91.

HOW TO GET AROUND. From the airport: Airport limousine service is available between the airport and Hartford hotels. Call 627–3210 for information concerning schedules and rates.

Car rentals: Several car rental agencies are located at Bradley International Airport; among them, Hertz, Avis, Dollar, National, and Thrifty.

Taxis: For cab service, call Yellow Cab, 522–0234, or Airport Taxi, 627–3210.

Urban bus lines: Connecticut Transit has an information center open daily except Sat. For schedules or information concerning their many routes in and around the city's suburbs, call 525–9181.

HOTELS AND MOTELS. Urban hotels in Hartford and the motels and inns in the capital region offer accommodations suited to every circumstance. Rooms are air-conditioned, have TV, and most have either indoor or outdoor pools or both. Accommodations are listed by average price per person, double occupancy: *Deluxe,* $75 and up; *Expensive,* $50–$69; *Moderate,* $30–$49; *Inexpensive,* $29 and less. Inquire concerning family or senior-citizen rates and wheelchair access.

Avon

Avon Old Farms Hotel, on Rte. 44., 06001 (677–1651). *Deluxe.* Medium-sized, with New England decor. Pool, pets. Across street from Avon Old Farms Inn. Restaurant and lounge.

East Hartford

Holiday Inn, 363 Roberts St., 06108 (528–9611). *Expensive.* Branch of chain. Restaurant, bar, indoor pool.

Enfield

Harley Hotel of Hartford/Springfield, Bright Meadow Blvd. I–91 Exit 49, 06082 (800–321–2323 or 741–2211). *Deluxe.* Lounge and restaurant, fitness center, airport limo service. Indoor-outdoor pool.

Farmington

Marriott Hotel, Farm Springs Rd., I–84, Exit 37, 06032 (800–228–9290 or 678–1000). *Deluxe.* Conference center and hotel, 10 min. from downtown Hartford. Lounge, restaurant, health club, indoor-outdoor pool, tennis, airport limo service.

Farmington Motor Inn, 827 Farmington Ave., 06032 (677–2821). *Expensive.* Restaurant, cocktail lounge. Nearby golf and tennis.

Hartford

Parkview Hilton, 1 Hilton Place, 06103 (249–5611). *Deluxe.* Two restaurants, lounges, health club. Parking garage. In center of downtown.

Sheraton-Hartford, 315 Trumbull St., 06103 (728–5151). *Deluxe.* Centrally located in Civic Center. Restaurants and lounge with entertainment. Cafe open for lunch and after-theater supper. Indoor pool and health club.

Summit Hotel, 5 Constitution Plaza, 06103 (278–2000). *Deluxe.* Main entrance overlooks Connecticut River. Free parking in adjacent parking garage (entrance direct to lobby). Restaurants and bar. Concierge floor. Airport limo service.

Ramada Inn, 440 Asylum St., 06103 (246–6591). *Moderate.* Family and weekend plans. Restaurant.

Susse Chalet Motor Inn, 185 Brainard Rd., I–91, Exit 27, 06114 (525–9306). *Inexpensive.* About 5 min. from downtown. One of chain.

Wethersfield

Ramada Inn, 1330 Silas Deane Pkwy., 06109 (563–2311). *Expensive.* Restaurant, lounge with entertainment evenings. Sauna. Pets. Golf and tennis nearby.

Windsor

Tobacco Valley Inn, 450 Bloomfield Ave., 06095 (688–5221). *Expensive.* New England country atmosphere in menu and dining room also. Bar. Seven mi. to airport, 5 mi. to downtown Hartford.

American Motor Lodge, 29 Windsor Ave., 06095 (525–1461). *Inexpensive.* Restaurant and coffee shop.

Windsor Locks

Sheraton Hotel at Bradley, Bradley International Airport 06096. Reservations via Sheraton reservation system (800–825–3535). *Deluxe.* Full-service hotel and restaurant open spring 1987. Attached to Bradley Airport with access to boarding gates.

Airport Ramada Inn, Airport Rd., 06096 (623–2441). *Expensive.* Seafood restaurant. Bar. Sauna. Airport limo service.

BED AND BREAKFASTS. More and more private homes are opening rooms and small suites as guest accommodations. Breakfast—from full menu to Continental to a serving only of coffee or tea—are offered. These accommodations are available through established referral agencies that handle all (including financial) arrangements. Owners vary—some take children, pets, or smokers. Some do not. Some have resident dogs or cats or both. Business people in the process of relocating find these accommodations comfortable and practical for interim periods. Because of the proliferation of these accommodations in the Hartford area, a registry would provide a suitable directory. In the Hartford area, contact the Nutmeg Bed & Breakfast, 222 Girard Ave., Hartford 06105 (236–6698).

RESTAURANTS. Restaurants of every description may be found in the Hartford area. With the redevelopment of the city, there are many new eating places. The supper club is back, and seafood as always is prevalent in most area dining rooms. Ethnic restaurants run the gamut of nationalities. Country inns in the capital region contribute another kind of ambience. Price ranges, based on a full meal, exclusive of alcoholic beverages, tax, and tip are: *Deluxe,* $30–$26; *Expensive,* $25 and up; *Moderate,* $15–$24; *Inexpensive,* under $15.

Avon

Avon Old Farms Inn, jct. Rtes. 44 and 10 (677–2818). *Moderate.* A typical Connecticut country restaurant. Several small dining rooms. Antique furnishings in this restored historic building.

Farmington

Champignon, in Marriott-Hartford Hotel, Farm Spring Rd. (678–1000). *Expensive.* Continental cuisine. Reservations necessary.
Reading Room. 40 Mill Lane (677–7997). *Moderate.* Located beside the Farmington River in a restored gristmill, reputedly the oldest in Connecticut. Gourmet menu. Reservations necessary.

Glastonbury

Blacksmith's Tavern, 2300 Main St. overlooking the Green (659–0366). *Expensive.* Several dining rooms with 18th-century emphasis on decor. 10 min. from downtown Hartford.

Hartford

L'Américain, 2 Hartford Sq. W. (522–6500). *Deluxe.* A handsome surprise in Hartford's south end. The decor is supplemented by soft music. Inspired French and American cuisine. Reservations necessary. Closed Sun.
Gaetano's Restaurant, Civic Center Plaza (249–1629). *Expensive.* French and Northern Italian cuisine. Elegant surroundings and distinctive service. Menu reflects quality ambience.
Carbone's Ristorante, 588 Franklin St. (249–9646). *Moderate.* Italian cuisine. Pleasant surroundings and good service in this family-owned and -operated restaurant featuring Italian specialties.

Frank's, 159 Asylum St. (527–9291). *Moderate.* Popular downtown restaurant. Continental atmosphere. Extensive Italian-American menu.

Honiss Oyster House, 440 Asylum St. (246–6477). *Moderate.* Open for breakfast, lunch, and dinner. Seafood specialties. A historic name among Hartford's best-known restaurants. Lounge with entertainment Fri. and Sat.

There are numerous restaurants in the **Civic Center** in downtown Hartford ranging from Gaetano's Restaurant to The Ice Cream Scene to Chuck's Steak House (one of a chain) serving charbroiled specialties. Prices range from expensive to very inexpensive, depending on the restaurant and the service provided.

Manchester

Cavey's of Manchester, 40 East Center St. (643–2751). *Expensive.* First-class family-operated restaurant. French cuisine downstairs in Cavey's Restaurant Francais, with choice wines. Italian menu upstairs in Cavey's Northern Italian, with veal and pasta specialties.

West Hartford

The Steak Club, 2537 Albany Ave. (233–4431). *Expensive.* Steaks, beef roasts, and seafood. Dinner only on Sunday.

Wethersfield

Steak Club, Ramada Inn, 1330 Silas Deane Hwy. (563–2344). *Moderate.* Lounge with entertainment evenings. Open seven days for breakfast, lunch, and dinner.

TOURIST INFORMATION. For information on tours and other events contact the Greater Hartford Convention and Visitors Center. One Civic Center Plaza, Hartford 06103 (728–6789). Pertinent information is included in their booklet, *Hartford and Southern New England,* available on request. Offices open Mon.–Fri. 8:30 A.M.–4:30 P.M.; Visitor Information, Old State House, 800 Main St., Hartford 06103 (522–6766). Open Mon.–Sat. 10 A.M.–5 P.M., Sun. noon–5 P.M. For Civic Center ticket information (727–8080), box office open daily 10 A.M.–6 P.M. and until showtime on events nights.

TOURS. Hartford abounds in historic houses, open to the public, state buildings, and museums—all offering tours. The Hartford Civic Center, at 1 Civic Center Plaza in the heart of downtown Hartford, could take a full day to explore. **Connecticut Transit** distributes a guide to the bus system and has its own information center at Main and State Sts. (525–9181).

Arrow Tours (528–9961), **Friendship Tours** (243–1630), and **NBT Tours** (828–0511) also have special itineraries of interest to visitors.

Dattco Tours (246–7950) offers a 1½-hour tour of the city. **Heritage Trails,** Box 138, Farmington 06034 (677–8867) for historical sites. Half-day, full-day, and dinner tours with narrations; maximum 10 people. Information on other bus tours may be obtained from the Greater Hartford Convention and Visitors Center.

The **Travelers Museum** in the Travelers Insurance Companies' building, 700 Main St. (277–5048) has displays of the companies' early history. The Travelers' 527-foot tower gives visitors an incomparable view of the city.

There is a 72-stair climb to the observation deck. (For information, 277–2431.) Free admission to both.

There are free guided tours weekday mornings at the **State Capitol** (240–0222).

SEASONAL EVENTS. May: Children & Family Services Horse Show and Country Fair in Farmington. In Hartford there's a food festival, A Taste of Hartford.

July: July 4th River Festival in Hartford.

October: Connecticut Antiques Show at the Hartford Armory.

November: Festival of Lights at Constitution Plaza in Hartford opens the holiday season.

PARKS. Several municipal parks in the city of Hartford have a variety of attractions. **Elizabeth Park,** 915 Prospect Rd., has 99 acres of rose gardens. **Keney and Goodwin Parks** have public golf courses among their recreational facilities. **Bushnell Park,** adjacent to the Capitol, is well-known because of its location in the heart of the city and for its 1914 carousel that operates mid-May–Sept.

SPORTS. Golf: In Hartford, there are two public 18-hole golf courses: Keney (722–6548) at the north of the city and Goodwin (722–2561) at the south. Goodwin also has a flat nine-hole course, picnicking facilities, playgrounds, and swimming. In the greater Hartford area: Tunxis Plantation Country Club (677–1367), and Westwoods Country Club (677–9192) in Farmington. Bel Compo Country Club (678–1358) in Avon. Rockledge Country Club (521–3156) and Buena Vista Country Club (523–1133) in W. Hartford, and Minnechaug Golf Course (643–9914) in Glastonbury. Greens fees range from $8 to $12, and courses are usually available to the public only on weekdays during the playing season.

Boating: There are boat-launching sites at E. Hartford, Windsor, and Wethersfield on the Connecticut River, Farmington River, and on Rainbow Reservoir and in New Hartford on West Hill Pond. Canoe trips on the Connecticut River are offered and include smooth water, white water, and weekend trips.

SPECTATOR SPORTS. Professional **soccer** and **basketball** games are played at the Hartford Civic Center, home of the N.H.L. Hartford Whalers. **Ice skating** spectaculars also take place here. There's **lawn bowling** in Elizabeth Park and **polo** at the Farmington Polo Grounds. The **Greater Hartford Open Golf Tournament** is held in July at the Edgewood Country Club in Cromwell and attracts many international celebrities. **Jai alai** is played at 89 Weston St., just off I-91, north of the downtown area (525–8611).

HISTORIC SITES. Mark Twain Memorial Building (1874), 351 Farmington Ave. (525–9317), home of the famous author when he wrote his famous works. Next to it is the **Harriet Beecher Stowe Home,** also open to the public. **The Butler-McCook Homestead** (1782) in the heart of downtown Hartford at 396 Main St. (522–1806) was occupied by four generations of one family and is furnished with original family possessions. An 1866 carriage house is a museum of vehicles, military uniforms, and sports equipment. **Hatheway House,** Main St. (Rte. 75), Suffield (247–8996) (built 1760–1795), is considered one of the finest examples of Connecticut architecture. Beautifully furnished. **Oliver Ellsworth Homestead,** 778 Palisado Ave., Windsor (688–8717); **Noah Webster Birthplace,** 227 S.

Main St., W. Hartford (521–5363), a saltbox house of around 1676, now a town museum.

In Wethersfield, the **Buttolph-Williams House,** Broad and Marsh Sts. (529–0460 or 247–8996); **Silas Deane House,** 209 Main St.; **Joseph Webb House** (1752), 211 Main St. (529–0612); General George Washington and Count de Rochambeau planned the Battle of Yorktown here in May 1781.

Old Newgate Prison and Copper Mine, Newgate Rd., East Granby (566–3005); the first copper mine in America (1707) and a prison 1775–1820. A National Historic Landmark. Open May 15–Oct. 15. Closed Mon. and Tues.

The **Connecticut State Library–Supreme Court Building,** 231 Capitol Ave. (566–3056), houses the Raymond E. Baldwin Museum of Connecticut History. The collections include the state's original Royal Charter (1662), clocks manufactured in Connecticut, and Colt firearms.

MUSEUMS AND GALLERIES. Wadsworth Atheneum, 600 Main St. (278–2670), with five connecting buildings, 36 galleries, conservation studio, 300-seat theater, art library, galleries for the handicapped, and shops.

Old State House (1796), 800 Main St. (522–6766). Bulfinch-designed brick and brownstone museum of state's legislative, executive, and judicial branches. A National Historic Landmark since 1961.

The Children's Museum of Hartford, 950 Trout Brook Dr., W. Hartford (236–1961), has a planetarium featuring daily shows, an aquarium, and a variety of special exhibits for children.

Museum of American Political Life, University of Hartford, W. Hartford (243–4090). More than 1500 items from the DeWitt Collection of Presidential Americana illustrate the candidates and the issues of presidential election campaigns from Washington (1789) to Bush (1989).

Real Art Ways, 100 Allyn St. (525–5521). Multimedia alternative art center. Varied schedule and special events.

Connecticut Historical Society Museum, 1 Elizabeth St. (236–5621). Over 100,000 items related to Connecticut history. Research library and genealogical collection. Open weekdays, 1–5 P.M.

The Historical Museum of Medicine and Dentistry, 230 Scarborough St. (236–5613). Exhibits document 200 years of development in the physical health sciences.

Hill-Stead Museum, 671 Farmington Ave., Farmington (677–4787). The former home of a Hartford collector of Impressionist paintings is now a museum. Guided tours are available on afternoons Wed.–Sun.

Farmington Museum (Stanley-Whitman House, c. 1660) 37 High St., Farmington (677–9222); **Old Academy Museum,** 150 Main St., Wethersfield (529–7656).

MUSIC AND THEATER. Bushnell Symphony Series: Distinguished orchestras at Bushnell Memorial, 166 Capitol Ave. (246–6807); **Connecticut Opera Association Series,** Bushnell Memorial; **Hartford Symphony Series,** guest artists throughout the winter, at Bushnell Memorial. **Symphony Band concerts** at Elizabeth Park (June–Sept.); **Trinity College Carillon concerts** (June and July); 527–3151 for information. **Chamber Music concerts** on summer Wed. evenings with a tour of the chapel following.

Hartford Stage Company, John W. Huntington Theater, 50 Church St. (527–5151), directly across the street from the Hartford Civic Center, is a professional repertory company, providing classics and modern works in its handsome theater. **Bushnell Memorial** across from the Capitol schedules operas, concerts, plays, films, recitals, lectures, and ballet. **Hartford Ballet Co.,** 308 Farmington Ave. (525–9396), performs at the Bushnell and may often be seen during tours to other parts of the state. **Coachlight Dinner Theatre,** Rte. 5, E. Windsor (522–1266), offers top musicals and comedies following a buffet dinner.

Colleges and universities in the area have ongoing theatrical and musical programs throughout the year. Little theater and community groups also present dramatic productions. Foreign films and revivals of classics are shown at the **Atheneum Theater** at Wadsworth Atheneum (268–2670).

SHOPPING. The **Hartford Civic Center** has many top-quality shops and boutiques, offering anything from petit-fours to the wooden spoons to mix the batter, clothes for every occasion or the fabrics to make them, and the accessories to go with them, plus sports and recreational merchandise. There are also numerous restaurants in the Civic Center with a wide variety of specialties.

Richardson Mall, 942 Main St., was created in a restored 1877 landmark with numerous shops and restaurants. It is located between the G. Fox and Sage Allen department stores, both of which are accessible from within the Richardson Mall.

The Pavilion, State House Sq., downtown. Vibrant design with 14 eateries and numerous shops and boutiques.

Suburban shopping centers have been developed in Glastonbury, Avon, Simsbury, Wethersfield, West Farms, and Bishop's Corner in W. Hartford. Most of the suburbs have at least one special shopping center to attract visitors. **Constitution Plaza,** in downtown Hartford, was one of the first redevelopment projects in the city. It started as a shopping mall, but now investment houses make this section of Hartford its "little Wall St." for those interested in shopping for money.

NIGHTLIFE AND BARS. Evening entertainment has been on the increase in the Hartford area. Taking the place of the old-style nightclubs are the discotheques and small cocktail lounges found especially in the larger hotels.

The major hotels in the city of Hartford have lounges where there is live entertainment. **Stage Cafe** at the Sheraton Hartford, the **Esplanade Lounge** at the Parkview Hilton, and the **Rendezvous Room** in the Summit Hotel are in this category.

Independent nightclubs can be found in downtown Hartford:

The Russian Lady, 191 Ann St. (525–3003). Live entertainment and dancing.

Boppers, 22 Union Pl. (549–5801). For dining and dancing. Open until midnight weeknights, later on weekends.

Other small bars and lounges with live music or jukeboxes are scattered throughout the city with new ones opening regularly. Inquiries should be made locally for the best choice at the time of the visit.

THE CONNECTICUT RIVER VALLEY

The Connecticut River valley, from Hartford down to the confluence of the river with Long Island Sound at Old Saybrook on the west and Old Lyme on the east, is a rural area that has remained unspoiled. The people who live here care about their surroundings sufficiently to insist on minimal development and the protection of their environment. The riverbanks are colorful and clean; the riverside villages maintain their historic land-scapes, and there are sites and attractions of interest to all ages.

Approaching the area from Norwich, one heads toward Middletown (downriver from Hartford) into Colchester on Route 16. Here the restored Nathaniel Foote House (1702) on the south side of Norwich Avenue has an interesting exhibit of colonial relics.

En route to Middletown, a side trip to the Salmon River State Forest promises a beautiful drive along the Salmon River. The Comstock Covered Bridge is one of the few remaining in Connecticut; this one is closed to traffic. South of the Salmon River is Day Pond State Park, with facilities for swimming, fishing, and picnicking.

At Westchester, Route 149 veers off toward Moodus, a summer vacation area with a sprinkling of resorts similar, in a small way, to those of New York's Catskills and Pennsylvania's Poconos.

Middletown

Portland is on the east side of the Connecticut River, opposite Middletown. From its quarries came most of the stone for the brownstone houses in New York City. Rockhounds often find beautiful specimens in old quarries here.

Middletown has several historic homes and an excellent historical society, yet its major attraction is Wesleyan University. The home of the Honors College, built in 1828 by the Russell family, was one of the grandest mansions in the state. The General Mansfield House has an interesting furniture collection.

As in most university towns, the center for cultural activities is at the university, and the schedules of special events offered by the university's various departments include a wide variety of programs. Schedules may be obtained from the university's public information office.

The campus overlooks the town and the river. Once the largest city in the state, Middletown was later surpassed by Hartford, New Haven, and Bridgeport. Today its major industry is the manufacture of marine hardware.

Haddam, East Haddam, Hadlyme, and Chester

From Middletown, south on Route 9, take Exit 7 to Route 82 across the Connecticut River to Goodspeed's Landing, an Historic District of East Haddam. The Goodspeed Opera House, an architectural gem built in 1876 and a true home of the American musical theatre, is open from March until December, presenting new and revival musicals. Several shows began their Broadway runs here. Tours of the theater are available in July and August on Mondays from 1 to 3 P.M. From the theater it is a short walk to interesting shops, craft coops in historic houses, and the East Haddam Historical Society Museum.

For a side trip, take Route 149 past the one mile of eighteenth- and nineteenth-century houses to Johnsonville Village, a private Victorian restoration. From Route 149, take Route 152 to Moodus Center to the Amasa Day House, an historical home open from mid-May to mid-October.

Route 82 leads to the Gillette Castle State Park in Hadlyme, where one of the few authentic castles erected in America still stands. It was built by William Gillette, the actor who made a fortune playing the role of Sherlock Holmes.

From Hadlyme, to go over to Route 9A on the east side of the river, follow signs to the Hadlyme-Chester ferry. This little ferry, one of two plying the Connecticut River, dates from the days before bridges spanned the river. It is now operated by the state, and for a minimal fee, one can cross in about five minutes—car and all.

From the ferry, continue on Route 148 to Chester, a village of small shops and restaurants. The National Theater of the Deaf and the Goodspeed Opera House satellite, Goodspeed-at-Chester, are here.

Farm Country

For a country road to New Haven, take Route 80 from Deep River to I–91. Route 80 winds through farm country, the communities of Winthrop, Killingworth, North Madison, North Branford, and Foxon, before connecting with I–91. By taking this route, one avoids the turnpike driving on Routes 9 and 95 to New Haven but also misses the historic little town of Essex, nestled on the river.

Essex: History and Marinas

Route 9A from Chester through Deep River is a beautiful rural road. It leads directly to the town of Essex, where bustling marinas are homeports for magnificent yachts. The main street, although filled with interesting shops and restaurants, appears primarily residential. Old sea captains' houses, which have been perfectly maintained over the years, give the town a prosperous appearance. Essex has been the home of the E. E. Dickinson Witch Hazel manufacturing plant for years. The Valley Railroad Steam Train, a popular tourist attraction, begins its trip north from tracks nearby.

Route 9 south dissolves into the main route from New York to Rhode Island, I–95, at Old Saybrook.

State parks and recreation areas are found throughout the valley, and scores of lovely old towns and villages—each with its own history and appeal—delight the tourists. Those towns included in this routing are fairly representative.

PRACTICAL INFORMATION FOR CONNECTICUT RIVER VALLEY

Note: The area code for all Connecticut is 203

HOW TO GET THERE AND AROUND. This part of Connecticut is accessible only by car. Hartford's Bradley International is the nearest major airport.

The package tours that come into the area are seasonal and not widely advertised. People with boats find marinas and yacht clubs along the river, and these are popular landing places during the boating season.

By car: Heading south, the access to this region from Hartford or Portland (across the river from Middletown) is Rte. 9. From the west, Rte. 66 joins Rte. 9 in Middletown, and heading north from I–95 Rtes. 9 and 9A parallel each other. Route 9 is a major highway; Rte. 9A a secondary road, a scenic route through towns and villages.

Major **car rental** agencies may be found in Middletown or Old Saybrook, as well as Hartford.

HOTELS AND MOTELS. This is not an area where one would find urban hotels; country inns and bed-and-breakfast facilities predominate.

Prices range from *Deluxe,* $70 and up; *Expensive,* $50–$70; *Moderate,* $30–$50; and *Inexpensive,* $30 and under.

Chester

The Inn at Chester, Rte. 148 at the Chester-Killingly line, 06412 (526–9541). *Deluxe.* A late 18th-century home, expanded to include guest rooms, facilities for small conferences, fitness facilities. Restaurant serving American cuisine. Reservations necessary.

Cromwell

Treadway Lord Cromwell Motor Inn, Rte. 72, 06416 (635–2000). *Expensive.* Between Hartford and Middletown. Restaurant. Indoor pool. Fine golf course nearby.

East Haddam

Klar Crest Resort and Motel, 11 Johnsonville Rd., 06469 (873–8649). *Expensive.* A summer resort catering to families; pool and participatory sports.

Middletown

Town Farms Inn, Silver St. and River Rd., 06457 (347–7438). *Deluxe.* Early 19th-century building overlooking the Connecticut River. Fine restaurant and lounge.
Middletown Motor Inn, 988 Washington St., 06457 (357–9251). *Expensive.* Nearby golf, shopping. Pets.

Moodus

Frank Davis Resort, Rte. 151, 06469 (873–8681). *Expensive.* A popular resort on 600-acre site with pool, stream, and sports facilities. American plan. Open May–Labor Day.

INNS, GUEST HOUSES, BED AND BREAKFASTS. Because of the expanding bed-and-breakfast opportunities and their growing popularity, travelers are advised to contact one of the bed-and-breakfast registries to assure a compatible, *moderately* priced accommodation. In this area, Nutmeg Bed & Breakfast, 222 Girard Ave., Hartford 06105 (236–6698) has an up-to-date list.

Following is a sampling of bed-and-breakfast inns in the area. All fall into the *Expensive* category.

Deep River

Selden House, 20 Read St., 06417 (526–9195) A lovely turn-of-the-century property with beautiful gardens makes this bed and breakfast ideal for relaxation. Continental breakfast.

East Haddam

Bishopsgate, Goodspeed Landing, 06423 (873–1677). An early 19th-century home beautifully restored and furnished with appropriate antiques. Full breakfast.

Moodus

The Fowler House, Plains Rd., Box 432, 06469 (873–8906) Late 19th-century home carefully restored and furnished with antiques of the period. Some rooms with fireplace. Afternoon tea and Continental breakfast.

DINING OUT. There are probably more fine restaurants in this immediate area than in any of the state's country areas. Many ethnic cuisines are represented, but most frequently found here are the seafood specialties and New England fare. Prices are not out of line with more urban restaurants, although some moderately priced meals may be found in some fine surroundings with careful searching. In general, price ranges for a complete dinner, without alcoholic beverages, tax, or tip, are: *Deluxe,* $30; *Expensive,* $25–$29; *Moderate* $15–$24; and *Inexpensive,* $14 and under.

Centerbrook

Finé Bouche, Main St. (767–1277). *Deluxe.* An unusual French menu prepared with care and distinction. Unpretentious surroundings. Luncheons and prix fixe dinners. Reservations required. Closed Sun. and Mon.

Chester

John B. Parmelee House, Rte. 148 (526–4961). *Expensive.* The restaurant in the Inn at Chester. Barn board interior, fresh flowers, Steinway grand piano music. American cuisine.

Restaurant du Village, 59 Main St. (526–5301). *Expensive.* Provincial and unadorned in the heart of the village. Simple but fine luncheons and dinners. Excellent fresh-baked breads and desserts. Daily specials. Reservations recommended.

Essex

Griswold Inn, Main St. (767–0991). *Expensive.* Catering to travelers for 200 years in rooms mellow with age. Walls covered with ship paintings, prints, and maritime memorabilia. New England fare, especially seafood and prime rib. Piano in taproom nightly and banjo music on weekends. Sun. hunt breakfast a feature.

Ivoryton

Copper Beech Inn, Main St. (767–0330). *Deluxe.* A restored inn with high standards. Fresh flowers, china, crystal, and snowy linen please the eye; and always an interesting menu. French-inspired cuisine. Closed Mon.

Middletown

Harbor Park, 80 Harbor Ave., Rte. 9 (347–9999). *Expensive.* A historic landmark on the Connecticut River, located in a converted boathouse. Lunch and dinner seafood specialties.

TOURIST INFORMATION. En route to Rte. 9 on I–95 there is, in Westbrook off the northbound side of the highway, a state-operated information center that is open seasonally, and information concerning the

Connecticut River valley would be available here. For year-round tourist information, contact the Connecticut Valley Tourism Commission, 70 College St., Middletown 06457 (347–6924).

TOURS. The Valley Railroad. Railroad Ave., Exit 3, Rte. 9, in Essex 06426 (767–0103), is probably the outstanding tourist attraction in the Essex area. A steam train runs from Essex to Deep River where passengers may change to a riverboat for the return to Essex. Open May–Oct. and weekends in Dec.

Connecticut River cruises: The *Eastern Clipper* and *Yankee Clipper* are run by N. E. Steamboat Line, Inc., 1 Marine Park, Haddam (345–4508).

SEASONAL EVENTS. Among the seasonal events taking place in the Connecticut Valley are the annual country fairs that are popular in most small towns in the state and take place usually on weekends. Antique, and arts and craft shows, as well as flea markets, are other featured events on weekends here. A list of these events is available from the Connecticut Tourism Office, 210 Washington St., Hartford 06106 (566–3385); or the Connecticut Valley Tourism Commission, 70 College St., Middletown 06457 (347–6924).

In **mid-July** in Deep River, the Ancient Muster of Fife and Drum Corps attracts these musical units from throughout the country. In **mid-September** in Essex, the Connecticut River Foundation has its annual Traditional Vessel Weekend, and in **mid-October** there is a Fall Foliage Bicycle Ride through the historic towns in the valley.

The fall foliage along the Connecticut River is second to none; visitors marvel at the changing colors along the riverbanks.

PARKS. Certainly the State Park that is unique here is the **Gillette Castle State Park** in Hadlyme, with the Gillette Castle the focus. Picnic grounds surround the castle, which is on a promontory overlooking the river. The **Devil's Hopyard** is in nearby East Haddam and covers about 860 acres of woodland.

There are fine hiking trails in **Chatfield Hollow,** Killingworth, where there are rocky ledge and natural caves. **Cockaponsett State Forest** is in Chester. There are camping facilities, and picnicking, fishing, and swimming.

SPORTS. Perhaps the most popular sports activities here have to do with proximity to the river and include yachting, canoeing, and fishing. **Canoes** are available at Downriver Canoes in Haddam (346–3308 or 345–8355).

The annual Greater Open Golf Tournament takes place in Cromwell, usually the end of June or 1st of July (Tournament Players Club, 522–4171).

Tennis courts can be found at campgrounds (see *Camping*).

FISHING. For saltwater fishing, charters are available in Old Saybrook at the Saybrook Point Marina. Call Capt. Phil Wetmore (399–9728 or 388–1143). Shad fishing is popular in the spring. For freshwater fishing information contact the Department of Environmental Protection, 165 Capitol Ave., Hartford 06106 (566–2304).

CAMPING. Numerous State Parks and Forests are in the Connecticut River valley; the Connecticut *Vacation Guide* issued free by the Tourism Division, Economic Development Commission, 210 Washington St.,

Hartford 06106 (566–3385) lists them all and charts the various facilities available including campsites.

Campsites, both public and private throughout this area, are listed in the *Vacation Guide* (see *Parks*), with the number of campsites at each, the services, the seasonal dates, and supplies. There are several in this area, including:

In East Haddam—**Wolf's Den Family Campsites** (225), Rte. 82, 06423 (873–9681).

In Higganum—**Little City Campground** (100), Little City Rd., 06441 (345–4192).

For information and reservation applications for campsites in State Parks and Forests, contact: Parks and Recreation Division, Department of Environmental Protection, 165 Capitol Ave., Hartford 06106 (566–2304).

HISTORIC SITES AND HOUSES. There are several interesting historic sites and restored homes in this area. Call ahead for days, hours, and admission charges.

Deep River

The Stone House, South Main St. (526–2609). A mid-19th-century restored house with exhibits ranging from Indian artifacts to local history. Seasonal.

East Haddam

Nathan Hale Schoolhouse, Main St. (Rte. 149) (873–9547). A one-room schoolhouse, named for its early teacher. Seasonal, and by appointment.

Essex

Pratt House, 19 West Ave. (787–0861). A mid-18th-century center-chimney home with early American antiques from the 17th, 18th, and 19th centuries. Interesting gardens. Seasonal, June–Sept. and at Christmas.

Hadlyme

Gillette Castle, Off Rte. 82 (526–2336). The hilltop castle built by the famous actor William Gillette in 1919. The interior furnishings reflect the eccentricities of the original owner. Now a state park. Open year-round except Thanksgiving.

Middletown

General Mansfield House, 151 Main St. (346–0746). An early 19th-century Federal house with period furnishings. Open Mon., Tues., and Sun. Closed major holidays.

Moodus

Amasa Day House, Moodus Green (873–8144). This house was built in 1816 and today has the furnishings of those generations who once lived in the house. May–Oct. daily.

MUSEUMS AND GALLERIES. In addition to museums exhibiting local history, there are several fine art collections. Call ahead for days, hours, and admission fees.

Chester

Connecticut River Artisans Cooperative, 9 Maple St. (526–5575). A gallery with works for sale and demonstrations, housed in a renovated woodworking mill. Closed Mon.

Essex

Connecticut River Foundation Museum, Main St. (767–8269). A maritime museum with local history housed in an 1878 riverside building. Apr.–Dec.

Hill's Academy Museum, 22 Prospect St. (767–0681). A variety of historic exhibits indigenous to the town. Open Wed.–Fri.

Middletown

Davison Art Center, High St. (347–9411, ext. 2253). At Wesleyan University. Excellent collections of paintings and prints. Alternating exhibits. Closed during university vacations.

Old Lyme

Florence Griswold House Museum, 96 Lyme St. (434–5542). This was the home of Florence Griswold, a well-known local lady whose home (1817) was the center for one of the country's early art colonies of Impressionist painters. Locally important furnishings and changing exhibits of paintings. Seasonal.

Lyme Academy of Fine Arts, 84 Lyme St. (434–5232). Housed in an early 19th-century building that is on the National Register of Historic Places, there are year-round changing exhibits and special classes.

Lyme Art Association, 70 Lyme St. (434–7802). This gallery has special shows during the summer only, and is closed Mon.

MUSIC, DANCE, AND STAGE. One of the leading small theaters dedicated to the American musical theater is in this valley in East Haddam. At the bridge that crosses the Connecticut River, and in the heart of the historic district, the **Goodspeed Opera House** has spawned several new shows that have been hits on Broadway, including *Man of La Mancha* and *Annie.* Each year productions include well-known musicals of decades ago. Because the theater is small (about 375 seats), tickets must be reserved well in advance. Goodspeed Opera House, Rte. 82, East Haddam 06423 (873–8668).

In Chester, Goodspeed has a satellite theater that is small and where new musicals are featured as well as special programs that are frequently presented during the year. For schedules and ticket information contact Goodspeed-at-Chester, North Main St., Chester 06410 (873–8668).

Also in Chester is the home of the **National Theater of the Deaf.** When not on tour this ensemble has occasional performances at their headquarters here or in the vicinity of Chester. For information contact National Theater of the Deaf, Chester 06410 (526–4971).

SHOPPING. The Connecticut River valley has some special shops that are for the most part individually owned. Some chains do locate in country centers, featuring casual clothes; these are found in some of the riverside towns. Antique shops and art galleries proliferate here. And if you are shopping for a yacht, there is probably no better place than Essex or Old Saybrook, both on the Connecticut River. You will find few if any major shopping centers, although some small enclaves of shops may be found; in cities, the downtown areas offer more diverse merchandise.

NORTHWESTERN CONNECTICUT:

LITCHFIELD HILLS

Riverton could be your first view of the area, and to reach this town one might travel from the Peoples' State Forest on Route 181, a popular summer recreational area for camping, hiking, fishing, and picnicking. On Route 20 at the northern edge of the Forest is Riverton, where the Hitchcock Chair Factory, founded in 1818, is still making chairs modeled from the original Hitchcock design. Through glass windows visitors may watch the "rushing" operation, the making of chair seats similar to those used in colonial times. The chairs and other colonial reproductions may be purchased in the adjacent salesroom. A fine country inn across the street, The Riverton, boasts an excellent restaurant.

Associated with the factory is the John T. Kenney Hitchcock Museum, specializing in nineteenth-century furnishings and artifacts, with special emphasis on Hitchcock originals.

Farther south on Route 8 is Winsted, a town known to sightseers for its Laurel Festival during the third week of June. The mountain laurel is the official state flower and is protected as such.

Route 8 leads to Torrington, where John Brown, the political abolitionist, was born. Although the house burned down some years ago, a ring of foundation stones and a plaque mark the site.

Halfway between Winsted and Torrington, on a side road off Route 8 leading to Burr Pond, Gail Borden concocted the world's first condensed milk. Only a plaque marks the spot where the creamery stood, the beginning of the giant Borden Corporation.

In December, Christmas Village attracts children and their parents. The village is a free, noncommercial venture in the Alvord Playground, and each child who visits receives a gift from Santa Claus.

Indian Lookout in Torrington· is a privately owned mountain field of laurel, a magnificent display of the flower when it's in bloom, in mid-June.

Elegant Litchfield

From the Torrington Valley, Route 202 leads into the Litchfield Hills, a beautiful rural section of Connecticut. It is six miles to Litchfield Green, dominated by the beautiful white-steepled Congregational Church. On both sides of the elm-shaded North and South streets are elegant white clapboard colonial homes with traditional black or green shutters. The area was declared an historic district by the state and in 1978 a National Historic Landmark.

On South Street (Route 63) stands the Tapping Reeve House, one of Litchfield's prizes. But the eye of history is on another building on the same property, a small structure that was America's first law school. Visitors can see the desks at which many distinguished American jurists studied, men like Aaron Burr (Tapping Reeve's brother-in-law) and John C. Calhoun, both vice-presidents of the United States; former Supreme Court justices Henry Baldwin, Leir Woodbury, and Ward Hunt; six cabinet members, more than 100 congressmen, 28 senators, and numerous governors and chief justices of states. All these, and others, went forth from a one-room building in a remote Connecticut village to practice law.

The birthplaces of three more famous Americans—Harriet Beecher Stowe; her father, Henry Ward Beecher; and Ethan Allen—all are on North Street.

A classical brick building houses the Litchfield Historical Society. It contains four galleries of exhibits depicting life in Litchfield during the past two centuries. A special "Please do touch" room is a children's exhibit.

The Haight Vineyard and Winery on Chestnut Hill, off Route 118 in Litchfield, is Connecticut's first vineyard-winery. Tours and tasting appointments may be made, May through October.

Bantam, Bethlehem, Washington

Route 202 leads to Bantam. Bantam Lake, on Route 209 to the south, is the largest natural lake in the state and a popular summer playground. While there is much private property on the lakeside, there is a public swimming pool at Sandy Beach. At least half of the lake is bordered by the 3,500-acre White Memorial Conservation Center. The White Memorial, on Route 202, is a bird and animal sanctuary that invites the public to hike, swim, picnic, camp, and ride through its 27 miles of bridle paths. There is also a launching ramp for boats. Cross-country skiing and snowshoeing are popular here on trails and wooded roads. On the property of the White Memorial Foundation, once a private house, there are nature displays and exhibits as well as a library and gift shop. Nature-education programs for all age groups and guided tours are available. Especially important here are the nature trails designed for the handicapped.

The White Flower Farm on Route 63 south has more than 25 acres of varicolored flowers in bloom in midsummer—a sight to behold! Hothouse plants are in vast greenhouses. Open to the public from April through December.

South on Routes 209 and 61 is Bethlehem, a pleasant rural community of colonial homes. It was in Bethlehem that the first theological school in this country was established. The founder of the school, Rev. Dr. Joseph Bellamy, was a distinguished and dynamic preacher who was born in 1719. A monument commemorating him is located on the site of the second Bethlehem Congregational Church at the north end of the small triangular green.

Washington (north again on Route 61 and then west on Route 109) has exquisite houses around a small green. The American Indian Archaeological Institute on Route 199 is a research and educational museum center for the study of prehistoric and historic man in Connecticut and New England. The numerous exhibits include a Paleo-Indian campsite, an indoor reconstructed longhouse, and an Indian garden. There are regularly scheduled weekend programs open to the public as well as courses and field trips.

New Preston is north of Washington, via Route 45 and Route 202. Nearby is Lake Waramaug and its spacious state park. The area has several fine country inns with restaurants of distinction and preparatory schools that draw their enrollments from every state in the Union and many foreign countries.

Hopkins Vineyard welcomes visitors with samplings of the award-winning wines in a restored nineteenth-century barn. A hayloft gallery shows the work of local artists and craftsmen.

Still farther along on Route 7 is Kent Falls State Park, a 275-acre preserve with a beautiful waterfall.

In the town of Kent, with a population of about 2,000, are three private schools and the Sloane-Stanley Museum, containing the Eric Sloane collection of early American tools. On the museum grounds one finds the remains of an early eighteenth-century blast furnace that once served the iron industry here.

Little Goshen, a farming village on Route 4, has a pretty main street lined with white clapboard houses. Commercial hard-cheese-making in America started in Goshen, and in early days its "pineapple" cheese was known throughout the country. There are large farms in this area. In fact, half of all Connecticut's dairy farms are in the Litchfield Hills.

In this part of the country, democracy in its purest form is a way of life. Rules, regulations, and ordinances are proposed by selectmen elected by the people, then approval must be obtained from the voters assembled in traditional town meetings where each has his say. Visitors may watch a town meeting in action from the balcony of the meeting place or at the rear.

New Milford and Cornwall

A short way from New Preston on Route 202 is New Milford, settled in the first decade of the eighteenth century by a group from Milford, Connecticut. Many of the houses overlooking the green in the center of town were built in the 1700s. Those of brick are said to have been constructed with bricks brought to this country from England. According to the New Milford Historical Society, the cargo ships came into New Haven and the bricks were delivered to New Milford by oxcart.

Cornwall, on Route 4 just off Route 7, is another colonial town that belongs on a calendar or postcard. Cornwall has attracted artists, writers, critics, and poets, and is a delightful, congenial community. The photogenic, historic Cornwall covered bridge—one of the few remaining originals—spans the Housatonic River here.

The far northwestern corner of Connecticut is dotted with lakes, mountains, state parks, forests, and lovely old colonial towns such as Sharon, Lakeville, Salisbury, and Canaan. Each has charming inns, its own historical society, perhaps the ruins of an early forge or foundry, a ravine, a gorge, or a hiking trail. There are often art shows, antiques sales, auctions, and country fairs on summer weekends.

Mohawk Mountain State Park, a popular ski area with tows, lifts, ski school, shops, and a warming house is in Cornwall. Since the area is in the lower snowbelt of New England, snowmaking machines supplement nature. The tows and lifts do not operate for sightseeing in summer, although picnicking and hiking are popular.

To the east from Thomaston via Route 72, families find a rare treat in America's oldest amusement park at Lake Compounce, Bristol, reopened in 1986 when the Hershey Corporation restored and expanded this genuine piece of Victorian Americana. It includes everything from a 1920s roller coaster to a state-of-the-art log flume ride carved out of the mountainside. Swimming, arcade games, live entertainment, even a water slide, and there are plenty of opportunities for either picnicking or obtaining food here. An alternative route is I–84, Exit 31, then north on Route 229. It is open May to September. For more information contact the Litchfield Hills Visitors Commission, Box 1776, Marbledale, CT 06777 (868–2214).

Returning to New Milford on Route 7, you will find Candlewood Lake, the largest artificial lake in the state. Much of the shore property is private, but there are public beaches and marinas. Squantz Pond State Park nearby is a popular swimming, boating, and picnicking area.

Danbury has an increasing number of corporate headquarters for major industries that have moved out to the suburbs from metropolitan areas. It was one of the cities burned by the British raiding parties during the Revolution. Several buildings, now part of the Scott-Fanton Museum and Historical Society, 43 Main Street, escaped the torch and may be visited. Huntington Exhibition Hall has frequently changing exhibits of art, science, and history. The rural Route 33 becomes the quaint, tree-lined Main Street of Ridgefield, a historic town.

Two other lovely old towns in this district are Woodbury and South-bury, off I–84. Woodbury is noted for its many antiques shops and for Curtis House, a mid-eighteenth-century inn, said to be the oldest in Connecticut; Southbury's Harrison Inn Conference Center is known to many of the state's corporate executives.

PRACTICAL INFORMATION FOR NORTHWESTERN CONNECTICUT

Note: The area code for all Connecticut is 203

HOW TO GET THERE AND AROUND. Although with a little research it might be possible to locate a train or motor coach schedule that would include a stop at a town in the Litchfield Hills, it would be best to plan on reaching the area **by car,** whether from New York via Rte. 44 or Massachusetts via Rte. 8. State highways within the region, Rtes. 7 and 8, primarily, run north from I–95 and the Merritt Parkway (Rte. 15).

By plane: Bradley International Airport in Windsor Locks is the one nearest Litchfield although there are smaller airports for private planes, such as the airport in Oxford.

By bus: Bonanza Bus Line serves the area with regular service from its transportation center in Southbury.

By train: Metro-North trains have a stop in Brewster, New York, which is the nearest train service for this area.

HOTELS AND MOTELS. This is country-inn country where renovated Victorian mansions, colonial homes, and Federal-style mid-19th-century houses rank among the better hotel accommodations in the state. Modern structures are also to be found, but generally in the guise of conference centers. Hotel-type accommodations are given first, followed by bed and breakfasts. Price ranges are based on double occupancy: *Deluxe,* $70; *Expensive,* $50–$69; *Moderate,* $30–$49; *Inexpensive,* under $30.

Cornwall

Cornwall Inn, Rte. 7 at Cornwall Bridge, 06754 (672–6884). *Moderate.* A 150-year-old building. Picturesque inn with good country dining. The pool is in a garden setting.

Danbury

Danbury Hilton and Conference Center, Old Ridgebury Rd., 06810 (794–0600). *Deluxe.* An extensive property with 14 meeting rooms. Indoor pool and sauna. Restaurant and coffee shop.

Kent

Club Getaway, S. Kent Rd., 06757 (For reservations call 927–3664). *Expensive.* An enclave of heated cabins with private baths, situated on 300 acres of woodland. Primarily singles, 20–40-year-olds. All meals. Lessons in most outdoor sports and equipment included. Weekend and weekly rates.
Fife 'n Drum, Main St., Rte. 7, 06757 (927–3509). *Expensive.* A small inn with rooms above a gift shop. Color TV, air-conditioning. Full bath. Complimentary coffee, tea, and fruit juice.

Lakeville

Interlaken Inn, Rte. 112, 06039 (435–9878). *Deluxe.* A resort and conference center on 26 acres between two lakes, in the Berkshire foothills. Seasonal rates, May–Oct., Nov.–Apr. Balconies with rural view. 5,000 sq. ft. conference space.

Litchfield

Litchfield Inn, Rte. 202, 06759 (567–4503). *Expensive.* An 18th-century country inn with elegant ambience throughout, compared with some of the more rustic accommodations. Noted French restaurant complemented by a superior wine cellar.
Toll Gate Hill Inn, Rte 202, 06759 (567–4545). *Expensive.* Built in 1745 and listed in the National Register of Historic Places. Continental breakfast served in elegantly furnished rooms. Lunch, cocktails, and dinner in the tavern room or formal dining room. The ballroom is for private parties.

New Preston

The Inn at Lake Waramaug, N. Shore Rd. 06777 (868–0563). *Deluxe.* Late 18th-century inn. Indoor pool. Seasonal sports and special events. Price includes dinner and breakfast.
Boulders Inn, New Preston 06777 (868–7918). *Moderate.* On Lake Waramaug. A Victorian mansion that has been an inn since 1950, furnished with antiques. American and European plans. Restaurant open every day. Open year-round.
Hopkins Inn, New Preston 06777 (868–7295). *Moderate.* In the Berkshire foothills, overlooking Lake Waramaug, this Federal-style mid-19th-century building has light and airy rooms furnished with country antiques. Seasonal. Open Apr.–Nov. No pets. Private beach for guests.

Norfolk

Mountain View Inn, Rte. 272, 06059 (542–5595). *Expensive.* A Victorian mansion located near the Norfolk Green. Furnished with antiques. Nearby antiquing. Downhill and cross-country skiing in winter; golf, tennis, fishing nearby. Daily specials on the restaurant dinner menu.

Salisbury

Under Mountain Inn, Rte. 41, 06068 (435–0242). *Deluxe.* Rooms with full English breakfast and British-flavored hospitality. Not suitable for children under six. No pets. Interesting antiques, books, and art in this inn built in the 1700s. Restaurant open Fri. and Sat. year-round features beef, kidney pie, and roast goose.

Southbury

Harrison Inn, Heritage Village, Exit 15, Rte 84 (264–8200). *Deluxe.* Although of recent vintage by comparison with other country inns nearby, there is a rustic charm that prevails, although the property has an adequate conference center. Most participant sports are available, and the Heritage Village Bazaar is also here. The Timbers Restaurant. Weekend entertainment.

Torrington

Yankee Pedlar Inn, 93 Main St., 06790 (489–9226). *Moderate.* Dating back to 1891, this country inn is charmingly casual. Furnished with antiques including four-poster beds and Tiffany lamps, it is geared to 20th-century convenience. Restaurant, bar, and banquet facilities.

Washington

The Mayflower Inn and Restaurant, Rte. 47, 06793 (868–0515). *Moderate.* Renovation of this century-old inn continued and rooms furnished are in contemporary country style. Children over eight welcome, pets are not. Property once owned by the Gunnery School in Washington.

INNS, GUEST HOUSES, BED AND BREAKFASTS. During the seasonal busy periods when visitors are flocking to this area, it is always best to have reservations for overnight and to make them well in advance. For bed-and-breakfast accommodations there are two registries serving this area: Covered Bridge Bed & Breakfast, Box 447, Norfolk 06058 (542–5944) and Nutmeg Bed & Breakfast, 222 Girard Ave., Hartford 06105 (236–6698).

The following bed-and-breakfast inns fall in the *Moderate–Expensive* range.

Bethlehem

Eastover Farm Bed and Breakfast, Guilds Hollow Rd., Rte. 132, 06751 (266–5740). Some shared-bath, other rooms with private bath in this late 18th-century farmhouse owned since 1929 by the same family. Near White Flower Farm in Litchfield and the White Memorial. Also near ski areas in the Berkshire foothills. Continental breakfast.

Bristol

Chimneyrest Manor, 5 Founders Dr., 06010 (582–4219). Bed-and-breakfast accommodations in a Tudor mansion. Suites, double rooms, efficiency; corporate and monthly rates. Reservations with deposit required.

Middlebury

Tucker Hill Inn Bed & Breakfast, 96 Tucker Hill Rd., 06762 (758–8334). Small colonial home with four guest rooms. Private and shared baths. Full breakfast.

New Hartford

Highland Farm, Highland Ave., 06057 (379–6029). A country bed-and-breakfast inn. Victorian farmhouse near Sundown ski area. Scenic environment and interesting antique shops nearby. Boating, fishing, canoeing also nearby.

Norfolk

Manor House Bed & Breakfast, Box 701, Maple Ave., 06058 (542–5690). A Victorian house built in 1898 and the elegance of the original period has been maintained. Full breakfast. Walking distance to Yale School of Music and Art. Near Tanglewood and Music Mountain. Children over 12 welcome. No pets.

Weaver's House, Rte. 44, 06058 (542–5108). A Victorian mansion, now a bed-and-breakfast home. The name, derived from the owner's craft, is evident throughout the home. Near Norfolk Chamber Music Festival site, Music Mountain, Tanglewood, Lime Rock, and summer theater. Skiing nearby in winter. Buffet Continental breakfast. No smoking and no pets. Shared bath. Short distance from Hawks' Nest Pub, a restaurant in the center of Norfolk featuring lunch and dinner specials.

Salisbury

Yesterday's Bed & Breakfast, Rte. 44 east, 06068 (435–9539). A mid-18th-century farmhouse with period furnishings. Full breakfast.

Woodbury

Curtis House, on Rte. 6 (263–2102). Connecticut's oldest inn in continuous operation, dates to 1754. In heart of state's antique center. Fine restaurant with country cooking. Continental breakfast.

RESTAURANTS. The variety of cuisines found throughout the state are also found here in the foothills of the Berkshires. Most of the country inns listed in the foregoing section have fine restaurants for which they are well known. Visitors to the area would do well to call ahead for reservations. Price ranges for a full meal exclusive of beverages, tax, and tip are: *Deluxe,* $30 and up; *Expensive,* $25–$29; *Moderate,* $15–$24; and *Inexpensive,* $14 and under.

Note: In addition to the listings that follow, elegant dinners can be had, usually at *deluxe* prices, in the restaurants of the country inns listed above.

Danbury

Bella Italia, 2 Padanarum Rd. (743–3828). *Moderate.* Ornate Italian decor. Three dining rooms: formal dining, trattoria, pizzeria. Excellent Northern Italian food prepared to order.

Kent

Kent Station Cafe, Kent Station Sq. (927–4751). *Expensive.* An interesting ambience in this restored railroad station. Closed Mon. and Tues. Reservations.

Litchfield

La Tienda Café, Rte. 202 (567–8778). *Moderate.* Offering award-winning Mexican menu, "mild, medium, or hot," as well as American dishes. Cantina, the cocktail lounge, is open for cocktails and snacks all day. Open 7 days. "To-go menu" also available.

Riverton

Old Riverton Inn, Rte. 20 (379–8678). *Moderate.* In center of town. Homey, friendly place. A stagecoach stop c. 1796. In rolling-hill country across the road from the Hitchcock Chair Factory.

Washington Depot

The Pantry, Titus Sq. (868–0258). *Moderate.* This unusual restaurant has tables scattered among shelves and stacks of kitchen tools and implements and packaged gourmet foods. A charcuterie adds to the ambience, with luncheon daily specials that can be taken out. Bakery on the premises and an assortment of cheeses.

West Cornwall

Freshfields, Rte. 128 (672–6601). *Expensive.* A charming country bistro near the famous Cornwall covered bridge. Distinctive American cooking featuring a wood-burning grill. Breads and desserts made on the premises. "Upstairs at Freshfields" for cocktails and light menu. Seating on deck, weather permitting. Closed Mon. and Tues., Nov.–Apr.

Winsted

The Tributary Restaurant, 19 Rowley St. (379–7679). *Expensive.* A restored property, "the old barn on Rowley St." built originally in mid-18th century, it has survived adversity, weather, and multiple uses. Now this restaurant in the renovated old structure is a veritable museum of local history. Lunch and dinner served daily except Mon., with a special Sun. dinner served at noon. Breads and desserts made on the premises.

TOURIST INFORMATION. For information on any of the towns in the Litchfield Hills area contact Litchfield Hills Visitors Commission, Box 1776, New Preston 06777 (868–2214).

TOURS. The **Litchfield Hills Travel Council** has created five self-guided automobile tours. These are published in a booklet available on request. These tours include routings, accommodations, and restaurants, as well as important sightseeing and tourist attractions.
Heritage Trails Tours, Box 138, Farmington 06034 (677–8867) has special tours within this area and a brochure with details is available on request.

Vineyard tours are offered by both Haight Vineyard and Winery, Chestnut Hill, Litchfield 06759 (567–4045), and Hopkins Vineyard, Hopkins Rd., Warren. The mailing address is New Preston 06777 (868–7954).

Maple Springs Farm Tours, Kenyon Rd. (567–8324). Two miles west of the junction of Rtes. 109 and 209. Offers barnyard farm tours by appointment only.

SEASONAL EVENTS. The Litchfield Hills region is one where the seasons are celebrated by various events, whether the coming of spring daffodils, laurel festivals, or apple blossom time. Summer events include numerous country fairs in the area and autumn of course is the foliage change which attracts visitors from throughout the United States. Winter is ski time and special winter sports events are scheduled throughout the hills.

For a calendar of information on country fairs, contact the Association of Connecticut Fairs, 190 South Rd., Box 363, Somers 06071.

May: Eastern Association of Women's Rowing Championship Regatta, Inn at Lake Waramaug, New Preston (mid-May); IMSA Camel GT Championship Auto Race, Lime Rock (late May).

June: Connecticut Wine Festival, Middlebury (early June); Laurel Festival, Winsted (mid-June). Antique horse-drawn carriage rally, Inn at Lake Waramaug, New Preston (late June).

July: SCCA Kendall Cup National Sports Car Racing, Lime Rock Park, (first weekend); Annual Open House Day with tours of local homes, Litchfield (mid-July).

September: Goshen Fair, Rte. 63, south of Goshen (early Sept.); Annual Huckleberry Finn Raft Race, Inn at Lake Waramaug, New Preston (early Sept.); Annual Vintage Fall Festival at Lime Rock State Park, Lime Rock (early Sept.); Family Nature Day at White Memorial Foundation, Litchfield (late Sept.).

October: Chrysanthemum Festival, Bristol (early Oct.); Antiques Fair at the Town Hall, Salisbury (early Oct.); Roseland Cottage Festival, Woodstock (mid-Oct.).

Late **November** through **December:** Holiday bazaars and fairs in towns and villages throughout the area. Also numerous musical events commemorating the season.

PARKS, FORESTS, NATURE CENTERS. State Forests in the area include: **Mohawk State Forest,** on Rte. 4 in Cornwall 06489 (672–6100), where, on Mohawk Mountain, there is one of the state's leading ski areas. This is also a wildlife sanctuary and there are hiking trails.

Topsmead State Forest on Buell Rd. in Litchfield 06759 (567–5694). There are 512 acres including a wildflower preserve and a 1920 Tudor mansion, Chase House, with original furnishings, which is open to the public.

Peoples State Forest with about 3,000 acres, on East River Rd., Barkhamsted, is near the Farmington River. Boating, backpack camping, fishing, and cross-country skiing are among the features here.

For specific information on parks, forests, and nature centers as well as ski areas in the northwestern section of Connecticut, contact the Parks and Recreation Division, Department of Environmental Protection, 165 Capitol Ave., Hartford 06106 or call 566–2304. The *Vacation Guide* issued by the Tourism Division, Department of Economic Development, 210 Washington St., Hartford 06106 (566–3385), has a concise listing of these areas with facilities available at each noted.

Other Attractions. In Litchfield, the **White Memorial Foundation** has a vast conservation center on Rte. 202 (567–0857) with nature trails and a museum.

White Flower Farm, Rte. 63 south (567–0801) has 40 acres of growing fields and 10 acres of display gardens.

In West Torrington, at **Indian Lookout** in the latter part of June, there is a vast display of the state flower, the mountain laurel.

VINEYARDS AND WINERIES.

Vineyards and wineries are being developed throughout the state, but two that began the trend are in the Litchfield area:

Haight Vineyard and Winery, Chestnut Hill, Litchfield 06759 (567–4045). "Connecticut's first established farm winery" established 1975. Open 7 days for guided winery tours and tastings. Closed major holidays.

Hopkins Vineyard, Hopkins Rd., New Preston 06777 (868–7954). Open seven days, May 1–Jan. 1. Weekends only, other months. Vineyard and winery tours and tastings. Gold Medal–winning wines.

SPORTS.

Golf courses in the area include: the Canton Golf Course on Rte. 44 with nine holes (693–8305) and, in Litchfield, the Stonybrook Golf Club on Milton Rd. 06759 (567–9977), also with nine holes. In New Milford, the Candlewood Valley Country Club, Rte. 7, 06776 (354–9359), is an 18-hole course.

Boating. Bantam Lake is noted for its sailboat regattas, and throughout the summer small boats may be launched or rented here, as well as at the area's other lakes, many of which are in local state parks or forests.

Downhill and **cross-country skiing** areas in the Litchfield Hills include: Mohawk Mountain, Rte. 4, Cornwall 06753 (672–6100); Ski Sundown, Rte. 219, New Hartford 06057 (379–9851); **Woodbury Ski and Racquet Area,** Rte. 47, Woodbury 06798 (263–2203).

FISHING.

Lake and pond fishing is popular here and well known for seasonal catches of trout, pickerel, bass, and shad. The Litchfield Hills Travel Council, Box 1776, Marbledale 06777 (868–2214) publishes a *Guide to Fishing* and it is available on request from the Council. Information is also available at any town clerk's office where licenses are also dispensed. The fishing season in Connecticut opens on the third Sat. in Apr. and runs through Mar. 31 the following year. During weekends when the town clerk's offices are not open, information and licenses may be obtained at fishing-tackle and bait shops: The Armoury, Rte. 202, Woodville 06777 (868–0001); the Wilderness Shop, Rte. 202, Sports Village, Litchfield 06759 (567–5905); and Sports Scene, Rte. 7, Kent 06757 (927–3852).

HUNTING.

Much small game is found in the Connecticut fields and forests; waterfowl in lakes and marshes along the rivers. Nov. and Dec. is bow-and-arrow deer-hunting season. Rules and other information are available from the Department of Environmental Protection in Hartford (566–2304).

SPECTATOR SPORTS.

National and regional **auto races** are staged during the summer at the Lime Rock Track. There is also stock-car racing in Salisbury close by.

Boating events take place on the area's lakes and rivers. For schedules of these events, inquire locally, as they vary each year.

HISTORIC SITES AND HOUSES. Litchfield was declared a historic district by the state in 1957. Most of the historic houses, monuments, and sites open to the public are owned or operated or both by local historical societies. Open hours, usually seasonal, depend on the availability of volunteers to act as hosts or hostesses. When telephone numbers are not listed, a call to the local Chamber of Commerce is the easiest way to obtain information. Or contact a historical society for information.

Litchfield

Litchfield Historical Society Museum, East and South Sts. (567–4501). The local history library, exhibits, and paintings. Open mid-Apr.–mid-Nov.

Tapping Reeve House and Law School, South St. (567–4501). The first law school in America (1784); its graduates include some of the great names in American history. Open mid-May–mid-Oct.

New Milford

New Milford Historical Society Museum, 6 Aspetuck Ave. (354–3069). Knapp House c. 1770. Early paintings, 18th- and 19th-century furniture, china, and costumes. Open Apr.–Oct.

Riverton

Hitchcock Museum, Rte. 20 (379–1003). An old church meetinghouse housing early Hitchcock furniture. Seasonal.

Torrington

Hotchkiss-Fyler House (1900), 192 Main St. (482–8260). A Victorian mansion with original furnishings. Greenhouse and carriage house.

Winsted

Solomon Rockwell House (1813), Lake and Prospect Sts. (379–8433). Furnished according to the period. Good examples of Connecticut craftsmanship in the furnishings. Open June–Sept.

Woodstock

Roseland Cottage (1846), Rte. 169 (928–4074). An excellent example of Gothic Revival architecture. Many original furnishings. Seasonal.

MUSEUMS AND ART GALLERIES. Museums and galleries in Connecticut reflect the lives of the people throughout more than three centuries of the state's history through exhibitions of fine art, decorative arts, furniture, and many of the industrial products for which Connecticut is well known. Call ahead to check days, hours, and admission fees.

Bristol

American Clock and Watch Museum, 100 Maple St. (583–6070). Connecticut-made clocks and watches dating back to the late 17th century and displayed in appropriate settings of handsome antiques. Apr.-Oct. Closed during winter.

Kent

Sloane-Stanley Museum and Kent Furnace, Rte. 7 (927–3849 or 566–3005). Tools and farm implements, some from the 17th century, interestingly displayed with appropriate backgrounds. Museum is on the site of the remains of the 19th-century Kent iron furnace.

Terryville

Lock Museum of America, 130 Main St. (589–6359). More than 20,000 locks and keys from early types to the present and exhibits of local industrial history.

Waterbury

Mattatuck Historical Society Museum, 119 W. Main St. (753–0381). A museum of local colonial and Victorian history; fine industrial arts. A collection of works by Connecticut artists.

MUSIC AND THEATER. Visitors to Litchfield Hills may find excellent productions by professional theater groups and musicians, especially during the summer. In Bristol—**Auberge d'Elegance Dinner Theater,** 140 North St. (589–7720).

In Danbury—**Charles Ives Center for the Arts at Western Connecticut University,** University Blvd. (797–4002). A variety of concerts offered July–mid-Aug.

In Norfolk—**Norfolk Chamber Music Festival,** Rte. 44 (542–5537 or 432–1966) at the Ellen Battell Stoeckel Estate.

In Southbury—**Southbury Summer Theater,** Oak Tree Rd. (264–8215).

SHOPPING. Shopping is not what one primarily goes to the Litchfield Hills for unless it's antiques you're looking for. There are also some interesting art galleries that sell works of local artists. Crafts, too, may be found in studios. Casual clothes suitable for country wear are in shops in most of the small towns. In Danbury, however, which is probably the "city" in the midst of this rural area, a vast shopping mall with over 150 shops and numerous restaurants is located on the site that was once the Danbury Fairgrounds. This shopping center is suitably named **Danbury Fair.**

NIGHTLIFE. In Winsted—**Gilson Café and Cinema,** 354 Main St. (379–5108) serves food and liquor. Movies on Wed. and Sun. nights.

In Torrington—**Warner Theater,** 69 Main St. (489–7180 or 489–1219). Live entertainment only.

In Bristol—**Lake Compounce,** Rte. 229 (582–6323). During the summer there is nightly entertainment at this amusement park, including special stage shows and bands. Open only until 10 P.M.

MAINE

By
JANE E. ZAREM

Jane E. Zarem, a born-and-bred New Englander, is a free-lance writer and editor who has traveled extensively throughout the region. She is a member of the New York Travel Writers Association.

One part or another of the marvelous state of Maine should appeal to nearly everyone. Maine is perfect for a vacation by the sea: for watching waves smashing on the rocky shore, fishing boats bringing home the day's catch, lighthouses blinking at passing gulls, islands dotting the horizon; for fishing and canoeing on crystal-clear mountain lakes, roaring rivers, and rushing streams; for hiking, camping, skiing and snowmobiling, or northwoods hunting. There are even inviting cottages on quiet coves where those who want to get away from it all can read, write, or paint.

Irregularly diamond-shaped, Maine is 320 miles from north to south and 210 miles from east to west at its widest point. The total land area is 33,215 square miles, which is just under half of all New England.

Like its neighbors in northern New England, Maine owes its dramatic, rugged beauty to eons of geologic action. Some 11,000 years ago the continental ice sheet melted, leaving a bedrock of sandstone, limestone, and shale. Over the centuries, the soft rock eroded into valleys and lowlands; the hard, more resistant rock formed Maine's western mountains, its rolling hills, and the random peaks found elsewhere in the state—Mt. Katahdin in north-central Maine and Cadillac Mountain on Mount Desert Island, for example.

The receding glaciers produced several mighty rivers and thousands of lakes, ponds, and streams as the ocean seeped inland. (Maine has more than 6,000 lakes and ponds and 5,100 rivers and streams.) The resulting coastline of what is now Maine consists of long stretches of sandy beach, tidal pools, quiet coves, and marshy lowlands from the New Hampshire border north to the Kennebec River. Down East from the Kennebec the coast is rugged and rocky, with scores of craggy peninsulas jutting into the ocean and countless offshore islands. Although the coast is just 230 miles long, if you were to follow the shoreline around all the bays and harbors, capes and peninsulas, you would travel some 3,500 miles—much of it spectacular.

Most of the land in the Pine Tree State is heavily wooded, with broad vistas of open wilderness between populated areas. Timber and wood lots cover 87 percent of the state.

Early Inhabitants

Burial mounds found in south-central Maine and shell heaps found along the coast near Damariscotta indicate that Indians inhabited the area well over 2,000 years ago. These early residents were the ancestors of the Abnaki Indians, descendents of whom are represented now on the Penobscot and Passamaquoddy reservations.

Norse, British, French, and Spanish explorers all visited what we know as Maine, but Pierre du Guast, le sieur de Monts, and Samuel de Champlain established the first French colony at the mouth of the St. Croix River in 1604. Shortly after arriving, Champlain explored the area to the west, naming it Mount Desert Island (Isle des Monts Desert) because of its bare mountaintops. The French colony was short-lived. In 1605, England's King James I included the Maine region in the land grant given the Plymouth Colony. The French then moved east, across the Bay of Fundy to Nova Scotia, and founded Port Royal, the chief town of Acadia.

Led by George Popham in 1607, the first English settlers arrived at what is now Phippsburg, at the mouth of the Kennebec River. The few survivors who endured the devastating winter of harsh weather and disease were forced to abandon the settlement in the spring of 1608.

In 1620, the Council for New England (successor to the Plymouth Colony) granted the territory between the Merrimack and the Kennebec rivers to English councilmen Ferdinando Gorges and Captain John Mason. By agreement of the two partners, the land was divided in 1629: Gorges took the area now known as Maine; Mason kept what became New Hampshire.

Gorges received a royal charter, confirming his grant, from King Charles I in 1639. In 1641, York became the first city chartered by England in the New World and the capital of the Province of Maine. After Gorges's death (1647), jurisdiction over the settlers in the territory fell to the Massachusetts Bay Company. Title was disputed for many years until, in 1677, Massachusetts purchased the rights to this land from Gorges's grandson.

Early settlers discovered Maine's abundant natural resources: excellent harbors and offshore banks teeming with fish; tall trees for ship hulls and masts; wildlife for food and fur; sand and stone for building materials. Navigable rivers enabled lumbermen and trappers to transport their harvests through the remote wilderness of the great north woods to the population centers along the coast. Lumbering camps and sawmills sprouted along the streams.

Sharing the land and its wealth with the native Americans resulted in bitter territorial battles. Struggles between the British and the French and

Indians continued, several very bloody wars being fought over French positions in the area east of the Penobscot River. The British ultimately prevailed, driving the French northward and eastward into Canada and wresting control of the land from the Indians.

In 1691, Massachusetts received a new charter for the Province of Maine and territorial problems settled down. A local government was instituted, with native-born Sir William Phipps as royal governor. As the eighteenth century began, only the settlements of Kittery, Wells, and York had survived the ravages of war and the Indian raids of the previous 25 years. Fishing, lumbering, and shipbuilding, though, led the devasted settlements to a relatively quick economic recovery.

Independence and Statehood

In America's struggle for independence, Maine men distinguished themselves by their leadership, fortitude, and sense of purpose. The first naval battle of the Revolutionary War took place unceremoniously off Machias, when local townspeople captured the armed British cutter *Margaretta.*

Along with the new nation came local agitation for statehood in the District of Maine. The displeasure of Maine residents over absentee ownership of land—and a basic political polarization between conservative Massachusetts and democratic Maine—added to the general dissatisfaction over what Maine felt was inadequate military protection by Massachusetts during the War of 1812. (It was not until the signing of the Treaty of 1814 that the British military presence was removed from Maine soil.)

The Missouri Compromise hastened the separation from Massachusetts; Maine was admitted to the Union as a free state in 1820 to balance the power between North and South on the issue of slavery. Portland became Maine's first capital; Augusta was made the permanent capital in 1832.

The final controversy in the establishment of the state was the northern border dispute, which nearly led to an Aroostook War in 1839 between Maine and Canada. The dispute was peacefully settled by the Webster–Ashburton Treaty in 1842, which set the present northern boundary.

Lumber, Boats, and Fishing

Timber, trade, and shipbuilding were primarily responsible for drawing new residents to coastal and river areas. As the Industrial Revolution took hold, manufacturing became predominant. The same rivers used so successfully for transportation provided a power supply for hundreds of mills. The production of textiles, leather goods, lumber, and wood products attracted workers and their families to the new sources of employment, and mill towns were created along the major rivers.

Today Maine's population of 1,173,000 is still concentrated along the coast and major rivers. Some early mills remain in operation, producing shoes, clothing, and wood products. The vast timber and wood lots of the north woods are owned by private corporations which operate pulp and paper mills.

The abundance of protected deep-water harbors ensures an involvement with the sea. Shipbuilding, important since 1800, remains relatively healthy in Maine. The proximity of forest to harbor encouraged the building of clipper ships in the early days; now production ranges from tankers and naval ships to private fishing and sailing boats. Commercial fishing also continues to be important to the state's economy. Maine fishermen

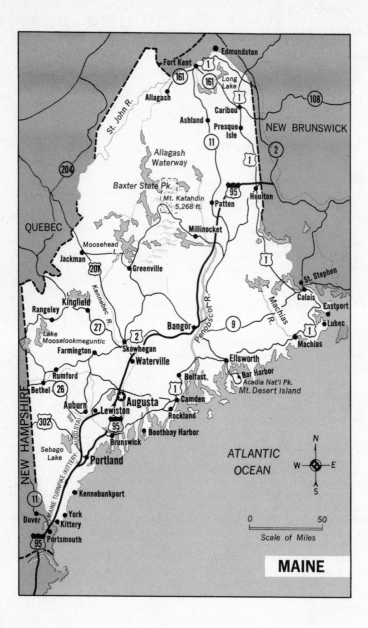

Edmundston
Fort Kent
161
1
161
Long
Lake
Allagash
108
1
Caribou
Ashland
Presque
Isle
NEW BRUNSWICK
Allagash
Waterway
11
St. John R.
204
Baxter State Pk.
Mt. Katahdin
5,268 ft.
95
Houlton
2
Patten
1
QUEBEC
Millinocket
Moosehead
L.
Jackman
201
1
St. Stephen
Greenville
Calais
Eastport
Rangeley
Kingfield
Penobscot R.
Machias R.
Lubec
Lake
Mooselookmeguntic
27
Kennebec R.
Bangor
9
Machias
1
Farmington
2
Skowhegan
Ellsworth
Rumford
Waterville
Belfast
Bar Harbor
Bethel
26
1
Acadia Nat'l Pk.
Mt. Desert Island
Auburn
Augusta
Camden
Lewiston
Rockland
302
95
ATLANTIC
OCEAN
Boothbay Harbor
Brunswick
Sebago
Lake
Portland
N
NEW HAMPSHIRE
MAINE TURNPIKE (KITTERY - AUGUSTA)
W
E
11
Kennebunkport
S
Dover
York
Kittery
0
50
95
Portsmouth
Scale of Miles

MAINE

bring in a varied catch, and the incomparable Maine lobster is world famous.

To stem the tide of economic fluctuations, the state's greatest resource—the natural beauty of its land—has been put to work. Tourism is a leading industry. Excellent interstate road systems allow easy access from the northeastern United States and southeastern Canada, winter and summer, to and through Maine. The climate is invigorating; healthful, clean air prevails because of the predominance of forest land. Thousands of acres of protected land are open for public recreation: national and state parks and forests, wildlife preserves, mountain trails, and waterfront.

Maine's busiest tourist season is summer, especially at the beach resorts and boating communities along the coast. Visitors can be assured of a cool summer holiday anywhere in Maine. An occasional day in mid-July can be hot and sticky, but average summer temperatures in the 70s make it more likely that you'll want a sweater, particularly in the evening.

Winters are long and cold, with temperatures averaging in the low 20s in January and February, yet winter days are usually sunny and crystal clear. The availability of excellent snow conditions is the payoff for alpine and cross-country skiers who make the trek to Maine.

Fall is hunting season, when sportsmen are lured to the wilderness areas. The magnificent autumn foliage peaks in late September.

And spring is for fishermen. The black flies can be a distraction, however, so come prepared!

Travel information is free and abundant, by mail or at information centers around the state. Colorful and comprehensive brochures and booklets are published by the Maine Publicity Bureau. Roads and highways are well marked with directions to towns and local attractions. Tourism is recognized as being vital to the economy, and tourists are always made to feel welcome.

Exploring Maine

THE SOUTHERN COAST

Most travelers to Maine enter the state at Kittery, its southernmost point, just beyond Portsmouth, New Hampshire. Here the decision can be made whether to take I–95 and the Maine Turnpike (the "fast route") north or to opt for scenic Route 1, which follows the coast. Whichever choice is made, the first stop for travelers should be the Maine Information Center, operated by the Maine Publicity Bureau. Accessible from both routes, this large hospitality center offers free information on accommodations, restaurants, tourist attractions, and activities for all parts of the state.

Kittery and the Berwicks

Kittery, first settled in 1623, is Maine's oldest community. Since those earliest days, the town has had an international reputation for its major industry, shipbuilding. English warships were constructed by local craftsmen; later, vessels were built for the Continental Navy. John Paul Jones set sail from Kittery on the 18-gun *Ranger* to defeat the British man-of-war *Drake* during the Revolution. Nowadays, submarine refitting is the major industry; the major employer, the Kittery-Portsmouth Naval Shipyard, was established in 1800 (no visitors). The Kittery Historical and Naval Museum, on Rogers Road off Route 1, has exhibits which portray Kittery's early history and its shipbuilding past.

Travelers and residents alike flock to the dozens of factory outlet stores concentrated along Route 1 in Kittery. Maine-made and imported products are sold at competitive or discounted prices.

At Kittery Point, across the Spruce Creek Bridge, the Lady Pepperell House (1760) is an eighteenth-century Georgian-style mansion built for the widow of Sir William Pepperell, the first person born in America to be made a baronet by the British crown. Farther along on Route 103 is Fort McClary (1690), a restored hexagonal blockhouse.

South Berwick, northwest of Kittery via Route 91, is the site of the first (1631) permanent settlement in Maine. The earliest sawmill run by water power was built here, on the Great Works River, in the 1640s. Long before the Revolutionary War, Maine timber was transformed in the Berwicks into pipe staves and ships. And on the slopes along the riverside, you can still see the terraced land where seventeenth-century colonists tried to grow grapes in the New World. Fine old homes in South Berwick have been preserved and are open to the public during the summer season. Hamilton House (1787), on Vaughan's Lane off Route 236, is a magnificently restored Georgian mansion with period furnishings. The Sarah Orne Jewett House (1774), 101 Portland Street, is lovingly preserved and worthy of the celebrated writer who chronicled Maine life.

The Yorks

Charming, colonial York Village was the first chartered city in America (1641). Prior to becoming a royal colony, it had been a popular summer playground for the Indians. The York Historic District includes a group of eighteenth- and nineteenth-century buildings and sites dating back to the days when the town was a colonial village and seaport. Some of the structures open to the public are: the Old York Gaol (1720), containing dungeons, cells, and jailer's quarters and built as the King's Prison for the Province of Maine; the beautifully furnished Emerson-Wilcox House (1742); Jefferd's Tavern (1750); the Old School House (1745); and the Elizabeth Perkins House (1731), a colonial home furnished as it was by its last occupants during the Victorian era. At the foot of Lindsay Street you'll find the John Hancock Warehouse, once owned by the bold signer of the Declaration of Independence.

While touring the Yorks, you're sure to cross Sewall's Bridge, a replica of the original built in 1761, the first pile drawbridge in America.

York Harbor is a fashionable resort colony. Boats are available for cruising and fishing. Farther north, York Beach is more family-oriented. There are shops and restaurants here and rides for the children at Wild Kingdom Amusement Park. Short Sands and Long Sands are both popular, hard-packed beaches that slope gently to the ocean.

Just past Long Sands Beach, Nubble Road is the turnoff for Cape Neddick, always a popular subject for artists and photographers. Visitors to the cape are rewarded with a fine view of the Atlantic, picturesque Nubble Light (1879), the northward-reaching Maine coast, and Boon Island and Light.

Ogunquit and Wells

Following the shore road to Ogunquit, majestic Bald Head Cliff towers 100 feet above the ocean. On a rough day you can see some fantastic surf; on any day you can marvel at the view.

Ogunquit is an Indian name meaning "beautiful place by the sea." The natural beauty of this charming coastal village draws thousands of summer visitors annually. Besides having a wonderful beach, Ogunquit has become famous as an artists' colony and the home of the Ogunquit Playhouse. Quaint Perkins Cove is fun to explore, with art galleries and artists' studios, gift shops and fishing boats. Or take a walk by the sea along Ogunquit's Marginal Way, a mile-long footpath that winds along the ocean and rocky cliffs. Gulls soar over the beaches and tidal pools along the way.

Wells, a seaside resort popular with families, has miles of sandy beach. Shoppers will find a concentration of brand-name factory outlet stores here, as well as flea markets, antique shops, and second-hand stores.

Wells is also the site of the Wells National Estuarine Research Reserve. A total of 4,000 acres of salt marsh has been set aside between Kittery and Portland to provide a sanctuary for many species of migrating birds. More than 1,600 acres of this marshland is in Wells, offering an excellent opportunity for birdwatching and photography.

The Kennebunks

The Kennebunks (Kennebunk, Kennebunkport, Kennebunk Beach, Cape Porpoise, Goose Rocks Beach, and Arundel) are popular summer vacation spots with more than their share of natural resources. Clean,

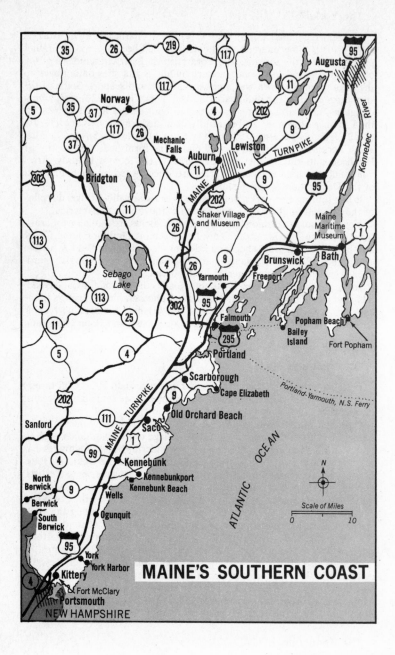

MAINE'S SOUTHERN COAST

sandy beaches, rocky coastline, calm harbors, and picturesque offshore islands attract the beachcomber, golfer, fisherman (river or deep-sea), yachtsman, artist, sightseer, and shopper.

On Main Street in Kennebunk, the Brick Store Museum (1825) shows marine artifacts and exhibits on early local shipbuilding. If you are heading toward the sea and Kennebunkport, the drive along Summer Street will take you past magnificent homes that date back to 1724. The architecture spans the colonial, Federal, Greek Revival, and Victorian periods. Certainly the most unusual house you will pass is the Wedding Cake House (privately owned—no visitors), built by a sea captain as a wedding present for his bride. Note that barns are attached to early Maine farmhouses, which made tending the animals easier for the farmers during cold winter months.

Kennebunkport is a colorful coastal community, a magnet over the years for many artists and writers. Here you will find a variety of tourist facilities, including comfortable inns and resorts, good restaurants, and a busy shopping area.

About three miles outside of town, on Log Cabin Road, kids (of all ages) will enjoy the Seashore Trolley Museum and a "ride back to yesteryear." The museum's collection represents a variety of mass-transit technology from the classic horsecar to latter-day streetcars. You can take a trolley ride: an adventure for the young, nostalgia for the young at heart. A restoration facility is on site, where artisans and aficionados return antique cars to working order.

Ocean Avenue, a scenic ocean drive, winds past stately seaside "cottages" (including that of President George Bush) on the way to Cape Porpoise and Goose Rocks Beach. At Cape Arundel, near Walker's Point, you will pass Spouting Rock, a spectacular ocean fountain, and Blowing Cave, a rock formation where the waves roar in with an explosive crash. (Look closely; they're unmarked.) Cape Porpoise is a quaint fishing village, the center of the area's lobstering activity. Goose Rocks Beach is a popular summer colony.

Old Orchard Beach and Prout's Neck

Old Orchard Beach, sometimes called the Coney Island of Maine, a seaside resort with one of the longest beaches on the Atlantic, is a favorite destination of families. The long stretch of white-sand beach provides safe swimming in a generally low surf; youngsters love the nearby amusement parks and the fast-paced atmosphere. More than any other location in Maine, Canadian visitors traditionally have preferred this resort area for their summer vacations. Many tourist facilities have bilingual staff to accommodate French-Canadian vacationers.

Just beyond Scarborough, on the western side of the Prout's Neck peninsula, there is a beautiful stretch of marshland where the colors change constantly as light and shadow play their tricks. At sunset the sight is magnificent. Winslow Homer used to live and paint at Prout's Neck.

The shoreline on Cape Elizabeth, north of Prout's Neck, is awe-inspiring. Cape Elizabeth Light (1827) overlooks a rocky promontory; the Atlantic Ocean pounds relentlessly at the jumble of rocks. The surf is wildest after a storm! Crescent Beach State Park has a 4,000-foot white-sand beach. Nearby, Two Lights State Park has scenic picnic sites. In clear weather there's a fine view of the famous Portland Head Light, constructed between 1785 and 1789 and ordered into commission in 1791 by George Washington. This is the oldest lighthouse on the Maine coast and the first lighthouse put into service in the United States.

Portland

Portland, where the Kennebec River empties into Casco Bay and the shoreline changes from marshy lowland to rocky coast, is the gateway to Down East Maine. The Eastern and Western promenades, beautifully landscaped esplanades at either end of the city, offer magnificent views of the bay and offshore islands to the east and the mountains to the west.

Bounded on three sides by water, Portland was an important shipbuilding city and port in the early days. Present-day Portland is the largest city in Maine and the cultural and commercial center of the state; it is still an important port. Over the last several years the city has undergone an economic surge due to extensive redevelopment and revitalization. Modern buildings have made their impact on the skyline, but the historic integrity of the bustling waterfront has been preserved in the Old Port Exchange. Here, just a few steps from the docks, nineteenth-century buildings and warehouses have been painstakingly restored and converted to an endless variety of shops, boutiques, bookstores, arts and crafts or antiques shops, theaters, and cafes and restaurants. Brick sidewalks, benches for tired shoppers and strollers, trees, and gaslights add to the ambience.

Boats are available for rent or charter, for fishing or sightseeing, at the waterfront. At Custom House Wharf, Casco Bay Lines runs daylight, sunset, and moonlight cruises to neighboring islands. Nearby, travelers can take the overnight ferry to Yarmouth, Nova Scotia.

The 9,000-seat Cumberland County Civic Center on Free Street, home of the Maine Mariners professional hockey team, presents a complete program of sports, music, and special events. Symphony Hall, at the City Hall building, houses the Kotzschmar Memorial Organ and is home to the Portland Symphony Orchestra. A full series of concerts is offered each year, including a Pops concert and summer recitals.

Definitely worth a visit is the Portland Museum of Art on Congress Square. The museum's Charles Shipman Payson wing, designed by I. M. Pei, houses a superb collection of American art. Its exhibit of works by Maine artists includes a fine collection by Winslow Homer.

The Wadsworth-Longfellow House (487 Congress Street), where the poet spent his boyhood, was the first brick building to be built in Portland (1785). The home of the author of *Tales of a Wayside Inn, The Song of Hiawatha,* and *Evangeline* is interesting, from its old-fashioned kitchen and lovely garden to its manuscript collection. The Maine Historical Society is next door.

At the junction of North and Congress streets at the east end of town, the octagonal Portland Observatory rises 82 feet above Munjoy Hill (and 223 feet above sea level). The last of the nineteenth-century signal towers on the East Coast, it kept the city alerted to approaching vessels and ships in distress. From its lantern deck, one gets a sweeping view of Casco Bay; looking inland on a clear day, one can see the Presidential Range of the White Mountains.

Stroudwater Village, three miles west of downtown, is unlike most of Portland, which has been rebuilt; much of the heart of Stroudwater has survived as an architectural unit. On a direct route to the Portland Jetport, and within earshot of the jets' roars, are the remains of mills, canals, and homes that date back nearly 250 years. In the center of the old village is Tate House. Built in 1755 with paneling brought from England, it overlooks the old mastyard where George Tate, Mast Agent to the King, prepared tall pines for the ships of the Royal Navy. In those years the king claimed all white pines in Maine measuring over 24 inches in diameter. No matter whose land a tree was on, once the royal agent put the "broad arrow of the king" on it, down it would come. The Tate House, restored by the Maine Society of Colonial Dames, is furnished as it was from 1755 to 1800.

In Falmouth, just north of Portland, Gilsland Farm is the headquarters of the Maine Audubon Society; the 6,000-square-foot building is heated by a solar and wood energy system. There are educational displays and natural history exhibits; guided tours and nature walks are available.

Freeport

Freeport is called the birthplace of Maine; in 1820, the documents that officially separated Maine from the Commonwealth of Massachusetts were signed here, and Maine became the twenty-third state of the Union.

In the heyday of wooden ships, Freeport more than held its own; today it is a shopper's mecca. No trip to Maine would be complete without a visit to world-famous L. L. Bean, which remains open 24 hours every day selling wilderness outfitting from clothing to canoes. More than 100 posh factory outlet stores have sprung up in town, attracted by L. L. Bean's success.

Freeport was the hometown of Admiral Donald B. MacMillan, who began his Arctic explorations with Admiral Robert E. Peary on the North Pole Expedition in 1908–09.

And for birdwatchers, a visit to the Audubon Wildlife Sanctuary, on Lower Mast Landing Road, is definitely worthwhile.

PRACTICAL INFORMATION FOR THE SOUTHERN COAST

Note: The area code for all Maine is 207

HOW TO GET THERE AND AROUND. By plane: National and regional airlines have scheduled flights between major cities in the northeast and Portland International Jetport. Intrastate flights are available between Portland and Augusta, Bangor, Lewiston/Auburn, Presque Isle, and Waterville. For information: Eastern Express (800–451–4221); Delta (800–221–1212); Business Express (800–345–3400); United (800–241–6522); Continental (800–525–0280); USAir (800–428–4322); or Valley Airlines (800–322–1008). Airport limousine service is available to and from Biddeford, Kittery, Portland, South Portland, Wells, and Westbrook.

By bus: Daily service is available from Boston to Portland on Greyhound Lines with intermediate stops at coastal towns. Canadian service is available from Quebec, New Brunswick, and Nova Scotia.

Portland Transit District (774–9351) provides local bus transportation.

By car: I–95 is the major highway entering Maine from the New Hampshire border, at Maine's southern tip. Canadian Rte. 173 from Quebec meets U.S. Rte. 201 near Jackman, in northern Maine, which leads to Augusta and the Maine Turnpike; from New Brunswick, travelers should take the connector from the Trans-Canada Highway to I–95 at Houlton, Maine, for the trip south.

Once in Maine, travelers may choose the "fast route" north via I–95 or the scenic coastal Rte. 1. The Maine Turnpike, a 100-mi. tollway from Kittery to Augusta, runs concurrent with I–95 from Kittery to Portland, with southern coast exits at York, Wells-Sanford, Kennebunk, Biddeford,

Saco, Scarborough, and Portland. Rte. 1 meanders along the coast through historic towns, offering glimpses of the ocean and easy access to local roads.

Car rentals: Major car rental companies are represented in Portland, Saco, Sanford, and York.

By boat: Daily passenger/auto ferry service is available (May–Oct.) on *Scotia Prince* between Portland and Yarmouth, Nova Scotia. The trip takes about 10 hrs. For information: Prince of Fundy Cruises, Ltd., Box 4216, Portland 04101 (800–341–7540).

HOTELS AND MOTELS. Lodgings on Maine's southern coast range from spectacular resorts to charming inns. Many hotels along the coast are closed Oct.–May; those that remain open lower their rates considerably during the winter months. Some require a minimum stay during the summer season.

Rates are based on double occupancy, in season: *Deluxe,* $100 and up; *Expensive,* $80–$100; *Moderate,* $60–$80; *Inexpensive,* $60 or less. There is a 7% Maine State Lodging Tax. Unless otherwise indicated, hotels are open year-round.

Kennebunkport

The Colony, Ocean Ave., 04046 (967–3331). *Deluxe.* Grand white clapboard resort hotel with motel annex; spectacular ocean view. Summer sports, pool, putting green, shuffleboard. Gracious dining; cocktail lounge with entertainment. Open June–Sept.

Village Cove Inn, S. Maine St., Chick's Cove, 04046 (967–3993). *Deluxe.* Rustic elegance, peaceful and quiet, overlooks private cove. Restaurant, bar, dancing; beaches, golf, fishing, tennis, and theater nearby. Indoor and outdoor pools. Open May–Oct.

Old Fort Inn, Old Fort Ave., 04046 (967–5353). *Expensive–Deluxe.* Luxurious resort in a secluded area of town. All rooms have kitchenette. Pool, tennis, walk to ocean. Continental breakfast. Open Apr.–Dec.

Inn at Goose Rocks, Dyke Rd., Goose Rocks Beach, 04046 (967–5425). *Expensive.* Surrounded by woods and saltwater marshes; a short stroll to the beach. Dining room serves breakfast and candlelight dinners. No children under five years of age.

Kittery

Charter House Motor Hotel, Rte. 1 Bypass, 03904 (439–2000). *Moderate.* Large family rooms available; pets permitted. Pool, summer sports. Restaurant next door.

Ogunquit

The Beachmere, Shore Rd., 03907 (646–2021). *Expensive–Deluxe.* Efficiency apartments, most with private balconies or terraces. Property is at water's edge, offering panoramic ocean views from most rooms. Apartments are in several buildings: the main inn, attached units, and cottages. Secluded bathing coves are steps from the lush lawn. Open Apr.–Dec.

The Cliff House, Bald Head Cliff, 03907 (646–5124). *Deluxe.* Original family inn and several motel units on nine acres. Panoramic ocean views. Near beach, shops, and theater. Tennis, water sports, pool, dining room. Open Mar.–Dec.

Sparhawk, Shore Rd., 03907 (646–5562). *Deluxe.* Fine accommodations, with ocean views from the balconies. Tennis, play area, golf near. Good restaurant. Open Apr.–Oct.

Old Orchard Beach

Brunswick Inn, West Grand Ave., 04064 (934–2171). *Deluxe.* Contemporary guest rooms or suites with kitchens adjacent to beachfront condominium complex. Condo facilities (gym and restaurant) available to guests of the inn.

Windsor Cabins, Ocean Park Rd., Rte. 5, 04064 (934–5514). *Inexpensive.* 23 fully equipped cabins in a pine grove. Pool, putting green, playground. Open May–Oct.

Portland

Sheraton Tara Hotel, 363 Maine Mall Rd., So. Portland 04106 (775–6161). *Deluxe.* Large, modern hotel. Indoor pool, good restaurant, entertainment. Convenient to airport and shopping.

Sonesta Hotel, 157 High St., 04101 (775–5411 or 800–343–7170). *Deluxe.* Luxurious in-town hotel with high standards of personal service. Pool, two restaurants, and "Top of the East" rooftop lounge. Complimentary airport transportation.

Holiday Inn–By-the-Bay, 88 Spring St., 04101 (775–2311); **Holiday Inn–West,** 81 Riverside St., 04103 (774–5601). *Expensive–Deluxe.* Full-service downtown hotel or suburban motel. Both have pools and restaurants.

Executive Inn, 645 Congress St., 04101 (773–8181). *Moderate.* Pleasant rooms, centrally located near tourist attractions. Pool. Pets. Free parking. Children free. Restaurant and lounge.

Scarborough

Black Point Inn, Black Point Rd., Prouts Neck 04074 (883–4126). *Deluxe.* Secluded oceanfront resort. Elegant and impressive; good service. PGA golf course, tennis courts, heated pool, sailing, beaches. Restaurant, bar, entertainment, dancing. American Plan. Open late May–mid-Oct.

Wells

Storer Garrison House, Rte. 1, 04090 (646–3497). *Expensive.* A 10-acre family resort surrounding a historic (1750) home. Overlooking the ocean, just 1 mi. from the beach. Motel, cottages, and guest rooms. Tennis, shopping, and restaurants within walking distance. Friendly and private. Open Apr.–Dec.

Sleepytown Motel and Resort, Rte. 1, 04090 (646–5545). *Expensive.* Resort motel and housekeeping cottages. Children's boating and fishing pond; pool and playground area. Restaurant and cocktail lounge. Open May–Nov.

York Harbor

Stage Neck Inn, Stage Neck Rd., 03911 (363–3850 or 800–222–3238). *Deluxe.* An inviting resort situated on a rocky point of land jutting into the ocean. Modern, attractive rooms with balconies. Saltwater pool and beach, golf, tennis, and fishing. Open May–Oct.

INNS, GUEST HOUSES, BED AND BREAKFASTS. Inns, guest houses, and bed and breakfasts are often the most charming and sometimes more reasonable accommodations. Most fall in the *moderate–expensive* categories, though in this area you'll find some that are *deluxe*. (See *Hotels and Motels* for rates and other information.)

The Maine Publicity Bureau (see *Tourist Information*) publishes an annual listing of bed-and-breakfast facilities; the local Chamber of Commerce will send names and addresses; or contact: Bed & Breakfast Down East, Ltd., Box 547, Eastbrook 04634 (565–3517).

Freeport

The Isaac Randall House Inn, Independence Dr., 04032 (865–9295). Restored Federal-style (1823) homestead, once a stop on the Underground Railway. Eight comfortable and attractive rooms. Evening snacks and hearty breakfast included. Five lovely acres for meandering. Walk to town.

Kennebunkport

Cape Arundel Inn, Ocean Ave., 04046 (967–2125). Small inn directly facing the ocean north of town. Excellent dining. Open Apr.–Dec.

Captain Jefferds Inn, Pearl and Pleasant Sts., 04046 (967–2311). Hospitable inn, beautifully furnished, built in 1804 by a wealthy sea captain. Close to Dock Sq.

The Captain Lord Mansion, corner Pleasant and Green Sts., 04046 (967–3141). An intimate Maine-coast inn, vintage 1812. Quiet elegance; fireplaces. Walk to shops and restaurants. Breakfast included.

English Meadows Inn, Rte. 35, 04046 (967–5766). Victorian farmhouse and carriage house furnished with antiques, wicker, and hooked rugs. Lovely grounds. Easy walk to Dock Sq. shops and waterfront; 1 mi. to beach. Full breakfast included. Open June–Oct.

Maine Stay Inn, Maine St., 04046 (967–2117). Restored 1860 inn, elegantly decorated with antiques and interesting furnishings. 11 efficiency cottages feature country prints. Easy walk to restaurants and shops. Open Apr.–Dec.

White Barn Inn, Beach St., 04046 (967–2321). 13 cozy rooms in a pre–Civil War farmhouse and surrounding cottages; six luxury suites with whirlpool. Continental breakfast. Near beach and village.

Ogunquit

The Colonial Inn, 71 Shore Rd., 03907 (646–5191). Large inn in the heart of town; rooms in the Victorian inn or in the more modern efficiencies or studios. Pool and picnic area. Coffee shop. Open May–Oct.

Old Village Inn, 30 Main St., 03907 (646–7088). In-town inn dates to 1833. Pleasant bedrooms and suites; TV in the living room; game room. Several comfortable dining rooms serve dinner. Closed Jan.

Portland

The Inn at Park Spring, 135 Spring St., 04101 (774–1059). Very small hotel in a three-story townhouse. Personal attention in the grand style. Help yourself to breakfast; traditional tea at 4 P.M.; evening brandy.

Yarmouth

Homewood Inn, Rte. 115, Drinkwater Pt., 04096 (846–3351). Informal, family-owned country resort inn on Casco Bay. Some housekeeping cottages. Many guest rooms with fireplaces. Boating, tennis, excellent seafood restaurant, clambakes, bar. Open June–Oct.

York Harbor

The Dockside, off Rte. 103, York Harbor 03911 (363–2868). Early Maine homestead with comfortable rooms.

Lilac Inn, Ridge Rd., York Beach 03910 (363–3930). *Moderate.* Bed-and-breakfast inn with Victorian charm. Attractively decorated, ocean views, and a large porch.

York Harbor Inn, Rte. 1A, Box 573, York Harbor 03911 (363–5119). Oceanside country inn. Some rooms have shared bath; one deluxe suite with spa.

RESTAURANTS. Travelers to Maine are guaranteed to find fresh Maine lobster featured in most restaurants. Just as consistently, diners will find warm, fresh-baked breads and desserts. The restaurants suggested below, except where noted, are open year-round, serve lunch and dinner, and accept major credit cards. Price ranges per person for a complete dinner excluding beverages, tax, and tip are: *Deluxe,* $35 and up; *Expensive,* $25–$35; *Moderate,* $15–$25; *Inexpensive,* $15 or less.

Falmouth

The Galley, 215 (rear) Foreside Rd., Rte. 88 (781–4262). *Expensive.* At active marina on Casco Bay. Chowder, salads, and seafood; best bets are steamed lobster and broiled chops. Casual dress; boaters welcome.

Kennebunk

The Kennebunk Inn, 45 Main St., Rte. 1 (985–3351). *Moderate–Expensive.* Gracious dining in classic Maine Coast inn (1799). International menu. Breakfast, lunch, and dinner. Reservations recommended.

The Unicorn and Lion, Portland Rd. (Rte. 1N) (985–2985). *Moderate–Expensive.* Restored turn-of-the-century barn serving Continental cuisine and regional Maine specialties. Piano bar in loft; dancing.

Kennebunkport

Olde Grist Mill, Mill Lane (967–4781). *Deluxe.* Historic mill (1749) on Kennebunk River. Traditional Maine dishes, from chowder to Indian pudding. Children's portions. Lunch, dinner. Country store adjacent. Open Apr.–Dec.

Cape Arundel Inn, Ocean Ave. (967–2125). *Moderate–Expensive.* Country inn overlooks spectacular rocky coast. Hearty New England breakfasts; native seafood, steaks, veal, and chicken dishes beautifully prepared for dinner. Open Apr.–Dec.

The Lobster Claw, Ocean Ave. (967–2562). *Moderate.* Delicious home cooking in a comfortable, informal atmosphere. Sidewalk cafe in summer. Seafood is the specialty; homemade soups, chowders, breads, and desserts. Children's menu.

Kittery

Warren's Lobster House, Rte. 1 (439–1630). *Moderate.* Pleasant ambience, fine seafood. Docking facilities.

Ogunquit

Whistling Oyster, Perkins Cove (646–9521). *Expensive.* Established 1907 in Queen Anne Victorian home. Elegant seafood and Continental dishes cooked to order; own baking. Proper dress required.

Jonathan's, 2 Bourne La. (646–4777). *Expensive.* Continental cuisine with flash. Casual. Dinner only.

Ogunquit Lobster Pound, Rte. 1 (646–2516). *Moderate.* Lobster (pick-your-own), clams, steaks, deep-dish pies; outdoors or in the rustic dining room. Open May–Sept.

Barnacle Billy's, Shore Rd., Perkins Cove (646–5575). *Inexpensive.* Dine outside on the deck or inside by the hearth. Sandwiches, salad plates, seafood, chicken, boiled lobster, lobster stew. Scenic cruises from the wharf. Open May–Oct.

Old Orchard Beach

Joseph's-by-the-Sea, 55 W. Grand Ave. (934–5044). *Moderate–Expensive.* Ocean-view dining. Seafood, steaks, roast beef, buffets. Family owned and operated. Open Apr.–Oct.

Portland

Raphael's, 36 Market St. (773–4500). *Expensive–Deluxe.* Fine northern Italian cuisine, extensive wine list. Reservations suggested.

Alberta's, 21 Pleasant St. (774–5408). *Expensive.* Eclectic menu—mesquite-grilled and Cajun specialties, pasta, and seafood. Dinner daily; lunch weekdays. Beer and wine only. No reservations.

The Baker's Table, 434 Fore St. (775–0303). *Expensive.* Informal bistro; imaginative entrees, using the freshest Maine ingredients.

Boone's, 6 Custom House Wharf (774–5725). *Expensive.* On the waterfront. Ocean-fresh lobster, fish, chowders, and stews, as well as steaks. Children's portions.

DiMillo's Floating Restaurant, 121 Commercial St. (772–2216). *Moderate–Expensive.* A former car ferry docked at Long Wharf. Attractive nautical decor. Fresh fish, lobster, shore dinners, steamers. Very popular.

Cap'n Newick's Lobster House, 740 Broadway, S. Portland (799–3090). *Inexpensive–Moderate.* Complete seafood menu at family prices. Also steaks and chicken. Informal.

Wells

The Grey Gull Inn, 321 Webhannet Dr., Moody Point (646–7501). *Expensive.* Quaint, chef-owned Maine Coast inn, serving lobster, seafood, and New England specialties. Spectacular ocean views.

Yarmouth

Camp Hammond, 74 Main St. (846–3352). *Expensive.* Despite the name, formal dining in an elegant, historic (1888) home. Continental specialties, including lamb, veal, bouillabaisse, and lobster. Garden dining.

Homewood Inn, Drinkwater Pt. (846–3352). *Expensive.* Shore dinners, chowders, delicious soups, and desserts. Weekly lobster bake. Open mid-June–mid-Oct.

York Harbor

Dockside Dining Room, Off Rte. 103 (363–4800). *Moderate.* Casual dining at early Maine homestead. Overlooks the marina. Duckling a specialty.

Bill Foster's Down East Lobster and Clambake, Rte. 1A (363–3255). *Moderate.* Clams, lobster, and all the "fixin's" (or steak or chicken). Features an old-fashioned sing-along. Reserve ahead. Summer only.

TOURIST INFORMATION. Colorful and informative folders, maps, and booklets may be requested by mail from the Maine Publicity Bureau, 97 Winthrop St., Hallowell 04347 (289–2423) and from the following Chambers of Commerce: Box 417, York 03909 (363–4422); Box 2289, Ogunquit 03907 (646–2939); Eldredge Road, Wells 04090 (646–2451); 105 Main St., Kennebunk 04043 (985–3608); Box 600, Old Orchard Beach 04064 (934–2091); 142 Free St., Portland 04101 (772–2811).

The Maine Publicity Bureau operates a major Tourist Information Center in Kittery, accessible from both I–95 and U.S. Rte. 1. Regional tourist information centers are located in Portland, at 142 Free St., and in Yarmouth on I–95.

TOURS. Boat tours: Casco Bay Lines, Custom House Wharf, Portland 04101 (774–7871), operates several daily cruises around the islands in Casco Bay. Longfellow Cruise Line, No. 1 Long Wharf, Portland 04101 (774–3578), operates several daily trips around Casco Bay on M. V. *Longfellow* (May–Dec.). Whalewatching cruises leave Arundel Wharf, Ocean Ave., Kennebunkport (May–Nov.). Indian Whale Watch (967–5912), June–Sept., leaves from Long Wharf in Portland. Sunset Whale Watch (975–0727 or 642–3270).

Bus tours: Greater Portland Landmarks, 165 State St., Portland (774–5561) hosts bus (and walking) tours of historic parts of the city.

Walking tours: Self-conducted tours have been outlined for both an Uptown Art Walk and the Old Port section in Portland, the Marginal Way in Ogunquit, and the historic district in York Village. Information is available at your hotel or from a local tourist information booth.

SEASONAL EVENTS. June: Old Port Festival, Portland (mid-June); Franco-American Festival, Biddeford (late June).

July: Yarmouth Clam Festival, Yarmouth (mid-July); Deering Oaks Family Festival, Portland (late July).

August: York Days Celebration, York (early Aug.); The Maine Festival of the Arts, Portland (late Aug.).

September: Cumberland Farmers Club Fair, Cumberland Center (late Sept.).

PARKS. Maine's state parks provide excellent facilities and a variety of outdoor experiences. Most open by May 15, and the season usually extends through mid-Oct. Leashed pets are allowed, but not on beaches. For information: Maine Bureau of Parks and Recreation, Station 22, Augusta 04333 (289–3824).

State parks in the Southern Coast area: **Bradbury Mountain** (Pownal)—camping, picnicking, hiking, play area, fun for families; **Crescent Beach** (Cape Elizabeth)—picnicking, swimming, fishing, snack bar; **Scarborough Beach** (Scarborough)—picnicking, swimming, fishing; **Two Lights** (Cape Elizabeth)—picnicking, swimming, fishing (only 9 mi. from Portland), magnificent scenery; **Wolf Neck Woods** (Freeport)—picnicking, hiking.

WILDLIFE. Maine Audubon Society, Gilsland Farm Rd., Falmouth (781–2330) organizes field trips to offshore islands to view the native vegetation and wildlife (mid-Apr.–mid-Nov.). The marshes at the **Wells National Estuarine Sanctuary,** at Wells (646–4521) are habitat for a variety of birds, mammals, and plants; nature walks are available. The **Maine Aquarium,** Rte. 1, Saco (284–4511) is a favorite of children.

BEACHES. Less than 75 miles of Maine's coastline is sandy beach, and most of that is reserved for local residents. Many beaches, especially along the Southern Coast, are also open to the public and have facilities for ocean swimming and surfing. Most charge a modest parking fee. York—Long Sands, Short Sands; Ogunquit—Ogunquit Beach; Wells—Wells Beach, Moody Beach, Drake Island Beach; Kennebunk—Parsons Beach, Kennebunk Beach; Kennebunkport—Gooch's Beach, Goose Rocks Beach; Biddeford—Fortunes Rocks Beach, Biddeford Pool, Hills Beach; Saco—Ferry Beach; Old Orchard Beach—Old Orchard Beach; Scarborough—Pine Point Beach, Higgins Beach; Cape Elizabeth—Crescent Beach.

SPORTS. Boating: At most coastal towns, boats are available for hire.
Golf: There is a public 27-hole golf course in Portland, the Riverside Municipal Course (797–3524); 18-hole courses in the area include Dutch Elm Golf Course in Arundel (282–9850); Purpoodock Club, Cape Elizabeth (799–1574); Gorham Country Club, Gorham (839–3490); Webhannet Golf Course, Kennebunk Beach (967–2061); Cape Arundel Golf Course, Kennebunkport (967–3494); Willowdale Golf Course, Scarborough (883–9351); and York Golf Club, York (363–2683). There are also nine-hole courses in Chebeague Island, Cumberland, Freeport, Guilford, Old Orchard Beach, Saco, Sanford, Scarborough, South Portland, and Westbrook.
Ballooning: Float along gentle air currents in a hot-air balloon, weather permitting. Six passengers per balloon; about an hour of air time per trip. Reservations recommended during the summer. Balloon Sports, 145 Glenwood Ave., Portland 04103 (772–4401), and Natural High Balloon Center, Lebanon (339–1565).

FISHING. A list of charter and head boats for deep-sea fishing is available from the Maine Publicity Bureau (see *Tourist Information*). No license is required for saltwater fishing.

CAMPING. In the *Maine Guide to Camping,* the Maine Publicity Bureau (see *Tourist Information*) provides a current listing of trailer parks, campsites, and conveniences available. Maine Campground Owners Association (MECOA), 655 Main St., Lewiston 04240 (782–5874).

SPECTATOR SPORTS. Hockey: At the Cumberland County Civic Center, on Free Street in Portland, the Maine Mariners play professional hockey Oct.–Apr. For information, call 775–3411.

Baseball: Maine Guides Baseball Club plays at The Ball Park, Old Orchard Beach from Apr.–Sept. For information: Maine Guides, Box 287, Old Orchard Beach 04064 (934–4561).

Auto racing: Stock-car racing is held Sat. nights early spring–Oct. at Beechridge Speedway, Holmes Rd., Scarborough.

Horse racing: Harness racing is held at Scarborough Downs, Scarborough 04074 and at Cumberland Raceway, Blanchard St., Cumberland 04021.

HISTORIC SITES AND HOUSES. Maine has designated many historic sites and districts to preserve its long history for future generations. Private interests have restored many historic houses.

Kittery

Fort McClary (1846), Kittery Pt. Rd. (Rte. 103). Restored hexagonal blockhouse, the last one built in Maine.

Portland

Portland Observatory, 138 Congress St. (774–5561). 19th-century signal tower; extensive views of Casco Bay and White Mts. from the Lantern Deck.

Tate House (1755), 1270 Westbrook St., Stroudwater Village (774–9781). Built by George Tate, King's Mast Agent; exceptional paneling and fine collection of 18th-century furnishings.

Victoria Mansion, 109 Danforth St. (772–4841). Victorian Italianate villa, with most of its original decoration and furnishings intact.

Wadsworth-Longfellow House (1785), 487 Congress St. (774–1822). Boyhood home of the famous poet contains many original furnishings.

South Berwick

Hamilton House (1787), Vaughan's Lane, off Rte. 236 (384–5269). Magnificently restored Georgian mansion with period furnishings.

Sarah Orne Jewett Memorial (1774), 101 Portland St. (384–5269). Preserved home of the famous writer, furnished with 18th- and 19th-century antiques.

York Village

Elizabeth Perkins House (1731), Sewall's Bridge (363–4974). Colonial home with Victorian furnishings.

Emerson-Wilcox House (1742), York St. (363–3872). Museum of local history and American decorative arts.

Jefferds Tavern (1750), 5 Lindsay Rd. (363–4974). 18th-century saltbox inn with period furnishings.

John Hancock Warehouse, Lindsay Rd. (363–4974). 18th-century warehouse with exhibits on local river history.

Marshall Store, Lindsay Rd. (363–4974). 19th-century store with many locally crafted items.

Old Gaol Museum (1720), York St. (363–3872). King's prison for Province of Maine, containing dungeons, cells, and jailer's quarters.

Old Schoolhouse (1745), Lindsay Rd. (363–4974). One-room school with 18th-century furnishings.

MUSEUMS AND GALLERIES. Maine's colorful and romantic history is carefully preserved in museums operated by local historical societies and private interests. Most museums charge admission or request a small donation. Call ahead for days and hours.

Kennebunk

Brick Store Museum (1825), 117 Main St. (Rte. 1) (985–4802). Local shipbuilding history and marine artifacts. Walking tour starts here.

Kennebunkport

Seashore Trolley Museum, Log Cabin Rd. (off Rte. 1) (967–2712). Vast collection of streetcars, including a restoration facility; ride on open trolleys.

Kittery

Kittery Historical and Naval Museum, Rogers Rd., off Rte. 1 (439–3080). Exhibits of local maritime history include ship models and dioramas.

Portland

Joan Whitney Payson Gallery of Art, Westbrook College, 716 Stevens Ave. (797–9546). Permanent collection of European and American masters; changing exhibits of contemporary art.

Portland Museum of Art (1882), Congress Sq. (775–6148). Important works of American art, much of it by Maine artists, and 19th-century American glass.

Wells

Wells Auto Museum, Rte. 1 (646–9064). Antique cars dating from 1900 are displayed; additional exhibits of motorcycles, bicycles, license plates, and antique toys.

THEATER. Maine, the birthplace of summer theater, offers professional productions of Broadway hits as well as non-Equity companies performing contemporary drama and comedy. Among the summer theaters are: **Hackmatack Playhouse,** Rte. 9, Berwick 03901 (698–1807); **Ogunquit Playhouse,** Rte. 1, Ogunquit 03907 (646–5511); **Maine Theatre,** Civic Center, Box 15002, Portland 04101 (871–7101); **Russell Square Theatre,** University of Southern Maine, 37 College Ave., Gorham 04038 (780–5483); and **Sanford Maine Stage Company,** Sanford 04073 (636–2222).

Several theater and dance groups in Portland give year-round performances. Theater groups: **Children's Theater of Maine** (854–0389), **Portland Lyric Theater** (799–1421), **Portland Performing Arts Center** (773–2562), **Portland Players** (799–7337), **Portland Stage Company** (774–0465), and **Portland Concert Association** (772–8630). Dance: **Casco Bay Movers** (871–1013), **Portland Ballet Company** (772–9671), and **Ram Island Dance Company** (773–2562).

The Portland Symphony Orchestra, 30 Myrtle St., 04101 (773–8191) presents classical and "pops" concerts at the Portland City Hall Auditorium from Sept. through spring.

SHOPPING. Kittery, Wells, and Freeport have a concentration of outlet stores, such as **G. H. Bass & Co.** (shoes) and **Hathaway Shirt Co.,** which sell their products at discount prices. For the hunter, camper, and lover of the outdoors, no trip to Maine is complete without a stop at world-famous **L. L. Bean,** Freeport (865–4761)—open 24 hours every day.

NIGHTLIFE. In resort towns along the coast, many of the large hotels, inns, and restaurants have cocktail lounges (some with entertainment on weekends). In Portland, there are many cafes and taverns in the Old Port section where people gather in the evening. Try **The Lounge at Holiday Inn West,** 81 Riverside St., the **Top of the East** at the Sonesta Hotel, 157 High St., or **Zootz,** 31 Forest Ave. For a more casual evening, try the **Seamen's Club,** 375 Fore St. In Kennebunkport, **Forefathers,** Log Cabin Rd., has live rock 'n' roll on weekends.

Much of the appeal of a Maine vacation, however, is the no-nonsense ability to commune with nature—either through active (or even rigorous) participation in, say, a long hike or by simply watching the sunrise against the craggy shore. The popular pattern throughout the state, therefore, is "early to bed, early to rise," with nightlife taking runner-up position.

THE MID-COAST REGION

The Mid-Coast region includes the coastal area from Brunswick to the mouth of the Penobscot River, near Bucksport. The ragged coastline and many long peninsulas characteristic of Down East Maine begin here, the result of the numerous tidal rivers that empty into the sea. The region is bisected by Route 1, the main route Down East.

Brunswick

Brunswick began as a fur-trading post known by the Indian name Pejepscot. The Pejepscot Historical Society Museum, on Park Row, is rich in regional Americana, and the society is accumulating a collection of military articles associated with General Joshua L. Chamberlain, the Civil War hero who later became president of Bowdoin College and governor of Maine.

Bowdoin College in Brunswick, founded in 1794 when Maine was still part of Massachusetts, was named for the governor, James Bowdoin. The governor's son, another James, collected paintings by Dutch and Italian masters during his tenure as U.S. minister to Spain and France. These paintings, along with valuable works by Winslow Homer, form the nucleus of the collection at the Walker Museum of Art on the Bowdoin campus. Special showings are arranged each summer.

Henry Wadsworth Longfellow, President Franklin Pierce, Nathaniel Hawthorne, Admiral Robert E. Peary, and Admiral Donald B. MacMillan were all graduates of Bowdoin. The Peary–MacMillan Arctic Museum, in Hubbard Hall on the Bowdoin campus, has exhibits and displays relating to their polar explorations.

The Stowe House (1806) on Federal Street, now an inn, is where Harriet Beecher Stowe lived while writing *Uncle Tom's Cabin.*

Bailey Island

A visit to one of Maine's lovely peninsulas is always a pleasant excursion, and a ride to Bailey Island offers such an opportunity. From Cooks Corner in Brunswick, Route 24 south will take you on a 16-mile drive through Great Island and Orr's Island to Bailey Island. The area is a popular but quiet summer colony dotted with picturesque fishing villages. A short bridge leads from Great Island to Orr's Island, where you can see the little white cottage, Pearl House, where Harriet Beecher Stowe summered and wrote *The Pearl of Orr's Island.* At Orr's Island the world's only cribstone bridge crosses from Will's Gut to Bailey Island. The 1,200-foot span, built in 1928, is constructed of great granite blocks laid lengthwise, then crosswise, in a honeycomb pattern; the blocks are held in place by their own weight, without mortar. This unique design allows the water from heavy tides and spring thaws to flow through the bridge freely.

Tuna fishing has become a major summer industry at Bailey Island. The annual Fishing Tournament takes place in late July. Giant bluefin tuna, often weighing 700 pounds or more, are caught and displayed. Deep-sea-fishing trips can be arranged on short notice.

Just off the coast, between Bailey Island and Harpswell to the west, you will spot Eagle Island, home of Admiral Peary. A pier is available to boaters, who can bring picnic lunches and visit Peary's residence.

Bath and the Kennebec

The mighty Kennebec River, flowing 150 miles from Moosehead Lake in the north to the Atlantic Ocean at Phippsburg, was one of the first rivers to be explored by Europeans. A main waterway for the early settlers, it became a lifeline for the commerce and industry that followed. About a century ago, one of the main cargos carried down the Kennebec was chunks of the frozen water itself. Ice harvests of the 1880s brought Kennebec ice to markets far and wide.

Bath is 12 miles inland on the Kennebec. Since its earliest days, Bath has been called the City of Ships. The area's maritime tradition dates to 1607, when the three-ton *Virginia of Sagadahock,* the first ocean-going English sailing vessel built in America, was launched at nearby Popham Colony. Since 1884, over 5,000 ships (wood, iron, and steel) have been built at Bath. During World War II, 244 Liberty ships were launched from Bath Iron Works (BIW) alone. BIW still turns out a number of steel-hulled vessels each year—guided-missile frigates and other U.S. Navy ships as well as containerized merchant ships. In 1930, J. P. Morgan's 343-foot turbine-electric yacht *Corsair IV* was built here, as was the successful America's Cup defender *Ranger* (1937) and the 125-foot bow section of the experimental tanker *Manhattan* that sailed to Alaska in 1969 via the Northwest Passage.

The Sewall House on Washington Street is one of several impressive nineteenth-century homes built by prosperous shipbuilders and sea captains. A four-block walking tour along Washington Street, between Front and Pearl, includes historic architecture representative of the major styles of the 1800s.

The Maine Maritime Museum, adjacent to the old Percy & Small Shipyard in South Bath, houses an outstanding collection of ship models, journals, photographs, and other artifacts related to over 300 years of Maine shipbuilding. The 142-foot Grand Banks fishing schooner *Sherman Zwicker,* one of the last of its kind, is on permanent display. The exhibit "Lobstering and the Maine Coast" is a multilevel, multimedia presentation. A boat ride along the Kennebec River on the 50-foot motor vessel *Sasanoa* is included in the admission during the summer months.

South of Bath, Route 209 through Phippsburg will bring you to the mouth of the Kennebec River and the site of the Popham Colony. This first attempt at a permanent settlement along the Maine coast by about 100 English settlers was short-lived. Disease and the harsh weather of their first winter caused the few survivors to return to England posthaste. Beyond this site is Popham Beach and Fort Popham, partially constructed in 1861. A climb to the top of the fort offers a sweeping view of the Kennebec's sparkling waters; down below are sandy salt marshes and the beaches of Popham Beach State Park.

Five Islands

On the east side of the Kennebec River, Route 127 takes you south across a group of heavily wooded islands to Reid State Park, a beautiful sandy beach and picnic area on the ocean, and Five Islands at the end of the peninsula. Round-trip from Route 1, the drive to Five Islands is about 30 miles. For those who love woodland and sea beautifully interwoven, it's well worth the trip. The warm scent of pines is in the air as you pass placid coves edged with evergreens on the trip south. Though you're at the coast, the pines and the still, reflecting waters of the area give a backwoods feeling.

At Five Islands the Maine coast becomes wilder. Here you begin to get an idea of the great tides and currents that affect the Down East coastline. Five Islands is at the mouth of the Sheepscot River, and its stilt-legged wharf is the center of peninsula life. Moored lobster boats bob on the sapphire and silver waters; speedboats zoom past on their way to privately owned islands; sleek schooners dip their sails as they round submerged rocks at the harbor entrance; gulls screech their complaints; the scent of wood smoke drifts by.

Wiscasset

Wiscasset, a town of great charm, is nestled on a western hillside overlooking the Sheepscot River, a dozen or so miles from the sea. This, too, was once a seafaring town, and many of its fine old homes were built by seafaring families.

Wiscasset is a prime example of the birth-death-rebirth cycle of many Maine communities. In the eighteenth century it was a busy shipbuilding and cargo-shipping community. Despite disease, war, and embargoes, trade in lumber and ice and the building of clipper ships carried Wiscasset through until new technology and disastrous fires destroyed it all. For a time Wiscasset was almost as derelict as the shipwrecked four-masted schooners, *Luther Little* and *Hester,* that still lie in the harbor. Now there is new industry, from the Maine Yankee Atomic Power Plant to the gathering and shipping of bloodworms and sandworms from the Wiscasset flats to sportsmen all over the nation.

Wiscasset has been lovingly preserved, and walking tours are offered by the Lincoln County Cultural and Historical Association.

The Lincoln County Fire Museum contains a collection of some of the country's oldest fire-fighting equipment, including an old hand tub dated 1830. The last of Maine's old-time stagecoaches is here, too. This museum

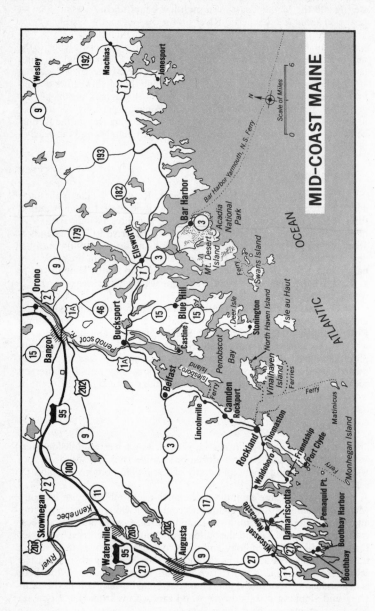

MID-COAST MAINE

is in the barn of the Nickels-Sortwell house, on the corner of Main (Route 1) and Federal streets, which is also open to visitors. One of Maine's most beautiful old homes, it was built by Captain William Nickels, a prominent shipmaster.

The old Lincoln County Jail (1809), constructed of three-foot-thick granite blocks, took over two years to build. The museum, next door in the jailer's house, displays 200 years of Maine arts and skills, as well as work of contemporary Maine craftsmen: weaving, pottery, toy-making, silk-screen printing.

At the Wiscasset Musical Wonder House, you'll find a nostalgic collection of antique music boxes, gramophones, pipe organs, player pianos, and similar items in a sea captain's home built in 1852.

Castle Tucker, on Lee Street, a mansion of 1807 with original Victorian furnishings and wallpaper—and a freestanding elliptical staircase—is open to the public.

North of Wiscasset on Route 27 is Dresden Mills, a tree-shaded village on the Eastern River. The Pownalborough Courthouse (1760), the oldest court building in Maine and the only one intact that predates the Revolution, is interesting for its architectural details and for its exhibits, including one on the Kennebec ice industry. The Old Alna Meetinghouse (1789), on Route 218, is filled with fascinating architectural details—including a pulpit leveler, a mechanism for elevating short-statured preachers.

The Boothbays

Boothbay and Boothbay Harbor are at the southern end of a peninsula between the Sheepscot and Damariscotta rivers; Route 27 south from Route 1 will take you to this busy summer resort area through North Edgecomb. Fort Edgecomb's two-story octagonal blockhouse (1808–1809) was built to protect Wiscasset's shipping industry from harassment by the English. Though this type of fortification proved inadequate during the War of 1812, it has been fully restored as a historic site.

Items relating to steam railroading are on display in a pair of restored railroad stations at Boothbay Railway Village, where you may take a ride on a narrow-gauge steam train. Several antique autos are exhibited as well. For the theater buff, the Boothbay Theater Museum has a collection of theater memorabilia from the eighteenth century to the present: costumes, autographs, portraits, playbills, models.

Boothbay Harbor, the Boating Capital of New England, is a pretty sight, sprinkled with sleek sailboats and backdropped by burly wharves, pleasant homes, pine-clad peninsulas, and church spires. In summer the narrow streets are often filled with visitors to the shops, art galleries, marinas, and restaurants. In mid-July, Windjammer Days is a festive event highlighted by a review of the windjammers that cruise the Maine coast during the summer months.

The best way to view the intricate network of islands, coves, rivers, harbors, and peninsulas is by boat. Excursion boats take passengers on morning, afternoon, or evening trips; points of interest may include Ocean Point (where at one spot you can see five lighthouses), Bath (up the Kennebec River), Five Islands, Seguin Light, Damariscove, Squirrel Island, Ovensmouth, Burnt Island Lighthouse, or Cape Newagen. Summer evening cruises aboard *Argo II* incorporate a Down East clambake. Take the "Balmy Days" cruise to Monhegan from Boothbay Harbor for a pleasant day trip (633–2284 for reservations). Boothbay Harbor is also a departure point for sport-fishing trips.

Back on land, take a trip down to Cape Newagen on Southport Island, where Scottish settlers first landed in the early 1600s. After many years of Indian raids, resettlement, then abandonment once again, the town in 1764 was incorporated into the town of Boothbay. At the town wharf you can watch the sea and the tides busily at work.

En route to the mainland, turn right in Southport just before crossing the drawbridge and proceed to McKown Point. (This drawbridge across Townsend Gut is the most often opened drawbridge in the state.) Here you can visit the Marine Aquarium, which is maintained by the State of Maine Department of Marine Resources. All manner of sea creatures are exhibited, including minute, newly hatched lobsters and playful seals in an outdoor pool. Next door to the aquarium is the Bigelow Laboratory for Ocean Sciences, a marine-life research facility known throughout the country as the authority on red tide.

Damariscotta and Newcastle

Damariscotta and Newcastle, twin villages along Business Route 1, are the gateway to the Pemaquid area. The two towns are separated by the Damariscotta River, famous for the running of the alewives each spring. There are notable churches and homes in this area. St. Patrick's Church in Newcastle, completed in 1808, is the oldest Catholic church in Maine. In the summer, services are sometimes held outdoors among the tall pines and flowering bushes.

Figureheads and other pieces by two famous early woodcarvers, William Southworth and Edbury Hatch, are displayed at the Chapman-Hall House on Main Street. Constructed in 1754, the Chapman-Hall House is believed to be Damariscotta's oldest remaining dwelling and is one of the few early houses that escaped the torch of Indian raiders. After looking at grander homes elsewhere, the early craftsmanship displayed here has a certain charm, a lived-in look.

Prehistoric oyster shell heaps east of the villages, on a state-owned archaeological site, suggest a long tradition of good eating. More than a million cubic feet of shells were piled up here during summer encampments of successive generations of Indians over the past 2,000 years. An annual Oyster Festival is held in Damariscotta in mid-July to celebrate the area's oyster cultivation business.

The Pemaquid Peninsula

Route 130 south from Damariscotta will take you down the Pemaquid Peninsula to famous Pemaquid Point Light. During the summer of 1965, amateur archaeologists, spades and pickaxes in hand, attempted to unearth an area near Pemaquid Beach. Old records indicated there had been a substantial trading post here in the mid-1600s. Some 14 foundations, believed to be those of seventeenth-century settlements, have been uncovered, along with hundreds of artifacts indicating earlier Indian settlement. The remains of an old customs house, a tavern, a forge, and several human skeletons were found. One skeleton was thought to be that of an Indian; another brought experts flying from all parts of the United States, for it was dressed in armor and sewn in a shroud of animal hide. The time of the burials could not be immediately determined, but archaeological experts have indicated that the man may have been a Viking, based on the armor he was wearing and the ancient Norse custom of sewing bodies in animal hide prior to burial. The State of Maine acquired the area of Colonial Pemaquid for preservation and restoration. Much of the material un-earthed in the dig is on display at an adjacent museum.

Fort William Henry, at New Harbor, is unique in having been a succession of four different forts. The first, built about 1630, fell to the pirate Dixey Bull two years later. The second, erected in 1677, was destroyed by Indians in 1689. Sir William Phipps built the third (the first one to be called Fort William Henry) in 1692, during King William's War. Four years later it was leveled by Indians under Baron de Castin. In 1729 the fourth fort was built, only to be destroyed during the Revolutionary War by locals who didn't want the British to occupy it. The present fort is a replica of the one Phipps built.

Pemaquid Point Light (1824), at the tip of the eastern fork of the peninsula, is one of the most painted, most photographed lighthouses in America. The Atlantic tosses its mane and pounds sonorously against the stratified rocks that form the shoreline. The former lightkeeper's cottage is now the Fisherman's Museum.

Christmas Cove, at the tip of the western fork of this peninsula (via Route 129), is a lovely, unspoiled area. Christmas Cove was named by Captain John Smith when he anchored here on Christmas Day 1614. In his report on the area, he noted: "More than 20 Iles overgrowne with good timber, of divers sorts of wood, which do make so many harbors as requireth a longer time than I had, to be well discovered. . . ." Present-day travelers have the same complaint.

Waldoboro, Friendship, and Thomaston

The earliest settlers in what became Waldoboro were Germans, led by General Samuel Waldo. A baleful inscription appears on a gravestone in the local cemetery: "This town was settled in 1748 by Germans who immigrated to this place with the promise and expectation of finding a prosperous city, instead of which they found nothing but wilderness." The Old German Church (1772), on Route 32 in Bremen, is well preserved, with square-benched pews and a pulpit shaped like a wine glass. The Waldoboro Historical Society Museum, on Route 220 near its junction with Route 1, is a complex of three buildings: the restored Boggs country schoolhouse, the town cattle pound (1819), and a farm kitchen.

Confirmed shunpikers and those interested in sailboats will want to take Route 220 and dip south to the charming village of Friendship, a seaport town famous for its gaff-rigged Friendship sloop. The old (1851) schoolhouse, at the junction of Route 220 and Martin's Point Road, is now the home of the Friendship Museum, where you can find historical information on the Friendship sloop. The annual Friendship Sloop Regatta is held in Boothbay Harbor in July; vintage sloops and present-day models join in the race.

Cushing is a summer community you may recognize from the paintings of Andrew Wyeth. It is on the coast, off Route 97 between Friendship and Route 1.

Thomaston, a village of attractive homes, flourished after the Revolution and grew into a major port and shipbuilding center during the first half of the nineteenth century. Today it is the location of the largest cement plant in New England and the Maine State Prison. At the Prison Store, open daily, visitors can buy furniture and other articles handcrafted by the prisoners.

High on a hill at the east end of Thomaston stands Montpelier, a reproduction of the magnificent Federal mansion built here in 1794 by General Henry Knox, Washington's chief of staff. General Knox was an artillery commander during the Revolution, the first Secretary of War, and he was instrumental in founding the U.S. Military Academy at West Point. Imposing Montpelier contains a bookcase of Marie Antoinette's (which Knox purchased after her execution), a traveling chest given him by Lafayette, and many pieces of rare china, family silver, and other personal effects of the general and his wife. The house is architecturally noteworthy for its flying staircase.

Port Clyde and Monhegan

Route 131 south from Thomaston takes you through the fishing village of Tenants Harbor to Port Clyde. There are fine shops and galleries to visit in Port Clyde, and Marshall Point Light overlooks splendid views of the ocean and nearby islands. You can take a boat to some of these islands, including Monhegan, 11 miles out to sea.

Monhegan Island, long a haven for artists, was discovered by Captain John Smith in 1614. There are dramatic cliff formations on this remote island, a lighthouse and museum, and majestic Cathedral Woods. Many of the hardy year-round residents are engaged in the hazardous occupation of winter lobster fishing.

Life on Monhegan is unhurried; cars are not permitted, and there is practically no electricity. (Ironically, Thomas Edison vacationed here.) Visitors are content to hike along the cliffs or in the woods, watch the birds, and visit the art galleries. There are many inns and guest houses on the island, but reservations are a must.

From Port Clyde, head north on Route 73 and take the road to Owl's Head Light. The proud little lighthouse, only 26 feet high, overlooks the sea from a red-and-yellow streaked headland. Nearby is the Owl's Head Transportation Museum. On many summer weekends you can see antique airplanes and automobiles in action; the display is almost as interesting on weekdays, when things are quiet.

Rockland

Rockland is Maine's largest fishing port and lobster distribution center—and the birthplace of the poet Edna St. Vincent Millay. You will find swimming, sailing, fishing, an art colony, arts-and-crafts shops, and festivals here.

The four-day Maine Seafood Festival occurs annually during the first weekend in August. There are marine exhibits, contests, and demonstrations—and thousands of lobster dinners served daily.

The William A. Farnsworth Library and Art Museum and the adjoining Farnsworth Homestead are impressive. One of the largest collections of the paintings of Andrew Wyeth, including *Her Room,* is in the gallery. The museum has dedicated one gallery to the works of Maine artists, including Winslow Homer and the elder Wyeth. Another gallery has a fine collection of works by other American artists.

The Shore Village Museum, in the Grand Army Hall on Limerock Street, has a permanent Coast Guard exhibit of lighthouse equipment, buoys, and lifesaving gear from search-and-rescue boats, coupled with a large collection of Civil War uniforms and artifacts.

In Rockland's harbor there are anchorages over 40 feet deep, accommodating anything from a freighter to a small pleasure cruiser. Windjammers, which take passengers on week-long cruises along the Maine Coast, sail from Rockland (as well as from nearby Camden, Rockport, and Belfast farther north). Day trips depart from the Maine State Ferry Terminal to the offshore islands of Vinalhaven, a busy fishing community with some tourist facilities, and North Haven, with a rugged shoreline and wooded headlands but no accommodations for tourists or campers.

Rockport and Camden

Approaching the Camden Hills, which rise to the northeast, you come to the virtual twin communities of Rockport and Camden.

Rockport, mainly a residential village, has a delightful harbor, assorted shops, and boatbuilding yards. Mrs. Efrem Zimbalist, one of the area's best-known summer residents, was responsible for the landscaping of the Rockport waterfront as well as that of the inviting Vesper Hill Chapel, which was landscaped according to biblical script. The historic lime quarries next to the Goose River bridge and the restored lime kilns have been designated landmarks.

Camden, with its incredible long-distance views of Penobscot Bay and its many islands, is a popular yachting center that has some of the best cruising waters anywhere in the world. This is home port for several windjammers that sail the Maine coast each summer, and there are boats on which you can cruise to nearby islands for the day.

Camden's Information Bureau is at the public landing; nearby there is a captivating view of the Camden River's waterfall, cascading into the harbor after running beneath Main Street. Visitors to Camden are charmed by the pretty flower baskets that grace the lampposts.

Musicians and music lovers have found Camden a favorite place to visit. Frequent musical programs and theater productions are presented at the outdoor amphitheater next to the Public Library at the top of Main Street.

Those interested in authentic colonial Maine farmhouses and barns will not want to miss Conway House (1780). Restored by the Camden–Rockport Historical Society, the house and barn have fascinating architectural details and old farm implements.

In the western part of town, off Hosmer Pond Road, is Ragged Mountain, where the Camden Outing Club maintains the Camden Snow Bowl—Maine's oldest ski area—for wintertime skiing, both downhill and cross-country, daytime and nighttime.

The Camden Hills, rising abruptly from Penobscot Bay, are a striking physical feature of this area. Camden Hills State Park has a family picnic area, and camping is permitted at the foot of the mountains. You can drive (toll road) or hike up to the 900-foot summit of Mt. Battie for a splendid panoramic view of the bay, the islands, and the peninsulas beyond. The view is breathtaking at night, too—a point to keep in mind at many places along the coast.

Lincolnville and Islesboro

Lincolnville Beach is north of Camden. Besides the sandy beach, there are seafood restaurants, antique shops, and gift shops.

From the Maine State Ferry Terminal, boats come and go between Lincolnville Beach and Islesboro. The ferry takes about 25 minutes for the trip and accommodates both cars and passengers. The island is worth visiting for its miles of rough country road and many snug harbors to explore. Warren Island State Park, reached only by private boat, is at the tip of Islesboro.

Belfast

Farther north on Route 1, Belfast is the next community. Follow the route marked Business District to see the Federal and Greek Revival homes built by merchant sea captains along the bay. If time allows, drive down a few of the cross streets to see still others. One of the centers of the state's poultry industry, Belfast is known as the Broiler Capital of Maine. A 15-acre city park that slopes to the shores of the bay is the site of the annual Belfast Bay Festival of mid-July, highlighted by a gigantic chicken barbecue.

Searsport

East of Belfast on Route 1 is the old seafaring town of Searsport, Maine's second largest deep-water port. Still busy with maritime commerce, Searsport is rich in the traditions of the sea. In the Penobscot Marine Museum there are portraits of 284 sea captains, all from Searsport. Indeed, 10 percent of all the nation's deep-water sea captains hailed from this town of 2,500 people in the 1870s and 1880s. The museum's exhibits, in seven buildings, include a whaling room and treasures from faraway lands where captains (and often their families) visited and traded. Paintings of famous ships, a collection of ship half-models, charts, logs, and navigational instruments are among the mementos of the days of the tall ships.

Today, Searsport's harbor is still very active. Lumber is brought from the northern woods to Searsport, via the Bangor & Aroostook Railroad, where modern freighters ship it to destinations far and wide.

With its concentration of antique shops and flea markets, Searsport also claims to be the antiques capital of Maine.

Fort Knox State Park

Continuing along Route 1, you turn onto Route 174 just before the suspension bridge over the Penobscot River to visit Fort Knox State Park. Fort Knox was built of granite by master craftsmen starting in 1844, one of the largest forts of its type in the United States. Maine Volunteers were garrisoned here during the Civil War; during the Spanish-American War, Connecticut troops were stationed at the fort. Some parts of the fort are underground and dark, so if you wish to see most of this huge structure, bring a flashlight or rent one near the park entrance.

From the fort there are impressive views of the Penobscot River. The mill on the opposite bank, in Bucksport, is the Champion International Paper Company, the area's main industry.

PRACTICAL INFORMATION FOR THE MID-COAST REGION

Note: The area code for all Maine is 207

HOW TO GET THERE AND AROUND. By plane: Commuter service is available into Rockland on Eastern Express (800–451–4221) and Valley Airlines (800–322–1008). Airport limousine service is available in S. Thomaston for the Camden-Rockport-Rockland area.

By bus: Daily service is available on Greyhound (via Portland) between major towns along the coast.

By car: For fast access to the mid-coast area: take the Maine Tpke./I–95 (toll road) to Exit 9 (where I–95 separates from the turnpike) and continue north on I–95 to Exit 22 (Brunswick) and Rte. 1, which follows the entire Maine coast. To reach the coast from points north, through Augusta: Rte. 3 goes to Belfast; Rte. 17 to Rockland; and Rtes. 9 and 27 to the Boothbay area.

State routes and local roads which cross Rte. 1 will take you either inland or down the many peninsulas.

Car rentals: Major car rental companies are represented in Brunswick, Camden, and Rockland.

By boat: Maine State Ferry Service, Box 645, 517A Main St., Rockland 04841 (594–5543), operates daily ferry service between Rockland and Vinalhaven, Rockland and North Haven, and Lincolnville and Islesboro; service is provided between Rockland and Matinicus Island one day a month. The ferry *Laura B* (372–8848) makes daily trips between Port Clyde and Monhegan.

HOTELS AND MOTELS. Lodgings range from full-service resorts, many offering boating and other sports activities, to small, comfortable inns. Some require a minimum stay during the summer, particularly on weekends. Many are closed Oct.–May; others remain open and lower their rates considerably during the winter.

Rates are based on double occupancy, in season: *Deluxe,* $100 and up; *Expensive,* $80–$100; *Moderate,* $60–$80; *Inexpensive,* $60 or less. There is a 7% Maine state lodging tax. Unless otherwise indicated, hotels are open year-round.

Bailey Island

Dockside Motor Inn, Mackerel Cove, 04003 (833–6656). *Moderate.* Small motel at water's edge. Marina, sundeck, snack bar, restaurant. Open June–Oct.

Bath–Brunswick

Stowe House, 63 Federal St., Brunswick 04011 (725–5543). *Moderate–Expensive.* Historic house (1807) near Bowdoin College with modern accommodations. Restaurant and tap room.

The New Meadows Inn, Bath Rd., W. Bath 04530 (443–3921). *Moderate.* Motor hotel and cottages geared to family vacations. Spacious pine-paneled rooms, colorfully decorated. Good restaurant.

Boothbay Harbor

Linekin Bay Sailing Resort, on Linekin Bay, 04538 (633–2494). *Deluxe.* Five large lodges and several cottages create an informal setting for sailboat enthusiasts. Sailboats are available for guest use; instructions for novices. Weekly regattas. Pool, tennis also. Full American Plan. Open June–Sept.

Topside, McKown Hill, 04538 (633–5404). *Deluxe.* Inn and newer motel. Picturesque setting—highest point in town, overlooking harbor and bay. Walk to all tourist and waterfront activities. Open late-May–Oct.

Smuggler's Cove Motor Inn, Rte. 96, E. Boothbay 04544 (633–2800). *Expensive–Deluxe.* Resort motel, right on the ocean, with fine accommodations. Boating, beach, pool. Restaurant. Open May–Oct.

Spruce Point Inn, Spruce Point Rd., 04538 (633–4152). *Expensive–Deluxe.* Picturesquely situated on wooded peninsula. Rooms in lodge or inn. Pools, putting green, tennis, beach, boats, fishing. Golf nearby. Lobster bakes, cocktail lounge, entertainment. Family units available. Meals included. Open June–Sept.

Fisherman's Wharf Inn, 42 Commercial St., 04538 (633–5090). *Expensive.* Large motel built on pier. Nicely decorated rooms overlook bay and dock. Downtown location, center of boating and shopping activity. Seafood restaurant, bar. Open Apr.–Nov.

Ocean Gate Motor Inn, on Rte. 27, Southport 04576 (633–3321 or 800–221–5924). *Expensive.* Modern motel nestled alongside harbor. Nicely decorated rooms. Boating, fishing. Pool. Restaurant, bar. Open June–Oct.

Tugboat Inn, 100 Commercial St., 04538 (633–4434). *Expensive.* The original tugboat *Maine* is the centerpiece of the inn's guest rooms, efficiency units, and apartments—all with a water view. Restaurant and marina.

Ocean Point Inn, Shore Rd., Rte. 96, E. Boothbay 04544 (633–4200). *Moderate.* Charming oceanfront inn and cottages. Down-east hospitality, home-cooked food. Boat trips leave from wharf. Pool. Open May–Oct.

Camden

Lord Camden Inn, 24 Main St., 04843 (236–4325). *Deluxe.* Spacious rooms with country-inn charm in a restored 1893 brick building on Camden's Main Street. Complimentary Continental breakfast.

Beloin's on the Maine Coast, Rte. 1, 04843 (236–3262). *Expensive.* Shorefront lodging on picturesque cliffs. Modern motel, mini-kitchen units available. Private beach. Nearby golf, shops, and restaurants. Open May–Oct.

Christmas Cove

Coveside Inn, Cove Rd., Rte. 129, S. Bristol 04568 (644–8282). *Moderate.* Shorefront inn-motel, marina, moorings. Restaurant and bar. Open Apr.–Oct.

Monhegan Island

Shining Sails, Box 44, 04852 (596–0041). *Moderate.* Five efficiency apartments, each with kitchenette and private bath. Beautiful ocean views; spectacular sunsets. Linens provided.

Rockland

Trade Winds, 303 Main St., 04841 (596–6661). *Expensive.* Modern units overlooking harbor. Indoor pool. Restaurant, bar, entertainment on weekends.

Rockport

The Samoset Resort, Warrenton Ave., 04856 (594–2511 or 800–341–1650). *Expensive.* Modern resort bounded on two sides by the Atlantic Ocean. Indoor and outdoor tennis and pools; golf course, health club, game rooms; restaurants and entertainment. Condo units available.

Sebasco Estates

Sebasco Lodge, Rte. 217, 04565 (389–1161). *Deluxe.* Water sports, fishing, and boating are featured at this 600-acre informal resort on Casco Bay. Comfortable rooms in lodge, lighthouse, or cottages. Saltwater pool, play area. Golf, tennis. Restaurant, entertainment, dancing. Open June–Sept.

INNS, GUEST HOUSES, BED AND BREAKFASTS. If you are hopscotching along the coast and are looking for a quiet, homelike setting with personalized service, inns, guest houses, and bed and breakfasts are often a good choice. Most are *moderate–expensive; some deluxe.* (See *Hotels and Motels.*)

The Maine Publicity Bureau (see *Tourist Information* below) publishes a listing; local Chambers of Commerce will send names and addresses; or contact: Bed & Breakfast Down East, Ltd., Box 547, Eastbrook 04634 (565–3517); Bed & Breakfast Society of Camden, Box 1103, Camden 04843; Maine Farm B&B Association, Box 4, Bristol Mills 04539.

Bailey Island

Driftwood Inn, Rte. 24, 04003 (833–5461). On the ocean; boating, pool, restaurant, lovely views. Open June–Oct.

Bath-Brunswick

Fairhaven Inn, N. Bath Rd., Bath 04530 (443–4391). A country inn built in 1790, nestled into the hillside overlooking the Kennebec River. New owners have added antique and country furnishings. Hiking, cross-country skiing, boating, beach, golf, restaurants nearby. Breakfast included.

Boothbay Harbor

Captain Sawyer's Place, 87 Commercial St., 04538 (633–2290). An old sea captain's home in the heart of town. Charming rooms with sitting areas and private baths—some with harbor views. Additional rooms in the annex. Open May–Oct.

Camden

Norumbega, 61 High St., 04843 (236–4646). Victorian stone castle overlooking Penobscot Bay. Distinctive service, elaborate public rooms, seven bedrooms with period furnishings, porches, and balconies. No children.

Whitehall, 52 High St., 04843 (236–3391). Historic colonial inn. Tennis, boat trips, concerts, entertainment. Gracious dining, cocktails. Open June–mid-Oct.

Camden Harbour Inn, 83 Bayview St., 04843 (236–4200). Spectacular harbor view. Authentic Victorian inn (1892) exudes old-fashioned charm; quiet and comfortable. Dining porch, lounge, entertainment.

Aubergine, Box 711, 04843 (236–6040). Cozy rooms available in lovingly restored Victorian inn on Belmont Ave. Swimming, boating, and golf nearby. Small, quiet, and classy. Excellent French restaurant.

Goodspeed's Guest House, 60 Mountain St., 04843 (236–8077). Small Federal-style (1879) guest house within walking distance of harbor. Attractively decorated rooms. Continental breakfast included. Open July–Oct; weekends-only in winter.

Islesboro

Dark Harbor House Inn, Dark Harbor, 04848 (734–6669). Informal elegance in a turn-of-the-century summer "cottage": a Georgian mansion, with beautifully decorated rooms, grand porches, and a sweeping lawn. Continental breakfast included. Open May–Sept.

Islesboro Inn, Dark Harbor, 04848 (734–2222). Guest rooms have dramatic views of the bay; some have fireplaces. Lovely public rooms. Relaxed atmosphere. Tennis, swimming. Meals included—picnic lunches prepared. Yachtsmen welcome. Ferry from Lincolnville Beach. Open May–Oct.

Monhegan Island

The Island Inn, 04852 (596–0371). Rather plain—both furnishings and food; for peace and quiet. Ideal location for birdwatchers, artists, and fishermen. No smoking. June–Sept.

Searsport

The HomePort Inn, Rte. 1, 04974 (548–2259). Bed and breakfast in an elegant New England sea captain's mansion (c. 1863). Warm, homey atmosphere.

Spruce Head

The Craignair Inn, Clark Island Rd., 04859 (594–7644). Not fancy, but a comfortable Maine coast inn in a small village at water's edge. Hiking, bicycling, birdwatching, fishing, boating, and swimming. Breakfast and dinner included.

Tenants Harbor

The East Wind Inn, Rte. 131, 04860 (372–6366). Restored 19th-century inn. Lovely view of the waterfront from the veranda. Perfect for a relaxing vacation. Weekly rates available. Hearty New England meals.

Westport

The Squire Tarbox Inn, Rte. 144, 04578 (882–7693). Very small restored country inn. Delightful and friendly. Antique furnishings, sumptuous dining. Open May–Oct.

RESTAURANTS. Reasonably priced seafood, fresh from the boat, tops the list on just about all menus—clams, salmon, trout, and the ubiquitous lobster. Once you taste a Maine lobster, you will never forget that ocean-fresh flavor. Chowders are featured at most restaurants, as are warm home-baked breads and desserts.

During your travels, particularly along the Mid-Coast, you will notice establishments called lobster pounds. The pound supplies local residents with fresh live lobster and also serves boiled lobster. At most pounds, you choose your own lobster and watch it go into a pot of boiling water. The lobsters are cooked in the open air, and most pounds have picnic tables outside where you can eat. (Many also have an indoor dining room for cold or rainy days.) Most diners order either New England clam chowder or steamed clams first. Then come the bibs, claw-crackers, picks, melted butter—and the lobster.

In summer, it is wise to call ahead for reservations at most restaurants. Those suggested below, except where noted, are open year-round, serve lunch and dinner, and accept major credit cards. Price ranges per person for a complete dinner excluding beverages, tax, and tip are: *Deluxe,* $35 and up; *Expensive,* $25–$35; *Moderate,* $15–$25; *Inexpensive,* $15 or less.

Bailey Island

Cook's Lobster House, Garrison Cove Rd. (833–2818). *Moderate–Expensive.* Lobster, steaks, and shore dinners served at water's edge overlooking the famous cribstone bridge. Open Memorial Day–Labor Day.

Mackerel Cove Marina Restaurant, Mackerel Cove (833–6656). *Moderate.* Dine or have cocktails overlooking the water. Open June–Oct.

Bath-Brunswick Area

22 Lincoln, 22 Lincoln St., Brunswick (725–5893). *Expensive.* The atmosphere is casual and friendly; the gourmet cuisine is artfully prepared; the elegant service is attentive, yet unobtrusive. Light suppers at the Side Door Cafe.

The Bowdoin Steak House, 115 Maine St., Brunswick (725–2314). *Moderate–Expensive.* Dine in a restored 1887 hotel. Casual and consistently good. Varied menu includes steaks, veal, and fresh seafood. Extensive wine list. Entertainment in the lounge on weekends.

New Meadows Inn, Bath Rd., W. Bath (443–3921). *Moderate–Expensive.* Serving Maine lobster and shore dinners since 1878. Varied menu includes steaks and vegetarian entrees. Fine view of cove from dining rooms.

Stowe House, 63 Federal St., Brunswick (725–5543). *Moderate–Expensive.* Near the Brunswick Music Theater. Enjoy prime ribs, Maine seafood, or nouvelle cuisine in this historic home of Harriet Beecher Stowe. Children's menu.

Montsweag Farm, Rte. 1, Woolwich (443–6563). *Moderate.* Charcoal-broiled steaks, lobster, and other seafood. Casual, nautical atmosphere. Cocktails.

Boothbay Harbor Area

Brown Bros. Wharf, Atlantic Ave. (633–5440). *Expensive.* Lobster from the tank and fresh local seafood; complete menu for landlubbers, too. Breakfast, lunch, dinner. Open June–Dec.

The Lawnmeer Inn Dining Room, Rte. 27, Southport (633–2544). *Expensive.* Traditional down-east cooking, excellent prepared and served in the spacious dining room. Open May–Oct.

Rocktide, 45 Atlantic Ave. (633–4455). *Expensive.* Three waterfront dining rooms; full menu, with seafood a specialty. Entertainment evenings. Open June–Oct.

Lake View's Greenhouse Restaurant, Lakeview Rd. (633–5381). *Moderate–Expensive.* Gourmet restaurant featuring lobster, steak, seafood, and Continental-style specialties. Open Apr.–Nov.

Tugboat Inn Restaurant, 100 Commercial St. (633–4434). *Moderate–Expensive.* Dine aboard the tugboat *Maine.* Fine seafood dinners, steak, and prime rib. Deckhouse lounge.

Andrew's Harborside, at Foot Bridge (633–4074). *Moderate.* Seafood, steak, sandwiches, and chowder. Homemade breads and pastries, wonderful cinnamon buns for breakfast. Informal. Open May–Oct.

Robinson's Wharf, at the drawbridge, Southport (633–3830). *Inexpensive.* Lobster, clams, and sandwiches to eat on the wharf or take out. Ice cream shop. Beer and wine. Open June–Sept.

Camden

Aubergine, 6 Belmont Ave. (236–6040). *Deluxe.* Intimate dining in beautifully renovated inn—or light supper in the bar. Classic French cuisine with a light touch and seasonal local ingredients. Reservations required.

Whitehall Inn, 52 High St. (236–3391). *Deluxe.* Gracious dining in a historic country inn; memorable meals; reservations requested. Open June–Oct.

Lobster Pound, Rte. 1, Lincolnville (789–5550). *Moderate–Expensive.* Pick your own lobster from the pool, have it boiled, then eat it on the deck overlooking the bay. Shore dinner, steak, ham, or turkey, also. Take-out service. Open May–Oct.

Peter Ott's Tavern and Steakhouse. 12 Bayview St. (236–4032). *Expensive.* Excellent steaks and seafood; salad bar; home-baked bread and desserts. Informal. Dinner only.

Waterfront Restaurant, Bayview St. (236–3747). *Moderate.* Lunch and dinner served on a deck overlooking the harbor. Regional seafood entrees, steaks, and sandwiches. Cocktails and raw bar. Outdoor dining in summer. No reservations.

Islesboro

Islesboro Inn, Dark Harbor (734–2221). *Expensive.* Marvelous view of the harbor. Extensive, varied menu. Cocktails. Open June–Oct.

Rockland

The Black Pearl, Harbor Park (594–2250). *Expensive.* Informal seafood and steak restaurant on the pier. Docking available. Nightly entertainment in the lounge. Open Apr.–Oct.

Rockport

The Sail Loft, Town Landing (236–2330). *Moderate–Expensive.* Harbor-view restaurant specializing in Maine shellfish. Cocktails. No credit cards.

Searsport

Nickerson Tavern, Rte. 1 (548–2220). *Moderate–Expensive.* Contemporary American dining in a sea captain's home of the 1830s. Homemade desserts.

Vinalhaven

The Haven, Main St., Carver's Harbor (863–4969). *Moderate–Expensive.* Restaurant overlooks the harbor. International cuisine served at dinner. Informal, family atmosphere. No liquor license. Breakfast and lunch, too. No credit cards.

Waldoboro

Moody's Diner, Rte. 1 (832–5362). *Inexpensive.* Busy "world-famous" diner—neon, chrome, linoleum. Home cooking, homemade pies, breakfast at any hour.

Wiscasset

Le Garage, Water St. (882–5409). *Expensive.* Dock and dine overlooking the Sheepscot River and the hulks of old shipwrecks. Traditional New England fare and Continental-style specialties using local ingredients. Home-baked breads and pastries.

TOURIST INFORMATION. Colorful and informative folders, maps, and booklets may be requested by mail from the Maine Publicity Bureau, 97 Winthrop St., Hallowell 04347 (289–2423) and from: Bath Area Chamber of Commerce, 45 Front St., Bath 04530 (443–9751); Brunswick Area Chamber of Commerce, 59 Pleasant St., Brunswick 04011 (725–8797); Pemaquid Area Association, New Harbor 04554 (No tel.); Boothbay Harbor Region Chamber of Commerce, Rte. 27, Boothbay Harbor 04538 (633–2353); Rockport-Camden-Lincolnville Chamber of Commerce, Box 919, Camden 04843 (236–4404); and Belfast Area Chamber of Commerce, Box 58, Belfast 04915 (338–2896).

There is a local information booth at the Town Landing in Camden.

TOURS. Boat tours: For a week's tour of the Maine coast, windjammers sail from Rockland, Rockport, and Camden during the summer season. Daily boat trips also depart from Camden. For information, write to the Chamber of Commerce, Box 246, Camden 04843 (236–4404), or Maine Windjammer Association, Box 317, Rockport 04856 (800–624–6380), for a list of cruises.

Out of Boothbay Harbor, excursion boats cruise the harbor islands and sheltered coves in the area. Some cruises are nature-oriented (whale-watching or seal-watching), others include a lobster bake, and still others venture farther out in the ocean to the outer islands. For brochures: Boothbay Harbor Region Chamber of Commerce (see *Tourist Information*).

Walking tours: Self-guided tours have been outlined for the historic districts of Bath, Brunswick, Wiscasset, and Camden-Rockport. Information can be secured at your hotel or through the local Chamber of Commerce (see *Tourist Information*).

Escorted tours: Northstar Escorted Tours, Box 186, Boothbay 04537 (633–6336), operates tours to rural and coastal Maine.

SEASONAL EVENTS. April: Fisherman's Festival, Boothbay Harbor (mid-Apr.).

July: Heritage Days, Bath (early July); Schooner Days (three-day celebration, Rockland (early July); Belfast Bay Festival, Belfast (mid-July); Windjammer Days, Boothbay Harbor (mid-July); Oyster Festival, Damariscotta (mid-July); Fishing Tournament, Bailey Island (late July); Friendship Sloop Days, Boothbay Harbor (late July).

August: Tuna Tournament and Fishing Rodeo, Boothbay Harbor (early Aug.); Maine Lobster Festival (three-day celebration), Rockland (early Aug.); Topsham Fair, Topsham (early Aug.); Downeast Jazz Festival, Camden (mid-Aug.); Bluegrass Festival, Brunswick (late Aug.).

October: Fall Foliage Weekend, Boothbay Harbor (mid-Oct.).

PARKS. Maine's State Parks provide excellent facilities and a variety of outdoor experiences. Most open by May 15, and the season usually extends through mid-Oct. Leashed pets are allowed, but not on beaches. For information: Maine Bureau of Parks & Recreation, Station 22, Augusta 04333 (289–3824).

State parks in the Mid-Coast area are:

Camden Hills (Camden)—camping, picnicking, snowmobiling, scenic drive, hiking trails; **Damariscotta Lake** (Jefferson)—picnicking, swimming, fishing; **Fort Point** (Stockton Springs)—picnicking, fishing; **Lake St. George** (Liberty)—camping, picnicking, swimming, boating, fishing, snowmobiling; **Moose Point** (Searsport)—picnicking; **Pemaquid Restoration** (Pemaquid)—picnicking, fishing, snack bar; **Popham Beach** (Phippsburg)—picnicking, swimming, fishing; **Reid** (Georgetown)—picnicking, swimming, fishing, snack bar; **Warren Island** (Islesboro)—camping, picnicking, fishing.

WILDLIFE. Marine Aquarium, McKown Pt., W. Boothbay Harbor 04575 (633–5572), is maintained by the State Department of Marine Resources. There are many exhibits, including newly hatched lobsters and playful seals. Open May–Oct.

The **Todd Wildlife Sanctuary** is the National Audubon Society's nature camp on Hog Island, off Bremen. It attracts students of nature from all over the country.

Merryspring (236–8831), a 66-acre nature park on the Camden-Rockport line, features marked trails through a varied landscape of wildflowers, shrubs, and trees indigenous to Maine.

At the **Montsweag Preserve,** in Woolwich, migrating waterfowl can be observed in the woods and tidal marshes. Also in Woolwich, the 180-acre **Robert P. Tristram Coffin Wildflower Sanctuary,** on Rte. 128, contains more than 200 species of flowers, grasses, trees, and shrubs.

BEACHES. Although most of Maine's sandy beaches are located along the Southern Coast, there are a few beaches in the Mid-Coast area that are open to the public: in Brunswick—Thomas Point Beach; in Phippsburg—Popham Beach State Park; in Lincolnville—Lincolnville Beach; in Rockport—Walker Park; in Camden—Laite Memorial Park; in Georgetown—Reid State Park; and in Bristol—Pemaquid Beach.

SPORTS. Boating: Maine's seemingly endless coastline and hundreds of miles of inland waterway offer perfect opportunity for boating of all sorts—cruising, sailing, or even rowing. Boats are for hire in most towns along the coast and charter fishing trips are available. Canoes can be rented for use on lakes and bays.

Hiking: A 1.4-mi. hike up to the 900-ft. summit of Mt. Battie, in the Camden Hills, provides an exhilarating climb and a splendid panoramic view of the bay.

Golf: 18-hole courses include Brunswick Golf Course, Brunswick (725–8224); Rockland Golf Course, Rockland (594–9322); and Samoset

Resort, Rockport (594–2511). There are nine-hole courses in Bath, Booth-bay, Brooks, Camden, Islesboro, North Haven, and Northport.

Skiing: Camden Snow Bowl, Ragged Mt., Camden 04843 (236–3438), has both aerial and surface lifts. It is the only major ski area in the Mid-Coast region and the oldest one in Maine. For ski conditions call 800–533–9595, in Maine 800–323–6330.

FISHING. For rugged and challenging year-round saltwater fishing, countless bays and inlets offer cod, Atlantic smelt, mackerel, halibut, flounder, pollock (the adult is known for its fighting spirit), haddock, striped bass, and tuna. Enthusiasts can fish from the wharves and rocks, or there are extensive boat-rental facilities available (advance reservations are recommended). A list of charter and head boats for deep-sea fishing is available from the Maine Publicity Bureau (see *Tourist Information*). No license is required for saltwater fishing except for lobstering.

CAMPING. Camping is available at many of the state parks in this area (see *Parks*). The Maine Publicity Bureau (see *Tourist Information*) pro-vides information on private facilities in their *Maine Guide to Camping*. Maine Campground Owners Association (MECOA), 655 Main St., Lewis-town 04240 (782–5874), also will provide a current listing of member campgrounds.

SPECTATOR SPORTS. Auto racing: Stock-car racing is held from early spring–Oct. at Wiscasset.

Boat races: Spectators may watch regattas during the active boating sea-son, spring–Nov. Friendship Sloop Races are held in Boothbay Harbor at the end of July.

HISTORIC SITES AND HOUSES. Several historic sites and houses in this area have been designated to preserve Maine's history and the mem-ory of the people who figured in it.

Alna

Old Alna Meetinghouse, Rte. 218 (586–5536). Meetinghouse from 1789, with fascinating architectural details, including a pulpit leveler and original box pews.

Bristol

Colonial Pemaquid Restoration, Rte. 130, Pemaquid Pt. (677–2423). Building foundations and artifacts indicating 17th-century Indian settle-ments.

Brunswick

Stowe House (1806), 63 Federal St. (725–5543). Where Harriet Beecher Stowe wrote *Uncle Tom's Cabin;* now an inn.

Camden

Conway House, Conway Rd., off Rte. 1 (236–2257). Authentic 1770 Maine farmhouse and barn, with period furnishings and utensils.

Damariscotta

Chapman-Hall House, Main St. (no tel.). Oldest remaining dwelling in Damariscotta (1754), with period furnishings, exhibits by local artisans, and an adjacent herb garden.

Dresden Mills

Pownalborough Court House, Rte. 128 (no tel.). Oldest court building in Maine (1761), with interesting architectural details and an exhibit on the Kennebec ice industry.

Harpswell

Eagle Island, Casco Bay (no tel.). Adm. Robert E. Peary's boyhood home, accessible only by boat from Mackerel Cove, Bailey Island; available to picnickers (Eagle Boat Tours, 774–6498).

North Edgecomb

Ft. Edgecomb (1808), Old Fort Rd., Davis Island (882–7777). Two-story octagonal blockhouse built to protect Wiscasset.

Phippsburg

Fort Popham (1861), Rte. 209 (no tel.). Granite fort built during the Civil War; near site of Popham Colony, early English settlement.

Prospect

Fort Knox, Rte. 174 (469–7719). Maine's largest fort, with underground stairways and interesting construction techniques.

Rockland

William A. Farnsworth Homestead, 21 Elm St. (596–6457). Victorian residence, fully furnished and preserved; adjacent to renowned Farnsworth Art Museum.

Thomaston

Montpelier, High St., Rte. 1 (no tel.). Replica of mansion built in 1794 by Gen. Henry Knox, advisor to George Washington and his Secretary of War.

Waldoboro

Old German Church (1772), Rte. 32 (no tel.). Well-preserved church with square-benched pews and a pulpit shaped like a wine glass.

Wiscasset

Castle Tucker, Lee St. (882–7364). An 1807 mansion built by Judge Silas Lee, with original Victorian furnishings and wallpaper—and a free-standing elliptical staircase.

Lincoln County Museum and Old Jail, Federal St. (Rte. 1) (882–6817). Museum is in the jailer's house (1837); examples of Maine arts and skills over the past 200 years are on exhibit. The Old Jail, next door, has granite walls more than three feet thick.

Nickels-Sortwell House (1807), cor. Main and Federal Sts. (Rte. 1) (882–6817). One of Maine's most beautiful old homes, built by Capt. William Nickels, a prominent shipmaster.

MUSEUMS AND GALLERIES. Specialized museums document Maine's shipbuilding and fishing industries; galleries proudly display the works of Maine artists and craftspeople. Most museums charge admission or request a small donation. Call ahead for days and hours.

Bath

Maine Maritime Museum, 963 Washington St. (443–1316). Exhibits of marine artifacts and an impressive multimedia/multilevel exhibit, "Lobstering and the Maine Coast," adjacent to a working boatyard; the Grand Banks fishing schooner *Sherman Zwicker,* and a boat ride along the Kennebec River aboard the *Dirigo.*

Boothbay

Boothbay Railway Village Museum, Rte. 27 (633–4727). Steam-railroading exhibits in a re-created New England village; ride on a narrow-gauge steam train.

Boothbay Theater Museum, Corey Lane (633–4536). Collection of theater memorabilia, costumes, playbills, posters, etc. Open June–Sept. by appointment.

Brunswick

Bowdoin College Museum of Art, Walker Art Bldg. (1894), Bowdoin Campus (725–8731). Collection of old masters, American colonial and Federal portraits, works of Andrew Wyeth, and an extensive collection of Winslow Homer memorabilia and paintings.

Peary-MacMillan Arctic Museum, Hubbard Hall, Bowdoin Campus (725–8731). Exhibits and memorabilia relating to Arctic explorations of Adm. Robert E. Peary and Adm. Donald B. MacMillan.

The Pejepscot Museum, 159 Park Row (729–6606). Exhibits on regional history, development, and 19th-century life. Also operated by the Pejepscot Historical Society are the Skolfield-Whittier House (1858), 161 Park Row, and the Joshua L. Chamberlain Civil War Museum, 226 Maine St., which have collections that detail local history.

Friendship

Friendship Museum (1851), jct. Rte. 220 and Martin's Pt. Rd. (no tel.). Historical information on the Friendship Sloop.

Monhegan Island

The Monhegan Museum, Lighthouse Hill (no tel.). Former lightkeeper's house includes displays of island plants, flowers, wildlife, and an art gallery.

Owls Head

Owls Head Transportation Museum, Rte. 73, Knox County Airport (594–4418). Collection of antique aircraft and automobiles (1900–1950), nearly all in operating condition; weekend demonstrations.

Rockland

William A. Farnsworth Art Museum, Rte. 1 (548–2529). Renowned collections of American and European art; changing exhibits.
Shore Village Museum, 104 Limerock St. (Grand Army Hall) (594–4950). Coast Guard exhibit of lighthouse equipment, buoys, and lifesaving gear from search-and-rescue boats, coupled with a large collection of Civil War uniforms and artifacts.

Searsport

Penobscot Marine Museum, Rte. 1 (548–2529). Collection of marine paintings, shipbuilding tools, and whaling memorabilia dramatically exhibited in several sea captain's homes.

Waldoboro

Waldoborough Historical Society Museum, Rte. 200 (near jct. Rte. 1) (no tel.). A complex of three buildings: a country school, town cattle pound, and a farm kitchen.

Wiscasset

Lincoln County Fire Museum, Federal St. (Rte. 1) (882–6817). Contains a collection of some of the country's oldest firefighting equipment, dating from 1803.
Musical Wonder House, 18 High St. (882–7163). Antique music boxes and player pianos in a restored house (1852). Summer candlelight concerts.

THEATER. Major professional summer theaters in the Mid-Coast area which offer Broadway musicals and contemporary drama are: The Performing Arts Center at Bath, 84 Washington St., Bath 04530 (442–8455); Maine State Music Theater, Pickard Theater, Bowdoin Campus, Brunswick 04011 (725–8769); The Theater Project, School St., Brunswick 04011 (729–8584); and Camden Shakespeare Co., Bok Amphitheater, Atlantic Ave., Box 786, Camden 04843 (236–8011). Camden Civic Theatre (594–4982) performs year-round at the Camden Opera House on Elm St.

At the Bowdoin Summer Music Festival, Bowdoin College, Brunswick 04011 (725–5000), Thurs. evening chamber concerts are presented. Bay Chamber Concerts (236–2823) presents concerts year-round at the Rockport Opera House.

The Carousel Music Theater, Boothbay Harbor 04538 (633–5297) and Boothbay Dinner Theater, McKown Hill, Boothbay Harbor 04538 (633–6186), are dinner theaters that present Broadway musicals mid-May–Oct.

SHOPPING. Local crafts are offered in many galleries and gift shops, especially in Boothbay Harbor and Camden.

Searsport is the "antiques capital of Maine." For a listing of dealers located throughout Maine, write: Antique Dealers Association, Inc., Box
178, Gorham 04038.

At the Maine State Prison Store, Rte. 1, Thomaston (354–2535), open
daily, the general public may purchase furniture and other gift items with
a nautical theme handcrafted by the prisoners.

But for the most delicious souvenir of your visit to Maine, many lobster
pounds in coastal towns will ship lobsters or pack them for travel.

NIGHTLIFE. Nightlife generally takes runner-up position with vacationers to Maine. However, there are some cafes and taverns, some with
live entertainment, in Boothbay Harbor and in Camden, where people
gather in the evening.

In Boothbay Harbor, try the **Tugboat Lounge**, 100 Commercial St.
(633–4434), or **Sullivan's Lounge** at Christiana's, 37 Atlantic Ave.
(633–6302).

In Camden, **Peter Ott's Tavern,** Bayview St. (236–4032), has a busy
bar; sea chanties and folk music fill the night at **The Thirsty Whale Tavern,**
Camden Harbor Inn, on upper Bayview St.

ACADIA

Acadia, that part of Down East Maine along the coast from Penobscot
Bay to Schoodic Point, is one of the most popular destinations of summer
vacationers and one of the more visually spectacular regions of the state.
There are mountain and ocean vistas, placid lakes and rushing streams,
offshore islands and rocky peninsulas, busy towns and sleepy fishing villages. The region stretches inland along the Penobscot River to Bangor,
the third largest city in the state, and Old Town, with its significant Indian
heritage.

The Bangor Area

Some 20 miles up the Penobscot River (about 10 miles north of Belfast
along Route 1A), Bangor was a bustling shipping center in the nineteenth
century. Because this was the frontier town between the great north woods
and the opening to the sea, fortunes were made here in lumber cargoes.
A trip to the Bangor Historical Society's museum, the Thomas Hill House
(1834), recalls those days of the 1850s when Bangor was the lumber capital
of the world. The 31-foot statue of the legendary Paul Bunyan, at Bass
Park near the Bangor Auditorium and Civic Center, suggests the brawn
of the Maine lumbermen; a large bronze statue near the public library memorializes Maine's river drivers.

Present-day Bangor, the Queen City of Maine, is the commercial, financial, and cultural center of northern and eastern Maine. The logging town
of the past has given way to modern shopping malls and industrial parks.
The city's heritage has been retained, however, by the carefully restored
mansions of the lumber barons in the Broadway Historic District.

At Bangor's Salmon Pool (opposite beautiful Grotto Cascade Park with
its 45-foot waterfall) each May and June, sea salmon weighing 10 to 30
pounds fight their way upstream. With proper licensing, fishermen can
try for that big one!

The Bangor State Fair takes place at Bass Park for 10 days in early August. Along with the midway and the cotton candy, there are agricultural exhibits, animal judging, and ox and draft-horse contests.

Orono, just north of Bangor on Route 2, is where you'll find the University of Maine's beautiful main campus along the Stillwater River. There is a planetarium on campus, the Maine Center for the Arts, and special exhibits on Maine Indians and Maine prehistory in the university's Anthropology Museum.

Following Route 1A north along the Penobscot River brings you to Old Town, hometown of the Old Town Canoe Company. Visitors are permitted to watch craftsmen construct the sleek-hulled canoes. Old Town is also the location of the Penobscot Indian Reservation, home to the remaining members of the tribe. The Penobscot National Historical Society Museum has items depicting the history of the Penobscot Indian tribe, members of the once-powerful Abnaki Nation so important to the early development of the region.

Naskeag Peninsula: Castine, Stonington, Blue Hill

Back on coastal Route 1, just beyond Bucksport, Route 175 south leads to a wonderland of Maine life. Those who seek the untrammeled byways will delight in the charming villages of the East Penobscot Bay Peninsula, or the Naskeag Peninsula, as it is often called.

Routes 166 and 199 loop the Castine cape. Castine today is a calm, peaceful settlement that belies a pugnacious past. For almost 200 years it was the object of dispute by English, French, Dutch, and colonial armies. Almost 100 signs posted throughout the town recount various events which occurred here in an attempt to piece together its past; reading the signs is an amusing pastime.

No one is quite certain when Castine's Fort George was originally built, but there were fortifications on the site as early as 1626. The fort was razed and rebuilt many times.

Just opposite Fort George and Witherle Park is the Maine Maritime Academy. The academy, which has been here since 1941, is one of five institutions in the United States which train young men and women for careers as Merchant Marine officers. Visitors can tour the *State of Maine,* training ship of the academy, when it is in port.

Brooksville, a tiny settlement along Route 175, is a favorite of yachtsmen; Bucks Harbor is one of the deepest harbors along the Maine coast. Farther south, the Deer Isle Bridge crosses Eggemoggin Reach.

Stonington, at the tip of Deer Isle, is the archetypal Down East fishing village and another favorite of artists and writers. The magnificent harbor, with the town climbing the surrounding hills, exemplifies the beauty of the Maine coast. Ames Pond, just west of Stonington, is blanketed with pink and white pond-lily blossoms in summer.

Stonington once had a flourishing granite quarry, the source of the stone used in New York's Triborough Bridge. Now the town is geared to the waterfront and lobstering, although quarrying is being revived.

Several boat trips are available in this area: A morning mail boat goes to Isle au Haut, a portion of which is part of Acadia National Park, and other cruises go to Vinalhaven and Swans Island. Stonington is a quiet but busy harbor; it is likely you'll see one of the windjammers that ply the Maine coast in summer.

From a distance you'll have no trouble recognizing Blue Hill. It not only dominates much of the scenery in the northern section of the peninsula, it is often blue! And in late summer and fall, when the leaves of the blueberry bushes turn, much of it becomes a brilliant, dramatic red. The Blue Hill area is dotted with fine estates and summer cottages. An ancient Norwegian coin, recently found in Blue Hill, has prompted archaeological digs to determine if the Vikings visited the area 900 years ago.

The Main Street parsonage of Jonathan Fisher, a highly talented individual who lived here in 1814—and the community's first minister—contains his manuscripts, his paintings, and his own homemade furniture. The Jonathan Fisher Memorial is open to visitors during the summer.

Kneisel Hall, a summer school for string and ensemble musicians, presents weekly chamber concerts.

At Rackliffe Family Potters and at Rowantrees Pottery you can watch potters work at their wheels.

Ellsworth

Ellsworth, which straddles Route 1 and is the business center of Hancock County, is a major crossroads: Bangor and the wilderness and farmlands are to the north via Route 1A; coastal Route 1 continues *way* Down East to rugged Washington County; and Route 3 south becomes the scenic causeway leading to popular Acadia National Park on Mount Desert Island.

At the outskirts of Ellsworth, north on Route 172, is the Colonel Black Mansion (1828). An elegant red-brick mansion of modified Georgian architecture, it is fully furnished. A visit gives one more the feeling of having paid a call than of having visited a museum.

Another point of interest in Ellsworth is the Stanwood Homestead Museum (1850), a memorial to Cordelia J. Stanwood, a pioneer ornithologist, photographer, and author. Adjacent is a 100-acre woodland sanctuary that includes eight trails and three ponds.

Mount Desert Island

In 1604, the French explorer Samuel de Champlain, noticing the bald mountain peaks on the island, called it L'Isle des Monts Deserts. In the mid-1800s, vacationers began coming to Mount Desert Island by rail and steamboat. Soon Bar Harbor and some of the smaller villages became colonies of spacious summer homes owned by wealthy people. As more and more families arrived, followed by merchants to serve them, privacy became threatened. In 1919, President Woodrow Wilson was persuaded to preserve much of the island as a national park. Descendents of those who once owned the great estates still come to Mount Desert Island.

Among the first summer residents of Bar Harbor, back in the 1800s, were artists attracted by the area's incredible natural beauty. The artists were followed by prominent East Coast families, such as the Astors and the Rockefellers, who built "cottages" to rival some of those in Newport, Rhode Island.

For about a century, until the Great Depression, Bar Harbor was a society resort. The Great Fire of 1947, coupled with the effects of the Depression, devastated the town. Many of the mansions burned, although some still exist, and some have now become inns. The Bar Harbor Historical Museum, in the basement of the Jesup Memorial Library on Mount Desert Street, has on display a large collection of photographs and other memorabilia of those early days.

Today, Bar Harbor is the commercial center of the island, an attractive village chock full of shops and restaurants, with a wide variety of accommodations available. Festivals, concerts, and special events are scheduled throughout the summer season.

The car/passenger ferry *Bluenose* departs from the terminal on Eden Street (Route 3), north of the center of town, for the six-hour journey to Yarmouth, Nova Scotia. Shorter excursions (sightseeing trips, sunset cruises, and deep-sea-fishing charters) leave from the Municipal Pier at West Street.

About three miles south of the village center, on Route 3, is the Jackson Laboratory, world-famous center for mammalian genetics research. Here scientists study inbred lab animals (mainly their own specially bred mice) for insight into behavior problems, aging, and human diseases—cancer, diabetes, birth defects. A one-hour lecture and film program is offered free of charge on certain afternoons each week during the summer.

Seal Harbor and Northeast Harbor, on the south coast of the eastern lobe of Mount Desert Island, are two villages where yachting is the main attraction. Summer residents and visiting yachtsmen gather for races, regattas, and cruises. Hundreds of boats of every size and shape can be seen at anchor in both harbors throughout the summer season.

From the public wharf in Northeast Harbor there is ferry service to the nearby Cranberry Isles. The Islesford Historical Museum, on Little Cranberry Island, has exhibits on the early history of Acadia.

Out of Northeast Harbor, Sargent Drive (passenger cars only) takes you to the fjord at Somes Sound. This is the only natural fjord on the East Coast, and the view is breathtaking.

Route 102 loops around the western lobe of Mount Desert Island—the quiet side of the island. Somesville, the first village you come to, is the oldest settlement on the island. The Acadia Repertory Theater stages several plays here each summer at the Masonic Hall on Route 102.

Southwest Harbor, farther south on Route 102, is another authentic Maine fishing village, its harbor crowded with lobster boats and its main street dotted with shops and galleries. The Mount Desert Oceanarium on Clark's Point Road has display tanks filled with all manner of live local sea animals. There are hands-on exhibits and workshops; fishing and lobstering demonstrations are presented. Kids will love the Oceanarium.

(The ferry between Northeast Harbor and the Cranberry Isles also stops at Southwest Harbor, at the Coast Guard Depot.)

Manset, Seawall (appropriately named, as you will see), and Bass Harbor are working fishing villages. From Bass Harbor, the *Vagabond* sails daily from the Town Dock for tours of the harbor. Ferries for Swan's Island run frequently; for Frenchboro, twice weekly.

For a change of pace (from boats to cars), the Seal Cove Automobile Museum has a collection of 150 or more antique autos that span the years from the early 1900s to the 1940s. There are also several restored fire trucks and pumpers. Seal Cove is on Route 102, on the western shore of Mount Desert Island.

The reader who wants to know more about this area should turn to Samuel Eliot Morison's *The Story of Mount Desert Island.*

Acadia National Park

These days, more than four million people annually visit Mount Desert Island. Often the main attraction is Acadia National Park. The 33,000-acre park has an air of vast, timeless beauty of mountain, sea, and shore. The Visitor Center is at the northern entrance to the park, at Park Headquarters, Route 3, Hulls Cove.

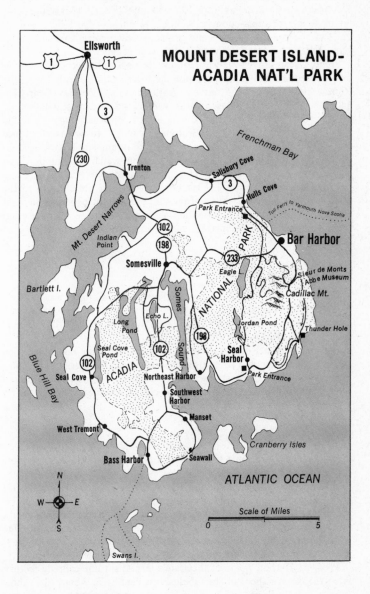

MOUNT DESERT ISLAND-
ACADIA NAT'L PARK

Acadia National Park is a 22-square-mile natural paradise with an extraordinary variety of wildlife and vegetation, woodland and rock formations, 18 mountains and numerous valleys, five large lakes, and magnificent ocean views. There are more than 50 miles of car-free carriage paths for bicycling (or cross-country skiing), 142 miles of footpaths, over 40 miles of bridle paths, 26 lakes and ponds, several picnic areas, and campsites. The park is open 24 hours a day, year-round.

Scenic Ocean Drive (one-way) follows the park's entire eastern perimeter. At Sieur de Monts Spring, near the beginning of Ocean Drive, the Robert Abbe Museum of Stone Age Antiquities has dioramas of early Indian life and Indian artifacts, a nature center, and gardens of wildflowers.

At various points along the 20-mile Park Loop Road (one-way traffic from Sieur de Monts Spring to Seal Harbor only; two-way between Seal Harbor and Hulls Cove) there are scenic lookouts and ample parking areas where you can stop to poke about, beachcomb, watch the pounding surf at Thunder Hole, and climb among great ragged cliffs and coves.

From Ocean Drive, at Seal Harbor, a park road heads north to the 1,532-foot summit of Cadillac Mountain, the highest point on the East Coast. The top of this bald mountain permits a 360-degree vantage point for sweeping views of the surrounding ocean, offshore islands, and rugged coastline.

Hancock and Sullivan

Back on Route 1, heading toward Washington County, music lovers will recognize Hancock as the site of the Pierre Monteux School of Music. Summer chamber concerts are held regularly. Begun in 1965, the Monteux Memorial Festival is a worthwhile event.

Farther east on Route 1, beyond Hancock and near Sullivan, a sign marks a scenic turnoff. From this spot you can look out on one of the most magnificent views of coastal America—a splendid panorama of Mount Desert Island, Cadillac Mountain, pine-clad offshore islands, and the far reaches of Frenchman's Bay.

Gouldsboro Peninsula

Winter Harbor, a quiet town and pretty harbor on the western shore of the Gouldsboro Peninsula, is the gateway to the 2,080-acre Schoodic Point section of Acadia National Park. A one-way road leading to the point is lined with pine and spruce forests. Pink granite rocks, caught between blue water and evergreen shore, make a memorable scene. Schoodic Mountain rises to an elevation of 500 feet above a terraced ledge. The view from Schoodic Head stretches east to the Bay of Fundy. The surf here is always spectacular; following a storm, it is awesome.

Prospect Harbor, home of the state's largest sardine canning factory, is on the eastern shore of the Gouldsboro Peninsula. About three miles farther east, on Route 195, is the village of Corea, a working harbor with trim lobster boats and long-legged wharves. Corea has two main paved streets: Each becomes a dirt road which peters out at the harbor's edge. Despite the peaceful scene, however, you sense that lobstering and fishing on this stern coast sometimes takes its toll.

PRACTICAL INFORMATION FOR ACADIA

Note: The area code for all Maine is 207

HOW TO GET THERE AND AROUND. By plane: National and regional airlines have scheduled flights between major cities in the northeast and Bangor International Airport (often via Portland). For information: Delta Airlines (800–221–1212); United (800–241–6522); Valley Airlines (800–322–1008); Business Express (800–345–3400); and Eastern Express (800–451–4221). Intrastate flights are available between Bangor and Augusta, Bar Harbor, Frenchville, Houlton, Portland, Presque Isle, Rockland, and Waterville via Eastern Express or Valley Airlines. Airport limousine service is available in Hermon, serving the Bangor area, and in Trenton, which serves Mount Desert Island.

By bus: Daily service to and from Bangor and between Bangor and Bar Harbor (via Ellsworth) is available on Greyhound. Connections from the south can be made in Portland; from New Brunswick or Nova Scotia, in Caribou. Canadian service is also available between Montreal and Bangor.

Bangor Citibus (947–0536) provides local service in that city. In Ellsworth, Downeast Transportation (667–5796) provides weekday service to Blue Hill and Stonington (timed with ferries to Isle au Haut) and to Schoodic Peninsula.

By car: I–95 is a direct route to Bangor from Portland and points south or from Houlton and Canada in the north; Rte. 1A connects Bangor with Ellsworth. The most efficient route from points south to the coastal resort areas is I–95 to Augusta, then Rte. 3 east to Belfast and Rte. 1. Scenic Rte. 1 follows the coast and passes through the gateway towns of Bucksport, Ellsworth, and Gouldsboro.

From Bucksport, Rte. 175 loops around the Naskeag Peninsula; Rte. 15, off Rte. 175, crosses Deer Isle to Stonington. From Ellsworth, Rte. 3 goes south to Mount Desert Island, Bar Harbor, and Acadia National Park; Rte. 102 loops around the western portion of Mount Desert Island. From W. Gouldsboro, Rte. 186 follows the perimeter of the Gouldsboro Peninsula.

Car rentals: Major car rental companies are represented in Bangor, Bar Harbor, and Trenton.

By boat: The passenger/car ferry *MV Bluenose* provides year-round service between Bar Harbor and Yarmouth, Nova Scotia, a six-hour trip. For information: Marine Atlantic, 121 Eden St., Rte. 3, Bar Harbor 04609 (800–341–7981).

Car ferry service to coastal islands is available between Bass Harbor and Swans Island (daily) and between Bass Harbor and Frenchboro (twice weekly) via Maine State Ferry Service, Box 645, 517A Main St., Rockland 04841 (594–5543 or 244–3254); passengers only on the boats between Stonington and Isle au Haut (367–5193). Daily ferry service between Northeast Harbor and the Cranberry Isles is provided June–Sept. aboard the *Sea Queen* by Beal & Bunker, Northeast Harbor (244–3575).

HOTELS AND MOTELS. Lodgings are abundant in Down East Acadia. The large chains are represented in the Bangor area; modern motels are available in Bar Harbor and in towns along Rte. 1. Reservations are recommended, especially during the summer season.

Many hotels and inns in the resort areas are closed Oct.–May; those that remain open lower their rates considerably during the winter. Rates are based on double occupancy, in season: *Deluxe,* $100 and up; *Expensive,* $80–$100; *Moderate,* $60–$80; *Inexpensive,* $60 or less. There is a 7% Maine state lodging tax. Unless otherwise indicated, hotels are open year-round.

Bangor Area

Bangor Airport Hilton, 308 Godfrey Blvd., Bangor 04401 (947–6721). *Expensive–Deluxe.* At Bangor Int'l. Jetport. Beautiful rooms and suites in this large, modern hotel. All amenities, excellent service, near shopping. Restaurant, cocktail lounge. Pool and sauna.

Holiday Inn, 404 Odlin Rd., Bangor 04401 (947–0101). *Expensive.* Comfortable motels. Restaurant, bar. Pets accepted. Pool.

University Motor Inn, 5 College Ave., Orono 04473 (866–4921). *Expensive.* Nicely decorated, with patio or balconies. Restaurant, bar. Pool. Walk to University of Maine.

The Phenix Inn, 20 West Market Sq., 04401 (947–3850). *Moderate.* Restored downtown hotel with modern facilities and Old World ambience. Convenient to business district.

Bar Harbor

Atlantic Oakes, Eden St., 04609 (288–5801). *Deluxe.* Handsomely decorated rooms, each with ocean view. Elegant, yet informal. Built on former estate. Pebble beach, boats, tennis, game room.

The Bayview on Frenchman's Bay, 111 Eden St., 04609 (288–5861). *Deluxe.* Artfully decorated rooms in Georgian estate and townhouses. Suites and efficiency units. Two dining rooms. Spacious, secluded grounds.

Bar Harbor Motor Inn, Newport Dr., 04609 (288–3351 or 800–248–3351). *Expensive–Deluxe.* Luxurious motor hotel, built in 1887, on the shore of Frenchman's Bay. Lovely grounds. Pool and sundeck. Restaurant and lounge. Open May–Nov.

Bluenose Motor Inn, 90 Eden St., 04609 (288–3348 or 800–445–4077). *Expensive–Deluxe.* Cliffside retreat overlooking the bay. Near ferry, town, and Acadia. No children under 13. Open May–Oct.

Wonder View Motor Lodge, Eden St., 04609 (288–3358). *Expensive.* Hilltop view of Bar Harbor and Frenchman's Bay. Pool. Restaurant, cocktail lounge. Close to town. Open May–Oct.

Cadillac Motor Inn, 336 Main St., 04609 (288–3831). *Inexpensive.* Pleasant motor inn close to town. Ideal for families. Convenient, comfortable. Some kitchenettes. Free transportation to and from airport, bus, or ferry terminal with prior arrangement.

Deer Isle

Goose Cove Lodge, Sunset (4½ mi. from Deer Isle Village), 04683 (348–2508). *Expensive.* Rooms in the lodge or in rustic cottages. Miles of nature trails on grounds overlooking Goose Cove. Private beach for swimming and boating. Weekly rates; family-style meals included. Open May–Oct.

The Captain's Quarters Inn and Motel, Main St., Stonington 04681 (367–2420). *Moderate.* Harborside location offers a panoramic view of the bay. Close to village. Rooms, suites, efficiencies, or apartments. Coffee shop.

Northeast Harbor

Asticou Inn, Rtes. 3 and 198, 04662 (276–3344). *Deluxe.* Grand turn-of-the-century resort hotel, filled with charm and tradition. Magnificent harbor view. Traditional or contemporary accommodations in inn, lodge, or housekeeping cottages. Pool, tennis, golf privileges. Breakfast and dinner included. Open June–Sept. Bed & breakfast in the Cranberry Lodge in spring and fall.

INNS, GUEST HOUSES, BED AND BREAKFASTS. A treat when vacationing in one of the small peninsula towns on Mount Desert Island is to stay in a comfortable Maine coast inn—or in a restored turn-of-the-century Bar Harbor "cottage." Residents of coastal villages have responded to the shortage of accommodations during the peak vacation season and have opened their homes to guests. Many have signs out front and advertise their services; many do not. The Maine Publicity Bureau (see *Tourist Information*) publishes a listing of bed-and-breakfast establishments; the local Chambers of Commerce will make recommendations; or contact: Bed and Breakfast Down East, Ltd., Box 547, Eastbrook 04634 (565–3517). Most of the inns that follow fall into the *moderate–expensive* category.

Bar Harbor

Manor House Inn, 16 West St., 04609 (288–3759). Turn-of-the-century decor in restored Bar Harbor "cottage." Quiet, comfortable guest house, yet convenient to town. Privileges at Bar Harbor Club across street—pool, tennis. Continental breakfast included. Open Apr.–Nov.

Stratford House Inn, 45 Mt. Desert St., 04609 (288–5189). Small, English Tudor inn styled after Shakespeare's birthplace and furnished with Jacobean-period antiques. Short walk to town center and waterfront. Continental breakfast included. Open May–Oct.

Cleftstone Manor Inn, 92 Eden St., 04609 (288–4951). Historic Victorian mansion at foot of Cadillac Mt. Gracious rooms, a well-stocked library, and a game room. Continental breakfast and afternoon tea included. No children under 12. No smoking. Open May–Oct.

Thornhedge Inn, 47 Mt. Desert St., 04609 (288–5398). Reminiscent of early Bar Harbor elegance. Downstairs sitting rooms. Spacious guest rooms. Congenial atmosphere. Complimentary breakfast. Walking distance to town. Open Apr.–Nov.

Blue Hill

Arcady Down East, South St., 04614 (374–5576). An elegant Victorian manse that exudes hospitality and charm. Bicycles available to guests. Continental breakfast included. Open June–Oct.

Blue Hill Inn, Main St., 04614 (374–2844). Very pretty landmark inn (1840) in the town center. Golf, tennis, and beaches nearby. Excellent dining.

Brooksville

Breezemere Farm Inn, Rte. 176, S. Brooksville, 04617 (326–8628). Lovely 1850 farmhouse and cottages on Orcutt Harbor. All amenities and numerous sports. Excellent restaurant. Open June–Oct.

Castine

Pentagoet Inn, Main St., 04421 (326–8616). Small, comfortable Victorian (1894) inn, right on the coast; warm, friendly atmosphere. Full dinner service. Open Apr.–Dec.

Castine Inn, Box 41, Main St., 04421 (326–4365). Traditional New England country inn (1898). Friendly service, comfortable accommodations. Complimentary home-baked rolls and pastries for breakfast. Open May–Oct.

Deer Isle

Pilgrim's Inn, Main St., 04627 (348–6615). Quiet colonial inn (1793) overlooks a millpond. Comfortable accommodations. Swimming and boating available. Weekly rates include meals. Open May–Oct.

Eggemoggin Inn, Little Deer Isle, 04650 (348–2540). A secluded inn perched on a point of land on Eggemoggin Reach. Oceanfront rooms, some with shared bath. Enjoy sailing, fishing, boating, and privacy. Continental breakfast available. Open May–Oct.

Lucerne-in-Maine

The Lucerne Inn, Rte. 1A, 04429 (843–5123). Farmhouse/stable has operated as an inn since 1814. Perched on a hill, overlooking Phillips Lake, it is half-way between Ellsworth and Bangor. Hiking, cross-country skiing, pool. Fine dining. Full breakfast included. No children.

Surry

Surry Inn, Rte. 172, 04684 (667–5091). Lovely, sprawling inn (1834) with a 60-ft. porch that overlooks sweeping lawns and Contention Cove. Swimming, boating, and lawn games in summer; cross-country skiing in winter. Delicious dining. Near Acadia National Park and Deer Isle.

RESTAURANTS. Dining choices in this busy resort area of Maine run the gamut from formal service and gourmet cooking to a casual seaside clambake. A variety of restaurants are concentrated in Bar Harbor, the major resort town. Regardless of the style you choose, however, you will doubtless be able to choose a fresh, steamed Maine lobster for your dinner.

The restaurants suggested below, except where indicated, are open year-round, serve lunch and dinner, and accept major credit cards. Price ranges per person for a complete dinner excluding beverages, tax, and tip: *Deluxe,* $35 and up; *Expensive,* $25–$35; *Moderate,* $15–$25; *Inexpensive,* $15 or less.

Bangor

The Greenhouse, 193 Broad St. (945–4040). *Moderate–Expensive.* Steaks, seafood, Continental specialties. Dining room decor features more than 400 plants. Reservations necessary.

Pilot's Grill, 1528 Hammond St., Rte. 2W (942–6325). *Moderate.* Family-owned and -operated. Home-style cookery, headed by delectable lobster, steak, and roast beef. Well-rounded bill of fare. Bar. Children's portions.

Seguino's Italian Restaurant, 735 Main St. (942–1240). *Moderate.* Full southern Italian menu with seafood and veal specialties. Pizzaria. Family operated. Patio dining in summer.

Bar Harbor

Bar Harbor Inn (The Reading Room), Newport Dr. (288–3351). *Deluxe.* Regional cuisine, fresh local seafood, baking on premises; extensive wine list. Formal service, white linen, fresh flowers. Picture windows overlook Frenchman's Bay.

George's, 7 Stevens La. (288–4505). *Expensive.* Early American decor in a comfortable home setting. Varied menu with daily specials. Dinner only. Jackets required for gentlemen. Open June–Oct.

Brick Oven, 21 Cottage St. (288–3708). *Moderate–Expensive.* Traditional American specialties served in dining rooms filled with memorabilia. Summer only.

Jordan Pond House, Park Loop Rd., in Acadia National Park (276–3316). *Moderate–Expensive.* Enjoy a lovely luncheon—or enormous popovers and homemade ice cream on the lawn for afternoon tea. Dinners are served in front of a crackling fire with classical music accompaniment. The view is magnificent during the day; the mood memorable in the evening. Open June–Oct.

Acadian Restaurant, Rte. 3, Hulls Cove (288–5493). *Moderate.* Seafood, chops, steak. Home-baked pies. Enjoy the panoramic water view while dining. Open for breakfast. Summer only.

Testa's, 53 Main St. (288–3327). *Moderate.* Grill Room and Garden Room. Steaks, shellfish, Italian specialties, inspired green salads; fresh fruit pies. Breakfast, too. Children's portions. Summer only.

Blue Hill

Firepond, Main St. (374–2135). *Expensive.* Gourmet dining in this historic building "by the old mill stream." Entrees prepared Continental style, with fresh seafood daily. Summer only.

Jonathan's. Main St. (374–5226). *Moderate–Expensive.* New American cuisine, daily menu changes. Extensive wine list. Reservations requested.

Castine

The Manor, Battle Ave. (326–4861). *Expensive.* In a turn-of-the-century mansion, innovative cuisine combines American specialties and a classic French treatment. Fine wines. Reservations requested.

Deer Isle

Pilgrim's Inn, Main St. (348–6615). *Expensive.* 200-year-old antique-filled inn serving international specialties. Prix fixe menu (children half-price). Reservations necessary. Open May–Oct.

Ellsworth Area

Le Domaine, Rte. 1, Hancock (422–3395). *Expensive.* Classic French country cuisine. Superbly prepared entrees and pastry. Open May–Oct.

Surry Inn, Rte. 172, Surry (667–5091). *Moderate–Expensive.* The French cuisine served in the pleasant dining room of this country inn is enhanced by the view of sweeping lawn and Contention Cove.

Northeast Harbor

Asticou Inn, Rtes. 3 and 98 (276–3344). *Expensive–Deluxe.* Attractive dining room overlooks the harbor. Prix fixe dinner. Traditional American menu. Jacket and tie required. Open June–Sept.

Southwest Harbor

Beal's Lobster Pier, Clark Pt. Rd. (244–3202). *Inexpensive.* Since 1930, diners have enjoyed lobsters, clams, crabmeat, shrimp, and fresh fish on the dock—from morning 'til sunset, weather permitting. No bar service, but you can bring your own.

TOURIST INFORMATION. Maps, booklets, and brochures may be requested by mail from the Maine Publicity Bureau, 97 Winthrop St., Hallowell 04347 (289–2423) and from the following local or regional organizations: Greater Bangor Chamber of Commerce, 519 Main St., Bangor 04401 (947–0307); Blue Hill Chamber of Commerce, Box 520, Blue Hill 04614 (no tel.); Deer Isle-Stonington Chamber of Commerce, Box 268, Stonington 04681 (348–2337); Ellsworth Area Chamber of Commerce, High St., Ellsworth 04605 (667–2617); Mount Desert Chamber of Commerce, Box 675, Northeast Harbor 04662 (276–5040); Bar Harbor Chamber of Commerce, Box 158, Cottage St., Bar Harbor 04609 (summer: 288–3415 or 288–3394; winter: 288–5103); Trenton Chamber of Commerce, Box 1111, Ellsworth 04605 (667–8548); and Winter Harbor Chamber of Commerce, Winter Harbor 04693 (no tel.).

Regional tourist information centers are open in the summer at Bass Park, 519 Main St., Bangor (945–5717); at the Ferry Terminal, Bar Harbor (288–3393); on High St., Ellsworth (667–2617); on Thompson's Island, Trenton (288–3411); and on Rte. 102 in Southwest Harbor (244–5718).

TOURS. Boat tours: Under the auspices of Acadia National Park, park naturalists conduct hourly or half-day cruises during the summer to and around offshore islands aboard privately owned boats out of Bar Harbor, Bass Harbor, and Northeast Harbor. For information: Park Information Center, Hull's Cove, Rte. 3, Bar Harbor 04609 (288–3338).

During the summer, a variety of sightseeing, lobster-fishing, seal-watching, and sailing trips around Mount Desert Island leave several times daily from Municipal Pier, West St., Bar Harbor, and from Sea St. Pier, Northeast Harbor.

Full-day whale-watching trips leave from Northeast Harbor aboard the *Island Queen* (288–9595), June–Sept, or with Bob Bowman's *Maine Whalewatch* (276–5803) July–Sept.

For a full day at sea, Marine Atlantic, 121 Ferry Terminal, Eden Street, Bar Harbor 04609 (288–3395) offers a 12-hour round-trip cruise to Yarmouth, Nova Scotia on the *Bluenose,* late June–Sept.

Bus/Limousine tours: Bar Harbor Limousine Service (288–5398) conducts personalized half-day historic and scenic tours of the area by reservation only. National Park Tours conducts a 2½-hr. bus tour of Acadia National Park, fully narrated by a park naturalist, that leaves twice daily from Testa's Restaurant, Main St., Bar Harbor. Inquire at the restaurant for particulars (288–3327). Bar Harbor Trolley Car Co., Town Pier (288–5741), runs frequent trips through Bar Harbor and Acadia National Park.

By air: Sightseeing flights can be arranged through Acadia Air, Inc., Bar Harbor Airport, Rte. 3, Trenton (667–5534) for an air tour over Acadia National Park and Cadillac Mt.

Industrial plant tours: The Maine Publicity Bureau (see *Tourist Information*) publishes a brochure listing several Maine businesses offering tours. In this area, Rackliffe Pottery, Rte. 172, Blue Hill 04614 (374–2297), and Rowantrees Pottery, Blue Hill 04614 (374–5535), welcome visitors to watch pottery and dinnerware being created; at the Old Town Canoe Co., 58 Middle St., Old Town 04468 (827–5513), you can see canoes and kayaks being constructed; and at Champion International Paper Co., Bucksport 04416 (469–3131) you can see fine printing paper and magazine stock manufactured. Advance notice is requested, but not always necessary.

SEASONAL EVENTS. February: Winter Carnival, Bangor.
June: Stonington Boat Races, Stonington (late June); Art Show and Music Festival, Bar Harbor (late June).
July: Seafood Festival, Bar Harbor (early July); Acadia Scottish Festival, Trenton (mid-July).
August: Bangor State Fair, Bangor (early Aug.); Retired Skipper's Race, Castine (mid-Aug.).
September: Hancock County Agricultural Fair, Blue Hill (early Sept.).

PARKS. Acadia National Park encompasses more than 30,000 acres on Mount Desert Island. Along spectacular scenic drives, visitors pass great ragged cliffs and sheltered coves, mountains, lakes, streams, and open ocean. A drive to the 1,530-ft. summit of Cadillac Mt. provides a 360° view of coastal and inland Maine. At Thunder Hole, the surf crashes with a fury into a rocky ravine. There are miles of hiking trails and car-free carriageways for bicycling, horseback riding, or cross-country skiing. Camping, trailer sites, and picnic areas are plentiful. Nature-guide service offers varied daily programs. Swimmers have a choice of salt or fresh water. Birdwatchers will spot everything from herons to eagles. Lots of wildlife, too—deer, beaver, raccoon, fox. The park is open 24 hours a day year-round. Additional sections of Acadia National Park are on Isle au Haut (boat from Stonington) and at Schoodic Pt. For information: Acadia National Park, Hulls Cove, Rte. 3, Bar Harbor 04609 (288–3338).

Maine's State Parks provide excellent facilities and a variety of outdoor experiences. Most open by May 15, and the season usually extends through mid-Oct. Leashed pets are allowed. For information: Maine Bureau of Parks and Recreation, Station 22, Augusta 04333 (289–3824).

State parks in this region are: **Holbrook Island Sanctuary** (Brooksville)—picnicking, hiking, nature study; **Lamoine** (Ellsworth)—camping, picnicking, fishing, boating.

INDIANS. The Maine Penobscot Indians are part of the Algonquin linguistic group. The Penobscots were the largest tribe in the Abnaki Nation and were very helpful to the American patriots during the Revolution. Indian crafts are sold at the Penobscot Indian Reservation on Indian Island near Old Town. The Penobscot National Historical Society Indian Museum (827–2271), also on Indian Island, has artifacts, photos, and religious items detailing the complete history of the Penobscot tribe.

WILDLIFE. Birdwatchers will sight many species in **Acadia National Park** on Mount Desert Island, the most important observation point for the Atlantic Flyway. Southwest Harbor is also nationally known for its variety of birds. Nature walks are scheduled morning, afternoon, and evening; inquire at the Park Information Center, Hull's Cove, Rte. 3; Bar Harbor 04609 (288–3338).

Birdsacre Sanctuary, adjacent to the Stanwood Homestead Museum, Rte. 3 (east of the town center), Ellsworth (667–8460), is a small wildlife refuge of about 100 acres. The museum, a memorial to Cordelia J. Stanwood, pioneer ornithologist, has an excellent collection of bird specimens; the sanctuary has trails, wildflowers, bird-nesting areas, ponds, and picnic grounds.

The 1,230-acre **Holbrook Island Wildlife Sanctuary** is at the northern end of Cape Rossier, on Deer Isle. There are no developed facilities, but the forests and meadows provide ample oportunity for hiking and nature study.

The **Mount Desert Oceanarium,** Clark Point Rd., Southwest Harbor 04679 (244–7330) is open to the public daily (except Sun.). Its "Please Touch" exhibits are fun for the entire family.

BEACHES. Ocean swimming can be bone-chilling in Down East waters, but enthusiasts will find saltwater beaches at Sand Beach, Acadia National Park, and at Lamoine Beach, Lamoine State Park (see *Parks*). Freshwater beaches are available to the public at Echo Lake, Southwest Harbor, and at Jenkins Beach, Green Lake (east of Bangor).

SPORTS. Boating: Sailboats, fishing boats, and other pleasure craft are available for hire in most towns along the coast, especially in Castine, Stonington, Northeast Harbor, Southwest Harbor, and Bass Harbor.

Hiking: In Acadia National Park, there are 142 mi. of footpaths and hiking trails and 17 mountains with paths to their summits. Climbs range from easy walks to precipitous cliff trails. Maps are available from Park Headquarters, Hull's Cove, Rte. 3, Bar Harbor 04609 (288–3338).

Mountain climbing: Climbers can tackle Blue Hill Mountain, Blue Hill, for a superb view of the bay; Cadillac Mt., Acadia National Park, at 1,530 ft., the highest mountain on the Maine coast; Penobscot Mt. and Sargent Mt., on Mount Desert Island; and Schoodic Mountain, Franklin.

Bicycling: Although bicycling on country roads throughout Maine is a popular pastime and mode of transportation, the safest location for cycling enthusiasts is Acadia National Park. There are over 50 mi. of car-free carriage paths in the main section of the park on Mount Desert Island and 6 mi. of one-way park roads out of Winter Harbor that follow the shore to Schoodic Point. Bicycle rentals are available locally.

Golf: 18-hole courses open to the public include Bangor Municipal Golf Course, Bangor (945–9226); Kebo Valley Golf Club, Bar Harbor (288–3000); Hermon Meadow Golf Course, Hermon (848–3741); Penobscot Valley Country Club, Orono (866–2423); and Bar Harbor Golf Course, Trenton (667–7505). There's a 15-hole course at Northeast Harbor; nine-hole courses at Brewer, Bucksport, Carmel, Castine, Deer Isle, Dexter, Ellsworth, Hampden, Kenduskeag, Newport, Southwest Harbor, and Winter Harbor.

Horseback riding: There is a 40-mi. system of bridle paths in Acadia National Park. Horses are available for hire in the park. Inquire at Park Information Center (see address under "Hiking").

Ballooning: Hot-air balloon trips can be arranged in Bangor through Daryl Young (843–7249).

Skiing: The roads and carriage paths of Acadia National Park are open to cross-country skiers in the winter.

FISHING. Deep-sea-fishing trips may be arranged out of Bar Harbor, Castine, Stonington, and most other coastal towns. Anglers may also fish from piers and rocks along the shore. No fishing license is required for saltwater fishing. Freshwater fishing at inland lakes and streams requires a license, available at most town halls. Try your luck at the Bangor Salmon Pool along the Penobscot River in Bangor (license required).

CAMPING. Acadia National Park permits fires and camping at designated sites only. Their two campgrounds are Black's Woods and Seawall. (There are private campgrounds outside park boundaries, as well.) Camping in the park is limited to 14 days.

The Maine Publicity Bureau (see *Tourist Information*) will send you their *Maine Guide to Camping,* which lists privately operated trailer parks, campsites, and conveniences available.

SPECTATOR SPORTS. Basketball: The Maine Lumberjacks, a professional basketball team, play at the Bangor Auditorium, 100 Dutton St., Dec.–Mar. Call 947–5252 for details.

Auto racing: Stock-car racing is held at Hermon, west of Bangor, early spring–Oct.

Horse racing: Harness racing is held at Bangor Raceway, Bass Park, Bangor, Memorial Day–July. Harness racing, with pari-mutuel betting, is a main attraction at the Bangor State Fair in early Aug. and the Hancock County Agricultural Fair, Blue Hill, in early Sept.

College sports: Sports activities at the University of Maine, at Orono, are open to the public: football, basketball, hockey, etc. For information call 581–7131.

HISTORIC SITES AND HOUSES. In Blue Hill—**Jonathan Fisher Memorial,** Main St./Rte. 15 (no tel.). Home of town's first minister (1814), with many of his homemade furnishings on display.

In Castine—**Fort George** (1779), Rte. 166A (no tel.). British-built fort with interpretive panels chronicling fort's history.

MUSEUMS. Local museums exhibit artifacts and memorabilia significant to the social history of the towns and the scientific importance of the coast. Most museums charge admission or request a small donation. Call ahead for days and hours.

Bangor

Bangor Historical Society Museum, 159 Union St. (942–5766). Exhibits of local memorabilia housed in historic Thomas Hill House (1834).

Bar Harbor

Bar Harbor Historical Society Museum, Jesup Memorial Library, 34 Mt. Desert St. (288–3838). Early photographs and memorabilia of Bar Harbor in the golden days before the fire of 1947.

The Jackson Laboratory, Rte. 3 (3½ mi. south of Bar Harbor) (288–3371). Active center for mammalian genetics research.

The Natural History Museum, College of the Atlantic, Bar Harbor 04609 (288–5015). Displays on whales, birds, and land mammals of the Mount Desert Island area; interpretive programs daily.

Robert Abbe Museum of Stone Age Antiquities, Sieur de Monts Spring, Acadia National Park (288–3519). Exhibits of Stone Age tools and early Indian life.

Castine

Wilson Museum, Perkins St. (no tel.). Geology, maritime, and North American Indian collections, plus artifacts dating back to prehistoric times.

Ellsworth

Col. Black Mansion, W. Main St. (667–8671). Georgian home furnished with period furniture; lovely gardens.

Stanwood Homestead Museum, Bar Harbor Road, Rte. 3 (667–8460). A memorial to pioneer ornithologist Cordelia J. Stanwood, with many bird specimens on exhibit; adjacent is a bird sanctuary with picnic grounds and walking trails.

Islesford

Islesford Historical Museum, Little Cranberry Island (no tel.). Exhibits on the early history of Acadia.

Old Town

Penobscot National Historical Society, Indian Island (827–2271). Exhibits detail the entire history of the Penobscot Indian Nation.

Orono

University of Maine Anthropology Museum, South Stevens Hall (581–1901). American Indian exhibits, especially Maine Indians and Maine prehistory; rotating exhibits from other museums.

University of Maine Planetarium, Wingate Hall (581–1341). Spectacular star shows available to the public.

THEATER AND MUSIC. Penobscot Theatre Company, Maine's only year-round professional theater company, performs Broadway hits and contemporary drama at Bangor in winter and, as **Acadia Repertory Company,** at Somesville (on Mount Desert Island) in summer. For information: Main St. at Union, Bangor 04401 (942–3333); Masonic Hall, Somesville 04679 (244–7260). **Cold Comfort Summer Theater** presents musicals and dramas at Emerson Hall, Castine 04421 (326–9041).

Bangor Symphony Orchestra, Union St., Bangor 04401, is the country's oldest continuing symphony orchestra.

The **Maine Center for the Arts,** at the University of Maine in Orono (581–1755), is a showcase for the arts Down East. A variety of musical and dance events are presented throughout the year in the modern, acoustically outstanding Hutchins Concert Hall.

The **Domaine School** for orchestra conductors (422–6251) presents public symphony concerts during the summer at Monteux Memorial Hall, Hancock.

SHOPPING. Bass, Hathaway, and other brand-name factory outlet stores are found in Bangor, Brewer, Dexter, and Ellsworth. At **H.O.M.E.,** on Rte. 1 in East Orland (469–7961), craftspeople rekindle the dormant skills of Maine's rural folks. There are weaving and pottery demonstrations; items handmade in Maine are for sale in the store.

WASHINGTON COUNTY

Washington County is one of the last undeveloped areas of the Atlantic Coast. Its 2,628 square miles make it larger than the states of Delaware and Rhode Island combined, and it is wild (1.47 million acres of woods, 133,000 acres of lakes and ponds, the rest cropland and pasture). Fondly called Sunrise County, this easternmost county in the United States is still a place where you can get away from it all to beachcomb, fish, hike, hunt, canoe, swim, paint, take photographs, seek antiques, study rocks and wildflowers, and camp out in the wilderness.

Machias Area

Route 1 east from Cherryfield to Machias (pronounced Match-EYE-iss), the county seat, passes by the headlands of several bays. The miles of meandering shoreline vary from stark, rocky ledge to quiet coves, making the area one of the most picturesque sections of the Maine coast. At Jonesport, fishing is the way of life—mainly for lobster but also for scallops, clams, and many types of fish.

There are broad stretches of blueberry barrens, starting between Columbia Falls and Machias and extending deep into the central part of the county. Ninety percent of the nation's low-bush crop is harvested right here. And this is spectacular fishing country. There are 46 trout streams in Harrington. The Pleasant River in Columbia Falls and the Machias River in Whitneyville are premier locations for Atlantic salmon fishing.

Fort O'Brien, in Machiasport five miles south of Machias on Route 92, was the site of the first significant naval engagement of the Revolution (five days before the Battle of Bunker Hill). The British schooner *Margaretta* was captured in 1775 by Jeremiah O'Brien and a motley crew of 40 colonists armed with swords and pitchforks.

Burnham Tavern (1770), at Main and Free Streets in Machias, the oldest building in eastern Maine, has been restored and is operated by the Daughters of the American Revolution as a museum. It contains period furnishings and items relating to the capture of the *Margaretta.*

If you follow Route 191 along the coast to Lubec, you pass through Cutler. This is the location of Radio Cutler, the U.S. Navy's Radio Transmitting Station. There are 26 towers, soaring up to 1,000 feet in the air, on the 2,800-acre site. It is the most powerful radio transmitting station in the world.

Lubec and Eastport

Lubec is a fishing and sardine-canning town, the gateway to Canada's Campobello Island and Roosevelt Campobello International Park. The park, on Route 774 in Welshpool, New Brunswick, is a 2,600-acre nature area with picnic sites, vistas, and a lookout at Friar's Head. The summer home (1897) of President Franklin D. Roosevelt has been preserved and contains many original family furnishings.

A main attraction of the Lubec area is a drive down to Quoddy Head State Park. Candy-striped West Quoddy Head Light (1807) stands on the easternmost point of land in the United States (hence the county's nickname, Sunrise County). Tides here are the greatest in the nation, a variation of some 20 to 28 feet between high and low tide.

Lubec and Eastport sit opposite each other, about three miles apart, at the mouth of Cobscook Bay. But to travel from one town to the other by land is a 40-mile trip. The bonus for making the circuit is a stop midway at Cobscook Bay State Park and the Moosehorn National Wildlife Refuge. The refuge, 22,565 acres of woods, fields, streams, and ponds, is home to deer, moose, beaver, mink, and an occasional seal. More than 190 species of birds make it a birdwatcher's paradise.

Eastport, located on Moose Island, was settled in 1772. During the War of 1812 it was captured by the British and held four years.

The birthplace of Maine's sardine business, Eastport no longer has fishing and canning plants, although the cool waters of Passamaquoddy Bay provide abundant sea life, from schools of herring to whales. The incredible movement of water here also generates some natural phenomena: The Old Sow Whirlpool, off the northeast tip of Moose Island, is the second largest of its kind; the Reversing Falls, in Cobscook Bay between Pembroke and Trescott, is caused by the outflow of two rivers meeting the incoming tide.

Quoddy Village, on the mainland just north of town, is a project started during the 1930s to harness the great ocean tides to generate electric power. Although there are continuing hopes that a great quantity of inexpensive power might still result, the project has never been fully developed. Part of the dam that was built underlies the present causeway linking Eastport to the mainland.

The Pleasant Point Indian Reservation, home of the Passamaquoddy Tribe of the Abnaki Indian Nation, is on Route 190 south of Perry. Many members of the tribe make their home here and sell intricately woven baskets to visitors. Perry, incidentally, is located halfway between the equator and the North Pole; a small stone marks the point at a roadside picnic area on Route 1.

Calais

Calais is a busy port of entry at the border between Maine and New Brunswick, Canada. If you're planning to visit Calais, the first thing you should know is that it is pronounced CAL-lus (not cal-LAY). Surrounded by forests and fields, lakes and streams, Calais is the commercial center of eastern Washington County. The major employer is Georgia-Pacific Corp., which operates a pulp, paperboard, and stud mill in nearby Woodland.

Calais and its sister city across the St. Croix River, St. Stephen, New Brunswick, have an unusually close community bond. They share essential municipal services, such as police and fire protection, and there is cooperative trade and commerce. The close bond is celebrated each August with a week-long International Festival.

St. Croix Island, about nine miles downstream from Calais, was named an international historic site in 1982 in a joint U.S.–Canadian ceremony. It was on St. Croix Island in 1604 that Samuel de Champlain and Sieur de Monts, along with about 100 soldiers and traders, tried in vain to found a permanent settlement. After one devastating winter, they moved east to Port Royal, Nova Scotia.

Sparsely populated central and northern Washington County has few roads, but you will find the rolling hills and woodlands perfect for a hunting or wilderness vacation or a canoe expedition. There are several lodges and sporting camps among the winding streams and sparkling lakes.

PRACTICAL INFORMATION FOR WASHINGTON COUNTY

Note: The area code for all Maine is 207

HOW TO GET THERE AND AROUND. By plane: Connections using private planes or charter flying services may be made between Bangor or Bar Harbor Airports and the local airports at Lubec, Machias, Princeton, and Eastport. For information on flying services operating in Washington County: Clinton Tuttle (853–4707), in Perry; Will Ketchen (454–2485) and Flying Ed Arbo (454–7461), in Charlotte; and Eastern Maine Aviation (853–4410), in Perry. (See *Acadia* "How To Get There and Around" for national and regional airlines serving Bangor and Bar Harbor airports.)

By bus: Bus service is available on Greyhound Lines between Bangor and St. Stephen, New Brunswick, with intermediate stops at towns in Washington County.

By car: From Portland and points south, I–95 to Bangor and Rte. 9 is the shortest route to Calais. Rte. 9 makes a beeline through the blueberry barrens and timberland of northern Washington County en route from Bangor to Calais.

Rte. 1 follows the coast and turns north at the Canadian border, passing through the major towns of Washington County and providing access to local highways and roads which lead to coastal towns and villages. From the Maritime Provinces of Canada, visitors take New Brunswick Rte. 1 to the border crossing between St. Stephen, N.B., and Calais.

HOTELS AND MOTELS. Nature lovers who are attracted to Washington County often plan a camping vacation. For those who are not so inclined, comfortable accommodations are available in motels and lodges.

Sporting camps catering to hunters and fishermen abound in the wilderness areas of northern Maine, beginning in the Grand Lake Stream area of northern Washington County. These camps are operated by people whose way of life is the great outdoors. Lodgings in the sporting camps may consist of housekeeping cabins or a central lodge with sleeping cabins. Meals are generally included, and guide service is available. Reservations are necessary.

Rates are based on double occupancy: *Expensive,* $50–$70; *Moderate,* $30–$50; *Inexpensive,* $30 or less. There is a 7% Maine state lodging tax. Unless otherwise indicated, hotels are open year-round.

Calais

Heslin's Motel and Cottages, Rte. 1, 04619 (454–3762). *Moderate–Expensive.* Informal motel and cottages overlook the St. Croix River and Canada. Pool. Restaurant, cocktail lounge. Canoeing, fishing, and wilderness expeditions available. Open June–Oct.

Grand Lake Stream

Leen's Lodge, Box 40, 04637 (796–5575). *Expensive.* From freshwater fishing to cocktail get-togethers, this family resort offers variety. Boats and guides available. Nicely furnished cottages have fireplaces or woodstoves. Excellent meals included. Open May–Oct.

INNS, GUEST HOUSES, BED AND BREAKFASTS. Travelers can find country inns in coastal towns. Some residents open their homes to overnight guests, offering both comfortable accommodations and an opportunity to meet local folks. The Maine Publicity Bureau (see *Tourist Information*) has a few area bed and breakfasts in their annual listing; the local Chambers of Commerce will also make recommendations.

The inns below fall into the *moderate* price category.

Cherryfield

Black Shutter Inn, Rte. 1, 04622 (546–2175). Riverside bed-and-breakfast inn. Large, comfortable home was built in the 1850s. Reservations recommended.

Dennysville

Lincoln House Country Inn, Rte. 1, 04628 (726–3953). Restored (1787) Georgian colonial offers seclusion, warm hospitality, peace and quiet. Choice birdwatching and Atlantic salmon fishing. Fine dining.

Eastport

Weston House, 26 Boynton St., 04631 (853–2907). Gracious bed-and-breakfast inn in 1810 historic homestead. Five comfortable rooms, elegantly furnished. Sumptuous breakfast; afternoon sherry or tea.

Lubec

Home Port Inn, 45 Main St., 04652 (733–2077). Pleasant accommodations and fine dining in a comfortable home (1880) in the historic section of town. No children under 7. No smoking. Open May–Nov.

RESTAURANTS. Dining in Washington County ranges from candlelight dinners to casual meals to do-it-yourself seafood feasts. Clams, lobsters, and mussels are available in abundance at stands along Rte. 1. Eat them on the spot, or—if you have a cooler in the car—take some along to cook later. Community suppers are scheduled at churches and halls in many small towns or villages and are open to the public. Look for posters in grocery or convenience stores and prepare yourself for a delicious covered-dish dinner—which often includes baked beans and home-baked pies.

The restaurants suggested below, except where indicated, are open year-round, serve lunch and dinner, and accept major credit cards. Price ranges per person for a complete dinner excluding beverages, tax, and tip are: *Expensive,* $20–$30; *Moderate,* $10–$20; *Inexpensive,* $10 or less.

Calais

Cold Spring Lobster House Restaurant, Rte. 1 south of town (454–3045). *Moderate.* At Cold Spring Lodge. Lobster, of course, and other local seafood. Open summer only.

Dennysville

Lincoln House, Rte. 1 (726–3953). *Expensive.* Restored 18th-century colonial, now an inn with two small dining rooms. Single seating for dinner. Limited menu changes nightly. Reservations required. Open Apr.–Dec.

Eastport

Cannery Restaurant, N. Water St. (853–4800). *Moderate–Expensive.* At the ferry landing. Live lobsters, fresh local seafood, and steaks. Dinner only. Reservations recommended. Informal meals and takeout orders are available at The Clam Kibben. Summer only.

Machias

Micmac Farm, Rte. 92, Machiasport (255–3008). *Expensive.* Casual dining in restored 1776 farmhouse on Machias River. Continental cuisine. No liquor license; setups provided. Reservations.

5 Water Street, 5 Water St. (255–4153). *Moderate.* Fine food and drink served by candlelight. Varied menu includes steaks and chops, as well as vegetarian dishes.

Helen's Restaurant, E. Main St. (255–8423). *Inexpensive–Moderate.* Family restaurant; good food at modest prices. Stop in for the pies.

Milbridge

Blueberry Goose Inn, Main St. (546–7533). *Moderate.* Continental cuisine served in New England inn with a view of the ocean from the dining room.

TOURIST INFORMATION. Maps, booklets, and brochures may be requested from the Maine Publicity Bureau, 97 Winthrop St., Hallowell 04347 (289–2423) and from the following local organizations: Washington County Regional Planning Commission, 63 Main St., Box 497, Machias 04654 (255–8686); Calais Chamber of Commerce, Box 368, Calais 04619 (454–2521); Eastport Area Chamber of Commerce, Box 254, 78 High St., Eastport 04631 (853–4644); Lubec Chamber of Commerce, School St., Lubec 04652 (733–2223); and Grand Lake Stream Chamber of Commerce, Box 76, Grand Lake Stream 04637 (796–5584).

The Maine Publicity Bureau operates a regional tourist information center on Main St., Calais, year-round.

A visitors center is operated by the National Park Service, on Rte. 1 just south of Red Beach (Calais), for information on historic St. Croix Island.

TOURS. Boat tours: From mid-June through mid-Sept., the Deer Island, N.B., car ferry makes hourly runs between Eastport and Campobello Island. En route, when the tide is right, passengers can view the Old Sow Whirlpool off the northeastern tip of Moose Island.

Whales, porpoises, seals, and puffins summer in the Bay of Fundy. Whale-watching expeditions depart from Lubec for daytrips during the summer on the *Seafarer* (733–5584); from Jonesport with Capt. Barna B. Norton, RR 1, Box 340, Jonesport 04649 (497–5933) June–Dec.; and from Machias for long weekends or a week's duration mid-June–Oct. with Seafarers Expeditions, Box 102, Machias 04654 (255–8816). Reservations are necessary, because the trips are popular; and the weather is often unpredictable.

Industrial plant tours: The Georgia Pacific Paper Mill, in Woodland (427–3311), operates tours of its plant on weekday mornings mid-June–Aug. No sandals, high-heels, cameras, or children under 12 are permitted. Tours start at the Administration Building.

["\n\n\n"]

In Cherryfield, Cherryfield Foods Inc. (546–7573) offers tours of its blueberry processing plant to small groups. Frozen blueberries are available at the factory.

Sardine-packing plants in Milbridge, Machiasport, Lubec, and Eastport are open to visitors. Inquire locally.

SEASONAL EVENTS. July: World's Fastest Lobster Boat Races, Jonesport (early July); Old Home Week Festival, Eastport (early July). **August:** Anniversary Celebration/Codfish Relay Race/Lobster Cookout, Milbridge (early Aug.); Passamaquoddy Tribe Ceremonial Day, Pleasant Point Eastport, (early Aug.); International Festival, Calais (mid-Aug.); Crafts Fair and Blueberry Festival, Machias (mid-Aug.).

PARKS. State Parks in Washington County provide a variety of outdoor experiences. Most open by May 15, and the season usually extends through mid-Oct. Leashed pets are allowed, but not on beaches. For information: Maine Bureau of Parks and Recreation, Station 22, Augusta 04333 (289–3824).

State parks in this region are: **Cobscook Bay** (Dennysville)—camping, picnicking, fishing, clamming, snowmobiling, hiking, boating, part of the Moosehorn National Wildlife Refuge is adjacent; **Quoddy Head** (Lubec)—adjacent to West Quoddy Head Light, easternmost point of land in the U.S., high and low tides vary by 20–28 ft., picnicking, shoreline hiking trail, beautiful spot for photography; **Roque Bluffs** (Roque Bluffs)—300-acre day-use park on Englishman Bay, picnicking, swimming, fishing.

INDIANS. The **Pleasant Point Indian Reservation,** on a piece of land that juts into the bay between Eastport and Perry, is home to the Passamaquoddy Tribe, part of the Abnaki Nation. About 200 members of the tribe that supported the colonists during the American Revolution have been honored with a monument erected at the cemetery by the Daughters of the American Revolution. Beautifully handcrafted baskets and souvenirs may be purchased on the reservation. All Passamaquoddy lands in eastern Maine, acquired through the Indian Land Claims Settlement of 1981, are administered at Pleasant Point.

WILDLIFE. Moosehorn National Wildlife Refuge, 6 mi. south of Calais at Baring (454–3521), consists of 22,775 acres of woods, fields, streams, and ponds. There are miles of trails and logging roads for an easy walk or backpacking—and wild blueberries for the picking. Nearly 200 species of birds and 39 species of mammals have been recorded.

Puffins, seals, and whales make their summer home in the **Bay of Fundy;** boat trips from Eastport, Lubec, and Machias are available for a close look at these wonderful creatures (see *Tours*).

BEACHES. Saltwater swimming is available at **Roque Bluffs State Park**—but it's cold! Freshwater swimming is also available at Roque Bluffs, as well as at several lakes. For example: **Reynolds Beach** on Meddybemps Lake, jct. Rtes. 191 and 214 south of Calais; **Six-Mile Lake,** on Rte. 192 north of Machias; **Gardners Lake,** Chases Mill Road off Rte. 1, East Machias.

SPORTS. Boating: For those who carry their boats on trailers, boat-launching ramps are located in many places along the shore and at nearly all the lakes. At villages all along the coast, boats are for hire for fishing or for sightseeing expeditions. Canoeists will enjoy a paddle around one of the numerous lakes in the region or a run down the Machias River. (Many think the Machias River is the state's premier river for canoeing; and it can be run throughout the summer.)

Hiking: Hiking trails are laid out for easy walks or backpacking excursions at State Parks in the county and at Moosehorn National Wildlife Refuge.

Golf: There is a nine-hole course open to the public in Jonesboro.

FISHING. Saltwater fishermen will find Atlantic smelt, cod, mackerel, halibut, flounder, pollock, haddock, striped bass, and tuna. For a rugged and challenging fishing experience, charter trips can be arranged in Milbridge, Jonesport, and Eastport. Saltwater fishing does not require a license.

The Dennys River, which empties into Cobscook Bay at Dennysville, is famous for Atlantic salmon fishing, as are Columbia Falls on the Pleasant River and Whitneyville on the Machias River. Maine is the only state where Atlantic salmon may be caught, and a special license is required.

At the hundreds of lakes and streams in Washington County, freshwater fishermen catch landlocked salmon, togue, brook trout, pickerel, smallmouth bass, and perch. There are 46 different trout-fishing streams in and around the town of Harrington. Grand Lake Stream, a 3-mi. stretch of rapid water, is very popular with fishing enthusiasts. All nonresident freshwater fishermen over the age of 12 require a fishing license; licenses are generally available at local sporting goods or hardware stores. Write to Department of Inland Fisheries and Wildlife, Station 41, State House, Augusta 04333 (289–2043) for information. For wilderness trips, guide service is recommended. Inquire locally or contact: Maine Professional Guides Association, Box 265, Medway 04460.

HUNTING. The many lakes, streams, and swamps in the area provide hunters with an abundance of deer, waterfowl, woodcock, and other wildlife. Strict hunting regulations are enforced for safety and to manage the wildlife. Licenses are required for all hunters 10 years old or over and may be purchased at local sporting goods or hardware stores. Applicants for adult firearms licenses must show proof of having previously held an adult license or having successfully completed an approved hunter safety course. Hunting on certain Indian territories is regulated by the tribes, and special permission must be obtained. For further information: Department of Inland Fisheries and Wildlife (see *Fishing*). Guide service is recommended for wilderness trips.

CAMPING. Camping is permitted at Cobscook State Park, in Dennysville. There are about 100 well-spaced campsites. Call 289–3824 for reservations.

Facilities in privately owned campsites range from simple basics in the wilderness to deluxe cabins. The Maine Publicity Bureau (see *Tourist Information*) will send you its *Maine Guide to Camping,* which lists privately operated trailer parks, campsites, and conveniences available.

HISTORIC SITES AND HOUSES. A rich heritage of international cooperation exists in the area of Maine adjacent to the Canadian border. Designated historic sites range from Maine's earliest settlement to a 20th-century presidential vacation home.

Calais

St. Croix Island, 9 mi. south on Rte. 1. The tiny island in the St. Croix River where Champlain and de Monts and about 100 others attempted a permanent settlement in 1604–5. Named an International Historic Site in 1982.

Columbia Falls

Ruggles House (1818), ¼ mi. off Rte. 1 (no tel.). Federal-style residence with intricately carved mouldings and a flying staircase that is a masterpiece.

Lubec

Roosevelt Campobello International Park, Welshpool, Campobello Island, N.B., Canada (506–752–2922). Lubec is the gateway to the island that became the summer home of Franklin Delano Roosevelt and his family from 1883–1921. The 34-room cottage with views of Passamaquoddy Bay, nature trails, and observation platforms is open to visitors in the summer.

Machias

Burnham Tavern (1770), Main and Free Sts. (Rte. 192) (255–4432). Pre-Revolutionary tavern (restored in 1907) with period furnishings and items relating to the initial naval battle of the Revolutionary War.
Fort O'Brien (1775), Rte. 92 (no tel.). Overlooking Machias Bay. Site of first naval battle of the Revolutionary War.

THEATER AND MUSIC. At the University of Maine at Machias, the **Stage Front Theater** presents a variety of summer programs: music, art, and cinema. For information: UMM Stage Front Theater, O'Brien Ave., Machias 04654 (255–3313).

Also in Machias, a series of summer chamber concerts is presented at the Center Street Congregational Church. For information: **Machias Bay Chamber Concerts,** Box 332, Machias 04654 (255–3889).

THE WESTERN LAKES AND MOUNTAINS

Fertile valleys, thick forest, rugged mountains, and sparkling lakes lie in store for travelers to the area along Maine's western boundary with New Hampshire. A wealth of recreational opportunities is available—both summer and winter—and there are few crowds. Life slips along at a leisurely pace, the tranquility is mesmerizing, the outdoor life reigns supreme.

Sebago Lake and Long Lake

Crystal-clear Sebago Lake, second largest in the state, is about 14 miles long and 11 miles wide. At points it reaches a depth of 400 feet. Spectacular fishing awaits the angler: land-locked salmon, trout, bass, and perch.

From Sebago Lake Village, at the southern tip of the lake, Route 114 follows the western shore through several waterfront villages to Naples. Route 35 follows the eastern shore of the lake from Sebago Lake Village to North Windham. (Thousands of Indian relics have been discovered here, as well as an Indian burial ground said to be one of the largest in the United States.) Route 302 continues along the eastern shore to South Casco, site of Nathaniel Hawthorne's boyhood home (1812) on Hawthorne Road.

Sebago Lake State Park, partly in South Casco and partly in Naples, is a 1,300-acre lakeside park that straddles the Songo River. The South Casco side is for day use only; the Naples side has camping facilities.

The Songo River connects Sebago Lake with Long Lake directly north. In the mid-1800s, the Cumberland-Oxford Canal was the important link between Portland and Harrison (at the northern tip of Long Lake). The railroad, coming into the area in the 1870s, made the canal obsolete, but one operating lock survives: Songo Lock, located on the Songo River between the two lakes. Pleasure boats keep the lock active, and boat rides through it are available from Naples.

Bridgton is at the head of Long Lake, on its western shore. This resort area attracts vacationers year-round: golf and tennis in the spring; swimming, fishing, and boating in the summer; foliage viewing, antiquing, and small-game hunting in the fall; and skiing, snowmobiling, and ice fishing in the winter. Bridgton has many waterfront campgrounds and cottage rentals. The Pleasant Mountain Ski Area, on Route 32, has 20 miles of trails and well-groomed slopes. The 4,000-foot chair lift takes you to the summit for skiing in the winter; in summer you can sweep down the mountain on the Alpine Slide.

Poland, Norway, Paris

Poland Spring, just off Route 26, is the source of the familiar mineral water. You can drive through the grounds of this once elegant resort, see the actual Poland Spring, and visit the State of Maine Building, built for the World's Columbian Exposition in Chicago in 1893 and reconstructed here on the grounds of the former Poland Spring Inn.

At the Cumberland/Androscoggin county line, also on Route 26, you will find the Shaker Museum. The members of this sect, established in 1793, continue their traditional lifestyle. There is a store and museum, with furniture, textiles, folk art, wooden objects, and farm tools on display and for sale.

Norway is a busy community famous for the manufacture of snowshoes and toboggans. Most of the snowshoes used by our armed forces in World War II were made here, and Admiral Peary trod to the North Pole on Norway snowshoes.

Just north of South Paris, be on the lookout for a small sign pointing east (an unnumbered route) to Paris Hill, once a main stop on the stagecoach route between Portland and Montreal. This is one of the prettiest towns in New England, with handsome houses and a wide, peaceful village green. Virtually unknown to the present-day traveler, it was once the business center of the area, and it retains a certain dignity. Hannibal Hamlin, Vice-President of the United States under Abraham Lincoln, was born here; you can see his childhood home next door to the Old Stone Jail.

Perham's Mineral Store, on Route 26 at Trap Corner, West Paris, attracts thousands of visitors annually to see and buy from the mineral and gem collection. Jane Perham, owner of this unpretentious but extraordinary shop, is a rock hound's friend who allows collectors to visit and chip away at the five mines she owns in the area. Maps and information are available at the store.

Bethel to Rumford

Bethel, an authentic nineteenth-century village nestled in the Oxford Hills, quiet and unpretentious, is the regional center of a thriving wood-products industry. Bethel is typically New England, with a common and handsome homes lining its streets.

The Bethel Inn, on the common, has put together a brochure outlining a walking tour of the town. Some of the highlights are: the Moses Mason Museum, a fully restored Federal-style house (1813); Gould Academy, one of the finest preparatory schools in the state; Dr. John G. Gehring Clinic, a Queen Anne-style house (1896) where Dr. Gehring studied and practiced the treatment of nervous disorders; several of the lovely homes located in the Broad Street Historic District and around the common; and the Bethel Inn (1833), a thriving year-round resort.

You will discover four-season recreation in the Bethel area—lake swimming and boating, golf, hiking, fishing, rock hounding, or skiing at Sunday River and Mount Abram ski areas. There are dramatic views of New Hampshire's White Mountains, for Bethel is near the edge of White Mountain National Forest.

Traveling north on Routes 5 and 26 brings you to Newry. The Artist's Covered Bridge (1872), which crosses the Sunday River near Newry, is the most photographed, most painted covered bridge in Maine. At Grafton Notch State Park, farther north on Route 16, sightseers and hikers are rewarded with incredibly lovely vistas and spectacular natural sights. Old Speck Mountain (4,150 feet), on the Appalachian Trail, has the highest forest lookout tower in Maine; Screw-Auger Falls is where the Bear River has drilled holes as deep as 25 feet into the rock riverbed.

Rumford, the largest community in the area, has a sizable business district. Boise Cascade, Rumford's predominant employer, operates one of the largest paper mills in the world, and it looms over the downtown landscape. The Ellis, Swift, and Concord rivers flow into the Androscoggin River at Rumford; Pennacook Falls can be viewed from the downtown business section of town.

Route 17 north from Rumford follows the rocky Swift River through meadow, woods, and sleepy towns. At Byron you are likely to see people wading among the rocks, sifting the sand of the river bottom as they pan for gold. Rent a kit along the roadside and try your luck!

Rangeley Area

Rangeley, the central town of this beautiful area, has a frontier quality; in a way, it is the last outpost before the pure wilderness that lies beyond. A chain of lakes and connecting streams create an area of more than 450 square miles of playground for sportsmen and lovers of the great outdoors: flyfishing, hunting, sailing, canoeing, swimming, hiking, camping, golfing, skiing, and snowmobiling. In and around the town of Rangeley, all manner of accommodations (resorts, hotels, lodges, camps, cottages) and a variety of restaurants are available.

The small town of Oquossoc is a few miles west of Rangeley along Routes 4 and 16. South of Oquossoc, on Route 17 at the Height of Land, a roadside turnoff provides a truly exquisite view. Lake Mooselookmeguntic, other lakes, islands, mountains, golden shores, patches of pine, the blue sky and water, form an unforgettable mosaic—one of the most extensive panoramic views in the state.

Rangeley Lake State Park, 691 acres of fragrant fir trees and mountain views, is on the south shore of Rangeley Lake with campsites, a boat-launching ramp, and a swimming and picnicking area.

Hikers have access to the Appalachian Trail where it crosses scenic Route 17 a few miles southwest of Rangeley Lake and again where it cuts across Route 4 about eight miles southeast of Rangeley.

From December through April you can ski Rangeley's Saddleback Mountain (4,116 feet). There are slopes and trails appropriate for all levels of competence from beginner to expert, including downhill racers. The Ski Nordic Touring Center at Saddleback offers 27 miles of scenic groomed trails through the wilderness.

More than 100 miles of trails are marked for safe, exciting snowmobiling. Rangeley Lake freezes solid in the winter, creating a further invitation to snowmobilers.

More and more travelers are visiting Rangeley each March to join in the excitement of the two-day, 30-mile Sled Dog Race. Contestants and teams come from all over northern New England, upper New York State, and Canada.

Rangeley is not far from Kingfield and the Carrabassett Valley. As you drive along Route 16, you can see the breathtaking vistas of mountains in this area. In the late afternoon you're likely to spot a moose by the side of the road.

Kingfield and the Carrabassett Valley

Kingfield is a busy little town in the Carrabassett River Valley, the hometown of F. E. and F. O. Stanley, inventors of the first steam-driven automobile, the Stanley Steamer.

The Carrabassett Valley area has become one of the East's leading four-season recreation spots. About 10 miles north of Kingfield, on Route 16, Sugarloaf/USA at Sugarloaf Mountain (4,237 feet, Maine's second-highest peak) is the largest winter resort in Maine. There are superb ski trails: novice, intermediate, and super steep; a 45-meter ski jump; and a Robert Trent Jones golf course and a modern Alpine village at the base. Enclosed four-passenger gondolas make the 9,000-foot (round-trip) ride to the summit, allowing magnificent views winter, spring, summer, and fall. Hunting and fishing opportunities are also available in the area in their respective seasons, and there are diversified winter activities in addition to skiing.

Farmington and Livermore

South of Kingfield and Rangeley, along Route 4, Farmington is a commercial center. The Nordica Homestead (1840), on Holley Road off Route 4, is the birthplace of the opera singer Lillian Nordica. A collection of her costumes, music, and programs are displayed at the museum. The Little Red Schoolhouse (1852), at the junction of Routes 4 and 2, serves as a local information booth.

Wilton, just south of Farmington on Route 4, is the home of the famous G. H. Bass Company, shoemakers.

Livermore and Livermore Falls are quiet communities situated among small ponds and streams in the hill country of Androscoggin County. It is primarily an agricultural area—apple country—although International Paper Company has enormous paper mills in Livermore Falls and in nearby Chisholm. Washburn-Norlands Center, on Norlands Road in Liver-more (just a mile or so north of Route 108), is a 430-acre working farm operated just as it would have been around 1870. The grounds of this living history center include the Washburn Mansion (1867), a one-room school (1823), a church (1828), and a stone library (1883).

Auburn and Lewiston

Auburn and Lewiston are twin cities on either side of the Androscoggin River, making up the second largest metropolitan district in Maine and a key commercial, industrial, and cultural center.

Residential Auburn has a diverse economic base. It is the agricultural trading center for the area on the one hand; on the other, there are several industrial parks housing a variety of businesses. Auburn remains a major shoe-manufacturing center as well. Lost Valley Ski Area is nearby, and just out of town, Lake Auburn is available for fishing, boating, and peaceful refreshment.

Lewiston is Maine's principal textile manufacturing town. The Bates Manufacturing Company, makers of bedspreads, draperies, and other linens, is located here. (An outlet store next door to the factory attracts bargain hunters.) Bates College, the well-known liberal arts institution, is located on 75 acres in Lewiston.

PRACTICAL INFORMATION FOR
THE WESTERN LAKES AND MOUNTAINS

Note: The area code for all Maine is 207

HOW TO GET THERE AND AROUND. By plane: Scheduled commuter service is available into Lewiston/Auburn on Valley Airlines (800–322–1008). Flying services provide "sports" with flights (float or wheel) to remote areas: in Rangeley, Mountain Air Services (864–5307); in Kingfield, Web-air (237–2701).

By bus: Service is available to Lewiston on Greyhound's Portland-Bangor run. Vermont Transit (207–772–6587) offers service between Portland and towns in Vermont through Naples, Bridgton, and Bethel.

Local service is available in the Oxford Hills area through Oxford Hills Transit, Norway (667–5796). Service is available between Auburn and Rumford and Auburn and Farmington (with intermediate stops on both routes) through Western Maine Transportation Services, Inc., Rumford (800–482–0170). Lewiston/Auburn local service is provided by Lewiston/Auburn Hudson Bus Lines (738–2033).

By car: Various exits along the Maine Turnpike/I–95 provide access to routes leading to the vacation centers of western Maine: Exit 8 (Portland) connects with Rte. 302 to Sebago Lake. From Exit 11 (Gray), Rte. 26 goes north through the Oxford Hills to Bethel, Grafton Notch State Park, and the mountains; Exit 12 (Auburn) connects with Rte. 4 north through Farmington to the Rangeley Lakes area; at Farmington, Rte. 27 north leads to Kingfield and the Carrabassett Valley. To approach this area through New Hampshire (from Canada, northern New England, or as an alternate route from the south), Rte. 302 leads through Fryeburg to Bridgton and Sebago Lake; Rte. 2 passes the White Mountain National Forest en route to Bethel, Rumford, and Farmington; and Rte. 16 is a scenic mountain road to Rangeley and Kingfield. Route 17 between Rumford and the Rangeley area is an especially scenic trip, as is the ride through the White Mountain National Forest on Rte. 113, which goes between Fryeburg and Gilead (near Bethel).

HOTELS, MOTELS AND COTTAGES. All manner of accommodations can be found in the Western Lakes and Mountains resort towns: ski resorts, cozy cabins nestled in the mountains, and sleek motels are all represented. Some lodgings around the Sebago Lake area close for the winter.

Sporting camps in the Rangeley Lakes area are popular for fishing and hunting vacations; meals are usually included, and guide and float-plane service can be arranged. For information: Rangeley Area Chamber of Commerce (see *Tourist Information*).

Rates are based on double occupancy, in season: *Deluxe,* $80 and up; *Expensive,* $60–$80; *Moderate,* $40–$60; *Inexpensive,* $40 or less. There is a 7% Maine state lodging tax. Unless otherwise indicated, hotels are open year-round.

Bethel

Bethel Inn and Country Club, On the Common, 04217 (824–2175). *Expensive–Deluxe.* Classic country resort, with lovely grounds. Rooms in main inn or adjacent buildings. Modern comforts, personal service, excellent cuisine, friendly atmosphere. Winter skiing, summer boating, tennis, golf course at the back door, fishing, swimming in the lake or pool, and more.

Bridgton

Tarry-A-While Resort, Ridge Rd., on Highland Lake, 04009 (647–2522). *Moderate–Expensive.* Hospitable lakeside resort—like stepping into Switzerland. All water sports, sandy beach, tennis; golf nearby. Rates include breakfast and dinner in the Switzer Stubli Dining Room. No credit cards. Open June–Sept.

Center Lovell

Quisisana, Rte. 5, 04016 (925–3500). *Deluxe.* Charming cottages scattered among the pines on lovely Lake Kezar. Sand beaches, boating, fishing, tennis, hiking. Superb food served in the dining room, adjacent to the main lodge. Staff includes performers from noted music schools who entertain in the evenings.

Westways, Rte. 5, 04016 (928–2663). *Deluxe.* Former corporate retreat on Kezar Lake, at the edge of the White Mountain National Forest. Rustic main lodge and surrounding cottages offer woodsy seclusion and magnificent lake views. Weekly rates available. Closed Apr. and Nov.

Kingfield–Carrabassett Valley

Sugarloaf Inn, at the foot of Sugarloaf Mt., Carrabassett Valley, 04947 (237–2701). *Expensive–Deluxe.* Modern, full-service inn. Exceptional skiing at your door in winter; pool, tennis, and Robert Trent Jones golf course in summer. Dining room and cocktail lounge.

The Herbert, Main St., 04947 (265–2000). *Expensive.* Gracious hotel restored and refurbished to its original 1913 style. Traditional New England dining.

Rangeley

Saddleback Lake Lodge, Box 620, 04970 (864–3627). *Expensive.* Individual log cabins nestled in the woods at the base of Saddleback Mt. Swim or fish in the lake outside your door. Delicious Maine fare included in rates. Central lodge with game room. Open mid-June–Oct.

Hunter Cove, Mingo Loop Rd. 04970 (864–3383). *Moderate.* Nine lakeside housekeeping cottages on six wooded acres each accommodate four to eight guests. Attractively furnished; some units have hot tubs. Boat rental available. Snowmobile from your door.

Town and Lake Motel, Main St., 04970 (864–3755). *Moderate.* On Rangeley Lake. Pleasant family resort with motel units and well-furnished housekeeping cottages. Beach area, boating, canoeing, play area. Winter skiing and snowmobiling. Pets permitted.

Rumford

Madison Motor Inn, Rte. 2, 04276 (364–7973). *Moderate–Expensive.* Nicely decorated, pleasant rooms (some with balconies or steam baths). Views of Androscoggin River. Restaurant, bar, dancing. Boating, fishing, hunting, skiing nearby.

South Casco

Migis Lodge and Cottages, Rte. 302, 04077 (655–4524). *Deluxe.* On Sebago Lake amid pine-tree forest. Small lodge and 25 cabins. Learn water skiing and enjoy boating at this waterfront resort. Fine beach. Open June–Oct.

Wilson's Mills

Bosebuck Mountain Camps, on Azicohos Lake, 03579 (243–2945). *Expensive.* Rustic cabins surrounded by 200,000 acres of remote wilderness. A choice area for hunters and fishermen. All meals included; guide service available. Family and package rates in summer.

INNS, GUEST HOUSES, BED AND BREAKFASTS. There are some lovely lakeside inns in the resort communities of western Maine. For recommendations on guest houses and bed and breakfasts in the Bridgton-Naples-Sebago Lake area and in Rangeley, contact the local Chamber of Commerce or the Maine Publicity Bureau for suggestions. (See *Tourist Information.*) The following inns generally fall into the *moderate–expensive* categories.

Bethel

Four Seasons Inn, Upper Main St. 04217 (824–2755 or 800–227–7458). A large bed & breakfast inn elegantly furnished with antiques. Near ski areas.

L'Auberge, Mill Hill Rd., 04217 (824–2774). Homelike country inn at edge of village. Spacious lawns and gardens lie just beyond the front porch. Mountains, lakes, and golf course nearby. Continental breakfast included. Dinners by reservation only.

The Sudbury Inn, Lower Main St., 04217 (824–2174). Charming inn in Bethel's historic downtown. 15 quaint and cozy guest rooms with private baths. Delicious contemporary cuisine in the dining room. Lounge with live entertainment. Closed Apr. and Nov.

Bridgton

Pleasant Mountain Inn, Mountain Rd., W. Bridgton 04009 (647–2431). Small Alpine inn on Moose Pond, offering boating, beach, fishing, hunting, ice skating, tennis. At base of Pleasant Mt. ski area. Dining room.

Kingfield

Winter's Inn, Winter's Hill, 04947 (265–5421). Restored Georgian mansion, offering beautifully decorated guest rooms and a fine French restaurant. View of surrounding mountains is spectacular. Pool, tennis, and skiing available. Closed Apr., May, Nov.

Naples

The Augustus Bove House, Rtes. 302 & 114, 04055 (639–6365). A reincarnation of a historical Hotel Naples. Colonial furnishings, relaxed atmosphere. Overlooks Long Lake. Full breakfast.

Rangeley

Country Club Inn, Country Club Rd., off Rte. 4, 04970 (864–3831). A delightful inn perched high on a hill overlooking Rangeley Lake. Magnificent view of lake and mountains. Good restaurant, golf course adjacent, pool. Fishing, water sports, skiing nearby. Closed Apr. and Nov.
Rangeley Inn, Main St., 04970 (864–3341). Pleasant turn-of-the-century lakeside inn with modern motel wing. Old-fashioned comfort and hospitality. Good restaurant; bar.

Waterford

Kedarburn Inn, Rte. 35, 04088 (583–6182). Small country bed-and-breakfast inn on the shore of Lake Keoka. Winter and summer sports available nearby. Fall foliage season is breathtaking. Full breakfast included; dinner served.
Olde Rowley Inn, Rte. 35, N. Waterford 04267 (583–4143). A former stagecoach stop. Comfortable "keeping room," with open-hearth fireplace. Cozy guest rooms decorated with folk art and period furniture. Full country breakfast included.

RESTAURANTS. Very fine dining is available in many of the small inns in western Maine which have dining rooms open to the public. Most offer a relaxed atmosphere with lovely mountain or lakeside views. The restaurants suggested below, except where noted, are open year-round, serve lunch and dinner, and accept major credit cards. Price ranges per person for a complete dinner excluding beverages, tax, and tip: *Deluxe,* $30 and up; *Expensive,* $20–$30; *Moderate,* $20–$30; *Inexpensive,* $10 or less.

Auburn

No Tomatoes Restaurant, 36 Court St. (784–3919). *Moderate.* Fine Continental cuisine. Lunches and light dinners in the Garden Lounge.

Bethel Area

Bethel Inn, On the Common (824–2175). *Expensive.* Superb cuisine served in the elegant dining room, in the Mill Brook Tavern downstairs, or on the veranda. Sun. brunch.

Olde Rowley Inn, Rte. 35, N. Waterford (583–4143). *Expensive.* A restored 1790s country inn. Delightful atmosphere in three cozy dining rooms. Fine cuisine, attractively prepared. Full menu, with daily specials, homemade breads and desserts.

The Sudbury Inn, Lower Main St. (824–2174). *Expensive.* Tasty, contemporary cuisine in the New England tradition. Light, airy dining room with lovely service. Lighter fare in the lounge.

Mother's, Upper Main St. (824–2589). *Inexpensive.* Gingerbread house with wood stoves and bookshelves in the dining room. Summer dining on the porch. Soups, salads, and sandwiches at lunch; lobsters and steamers featured in the evening.

Bridgton Area

Oxford House Inn, Main St., Fryeburg (935–3442). *Expensive,* Country elegance and pleasant atmosphere enhance dinner, exquisitely prepared with fresh local ingredients. Cocktails on the piazza.

Switzer Stubli Restaurant, in Tarry-a-While Resort, Ridge Rd., Bridgton (647–2522). *Moderate–Expensive.* Specialties prepared by Swiss chef: wiener schnitzel, raclette, fondue. Home-baked breads and pastries. Open June–Sept.

Kingfield–Carrabassett Valley

Le Papillon at The Winter's Inn, Winter's Hill (265–5421). *Deluxe.* Lovely inn with marvelous mountain views. French cuisine, prepared with care. Reservations required.

One Stanley Avenue, 1 Stanley Ave. (265–5541). *Expensive.* Queen Anne-style Victorian inn. Continental and regional cuisine includes interesting preparations of veal, chicken, pork, and beef—as well as seafood. Delicious desserts.

Tufolio's, Rte. 27, Carrabassett Valley (235–2010). *Moderate–Expensive.* Italian-American cuisine, seafood specialties. Casual family restaurant. No reservations.

The Herbert, Main St. (265–2000). *Moderate.* Traditional American fare served in three dining rooms of hotel restored to 1913 ambience.

Naples

The Epicurean Inn, Rte. 302 (693–3839). *Expensive.* Classical French and new American menu. Originally a stagecoach stop, this popular restaurant changes its menu weekly. Reservations necessary.

Rangeley Lakes Area

Country Club Inn, Rtes. 4 and 16, Rangeley (864–3831). *Expensive–Deluxe.* Fine dining, pleasant service, magnificent view of lake and surrounding mountains. Traditional American fare with delightful service. Nightly specials.

Rangeley Inn, Main St., Rangeley (864–3341). *Expensive.* Fine food served in dining room of turn-of-the-century inn. Live entertainment and dancing.

The Oquossoc House, Rtes. 17 and 4, Oquossoc (864–3881). *Moderate.* Family restaurant, rustic decor. Charcoal-broiled steaks, seafood, daily specials.

The Red Onion, Main St., Rangeley (864–5022). *Inexpensive.* Informal restaurant and bar. Italian specialties, burgers and fries. Outdoor dining on the deck in summer.

TOURIST INFORMATION. Maps, folders, and brochures may be requested from the Maine Publicity Bureau, 97 Winthrop Street, Hallowell 04347 (289–2423) and from the following: Bridgton-Lakes Region Chamber of Commerce, Box 236, Bridgton 04009 (647–3472); Naples Business Assoc., Box 412, Naples 04055 (693–3285); Bethel Area Chamber of Commerce, Box 121, Bethel 04217 (824–2282); Rangeley Lakes Region Chamber of Commerce, Box 317, Rangeley 04970 (864–5364); or Sugarloaf Area Chamber of Commerce, Box 2151, Carrabassett Valley 04947 (235–2500).

The Maine Publicity Bureau operates regional tourist information offices during the summer months west of Bethel, at the junction of Rtes. 2 and 113, and in Fryeburg, on Rte. 302.

TOURS. Boat tours: In the Sebago Lakes area, the stern paddle wheeler *Songo River Queen II* cruises through the Songo Lock or around Long Lake for a half-day trip from the Causeway, Rte. 302, Naples (693–6861). Boat tours of Rangeley Lake are available through C. Bollette in Rangeley (864–3791)—and of Mooselookmeguntic Lake through Sundown Lodge, Bald Mt. Road in Oquossoc (864–3650).

By air: Seaplane rides are available in Naples, at the Causeway, and in Rangeley at Steve's Air Service, Main St. Scenic rides are also available at Sugarloaf Regional Airport, Rte. 27 north of Kingfield.

Walking tours: A self-conducted walking tour has been outlined for the historic district of Bethel. A brochure is available from the Bethel Chamber of Commerce or The Bethel Inn.

Industrial plant tours: For tours of pulp and paper mills, contact Paper Industry Information Office, 133 State St., Augusta 04330 (622–3166).

Fall foliage: Country fairs, apples, and pumpkins at roadside stands, and a crispness in the air mark autumn in Maine and spectacular foliage viewing mid-Sept.–early Oct. The sweeping views one gets in the mountains of western Maine offer the most striking panorama of brilliant fall colors. The 9,000-ft. gondola ride at Sugarloaf/USA, Kingfield, operates daily in the fall and provides a perfect vantage point.

SEASONAL EVENTS. January: Sled-dog Races, Rangeley (early Jan.); Winter Carnival (Sugarloaf/USA), Kingfield (mid-Jan.).

February: Winter Carnival, Bethel (Sunday River, mid-Feb.). Winter Carnival, Bridgton (late Feb.).

March: 30-mile Sled-dog Race, Rangeley (mid-Mar.).

May: Upper Dead River Whitewater Canoe Race, Kingfield (late May).

July: "Oxford 250" auto race, Oxford (mid-July); Wild Mountain Time (mid-July); Oxford Hills Beanhole Bean Festival, Oxford (late July); Franco-American Festival, Lewiston (late July).

September: Blue Mountain Arts and Crafts Festival, Bethel (late Sept.).

October: W. Oxford Agricultural Fair, Fryeburg (early Oct.).

PARKS. The five state parks in this area of Maine provide a variety of outdoor experiences in scenic environments. At **Grafton Notch State Park** (Upton and Newry), picnickers, hikers, and mountain climbers are rewarded with panoramic views of Old Speck and Baldpate mts. and a close-up look at Screw Auger Falls. At **Mount Blue State Park** (Weld), visitors may picnic, swim, fish, hike, camp, and mountain climb. **Rangeley Lake State Park,** on the eastern shore of the lake, has campsites and a pleasant lakeside spot for picnicking, swimming, fishing, and boating. **Sebago Lake State Park** (Naples) provides camping, picnicking, swimming, fishing, and boating; Songo Lock is operated daily for Sebago Lake–Songo River boat trips. Picnicking, swimming, fishing, and boating are available at **Range Ponds State Park** (Poland).

NATIONAL FOREST. White Mountain National Forest is partly in Maine, southwest of Bethel. There are campsites, hiking trails, picnic grounds, and magnificent mountain scenery. For information, contact: Ranger, White Mountain National Forest, Bethel 04217 (824–2134).

WILDLIFE. The **Fish and Wildlife Center** (657–4977), off Rte. 26 at Dry Mills (near Gray), has exhibits of native animals and birds and a fish hatchery. In **Standish,** just south of Sebago Lake, there is a state game preserve where deer and other wildlife have sanctuary. The **Rumford Wild Animal Farm** (364–7043), on Rte. 2 at Rumford Pt., is a hit with the kids; animals and birds from around the world are on display (summer only). **Hunter Cove Wildlife Sanctuary,** opposite Dodge Pond on Rte. 4 north of Rangeley, has walking trails for viewing the region's wildlife and natural history. **Bigelow Game Preserve,** off Rte. 27 in Bigelow (west of Carrabassett Valley), is a vast wooded area where large and small game roam free.

SUMMER SPORTS. Boating: Boating is a popular sport on the large lakes of the area—Sebago, Long, and Rangeley. Boats are for hire at lakeside.

Canoeing/Rafting: Maine has, undoubtedly, the best wilderness canoeing and white-water rafting in the East. Early summer is the best time for this sport—when the water is high. Guided trips are available along the northern reaches of the Kennebec, Dead, Androscoggin, and Penobscot's West Branch. The Maine Publicity Bureau (see *Tourist Information* above) publishes a list of licensed outfitters.

Hiking/Mountain climbing: Trails in the White Mountain National Forest, near Bethel, connect with the 280-mi. stretch of the Appalachian Trail that traverses Maine northeast over Saddleback Mt. to Mt. Katahdin. The Maine Appalachian Club, Box 283, Augusta 04330 publishes a map and trail guide; volunteers maintain the trail. Also, good climbs can be made at Evans Notch in the White Mountain National Forest, at Grafton Notch north of Newry, and at Mt. Blue in Weld.

Golf: 18-hole courses open to the public include Prospect Hill Golf Course, Auburn (782–9220); Sugarloaf Golf Course (designed by Robert Trent Jones), Carrabassett Valley (237–2000); Fairlawn Golf Club, Poland (998–4277); Poland Spring Country Club, Poland Spring (998–4352); Mingo Springs Golf Course, Rangeley (864–5021). There are nine-hole courses at Bethel, Bridgton, Hollis, Lewiston, Livermore, Lovell, Mexico, Norway, Paris, Parsonfield, Poland, and Wilton.

WINTER SPORTS. Skiing: Skiing in Maine begins in mid-Nov. and lasts through April. Slopes are less crowded and lift lines are shorter than in neighboring states, and snow conditions and facilities easily can compete. Maine's premier ski country is in the western mountains: Pleasant Mt., Rte. 302, Bridgton (647–8444); Mt. Abram, Rte. 26, Locke Mills (875–2601); Sunday River, Rte. 26, Bethel (824–2187); Saddleback Mt., Rte. 4, Rangeley (864–3380); and Sugarloaf/USA, Rte. 27, Kingfield (237–2000). All have downhill trails ranging from easy to difficult; all have cross-country touring centers. For skiing information: Ski Maine Association, 21 Elm St., Camden 40843. For ski conditions: 800–533–9595; in Maine, 800–323–6330.

Snowmobiling: Snowmobiling is a winter way of life in Rangeley and other northern towns. The large lakes freeze solid, inviting enthusiasts, and the miles of groomed and marked trails through the wilderness are perfect for a guided snowmobile safari. Races are held in Rangeley during the winter months, and machines are readily available for rent. For information on the nearly 8,000-mile Interconnecting Trail System: Maine Snowmobile Assoc., Box 77, Augusta 04330. For trail conditions: 800–462–1019. Snowmobiles can be rented in Rangeley.

FISHING. At the first croak of spring, when the ice melts and the season opens, fishermen flock to the lakes and streams throughout the region—and the state—to try their luck. The Rangeley area is a fly-fisherman's paradise; the innumerable ponds and streams support large populations of native trout and land-locked salmon. All nonresident freshwater fishermen over the age of 12 require a fishing license; licenses are generally available at local sporting-goods or hardware stores. For further information: Department of Inland Fisheries and Wildlife, 284 State St., Augusta 04333 (289–2043). For wilderness trips, a professional Maine Guide is recommended. Inquire locally or write: Maine Professional Guides Association, Box 265, Medway 04460.

HUNTING. Open season on game birds, including woodcock and partridge, attracts hunters to Rangeley and other northern towns in Oct. By Nov., skilled sportsmen are guided into the deep woods after deer and bear. Strict regulations are enforced; licenses are required for all hunters 10 years old or over and may be purchased at local sporting-goods or hardware stores. Applicants for adult firearms licenses must show proof of having previously held an adult license or having successfully completed an approved hunter safety course. Maine Guide service is recommended for wilderness trips. (For further information, write to addresses mentioned in *Fishing*.)

CAMPING. Campsites are available in some state parks. An enormous number of private campgrounds exist throughout Maine, offering a vast range of amenities—from simple comforts (like hot water and electricity) to deluxe facilities, rental boats, playgrounds, etc. For a statewide listing of private campgrounds, contact: Maine Campground Owners Association, 655 Main St., Lewiston 04240 (782–5874), or request the *Maine Guide to Camping* from the Maine Publicity Bureau (see *Tourist Information*).

SPECTATOR SPORTS. Auto racing: Oxford Plains Speedway Inc., Oxford, is the site of one of New England's foremost auto-racing tracks, with summer stock-car racing and a drag strip.

Horse racing: Harness racing is held at Lewiston Raceway, 729 Main St., Lewiston 04240, in summer.

HISTORIC SITES. The peace and tranquility of western Maine is as real now as it was in the past. The significant history of this region is more involved with people and commerce than with battles and strife.

Naples

Songo Lock, on Songo River (693–6861). Only surviving operating lock of Cumberland-Oxford Canal; boat trips available.

Paris Hill

Hannibal Hamlin Memorial Hall and Old Stone Jail. (no tel.). Jail now houses a library and museum of American primitive art, local minerals, and artifacts from the Hamlin family. Hamlin home, next door, is now privately owned and not open to visitors.

South Casco

Nathaniel Hawthorne's Home (1812), Hawthorne Rd., off Rte. 302 (no tel.). Boyhood home of the famous author, now a community hall.

MUSEUMS. Early Maine life is depicted at several museums in the area. Call ahead for days, hours, and admission fees.

Bethel

Moses Mason Museum, 15 Broad St. (824–2908). A fully restored Federal-style house (1813) with period furnishings and special local historical exhibits year-round.

Farmington

Nordica Homestead, Holley Rd., off Rte. 4 (778–2042). Birthplace of the opera singer Lillian Nordica (née Norton); home dates from 1840, and her costumes, music, programs, and other memorabilia are displayed.

Livermore

Washburn-Norlands Center, Norlands Rd., north of Rte. 108 (897–2236). Living history programs where visitors can sample 19th-century living on a 430-acre working farm. Grounds include a school, church, library, and homestead.

New Gloucester

The Shaker Museum, Rte. 26 (926–4597). Exhibits of furniture, crafts, and folk art depict the Shaker community in Maine. Established in 1793, the Shaker community in New Gloucester is one of the oldest and most active remaining in the U.S. and the last in Maine.

Newfield

Willowbrook at Newfield, Main St., off Rte. 11 (793–2784). Re-creation of a complete 19th-century village; 33 structures illustrate village life, tools, vehicles, household implements, and trades of yesteryear.

Rangeley

The Wilhelm Reich Museum, Rte. 4 west of town (864–3443). Exhibits cover the life and work of the Austrian-born psychiatrist whose theories on biological energy landed him in prison.

THEATER. In Lewiston, the **Maine Acting Company** presents a variety of programs at the Performing Arts Center, Lisbon St. (784–1616), year-round.

SHOPPING. Bridgton is the antique center of the Lakes Area, with more than a score of shops and a number of auctions in the summer. Snow-shoes and snowshoe furniture are manufactured in Norway and can be purchased at the **Sno-craft** factory, Tannery St. Handmade-in-Maine (mostly wood) products—toys, lamps, birdhouses, pottery, boxes, and shelves—are sold through **Maine Line Products,** Main St., Bethel. **Bonne-ma Potters,** Lower Main St., Bethel, offers the creative works of local arti-sans. **Groan & McGurn,** Rte. 2, W. Bethel, sells original T-shirts and other Maine souvenirs. Rockhounds must stop at **Perham's Mineral Store,** Trap Corner, jct. Rtes. 26 and 219, West Paris, where a large variety of local minerals, gems, and jewelry are for sale, and five nearby quarries where you can dig your own gemstones. The **Bates Factory Outlet,** Canal St., Lewiston (784–7311), has good buys on bedspreads, draperies, and other linens.

THE KENNEBEC VALLEY

The Kennebec Valley is located in the center of the most populated part of the state. The concentration of industrial towns along the river is testi-mony to the Kennebec's early history, when it was the means for shipping lumber and ice harvests to markets worldwide. The capital city, Augusta, straddles the Kennebec; Waterville and Skowhegan are farther north. Three popular vacation areas are located in the valley, among the rolling hills, fertile farmlands, and countless lakes and streams: Belgrade Lakes, China Lake, and Winthrop.

Augusta

Augusta, the capital city, and nearby Hallowell offer history and antique buffs many hours of interesting exploration.

The State House (1829), on State Street in Augusta, was designed (as were many official buildings in New England) by the Boston architect Charles Bulfinch and constructed of Hallowell granite. The State House, Blaine House (the governor's residence), the State Archives, the Library, and the Maine State Museum are all open to the public. The museum has exhibits relating to Maine's heritage, its traditional industries, and local natural history.

As far back as 1628, the Plymouth Colony of Massachusetts had a trad-ing post near the present site of Fort Western, on Bowman Street. Fort Western was built in 1754 for protection against Indian raids. Benedict Arnold's army of men regrouped and transferred to bateaux here while on their historic but unsuccessful march to Quebec. The barracks rooms are furnished in keeping with the early days, and there are exhibits devoted to military and naval articles. The fort was restored in 1921.

Though more than 30 miles from the sea, Hallowell, just down river from Augusta, was once a busy port and shipbuilding center. Hallowell is an antique center today, with many shops along Water Street. Many of the residences on the streets that reach uphill from the riverfront are fine examples of varied and interesting architectural styles—Federal, Greek Revival, Victorian, wooden row houses—which suggest Maine's cultural, economic, and social heritage.

A Chain of Lakes

In the valley on either side of the Kennebec River there are chains of lakes that have become popular cottage communities and recreation areas.

Winthrop Lakes is just west of Augusta; the 200-square-mile area of rolling hillsides, ponds, and lakes are inviting to vacationers and fishermen. The larger towns in this vicinity are Winthrop and Monmouth.

China Lakes, on the east bank of the Kennebec, is a vacation area especially popular with families who own cottages or rent them for (or during) the summer. Fishermen are attracted by the challenge of catching landlocked salmon and smallmouth bass in the many lakes.

Belgrade Lakes, the farthest north of these three recreation areas, is just west of Waterville. The area's seven large lakes are famous fishing areas—for bass, salmon, and trout—and also attract cottagers looking for a peaceful respite in summer.

In all three lake locations there are motels and campsites available to vacationers, as well as weekly cottage rentals.

Waterville

Waterville, the Elm City, was a summer residence of the Abnaki Indians in its earliest days. More recently the town has played a key role in the industrial development of the Kennebec River Valley; the Hathaway Shirt Company is its best-known industry. Colby College, established in 1813, has an impressive 500-acre campus on Mayflower Hill.

The Two-Cent Bridge, between Waterville and Winslow on Front Street, is the only known footbridge in the country that, until recently, collected a toll.

Skowhegan

Skowhegan is the county seat and a major crossroads in northern Kennebec County. The largest town in the area, it is the commercial center of a rich farming region. The major industry here is Scott Paper Company's vast paper mill. (Tours are available in summer.) The Skowhegan State Fair, in mid-August each year, is one of the largest agricultural fairs in Maine. You can't miss the 65-foot statue of an Abnaki Indian in town; it was handcarved by the late Maine sculptor Bernard Langlais and erected in 1960 to commemorate the area's first inhabitants. Skowhegan is the birthplace of Margaret Chase Smith, who was Maine's well-known U.S. Senator for over 30 years. Memorabilia documenting her life and career are on display at the Margaret Chase Smith Library Center, Norridgewock Ave.

PRACTICAL INFORMATION FOR THE KENNEBEC VALLEY

Note: The area code for all Maine is 207

HOW TO GET THERE AND AROUND. By plane: Commuter service is available via Eastern Express (800–451–4221) between Augusta and Portland, Lewiston, Waterville, or Bangor; and via Valley Airlines (800–322–1008) between Augusta and Bangor, Frenchville, or Presque Isle.

By bus: Daily service to Augusta and Waterville is available on Greyhound's Portland-Bangor run.

By car: I–95 cuts through the region diagonally, providing access to most towns and recreation areas. The Maine Turnpike (toll road) ends in Augusta (Exit 15). From Augusta, Rte. 202 west goes to the Winthrop Lakes area; Rte. 202 east goes to China Lakes; and Rte. 23 leads to the Belgrade Lakes.

Car rentals: Major car rental companies are represented in Augusta and Waterville.

HOTELS, MOTELS, AND COTTAGES. Accommodations in the Kennebec Valley region are found in motels and motor inns in the major towns or cities; in the lake resort areas, cottage or "camp" communities are available by the week. Motels and motor inns are generally open all year; some cottages in the resort areas are open only for the summer vacation season.

Rates are based on double occupancy, in season: *Expensive,* $60–80; *Moderate,* $40–60. There is a 7% Maine state lodging tax.

Augusta

Best Western Senator Inn, 284 Western Ave. at I–95, 04330 (622–5804). *Expensive–Deluxe.* Large, full-service Best Western Motor Inn. Comfortable guestrooms, decorated in contemporary style. Pool, popular restaurant, evening entertainment in lounge.

Belgrade Lakes Area

Embden Resorts, Box 189, N. Anson 04958 (566–5301). *Expensive.* Guest cottages or duplex motel units in a rustic setting on Embden Pond. All have efficiency kitchens and wood stoves. Restaurant and lounge in the lodge, with dancing weekends. Complete recreational facilities. Some or all meals included.

Castle Island Camps, Mt. Vernon Rd., Long Lake, Belgrade Lakes 04918 (495–3312). *Moderate.* Fully furnished cottages, ideal for a family vacation. Beautiful pine-forest setting. Community building for dining and recreation. Excellent fishing and swimming in lake—at your doorstep. Boats available. Daily or weekly rates, meals included. Open May–Sept.

China Lake Area

Willow Beach Camps, Rte. 202, China 04926 (968–2421). *Moderate.* Cozy, fully equipped cabins among the trees on the shore of China Lake. Home-style meals in the dining room. Fishing, swimming, and varied recreational facilities. Weekly rates. Summer only.

Skowhegan

The Towne Motel, 248 Madison Ave. 04976 (474–5151). *Moderate.* Comfortable motel with all modern conveniences and colonial decor; some kitchenettes. Pleasant grounds, pool, and patio. Close to restaurants and local attractions. Continental breakfast included.

Waterville

Holiday Inn, 375 Upper Main St., 04901 (873–0111). *Expensive.* The usual pleasant accommodations, with all amenities. Pool, pets accepted; Irish restaurant and pub.

RESTAURANTS. Many vacationers to the Kennebec Valley region rent cottages or camp and are, therefore, self-sufficient. Augusta, the capital city, and Waterville, a college town, do have interesting restaurants.

The restaurants suggested here are open year-round, serve lunch and dinner, and accept major credit cards. Price ranges per person for a complete dinner excluding beverages, tax, and tip: *Expensive,* $20–$30; *Moderate,* $10–$20.

Augusta-Hallowell

Oyster Bar & Grille at The Senator Inn, Western Ave., Augusta (622–0320). *Expensive.* Fresh Maine seafood and other well-prepared specialties; homemade breads, excellent desserts. Sunday brunch. Nightly entertainment in the Bistro.
Hazel Green's, 349 Water St., Augusta (622–9903). *Moderate.* Informal pub. Steak, seafood, fine prime ribs, salad bar.
Slate's, 167 Water St., Hallowell (622–9575). *Moderate.* Attractive, candlelit dining room at dinner; salads and sandwiches all afternoon in the bar. Varied menu with a French touch.

Waterville

Johann Sebastian B., 40 Fairfield St., Oakland (465–3223). *Moderate–Expensive.* Victorian house near Belgrade Lakes. German-American specialties include schnitzel, homemade pastries.
Weathervane Seafoods, 470 Kennedy Memorial Dr. (873–4522). *Moderate.* Popular family restaurant with colonial atmosphere. Full menu for lunch and dinner, including fresh seafood and roast beef. Bar. Children's portions.

TOURIST INFORMATION. Information may be requested from the Maine Publicity Bureau, 97 Winthrop St., Hallowell 04347 (289–2423) or from the following regional organizations: Maine Chamber of Commerce, 126 Sewall St., Augusta 04330 (623–4568); Belgrade Lakes Region, Inc., Box 426, Oakland 04963 (495–3444); China Area Chamber of Commerce, Box 189, South China 04358 (923–3355); and Mid-Maine Chamber of Commerce, Box 142, Waterville 04901 (873–3315).

A local tourist information booth is open during the summer months on Rte. 27, Belgrade.

SEASONAL EVENTS. July: The Great Kennebec River Whatever Week and Race, Augusta (early July).

August: Skowhegan State Fair, Skowhegan (mid-Aug.); Logging day, Skowhegan (late Aug.).

PARKS. Picnicking, swimming, and fishing and available at the **Peacock Beach State Park** in Richmond, about 10 mi. north of Augusta on Rte. 201.

SPORTS. Boating: The many lakes in the region offer endless opportunity to boating enthusiasts. Power boats, small sailboats, rowboats, or canoes are generally available for rent—for fishing or just putting around the lake.

Golf: 18-hole golf courses open to the public include Springbrook Golf Course, Leeds (933–4551); Augusta Country Club, Manchester (623–3021); Natanis Golf Course, Vassalboro (622–3561); Waterville Country Club, Waterville (465–7773). There are nine-hole courses in Augusta, Burnham, Farmingdale, Madison, Monmouth, Palmyra, Waterville, and Wilton.

Fishing. Fishing is the name of the game in this region. Huge numbers of large bass, trout, salmon, pickerel, and perch are caught. All nonresident freshwater fishermen over the age of 12 require a fishing license; licenses are generally available at local sporting-goods or hardware stores. For further information: Department of Inland Fisheries and Wildlife, 284 State St., Augusta 04333 (289–2043).

HISTORIC SITES AND MUSEUMS. In Augusta—**Fort Western** (1754), Bowman St. (623–2385). Built to defend the Kennebec River during French and Indian War; stopping place for Benedict Arnold on his march to Quebec. Restored blockhouse and stockade.

Maine State Museum, State St. (Capitol complex), Augusta (289–2301). Various exhibits depicting Maine's natural and cultural history; "Made in Maine" exhibit focuses on Maine industries and products.

In Waterville—The collection of the **Colby College Museum of Art,** Bixler Art & Music Center (872–3228), has works of Winslow Homer and John Marin.

In Skowhegan—**Margaret Chase Smith Library Center,** Norridgewock Ave. (474–7133), has exhibits covering the senator's life and career.

THEATER. Summer theater productions of Broadway musicals and contemporary drama can be seen at The **Theater at Monmouth,** Cumston Hall, Monmouth 04259 (933–2952); **Lakewood Theater,** Rte. 201, Skowhegan 04976 (474–0080); and **Waterville Summer Music Theater,** Waterville Opera House, Waterville 04901 (872–2707).

THE NORTHERN LAKES AND FORESTS

Much of Maine is uninhabited and inaccessible—square mile after square mile of forest and timberland, broken only by lakes and ponds and crisscrossed by long, straight logging roads. Nowhere is this more evident than in the northern and north-central regions of the state.

The folks who live in the towns and villages along the rim of this vast, unspoiled wilderness are hardy souls who face arctic winds and up to 20 feet of snow in the winter. Logging roads that turn impassable become cross-country ski or snowmobile trails. At ice-out in May, the streams begin to flow again, and local guides lead fishermen to remote areas to fill their creels with trout. Summer offers canoe and white-water rafting enthusiasts some of the best waters to be found anywhere; on the Allagash, the Kennebec, and the West Branch of the Penobscot there are "runs" suitable for novice or expert. Hunters come in the fall, along with magnificent foliage, and the cycle begins again.

Moosehead Lake, Greenville, Rockwood

Crystal-clear Moosehead Lake—so named because of its resemblance to the state's favorite animal—is Maine's largest lake. Over 40 miles long and, in some places, 20 miles wide, it has many islands and bays. The 420 miles of shorefront, owned almost entirely by paper companies (about 97 percent), is virtually uninhabited. Logging roads provide access to some of the remote areas, but much of the shorefront is accessible only by float-plane, boat, or canoe. The area is popular for fishing, cruising, camping, and hunting, as well as for finding fossils and Indian artifacts. Moose watching is also a popular sport, particularly in the evening!

Greenville is the starting point for trips into this fantastic fishing and hunting country. The lake front is busy with the pontoon planes of local air services that fly sports enthusiasts to even more remote sites. There are ample accommodations and restaurants in and around the village.

The Moosehead Marine Museum on Pritham Avenue has displays of artifacts and photographs of the steamboat era and the logging industry at Moosehead Lake. The restored lake steamer *Katahdin* (1914) offers summer excursions up and down the lake, much as she did in her heyday when wealthy vacationers and sportsmen would take the "Kate" to reach hotels and sporting camps around the lake.

North on Routes 6 and 15 brings you to Big Squaw Mountain (3,267 feet) with its panoramic view of Moosehead Lake. Big Squaw Mountain Ski Area has resort facilities and downhill and cross-country ski trails.

A few miles farther north is Rockwood, a resort village for nature lovers. The rivers, brooks, and streams here are a paradise for fishermen; the wildlife areas are among the best hunting grounds for deer, bear, partridge, and small game. There are well-maintained snowmobile trails, snowshoeing, and ice fishing for the cold-weather vacationer. During the warmer months, canoe trips and white-water rafting provide thrilling expeditions along picturesque rivers (or through boiling rapids).

One of the great sights for travelers to this area is Mt. Kineo, a sheer cliff that rises out of the lake to a height of 1,860 feet. A geological oddity, it is a solid piece of green flint. Indians sought the flint to make arrowheads and stone tools. A boat tour is available.

Jackman

If you love wilderness scenery and want to see more than you have seen so far, take Routes 6 and 15 about 30 miles west to Jackman. Jackman is only 16 miles from the Canadian border.

Like Greenville, Jackman is a jumping-off place for deep-woods fishing, hunting, ski touring, and snowmobiling—and a station on both the Moose River and Attean Lake canoe routes. With many mountain ranges forming a backdrop, Jackman caters to outdoor interests and casual vacationers year-round. Sporting camps, restaurants, and other accommodations are available in the region.

Route 201 south from Jackman becomes the Maine Scenic Highway from The Forks (named because it marks the confluence of the Dead River and the mighty Kennebec) to Solon, 32 miles away. Back in 1775, this route was a portion of the trail Benedict Arnold and his men followed on their march to Quebec. (There are several commemorative markers along the roadside.) Today this area is one of the state's most exciting canoeing and rafting sites.

Millinocket and Baxter State Park

Millinocket, in the heart of timber country, is a newsprint manufacturing center and the home of Great Northern Paper Company. It is also the primary gateway to Baxter State Park and Mt. Katahdin, about 16 miles northwest of town. Don't be disturbed that much of the road skirting the park is marked "private" on the map; it belongs to Great Northern, but the public is permitted access.

Baxter State Park is a wilderness preserve that covers more than 200,000 acres of land collected over a period of 30 years by former governor Percival P. Baxter "for the benefit of the people." In 1930, Baxter deeded the land to the state to be held in trust "as a state forest, public park, and for public recreational purposes . . . to be kept in its natural wild state and as a sanctuary for wild beasts and birds."

And a true wilderness it is. Roads in the park are narrow, winding dirt roads, with tall stands of pine and fir on either side. Moose, white-tailed deer, and bear roam freely here. A growing number of hikers and mountain climbers are attracted each year to Baxter State Park's miles of footpaths and more than 45 peaks.

Mt. Katahdin (the Indian word means "greatest mountain") in the park is the highest point in Maine (5,268 feet, with a 4,000-foot vertical drop) and one of the highest points in the United States east of the Rockies. Baxter Peak, Katahdin's summit, marks the northern terminus of the Appalachian Trail, which extends 2,050 miles south to Mt. Oglethorpe in north Georgia.

There are several campgrounds in Baxter State Park; some are accessible by car, others only by foot. Large house trailers are not permitted in the park because they cannot traverse the narrow roads. Reservations for camping must be made and paid for in advance. Hikers and other park visitors must have permits to use or to travel through the park. No food, fuel, or supplies are available once visitors are inside, so you must be sure to come fully equipped.

PRACTICAL INFORMATION FOR
THE NORTHERN LAKES AND FORESTS

Note: The area code for all Maine is 207

HOW TO GET THERE AND AROUND. By plane: Commercial flights are available to Bangor (see *Acadia*). From Bangor, charter flights can be arranged with flying services for transportation to local towns or remote areas.

Flying services also provide charter flights between towns or floatplane (and even ski-plane) service to just about anywhere. For example: Currier's Flying Service, Greenville Jct. (695–2778); Folsom's Air Service, Greenville (695–2821); Jack's Flying Service, Greenville (695–3020).

By train: Maine's only passenger rail service is offered by VIA Rail, whose service between Montreal and Halifax, Nova Scotia, makes stops in Maine at Jackman, Greenville, Brownville Junction, Danforth, and

Vanceboro. For information: VIA Rail, Box 8116, 2 Place Ville-Marie, Montreal, Quebec H3B 2G6. In the United States, contact your local AMTRAK office.

By car: To the Moosehead Lake area: Use I–95 to Newport, Rte. 7 to Dexter, Rte. 23 to Guilford, and Rtes. 6 and 15 to Greenville. To Jackman: I–95 to Exit 36 at Fairfield, then Rte. 201 directly to Jackman. Canadian Rte. 173 from Quebec becomes U.S. Rte. 201 to Jackman. To the Baxter State Park area: Use I–95 to exit 56 at Medway; then Rtes. 11 and 157 west to Millinocket.

From Millinocket (south), Baxter Park Road is a 16-mi. dirt road northwest to the park entrance; from Greenville (west), Great Northern Paper Co.'s private road (open to the public except when closed by winter weather) passes through Lily Bay and Kokadjo en route to the park 59 mi. away; and from Patten (northeast), Rte. 159 to Shin Pond becomes a private road to the park about 30 mi. away.

Rtes. 6 and 15 are the east-west routes connecting Jackman, Rockwood, Greenville, and Dover-Foxcroft; Rtes. 6 and 11 connect Dover-Foxcroft and Millinocket. Rte. 201 is the scenic route from the Kennebec Valley area north through The Forks and on through the wilderness to Jackman.

There are few public roads in the wilderness area of the northwest. Logging roads are privately owned by paper companies, but many are available for public use (weather permitting). Some require permits, some have road-access fees. For information: North Maine Woods, Inc., Box 382, Ashland 04732 (435–6213).

HOTELS, MOTELS, AND COTTAGES. Accommodations are available in hotels, motels, and wilderness resorts in or near the larger towns and villages. Visitors to this area, however, are often sportsmen who arrange to stay in sporting camps, with meals included and guide service either included or available; lodgings can be simple cabins or more elaborate quarters. Reservations are necessary at the sporting camps.

Rates are based on double occupancy: *Deluxe,* $60 and up; *Expensive,* $50–$60; *Moderate,* $40–$50; *Inexpensive,* $40 or less. Weekly rates are generally available, averaging about $300 per week for a small cabin (2–4 people); higher rates for larger facilities. There is a 7% Maine state lodging tax. Unless otherwise indicated, hotels are open year-round.

Dover-Foxcroft

Blethen House Inn, 37 E. Main St., Rte. 15, 04426 (564–2481). *Moderate.* Downtown hotel built in 1842, with adjoining modern motel units. Dining room and cocktail lounge. Central location for trips to Sebec Lake area.

Greenville

Little Lyford Pond Lodge, Box 1269, 04441 (695–2821). *Deluxe.* Secluded log cabins and lodge near Gulf Hagas Gorge. No vehicles allowed: in summer, fly in or drive on logging roads to within one-third mile of the lodge; in winter, fly or ski in. No phones. All meals included. Good library. Boats provided; licenses available.

Penobscot Lake Lodge, Penobscot Lake (north of Greenville near Quebec border), 04441 (695–2786). *Deluxe.* Wilderness sporting camp reached by floatplane from Greenville, a 50-mi. trip. No direct access by road. Rates include full meal service and use of boats, canoes, fishing tackle.

Accommodations are in private log cabins, with lodge for socializing and dining. Fishing is the main attraction. Open late May–Sept.

Greenville Inn, Norris St., 04441 (695–2206). *Expensive.* Former lumber baron's home (1895). Rooms, cottages, a carriage house apartment. Snowmobile trails, skiing, golf, and tennis nearby; boating and water sports at Moosehead Lake. Lake view from dining room.

Squaw Mountain Lodge, Greenville Jct., 04441 (695–2272). *Expensive.* Four-season mountainside/lakeside family resort. Offers full range of water sports, plus tennis, riding, lawn games in summer; snowmobiling, skiing, and hunting in winter. Play area for children. Restaurant, bar; entertainment, dancing on weekends.

Chalet Moosehead, on Moosehead Lake, just off Rtes. 6 and 15, 04441 (695–2950). *Moderate.* Motel with two-room efficiencies. Attractive grounds overlook the lake. Private beach, boating, fishing, and hiking available. Free use of canoes. Golf, tennis, and skiing nearby.

Jackman

Attean Lake Resort, off Rte. 201 on Attean Lake, Jackman 04945 (668–3729). *Moderate.* Rustic log cottages with fireplaces. Fishing, mountain climbing, water sports, hiking, and nature walks all at your doorstep. Great family vacation spot. All meals included.

Millinocket

Pamola Motor Lodge, 973 Central St., 04462 (723–9746). *Moderate.* Modern motel rooms or efficiencies at the gateway to Baxter State Park. Pool, dining room, cocktail lounge.

Rockwood

The Birches, 2 mi. north of Rockwood on Moosehead Lake, 04478 (534–7305). *Moderate.* Main lodge and 17 log cabins among the birch trees. Housekeeping facilities or full meal service available by the week only. Private marina. Only six cabins open during the winter for cross-country skiing and snowmobiling. (Dining room closed Dec.–Apr.)

Rockwood Cottages, on Moosehead Lake opp. Mt. Kineo, 04478 (534–7725). *Moderate.* Eight shorefront cottages—neat, fully equipped, and comfortable—for quiet, peaceful north woods family vacation or hunting and fishing. All water sports in summer; ice fishing, skiing, and snowmobiling in winter.

Tomhegan, Box 8, 04478 (534–7712). *Inexpensive.* Woodland hideaway. Ten hand-hewn log housekeeping cottages and four lodge rooms on Moosehead Lake. No meal service. Weekly rates. Expert outfitters and guides for hunting, fishing, cross-country skiing, and ice fishing. Boats and licenses available.

The Forks

Northern Outdoors, Box 100, Rte. 201, 04985 (663–4466). Four-season, full-service log lodge on the Interconnecting Trail System (snowmobiles). Huge stone fireplace, modern rooms, hot tub and sauna, restaurant, and bar. Trails lead from the back door to wilderness lakes. Snowmobiling, cross-country skiing, canoeing, and rafting trips arranged.

RESTAURANTS. Meals are often included in the camps or lodges where many visitors stay. Hotel dining rooms are open to the public and offer pleasant dining and rustic charm.

The restaurants suggested below, except where indicated, are open year-round, for lunch and dinner and accept major credit cards. Price per person for a complete dinner excluding beverages, tax, and tip: *Deluxe,* $30 and up; *Expensive,* $20–$30; *Moderate,* $10–$20; *Inexpensive,* $10 or less.

Dover-Foxcroft

Brown's Mill Restaurant, 16 Vaughan St. (564–8614). *Moderate.* Upstairs in an old mill on the Piscataquis River. Simple, traditional New England fare, from hot dogs and beans to steamed salmon steak.

Greenville

Lake View Manor Restaurant, Lily Bay Rd. (695–3810). *Expensive.* French haute cuisine in cozy dining room before a crackling fire. Closed Mon. and Tues. Dinner only.

Greenville Inn, Norris St. (695–2206). *Moderate.* A former lumber baron's home on Moosehead Lake. Changing menu includes Austrian specialties. Dinner only. Reservations requested.

Rockwood

The Birches, On Moosehead Lake (534–7305). *Moderate.* Plentiful home-cooked meals. Weekend specials. Fresh vegetables and homemade desserts. Lounge. Reservations requested. Open May–Nov.

TOURS. By air: Flying-service operators offer year-round scenic and fire-patrol rides on wheel, float, or ski planes. (See *How To Get There and Around* for suggested flying services.)

By boat: In Greenville, the restored lake steamer *Katahdin* (1914) offers excursions around Moosehead Lake during July and Aug. For information: Moosehead Marine Museum (695–2716).

TOURIST INFORMATION. The Maine Publicity Bureau, 97 Winthrop St., Hallowell 04347, can provide information on sporting camps and wilderness expeditions.

Local information can be requested from: Moosehead Lake Region Chamber of Commerce, Box 581, Greenville 04441 (695–2702); Moosehead Vacation and Sportsmen's Association, Box A, Rockwood 04478 (534–7300); Baxter State Park Authority, 64 Balsam Dr., Millinocket 04462 (723–5140); Jackman/Moose River Chamber of Commerce, Box 368, Jackman 04945 (668–2111); Millinocket Chamber of Commerce, Box 5, Millinocket 04462 (723–4443).

SEASONAL EVENTS. September: International Seaplane Fly-in, Greenville (early Sept.).

PARKS. Lily Bay State Park, north of Greenville, is open from ice-out (early May) until mid-Oct. and offers camping (reservations accepted), picnicking, swimming, fishing, and boating. Snowmobiling is permitted in the winter months.

Peaks-Kenny State Park, north of Dover-Foxcroft, is open mid-May–mid-Oct. and offers camping, picnicking, swimming, fishing, and hiking.

Baxter State Park, north of Millinocket, is Maine's premier park. A 200,000-acre wilderness preserve, with more than 150 mi. of footpaths and 46 peaks, visitors enjoy camping, fishing, hiking, and mountain climbing. Roads are narrow, dirt, and winding, excluding large trailers. Neither motorcycles nor pets are permitted. Camping is permitted mid-May–mid-Oct. (Day use only at other times, except with special permission.) Facilities for camping range from basic campsites with lean-tos to bunkhouses or cabins; there are some remote campsites available to backpackers. Reservations for camping must be made and paid for in advance. The Appalachian Trail terminates in the park at Mt. Katahdin (5,268 ft.), the highest point in Maine. Hikers and other park visitors must have permits to use or to travel through the park. No food, fuel, or supplies are available once visitors are inside, so you must be sure to come fully equipped. For maps, permits, and other information, write: Baxter State Park Authority, 64 Balsam Dr., Millinocket 04462 (723–5140). (See *How to Get There and Around* for access routes.)

SUMMER SPORTS. Canoeing: Fully outfitted and guided canoe/camping trips can be arranged with licensed outfitters for thrilling expeditions along the Allagash Wilderness Waterway, the West Branch of the Penobscot River, or on some of the large lakes in the area. Trips may last for a few days or for more than a week; some are designed for beginners, others for experts. For a list of canoe trips and licensed outfitters, write: Maine Publicity Bureau (see *Tourist Information*) or Maine Department of Inland Fisheries and Wildlife, 284 State St., Augusta 04333 (289–2043).

White-water Rafting: Through steep-walled canyons and gorges, the Kennebec and Penobscot rivers rush downstream, carrying rubber rafts full of adventurers on a thrilling ride. Licensed outfitters arrange and guide these trips along some of the most spectacular waters in the nation, certainly in the East. Minimum age for participants is generally 12 years. For a list of licensed outfitters, contact: Department of Inland Fisheries and Wildlife (see above for address and telephone).

Hiking: The final 5 mi. of the Appalachian Trail wind through Baxter State Park to the summit of Mt. Katahdin. About 140 mi. of additional trails and footpaths are in the park, suitable for the casual walker or the serious backpacker. Shelters are situated throughout the park for the use of hikers. Permits are required to use the park. (See *Parks* for further information.)

Mountain Climbing: Mount Katahdin, in Baxter State Park (see *Parks*), is the destination of serious mountain climbers. Nearly a mile high, Katahdin has a 4,000-ft. vertical drop. With special permission, experts can attempt ice climbing in the winter months.

Golf: There are nine-hole courses open to the public in Dover-Foxcroft, Greenville, Millinocket, Milo, and Moose River.

WINTER SPORTS. Skiing: In its five-month winter, northern Maine gets up to 20 ft. of snow. Miles of groomed ski-touring trails and open trails on old logging roads stretch from Quebec to Katahdin. Big Squaw Mountain Ski Resort, Greenville (695–2272), is a family vacation spot, with downhill trails for all levels of experience and a 25-mi. cross-country trail system. For ski conditions, call 800–533–9595, in Maine 800–323–6330.

Snowmobiling: When the ground is covered with snow, between Thanksgiving and Apr., snowmobiles emerge. An extensive network of groomed snowmobile trails, part of the Interconnecting Trail System, continues into Canada. For trail conditions, call 800–462–1019. Unlimited possibilities exist for exploring the pristine wilderness on miles of logging roads. Rentals are available in Millinocket.

FISHING. When the season opens in the spring, lakes and streams come alive with fishermen angling for trout and salmon. This area of Maine is known worldwide by fishing enthusiasts for the size and fighting spirit of the fish, its endless opportunity, and its incredible beauty. All nonresident freshwater fishermen over the age of 12 require a fishing license; licenses are generally available at local sporting-goods or hardware stores. For further information: Department of Inland Fisheries and Wildlife (address above). For wilderness trips, a professional Maine Guide is recommended. Sporting camps often provide guides or will certainly recommend one. Inquire locally or write: Maine Professional Guides Association, Box 265, Medway 04460.

In winter months, ice fishing is popular on the numerous frozen lakes. Equipment and ice huts are available for rent. Special licensing is required.

HUNTING. Fall brings hunters to the uninhabited forest and swamp areas of northern Maine. With bow and arrow, firearms, or traps, hunters seek deer, bear, moose (limited by lottery), pheasant, partridge, and other game. Strict regulations are enforced; licenses are required for all hunters 10 years old or over and may be purchased at local sporting-goods or hardware stores. Applicants for adult firearms licenses must show proof of having previously held an adult license or having successfully completed an approved hunter safety course. Maine Guide service is recommended for wilderness trips. (For further information, write to addresses mentioned in *Fishing.*)

CAMPING. Camping is permitted in the region's State Parks: at Peaks-Kenny (Dover-Foxcroft) and at Lily Bay (Greenville) by reservation (695–2700) or on a first-come, first-served basis. For information on camping at Baxter State Park, see *Parks.*

Information on campsite and campground availability—as well as the prevalence of sporting camps—in the Northern Lakes and Forest region is similar to that of the wilderness areas in northwestern Aroostook County. (See *Camping* for Aroostook County.)

HISTORIC SITES AND MUSEUMS. Katahdin Iron Works (1843), 6 mi. down a gravel road off Rte. 11, 5 miles north of Brownville Jct. Once a mine and smelting mill, now has a restored stone blast furnace and charcoal kiln on site.

Moosehead Marine Museum and *S/S Katahdin* (695–2716) in Greenville. The restored steamship *Katahdin* is a floating museum, with exhibits on the local logging industry and the steamship era around Moosehead Lake. (Open Memorial Day–Columbus Day.)

In Patten—**The Lumberman's Museum,** Rte. 159, west of Patten (528–2650). More than 3,000 artifacts pay tribute to Maine's lumbering industry and include models, dioramas, tools, heavy equipment, and a replica of an 1820 logging camp. (Open Memorial Day–Labor Day.)

AROOSTOOK COUNTY

The County, as it is referred to in Maine, is the state's largest; bounded on three sides by Canada, it covers an area of 6,453 square miles. Most of the population lives along the eastern edge of the county and in the St. John River Valley in the north. Many residents are descendents of Micmac and Malicite Indians, Acadian French, and Swedish settlers.

In southern and eastern Aroostook, from Houlton to Presque Isle and on up to Fort Kent, the low rolling countryside, rich and green, yields five million bushels of potatoes a year. In addition to the harvest's economic importance to the region, the potato fields in summer burst forth acres of varicolored blossoms—a sight to behold.

Nearly all the northwestern portion of the county is wilderness. There are some four million acres of forest, nearly all privately owned by five paper companies whose pulp and paper mills produce lumber and wood and paper products. With proper permits and licensing, this wilderness area is a sportsman's paradise of fishing, hunting, camping, hiking, canoeing, swimming, boating, skiing, and snowmobiling.

Houlton

Houlton, the oldest community in the county and the county seat, is at the junction of Route 1 and I–95, about 100 miles north of Calais. (I–95 begins in Houlton and continues south to Florida.) This is the center of southern Aroostook County's potato farming area and the primary port of entry to Canada's Maritime Provinces.

Settled in 1805 by Joseph Houlton, Houlton earned a special place in Maine's history. Hancock Barracks, on Garrison Hill, was troop headquarters during the "Bloodless Aroostook War," the northern border dispute (1839) settled by treaty before a shot was fired. The site is now a pleasant park and picnic area.

Substantial homes, built during Houlton's population expansion in the 1890s when the Bangor & Aroostook Railroad was extended to town, are still evident on the residential streets. Several structures have been included in an Historic Business District. Local history has been preserved in the displays and exhibits at the Aroostook Historical and Art Museum on Main Street.

Presque Isle, Fort Fairfield, Caribou

Presque Isle, Aroostook's largest city, is the business, industrial, and cultural center—and the primary potato shipping point—of the county. It is also where the first successful transatlantic hot-air balloon, *Double Eagle II,* was launched in August 1978. Each August the Northern Maine Agricultural Fair is held at the fairgrounds, a week-long event with agricultural exhibits, horse shows, contests, and harness racing. Adjacent to the fairgrounds is the Northern Maine Forum and Civic Center, where special events are regularly scheduled. Just south of town, the 430-acre Aroostook State Park offers camping, swimming, boating, nature walks, and skiing. Or follow the hiking trail to the 1,213-foot summit of Quoggy Joe Mountain.

Fort Fairfield, which straddles Route 1A by the Canadian border northeast of Presque Isle, is another town that is busy growing and shipping potatoes. There are recreational opportunities in or near the town, including hunting, fishing, camping, winter sports, and golf. Each July the town hosts the Potato Blossom Festival, with a parade, a queen, and other activities including mashed-potato wrestling!

Caribou, the third town of the triangle, is located northwest of Fort Fairfield and north of Presque Isle. In addition to the major crop—potatoes—peas, hay, and oats are grown in the area. The Nylander Museum, on Route 161, is a natural history museum with exhibits of rocks, minerals, marine life, prehistoric tools, and specimens of mounted birds and insects from all over the world. Loring Air Force Base, northeast on Route 89 toward Limestone, is a sprawling complex half of whose installations are underground.

Fort Kent

The area from Van Buren to Fort Kent was settled during the mid-eighteenth century by Acadian refugees expelled from Nova Scotia. The spirit of those Acadians, as immortalized by Henry Wadsworth Longfellow in his poem *Evangeline,* has been preserved at the Acadian Village on Route 1 in Van Buren. The group of 16 reconstructed buildings includes houses with period furnishings, barns, a railroad station, a school, a blacksmith shop, a general store, and several other structures.

Van Buren itself is a small manufacturing (tennis racquets), farming (potatoes and sugar beets), and lumbering town.

Madawaska, an industrial community, is the northernmost town in Maine. Just south on Route 162, Long Lake is a major recreation area famous for landlocked salmon fishing, hunting, canoeing, and snowmobiling. There are many sporting camps here.

Fort Kent is probably best known as the beginning of U. S. Route 1, which ends in Key West, Florida. It is also a port of entry into the U.S. from Canada; Quebec City is just 169 miles away. There is fishing in the St. John and Allagash rivers and hunting for bear, deer, and grouse in the vast hinterlands. Fort Kent is the downstream terminus of the famous St. John-Allagash canoe trip, which begins 156 miles away at Moosehead Lake.

The Fort Kent Blockhouse (1839) was built to protect timber interests during the "Aroostook War" with Canada. The fort was never used, as the border dispute was settled peacefully by the Webster-Ashburton Treaty of 1842.

Fort Kent is the gateway to northwest Aroostook's vast wilderness and recreation region. This is wild country, some of it still not thoroughly explored. With the exception of a route that goes to Allagash out of Fort Kent, there are no public roads in this remote area, only private logging roads.

Allagash Wilderness Waterway

Route 161 follows the St. John River about 40 miles west along Maine's northern border from Fort Kent to Allagash. At the confluence of the St. John and Allagash rivers, Allagash Village marks the terminus of the Allagash Wilderness Waterway. This 92-mile-long corridor through 200,000 acres (30,000 of them water, the rest woods) is the result of creative cooperation. The state and federal governments funded the project jointly; the

Maine Department of Parks and Recreation administers it. Access to this area is limited, and all parties must be registered.

Although Allagash has been very popular for its white-water canoeing, camping, and fishing in the warmer seasons, the snowmobile has now increased winter use. Yet the area can be enjoyed only when there has been advance planning about entry, registration, rules, and regulations.

Portage, Ashland, Patten

From Fort Kent, the Aroostook Scenic Highway (Route 11) is a 50-mile drive south through a wooded paradise with dense forests, mirror lakes, and turbulent streams. Picnic sites and camping areas are provided by the state along the route.

Portage is a lumbering and recreation center with sporting camps and floatplane service to remote areas; it is the southern terminus of the Fish River Chain of Lakes canoe trip.

Ashland, just 10 miles south on Route 11, is the largest lumbering town in the county. American Realty Road begins in Ashland, a 50-mile gravel road that stretches westward into the forest. The three-day Lumberjack Roundup in early July is a festival of competitive contests where lumbermen can show their skill and stamina.

Patten, farther south, is a commercial center and logging town. The outstanding Patten Lumberman's Museum on Route 159 is a group of eight buildings that tell the story of Maine's logging history. There are more than 2,000 artifacts, log haulers, tractors, a re-creation of a logging camp, and several other machines and exhibits. Route 159 west leads to the northern entrance to Baxter State Park, 30 miles away.

PRACTICAL INFORMATION FOR AROOSTOOK COUNTY

Note: The area code for all Maine is 207

HOW TO GET THERE AND AROUND. By plane: Scheduled commercial service is available to Houlton International Airport (with customs service available), Frenchville, Madawaska, and Presque Isle via Portland, Bangor, or Augusta. For information: Valley Airlines (800–322–1008), or Eastern Express (800–451–4221).

Flying services are located in Ashland, Caribou, Fort Kent, Frenchville, Houlton, Patten, Presque Isle, Shin Pond, Sinclair, and St. Francis for small-plane or seaplane transportation to smaller towns and remote areas. For example: Jerry's Flying Service, Caribou Airport (496–7601); Daigle Flying Service, Fort Kent (834–5313); Valley Airlines, Frenchville (543–7322); Larson's Flying Service, Houlton International Airport (532–9489); and Air-Tech Aviation, Presque Isle Airport (764–3368).

By bus: Bus service is provided by Bangor and Aroostook Bus Service between Bangor and towns in Aroostook County.

By car: I–95 cuts across southern Aroostook County, terminating at Houlton near the Canadian border. The Trans-Canada Highway follows the border on the Canadian side, with international access at several locations.

Routes 1 and 1A follow the Canadian border, passing through the major towns of the county between Washington County and Fort Kent. Route 11, the "Aroostook Scenic Highway," is the inland north-south route between I–95 and Fort Kent. There are very few public roads in the wilderness areas of the northwest. Logging roads are privately owned, but many are available for public use (weather permitting). Some require permits, some have road-access fees. For information: North Maine Woods, Box 382, Ashland 04732 (435–6213).

Car rentals: Major car rental companies are represented in Presque Isle.

HOTELS, MOTELS, AND COTTAGES. Tourist accommodations are available, but many visitors to Aroostook County spend their time fishing or hunting in remote areas; lodges and sporting camps, therefore, cater specifically to these folks. Accommodations range from very simple to quite elaborate, a stay of a week or more is expected, all meals are usually included, and guides and floatplane service are either provided or available. Reservations are necessary at the sporting camps.

Rates are based on double occupancy: *Expensive,* $50–$70; *Moderate,* $30–$50. There is a 7% Maine state lodging tax. Unless otherwise indicated, hotels are open year-round.

Caribou

Caribou Motor Inn, Jct. Rtes. 1 and 164, 04736 (498–3733). *Expensive.* Large luxury motel with pool, gym, tennis. Some efficiencies, suites with whirlpool baths. Dining room.

Fort Kent

Jalbert's Allagash Camps. Box 126, 04743 (834–5015). *Moderate.* Located in Allagash Wilderness Waterway area. Comfortable cabins, tasty food. Camps reachable by canoe only; equipment and guides provided. Variety of "deep-woods" vacation trips available—mainly trout fishing and canoeing. Open May–Oct.

Rock's Motel, Main St., opp. International Bridge at start of U.S. Rte. 1, 04743 (834–3133). *Moderate.* Convenient resting place in hunting, fishing, canoeing, and snowmobiling area.

Houlton

Shiretown Motel, North Rd. at jct. Rte. 1 and I–95, 04730 (532–9421). *Moderate.* Full-service motor inn, comfortable and convenient. Two restaurants; kitchenettes available. Indoor pool, sauna, exercise room, tennis courts. Pleasant dining.

Patten

Mount Chase Lodge, Shin Pond Rd. 04765 (528–2183). *Expensive.* Family accommodations in the wilderness country of northern Maine at the north entrance to Baxter State Park. Bathing, fishing, canoeing, hiking, and floatplane service available. Family-style meals.

RESTAURANTS. Given the sparsely populated nature of much of Aroostook County, the best bet for dining out is to patronize the restaurants in motels in which you're staying. Most serve breakfast, lunch, and dinner and are generally inexpensive. The other alternatives are small, in-town restaurants and grills or quick-lunch shops. Most travelers to this area are campers and are self-sufficient. Sporting camps provide meals.

TOURIST INFORMATION. The Maine Publicity Bureau, 97 Winthrop St., Hallowell 04347, can provide brochures on sporting camps and wilderness experiences. The bureau operates a regional tourist information center in Houlton, on Ludlow Rd. near the jct. of I–95 and U.S. 1.

Information on local attractions can be requested from the Aroostook County Commissioners, Box 846, Caribou 04736 (493–3318), or from Caribou Chamber of Commerce, Box 357, Caribou 04736 (498–6156); Fort Kent Chamber of Commerce, Box 430, Fort Kent 04743 (834–5148); Houlton Chamber of Commerce, 109 Main St., Houlton 04730 (532–4216); and Presque Isle Chamber of Commerce, Box 672, 572 Main St., Presque Isle 04769 (764–6561).

TOURS. Most flying-service operators offer scenic rides (see *How to Get There and Around*).

SEASONAL EVENTS. January: Drag-sled races, Caribou (through March).

February: Winter carnival, Caribou (mid-Feb.); snowmobile races, Fort Kent (late Feb.).

June: Acadian Festival, Madawaska (late June).

July: Northern Maine Lumberjack Roundup (log rolling, canoe tilting, tree-cutting contests), Ashland (early July); Maine Potato Blossom Festival, Fort Fairfield (mid-July).

August: Northern Maine Fair, Presque Isle (early Aug.); Potato Feast and Arts and Crafts Festival, Houlton (late Aug.).

PARKS. Aroostook State Park, in Presque Isle, offers camping, picnicking, swimming, boating, fishing, snowmobiling, and hiking.

Allagash Wilderness Waterway is a 92-mi. corridor of lakes and rivers from Moosehead Lake to the far north near Fort Kent. The waterway is famous for canoeing, but visitors also enjoy picnicking, fishing, and snowmobiling. The busiest time for visitors is during the early summer, but the fall foliage in this wilderness area makes an autumn trip very pleasant indeed. If you plan to visit the area or make the canoe trip, registration is required. For information: Maine Bureau of Parks and Recreation, State House Station 22, Augusta 04333 (289–3821).

SUMMER SPORTS. Canoeing: The more than 2,000 lakes, streams, rivers, and ponds of the county offer the canoeing enthusiast opportunities of an incredible scope: from a casual paddle in a calm pond—to a frenetic running of the rapids—to a full-blown expedition down the mighty St. John River or along the Allagash Wilderness Waterway. Canoes are available for rent in most towns. For wilderness expeditions or major river trips, a guide is recommended. Specialized gear can be obtained from a wilderness outfitter. For listings of canoe trips and licensed outfitters, write: Maine Publicity Bureau (see *Tourist Information*) or Maine Department of Inland Fisheries and Wildlife, Station 41, Augusta 04333 (289–2043), or a local Chamber of Commerce.

Golf: There is an 18-hole course open to the public at Fort Fairfield—Aroostook Valley Country Club (476–6501); nine-hole courses at Caribou, Fort Kent, Hartford, Houlton, Island Falls, Madawaska, Portage, and Presque Isle.

WINTER SPORTS. Snowmobiling: From early Dec. through Mar., the snow-covered fields, lakes, and forest trails become a snowmobile heaven. There are hundreds of miles of supervised trails available to the casual "Sunday driver" or the serious speedster. The Allagash Wilderness Waterway offers 100 mi. of trails for experienced riders or with guides.

Skiing: Alpine skiing is available at Big Rock Mt. in Mars Hill (425–6711), at Ski Tow in Fort Kent (834–5202), and at Quoggy Joe Mt. in Presque Isle (764–3248). Miles of cross-country ski trails are provided in Caribou, Fort Fairfield, Fort Kent, Frenchville, Houlton, Madawaska, Mars Hill, Presque Isle (Aroostook State Park), and Stockholm.

FISHING. From ice-out in early May, landlocked salmon and trout attract sportsmen to the great north woods for a week or more of fishing in the wilderness. Sporting camps abound in Aroostook County, with guides, gear, and "secret spots." Floatplane service is available—and often necessary. Licenses are required for all freshwater fishermen over the age of 12 and may be purchased at many sporting-goods or hardware stores. For more information on fishing regulations, write Maine Dept. of Inland Fisheries and Wildlife (address above). In winter, fishermen set up ice-fishing huts on the hard-frozen lakes. Special regulations and licensing apply.

HUNTING. Hunting wild birds and animals is a major autumn attraction in Maine's millions of acres of wilderness. Moose (limited by lottery), grouse, and deer are special attractions to hunters in Aroostook County. Strict regulations are enforced for hunting with bow and arrow, firearms, and traps for safety and to manage the abundant wildlife. Licenses are required for all hunters 10 years old or over. Applicants for adult firearms licenses must show proof of having previously held an adult license or having successfully completed an approved hunter-safety course. Hunting on certain Indian territories is regulated by the tribes, and special permission must be obtained. For information on hunting regulations, write Department of Inland Fisheries and Wildlife (see *Summer Sports*). Professional guide service is recommended for wilderness trips. Contact Maine Guide Association, Box 265, Medway 04460. Sporting camps usually provide guides along with accommodations.

CAMPING. The clean air, sparkling waters, and endless wilderness of northern Maine are lures to those who enjoy camping. Campsites are available at Aroostook State Park in Presque Isle on a first-come, first-served basis. Primitive back-country campsites, mostly on lakes and rivers in the northwestern wilderness, are available at no charge and on a first-come, first-served basis; maps and information are available from the Maine Forest Service, Department of Conservation, State House Station 22, Augusta 04333 (289–2791). Many wilderness campsites are maintained throughout the commercial forest land by North Maine Woods, Inc., Box 382, Ashland 04732 (435–6213); early reservations are suggested for these campsites.

Facilities in privately owned campsites range from simple basics in the wilderness to deluxe cabins and cottages for rent—sometimes including canoe and boat rentals, automatic laundry equipment, snack bars, and recreation halls.

In its *Maine Guide to Camping,* the Maine Publicity Bureau (see *Tourist Information*) publishes a current listing of cottage rentals, campsites, and conveniences.

For a detailed list of private campgrounds catering primarily to people with camper-trailers, contact: Maine Campground Owners Association, 655 Main St., Lewiston 04240 (782–5874).

SPECTATOR SPORTS. Auto racing: At Aroostook County International Speedway, in Caribou, there are stock-car races, go-cart races, and truck pulling Sat. nights Memorial Day–Labor Day.

Horse racing: Harness racing is part of the action at the Northern Maine Fair, Presque Isle, in early Aug.

HISTORIC SITES. In Fort Kent—**Fort Kent Memorial** (1840), Block House St., off Rte. 1 (no tel.). Blockhouse built in preparation for Aroostook War; never used, since dispute was solved by treaty.

In Presque Isle—**Double Eagle II Monument.** (no tel.). Commemorates the first successful transatlantic hot-air balloon flight, launched at Presque Isle on Aug. 11, 1978.

MUSEUMS. Specialized museums in the region document Maine's important lumbering industry, its earliest settlers, and its natural history. Call ahead for days, hours, and admission fees.

In Ashland—**Ashland Logging Museum,** Garfield Rd. (435–6663). Exhibits relating to lumbering industry, including several buildings and heavy equipment.

In Caribou—**Nylander Museum,** 393 Main St. (493–4474). Exhibits of Indian items, shells, and marine life—and over 6,000 specimens of native animals and plants.

In Patten—**The Lumberman's Museum,** Rte. 159, west of Patten (528–2650). 2,000 artifacts related to Maine's lumbering industry, including heavy equipment and an 1820 logging camp.

In Van Buren—**Acadian Village,** Rte. 1 (868–2691). Sixteen reconstructed buildings depicting the Acadian culture, all with period furnishings.

MASSACHUSETTS

By
WILLIAM G. SCHELLER and CHRISTIE LOWRANCE

Christie Lowrance, who wrote the Cape Cod section of this chapter, is a free-lance writer who has been a full-time stringer for the Cape Cod Times *and a frequent contributor to* Cape Cod Life. *She has lived in Falmouth and Mashpee and now resides in Sandwich.*

Although the face it wears is still largely one of clapboard and old brick, Massachusetts, on the threshhold of the 1990s, has embarked on a bold new phase of its history. Yes, cities like Brockton and Lynn may be fighting to find a place for themselves now that the shoe factories have mostly gone, but the computer wizards who work in Lowell, Marlborough, and along Route 128 in the Danvers-to-Dedham crescent (which calls itself America's Technology Region) are busy fashioning the slivers of silicon that add, subtract, digest, file, remember, and amuse and propel us into the twenty-first century. Surely, much of the old landscape has changed; but drive up the coast to Salem, Marblehead, or Newburyport, out to Concord and Deerfield, or along the South Shore to Duxbury and Cohasset, and you will find that prosperity has made possible as careful a husbanding of history as you will find in the United States.

It wasn't so long ago that the Commonwealth of Massachusetts seemed to have more of a history than a future. Wise observers said that the American economy was moving west and south, that old industrial New England was done for, and that the Bay State would descend into a shabby gentility with only its books and its tourists for company. The wise observers were wrong, of course, and today the Massachusetts economy is the hottest in the nation. This *is* America's technology region (however clumsy a phrase that might be), but if it hadn't been high-tech it would have been something else. Massachusetts has been around too long, and has learned too much, to give up quite as easily as the Sunbelt boosters may have expected. After all, this state began as an experiment—one of the most radical and portentous in history—and an experiment it remains. That patina of age conceals a lively community indeed, one which is still developing in keeping with the restless and inquisitive spirit that has characterized Massachusetts for over 350 years.

How Massachusetts Got Started

The men and women who came to Plymouth and Boston in the early 1600s were the vanguard of a new spirit in the West. For the most part, they were the members of a new social order: the middle class. The tremendous surge of mercantile activity that followed the breakdown of feudalism had created this class, but the scheme of European politics had not kept pace with the new economics. As a result, many of the new merchants and professionals and yeoman farmers felt disenfranchised in a system that made few allowances for a middle.

This disillusioned class embraced a religion, Puritanism, that was morally conservative yet politically radical. In opposing the lax, quasi-Romanized Anglican establishment of their day, the Puritans were also reacting against the English king and aristocracy. In England their movement triumphed temporarily during the regime of Oliver Cromwell, following the civil war of the mid-seventeenth century, but by this time the most zealous and impatient of the Puritans had left for Massachusetts. Here, neither political nor religious hierarchies could impede their establishment of a New Canaan, whose chosen people were themselves and whose promised land was the vast American continent—or at least that portion of it not already claimed by the Roman Catholic French.

Although the political order which they established in Massachusetts during the seventeenth century might seem a dreadfully oppressive theocracy to us today, it was in many ways a quite radical departure from the modes of government then prevailing in Europe. The Mayflower Compact, drawn up by the Pilgrims as their ship lay at anchor in Plymouth Harbor in 1620, respected the will of the majority as the foundation of governmental authority—a precept which would be echoed in the constitution of the Commonwealth of Massachusetts and the United States Constitution over a century and a half later. The rights of minorities, particularly religious minorities such as the Quakers, were a consideration whose time had not yet come in the Massachusetts of the 1600s. Men and women like Roger Williams, the founder of Rhode Island, and Anne Hutchinson, another religious dissenter, were forced to leave the colony; the Quaker Mary Dyer, twice banished from Boston for practicing her religion, was hanged for her nonconformity. In the most potent and deadly convergence of clerical authority and mob psychology, 14 men and women were put to death as witches in the Salem of the 1690s.

Yet, however rudimentary and imperfect the Puritans' governmental institutions in their new homeland might have been, however unjust their concept of religious freedom for themselves and no one else, the die had nonetheless been cast for a system which would evolve away from arbitrary, centralized authority toward a concept of government by the consent of the governed. When in 1686 James II revoked the individual charters of the New England colonies and installed Sir Edmund Andros as

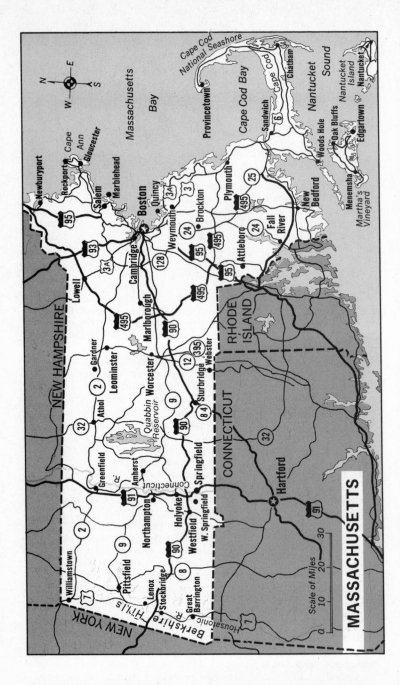

royal governor of the entire region, the colonial populace howled in protest. When James was deposed two years later, Bostonians took the cue and threw Andros into jail. This wasn't to be the last time that London's high-handedness would fan the flames of rebellion in Massachusetts.

By the end of the seventeenth century, 80,000 settlers had made the voyage from England to Massachusetts. The sheer numbers of these pioneers and their progeny, scattered across the countryside of Massachusetts and concentrated in the great trading centers of Salem and Boston, made it as difficult for the clergy to govern New England as it was for a distant king. Part of the reason for the secularization of New England life was the growing acceptance of the ideas generated in the Age of Reason; ironically, the very emphasis placed by the Puritans on education made for a populace more receptive to ways of thinking not necessarily sanctioned by the ruling divines. But far more important was the material comfort and expansiveness that comes with economic growth. It's one thing to maintain a community of the spiritually elect in a ring of huts surrounded by a howling wilderness; it's quite another matter to steer clear of the ways of the world in a minimetropolis filled with bustling craftsmen and merchants, men who plied their trades not only out of the Puritan love of useful toil but also because they might want bigger houses, silks for their wives, or a better quality of Madiera on their tables. Massachusetts in the eighteenth century became less an outpost for religious dissenters and more a New World foothold for mainstream English civilization.

The Coming of the Revolution

However strong the cultural connections, the mother country's political hold on the colonies became more and more strained as the century wore on. The governments of George II and George III sought to reimpose the authority previously ceded to the colonists, at first through a series of restrictions on colonial trade. The Acts of Trade and Navigation required the colonies to conduct trade only with English sources and markets. They were followed by the Stamp Act of 1765, the Tea Act of '73, and the so-called trade-restricting Intolerable Acts of the following year. At first the idea of outright rebellion, let alone secession, seemed unthinkable to all but the most radical political elements. But as George III and his ministers turned the screws ever tighter, firebrands like Samuel Adams were able to turn indignation to outright hostility. The muskets finally spoke on Lexington Green at dawn on April 19, 1775. Although the battles there and at Concord later the same day and at Bunker Hill (actually Breed's Hill) in Charlestown two months later were virtually the only Revolutionary struggles fought on Massachusetts soil, the old bay colony was clearly the place where the rhetorical groundwork for the war had been accomplished. And it was Massachusetts men like John Adams and John Hancock who would go on to take an important part in the political follow-through to the war, the framing of the United States Constitution.

The period immediately following the Revolution, prior to the establishment of a strong federal government, was a time of uncertainty and instability in Massachusetts. This was the era of Shays' rebellion, an uprising of farmers protesting high taxes and mortgage foreclosures. The 1790s, however, ushered in a period of unbridled prosperity for the state—or at least for those elements connected with trade and finance. This was the Federal, or Federalist era, so named after the ascendant Federalist political party that Massachusetts so strongly supported. Between 1790 and the War of 1812 Yankee ships roamed the globe; so numerous were the merchantmen of Salem in the harbors of distant China that Chinese traders

thought Salem was a magnificent country of its own. They were right
about the magnificence; Salem's merchant princes, including America's
first millionaires, lived in lovely Federal mansions designed by the likes
of Samuel McIntire; many of these beautiful homes survive today. In Boston, the peerless Charles Bulfinch, America's first important architect, was
busy translating prosperity into stone and brick, as in the Massachusetts
State House (1799) and the three Harrison Gray Otis houses (1796–1804).

Industry's Reign in Massachusetts

The dominance of such ports as Salem ended with the War of 1812 and
its interruption of foreign trade. But soon New England, and Massachusetts especially, was to discover a source of prosperity undreamed of in
the days before the Revolution. At the center of the new golden age was
the power loom, brought to life by the waters of the Merrimack in Lowell
and dozens of other rivers throughout the region. The Industrial Revolution in America had begun.

Manufacturing was king in Massachusetts during the middle and latter
part of the nineteenth century. In Lowell and Fall River it was textiles;
in Haverhill and Brockton and Lynn it was shoes; in Waltham it was
watches. Taunton turned out locomotives, and Gardner made furniture.
Not that Massachusetts had turned its back on the sea; Donald McKay
built his great clipper ships in Newburyport and East Boston in the 1850s,
and whalers sailed out of New Bedford and Nantucket well into midcen-
tury. The fishing fleets of Provincetown and Gloucester worked hard then,
as they do today.

Although Boston had its own busy factories and wharves, its principal
role was that of financial and political nerve center during the boom years
of the 1800s. A certain class of Bostonians, scions of the great trading and
manufacturing fortunes, came to dominate the social and financial life of
the city. These were the "Proper Bostonians" documented in the informative nonfiction book of that title by Cleveland Amory, and in John P. Marquand's satiric novel *The Late George Apley*. Ensconced in their brownstone rowhouses in the Back Bay and their offices on State Street, the
members of the so-called Brahmin class acquitted themselves admirably
in the endowment of enduring cultural institutions such as the Boston
Symphony and Museum of Fine Arts but seemed to suffer a loss of nerve
or interest when it came to playing the capitalist game with vigor. For
whatever reason, New York eclipsed Boston as the nation's financial center well before the close of the nineteenth century, and a number of re-
verses—chief among them the cheap-wage textile industry rivalry of the
South—caused a decline in Massachusetts's economic fortunes that per-
sisted well into the twentieth century. By the 1960s the great mills were
mostly silent; the racket of flying shuttles and shoe-stitching machines had
all but ceased except in the smaller specialty shops.

Fortunately, Massachusetts had one ace up its sleeve: the tremendous
commitment to education which had been a legacy of the Puritans. With
over 50 institutions of higher learning in the greater Boston area alone,
led by giants such as Harvard, the Massachusetts Institute of Technology,
and Boston University, the commonwealth had plenty of brainpower to
draw upon when the high-tech revolution began in earnest. Today the
firms that make news on the business pages of the *Boston Globe* not only
have names no one had heard of in 1950, but they deal in products that
were unknown a generation ago. Massachusetts entrepreneurs and their
companies pioneer in semiconductors and office computer systems, in
computer software, in biotechnology, and in photovoltaics—the science

of creating electrical energy from sunlight. If this decade is remembered as the Roaring Eighties, Massachusetts business will be remembered as having been on its cutting edge.

We would be remiss, however, if we were to suggest that everyone in this state is riding the crest of the boom. Massachusetts's oldest industry, fishing, is not having the best of times; some Gloucestermen are letting their boats lie at anchor in the face of impossibly high insurance premiums, and the scallop catch is off everywhere but on the banks off Nantucket. The state's farmers have retreated before the onslaught of suburban development, although they are now assisted by a still underfunded open-land preservation program and more favorable property tax status. Workers in the traditional manufacturing industries cannot be certain about the security of their jobs. Those whom the boom economy has left behind are stymied by a superheated real-estate market; what might have been an affordable apartment for a factory worker and his family 10 years ago is now an expensive condominium. The challenge for Massachusetts, for its politicians and its economic managers, will be to see that all boats rise in a favorable tide.

The Lay of the Land

It isn't a very large piece of territory on which this history has been played out. Massachusetts is only 45th in size among the nation's 50 states, with an area of 8,257 square miles. But the terrain is varied and appealing, with an environment—urban decay and suburban sprawl notwithstanding—that is among the most architecturally and historically interesting in the nation.

Like the Pilgrims, who made a landfall at what is now Provincetown even before they reached Plymouth and its now-famous rock, many modern visitors get their first look at Massachusetts on a trip to Cape Cod. The Cape is representative of much of the coastal topography of the state, particularly along the coast south of Boston. The foundations of the "upper" Cape (don't be confused; this term refers to the part closest to the mainland, before you reach the "elbow" at Chatham) and of Martha's Vineyard and Nantucket are glacial moraines—the geologist's term for the accumulation of material that marked the southernmost stopping point of the vast glaciers of the last ice age. These landforms have been built upon, over the years, by the action of wind and tides to create the shifting dunes of the barrier beaches at Cape Cod's Monomoy Island, Nauset Beach, and Race Point, and at Great Point on Nantucket. The more stable interior dunes are covered with scrub brush and heather, lovely in the autumn of the year, while the Cape's bay side features fertile salt marshes.

North of the scrubby, marshy country around Plymouth (Massachusetts's famed cranberry bogs are located near here), the land becomes hillier; the Blue Hills, located just south of Boston on the state reservation of the same name, are the highest points along the Massachusetts coast. The now-enlarged peninsula on which Boston was built once featured three steep hills, of which Beacon Hill is the only remaining vestige. Heading north across the urbanized lowlands of southern Essex County, you will reach rocky Cape Ann, at the eastern tip of which the old fishing ports of Gloucester and Rockport jut into the cold Atlantic. Farther north still, between Cape Ann and the New Hampshire border, picturesque salt marshes are crisscrossed by tidal estuary streams. The elongated barrier beach of Plum Island, much of it set aside as the federal Parker River Wildlife Refuge, protects these peaceful marshes from the open ocean.

Gently undulating hills characterize interior Massachusetts just beyond the coastal plains. This is old farm country, now dotted with mill towns and burgeoning Boston suburbs, drained by the Merrimack, the Mystic, the Charles, and the Concord rivers. Beyond Fitchburg and Worcester the state's topography takes on more of the character of upland New England, similar to southern Vermont or New Hampshire. Forests surround huge, man-made Quabbin Reservoir at the center of the state. Now vistas widen as the valley of the Connecticut, New England's longest river, finally comes into view. Springfield, a historic manufacturing center, is the capital of this region; along with the college towns of Amherst and Northampton, and historic Greenfield and Deerfield to the north, it forms the population nucleus of what is known as the Pioneer Valley, after the settlers who made their way from the coast into this wilderness more than 300 years ago.

From the Pioneer Valley to the New York State border the direction is west—and up. These are the Berkshire Hills, old, rounded peaks of the Appalachian range. If you've been to Tanglewood in the summer to hear the Boston Symphony, you've been to the Berkshires; yet there's a lot more to the area than even its admirable array of seasonal cultural activities, and any visit ought to include a day or so spent getting lost on the back roads among the last of the hill farms.

Exploring Massachusetts

BOSTON

Boston is a walker's city. True, patterns of suburban annexation in the last century have made for a municipality with borders lying far to the west and south of the central city; but the area containing most of the points of historical and architectural interest is quite compact, and most sites are easily accessible by foot or public transportation. An automobile is a liability when you are sightseeing in Boston neighborhoods such as Beacon Hill, the North End, and Back Bay. Downtown, the streets are seventeenth-century village lanes that happen to have skyscrapers along them, and traffic moves at a crawl. Free parking is nonexistent, meters run out before you walk to the end of the block, and garages are extremely expensive. The multiyear project to reconstruct the Central Artery in downtown Boston, scheduled to begin in 1990, will create further problems for motorists. Walk Boston and you will like it—drive it, and you won't.

The Freedom Trail

A good introduction to downtown Boston and its principal historical attractions is the Freedom Trail, a mile-and-a-half route which leads past 16 famous sites. The Freedom Trail is a walk not only into the heart and history of Boston, but into the events surrounding the birth of the American nation. The Trail begins at the Freedom Trail Information Center on Boston Common, near the Park Street subway station. There you can obtain a booklet with a map and descriptions of the sites along the way, as well as information about other Boston points of interest.

From Park Street station, the Freedom Trail leads up through Boston Common, once a common pasture set aside for the use of Boston's colonial citizens and the oldest park in the nation, to the "new" State House. This magnificent structure, considered by many to be the finest example of classical architecture in the United States, was designed by Boston native Charles Bulfinch and completed in 1799. (Only the red-brick center section, with its gilded dome, is original; the stone wings on either side were added in 1918, and the yellow brick extension in the rear dates from late Victorian times.) Free guided tours of the State House include the Hall of Flags, the General Court (legislature) chamber with its "Sacred Cod" commemorating the importance of the state's fishing industry, and the Archives, containing such priceless documents as Governor Bradford's *History of Plimoth Plantation* and the original Massachusetts Bay Company charter, along with original plates and engravings by Paul Revere depicting the Boston Massacre.

From the State House, the Trail heads back down Park Street to the Park Street Church, designed by Peter Banner in the Georgian style and built in 1809. The spire was influenced by the work of the great English

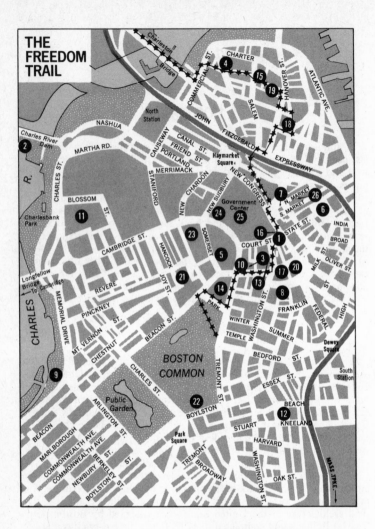

THE
FREEDOM
TRAIL

Points of Interest

1) Boston Massacre Site
2) Boston Museum of Science
3) Old City Hall
4) Copp's Hill Burying Ground
5) Court House
6) Custom House
7) Faneuil Hall
8) Franklin's Birthplace Site
9) Hatch Memorial Concert Shell
10) King's Chapel
11) Massachusetts General Hospital
12) Tufts New England Medical Center
13) Old Corner Book Store
14) Park Street Church and Old Granary
     Burying Ground
15) Old North Church (originally Christ
     Church)
16) Old State House
17) Old South Meeting House
18) Paul Revere's House
19) Paul Revere Statue
20) Post Office
21) State House
22) Central Burying Ground
23) State Office Building
24) John F. Kennedy Federal Building
25) New City Hall
26) Faneuil Hall Marketplace

architect Sir Christopher Wren. Park Street Church has been the site of much inspirational political and religious oratory, but perhaps its most important moment was on July 4, 1829, when the great abolitionist William Lloyd Garrison gave his first public speech in Boston against slavery.

Adjacent to Park Street Church, on Tremont Street, is the Old Granary Burying Ground. This hallowed cemetery contains the graves of John Hancock, Robert Treat Paine, and Samuel Adams, all signers of the Declaration of Independence; Paul Revere and Peter Faneuil; the parents of Benjamin Franklin (Franklin is buried in Philadelphia); nine early governors of Massachusetts; and the victims of the Boston Massacre, which occurred when an angry mob was fired upon by British sentries at the Old State House on March 5, 1770. Future president John Adams offered legal defense for the soldiers, two of whom were found guilty of manslaughter, but Samuel Adams and Paul Revere ground a great deal of revolutionary propaganda out of the incident.

Farther down the Trail, at the corner of Tremont and School streets, is King's Chapel, Boston's first Episcopal Church. Built in 1749, it never received the steeple which architect Peter Harrison had intended, yet it contains one of the most austerely beautiful Georgian interiors in New England. As fine a building as King's Chapel is, the Puritan-descended Congregationalists of eighteenth-century Boston resented its presence as a symbol of the old, royalist Anglican religion their forebears had fled. In 1789, after a good part of Boston's Anglican population had packed its bags and Tory sympathies and left for Canada or England, the church became Unitarian, and so it remains to this day.

The Burying Ground beside King's Chapel predates the church by a century and is in fact the oldest in Boston. Here lie the remains of several of the colony's early governors and other early citizens, beneath headstones carved with primitive death's heads and epitaphs admonishing the living. One stone here is of particular interest to students of American literature. It marks the grave of Elizabeth Pain, whom Nathaniel Hawthorne used as the model for Hester Prynne in *The Scarlet Letter*.

The Freedom Trail continues down School Street past the old City Hall, which once concealed the labyrinths of power managed by the legendary James Michael Curley and now houses a cafe and French restaurant. The statue in front is of a man who knew a bit about power and no doubt enjoyed French restaurants: Benjamin Franklin, born a few blocks from here in 1706. The statue, sculpted by Richard S. Greenhough and dedicated during the Franklin sesquicentennial year of 1856, cleverly reveals both the serious and puckish sides of the great man's personality.

Continue down School Street toward the business district to reach Washington Street. Here, at the corner of School and Washington, are two historic structures. The smaller of the two is the Old Corner Bookstore, built about 1718 as an apothecary's shop and now one of the oldest brick buildings in Boston. The ground floor went into use as a bookstore as early as 1829, but the upstairs rooms were famous not for books but for the men who wrote them. Here were the offices of William D. Ticknor and James T. Fields, perhaps the most influential publishers of their day. Their premises became New England's principal literary salon, frequently visited during the mid-nineteenth century by Emerson, Longfellow, Hawthorne, Holmes, Harriet Beecher Stowe, Whittier, and Julia Ward Howe. Today both floors have been restored and are operated as a bookstore by the *Boston Globe*. The store has a fine selection of books about New England and by New Englanders.

Diagonally across Washington Street from the Old Corner Bookstore is Old South Meeting House (1729), a plain brick church with a graceful wooden steeple. The Old South was where many of colonial Boston's most impassioned anti-British meetings took place, culminating in the gathering on the night of December 16, 1773. It was then that the incendiary Samuel Adams stirred his listeners into heading down to a nearby pier and throwing a shipment of heavily taxed tea into Boston Harbor. Boston had its Tea Party, and the Revolution was that much closer. So was the despoilation of the Old South Meeting House, which was stripped of its pews and turned into a riding stable by the British during the occupation. Restored by a citizens' campaign in the mid-1800s, the old church now houses a collection of Revolutionary era relics.

From the Old South, the Freedom Trail winds through Boston's financial district to the old State House. Built in 1713, this diminutive brick structure was the seat of government during the colonial era and naturally became the focus of considerable animosity as the Revolution drew nearer. After the war was over, it became the seat of the new Massachusetts state government until Bulfinch's grand new edifice on Beacon Hill was completed. Used for commercial purposes throughout much of the nineteenth century, the building has been carefully restored and now houses an interesting collection of maritime artifacts as well as historical exhibits. Even the colorful lion and unicorn, symbols of British imperial power pulled down during the Revolution, have been restored to their places at the building's east gable ends. But the Boston Massacre, the site of which is marked by a circle of cobblestones in the street just below, has not been forgotten.

The next stop on the Freedom Trail is Dock Square (right behind the new City Hall), which is dominated by a statue of Samuel Adams and by historic Faneuil Hall. Donated in 1742 by the wealthy Boston merchant Peter Faneuil and enlarged to a design by Charles Bulfinch in 1805, Faneuil Hall earned the name Cradle of Liberty because of the many Boston town meetings held here between 1763 and the outbreak of the Revolution. The tradition begun by Samuel Adams and James Otis continues; to this day, any legitimate citizens' group may, upon petition, use Faneuil Hall as a forum for discussion and debate. Individuals, of course, are always welcome here. The main hall contains a number of interesting paintings, and the top floor houses the headquarters and museum of the ceremonial Ancient and Honorable Artillery Company, the nation's oldest militia. Arms, uniforms, and other historical artifacts are on display.

The grasshopper weathervane on top of Faneuil Hall, once the symbol of Boston to returning mariners when the three-story building was a fixture on the low-rise city's skyline, is now the symbol of one of the most ambitious urban "recycling" projects ever. This is Faneuil Hall Marketplace, also known as Quincy Market because that was the original name of the three granite arcades built in 1826 between Faneuil Hall and the harbor. Conceived as a central market for butchers, greengrocers, and other victualers, Quincy Market served this purpose well into the present century, but by the 1970s the complex and the area around it had become seedy around the edges. However, the great gentrification of Boston was about to begin, and this was to be its centerpiece. The bicentennial year of 1976 found Quincy Market reborn as a "festival marketplace," chockfull of food stalls, specialty retailers, restaurants, bars, and dispensers of designer chocolate chip cookies. Even some of the market's pre-renovation tenants, such as Berenson the butcher and Doe, Sullivan the cheese seller, are back at their old vastly refurbished locations. The place has become Boston's biggest tourist draw, at least in terms of revenue (people don't spend money at Paul Revere's House), and it has inspired a raft of imitators in every city that has more tatty old downtown buildings than it knows what to do with.

Just to the right of Quincy Market, at the end opposite Faneuil Hall, stands one of Boston's odder buildings. This is the Customs House, the lower part of which was built in 1847 in the Greek Revival style then popular. The classically inspired skyscraper addition was appended in 1915, at which time this became the city's tallest building. Recently the federal government decided to move the Customs Service elsewhere and sold the old tower to the city. When the funds for development have been found, the base of the tower will become home to the New England Sports Museum and the tower itself will be converted to office space.

Downtown, the Waterfront, and the Harbor Islands

Adjacent to the Quincy Market area, and off the Freedom Trail (except for the Old South Meeting House and old State House described above) are Boston's financial and main shopping districts whose looping and frequently confusing streets grow ever more congested as one high-rise office tower after another contributes to what has been called the Manhattanization of this old city. Most downtown shopping is along Washington Street. Here's where you'll find the venerable department stores, Filene's and Jordan Marsh, as well as the shops of Lafayette Place and narrow side streets selling used books, fine cutlery, leather luggage, and just about anything else you can think of. On the other side of the Central Artery (an elevated expressway) from the financial district are the buildings of Boston's restored waterfront. The prime attraction here is the superb New England Aquarium, with its huge, cylindrical ocean tank housing dozens of species of marine creatures and its outdoor porpoise and sea lion shows. South of the aquarium, at Rowe's Wharf, Boston Harbor sightseeing boats depart for tours of the harbor and its islands. (Other tours, including, in summer, boats to Provincetown, on Cape Cod, depart from nearby Long Wharf.) Most of the harbor islands have been gathered into the new Boston Harbor Islands State Park, which affords visitors and natives the opportunity to "get away" from the city while still keeping its skyline well in view. Camping, hiking, swimming, and exploring old military ruins are favorite harbor islands pastimes. There is regular boat service (daily in summer; weekends in the spring and fall) to George's Island, site of a Civil War fort; from George's, a free water taxi connects with the other islands.

Boston's Oldest Neighborhood: The Italian North End

The Freedom Trail passes around Haymarket Square (a riot of open air fruit and vegetable stalls on weekends) and under the Fitzgerald Expressway to emerge in Boston's North End. Although the city's renovated Central Artery will pass near the North End, planners guarantee that no existing buildings will be lost. The narrow, winding streets of the North End are Boston's oldest; up until the end of the eighteenth century, this was almost all there was to the city—the rest of it was yet to be reclaimed from the harbor and the mudflats of the Charles, and Beacon Hill was still a steep tangle of shrubbery. As the 1800s wore on, fashionable folk moved to the city's newer neighborhoods and left the North End to successive waves of immigrants. The Irish had their day here, as did the eastern European Jews. The Italians arrived around 1900, and they did something different: they stayed. To this day, despite the encroachment of expensive condominiums inhabited by decidedly nonethnic types (their grandparents may have been, but they buy their clothes at Brooks Brothers and Bonwit

Teller), the flavor of the North End is decidedly Italian. You will still hear Neapolitan and Abruzzese dialects spoken in this neighborhood, and on summer weekends the patron saints of various old-world clubs and civic associations are honored with parades and street festivals. There are dozens of Italian restaurants in the North End, many of them old-line places that honor the tradition of tomato sauce on everything.

Underneath this deep Mediterranean patina, however, are several of the historical icons of colonial Boston. The Freedom Trail heads up Hanover Street, the area's main shopping strip, and turns right on Richmond and left on North Street to reach the Paul Revere House. The silversmith-patriot lived here with his large family from 1770 to 1780, and it was from here that he set off on his famous ride on the night of April 18, 1775. The house, which was already a hundred years old when Revere bought it, is Boston's oldest wooden building. It had become a slum dwelling by the turn of the present century, when it was rescued and more or less faithfully restored to its original (seventeenth-century) appearance. Inside, the first floor has been arranged as it might have been well before Revere's tenancy, with the wide hearths and simple furniture of the earliest period of settlement. The second floor reflects the style of Revere's own age. Although the furniture is not his own, there is a collection of some of his engravings and personal belongings.

From the Revere House the Trail leads to the Old North Church by way of the Paul Revere Mall, the main feature of which is an equestrian statue of American history's most famous mounted messenger by Cyrus Dallin. The Church itself, even if we set aside its historical connections, is a magnificent work of Georgian architecture. This oldest of Boston's houses of worship was built in 1723 as Christ Church, and it still houses the second Episcopal Congregation in Boston. The bells in the steeple, which Paul Revere rung as a boy, were the first cast for Britain's colonies in the New World, but this steeple is famous for another reason. Here, on the night of Revere's ride, his friend Robert Newman hung two lanterns to warn the citizens of Charlestown of the approach of British troops by water. Revere already knew that; the lanterns weren't for his information, despite Longfellow's poem.

Just down Hull Street from the Old North is Copp's Hill Burying Ground, where many of Boston's colonial era families had their plots; the most famous of them is the Mather clan, of which Cotton and Increase Mather were scions. Shady Copp's Hill is a pleasant place for walking, especially if you enjoy deciphering the ancient inscriptions on chipped and mossy gravestones. Leaving the burying ground, you can walk downhill to Commercial Street, turn left at the intersection of Commercial and Charter, and head for the bridge that will take you across to Charlestown.

Charlestown, separated from the rest of Boston by the Charles River, is the site of the decommissioned navy yard where the navy's oldest commissioned ship, the USS *Constitution,* is permanently moored. (You can also reach the navy yard by bus or subway from the Haymarket station.) The USS *Constitution,* affectionately known for generations as Old Ironsides, was launched in Boston in 1797 and never lost a naval engagement. The stout wooden man-of-war is open to visitors, as are several museums on the grounds of the vast and once-important navy yard.

Beyond the navy yard you can see the granite shaft of the Bunker Hill Monument, erected to commemorate the battle fought here on June 17, 1775. The monument actually stands on Breed's Hill, where the misnamed battle took place; Bunker Hill is just to the north. Diorama exhibits explain the fighting; climb the tower (no elevator) for a fine view of the city and harbor.

Beacon Hill

To many visitors, Boston is best symbolized by the gracious brick row houses and narrow, gaslit streets of Beacon Hill. Bordered along Boston Common by Beacon Street, dubbed by Oliver Wendell Holmes, Sr., as "the sunny street that holds the sifted few," Beacon Hill was the home of the city's most prominent families during the first half of the nineteenth century. Even after the center of residential fashion shifted to the Back Bay, Beacon Hill retained its reputation as the bastion of Brahmin propriety, the very seat of Brahmin Boston. Although many of the old row houses have been broken up into apartments and condominiums (the remaining single-family homes are priced at well over a million dollars in most cases), the elegance and harmony of the Federal era facades have been preserved by zoning ordinance and the all-powerful Beacon Hill Civic Association.

The hill takes its name from a harbor beacon placed on the summit in the earliest years of settlement. At that time, Beacon Hill was much higher and steeper, but the leveling that was done in the 1790s to accommodate the new State House (the fill was used to make dry land of the area around Charles Street, not—as is sometimes believed—the Back Bay) created some highly developable real estate. By 1800, the newly tamed slopes of the hill were beginning to sprout handsome row houses and freestanding mansions. Row-house design prevailed as the neighborhood became more popular—this acreage was too valuable for broad lawns, although open space survives in many lovely concealed backyard gardens and of course in the stately, iron-fenced quadrant around which Louisburg Square was built in the 1830s and 1840s.

Singling out the most interesting houses on Beacon Hill is a tricky business, since the best way to appreciate the place, on a first visit at least, is in its ruddy-bricked totality. Yet certain structures do stand out. Numbers 39 and 40 Beacon Street were designed by Charles Bulfinch and Alexander Parris for Nathan Appleton and Daniel Parker. Today they belong to the Women's City Club of Boston, which conducts guided tours by appointment. In addition to Parris's splendid Greek Revival interiors, the houses—like certain others on the hill—are notable for containing several panes of mauve-tinted glass on their Beacon Street facades. The color was produced accidentally, by the action of sunlight on imperfections in the imported glass. In its age and rarity, the old glass has become a trademark of Beacon Hill.

Farther down Beacon Street toward Charles Street is No. 45, built in 1804. This was the last of three Beacon Hill houses designed by Charles Bulfinch for Harrison Gray Otis, congressman, Boston mayor, and one of the hill's original developers. The other Bulfinch Otis houses are at 85 Mt. Vernon Street (built in 1800) and 140 Cambridge Street (built in 1796); the Cambridge Street address is the headquarters of the Society for the Preservation of New England Antiquities, and its restored period rooms are open to visitors. Other Bulfinch-designed houses on the hill (all private) are at 6, 8, 13, 15, and 17 Chestnut Street.

The area north of Pinckney Street, generally known as the "back" or "north slope" of Beacon Hill, was never as fashionable as the side facing the Common. But its steep, narrow streets make for an interesting walk, and many tiny, circa 1800 row houses may be found among its later three- and four-story apartment buildings. This was once Boston's black neighborhood; an early black meetinghouse has been preserved on Smith Court, off Joy Street. Also interesting are the north slope's tiny cul-de-sac streets, with their iron gates and cobblestones.

Beacon Hill's western boundary is Charles Street, which constitutes the neighborhood's retail and restaurant center. Here, and along the streets between Charles and the river which comprise the "flat side" of the hill, are a number of fine antique shops. At the foot of the south slope of the hill is Cambridge Street; take a right here and you will soon find your way to Government Center.

A lot has been said and written about Government Center since it was built in the early and mid 1960s, and as the years go by more and more of it is negative. It's still easy to find apologists for the inverted-ziggurat concrete City Hall, but the acres of sterile, brick-paved mall which surround this and the Center's other structures now seems a poor replacement for the residential streets of the old West End, which was obliterated for the government buildings and the expensive Charles River Park high-rise residential development. In an ironic recent turn of events, the Hurley Building—a concrete behemoth that sprawls just west of the twin Gropius-designed towers of the Kennedy federal office building—has been declared surplus state property, and plans are afoot to convert it to low- and middle-income apartments. Priority for rental applications would be given to none other than the families who were bulldozed out of the West End 25 years ago. We live and learn, and the 1960s were one of the most costly learning experiences for American municipal governments.

The Back Bay and South End

Beyond Charles Street and the westward limits of Boston Common lies a vastly more successful experiment in grand-scale urban planning, the Back Bay. Up until the middle of the nineteenth century the land stretching between here and present-day Kenmore Square lay under a backwater of the Charles River. Cut off first from the river by a milldam topped by an extension of Beacon Street, and later crisscrossed with rail lines and sullied with sewage, this "back" bay was by 1850 beyond salvation as a water resource. The landfill began at the eastern end, with the creation of the beautiful Public Garden and its lagoon, where the famous swan boats have paddled for over a hundred years. From spring through autumn, the formal plantings in the Public Garden are magnificent. Stroll around the lagoon and past the equestrian statue of George Washington to Arlington Street, and begin your tour of the Back Bay at the beginning of Commonwealth Avenue.

The first thing you'll notice about this part of town, as you look down the tree-lined expanse of Commonwealth, is that the streets are, for Boston, uncharacteristically straight. The whole neighborhood, in fact, is a neat grid, bordered on the west by the Charles River and its delightful pedestrian Esplanade. (Near the Beacon Hill end of the Esplanade is the famous Hatch Memorial Shell, where the Boston Pops presents its free outdoor concerts in summer.) Between the river and the shopping district of Boylston Street, the next mile is filled with the rich architectural and historical traditions of the Back Bay.

The reason the Back Bay is so evenly laid out is that its planners, a hundred years ago and more, were consciously imitating the newly built boulevards of Paris. As the new streets were graded, Bostonians of means were quick to buy lots and build the stately brick and brownstone row houses which still give the district its character. Most of these four-story mansions have long since been converted to condominiums and apartments, yet their exterior dignity and restrained but diverse architectural styles still reflect the era—from about 1870 to 1930—when this was *the* place to live in Bos-

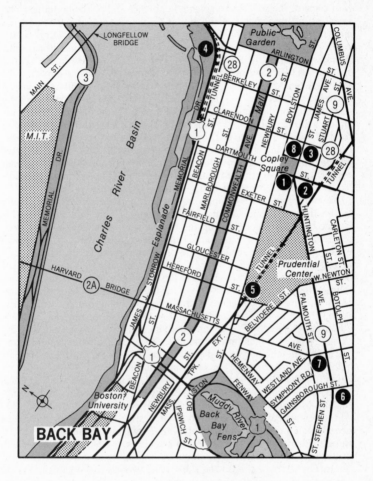

Points of Interest

1) Boston Public Library
2) Copley Place
3) Hancock Tower
4) Hatch Memorial Shell
5) Hynes Auditorium
6) New England Conservatory of Music (Jordan Hall)
7) Symphony Hall
8) Trinity Church

ton. And people will still pay a premium rent or purchase price for a Back Bay address.

As the Brahmins built their new houses, they furnished the Back Bay with some of the city's most splendid churches and public buildings. The architectural focal point of the area is Copley Square, site of two of the most important American buildings of the late nineteenth century: Henry Hobson Richardson's Trinity Church (1877) and McKim, Mead, and White's Boston Public Library (1895). Trinity Church is the quintessential expression of Richardson's Romanesque Revival style, inspired by churches of France and Spain. The great stone mass of Trinity centers on a bold central tower modeled after that of the cathedral in Salamanca, Spain; the sheer weight of the building's presence is made less ponderous by the architect's use of multicolored masonry, buff and brown with graceful stone rosettes. But don't limit your appreciation of Trinity to the building's exterior. Inside are magnificent works in stained glass by Edward Burne-Jones and paintings—indeed, an entire interior color scheme—by the American master John LaFarge. The ornamentation of the vaulted ceilings, unequalled in the United States, is easily worth a stiff neck.

Facing Trinity across Copley Square is the grand Renaissance facade of the Boston Public Library. Walk through Daniel Chester French's bronze bas relief doors and up the marble stairs of this elegant palazzo to the main reading room, Bates Hall, one of Boston's most impressive public spaces. In the adjacent book-processing room are Edwin Abbey's murals depicting the search for the Holy Grail; the paintings at the head of the staircase, by the French artist Puvis de Chavannes, portray the nine muses. Upstairs, in the anterooms of the fine arts collections, is the Boston painter John Singer Sargent's mural series on Judaism and Christianity. If you return to the first floor and follow the corridor to the 1972 library addition designed by Philip Johnson, you will pass through a lovely enclosed garden in which flowers bloom in spring and summer around a central fountain. The library is planning a major renovation to celebrate its 100th anniversary and preserve its magnificence.

One of the most important cultural landmarks in the United States stands in the southern corner of Back Bay at the intersection of Huntington and Massachusetts avenues. This is Symphony Hall, home since 1900 of the renowned Boston Symphony Orchestra. Although the building's neo-Georgian exterior, another McKim, Mead, and White design, is distinguished, Symphony Hall's greatest asset is its wonderful acoustics. Each of the hall's 2,500 seats is a good one from which to hear the Boston Symphony Orchestra or the Boston Pops. (The two musical organizations are composed of essentially the same personnel.)

Modern architects have provided a number of dramatic foils to the traditional building styles of the Back Bay, with an array of new development complexes along the eastern "spine" of the neighborhood. The earliest of these was the mid-60s Prudential Center, which lies between Boylston Street and Huntington Avenue adjacent to the newly enlarged Hynes Auditorium. The Pru, as locals call it, is a 52-story office tower surrounded by a shopping plaza, luxury hotel, and high-rise apartments. One of its principal attractions is the central tower's top-floor Skywalk, an observatory offering fine views of Boston, Cambridge, and the suburbs to the west and south. One of the more interesting sights to be seen from this lofty perspective is the adjacent Christian Science Center, containing the world headquarters and mother church of the Christian Science religion, as well as the church's publishing operations, including the *Christian Science Monitor*. Seen from above, the geometry of I. M. Pei's design is fascinating.

Visitors can take guided tours of the center, a highlight of which is the Maparium, a walk-in translucent globe.

Just back of the library, and practically rubbing elbows with the Prudential Center, is the lavish new shopping center–hotel complex called Copley Place. Time was when no one thought Boston would have its own branch of the flashy Texas retailer Neiman-Marcus, but here it is, along with an impressive array of posh and down-to-earth shops including Ralph Lauren, Louis Vuitton, Mark Cross, Gucci, Tiffany, Godiva Chocolates, Victoria's Secret, and a Rizzoli bookstore. To make a grand entrance into Copley Place, use the Westin Hotel door at Dartmouth Street and St. James Avenue and ascend past the indoor waterfalls.

Another fine view of the city and its suburbs may be had from the top-floor observatory of the 62-story John Hancock Tower, tallest building in New England and easily the most reflective. It's fun to watch the rest of the neighborhood, including Trinity Church, undulate along with the cloudscapes in the Hancock's sheer walls of blue mirror glass. As to whether the rhomboidal skyscraper makes an appropriate neighbor for Richardson's fine old pile—well, you'll have to answer that question for yourself.

Copley Place and the Prudential Center tend to wall off one of Boston's most interesting neighborhoods, the South End. Here the brick row houses are almost uniformly bowfronted, with high front steps and ornate cast iron railings. The side streets—Rutland Square and Union Park are among the most attractive—have more of the feeling of London than of Paris about them; it's altogether a more intimate neighborhood than the Back Bay and a great place for an aimless stroll. The South End is interesting, too, in that it is only partly gentrified; magnificent restorations stand not far from buildings that still speak of the area's mixed socioeconomic and racial roots. Many people feel that this makes for a more appealing sense of place, one that is less homogenized and glossed over. Don't count on it to last.

The Emerald Necklace

When the master planners of the late nineteenth century gave Boston much of its present-day appearance, they weren't working only in bricks and mortar. One of the great glories of the city is its Emerald Necklace, the chain of parks and green spaces largely designed by the great landscape architect Frederick Law Olmsted. Although the "necklace" can be said to begin at the older Boston Common and Public Garden and continue along the Commonwealth Avenue Mall, Olmsted's influence really comes into play at the Back Bay Fens, a naturally landscaped park surrounded by Park Drive and the Fenway, just a short walk from busy Kenmore Square and that temple of unanswered prayers, the Red Sox' Fenway Park. In one section of the Fens, marsh reeds still grow along the banks of the Muddy River; elsewhere there are rolling lawns, meandering footpaths, and even a formal rose garden.

Two of Boston's finest art museums are located adjacent to the fens. The Museum of Fine Arts (main entrance on Huntington Avenue) is one of the nation's most important collections, strong in Impressionist painting; colonial American painting, furniture, and silver; and Greek, Roman, and Egyptian art. The Isabella Stewart Gardner Museum is a far more idiosyncratic institution, the legacy of the turn-of-the-century collector and socialite Mrs. John Lowell Gardner. Mrs. Jack, as she was called, built the Venetian palazzo as her private home and the home of her collection; after her death, the terms of her will specified that it be maintained exactly

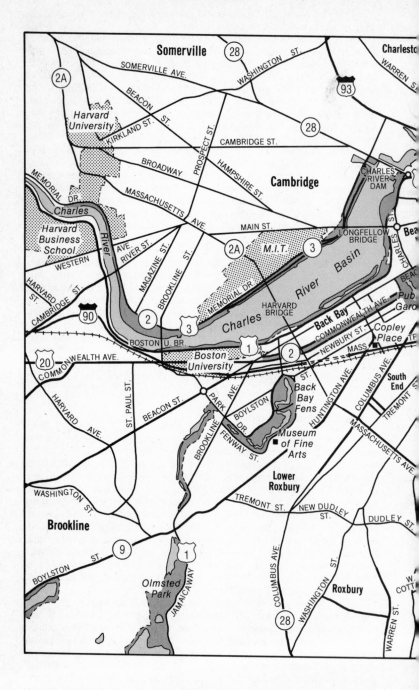

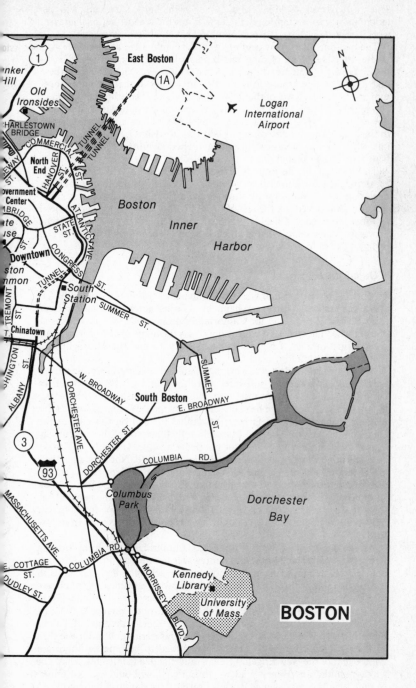

East Boston

1A

Logan
International
Airport

N

nker
Hill

Old
Ironsides

CHARLESTOWN
BRIDGE

COMMERCIAL ST.

North
End

HANOVER ST.

overnment
Center

BRIDGE

TUNNEL
TUNNEL

Boston

Inner

Harbor

ATLANTIC AVE.

STATE ST.

te
use

Downtown

CONGRESS

ston
mon

TUNNEL

South
Station

SUMMER ST.

Chinatown

TREMONT ST.

HINGTON ST.

ALBANY ST.

W. BROADWAY

DORCHESTER AVE.

South Boston

E. BROADWAY

SUMMER ST.

3

93

DORCHESTER ST.

COLUMBIA RD.

MASSACHUSETTS AVE.

Columbus
Park

Dorchester
Bay

E. COTTAGE
ST.

COLUMBIA RD.

DUDLEY ST.

MORRISSEY BLVD.

Kennedy
Library

University
of Mass.

BOSTON

as it was when she lived here. Each floor of the house surrounds a lovely indoor courtyard brimming with flowers, but the real attractions here are works by Rembrandt, Titian, Cellini, Raphael, and other masters.

The tree-lined Riverway leading from the Fens widens at Olmsted Park, where there is a chain of three small ponds followed by the broad, park-lined expanse of Jamaica Pond. Farther south along the Arborway (best take a car or public transportation; it's a long walk) is the Arnold Arboretum, the botanical jewel of the Boston park system. The arboretum, owned and managed by Harvard University, is open to the public each day from dawn to dusk. Its 223 acres contain over 6,000 trees and shrubs native to the North Temperate Zone. The best time to visit is between spring and fall, when a succession of azaleas, lilacs, rhododendrons, magnolias, and fruit trees are in bloom. The bonsai collection is superb.

The last link in the Emerald Necklace is Franklin Park, an Olmsted creation best known to visitors as the home of the Boston Zoological Gardens. The zoo features a walk-through aviary and a special children's section. But don't overlook the rest of Franklin Park, much of which has been restored after years of neglect thanks to an energetic, grass-roots citizens program. As for safety—avoid all parks after dark, and keep in pairs when exploring remote areas.

Cambridge

More people are familiar with Cambridge than with most small industrial cities, and not just because it happens to lie just across the Charles River from Boston. The reason for Cambridge's prominence, of course, is that one of those "industries" is education: this is the home of two of America's greatest institutions of higher learning, Harvard and the Massachusetts Institute of Technology.

Although Cambridge is a working-class city making everything from hard candy to computer software, and "town and gown" controversies have flared here throughout the past 350 years, the histories of the settlement and its schools have been closely intertwined. Within six years after a small group of Puritan farmers first tilled the soil on this side of the Charles, the General Court of Massachusetts (ancestor of the present-day legislature) chartered a college for the fledgling colony, and New Towne, as Cambridge was then called, was chosen as the site. Not long after that, a Cambridge-educated minister, young John Harvard of Charlestown, died and left half of his library and half of his estate to the new school. In gratitude its overseers named it Harvard and changed the name of the town to Cambridge. Who knows; if John Harvard had gone to a different university in England, Boston might have been across the river from Oxford.

As the eighteenth century progressed, Cambridge grew from farming hamlet to small town to elegant country seat for wealthy Boston families, and Harvard changed from the tiny divinity school it had started as in the 1600s to an institution reflecting the growing stratification of classes in a more sophisticated New England. In the Harvard of the mid-1700s, one's place on the class roster was determined not alphabetically or by academic accomplishment but according to social standing. Religious bickering also weakened the school during this period, but after the turn of the nineteenth century Harvard was poised to become an important component of the New England Renaissance, with a faculty graced, at one time or another, by Henry Wadsworth Longfellow, Louis Agassiz, Oliver Wendell Holmes, and James Russell Lowell. The Harvard of the last century was a place where tremendous strides were made in the teaching of medicine and law, and indeed these disciplines are still among the bulwarks of the modern university that celebrated its 350th anniversary in 1986.

Cambridge, meanwhile, followed its own patterns of growth and change. A stronghold of the Patriots during the Revolution, this is where George Washington took command of the Continental Army. After the war, the farms and estates on the outskirts of Cambridge began to take on the aspect of genteel suburbs, while those parts of the city nearer Harvard Square and the Charles became a sizeable town. Cambridgeport, just across the river from Boston, was a busy industrial center by the late nineteenth century. Here in 1916, a vast campus was dedicated for an engineering college that had outgrown its old location in Boston's Back Bay. The serene, classical buildings that line the riverbank along Memorial Drive are the home of M.I.T., one of the world's centers of scientific learning and a major force in the ascendancy of greater Boston in the world of high technology. The phrase "They're working on it at M.I.T." has entered the language—and if it's worth working on, they probably are.

If you're approaching Cambridge from Boston and would prefer not to race down Memorial Drive and start your explorations at Harvard Square, enter the city by crossing the Charles at the Massachusetts Avenue Bridge. (An alternative is the MBTA Red Line subway to Kendall Square.) This will bring you virtually onto the M.I.T. campus, tours of which are given each weekday (inquire at Building 7, on Massachusetts Avenue). Two outstanding buildings are the Kresge Auditorium and the school's Interdenominational Chapel, both designed by Eero Saarinen. From M.I.T., head up Massachusetts Avenue through Central Square, the shopping district of a neighborhood that is rapidly changing from working class to young urban professional. Beyond Central Square the shops grow trendier, the bookstores more esoteric, and soon the black iron gates and red brick buildings of Harvard come into view. Harvard Square and Harvard Yard are two very different places. The former is a busy commercial center, clustered around the venerable Harvard Coop (Cooperative Society, that is; it's a department store) and the lively out-of-town newspaper and magazine stand in the middle of the square. Nearby you can buy records, jeans, computers, and everything else a successful undergraduate needs, and you can feast on the cuisines of at least two dozen nations. Harvard Square is a little more upscale and self-consciously chic these days, but it is still a polyglot and a true crossroads.

Enter those gates, though, and a change in climate is immediately apparent. Harvard Yard is surrounded by monuments not to commerce but to the life of learning: vast Widener Library, which with its satellite collections forms the largest university library in the world; stately Massachusetts Hall (1720) and Harvard Hall (1766), two of the oldest college buildings; and the chaste Georgian spire of Memorial Church. Alongside the Widener, not far from the entrance to the yard from Harvard Square, is Daniel Chester French's statue of the seated John Harvard, whose bequest has grown by so many hundredfold.

Not all of this vast university, of course, is clustered around so small a space as the Yard. Just beyond (in the opposite direction from the Square) are the Fogg (European and American) and the Sackler (Islamic and Oriental) art museums; the Peabody Museum of archaeology and ethnology, with separate collections dedicated to comparative zoology, minerals, geology, and botany (don't miss the glass flowers); and the recently refurbished Victorian gothic extravaganza of Memorial Hall, built as a monument to Harvard's Union dead in the Civil War but now famous as the site of the acoustically impressive Sanders Theater. Beyond here are the buildings of the Harvard Law School and Radcliffe College, once a separate school for women but now fully integrated into Harvard life. The famed Harvard Business School is across the river, on the Boston side.

Don't make the mistake of thinking that this part of Cambridge is all Harvard and nothing but. Walk out Brattle Street, past the Loeb Drama Center (yes, another Harvard institution), to the residential blocks of Tory Row, so called because of the upper-class pro-British families that lived in its Georgian mansions in the years before the Revolution. Some of the most beautiful homes in the Boston area line this street, serene amidst their landscaped gardens. Among the more interesting, particularly for visitors, are the Hooper-Lee-Nichols House (159 Brattle Street), headquarters of the Cambridge Historical Society and open on Thursdays, and the Long-fellow House (105 Brattle Street), an impressive Georgian mansion that was the home of the poet during the latter part of his life. It's now a National Historic Site, maintained by the U.S. Department of the Interior.

Like a good many others who have come this way during the past 350 years, you'll find that it's hard to leave Cambridge without having learned something.

PRACTICAL INFORMATION FOR BOSTON

HOW TO GET THERE. Given its location at the northern end of the Eastern Seaboard's "megalopolis" that begins at Washington, D.C., Boston is well served by air, rail, and bus lines as well as the interstate highway system.

By plane: Boston's airport is Logan International, one of the nation's busiest. Located across the harbor from downtown in East Boston, it is accessible by car, via the often-congested Sumner and Callahan tunnels; by ferry, the Airport Water Shuttle from Rowes Wharf in downtown Boston, with connecting boats from Quincy, Hingham, and Hull (800–235–6426); by taxi (average fare, about $12 including tip); and by subways operating along the MBTA's Blue Line. For subway information, call 617–722–3200 weekdays, 617–722–5000 nights and weekends. A Massport shuttle bus connects the subway station with airline terminals. Dozens of major carriers serve Logan, including American, Continental, Delta, Eastern, Northwest, Pan Am, Piedmont, TWA, United, and US Air.

By train: Boston is the northern terminus of Amtrak's Northeast Corridor. The point of arrival and departure for Amtrak trains connecting the city with New York, Philadelphia, Washington, D.C., and points south and west is South Station on Atlantic Avenue, downtown; Back Bay Station, near Copley Square, 145 Dartmouth St., Route 128 Station, on the city's southern periphery, serves the high-tech belt along Rte. 128. South Station is also the point of arrival and departure for the daily Amtrak *Lake Shore Limited,* connecting Boston with Chicago by way of Springfield, Massachusetts, Albany and Buffalo, New York, and Cleveland, Ohio. (For information on Amtrak trains, call 800–USA–RAIL.)

By bus: The two major national carriers, Trailways and Greyhound, connect Boston with major cities throughout the United States and Canada. The Greyhound/Trailways station is on St. James Ave. near Park Sq. (423–5810); the Boston station serving regional carriers, such as Peter Bus Lines and Concord Trailways, is at 555 Atlantic Ave. (6–7838). These two terminals are also the points of arrival and departure for other smaller regional bus lines affiliated with the larger car-

By car: The primary auto routes leading into Boston are the Massachusetts Turnpike, which runs east–west between the metropolitan area and the New York State border near Albany (this is a toll road); the north–south I–95, providing a direct connection with Providence, Rhode Island, and New York City to the south and Portland, Maine, to the north; and I–93, which heads north out of Boston towards points in New Hampshire and connections with I–91 and I–89 to Vermont and Canada. In addition to these limited-access routes, the Greater Boston area is crisscrossed with primary and secondary highways, all of which are amply provided with travel services.

HOW TO GET AROUND. From the airport: In addition to the options for traveling between downtown and the airport mentioned above, there are several airport-based shuttle and limousine services. Airways Transportation Co. (617–267–2981) serves major downtown hotels, Greyhound/Trailways bus stations, and Hanscom Field (commuter air terminal) in Bedford, Massachusetts. Hudson Bus Lines (617–395–8080) serves cities and towns north and west of Boston, including several New Hampshire points. Southern New Hampshire points are also served by C & J Limousine Service (800–258–7111).

Car rentals may be arranged at all passenger terminals. The major firms represented at Logan include Avis (617–424–0800 or 800–331–1212), Budget (800–527–0700), Dollar (617–569–5300 or 800–421–6868), Hertz (617–569–7272 or 800–654–3131), and National (617–569–6700 or 800–227–7368).

Public transportation: Subway, bus, and trolley service in Boston and environs is provided by the Massachusetts Bay Transportation Authority (MBTA). (For information, call 617–722–3200 weekdays, 617–722–5000 nights and weekends.) The four subway/trolley lines—Red, Green, Orange, and Blue—connect Boston and Cambridge with the nearer suburbs; outlying areas, as well as points within the central city, are served by bus. For route maps, stop at Park Street Station, corner of Park and Tremont Sts. at Boston Common. The MBTA also runs suburban commuter train lines out of South Station (trains to southern suburbs) and North Station, located on Causeway St. near Government Center. Trains from North Station connect Boston with North Shore points (Gloucester, Salem, Ipswich) and western cities and towns (Concord, Fitchburg, Leominster, Haverhill, Lowell). For information, call Commuter Rail (part of Amtrak and MBTA) at 617–227–5070.

By boat: Mass Bay Lines, 344 Atlantic Ave., (617–749–4500), runs commuter boats between Hingham, on the South Shore, and downtown piers. In summer, Bay State Cruises, Commonwealth Pier (617–723–7800), provides boat service between Boston and Provincetown, on Cape Cod.

By foot: If your travels are largely limited to central Boston (downtown, Beacon Hill, the North End, Back Bay, and the South End) or to areas such as Harvard Sq. in Cambridge, don't forget that this is first and foremost a walker's city. The traffic is terrible, the parking is worse, and points of interest are packed very closely together. All you need are a good street map and a pair of comfortable shoes.

HOTELS AND MOTELS. Over the past 12 years, Boston and her immediate environs have been the focus of an incredible boom in hotel building. Where once only the venerable Ritz-Carlton, Copley Plaza, and Parker House dominated the trade, today's traveler has a choice of brand-new hostelries large and small. Unfortunately for budget-minded tourists, most of the new hotel development has been at the upper end of the scale; however, even the priciest places usually offer attractive weekend packages. For real savings, of course, the best bet is a motel or chain hotel in the suburbs (other than those that cater primarily to an executive expense-account trade)—but this will necessitate back-and-forth travel costs and, if you are driving, expensive parking arrangements.

The following ranges pertain to double occupancy in Boston and Cambridge hotels and motels: *Deluxe,* $145 and up; *Expensive,* $100–$145; *Moderate,* $80–$100; *Inexpensive,* $45–$80. (*Note:* Rate categories apply to weekday accommodations; for a weekend stay, a *deluxe* rate may drop to *expensive.*)

Boston

Deluxe

Back Bay Hilton, 40 Dalton St., 02115 (617–236–1100). High-rise hotel across the street from Prudential Center; convenient to Hynes Auditorium and Copley Place shops. Pool; restaurant and lounges.

Bostonian, Dock Sq., 02109 (617–523–3600). A new, small, "European style" hotel located near Faneuil Hall Marketplace and the North End. Some rooms feature fireplaces and Jacuzzis; restaurant is excellent.

Colonnade, 120 Huntington Ave., 02116 (617–424–7000). Just across from Prudential Center; convenient to Copley Place and Hynes Auditorium. Pool (summer only). Restaurants, bars, entertainment.

Copley Plaza, 138 St. James Ave., 02116 (617–267–5300). A *Grande Dame* of the Back Bay, overlooking Copley Sq. for 75 years. Fine restaurants; Plaza Bar with entertainment.

Four Seasons, 200 Boylston St., 02116 (617–338–4400). A sumptuous new hotel overlooking the Public Garden—spacious rooms, elegant public areas, indoor pool and health club, outdoor cafe, fine restaurant.

Lafayette, 1 Ave. de Lafayette, 02110 (617–451–2600). A new Swissotel in downtown's Lafayette Place development. A sedate oasis in the Federal style. Outdoor pool and terrace; excellent restaurant.

Long Wharf, 296 State St., 02109 (617–227–0800). A Marriott property on the downtown waterfront. Striking architecture features four-story atrium; terrace dining overlooking harbor. Indoor pool.

Marriott at Copley Place, Copley Pl., 02116 (617–236–5800). One of the largest of the new generation of Boston hotels, with over 1,100 rooms. Full convention facilities and the city's largest ballroom. Three restaurants, cocktail lounges.

Meridien, 250 Franklin St., 02110 (617–451–1900). Bold renovation of old Federal Reserve building and modern addition make this a unique hotel. Some rooms are loft suites. Located right in the financial district. 24-hour room service; fine restaurant.

Omni Parker House, 60 School St., 02108 (617–227–8600). Boston's oldest and most centrally located hotel has been completely refurbished and is in top shape. Convivial bars and fine restaurant.

Ritz-Carlton, 15 Arlington St., 02117 (617–536–5700). Elegant and understated, a favorite of the Old Guard. Many rooms overlook public garden; older section has fireplaces in suites. Elegant dining and renowned bar.

Sheraton-Boston, 39 Dalton St., Prudential Center, 02199 (617–236–2000). Luxurious high rise, adjacent to recently enlarged Hynes Auditorium. Indoor and rooftop pools; plenty of restaurants and bars.

Westin, Copley Pl., 02116 (617–262–9600). A striking high rise with indoor acess to all of the Copley Place shops. Upper-story rooms have some of Boston's best views. Indoor pool; health club. Bars, three restaurants.

Expensive

Hilton Inn at Logan, Logan International Airport, 02128 (617–569–9300). Avoid tunnel traffic. Outdoor pool. Restaurants, bar, entertainment, airport limo. Pets OK.

Holiday Inn–Government Center, 5 Blossom St., 02114 (617–742–7630). Convenient to Government Center, Boston Garden, and Beacon Hill. Dining; rooftop lounge with entertainment. Pets OK.

Howard Johnson, 200 Stuart St., 02116 (617–482–1800). Downtown, near theater district and Park Sq. Indoor pool, sauna. Restaurant, bar.

Park Plaza, Park Sq., 02117. (617–426–2000). An old Boston standby, renovated and up-to-date. *Moderate* rates on lower floors, "Towers" rooms are *deluxe*. Restaurant, bars.

Moderate

Eliot, 370 Commonwealth Ave., 02215 (617–267–1607). Small, convenient Back Bay hotel.

Howard Johnson Kenmore Square, 575 Commonwealth Ave., 02115 (617–267–3100). At Kenmore Sq., and convenient to Boston University and the Fenway. Indoor pool.

Lenox, 710 Boylston St., 02116 (617–536–5300). A small, comfortable hotel near Copley Place and all Back Bay attractions, without big-time rates. Restaurant; popular piano bar.

Ramada Inn–Airport, 225 McClellan Hwy., 02128 (617–569–5250). East Boston location is convenient to airport. Indoor pool; play area. Restaurant, bar, entertainment.

Inexpensive

Copley Square, 47 Huntington Ave., 02116 (617–536–9000). Right across from Copley Sq. but miles away in price. Economy rooms, without bath, are a great bargain. Restaurant, bar.

Howard Johnson Fenway, 1271 Boylston St., 02115 (617–267–8300). Next to Fenway Park. Pool. Free parking. Restaurant and bar.

Howard Johnson, 407 Squire Rd., Revere, MA 02151 (617–284–7200). Just north of Logan Airport. Outdoor pool, lounge, 24-hour coffee shop, and Japanese steak house.

Quality Inn, 275 Tremont St., 02107 (617–426–1400). A rehab of the old Hotel Bradford. Good downtown location, near theater district. Restaurant; nightclub; health club.

Ramada Inn, 1234 Soldiers' Field Rd., Brighton (Boston) 02135 (617–254–1234). A short drive from downtown. Outdoor pool, play area. Restaurant and lounge.

Susse Chalet, 800 Morrissey Blvd., 02122 (617–287–9100). Member of economical regional chain. Outdoor pool and play area. Restaurant near.

Terrace Motor Lodge, 1650 Commonwealth Ave., 02135 (617–566–6260). All rooms have kitchenette. Trolley ride to downtown. Low weekly rates.

Cambridge

Deluxe

Cambridge Center Marriott, Cambridge Center, Kendall Sq., Cambridge 02142 (617–494–6600). This latest area Marriott features a pool and health club, deluxe "Concierge Level," restaurant and lounge, and airport limo. Near M.I.T. and new Kendall Sq. business district.

Charles Hotel, 1 Bennett St., Cambridge 02138 (617–864–1200). Deluxe new hotel near Harvard Sq. features bathroom TV and phones. Restaurant, outdoor cafe, top jazz artists in nightclub.

Hyatt Regency, 575 Memorial Drive, Cambridge 02139 (617–492–1234). Striking modern design typical of the Hyatt chain, with a 14-story atrium and revolving rooftop lounge. Two restaurants. Convenient to Harvard and M.I.T.; nice river views.

Expensive

Sheraton-Commander, 16 Garden St., Cambridge 02238 (617–547–4800). Older, nicely renovated hotel in quiet location on Cambridge Common. Restaurant, bar. Convenient to Harvard Sq.

Royal Sonesta, 5 Cambridge Pkwy., Cambridge 02142 (617–491–3600). Cambridgeport location just across from Boston's Government Center. Pool. Restaurants, bar, entertainment. Pets OK.

Moderate

Howard Johnson, 777 Memorial Dr., Cambridge 02139 (617–492–7777). Outdoor pool and platform tennis. Views of Boston and Charles River. Japanese steak house.

Inexpensive

Quality Inn, 1651 Massachusetts Ave., Cambridge 02138 (617–491–1000). Near Harvard Law School. On bus line, 10-min. walk from Harvard Sq. Parking. Restaurant, lounge.

BED AND BREAKFASTS. More and more Bostonians and residents of nearby communities have been opening their homes to guests on a bed-and-breakfast basis. Rates are reasonable (generally what you might expect to pay for a room in one of the commercial establishments in the *Moderate* category), and you may have a chance to stay in a home in a quiet part of Cambridge, or even in a Back Bay townhouse. Reservations for bed-and-breakfast accommodations are handled through central information and booking organizations. Here are several: Bed & Breakfast Agency of Boston, 47 Commercial Wharf, Boston 02110 (617–720–3540); Bed and Breakfast Areawide Cambridge and Greater Boston, Box 665, Cambridge 02138 (617–576–1492); Bed and Breakfast Associates Bay Colony Ltd., Box 166, Boston 02157 (617–449–5302); Bed and Breakfast Brookline/Boston, Box 732, Brookline 02146 (617–277–2292); Host Homes of Boston, Box 117, Boston 02168 (617–244–1308); New England Bed and Breakfast, Inc., 1753 Massachusetts Ave., Cambridge 02138 (617–498–9819).

HOSTELS. For information on the even less expensive accommodations offered at hostels affiliated with American Youth Hostels, contact the Greater Boston Council of A.Y.H. at 1020 Commonwealth Ave., Brookline 02146 (617–731–5430).

RESTAURANTS. The tradition of dining out in Boston dates back to the 18th century, when the city's first restaurant was established by a French emigré. Over the period that followed, however, Boston restaurants clung tenaciously to a meat, potatoes, and codfish repertory despite inroads made by a few French, Italian, and Chinese chefs. So things stood until about 10 years ago, when Boston acquired a new restaurant sophistication almost overnight. Nowadays, one hears about a new place opening almost every week, and menu offerings include the trendiest of European and "New American" dishes, from black fettucini to incendiary Cajun specialties. Underneath it all, you can still find a decent chop or a nice piece of scrod.

The cost of an à la carte dinner, exclusive of liquor, wine, and tips, is the basis of our price classifications: *Deluxe,* $30 and up; *Expensive,* $22–$30; *Moderate,* $16–$22, *Inexpensive,* under $16. Remember that there are plenty of places with prices even lower than the *inexpensive* category, as well as superdeluxe establishments that will make our $30 *deluxe* classification seem a pittance. Most restaurants accept credit cards, especially in the higher price brackets; however, we strongly advise you to call ahead and double-check. It's also wise to make reservations, if restaurant policy permits, especially on weekends.

Boston

American International

The Colony, 384 Boylston St. (617–536–8500). *Deluxe.* The traditional cuisine of New England, reinvented and made more subtle: lobster with hot pepper butter; halibut and scallops in a buttery cider sauce; three-berry cobbler. A la carte or prix fixe dinner ($52 for 5 courses).

Locke-Ober, 3 Winter Pl. (617–542–1340). *Deluxe.* A bastion of Victorian Boston, serving Victorian Boston fare: oyster stew, steaks and chops, sweetbreads. The bar was carved in Germany and shipped here 100 years ago.

Parker's, Parker House Hotel, Tremont St. (617–227–8600). *Deluxe.* An updated Yankee menu strong on seafood and veal—and a sumptuous Sun. brunch. Parker House rolls, of course.

Ritz-Carlton, 15 Arlington St. (617–536–5700). *Deluxe.* There are trendier places to eat in Boston, and far more innovative kitchens—but the Ritz keeps its standards high and is certainly the most elegant restaurant in town. Serene and elegant, like the hotel itself, with a French-inspired traditional menu.

Seasons, Bostonian Hotel, Dock Sq. (617–523–3600). *Deluxe.* Consistently cited as one of the city's best restaurants, with a menu that changes, as you might suspect, with the seasons.

Arne's, Copley Place (617–267–4900). *Expensive.* An ambitious seafood restaurant serving an impressive variety of fresh fish and shellfish, conveniently located for Copley Place shoppers. Start with the escargot ravioli in garlic butter.

Hamersley's Bistro, 578 Tremont St. (617–267–6068). *Expensive.* Memorable versions of familiar dishes (roast chicken, pork tenderloin with mashed potatoes) in a small, chic South End spot.

Landmark Cafe, Brasserie Les Halles, Boston Beach Club—three in one building. North Market Bldg., Quincy Market (617–227–9660). *Expensive.* Landmark serves salads and sandwiches; Brasserie French cuisine combined with fine dining; Beach Club food plus entertainment nightly.

Saint Cloud, 557 Tremont St. (617–353–0202). *Expensive.* A new South End spot that proves "trendy" food can be hearty and satisfying—witness the squid-ink pasta with scallops, or Cornish hen stuffed with wild rice and pecans. Near Boston Center for the Arts.

Bnu, 123 Stuart St. (617–367–8405). *Moderate.* Near the theater district. Paint and lights suggest the courtyard of an ancient villa; the eclectic Italianate menu offers small, fanciful pizzas and gorgeous desserts.

Chart House, 60 Long Wharf (617–227–1576). *Moderate.* A basic steak-and-seafood menu, served up in restored colonial wharf building.

Durgin Park, Faneuil Hall, Quincy Market (617–227–2038). *Moderate.* The Boston fare of legend—huge slabs of roast beef, baked beans, Indian pudding—served at long communal tables. A local tradition. Also in Copley Place (617–266–1964).

Legal Seafoods, Park Plaza Hotel, Park Sq. (617–426–4444). *Moderate.* Long a local favorite, and now the flagship of a growing chain, "Legal" serves up the freshest Atlantic seafood. Selections reflect the market; look for some unusual varieties.

Brandy Pete's, 267 Franklin St. (617–439–4165). *Inexpensive.* Plain and simple; a downtown bargain. Roast turkey; seafood; veal parmigiana. Good drinks.

Cornucopia, 15 West St. (617–338–4600). *Inexpensive.* Pricier upstairs, but go for the first-floor cafe menu. Tasty soups, unusual entrees, great desserts.

Souper Salad, five locations in downtown, Back Bay, and Cambridge. *Inexpensive.* Soups, sandwiches, quiche, a few hot specials, and a top-drawer salad bar.

Chinese

Chau Chow, 52 Beach St. (617–426–6266). *Inexpensive.* A Chinatown spot that specializes in seafood. Try clams or squid in black bean sauce, lobster with ginger and scallion, or the fine steamed sea bass. Plenty of good nonseafood dishes, too.

Imperial Tea House, 70 Beach St. (617–426–8439). *Inexpensive.* A respectable dinner menu, but the real fun is at lunchtime, when the *dim sum* carts make the rounds. Just point at what you want, and keep eating.

French

Aujourd'hui, Four Seasons Hotel, 200 Boylston St. (617–451–1392). *Deluxe.* A new spot starting out strong—it's nominally French, but specialties run to imaginative "New American" as well as continental treatments.

Julien, 250 Franklin St. (617–451–1900). *Deluxe.* Julien's approach to nouvelle cuisine is faithful without being dogmatic, and this new hotel restaurant (it's at the Meridien) is already one of Boston's best. Recent offerings have included salmon and sole mousse, veal kidneys with red wine butter, and medallions of duck. The desserts are excellent, as is the service.

Le Marquis de Lafayette, Lafayette Hotel, 1 Ave. de Lafayette (617–451–2600). *Deluxe.* An ambitious and successful offering of updated haute cuisine; duck and salmon dishes are exceptional.

L'Espalier, 30 Gloucester St. (617–262–3023). *Deluxe.* At or near the top of everyone's "best" list for Boston. All dinners are prix fixe and might include venison, quail salad, or *escalope de saumon,* depending on the chef's current interests and the availability of ingredients. A cheese course is served.

Another Season, 97 Mt. Vernon St. (617–367–0880). *Expensive.* Popular with Beacon Hill neighborhood crowd. Menu changes every other week. A tasteful blend of ethnic cuisines, with a French bias. Good fish dishes, and always a vegetarian selection.

Icarus, 3 Appleton St. (617–426–1790). *Expensive.* An intimate South End spot. The food runs to revisionist French provincial or what's called "New American"—examples are artichoke and red onion tart with goat cheese, smoked tenderloin of pork braised in cider with cabbage and pears.

Lily's, Faneuil Hall Marketplace (617–227–4242). *Expensive.* Don't mistake the sidewalk cafe for the restaurant of the same name, located just indoors and a world away.

Maison Robert, 45 School St. (617–227–3370). *Expensive.* Two restaurants in Boston's Old City Hall: Bonhomme Richard offers elegant variations on classic cuisine, such as lobster with caviar butter; Ben's Cafe serves outdoors in season.

German

Jacob Wirth's, 31 Stuart St. (617–338–8586). *Inexpensive.* As much a bar as a restaurant, but the only place in town that serves up big platters of wurst, kraut, and boiled meats Milwaukee style. It owes its old-time look not to a decorator, but to time itself.

Greek–Middle Eastern

Aegean Fare, Faneuil Hall Marketplace (617–742–8349) and two other Boston locations. *Inexpensive.* Boston loves Greek salad, and this restaurant is largely responsible. Baklava is also featured.

Indian

India Quality, 536 Commonwealth Ave. (617–267–4499). *Inexpensive.* An intimate little Kenmore Sq. spot serving traditional vegetarian and nonvegetarian Indian cuisine. Lunch specials are a good value.

Kebab-n-Kurry, 30 Massachusetts Ave. (617–536–9835). *Inexpensive.* Authentic Indian cuisine served at lunch and dinner.

Italian

Davio's, 269 Newbury St. (617–262–4810). *Expensive.* Easy to pass by, but don't. Extensive northern Italian menu. Fettuccine Alfredo, mozzarella in carozza. Light, flavorful sauces.

Venezia, 20 Ericson, off SE Expwy. in Dorchester (617–436–3120). *Moderate–Expensive.* Great harbor views—it's even accessible by boat! Northern Italian cuisine, with fine repertory of veal and seafood dishes. Handy if you've been to Kennedy Library or Bayside Expo Ctr., but get directions first.

Cafe Amalfi, 8–10 Westland Ave. (617–536–6396). *Moderate.* Just around the corner from Symphony Hall, Amalfi has been around a long time serving up solid Southern Italian fare—with a respectable nod to the currently popular lighter Northern specialties. A nice way to begin an evening at Symphony or Pops.

Felicia's, 145A Richmond St. (617–523–9885). *Moderate.* House specialty is Chicken Verdicchio, with artichoke hearts and dry white wine. Beer, wine. Closed holidays.

The Romagnolis' Table, North Market Building, Quincy Market (617–367–9114). *Moderate.* Good homemade pasta and sauces—try the tortellini in cream sauce with walnuts. Veal, chicken. Nice desserts. Owned by famous TV cooks.

Pat's Pushcart, 61 Endicott St. (617–523–9616). *Inexpensive.* Not a pushcart exactly, but a cozy and inviting little spot. Good sandwiches at lunchtime; full dinner menu.

Japanese

Agatha, 142 Berkeley St. (617–262–9790). *Expensive.* Charcoal grilling Kyoto style is a specialty; sushi and tempura.

Gyuhama, 827 Boylston St. (617–437–0188). *Expensive.* Opposite Prudential Center. Traditional Japanese dishes, extensive selection of appetizers. Sushi and sashimi.

Mexican

Casa Romero, 30 Gloucester St. (617–536–4341). *Moderate.* More sophisticated than the usual Tex-Mex menu one usually finds this far north; the marinated seafood and green chili-flavored pork dishes are excellent.

Thai and Burmese

Montien, 63 Stuart St. (617–338–5600). *Inexpensive.* Spicy yet subtle, Thai cuisine is gaining recognition locally. Spices such as tamarind, chili, and lemon grass flavor interesting beef, duck, and shrimp dishes. Some heavily spiced items are for the brave.

Mandalay, 329 Huntington Ave. (617–247–2411). *Moderate.* Long a neighborhood favorite, now in a second Cambridge location. Burmese cuisine has affinities with both Chinese and Thai; coriander, lemon grass, and hot spices are frequent flavorings. Distinctive noodle dishes and cold salads.

East Boston

Blazing Saddles, 940 Saratoga St. (617–569–2020). *Inexpensive.* Tasty, hearty portions of baby back ribs, sirloin tips, steak. The onion ring loaf is superb—but make sure you're hungry. A good place to stop when you're early for a flight out of Logan.

Brookline

Chef Chang's House, 1004–1006 Beacon St. (617–277–4226). *Inexpensive.* Mandarin, Szechuan, and Shanghai specialties, including Peking duck.

Sol Azteca, 914A Beacon St. (617–262–0909). *Inexpensive.* A small, chef-owned Mexican spot that does a creditable job with the standard south-of-the-border (and Tex-Mex) repertory.

Cambridge

American International

Harvest, 44 Brattle St. (617–492–1115). *Expensive.* American nouvelle, featuring salmon in season, duck breast with papaya, homemade pâtés. Outdoor cafe.

Peacock, 5 Craigie Circle (617–661–4073). *Moderate.* French provincial dishes, such as roast duck with red cabbage. Excellent desserts. Closed Sun. and Mon.

Casablanca, 40 Brattle St. (617–876–0999). *Moderate.* Enter from the side alley. A cozy upstairs spot featuring good soups, steaks, pasta, daily specials. Bar. The murals depict scenes from a certain movie . . .

Pentimento, 344 Huron Ave. (617–661–3878). *Inexpensive.* Old oak furniture and down-home cooking in a quiet corner of Cambridge. Ratatouille, chicken potpie, vegetable curry, rich desserts. No smoking.

Peppercorn's, 154 Prospect St. (617–661–2022). *Inexpensive.* Tasty steak, seafood, chicken, and other traditional entrees served at remarkably low prices. Chili, burgers, homemade soups.

Chinese

Lucky Garden, 282 Concord Ave. (617–354–9514). *Inexpensive.* A restaurant with a following. Steamed and fried dumplings, chicken and peanuts in spicy sauce, Peking duck, plus many other authentic dishes.

French

Chez Jean, 1 Shepard St. (617–354–8980). *Moderate.* 10 minutes from Harvard Sq.; traditional dishes (onion soup, coq au vin) in a quietly comfortable setting.

Cajun

The Cajun Yankee, 1193 Cambridge St. (617–576–1971). *Moderate.* The real thing—gumbo, jambalaya, shrimp remoulade, crayfish etouffee. Small—reservations a must.

Greek

Averof, 1924 Mass. Ave. (617–354–4500). *Inexpensive.* Greek cuisine and entertainment; luncheon buffet is one of area's best bargains.
Middle East, 472 Massachusetts Ave. (617–354–8238). *Inexpensive.* Shish kebabs, salads, and daily specials; the pumpkin kibby and eggplant dishes are good choices for vegetarians. Music on weekends.

Indian

India, 1780 Mass. Ave. (617–354–0949). *Inexpensive.* An assortment of curries; Indian bread and desserts.
Oh Calcutta, 468 Massachusetts Ave. (617–576–2111). *Inexpensive.* Meat and vegetable curries; Indian breads and condiments.

Italian

Michaela's, 1 Athenaeum St. (617–225–3366). *Expensive.* Northern Italian cuisine in one of the city's new high-tech neighborhoods. Seafood ravioli a specialty.

Japanese

Bisuteki, Howard Johnson Motor Lodge, 777 Memorial Dr. (617–492–7777). *Moderate.* Japanese steak house features *tepinyaki* tableside cookery. Sakura lounge.
Little Osaka, Concord Ave., off Fresh Pond Circle (617–491–6600). *Moderate.* Sushi, traditional dishes. Popular with visiting Japanese.

Portuguese

Casa Portugal, 1200 Cambridge St. (617–491–8880). *Moderate.* An ethnic cuisine not to be overlooked. The Portuguese have an especially fine touch with pork and seafood dishes.

Watertown

Le Bocage, 72 Bigelow St. (617–923–1210). *Expensive.* Tournedos of beef, French provincial cuisine. Informal and intimate.
Glenda's Kitchen, Lexington St. (617–926–3222). *Moderate.* Spanish/Mexican dishes, including enchiladas and seafood platters. Pitchers of sangria. Luncheon specials a good value.

TOURIST INFORMATION. There are three places to go to for general tourist information in Boston. One is the booth near the Tremont St.–Park

St. corner on Boston Common. The other two are both at 15 State St.,
downtown, near the old State House. Here you'll find the reception center
of the Greater Boston Convention and Visitors' Bureau, the mailing address of which is Box 490, Boston 02149 (800–858–0200). 15 State is also
the headquarters of the National Park Service's Boston National Historic
Park, which manages most of the major historic sites in the area
(617–242–5642).

TOURS. Gray Line of Boston offers tours of greater Boston and historic
suburbs leaving from many of the city's hotels. Tour No. 1, three hours,
covers highlights of old and new Boston; Tour No. 2, three hours, takes
sightseers to Lexington and Concord, including battlefields, by way of
Harvard Square; Tour No. 3, seven hours, is a "grand combination" of
the above excursions, with a lunch stopover (price of meal not included)
at Longfellow's Wayside Inn in Sudbury. For schedules and prices, call
or write the Gray Line, 275 Tremont St., Boston 02116 (617–426–8805).

SPECIAL-INTEREST TOURS. Bay State Cruises, 20 Long Wharf
(617–723–7800), offers cruises around Boston Harbor and to George's Island, where there is a Civil War fort. From George's, take free water taxi
to other harbor islands. Also boats to Provincetown; lunch cruises. Weekend schedule begins Memorial Day, ends Columbus Day. Daily schedule
June–Labor Day. **Mass. Bay Lines,** 344 Atlantic Ave. (617–749–4500),
offers similar itineraries from Rowe's Wharf (no Provincetown service);
also, lunch, dinner, and sunset cruises. Weekend schedule Memorial
Day–Labor Day; daily schedule starts 4th of July. Private charters are
available.
   Beacon Hill Tours: Tours of some homes may be arranged through the
Women's City Club of Boston, 40 Beacon St. (617–227–3550).
   Harborwalk highlights maritime and mercantile history; brochures are
available at the information center on Boston Common.
   Bicycle Tour: Planned and frequently ridden by famed heart specialist
Dr. Paul Dudley White, marked 11-mi. path begins and ends at Eliot
Bridge across Charles River. Bike rentals at Community Bike Shop, 490
Tremont St., Boston (617–542–8623).

SEASONAL EVENTS. January: Chinese New Year, celebrated in
streets of Chinatown (late Jan.–early Feb.; date depends on Chinese calen-
dar).
   February: New England Boat Show, Bayside Expo Center, off Southeast
Expressway.
   March: Flower Show, Bayside Expo Center; Home Show, Bayside Expo
Center; *Boston Globe* Jazz Festival, various locations; St. Patrick's Day
Parade, South Boston.
   April: Boston Marathon, finish line in Back Bay (third Mon. of Apr.).
   May: Beacon Hill Garden Tour.
   June: Bunker Hill Day celebration, Charlestown (Sunday before June
17); Cambridge River Festival, Memorial Drive on the Charles River
(early June).
   July: Harborfest, first week of July, including waterfront concerts, July
4th concert by Boston Pops on Esplanade.
   August/September: August Moon Festival, Chinatown, dates depend
on Chinese calendar; Charles Street Fair, Beacon Hill (early Sept.).
   October: Head of the Charles Regatta, rowing races on Charles River
(late Oct.).

December: Boston Tea Party Reenactment, Fort Point Channel; Christmas Tree Lighting, Prudential Center; First Night, New Year's Eve celebration throughout downtown and Back Bay features indoor and outdoor entertainment.

PARKS. Boston Common, America's oldest public park, bounded by Beacon, Park, Tremont, Boylston, and Charles Sts., features summer concert series, Frog Pond for children's wading and skating; historic burying ground. **Back Bay Fens** incorporate marshes and lawns in Olmsted design near Kenmore Sq. and Museum of Fine Arts; **Storrow Embankment** stretches along Charles River; **Franklin Park,** bordering Roxbury and Jamaica Plain, is a vast Olmsted park featuring golf course, bridle trails, zoo.

STATE PARKS. Boston Harbor Islands State Park manages the islands of the harbor, most of which are accessible to visitors via water taxi from Long and Rowe's wharves, downtown. For information on access, activities, and camping permits for those islands on which overnight stays are permitted, contact Boston Harbor Islands State Park, 349 Lincoln St., Bldg. 45, Hingham 02043 (617-740-1605).

GARDENS. Public Garden, next to Boston Common, has formal gardens, rare trees, and in spring a wondrous display of tulips. **The Arnold Arboretum,** Jamaica Plain, offers a nonstop, year-round show of flowers, shrubs, trees—one of the best in the country. You can pick up a pamphlet at the office for a self-guided tour.

ZOOS. Franklin Park Zoo, Blue Hill Ave. and Columbia Rd. (617-442-2002) has zebras, camels, African range animals, a walk-through aviary, and a children's zoo. Open daily except Christmas and New Year's, 9 A.M.–4 P.M. in winter, till 5 P.M. in summer. $1 per person. Children's Zoo free. The Metropolitan District Commission also maintains the **Stone Memorial Zoo,** a somewhat more comprehensive facility, in north suburban Stoneham; Pond St., off I-93 (617-438-3662).

SUMMER SPORTS. For a compact urban area, Boston offers its share of outdoor summer activities. **Bicycling** is popular, particularly along the Paul Dudley White Bikeway, an 18-mi. route running along both the Boston and Cambridge sides of the Charles. Rent bikes at Community Bike Shop, 490 Tremont St. (617-542-8623).

Tennis enthusiasts can use the Metropolitan District Commission courts at Charlesbank Park, Charles St.; permits can be obtained from the MDC office at the Lee Pool, Charles St. (617-523-9746). Open Apr.–Nov. The MDC also operates a number of **swimming pools** in the area; those closest to downtown are the Lee Memorial, Charles St. (617-523-9746), and the Veterans Memorial, 719 Memorial Dr., Cambridge (617-354-9381). MDC-operated **beaches** along the harbor in Dorchester and South Boston are open when water quality permits; call the Harbor District office at 617-727-5118 for information.

Jogging (running, if you're serious) is big in Boston; join the locals along the Charles River Esplanade, or alongside Memorial Dr. on the Cambridge side of the river.

WINTER SPORTS. Although you can **ice skate** on the lagoon in the Public Garden, you'll find the ice better maintained at the MDC rinks on Commercial St. in the North End (617-523-9327) and Cleveland Circle, Brookline (617-277-7822). **Skiing** is the favorite winter activity at the

Blue Hills Reservation; the slopes aren't in the same league as those in Vermont and New Hampshire, but the Reservation is close to Boston, on Rte. 138 in Canton, just off Rte. 128 (617–828–5070).

SPECTATOR SPORTS. Suffolk Downs Race Track, Rte. 1A, E. Boston (617–567–3900) has thoroughbred racing year-round. Greyhounds are raced at Wonderland Park, 190 VFW Parkway Revere (617–284–1300).

The Red Sox play baseball at Fenway Park; the Celtics, basketball, and Bruins, hockey, at Boston Garden; and the Patriots, football, at Sullivan Stadium in suburban Foxboro. For information: *Red Sox,* 617–267–8661; *Celtics,* 617–523–3030; *Bruins,* 617–227–3200; and *Patriots,* 617–262–1776 or 800–543–1776.

HISTORIC SITES AND HOMES. Many of the Boston area's historic sites are administered by the U.S. Interior Department under the authority of the Boston National Historic Park. For general information on these sites, which are described below, visit the park's headquarters at 15 State St. (617–242–5642).

Freedom Trail. Booklet outlining walking tour is available at Tremont St. Information Center; the Greater Boston Chamber of Commerce, Prudential Plaza, Box 490 (617–227–4500), from the Greater Boston Convention and Tourist Bureau, Prudential Plaza (800–858–0200), and at points along the way.

John F. Kennedy National Historic Site, 83 Beals St., Brookline (617–566–7937). Birthplace of Pres. Kennedy. Closed Jan. 1, Thanksgiving, Dec. 25.

Bunker Hill Monument, Monument Sq., Lexington and High Sts., Charlestown (617–242–5641). Spiral staircase to top off 221-ft. obelisk. Closed Thanksgiving, Christmas, and New Year's.

Longfellow House National Historic Site, 105 Brattle St., Cambridge (617–876–4491). Closed Jan. 1, Thanksgiving, Dec. 25.

Dorchester Heights National Historic Site, 456 W. 4th St., South Boston (617–269–4275).

Frederick Law Olmsted National Historic Site, Warren St., Brookline (617–566–1689). Landscape architect's home and studio. Closed Thanksgiving, Christmas, and New Year's.

State House, corner of Beacon and Park Sts. (617–727–3676). Classic Bulfinch structure is seat of Massachusetts government. Free tours Mon.–Fri. 10 A.M.–4 P.M.

Park St. Church, 1 Park St. (617–523–3383). Built in 1809; site of Garrison's anti-slavery speeches. Open daily, except Mon. services Sun.

Old Granary Burying Ground, Tremont St., adjacent to Park St. Church. Burial site of Paul Revere, Sam Adams, other patriots. Open daylight hours.

King's Chapel, 58 Tremont St. (617–523–1749). Earliest home of Church of England in Boston; historic graveyard. Open daily, except Mon. services Sun.

USS *Constitution,* Charlestown Navy Yard, across Charlestown Bridge from North End (617–242–5601). "Old Ironsides" is star attraction of decommissioned Navy Yard, now a National Historic Site featuring museum, maritime history exhibits. Open daily, 9:30 A.M.–3:45 P.M. Free tours of ship; museum. (617–426–1812). $2 adults; $1.50 seniors; 50 cents children.

Old South Meeting House, corner of Washington and School Sts. (617–482–6439). Where the Tea Party began. Free daily lectures on the half hour during summer months.

Faneuil Hall, Dock Sq. (617–565–8535). "Cradle of Liberty" has shops on first floor, great hall above. Open daily.

Paul Revere House, 19 North Sq. (617–523–1676). Home of patriot and oldest wooden house in Boston. Open daily year-round, except Mon., Jan.–Mar. $2 adult, $1.50 students, seniors, 50 cents children.

Old North (Christ) Church, 193 Salem St. (617–523–6676). One if by land, two if by sea: this is the church. Free tours daily, year-round.

Copps Hill Burying Ground, Hull and Snowhill Sts., North End. 1659 graveyard is burial place of Mather family, other colonial notables. Open daylight hours.

Appleton House, 40 Beacon St. (617–227–3550). Home of Women's City Club of Boston. Tours Wed. by appointment, year-round. $2.00 fee.

Harrison Gray Otis House, 141 Cambridge St. (617–227–3956). 1796 home of patriot and Beacon Hill developer, designed by Bulfinch. Tours Tues.–Sat. year-round. $3 adults, $1 children.

Old West Church, 131 Cambridge St. (617–227–5088). Designed by Asher Benjamin. Open daily.

Boston Massacre Site, in front of Old State House, at the head of State St. circle of cobblestones marks site where five colonists died in hail of British gunfire.

Trinity Church, Copley Sq. (617–536–0944). Richardson's Romanesque masterpiece. Tour guides available daily in summer, 10:30 A.M.–3:30 P.M.; call for appt. rest of year. No set charge; donations accepted.

City Hall, 1 City Hall Sq., (617–725–4000). Striking modern structure at heart of Government Center. Tour guides available for groups.

Hooper-Lee Nichols House, 159 Brattle St., Cambridge (617–547–4252). Home of Cambridge Historical Society. Open Tues.–Thurs., 2–5 P.M.

LIBRARIES. Boston Public Library at Copley Sq. is an impressive Italian renaissance building with rare book collections, priceless paintings, and the only Chavannes murals outside of France. See the library's beautiful enclosed courtyard, with its fountain and formal garden. **Bapst Library,** Boston College, has a rare book section, a collection of Irish literature. Free. **John F. Kennedy Library,** overlooking the harbor at Columbia Pt., Dorchester, houses late president's papers and effects; film on JFK's life shown daily; library also houses Hemingway papers, accessible to scholars. Harvard's **Widener Library,** in Cambridge, shows a Gutenberg Bible and changing exhibitions.

MUSEUMS. Museum of Fine Arts, 465 Huntington Ave. (617–267–9300). American, European, Oriental collections; period rooms, musical instruments, silver. The Evans Wing houses masterpieces of American art. Lectures, films, special children's programs. Closed Mon., Jan. 1, July 4, Christmas. The Museum is proud of its fine new West Wing, designed by I. M. Pei.

Isabella Stewart Gardner Museum, 280 The Fenway (617–734–1359). Paintings, sculpture, concerts. Closed Mon. and major holidays.

Fogg Museum, 32 Quincy St., Cambridge (617–495–2387). Paintings, sculpture; all periods. Closed Mon., legal holidays. Free Sat. mornings.

Peabody Museum, 11 Divinity St., Cambridge (617–495–2248). Artifacts of ancient civilizations. The Botanical Museum in this complex houses the famous Ware Collection of hand-blown glass flowers. Closed Jan. 1, Thanksgiving, Christmas.

Arthur M. Sackler Museum, 485 Broadway, Cambridge (617–459–0799). Oriental, Classical, Islamic art. Closed Mon. Free Sat. mornings.

Museum of Science, Science Park (617–723–2500). Do-it-yourself exhibits, Talking Transparent Woman, physical science demonstrations, medical science displays. Separate admission charge for the popular Omni Theater. Closed Mon., legal holidays.

Charles Hayden Planetarium, part of Museum of Science. 45-min. shows.

Children's Museum, Museum Wharf, downtown Boston (617–426–8855). Hands-on exhibits. Closed Mon., Thanksgiving, Christmas, New Year's.

Museum of Transportation, 15 Newton St., Brookline (617–522–6140). Old cars; public transportation exhibits. Closed winters.

New England Aquarium, Central Wharf (617–973–5200). More than 2,000 species; daily dolphin and sea lion shows. Closed Christmas, Thanksgiving.

Nichols House Museum, 55 Mt. Vernon St. (617–227–6993). Home of Miss Rose Nichols, philanthropist; exquisite 19th-century furnishings. Also home of International Visitors Center. Seasonal hours—call first.

Bostonian Society Historical Museum, 15 State St. (State St. entrance, Old State House) (617–720–3290). Focus is on Colonial and early republican Boston. Closed Thanksgiving, Christmas, New Year's, Easter.

Computer Museum, Museum Wharf (617–426–2800). Computer graphics, hands-on stations, multimedia robot show. Closed Mon. except holidays and Boston school vacation weeks.

MUSIC, DANCE, AND THEATER. Boston Symphony Orchestra winter season begins the end of Sept. with concerts in Symphony Hall, Massachusetts and Huntington aves., Fri. afternoon, Sat., Tues., and Thurs. evenings. Several rehearsals open. **Pops Concerts** in Symphony Hall, late Apr.–late June, and Christmas season. Outdoor Esplanade Concerts in Hatch Memorial Shell, along Charles River, end of June–mid-July. For BSO and Pops information, call 617–266–2378. See *Boston Globe* Calendar, Thurs., for programs at John Hancock Hall, New England Mutual Hall, Boston University Concert Hall, Jordan Hall, Berklee College, New England Conservatory of Music, and museums. The **Opera Company of Boston,** under the direction of the renowned Sarah Caldwell, performs during winter opera season at the Opera House (617–426–2786), 539 Washington St., in downtown Boston; check newspapers for schedules, or call 617–426–5300. Oldest U.S. active choral group, Boston's **Handel and Haydn Society,** performs in Boston and Philharmonic Hall, New York. **Boston Ballet** has been widely acclaimed; tickets at Wang Center, or call 617–542–1323.

There are frequent chamber music performances in Harvard's **Sanders Theater;** watch local papers for details.

Boston has three major downtown theaters famous for pre-Broadway premieres. They are the **Wilbur,** 246 Tremont St. (617–426–1988); the **Shubert,** 265 Tremont St. (617–426–4520); and the **Colonial,** 106 Boylston St. (617–426–9366). The **Wang Center,** 268 Tremont St. (617–482–9393), offers occasional theatrical presentations as well as concerts. Smaller theaters include the **Alley Theater,** 1253 Cambridge St., Cambridge (617–491–8166); **Charles Playhouse,** 74 Warrenton St. (617–426–6912); **Lyric Stage,** 54 Charles St. (617–742–8703); and **New Ehrlich Theatre,** 551 Tremont St. (617–482–6316). The **Boston Shakespeare Company** is at 52 St. Botolph St. (617–267–5600). Presentations by **college drama groups,** such as those at Tufts, Boston University, Emerson College, and **Loeb Drama Center** at Harvard, are scheduled throughout the year. Boston University Theatre houses the **Huntington Theatre Company,** 264

Huntington Ave. (617–266–3913), which does five productions a year. The Loeb, 64 Brattle St., Cambridge (617–547–8300), is the home of the **American Repertory Theater.** For tickets, call box offices, Ticketron (617–720–3434), or stop at the Quincy Market kiosk of Bostix (617–723–5181), which is closed Mon.

ART GALLERIES. Boston's major concentration of art galleries is on and around Newbury St., in the Back Bay. Most specialize in contemporary art, although you will have no trouble finding marine, sporting, and other more traditional subjects. Exhibits and sales of fine photography are also becoming more common. Most galleries are closed on Sun. and Mon. For information on the latest openings, check the Calendar section of the *Boston Globe,* which appears as an insert every Thurs.

Alpha Gallery, 121 Newbury St., Back Bay; 617–536–4465. Contemporary American and European painting, sculpture, and master prints. Call for hours.

Art Institute of Boston, 700 Beacon St., Kenmore Sq.; 617–262–1223. Changing monthly exhibits of students' work. Open 9 A.M.–5 P.M. weekdays.

Bromfield Gallery, 90 South St.; 617–451–3605. Oldest artist-owned gallery in Boston shows work of New England artists early in career. All media. Open Tues.–Sat. 10:30 A.M.–5 P.M.

Childs Gallery, 169 Newbury St., Back Bay; 617–266–1108. American and European paintings, prints, drawings, sculpture. Open Tues.–Fri. 9 A.M.–5 P.M., Mon. and Sat. 10 A.M.–5 P.M.

Copley Society of Boston, 158 Newbury St., Back Bay; 617–536–5049. Nonprofit membership organization founded in 1879 features the work of well-known and aspiring New England artists. Open Tues.–Sat., 10 A.M.–5 P.M.

Eugene Galleries, 76 Charles St., Beacon Hill; 617–227–3062. Specializing in prints, etchings, old maps, and city views. Also books. Call for hours.

Gallery NAGA, 67 Newbury St., Back Bay; 617–267–9060. Contemporary works featuring local artists; some photography. Open Tues.–Sat., 10 A.M.–5 P.M.

Haley and Steele, 91 Newbury St., Back Bay; 617–536–6339. 18th- and 19th-century prints on sporting and botanical subjects. Open Mon.–Fri., 10 A.M.–6 P.M. and Sat., 10 A.M.–5 P.M.

Harcus Gallery, 210 South St.; 617–262–4445. Contemporary sculpture, painting, graphics, and drawings, including work by Nevelson, de-Kooning, Albers, and Caro; some local and less-famous artists are also featured. Open Tues.–Sat., 9:30 A.M. to 5:30 P.M.

New England School of Art and Design, 28 Newbury St., Back Bay; 617–536–0383. Student and faculty exhibits of graphics, sculpture, drawings, paintings, and photography. Open weekdays, 9 A.M.–5 P.M.

New England School of Photography, 537 Commonwealth Ave., Kenmore Sq.; 617–437–1868. Gallery of students' photography. Open daily, 9 A.M.–5 P.M.

Vision Gallery, 216 Newbury St., Back Bay; 617–542–8191. Some 19th-century but mostly the work of such 20th-century photographers as Alfred Stieglitz, Joel Sternfeld, and Olivia Parker; also books, prints, and posters. Call for hours.

Vose Gallery, 238 Newbury St., Back Bay; 617–536–6176. 18th- and 19th-century American and European paintings. Open Mon.–Fri., 8 A.M.–5:30 P.M., and Sat., 9 A.M.–4 P.M.

SHOPPING. Filene's, 426 Washington St., Boston's most famous store, includes **Filene's Basement,** a bargain-hunter's paradise. **Jordan-Marsh Co.,** 450 Washington St., has everything from records to designer dresses. Newbury St., in the Back Bay, is lined with art galleries, haute couture shops, and branches of exclusive New York stores such as **Bonwit Teller, Brooks Brothers,** and **F.A.O. Schwartz.** On nearby Boylston St., you'll find **Louis** and **Roots,** two of Boston's best men's shops, and the venerable jewelry, tableware, antiques, and gift emporium of **Shreve Crump and Low.** The new **Copley Place** complex features **Nieman Marcus, Gucci, Charles Jourdan, Louis Vuitton, Tiffany, Rizzoli Books, Ralph Lauren, Saint Laurent Rive Gauche, Godiva Chocolatier,** and several dozen other posh shops. In the Prudential Center, you'll find **Lord and Taylor, Saks Fifth Avenue,** and many smaller specialty shops.

The Faneuil Hall-Quincy Market complex is a colorful and eclectic bazaar; visit when you're hungry.

Downtown at 29 School St., near the old City Hall, is **Brookstone,** which sells ingenious, high quality tools and gadgets for home, car, and garden. Outdoorspersons will enjoy **Eastern Mountain Sports,** 1041 Commonwealth Ave. near Boston University and at Winthrop Sq. downtown.

The Harvard Coop, in Cambridge and downtown Boston, has outstanding record and book selections, and Harvard Sq. is home to some 25 bookstores. Visit **Crate & Barrel,** Brattle Square, Cambridge, for housewares.

NIGHTLIFE. For *Jazz:* **The Plaza Bar,** Copley Plaza Hotel, Copley Sq. (617-267-5300), is the home of jazz piano great Dave McKenna from autumn through spring. An elegant, comfortable room. No cover. **Saffi's New Orleans North,** 835 Beacon St. (617-424-6995), is a room devoted to traditional jazz sounds—Cajun and Dixieland. No cover. Cambridge, **Regattabar** in the posh new Charles Hotel, 1 Bennett St. (617-876-7777), features top local and national jazz acts, great vocalists. Cover.

For *Rock:* **The Channel,** 25 Necco St., near Fort Point Channel (617-451-1905), showcases the area's hot new bands. Cover. Kenmore Sq. rocks on with the new clubs **Axis** and **Citi** (formerly Metro), both at 13 Landsdowne St. (617-262-2424). The **9 Landsdowne Club** (617-421-9595) features occasional concerts. **The Rat,** 528 Commonwealth Ave., (617-536-9438), yet another popular Kenmore Sq. spot and a landmark punk club, books local and national talent.

A selection of *bars,* some with music, some without: **The Black Rose,** 160 State St. (617-732-2286), dispenses draft stout and offers Irish folk music nightly. Lunch and dinner. **Clarke's,** 21 Merchants Row (617-227-7800) is a popular after-work spot in Boston's financial district. **Friday's,** Newbury at Exeter St. (617-266-9040), occupies a sidewalk greenhouse attached to the old Exeter Street Theater. The bar at the **Lenox Hotel,** 710 Boylston St. (617-536-5300), features popular piano singalongs. **Hampshire House,** 84 Beacon St. (617-227-9600), features two taprooms—an upstairs parlor decked out like a 19th-century mens' club, with a lovely view of the public garden, and the **Bull and Finch Pub,** a more informal (and louder) cellar bar. This is the bar on which the TV show "Cheers" is based. **The Last Hurrah,** at Dunfey's Parker House, Tremont St. (617-227-8600), also serving lunch and dinner, is hung with photos of old-time politicos. Swing orchestra often featured. **Lily's,** in the Faneuil Hall Marketplace (617-227-4242), has jazz in both cafe and bar settings. **The Ritz Bar,** in the Ritz Carlton Hotel (617-536-5700), is perhaps Boston's most famous spa and surely its quietest and most intimate. Luncheon and hors d'oeuvres served. Recently remodeled; looks more like it did pre-1970. Another quiet, dressy spot for cocktails—with a spectacular view—is the lounge at the **Bay Tower Room,** 60 State St. (617–723–1666).

THE NORTH SHORE

Massachusetts's North Shore, as the area along the coast between Boston and the New Hampshire border is known, combines classic New England scenes of waves crashing on granite and of peaceful salt marshes with the rich legacy of three and a half centuries of settlement and seafaring. Begin your North Shore explorations by heading out of Boston via the Callahan Tunnel, staying on Route 1A through Revere Beach and the old shoe manufacturing city of Lynn. Just past Lynn is Swampscott; here, bear right on Route 129 and continue into Marblehead.

Marblehead

Marblehead, with its ancient clapboarded houses and narrow, winding streets, retains much of the character of the village founded by fishermen from Cornwall and the Channel Islands in 1629. Today's fishing fleet is small, however, compared to the armada of pleasure craft that anchors in Marblehead's fine harbor. This is one of New England's premier sailing capitals, and Race Week—usually held in the last week of July—brings boats from all along the Eastern seaboard. But the men who made Marblehead prosper in the eighteenth century were merchant sailors, not weekend yachtsmen, and many of their gracious Georgian mansions still line the downtown streets.

Abbott Hall, Marblehead's municipal building, houses A. M. Willard's famous 1876 painting *The Spirit of '76,* one of America's most treasured patriotic icons. Many people, familiar since childhood with the depiction of the three Revolutionary veterans, with fife, drum, and flag, are surprised to find the original in an otherwise unassuming town hall—but of such surprises are Massachusetts travels made. Other notable Marblehead sites are the Old Town House on Mugford Street (1727) and St. Michael's Church (1714) with its Paul Revere bell.

Salem

After visiting Marblehead Neck and the lighthouse at the entrance to the harbor, head back inland on Route 114 and follow the signs for Salem. Here is a small city that once loomed very large indeed in the minds and ledgers of merchants throughout the Orient, a city that, many years before the era of mercantile prowess, witnessed the unfolding of a tragic episode in American history, one that involved the imagined threat of witchcraft and the very real terror of mob psychology.

The Salem witchcraft hysteria of the 1690s actually began in Salem Village, now a part of nearby Danvers. It all started when a West Indian slave named Tituba told fireside tales of sorcery and voodoo to a pair of impressionable young girls, whose subsequent nightmares were taken as a sure sign of enchantment. They accused Tituba of acquainting them with the devil, and soon no one—particularly unpopular old women—was safe from the hysteria which gave rise to the term "witch hunt." By the end of 1693, 19 persons had been hanged and one pressed to death in Salem (no one was burned at the stake). The witchcraft trials came to an abrupt

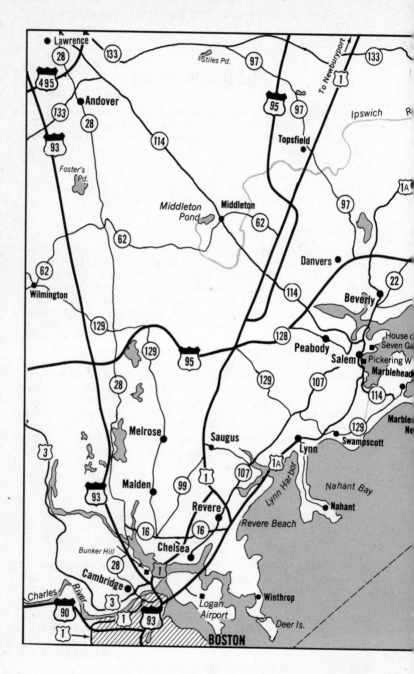

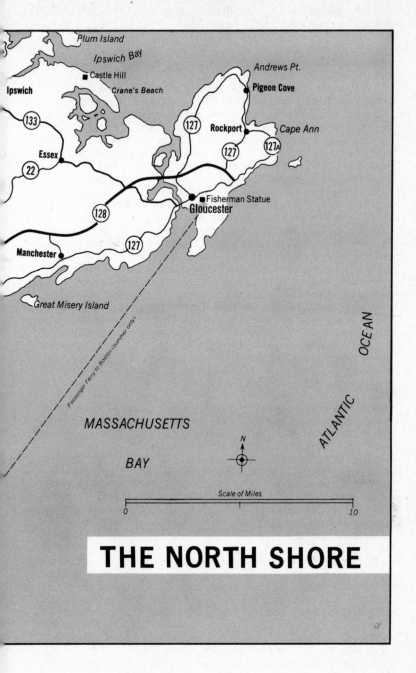

THE NORTH SHORE

halt when the wife of Governor Phipps and the saintly Mrs. Hale, wife of a minister, were accused.

Three hundred years later, this dreadful behavior on the part of clergy-ridden settlers still groping their way out of the Middle Ages has become somewhat of a tourist industry. Visitors flock to the Salem Witch Museum and to the "Witch House," the restored home of Jonathan Corwin, one of the judges who presided over the trials. Original court documents, some of them on display, are kept at the Essex Institute in downtown Salem.

A hundred years later, the years following the Revolution proved to be brighter ones for Salem. This was the home port of the sea captains who made fabulous fortunes in the China Trade, and here they built the fine, Federal-style mansions that still speak volumes about the way they lived. The Essex Institute maintains a half-dozen homes, open to the public in summer, that typify this as well as earlier eras. And Chestnut Street, within a few blocks of downtown, boasts a magnificent architectural harmony, all circa 1800. The merchant princes who lived here created one of the most beautiful streets in America.

Before you leave Salem, be sure to visit the Peabody Museum, a treasure house of maritime history as well as of Oriental art and artifacts (remember, Salem was the seat of the China Trade). Reminders of the city's glory days may also be found at the Salem Maritime National Historic Site, which includes the Custom House where Nathaniel Hawthorne worked as a young man.

Heading north out of Salem on Route 1A, you will cross the harbor bridge and come into Beverly, known as the "birthplace of the American Navy." Here, in 1775, the schooner *Hannah* was armed and sent out to menace British shipping. She returned with her first prize on September 7, just two days after her commission.

Cape Ann

Route 1A continues north through the "hunt country" of Hamilton and Wenham, where folk still ride to the hounds on autumn mornings, but if your time is limited and you've never seen Cape Ann, by all means bear right at Beverly onto Route 127. This shore road will take you through Beverly Farms, Pride's Crossing, Manchester-by-the-Sea, and Magnolia, where many of Boston's Brahmin families built their summer retreats. Head down Hesperus Avenue in Magnolia for a look at Norman's Woe Rock, made famous by Longfellow in "The Wreck of the Hesperus." (The best view is from the fanciful ersatz castle built by the inventor John Hammond, now a museum.) Hesperus Avenue rejoins Route 127, which crosses the Annisquam River and takes you into the old fishing port of Gloucester.

If you enter the city by this route, virtually the first sight you'll see will be the statue that symbolizes Gloucester and memorializes the Gloucestermen who have gone "down to the sea in ships" for the better part of four centuries. This is the famous Gloucester fisherman, bent over his wheel, eyes on the horizon—the type of monument that is all too uncommon, dedicated as it is to the anonymous souls who do the work of the world. And dangerous work it often is; hardly a year or two goes by without word of a Gloucester boat and her crew lost at sea.

Workaday Gloucester is downtown, near the docks. For a different look at the city, head out to the artists' colony on Rocky Neck, and to Eastern Point where a number of magnificent mansions stand above the granite shore. Both are just short side trips off the main route, 127.

Rockport, at the very tip of Cape Ann, derives its name from those same granite formations; many a Boston-area structure was built with stone from the town's long-gone quarries. Today, Rockport is known primarily as a tourist's town, although one which has kept itself to a comfortable human scale and not gone totally overboard on T-shirt emporia and other accoutrements of a summer economy. The best time to visit Rockport is in the off-season; many of the shops are open but the crowds are gone, and it's possible to see the place for what it is—a lovely New England sea-coast town. Walk out to the end of Bearskin Neck (there's a strudel shop along the way worth your attention) for an excellent view of the open Atlantic and of the nearby lobster shack affectionately known as Motif No. 1 because of its favor as a subject for amateur artists.

Route 127 continues past Rockport along the north coast of Cape Ann, affording fine ocean views as it winds its way to meet Route 128. Don't stay on 128 long—get off on Route 133 and head for the old shipbuilding town of Essex, which has a whole afternoon's worth of antique shops on its main street. There are a number of places in Essex to buy fried clams, which were supposedly invented here, and an interesting shipbuilding museum. Essex is one of those pretty little towns that looks to have an excellent chance of staying that way, for most of the land not already built on is tidal marsh that is by law protected from development.

Ipswich, Newburyport, Salisbury

Four miles north of Essex is Ipswich, an unimposing town that was settled in 1633 and is said to have more seventeenth-century houses still standing and lived in than any other place in America. The Whipple House, a brooding, almost medieval dwelling built around 1640, is filled with antiques and open to the public. It's on the common, at the intersection of 133 and 1A. Nearby is the turnoff onto Argilla Road, which leads to the Crane Memorial Reservation. The attractions here are a pristine 10-mile beach and an imposing mansion, Castle Hill, built in the 1920s by the plumbing-fixture baron Richard Crane. A program of concerts is held on the great lawn of the estate in summer.

From Ipswich, continue north on Route 1A for 12 miles, past the salt marshes of Rowley and Newbury, until you reach Newburyport. Route 1A becomes High Street, which is lined with some of the finest examples of Federal-style (roughly 1790–1810) mansions in New England. You'll notice "widow's walks," which afford a view of the port and farther out to sea, perched atop many of these fine houses. Like those in Salem, they were built for prosperous sea captains who lived in this city, which also once thrived as a leading port and shipbuilding center. Although Newburyport's maritime significance ended with the day of the clipper ships, some of the best of which were built here, an energetic downtown renewal program has brought new life to the town's brick-fronted center. Renovated buildings now house an assortment of restaurants, taverns, and shops, selling everything from nautical brasses to fine antique oriental rugs. These civic improvements have been matched by private restoration of the town's housing stock, much of which dates from the eighteenth century, with a scattering of sixteenth-century homes in some neighborhoods.

A causeway leads from Newburyport to Plum Island, a narrow spit of land harboring a summer colony at one end and a fine, carefully managed wildlife refuge at the other. The beaches on the refuge are open to bathers and fishermen (gates close when parking lots are filled), and the self-guided trails through dunes and marshes offer the North Shore's most rewarding setting for birdwatching.

The last town in Massachusetts before you get to the New Hampshire border is Salisbury, just across the Merrimack River from Newburyport and light years away from the upscale, brass-and-brick character of its neighbor. Salisbury's claim to fame is Salisbury Beach, a picture-perfect survivor of the great age of boardwalk honky-tonks, pizza joints, Skee-ball arcades, Ferris wheels, and kiddie rides. You've seen a lot of authentic Americana since leaving Boston; before heading back down Route 95 or continuing north, why not take in some more—circa 1955.

PRACTICAL INFORMATION FOR THE NORTH SHORE

HOW TO GET THERE AND AROUND. The entire North Shore area lies within 40 mi. of Boston, an easy day trip by car or train. Several Boston-Gloucester cruises allow sightseeing stopover time; call A. C. Cruise Line, Pier 1, Boston (617–426–8419).

By plane: Logan Airport, Boston, is the nearest commercial airport for North Shore points. (See *Practical Information for Boston.*)

By train: A number of North Shore points are served by the MBTA commuter lines. Trains leave North Station, Causeway St., Boston for Salem, Beverly, Gloucester, Rockport, and Ipswich. Call 617–227–5070 for information.

By bus: Bus service from Boston to North Shore points is sketchy. There is some MBTA service to the more southern locations; call 617–722–3200 for information. Greyhound service to Maine and eastern Canada points includes a Newburyport stop, about 3 mi. out of town; call 617–423–5810 for information.

By car: The primary north–south routes through the North Shore region are I–95, which runs from Danvers to the New Hampshire border; Rte. 1, from Boston to New Hampshire by way of Danvers and Newburyport; and Rte. 1A, the most scenic route, which follows the coast (except for Cape Ann) by way of Salem, Beverly, Ipswich, and Newburyport. Route 128 is the quick way to Gloucester, on Cape Ann; Rte. 127 is the more scenic, roundabout route. Rte. 133 connects Gloucester with Rte. 1A at Ipswich by way of Essex.

HOTELS AND MOTELS. There are plenty of accommodations available on the North Shore, from overnight motels along Rte. 1 to cozy inns and oceanfront motor hotels on Cape Ann.

The following rates are based on double occupancy: *Deluxe,* $95 and up; *Expensive,* $70–$95; *Moderate,* $55–$70; *Inexpensive,* under $55. Remember that summer rates along the coast, particularly on Cape Ann, will be higher than in the off-season.

Andover

Sheraton Rolling Green Motor Inn, 311 Lowell St. at I–93, Exit 43, 01810 (508–475–5400). *Deluxe.* Attractive rooms. Pools. Tennis, golf, cross-country skiing. Play area. Restaurant. Bar, entertainment, dancing weekends.

Andover Inn, Chapel Ave., 01810 (508–475–5903). *Moderate.* Restaurant, bar, entertainment, dancing. Play area, rec room. On campus of Phillips Academy.

Merrimack Valley Motor Inn, Chickering Rd., 01810 (508–688–1851). *Moderate.* Restaurant, bar, entertainment.

Danvers

Sheraton Tara, I–95 at Rte. 1, 01923 (508–777–2500). *Deluxe.* Country club setting. Restaurant, lounge. Golf, cross-country ski trails. Package plans avail.

King's Grant Inn, Trask Lane, Rte. 128 at Exit 21N, 01923 (508–774–6800). *Expensive.* Very inviting quarters. Good restaurant, bar, entertainment. Pool.

Hathorne Motor Inn, 225 Newbury St. 01923 (508–774–6500). *Moderate.* Outdoor pool. Pleasant spacious rooms. Restaurant, bar.

Gloucester

Best Western Manor Motor Inn, Atlantic Rd. on Scenic Shore Dr., 01930 (508–283–7500). *Deluxe.* Pool. Restaurant, bar, entertainment. Play area, rec room, near beach. Open Feb.–Nov.

Bass Rocks Motor Inn, 89 Atlantic Rd., 01930 (508–283–7600). *Expensive.* Pool, beach near. Private balconies overlook ocean. Serves breakfast. Open Apr.–Oct.

Vista, Thatcher Rd., 01930 (508–281–3410). *Expensive.* Private patios or balconies overlook ocean. Near restaurant.

The Anchorage, 5 Hawthorne Lane, beyond Rocky Neck, 01930 (508–283–4788). *Moderate.* Overlooks harbor. Near beach. Free coffee and rolls. Near restaurant.

Newburyport

Garrison Inn, 11 Brown Sq., 01950 (508–465–0910). *Expensive.* An 1809 inn, recently restored and reopened. 24 rooms, several suites. Two restaurants, tavern. Near shops, waterfront.

Rockport

Seaward Inn, 62 Marmion Way, 01966 (508–546–3471). *Deluxe.* Attractive inn on rocky coast with resort atmosphere. Golf, tennis near. Planned entertainment. Near beach, bird sanctuary. Open mid-May–mid-Oct. American Plan, Modified American Plan available.

Yankee Clipper Inn, 96 Granite St., 01966 (508–546–3407). *Deluxe.* Popular quiet hotel overlooking ocean. Pool. Restaurant serves dinner Fri.–Sat. and Sun. brunch. Meeting facilities.

Captain's Bounty Motor Inn, 1 Beach St., 01966 (508–546–9557). *Expensive.* Near private beach. Near restaurant. Open Apr. 1–Oct., weekends in Nov.

Bearskin Neck, Bearskin Neck, 01966 (508–546–6677). *Moderate.* Small two-story motel on ocean. Near restaurants. Open Apr.–Dec.

Tuck-Inn Lodge, 17 High St., 01966 (508–546–6252). *Moderate.* Quiet area near town. Pool. Breakfast available. Near restaurant.

Turk's Head Motor Inn, 283 South St., 01966 (508–546–3436). *Moderate.* New motel located a short walk from beach. Pool. Coffee shop.

Salem

Hawthorne Inn. 18 Washington Sq., 01970 (508–744–4080). *Expensive.* Homelike atmosphere, many antiques. Restaurant, bar, entertainment.

INNS, GUEST HOUSES, BED AND BREAKFASTS. The more northerly coastal towns of the North Shore area are sprinkled with comfortable inns, often occupying graceful old structures dating back to the Federal era. Bed-and-breakfast homes offer accommodations at more modest prices; reservations are handled by organizations such as New England Bed and Breakfast, 1045 Centre St, Newton (617–244–2112). The Greater Boston Council of American Youth Hostels, 1020B Commonwealth Ave., Brookline 02146, can give information on the summer-only Youth Hostel located at the YMCA in Amesbury. Call 508–388–3873.

Most inn accommodations will fall into the *moderate* category, as outlined above under "Hotels"; in summer, rates are often higher.

Newburyport

Essex Street Inn, 7 Essex St., 01950 (508–465–3148). On a quiet side street near downtown and the waterfront. Most rooms have phones and TV; larger suites have fireplaces. Continental breakfast available.

Rockport

Eden Pines Inn, Eden Rd., 01966 (508–546–2505; during off-season, write 8 Cakebread Dr., Sudbury 01776). Rambling, shingled building overlooking ocean; some rooms have private decks. Continental breakfast and cocktails on porch. Open mid-May–mid-Nov.

Old Farm Inn, 291 Granite St., Pigeon Cove 01966 (508–546–3237). Family-run in secluded setting next to Halibut Point State Park. Breakfast included. Open Apr.–Dec.

Ralph Waldo Emerson Inn. Pigeon Cove, 01966 (508–546–6321). Pool, play area. Traditional, quiet hotel. Restaurant. Open May–Oct., weekends Apr. and Nov. Modified American Plan; European Plan off-season.

Salem

Coach House. 284 Lafayette St., 01970 (508–744–4092). Old inn with memorabilia of clipper ship days. Continental breakfast.

RESTAURANTS. North Shore restaurants have long been noted for fresh seafood. While lobster and scrod still hold sway, along with the ubiquitous fried clams, more sophisticated menus have also begun to proliferate.

The cost of an à la carte dinner, exclusive of drinks and tip, is the basis of our price ranges: *Expensive,* $20 and up; *Moderate,* $10–$20; *Inexpensive,* under $10.

Andover

Andover Inn, on Phillips Academy campus (508–475–5903). *Expensive.* Relaxed atmosphere, good service. Rijsttafel—the Dutch Indonesian buffet—is a Sun. tradition.

Backstreet, 19 Essex St. (508–475–4411). *Moderate.* Veal Oscar; French onion soup; fresh vegetables. Good wine list.

Danvers

Cherrystones, Rte. 1 at Rte. 114 (508–774–3300). *Moderate.* Serving an impressive variety of fresh fish and shellfish. Raw bar at cocktail time; great Sun. brunch.

Gloucester

White Rainbow, 65 Main St. (508–281–0017). *Expensive.* In a registered landmark building. Prix fixe dinner only. Bar, entertainment weekends. Menu changes, but fresh vegetables, fine soups and pâtés, and imaginative entrees are a standby. Sun. brunch.

Captain Courageous, 25 Rogers St. (508–283–0007). *Moderate.* Popular locally. New England specialties, plus steak, prime ribs.

Easterly, 87 Atlantic Rd. (508–283–0140). *Moderate.* Dover sole meuniere, veal scallopine Marsala. Overlooks ocean. Lounge, entertainment in summer. Closed Nov. 1–early Apr.

Gloucester House, Rte. 127 (508–283–1812). *Moderate.* At Seven Seas Wharf, overlooking harbor. Excellent seafood. Bar. Children's portions. Dancing in summer.

The Rudder, 73 Rocky Neck Ave. (508–283–7967). *Moderate.* Steaks, roast beef, plus delicious baked clams farcis, filet of sole hollandaise. Children's portions. Closed Mon., Tues., and Nov.–mid-May.

Marblehead

Rosalie's, 18 Sewell St. (617–631–5353). *Moderate.* Homemade pasta, tender veal, and consistently good renditions of the Northern Italian repertory.

Newburyport

Scandia, 25 State St. (508–462–6271). *Moderate.* Small, intimate restaurant with new American cuisine. The seafood is always good, *especially* the chowder.

The Grog, 13 Middle St. (508–465–8008). *Inexpensive.* Two floors of dining, two bars, and jazz music in the basement. Menu includes burgers, prime rib, daily seafood specials, and an assortment of Mexican dishes.

Rockport

Blacksmith Shop, 23 Mt. Pleasant St. (508–546–6301). *Moderate.* Charming restaurant overlooks harbor. Children's portions. Open mid-May–mid-Oct.

Oleana-by-the-Sea, 27 Main St. (508–546–2049). *Moderate.* Scandinavian-American specialties. Smorgasbord. Open mid-Jan.–mid-Dec. Closed Mon.

Peg Leg, 18 Beach St. (508–546–3038). *Moderate.* Lobster, seafood, steak, roast beef served in greenhouse overlooking ocean. Closed mid-Nov–Mar. Children's portions.

Salem

Chase House, Pickering Wharf (508–744–0000). *Expensive.* 100-year-old restaurant. Mako shark, halibut, swordfish, haddock creole, steak. Weekend entertainment nightly. Cozy traditional atmosphere.

Lyceum, 43 Church St. (508–745–7665). *Expensive.* Veal, duckling, good variety of local seafood. Excellent dessert selection.

Swampscott

General Glover House, Salem St. (617–595–5151). *Moderate.* Home of Gen. John Glover, father of U.S. Navy. Steaks, roast beef. Cocktails.

Hawthorne-by-the-Sea, 153 Humphrey St. (617–595–5735). *Moderate.* Waterfront restaurant featuring lobster stuffed with lobster.

TOURIST INFORMATION. In addition to the Chambers of Commerce of the individual towns along your itinerary, a good source of North Shore touring information is the North of Boston Tourist Council, Box 3031, Dept. MA, Peabody 01960 (508–532–1449).

TOURS. The **Gray Line,** 275 Tremont St., Boston 02116 (617–426–8805), offers several North Shore tours. These include a six-hour Cape Ann tour, with dinner at a Rockport restaurant; a four-hour Salem tour, including Marblehead; and an eight-hour seacoast tour that takes in Newburyport, Portsmouth, New Hampshire, and York, Maine. All tours begin in Boston.

Special-Interest Tours. In recent years, the most popular specialty tours along the North Shore have been **whale-watch** cruises. While whale sightings can't be guaranteed, cruise patrons nearly always see humpbacks and other species. Reputable cruise operators include Captain's Fishing Parties, Plum Island Point, Newburyport (508–462–3141); Cape Ann Whale Watching, 415 Main St., Gloucester (508–283–5110); and Captain Bill's Deep Sea Fishing, 9 Traverse St., Gloucester (508–283–6995).

SEASONAL EVENTS. May: Antique Flea Market, Topsfield Fair Grounds, Topsfield.

June: Blessing of the Fishing Fleet, Gloucester.

July: Yankee Homecoming, Newburyport; Olde Newbury Horse Show, Plum Island Tpke., Newburyport.

August: Newburyport Waterfront Festival, Plum Island Tpke., Newburyport.

October: Topsfield Fair, Topsfield; 17th-Century Day, Ipswich; Myopia Hunt Club Four-in-Hand Event, Hamilton.

PARKS AND FORESTS. Bradley Palmer State Park, on Rte. 1 in Topsfield, is relatively undeveloped but has an extensive system of trails for hiking and cross-country skiing. Skiers and hikers will also enjoy the new **Maudslay State Park** along the heights above the Merrimack River in Newburyport, near the Rte. 113 exit off I–95. The **Salisbury Beach State Reservation,** off Rte. 1A in Salisbury, has ocean beaches, camping. For information on all state parks, including activities and permits, contact the Massachusetts Department of Environmental Management, 100 Cambridge St., Boston (617–727–3180).

WILDLIFE REFUGES. The North Shore is the home of one of the nation's most famous wildlife refuges, the **Parker River National Wildlife Refuge.** Popular with birders throughout the year, the refuge occupies the southern two-thirds of Plum Island, a barrier beach of windblown dunes and scrub thickets accessible by road from Newburyport. Hours are dawn to dusk; in summer, parking lots fill quickly and the refuge takes in no more autos until visitors begin to leave, later in the afternoon. Greenhead flies may make you wish for insect repellent, mid-July–mid-Aug. For information, call the U.S. Fish and Wildlife Service, Plum Island (508–462–1044).

BEACHES. The North Shore is famous for its beautiful sandy beaches, but you'd better appreciate the bracing feel of cold North Atlantic water if you plan to take a dip. Among the more popular beaches are the **Singing Beach** in Manchester (named for the sound the wind makes in the sand), just off Rte. 127; **Wingaersheek Beach,** Gloucester; and Crane's Beach, off Argilla Road in Ipswich. This beach is part of the beautiful Crane Reservation, operated by the private Trustees of Reservations; upkeep forces the Trustees to charge a hefty parking charge in summer ($8 per car). The above-mentioned **Parker River Refuge** and **Salisbury State Reservation** also have fine, unspoiled beaches; town beaches in Newburyport (on Plum Island) and Salisbury are also popular. The water along the North Shore is warmest in Aug.

SUMMER SPORTS. As one might expect, water sports lead the list of summer activities on the North Shore. **Boating,** especially sailing, is big—many towns have waiting lists of several years for moorings. If you're bringing your boat along, though, you should have no trouble finding public launch ramps. The best bet is to call the harbormaster of the town you're planning to launch from, or stop at a local marina. Town harbormasters will also be able to tell you what the nightly fees are for tying up at public docks, when spaces are available.

Canoeing involves less complicated logistics than getting a sailboat in the water; the Ipswich and Parker rivers are both popular. For saltwater canoeing, try the calm, protected waters of the Essex River estuary, in Essex.

Golfers have a choice of a number of fine courses on the North Shore. The Salem Country Club, Peabody (508–532–2540); Middleton Golf Course, Rte. 114, Middleton (508–774–4075); and Rowley Country Club, Dodge Rd., Rowley (508–948–2731), are all open to the public.

WINTER SPORTS. Cross-country skiing is the dominant winter sport in an area that doesn't boast any downhill areas; most golf courses are open to skiers, as are the locations listed above under parks and forests.

FISHING. Although fishing party boats depart from piers in Newburyport and Gloucester, the most popular form of saltwater fishing on the North Shore is surfcasting. Bluefish, pollock, and the all-too-elusive striped bass can be taken from the ocean shores of Plum Island; permits to remain on the beach of the Parker River Wildlife Refuge after dark may be obtained free of charge by anyone entering the refuge with fishing equipment during daylight hours. Permits aren't necessary to fish from the public beaches on Plum Island; the action can be especially good at the mouth of the Merrimack River. Freshwater fishing spots include the Parker and Ipswich rivers, both stocked with trout each spring.

HUNTING. The more southerly sections of the North Shore are too built up for hunting, but small-game hunters can go out after rabbit, pheasant, and grouse on state wildlife management areas in Newbury and Rowley. Contact the Fisheries and Wildlife Department, 100 Cambridge St., Boston (617–727–3151) for rules and regulations. Duck and geese hunters favor the salt marshes at the mouth of the Parker River and Plum Island River; for information, call the above number as well as the headquarters of the Parker River National Wildlife Refuge (508–462–1044). (Refuge managers allow waterfowl hunting along certain peripheral areas at select times.)

CAMPING. Campsites are few and far between in this part of Massachusetts, although a few spaces are available at the Salisbury Beach State Reservation and Bradley Palmer State Park. (See *Parks and Forests.*)

SPECTATOR SPORTS. The one spectator sport of note on the North Shore is an unusual one—**polo.** The Myopia Hunt Club stages polo matches on Sundays, late May–early Oct., on its grounds along Rte. 1A in Hamilton. For schedules, write the club: Myopia Hunt Club, Polo Promotions, Box 2103, South Hamilton, 01982 (508–468–4433).

HISTORIC SITES AND HOUSES. As one of the earliest settled areas in the United States, the North Shore has no shortage of historic places, many dating back to the 1600s. The area's rich maritime history is also well documented.

Beverly

Balch House, 448 Cabot St. (508–922–7076). Open Memorial Day to Oct. 15, Wed.–Sat. This house (1636) is one of the oldest in New England.

Gloucester

Fisherman Statue, Rte. 127, Gloucester. Commemorates over three centuries of Gloucestermen who went "down to the sea in ships."

Ipswich

Whipple House, South Village Green, Ipswich (no tel.). Open Apr. to Nov., Tues.–Sun. A fine example of a "First Period" house (1640). Exquisitely restored and furnished with antiques.

Magnolia

Norman's Woe Rock, Hesperus Ave. Immortalized in Longfellow's poem "Wreck of the Hesperus."

Marblehead

Abbott Hall, Washington St. (617–631–0528). Open Mon.–Fri.; weekends in summer. Marblehead's Town Hall houses famous painting *The Spirit of '76.*

Jeremiah Lee Mansion, 161 Washington St. (617–631–1069). Elegant Georgian building (c. 1768) is home of the Marblehead Historical Society. Open mid-May–mid-Oct.

Rockport

Paper House, 52 Pigeon Hill St. (508–546–2629). Open daily July and Aug.; by appt. rest of year. 60-year-old house built of over 100,000 newspapers.

Salem

The Salem Maritime National Historic Site, 174 Derby St. (508–744–4323). The 9-acre site includes a visitor center, the Custom House on Derby St., that was the shipping center of Salem from 1760 to 1860, and a West India Goods Store. Open daily, except Christmas, Thanksgiving, New Year's. Scale House and Bonded Warehouse have seasonal hours. Free.

Derby House, restored and furnished, is open year-round. Daily tours by reservation.

Jonathan Corwin House, Essex St. (508–744–0180). Open daily Mar. 15–Dec 1. Call for hours. Restored home of witch-trials judge.

Saugus

On the grounds of the **Saugus Iron Works National Historic Site** on Central St. (617–233–0050) are restorations of an ironmaster's house, blast furnace, forge slitting mill. There is also a museum. Grounds open all year; tours conducted daily, Apr.–Oct.

MUSEUMS AND ART GALLERIES. There are several specialized museums in this area. Call ahead to check days, hours, and fees.

Andover

Addison Gallery of American Art, Rte. 28 (508–475–3403). Works of American artists, glassware, sculpture, ship models. Tues.–Sat., 10 A.M.–5 P.M.; Sun., 2:30–5 P.M.. Closed Mon. and holidays. Free to public.

Gloucester

Beauport, Eastern Point Blvd. (508–283–0800). Early American furniture and decorative arts. Mon.–Fri., May 15–Oct. 31.

Magnolia

Hammond Museum, 80 Hesperus Ave. (508–283–2080). Castle-styled home with art and historic exhibits; famed for one of world's largest pipe organs; concerts in summer.

North Andover

Museum of American Textile History, 800 Mass. Ave. (508–686–0191). Old tools, photos, documents show growth of U.S. textile industry. Library. Spec. demonstrations Sun. Closed Mon. and holidays.

Salem

Essex Institute, 132 Essex St. (508–744–3390). Regional museum with historic houses, gardens, museum galleries, research library, shop. Includes Gardner-Pingree House (1804), John Ward House (1684), Pierce-Nichols House (1782), Crowninshield-Bentley House (1727), Cotting-Smith Assembly House (1782). Closed Mon. in winter. Historic homes open June 1–Oct. 31.

House of the Seven Gables, 54 Turner St. (508–744–0991), built 1668; made famous in Hawthorne novel. Also on grounds are Hawthorne's birthplace and other 17th-century dwellings. Closed Thanksgiving, Christmas, New Year's Day and last two weeks in Jan.

Peabody Museum of Salem, East India Sq. (508–745–9500). Natural history exhibits, artifacts from clipper trade, orientalia. Asian Export Art Wing opened May 1988. Mon.–Sat., 10 A.M.–5 P.M.; Sun., 12–5 P.M. Closed Thanksgiving, Christmas, New Year's Day.

Salem Witch Museum, 19½ Washington Sq., N. Salem (508–744–1692), with re-creations of witch trials. Open year-round, 10 A.M.–5 P.M. in winter; 10 A.M.–7 P.M. in summer.

Wenham

Wenham Museum, 132 Main St., Wenham (508–468–2377). Fine antique doll collection; restored 17th-century house. Closed early Feb. and major holidays.

MUSIC, DANCE, AND STAGE. In Ipswich—**Castle Hill Festival,** July, Aug. at Castle Hill estate, Crane Reservation (508–356–4070).

In Beverly—**North Shore Music Theater,** summer theater and pop concerts (508–922–8500).

In Gloucester—**Gloucester Stage Company,** 267 East Main Street, theatre open April–Dec. (508–281–4099).

In Newburyport—The **Theater of Newburyport,** year-round theater company, 75 Water St. (508–462–3332).

In Rockport—**Rockport Chamber Music Festival,** Rockport Art Association, 12 Main St. (508–546–7391). Spring program.

SHOPPING. From candles and mugs to fine art, the cities and towns of the North Shore offer a tremendous variety of shopping experiences. If you like to browse in antique shops or do some serious shopping, your best bet is the half-mile main street of tiny Essex, where at least a half-dozen dealers have shops. **Bearskin Neck,** Rockport, is a good place to search for souvenirs and crafts, but don't overlook the shops downtown on either side of the neck. In Newburyport, **Market Square, State Street,** and the **Inn Street Mall** are crowded with shops selling clothing, crafts, nautical brass, jewelry, toys, leather, and kitchen paraphernalia. In Salem, a number of interesting shops are clustered on **Pickering Wharf;** also, the gift shop at Salem's **Peabody Museum** is one of the best of its kind.

NIGHTLIFE. Grover's, 392 Cabot St., Beverly, showcases rock bands, cover charge after 9 P.M. (508–927–7121); the **Blue Star Lounge,** Rtes. 1 and 99, Saugus, is a country music and rockabilly roadhouse on a busy strip (617–233–8027); the **Grog,** 13 Middle St., Newburyport, is a small basement room (restaurant upstairs) with a big sound, featuring everything from blues to rock to whatever-happened-to name acts, cover charge (508–465–8008); the **Me and Thee Coffeehouse,** 28 Mugford St., Marblehead, is a folksy cofeehouse in a Unitarian Church, half-price admission after 6 P.M. (617–631–8987). Also in Marblehead, **Frankie's Place** features rock bands and varying cover charges; 12 School St. (617–631–9894).

THE SOUTH SHORE AND BRISTOL COUNTY

The paths leading southward out of Boston run, as far as the tourist is concerned, in two general directions. If you cling to the Atlantic and

Cape Cod Bay shores along Route 3 or the more interesting side roads, you'll be heading toward Plymouth, the Cape Cod Canal, and the Cape itself. Take I–93 south to Route 24, however, and you'll follow an inland route leading to the old seaports of New Bedford and Fall River. (Farther west, I–95 is the direct route to Providence, Rhode Island.) The following pages are about this southeastern corner of Massachusetts, an area too often overlooked by travelers in a hurry to get to Cape Cod and the islands.

Along the Coast from Quincy to Plymouth

The first large city south of Boston is Quincy, located just across the Neponset River via I–93 or Route 3A. Quincy is the only city in America where you can see the birthplaces, homes, and final resting places of two Presidents. On Hancock Street at the corner of Washington is the First Parish Church, which was built in 1828 of Quincy granite and contains the crypt of the Adams family. Here are buried the remains of John Adams and his wife, Abigail, as well as those of John Quincy Adams and his wife, Louisa Catherine. A little beyond the church on Hancock Street, turn right on Franklin Street for the Adams National Historic Site, the home of four generations of the Adams family. Filled with priceless heirlooms and antiques, it is open to the public. The family presented the home to the United States government in 1946. Also located on Hancock Street is the home of Dorothy Quincy, wife of John Hancock. The Quincy family, long prominent in colonial politics and trade, were prosperous New England shipbuilders. Visitors are welcome at the Quincy home.

Quincy, in its early days, was well known for its granite, with which the Bunker Hill Monument and King's Chapel were built. The first railroad in the U.S. was built to haul Quincy granite in the 1820s, but the motive power was draft animals rather than steam. You may return to Route 3 from here, or if you have time, remain on Route 3 Alternate, through the pleasant seaside towns of Hingham, Cohasset, Greenbush, and Marshfield. This route runs close to the ocean, and many public beaches can be enjoyed by turning left on almost any of the small roads. The community of Duxbury was established by the Pilgrims shortly after the settlement of Plymouth, and you may visit the John Alden House there. Route 3 Alternate rejoins and crosses the superhighway (Route 3), but visitors should stay on the smaller road to Kingston. The history of this town almost coincides with that of Plymouth, of which it was a part until 1726. The Bradford House contains many of the original furnishings, dating back to 1674, when it was built. Route 3 Alternate continues four more miles to Plymouth.

Bristol County: Fall River and New Bedford

Although no longer a prime port, New Bedford is a busy center of fishing and textile manufacturing. From 1820 until the discovery of oil in Pennsylvania almost 40 years later, New Bedford vied with Nantucket for preeminence in American whaling. Today the industry which once employed 10,000 seamen is commemorated in museums like the one on Johnny Cake Hill in New Bedford. Here you can see the square-rigged whaler *Lagoda,* a half-scale (89 feet) replica of the sort of ship that once crowded the docks of New Bedford. And there are prints and paintings, ship carvings and scrimshaw, and the world's largest collection of whaling gear. Nearby is the seamen's Bethel, vividly pictured by Melville in *Moby Dick.* The Bethel (chapel) was built in 1832 for the spiritual edification of the sailors who shipped out from New Bedford. Melville, whose brief whaling career began here, first visited the chapel when it was but eight years old. The pew where he sat is marked with a commemorative plaque.

New Bedford was once the home of a flourishing glass industry, the products of which are displayed in a recently opened glass museum which occupies the restored Rodman House just one block from the Whaling Museum on North 2nd Street. New Bedford glass is not just a well-kept memory; after a 20-year absence, the Pairpoint Glass Company has returned to a new plant near the museum.

Fall River is a short ride west from New Bedford on Interstate 195. Here is a classic scene in the Massachusetts story, a once-booming textile town struggling to make a comeback from the southward movement of the mills. Like New Bedford, Fall River has a large Portuguese community as well as many French-Canadians.

Here the great veteran of World War II naval action, the USS *Massachusetts,* is berthed, along with other historic fighting ships. It's open all year from 9 A.M. to dusk. Just a short walk from the battleship is Fall River's Marine Museum, with an interesting collection of ship models, steam engines, and material related to the old Fall River line and other ships of the steamboat era. Bargain hunters should note that Fall River has become a major factory outlet center—at last count, there were 51 outlets in the city, most concentrated in one area. If you'd like to see some lively dog racing, take State 24 north to Taunton Dog Track and Raynham Park.

PRACTICAL INFORMATION FOR THE SOUTH SHORE AND BRISTOL COUNTY

HOW TO GET THERE AND AROUND. By plane: Boston's Logan International is the closest major airport to South Shore and Bristol County points. New Bedford Municipal Airport (508–991–6160) is served by Continental/PBA (800–525–0280) and charter services.

By bus: Quincy and Braintree may be reached from Boston on the buses of the Massachusetts Bay Transportation Authority (MBTA). Call 617–722–3200 for information. Both cities are also served by the MBTA's Red Line elevated trains. Boston–New Bedford service is provided by American Eagle (508–993–5040); buses depart Boston from the Trailways station, Atlantic Ave.

By car: The coastal expressway connecting Boston with Plymouth and Cape Cod is Rte. 3, which connects with I–93 at Braintree, near Quincy. Route 3A is the slower but more scenic coast road. Route 24, which connects with Rte. I–93 in Milton, south of Boston, runs north-south between that point and Fall River (turn onto Rte. 140 at Taunton to reach New Bedford). New Bedford and Fall River are connected by I–195.

HOTELS AND MOTELS. This part of Massachusetts isn't all that liberally sprinkled with accommodations—it seems to be assumed that most people are on their way to Providence or the Cape—but you shouldn't have any problem finding a place to stay. The following price ranges are based on double occupancy: *Expensive,* $70–$95; *Moderate,* $45–$70; *Inexpensive,* under $45.

Dedham

Comfort Inn, 235 Elm St., 02026 (617–326–6700). *Moderate.* Just off Rte. 128/I–95, near Rte. 1. Restaurant, lounge; entertainment.

Quincy

Howard Johnson, 150 Granite St., Braintree 02184; Rte. 128 Exit 6 (617–848–8500). *Expensive.* Indoor pool, lounge, and Mexican restaurant.
Sheraton Tara, Rte. 128, Exit 6, Braintree 02184 (617–848–0600). *Expensive.* Pools, sauna, raquetball, exercise facilities. Restaurant, bar, entertainment. Recently doubled capacity.
Boston, 655 Washington St., Weymouth 02188 (617–337–5200). *Moderate.* Pool, play area. Restaurant, bar.
Susse Chalet Motor Lodge, 125 Union St. (at Rte. 3), Braintree 02184 (617–848–7890). *Inexpensive.* Member of popular budget chain. Convenient to Boston and Cape.

New Bedford

Durant Sail Loft Inn, 1 Merrill's Wharf, 02740 (508–999–2700). *Moderate.* In restored, historic Bourne Counting House. Views of historic working waterfront. Restaurant, bar, conference and function rooms.
Skipper, 110 Middle St., Fairhaven 02719 (508–997–1281). *Moderate.* Pool. Pets. Restaurant, bar, entertainment. Marina, health spa.

INNS, GUEST HOUSES, BED AND BREAKFASTS. For statewide bed-and-breakfast listings, contact the Massachusetts Department of Commerce, Division of Tourism, 100 Cambridge St., Boston 02202. As for inns—well, the phenomenon hasn't quite caught on in this part of the state.

RESTAURANTS. As on the North Shore, the restaurants south of Boston make much ado about seafood. Nowadays, however, you're likely to find it in *seviche* as well as in a fried platter. The cost of an à la carte dinner, without drinks or tip, is the basis of our price classifications: *Expensive,* $22 and up; *Moderate,* $12–$22; *Inexpensive,* under $12.

Cohasset

Golden Rooster, 78 Border St., N. Scituate (617–545–1330). *Moderate.* Prime ribs, baked stuffed lobster. Children's portions.
Hugo's Lighthouse, 44 Border St. (617–383–1700). *Moderate.* Ocean-fresh seafoods, steaks, chops. Cocktails.

Fall River

Moby Dick Wharf, 1 Bridge Rd., Westport Point (508–636–4465). *Moderate.* Right on the water. Favorites such as steamers and lobsters, along with steaks and Cajun specialties. Outdoor jazz on summer weekends.

New Bedford

Candleworks Cafe, 72 N. Water St. (508–992–1635). *Moderate.* A nicely restored building near the harbor, featuring an international seafood menu.

Quincy

Rafael's, 1 Monarch Dr. (617–328–1600). *Expensive.* Art deco decor; seafood, chicken, veal, homemade pasta, pastries.
La Paloma, 195 Newport Ave. (617–773–0512). *Inexpensive.* A small, pleasant Mexican spot; the Tex-Mex standards are handled well.

Weymouth

Great Escape, 500 Washington St. (617–337–7732). *Moderate.* "Good time" ambience, with big sandwiches and light entrees; Sun. brunch.

TOURIST INFORMATION. Coastal South Shore information is handled by the Plymouth County Development Council, Box 1620, Dept. MA., Pembroke 02359 (617–826–3136). For New Bedford and Fall River information, try the Bristol County Development Council, 70 North Second St., New Bedford 02740 (508–997–1250).

TOURS. The **Gray Line,** 275 Tremont St., Boston 02116 (617–426–8805), includes Quincy and the Adams Mansion as part of its four-hour Plymouth tour, Apr.–Oct. **Yankee Holidays,** 20 Spring St., Saugus 01906 (617–231–2884), offers a four-day tour that takes in South Shore sights.

SEASONAL EVENTS. August: Marshfield Fair, Marshfield. **September:** Cranberry Festival, Carver; Rehoboth Fair, Dighton. **December:** Christmas festivities, Edaville Railroad, Carver.

PARKS AND FORESTS. One of Massachusetts's largest state forests, **Myles Standish State Forest,** is located just inland from Plymouth; take Exit 5 off Rte. 3. The forest offers an interesting look at a pine barrens ecosystem, characterized by sandy soil and scrub evergreens. Other state properties in Massachusetts's southeastern corner include **Massasoit State Park,** near Middleboro; **Horseneck Beach State Park** and **Demarest-Lloyd State Park,** on Rhode Island Sound near Westport, and **Wompatuck State Park,** Hingham. Call Massachusetts Division of Forest and Parks Southeast (508–866–2580).

BEACHES. With many miles of coastline on Cape Cod Bay and Rhode Island Sound, **swimming** is a top summer activity on the South Shore. In addition to numerous town beaches (be sure to check local parking restrictions), two of the best spots are Nantasket Beach in Hull, and Fort Phoenix State Beach, on Apponagansett Bay near New Bedford. Horseneck Beach State Park, Westport Point, is also popular.
Golf: The Kittansett Club, Marion, is located halfway between New Bedford and the Bourne Bridge leading to Cape Cod.
Southeastern Massachusetts's flat terrain is not conducive to downhill skiing development, but if the snow cover is good you may well find decent **cross-country skiing** at Wompatuck State Park, Cohasset, and Myles Standish State Forest, Plymouth. Although trail systems are extensive in these parks, the latest state information does not indicate that trails are systematically groomed. Unless local skiers have smoothed the way, you may be in for some powder plowing.

FISHING. The best fishing in this part of the state is surf fishing, on the waters of Cape Cod Bay and Rhode Island Sound. Quincy Bay, just south of Boston, is one of the nation's flounder-fishing capitals; this sport generally requires a small boat, although shore fishermen can be successful. Bayswater Boat Rental, 15 Bayswater Rd., Quincy (617–471–8060), rents small craft and sells bait and tackle. Elsewhere along the coast, striped bass and bluefish are the main attraction for anglers.

CAMPING. The best camping facilities on the South Shore are at Myles Standish State Forest, Plymouth. There are even cabins for rent. For camping and cabin rental information, call the Massachusetts Department of Environmental Management, 100 Cambridge St., Boston 02202 (617–727–3180).

SPECTATOR SPORTS. Sullivan Stadium, Foxboro, is the home of the New England Patriots professional football team. (For schedules of games and ticket information, call 617–262–1776.)

HISTORIC SITES AND HOUSES. In Quincy—**Adams National Historic Site,** 135 Adams St. (617–773–1177). Original furnishings. Open mid-Apr.–mid-Nov.
In Fall River—**USS *Massachusetts,*** Battleship Cove (508–678–1100). Surviving battlewagon of WW II; 16-inch guns and all. Open daily. Closed major holidays.

MUSEUMS. There are several specialized museums in this area. Call ahead to check days, hours, and admission charges.

Carver

Edaville Railroad, S. Carver (508–866–4526). Railroads and early Americana, with an actual narrow-gauge train chugging through a working cranberry bog. Open daily in summer; evenings Nov.–Jan.; weekends only in spring. Restaurant and picnic grounds.

Fall River

Marine Museum, 70 Water St. (508–674–3533). Ship models and steamboat memorabilia. Open daily.

Milton

Captain Robert Bennet Forbes House, 215 Adams St. (617–696–1815). Home of a family prominent in the China trade, restored to the last 3 decades of the 19th century. Open Wed. and Sun., 1 P.M.–4 P.M.

New Bedford

Whaling Museum, 18 Johnny Cake Hill (508–997–0046). Whaling artifacts and an 89-foot whaleship model to climb aboard. Open daily. Closed Jan. 1, Thanksgiving, Christmas.
Glass Museum, 50 N. 2nd St. (508–994–0115). Displays of glass from the days when this industry flourished in New Bedford. Closed Mon. Jan.–Apr.; open daily in summer.

North Middleboro

A&D Toy-Train Village and Railroad Museum, 49 Plymouth St. (508–947–5303). Over 30 operating toy trains; exhibits of antique toy trains in all gauges. Terrific layouts. Open daily 10 A.M.–6 P.M. Closed Jan. 1, Thanksgiving, Christmas.

MUSIC, DANCE, AND STAGE. The big name in summer theater and concerts on the South Shore is the **South Shore Music Circus,** Cohasset. For information on performances, call 617–383–1400.

CAPE COD AND THE ISLANDS

The Cape, like Boston and much of Massachusetts's South Shore, has figured in American history from the start. It was explored in 1602 by the English navigator Bartholomew Gosnold, who named it after the great schools of codfish he found in the bay. Eighteen years later, the Pilgrims first landed in Provincetown before continuing on to Plymouth. Although the sand and marshes these early settlers found did not support much farming, prosperous whaling and fishing industries developed and flourished. Salt works had been established on the Cape during Pilgrim times, and in the early 19th century came the glass industry of Sandwich. But the Cape never developed as a major industrial center, with the exception of the early 1900s when the Keith Car and Manufacturing Company in Sagamore made railroad cars. At one time this company was the largest employer in New England. Manufacturing began to decline in the mid-19th century, and the Cape entered a period of economic depression.

In the 1920s, a new industry and a new way of life were born in tourism. Although the fishing, boatbuilding, cranberry and light industries are still alive, tourism is by far the biggest industry on the Cape today. With its miles of varied beaches and temperate waters, with its charming old New England villages of white clapboard homes and steepled churches and silver-shingled Cape Cod cottages, with its pine woods, grassy marshes, and rolling dunes, Cape Cod has been one of the country's most loved vacation spots for many years. Inescapably, the new prosperity brought by the tourists who flock there in ever-increasing droves has significantly altered the appearance, the way of life and the ecological balance of the Cape. The great danger is that the primitive natural beauty that draws travelers to the Cape will be destroyed by the persistent growth of tourism. Or, the Cape may gradually be transformed into a southern suburb of Boston, a process that has already begun in the burgeoning Upper Cape. At any rate, the Cape is not what it was 20 years ago, and it will undoubtedly continue to change for some years to come. However, despite summer crowds and overdevelopment of the most frequented resorts, much of the Cape remains compellingly beautiful.

The Cape is convenient to Boston, and under ideal conditions you can travel by car to Sandwich in one hour or to Provincetown in two and a half hours. Although you can make a complete circuit of it in about two days, the Cape is really a place for relaxing—for swimming and sunning; for fishing, boating and playing golf or tennis; for attending the summer theater, antique hunting and making the rounds of the art galleries; or for leisurely walking and exploring. So if you like sand and sea and have time, it's a good idea to spend at least a few days there. You can find all sorts of accommodations, from guest houses to resort motels or housekeeping cottages and cabins. Summer travelers should always reserve several months in advance, and even off-season lodging is getting harder to come by without reservations. But there is still plenty of elbow room on the Cape in the fall and spring, and you may even find the Cape's visual appeal enhanced during those seasons, although swimming and sunbathing must often be forsaken. A Cape Cod resort directory may be obtained at the Cape Cod Chamber of Commerce information booths at Bourne and Sagamore, where the two bridges cross the Cape Cod Canal. Or, write the Chamber of Commerce at Hyannis, MA 02601 (508-362-3225). If possible, it's a good idea to avoid travel to and from the Cape on crowded Fridays and Sundays when traffic jams sometimes occur on Route 3 from Boston and on Route 6 on the Cape.

Plymouth

Historic Plymouth is a major attraction on the way to the Cape. Plymouth was one of the first English-speaking settlements in the New World. Today, it is visited annually by thousands who want to know about the origins of American history. Since that historic day in December 1620, when the weary, weakened Pilgrims landed there in the *Mayflower,* Plymouth has grown and thrived, and it is now a busy city. But thanks to the many restorations and museums, imaginative visitors to Plymouth will find that sense of the past they seek. To enjoy this town you must first close your eyes and picture the 102 *Mayflower* voyagers sailing anxiously into the quiet harbor of an unknown region, to what they hoped would be their new home. The first winter was hard and took the lives of half the group. When the *Mayflower* departed for England in the spring, however, not a single survivor returned with her.

Turn off Route 3A, left on North Park Avenue, and continue to the waterfront, where Plymouth Rock now rests under a canopy of granite to protect it from souvenir hunters. Not far from the hallowed boulder is the *Mayflower II,* a replica of the original ship, which was built in England and sailed across the Atlantic in 1957. Visitors are welcome aboard. From the rock, climb the stairway leading to Cole's Hill. This is where the Pilgrims buried their dead by night, so the Indians could not calculate the number of survivors. If it had not been for the friendship of Massasoit, the great chief of the Wampanoags, they would have all perished. A statue of him stands near the sepulcher. On Leyden Street is the First Parish Church, home of a congregation begun by the Pilgrims. The original building was erected in 1683 and the present church is the fifth on this site. Walk up the stone steps beside the church to Burial Hill, which overlooks the square. The fort was built in 1621 and contained five cannons. Nearby are the graves of such early settlers as William Bradford, Edward Gray, Thomas Clark, and John Cotton. Also of interest is the town brook, which furnished water to the Pilgrims. The town established Brewster Gardens, nearby, on the site of the settlers' original gardens.

If you continue north along Water Street and turn left on Chilton Street, you will arrive at the Pilgrim relics and paintings. Located nearby, off Court Street, is the visitor information booth. After leaving the Plymouth waterfront, follow Route 3A south about half a mile to Plimoth Plantation, a recreation of the original Pilgrim colony as it probably looked in 1627. The first census was taken in 1627; in that year, the herd of cattle, which had previously been owned in common, was apportioned. Surviving records of these efforts tell us who lived in each of the houses. Costumed men and women enact the day-to-day life of the Pilgrims and provide fascinating conversation that highlights the similarities and contrasts between the seventeenth and twentieth centuries. A Wampanoag Indian summer encampment is staffed by trained interpreters, some of whom are Native Americans.

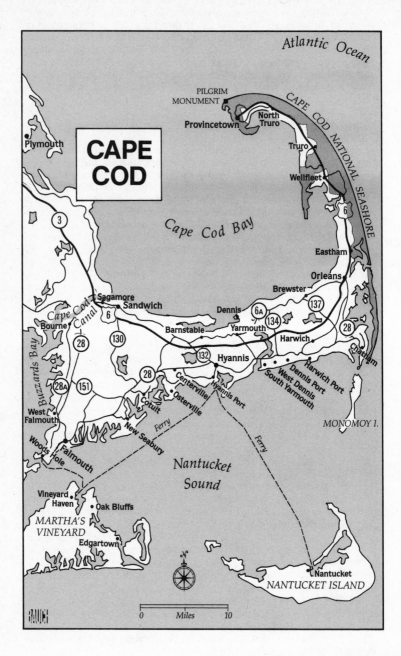

The Cape

Next, follow Route 3 to the Cape Cod Canal, which separates the Cape from the mainland and is crossed on the eastern side by the Sagamore Bridge and from Route 28 on the Buzzards Bay side by the Bourne Bridge. The canal was dug between 1909 and 1914 by the U.S. Army Corps of Engineers, 300 years after Myles Standish first proposed it to eliminate the dangerous trip around the shallows off Provincetown.

From the canal to the elbow (Cape Cod resembles a crooked arm), the Cape is traversed by three major roads: Route 6A to the north, Route 6 down the middle, and Route 28 along the southern shore. The roads all join at Orleans and from there Route 6 continues up the forearm to Truro and Provincetown. The Cape's townships are oddly formed, often extending from the North Shore down to the South. The township of Dennis, for example, consists of the villages of Dennis and East Dennis on the North Shore, South Dennis in the center, and West Dennis and Dennis Port on the South Shore. Because of the large number of similarly named villages, it's always a good idea to check your directions.

The three main highways traverse contrasting regions. Route 6 passes through the relatively unpopulated center of the Cape, which is characterized by an undulating landscape of scrub pine and scrub oak. It is the fastest route east and visitors with specific destinations on the North or South shores or who want to travel directly to the National Seashore are advised to take it to the appropriate exits. You may wish to drive east on Route 6 to the Yarmouth or Dennis exits and then swing south to Route 28, thereby avoiding the more congested areas around Hyannis.

The southern side of the Cape, reached by Route 28, is heavily populated and the major center for tourism. Its growth as a resort area has been abetted by its abundance of scenic harbors overlooking Nantucket Sound and its fine beaches with white sand and gentle surf. At the extreme southwestern corner is Woods Hole, where car ferries for Martha's Vineyard and Nantucket depart. It is also the location of the Woods Hole Oceanographic Institute (WHOI), the Marine Biological Laboratories, and the National Marine Fisheries Service, a branch of the U.S. Department of Commerce, among the world's largest and most prestigeous centers for marine research. The successful search for the Titantic led by WHOI staff and research vessels was launched from Woods Hole in 1986. Falmouth's eight villages constitute one of the Cape's main commercial and resort areas. Falmouth was settled in 1661 by a group of Quakers and was an active center of trade and shipping. The Congregational church, opposite the green, contains a bell made by Paul Revere.

Mashpee is the home of the Cape's Wampanoag Indians and recently developed South Cape Beach, open to the public. Hyannis, with its fashionable satellite resort towns, is the commercial hub of tourism on the Cape. Hyannis Port is famous as the site of the Kennedy family compound. Although tourists are not allowed near the compound, which is surrounded by a high fence, traffic is heavy with sightseers. Lewis Bay, farther east, is a focal point of boating activity and the point of departure for summer passenger ferries to Martha's Vineyard and Nantucket. The proliferation of motels, restaurants, and antique shops continues past Hyannis on the South Shore but thins out somewhat as you go east. There are fine sea captains' mansions in South Yarmouth. You may want to take Lower County Road from West Dennis to Harwich Port, where it rejoins Route 28 and passes by scenic Wychmere Harbor.

Noncommercial Chatham to Orleans

Chatham is a seaside Cape Cod town that is relatively free of the development and commercialism that one finds elsewhere on the Cape. It also boasts the largest public beaches on the Cape. You can watch the boats unloading their catch around noon at the Fish Pier. Every Friday night during the summer, the Chatham band gives a concert in a natural amphitheater located just off Main Street. Children will enjoy the programs, which are planned with them in mind.

The view of the ocean from the Chatham Lighthouse is spectacular. South of Chatham, trailing off from the "elbow" of the Cape, lies Monomoy Island, accessible only by boat. This fragile spit of land now enjoys protection as a federally designated wilderness area—although this political distinction did nothing to mitigate the ravages of the freak tides that accompanied the blizzard of 1978 as well as more recent storms. In the words of an Audubon Society official, there are now "two Monomoys." The entire eastern coast, from Monomoy up past Chatham Lighthouse to Nauset Beach and the Cape Cod National Seashore, has been the scene of countless shipwrecks, and there are many stories of vessels helplessly dashed against the coast by the unchecked force of fierce northeasters. In one of the most famous of these wrecks, the British man-of-war *Somerset* ran aground in 1778. She figures in Longfellow's *The Midnight Ride of Paul Revere* as the ship Paul had to row past in order to reach Charlestown. Every half century or so, the sands shift to uncover the *Somerset*'s remains.

From Chatham, Route 28 curves north and joins 6 and 6A at Orleans on the northern part of the Cape. In Orleans, you can follow Rock Harbor Road to the town landing. Here, in 1814, the militia of Orleans routed a British landing party. The Captain Linnel House on this road resembles a country home in southern France. From Orleans, go east on Nauset Beach Road to Nauset Beach, one of the finest barrier beaches along the East Coast. It is the anchor end of a 40-mile stretch of beach extending to Provincetown. This is the "Great Beach" of which Thoreau wrote so movingly in *Cape Cod*. Visitors can still walk its length, as Thoreau did, although the writer's path is now under water: each year, the Atlantic claims more of the Cape's eastern shore.

National Seashore

Three miles north on U.S. 6 is the town of Eastham; just beyond the village is the headquarters building of the Cape Cod National Seashore, established in 1961 to preserve the Cape's natural and historic resources. Four major areas of the park have been developed for visitors: Nauset, Marconi Station, Pilgrim Heights and Province Lands. Within them you can find superb ocean beaches; great rolling, lonely dunes; various types of swamps, marshes and wetlands; austere scrub and grasslands; and all kinds of wildlife. The headquarters building at Nauset Center in Eastham has displays, literature racks and an auditorium for nature lectures. Turn right here for the Coast Guard area and the Nauset Beach Lighthouse. The beach has parking and bathhouse facilities. During the season, park guides offer daily nature walks and lectures. There is the special Buttonbush Trail for the Blind with handropes and braille inscriptions; other trails lead to a red maple swamp, a salt pond and Nauset Marsh. The high bluffs in this area provide excellent views. Although these sand cliffs tempt visitors to make a quick, well-cushioned descent, climbing or sliding is discouraged because of its contribution to the already serious erosion problem.

Five miles beyond, on the same route, is the Marconi Station Area of the park. Here are the remains of the first transatlantic wireless station erected on the U.S. mainland. From here, Guglielmo Marconi sent a radio message to Europe on January 18, 1903. Most of the site has given way to the relentless waves that each year erode more of the shore and that, hundreds or thousands of years from now, may break through to Cape Cod Bay. In 1717, the pirate ship *Whydah* was blown ashore in the surf three-quarters of a mile northeast of the Marconi Area, spilling her crew and their ill-gotten wealth into Cape Cod waters. In 1984, after years of searching for the fabled ship, Barry Clifford located it, and divers began to recover the *Whydah*'s gold.

Route 6 continues on through Wellfleet, once the location of a large oyster industry and, along with Truro to the north, a colonial whaling and codfishing port. Wellfleet is one of the more picturesque and tastefully developed Cape resort towns. The village contains a number of fine restaurants, inns and historic homes. A foot trail leads through a sandy wilderness to the tip of Great Island, the promontory that forms Wellfleet Harbor. Truro, a town boasting huge dunes, is popular with artists and writers. The most prominent painter to have lived here was the late Edward Hopper, who found the Cape light ideal for his austere brand of realism. Up Route 6, a bit farther on the right, is the Pilgrim Heights Area of the National Seashore. Lectures on the early history of this region are given daily at the shelter, and there are parking and picnic areas. Close by is the spring from which the Pilgrims refilled their casks before sailing on to Plymouth. There is also a self-guided trail to Small's Swamp. From here, you can follow U.S. 6 to the Province Lands Area of the Park or U.S. 6A to Provincetown. The Province Lands Area comprises Race Point and Herring Cove beaches, a picnic area, bicycle trails and the Beech Forest Nature Trail.

Provincetown

Provincetown, or P-town as Cape Codders call it, stands by itself; what attracts one visitor to Provincetown may cause another visitor to raise an eyebrow. The town enjoys spectacular, windswept beaches and dunes and offers opportunities for many forms of outdoor recreation, from surf fishing to horseback riding. In Provincetown's commercial district, Portuguese-American fishermen mix with whale watchers from Boston and tourists from Quebec. The town has attracted a variety of painters, poets, and writers. P-town has also become a popular resort town for gays.

European fishermen and explorers first came to what is now Provincetown in the 1500s. In 1620, the Pilgrims' first landfall in the New World was at the tip of Cape Cod. The 252-foot stone tower called the Pilgrim Memorial, located at the juncture of Commercial Street and Beach Highway, commemorates the *Mayflower*'s brief visit to the area before it sailed on to Plymouth. Provincetown has always been unconventional, and by the early 1700s, Provincetown had gained its reputation for being an "outlaw town"—pirates, privateers, smugglers, and their doxies all found refuge close to the harbor. Later, honest fisherfolk—first Yankees, then Portuguese-speaking immigrants—arrived to tame the Cape's frontier.

During the early 1900s, Provincetown became known as "Greenwich Village North." Long before the 1960s and the age of "the counterculture," local Bohemians were shocking the more staid members of Provincetown society. Inexpensive summer lodgings, close to unspoiled beaches, attracted a variety of young rebels and artists, including Jack Reed, Mabel Dodge, Louise Bryant, Sinclair Lewis, and Eugene O'Neill. Many of O'Neill's early plays were presented in a tiny wharfside theater. The Provincetown Playhouse still builds its repertory around O'Neill's works.

Thousands of visitors make the trek to Provincetown each summer. In mid-July, Commercial Street, in the center of town, is packed with sightseers. Rental fees for studio space soar into the stratosphere. In the spring and fall, however, the rents are down and P-town regains its quiet charm.

There is an underlying stability to Provincetown: It is a fishing village, with classic Victorian homes, from which fishermen venture out each morning to confront the rough Atlantic. The artists, too, seem to be well rooted in P-town. And, in their own way, the summer crowds, the waitresses, and the candy makers, all seem to be part of a familiar Provincetown pageant.

Bay Side

The northern shore of the main part of the Cape, reached by Route 6A, is quite different from the southern shore and the forearm. This coastline, known as the Bay Side, tends to be marshy, and the water in the protected bay is far calmer than that of Nantucket Sound and the Atlantic. The Bay Side is generally far less developed than the other sections. Here restaurants and motels are fewer, and, for the most part, the only commercial establishments you will see along Route 6A are decorous craft and antique shops. The towns have retained more of their original quality; their main streets are lined with the stately white clapboard mansions of sea captains and the fine old shade trees that were planted to set them off. Brewster has several such mansions, as well as saltbox Cape Cod cottages. In West Brewster you can visit a working corn mill, a museum of natural history and Sealand of Cape Cod, which features a marine aquarium, seal pool and trained dolphins.

While you are driving along 6A, watch for signs pointing out town landings; if you have time, visit these and watch the local fishermen unload their catches. West of Brewster, the town of Dennis, along with Sandwich and Harwich is one of the centers of cranberry culture on the Cape. In early autumn, travelers along 6A can see the berries being harvested in shallow, red-splotched bogs. Dennis also boasts Scargo Hill, the highest spot in the mid Cape, all of 160 feet tall. From here the view of Cape Cod Bay is spectacular. Yarmouth and Yarmouth Port are particularly lovely old seafaring towns, and some of the captains' homes in the latter are open to the public.

Barnstable and Sandwich

As you continue west on 6A past fine views of meadows and the bay, you will come to Barnstable, the site of the Liberty Pole. Here the colonists held many freedom meetings. When the pole disappeared from the village green, suspicion centered on one Aunt Freeman, a defiant Tory who had threatened to tear down the patriots' pole. Aunt Freeman was tarred and feathered and ridden out of town on a rail. Barnstable is now a lovely town of large old homes, many built when the town had a large trade in codfish, rum, and molasses. Great salt marshes extend into the bay. Sturgis Library, dating to 1645, is a fine example of the Cape Cod house.

Sandwich is the oldest town on the Cape and one of the most interesting and charming. It remains famous for the beautifully colored glass that bears its name and was produced there from 1825 until 1888 when compe-

✗N

VISA

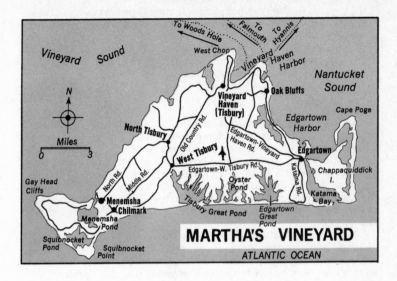

MARTHA'S VINEYARD

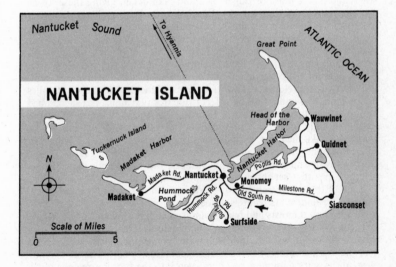

NANTUCKET ISLAND

tition with glassmakers in the Middle West closed the factory. The Sandwich Glass Museum on Main Street contains relics of the early history of the town, as well as an outstanding collection of pressed and lace glass. You may visit the nearby Hoxie House, a seventeenth-century shingled saltbox restoration, and see the Dexter Gristmill in operation. Heritage Plantation, situated on the beautifully landscaped grounds of the Dexter Estate, is a complex of various museum buildings and craft exhibits and has an extensive collection of rhododendrons.

The Islands

Martha's Vineyard, Nantucket, and the Elizabeth Islands, known collectively as "the Islands," were formed some 100,000 years ago when a retreating glacier left behind its ragged collection of clay, sand, and rocky debris. Most of this glacial moraine became Cape Cod, but the outermost protrusions formed a series of islands as the glacier melted and the sea level rose. Some of the Elizabeth Islands, a small chain located off Woods Hole and parallel to the west coast of Martha's Vineyard, remain much as they were then. They are, for the most part, privately owned and not easily accessible.

Thomas Mayhew, after buying Martha's Vineyard, Nantucket, and the Elizabeth Islands in 1641 for the grand sum of 40 pounds, settled the Vineyard the following year at what is now Edgartown. Nantucket was settled several years later, largely by Quakers retreating from the repressive religious authorities of the Massachusetts mainland. For a while, the rolling grassy heath of the two islands was used for farming and raising sheep, but in the eighteenth century their economies shifted to whaling, and both became major whaling centers. Mansions built by wealthy sea captains still stand in the ports of Edgartown and Nantucket, giving these towns a brooding aura of the past. As the whaling and shipbuilding industries died out, the Islands were slowly depopulated and nearly forgotten. But, like Cape Cod, they were reborn as resort areas in the first decades of the twentieth century. Because they are only accessible by ferry, private boat, or airplane, however, they have changed less radically and more slowly. Many summer visitors return year after year, and close-knit summer communities have developed, each with its own character. Nantucket, 30 miles at sea and a two-and-a-half-hour ferry ride from Hyannis, has succumbed less to the influences of tourism than has Martha's Vineyard, thanks to extremely tight local zoning regulations, as well as its distance from the mainland. Like the Cape, the Islands attract visitors because of their magnificent beaches, harbors, and bays; the lure of the sea; and the appeal of the old towns and weathered gray cottages. But the Islands have distinctive qualities that set them apart from the Cape and from each other.

Each of the villages on Martha's Vineyard has its own personality and appearance and tends to attract year-round and summer residents who have common interests and backgrounds. There is a remarkable diversity in the landscapes of the Vineyard, which include verdant heath, scrub oak woods, flat meadows, salt and fresh water ponds and marshes, clay cliffs, busy harbors, and lonely ocean beaches pounded by surf. The sea is omnipresent, its salty dampness reaching even into the farming regions of the interior.

Nantucket is wilder and more isolated than Martha's Vineyard. Its hilly moors seem primitive and more open to the fury of the sea. The town of Nantucket, with its cobblestone streets, old captains' mansions and gray weathered cottages, hardly seems changed since whaling days. Salt breezes carry the smell and feel of the sea everywhere. Nantucket serves as a reminder that human settlement and natural beauty are not necessarily incompatible. Travelers eager to escape the summertime crowds on the Cape may enjoy making a day trip to Nantucket from Hyannis. Leave your car on the Cape.

Martha's Vineyard

Passenger ferries to Martha's Vineyard depart frequently from Woods Hole, Falmouth, Hyannis Port, and, in summer, New Bedford and land either in Vineyard Haven or nearby Oak Bluffs. Bus tours of the island leave from stations near the ferry landings, and there is summer bus service between Oak Bluffs, Vineyard Haven, and Edgartown. Bicycling is a popular and healthful way of getting around the island, and bicycles may be rented in the three main towns or brought over on the car ferries. Automobiles are not essential, unless you wish to travel quickly from town to town. But why rush on the Vineyard? You may rent a car near the ferry landings or bring your own on the Woods Hole ferry. However, car space on the ferries is limited and you need to make automobile reservations well in advance; contact the Woods Hole, Martha's Vineyard, and Nantucket Steamship Authority, Box 284, Woods Hole, MA 02543.

Most of the island's visitors land at Vineyard Haven, the main port, shopping center, and winter community. Because much of the old whaling and fishing town was destroyed by the Great Fire of 1883, Vineyard Haven lacks the architectural and historical interest of Edgartown, the other whaling port. But its busy harbor and a varied and attractive shopping district make it a pleasant place to visit. You may also visit a restored sailors chapel near the main wharf and discover a few old buildings that escaped the fire's destruction.

Oak Bluffs, where the rest of the ferries dock, is located across the harbor from Vineyard Haven. It, too, was settled in the seventeenth century, but its fascinating architecture dates from the nineteenth century, when it became the center for Methodist camp meetings. These meetings began as tent revivals, but as more and more worshippers attended, permanent buildings were erected. A great conical ironwork tabernacle was built in the center of the campground. Around it, arranged in concentric circles, is a fantastic array of tiny Victorian gingerbread cottages, each striving to outdo its neighbors with the ornateness of its patterned shingles and colorful decorative moldings. The cottages are brightly colored and neatly kept. Once every summer, on the holiday known as Illumination Night, their owners festoon them with brilliant Japanese paper lanterns, turning the campground into a veritable fairyland.

Many of the other houses in Oak Bluffs were built in the same era as the campground cottages and were influenced by their design. The predominance of these whimsical pastel-colored dwellings gives the whole community the look of a seaside toyshop. In addition to being a Methodist center, Oak Bluffs is also one of the oldest black resort communities in the United States. Oak Bluffs has many of the island's restaurants and a popular harbor with berths for pleasure boats.

The oldest town on Martha's Vineyard, and a famous whaling port in the eighteenth and nineteenth centuries, Edgartown is now characterized by the beautiful old houses and tree-lined streets of its past and the elegant stores, fine hotels and restaurants that make it the most fashionable summer resort on the island. This combination makes it a superb spot for walking and window shopping. You might wish to start at the Thomas Cooke House on Cooke Street, headquarters of the Dukes County Historical Society. The house, built in 1765 by shipbuilders, now houses a whaling and historical museum. At the end of Cooke, the island's oldest street, is the Edgartown Cemetery. North and South Water streets are lined with captains' houses, some with widow's walks on their roofs. Main Street, lined with fine shops, ends at the town dock, where you catch the little ferry, *On Time,* to nearby Chappaquiddick, a sandy island with the Cape Poge Wildlife Reservation, a good spot for birdwatching. Chappaquiddick lacks stores and restaurants, so pack a snack for your expedition.

The south shore of Martha's Vineyard faces the ocean, and along its entire length there are fine surf beaches with unusually warm water. The county beach that extends across Katama Bay is open to the public. At the western end are smaller beaches reserved for residents of Chilmark. Behind the beaches are saltwater ponds and marshes.

The west end of Martha's Vineyard, known by residents as "up-island," is more rural and wild than the east end. The winter winds blow with such bitterness that some of the year-round islanders who live here in the summer move to sheltered Vineyard Haven when it gets cold, even though the moderating influence of the sea keeps Martha's Vineyard from getting much of the snow that falls farther north on the mainland. But in the summer, "up-island" is a favorite vacation spot for nature lovers, writers, educators and other professionals who return year after year and have established close ongoing summer communities.

West Tisbury, which occupies the central swath of the island, includes a charming New England village, a small settlement at Lambert's Cove and surrounding farms and summer homes. Visitors may go bird watching or walk through the woods to a freshwater pond on Cedar Tree Neck, situated along the north shore. Chilmark, to the west, has always been less developed, although its oak woods now hide summer homes. Its roads afford a succession of scenic views of the ocean or Vineyard Sound and two beautiful ocean beaches are open to residents. To the north, on the stretch of cold, swift water called the Menemsha Bight, is the fishing village of Menemsha. A small collection of fishermen's weathered shanties and sturdy fishing boats ranged along either side of the channel that connects Menemsha Pond to the Bight, this little town makes what many consider the most picturesque scene on the island. But the piled-up lobster traps and fishy odor attest to the fact that this beautiful village has not been built for show. You may purchase fresh fish or eat in a nearby seafood restaurant. The Menemsha Beach, open to the public, is located right next to the docks.

Gay Head

When the first colonists came to Martha's Vineyard in the mid-seventeenth century, they found the island's earliest settlers, the Wampanoag Indians, living at the western tip, which is now called Gay Head. The Indians taught the colonists how to kill whales and plant corn and where to fish. Later on, the Gay Head Indians were hired by whalers; in *Moby Dick,* Melville describes Gay Head as "a village which has long supplied the neighboring island of Nantucket with her most daring harpooners." The descendants of the Wampanoags still live and work in the area. You may see some of them at the concessions on the way up to the Gay Head Cliffs, brilliantly colored clay bluffs on the extreme western tip of the island. Unfortunately, the sea that first carved out these bands of ochre, gray, rust, and white is now reclaiming them. Until recently, visitors could descend them to the colored beaches below, but their trampling hastened the process of erosion and now the cliffs must be enjoyed from a roped-in area above or by walking around to the beach from a marked path to the south. The cliffs have greatly diminished in size in recent years, and since no feasible means of preserving them has been discovered, no doubt they will eventually crumble away altogether in a few centuries.

Nantucket

The name Nantucket is a corruption of the Indian word *Nanticut*, "faraway land," a description that seems quite apt as you near the end of the long ferry ride there. Your first glimpse of the town, as the ferry pulls into the safe enclosure of Nantucket Harbor, is likely to be obscured by fog. You may be able to distinguish the silvery brown of weatherbeaten shingles. The oft-shrouded island has been called "the gray lady." You have to be on the island a while to understand another of its Indian names, *Canopache*, "the place of peace." Its small size and geographic isolation, along with the contrast between the snug brick-and-clapboard village of Nantucket and the bleak, exposed moors nearby, gives the island a dreamlike quality.

There are a number of summer colonies on the island, but Nantucket is the only real town. Its great whaling saga began when Nantucketers caught their first whale in 1672 off the shores of the island. Old South Wharf still stands as a nostalgic emblem of the era when Nantucket was the greatest whaling port in the world. The best place to begin exploring Nantucket is the marvelous Whaling Museum on Broad Street. The museum's fascinating exhibits on whales and the various operations involved in catching and processing them, its displays of whaling artifacts, its collection of captains' portraits, and a library of books about Nantucket will enable you to peer into the past and to see the town's cobblestone streets and historic dwellings as they were 150 years ago, when the town ranked third in commerce in Massachusetts.

From the museum, walk back to Main Street in the center of Nantucket. Lined with white clapboard captains' mansions and shaded by elm trees, this beautiful street reflects the affluence enjoyed by the town at the peak of its whaling trade. The elegant Hadwen-Satler Memorial House at 96 Main Street is open to the public. It is one of the exhibits of the Nantucket Historical Association, which administers the Whaling Museum and maintains several original buildings as public museums. The Historical Museum at 8 Fair Street, just off Main Street, consists of a collection of primitive portraits and period furniture and a wing of the Friends Meeting House. The Jethro Coffin House was built in 1686 and is the oldest house on Nantucket. It is located on Sunset Hill, at the northern end of the town, and contains period furniture. On Old Mill Hill, on the southwestern side of town, stands the Old Mill, built by Nathan Wilbur in 1746 from the wood of shipwrecks, and still used to grind corn. Nearby on Mill Street is the 1800 House, a restored early-American dwelling dating from Nantucket's early whaling days.

Other buildings of interest in Nantucket are the Maria Mitchell House, 1 Vestal Street, birthplace of America's first woman astronomer and discoverer of Mitchell's Comet; the adjacent observatory and Mitchell Memorial Library; and the old jail, farther west on Vestal Street.

These buildings are restorations open to the public, but because of ironclad laws regulating the exteriors of both houses and businesses, the entire town of Nantucket is like a living museum. The laws are so strict that permission is needed to make the smallest exterior changes, and all signs must be approved. In addition to the houses maintained by the historical association, there are periodic tours of privately owned historic homes.

A recent addition is the luxurious Nantucket Boat Basin, planned and constructed by Walter Beinecke, who, along with his father, established the Nantucket Historical Trust in the 1950s to restore the town's landmark buildings. Beinecke enlarged the docks and built little gray shingled houses on them, making an attractive facility for sailing and motor yachts.

Lonely Moors and Summer Colonies

Beyond the town are the moors, covered with bayberry, wild roses, brambles and cranberry vines, still colorful with flowers in the autumn. Scattered among them are the small summer colonies of Madaket Polpis and Wauwinet. Siasconset, the largest of these, is an artists' colony with little houses and delightful rose gardens. Like Martha's Vineyard, Nantucket has beaches for all tastes. The south shore looks out on the Atlantic, which crashes on the wide sandy beaches in powerful breakers. The ocean is wildest on the Madaket side. The water on Nantucket Sound is calmer, and the harbor's beaches are the most placid of all. Great Point, the tip of the northern peninsula, is a good area for surf casting and bird watching. It is accessible only by four-wheel-drive vehicles or on foot, and makes a perfect destination for an all-day round-trip hike.

The last word on Nantucket belongs to Melville:

The Nantucketer, he alone resides and riots on the sea; he alone, in Bible language, goes down to it in ships; to and fro ploughing it as his own special plantation. *There* is his home, *there* lies his business. . . . For years he knows not the land; so that when he comes to it at last, it smells like another world, more strangely than the moon would to an Earthsman (*Moby Dick,* Chapter XIV, "Nantucket").

PRACTICAL INFORMATION FOR CAPE COD AND THE ISLANDS

HOW TO GET THERE. By plane: Barnstable Airport in Hyannis, Provincetown Municipal Airport, Martha's Vineyard Airport, and Nantucket Memorial Airport are served from New York and Boston by Eastern (800–327–8376) and Delta (800–221–1212). Nantucket Airline (800–635–8787) has frequent flights daily between Nantucket and Hyannis.

By ferry: Car ferries operate year-round to Martha's Vineyard from Woods Hole and to Nantucket from Hyannis. Summer car reservations should be made well in advance. Contact Steamship Authority, Box 284, Woods Hole, MA 02543 (508–540–2022). Parking is available for ferry passengers. Passenger ferries operate from Hyannis to Martha's Vineyard (Oak Bluffs) and Nantucket in season; contact Hy-Line, Ocean Dock, Hyannis 02601 (508–775–7185). Between Falmouth and Oak Bluffs, *Island Queen,* Pier 45, Falmouth 02540 (508–548–4800). Passenger service from Boston to Provincetown is also available during the summer. Contact Bay State–Spray & Provincetown Steamship Co., 20 Long Wharf, Boston 02110 (617–723–7800). Passenger-only ferry service between New Bedford and Martha's Vineyard (Vineyard Haven) is provided from May through October on *Schamonchi* by Cape Island Express, Leonard's Wharf, New Bedford, MA 02740 (508–997–1688). From Plymouth to Provincetown: Plymouth & Provincetown Steamship Co., State Pier, Plymouth 02360 (508–747–2400).

By train: Cape Cod and Hyannis Railroad runs from Hyannis to Sandwich, Buzzards Bay, and Boston, Mid-Apr.–early Sept. 252 Main St.,

Hyannis 02601 (508–771–1145). Excellent sightseeing opportunity. AMTRAK links New York and Boston with Hyannis on weekends, late May–early Sept. (800–USA–RAIL).

By bus: Plymouth and Brockton (P&B) has service to Boston and Logan Airport from Hyannis and Sagamore. For information, call 508–775–5524. Bonanza Bus Lines (800–556–3815) offers service from cities in New York and New England to Falmouth and Buzzards Bay with ferry connections to the Islands.

By car: You will arrive at the Cape by crossing either the Sagamore (Rte.6) or the Bourne (Rte.28) bridge. Rte. 28 takes you to Bourne, Falmouth and the Islands, whereas Rte. 6, the Cape's major highway, extends from the canal to Provincetown. It is the fastest route, but Rtes. 6A and 28A, though slower, offer the opportunity to see and explore salt marshes, old homes, historic markers and quaint shops that characterize the Cape.

HOW TO GET AROUND. By car: Public transportation on the Cape is close to nonexistent. If you want to travel around, plan on bringing a car or renting one. There are a number of car rental companies in Falmouth, Hyannis, Chatham and Provincetown. It is expensive to transport a car to the Islands on the ferry, and reservations are essential. Both Martha's Vineyard and Nantucket have car rental service, frequent shuttle bus service between towns, and taxis available near the ferry slips.

By bike: Extensive bike trails, including the service road along the canal, Shining Sea Bikepath in Falmouth, Cape Cod Rail-Trail in Dennis and state bike paths. Rentals and bike shops in most towns.

By moped: Rentals at the Outdoor Shop in South Yarmouth and at several locations in Oak Bluffs and Vineyard Haven on Martha's Vineyard.

HOTELS AND MOTELS. The area offers a wide range of accommodations, from luxurious seaside resorts to the most basic motel. Many accommodations close down during the off season; others offer much lower prices. Unless noted, those listed are open year-round. Our price rating is based on double occupancy, European plan, in season. *Deluxe,* $100 and up; *Expensive,* $75–$100; *Moderate,* $50–$75; *Inexpensive,* $35–$50.

In general, prices on the Islands are higher than on the Cape. Cape Cod Reservation Center, 76 Enterprise Rd., Hyannis 02601 (508–790–3131 or 800–272–4343) will make bookings at oceanfront resorts, hotels and motels, cottages and B&Bs, townhouses and condos.

PLYMOUTH

John Carver Inn, 25 Summer St., 02360 (508–746–7100 or 800–447–7778). *Expensive.* In-town location. Restaurant and lounge.

Pilgrim Sands Motel, 150 Warren Ave., 02360 (508–747–0900). *Expensive.* Across from Plimoth Plantation. Private ocean beach, pools, coffee shop.

Sheraton Plymouth at Village Landing, 180 Water St., 02360 (508–747–4900 or 800–325–3535). *Expensive.* Pool, restaurant, lounge, pub, 175 rooms, some with balconies overlooking pool or harbor. In-town location, near historical sites, shopping, restaurants. Open year-round.

The Sleepy Pilgrim, 182 Court St., 02360 (508–746–1962). *Moderate.* Small motel ½ mi. from Plymouth Center. Cafe nearby. Open Apr.–Nov.

CAPE COD

Barnstable

Lamb and Lion, Rte. 6A, 02630 (508–362–6823). *Expensive.* Pleasant motel that tries to be "as noncommercial as possible." Efficiencies available. Large swimming pool and sundecks. Daily and weekly rates. Off-season rates.

Bass River (South Yarmouth)

Blue Water, 291 S. Shore Dr., 02664 (508–398–2288). *Deluxe.* Large resort motel. Indoor and outdoor pools, private beach, tennis, and putting green. Some efficiencies. Cafe, bar, dancing weekends.

Red Jacket Beach Motor Inn, S. Shore Dr., 02664 (508–398–6941). *Expensive–Deluxe.* Indoor and outdoor pools, beach. Private balconies. Tennis, play area. Saunas, putting green. Restaurant. Open Apr.–Oct.

Ambassador Motor Inn, Rte 28 (508–394–4000). *Expensive.* A large motel with restaurant and lounge. Pools, near shops and restaurants.

Ocean Mist, 97 S. Shore Dr., 02664 (508–398–2633). *Expensive.* Pleasant motel on private beach. Pool, play area. Kitchen units available. Open Mar.–Nov.

Surfcomber, S. Shore Dr., 02664 (508–398–9228). *Expensive.* On the ocean with private beach. Efficiencies available. Pool. Lawn games. Open mid-May–early Oct.

Village Green, S. Shore Dr., 02664 (508–398–2167). *Moderate.* Pleasant motel opposite beach. Pool, play area. Some efficiencies. Children welcome. Open Apr.–mid-Oct.

Windjammer, S. Shore Dr., 02664 (508–398–2370). *Moderate.* Beach just a step away. Pool. Package plans available. Open late Mar.–Oct.

Bourne

Inn at Buttermilk Bay, 23 Nick Vedder Rd., Buzzards Bay, 02532 (508–759–6736). *Expensive–Moderate.* Period furnishings in inn rooms, modern motel with balconies and water view. Near Cape Cod Canal, shops, restaurants, fishing, railroad. Restaurant and lounge.

Mashnee Village, Mashnee Village Rd., 5 mi. E. of bridge, off Rte. 28, 02532 (508–759–3384). *Moderate.* Pool, tennis, play area, beach. Two-bedroom cottages with kitchen, apts. Fishing, boating. Bar. Pets. Open mid-May–mid-Oct.

Windmill Motel, Mid-Cape Hwy., 02532 (508–888–3220). *Moderate.* Pool. Restaurant. Near shopping and canal.

Redwood Motel, Buzzards Bay, 02532 (508–759–3892). *Inexpensive.* Unpretentious and clean. Near shops, restaurants, canal, train station. Year-round.

Yankee Thrift Motel, Rte. 28, Bourne Rotary, 02532 (508–759–3883). *Inexpensive.* Indoor and outdoor pool; 55 units, including 20 with full kitchen. Near canal, bike path, fishing, recreational facilities.

Centerville

Trade Winds Inn, 780 Craigville Beach Rd., 02636 (508–775–0365). *Deluxe.* Private beach. Dining room. Open Apr.–Nov.

Centerville Corners Motor Lodge, 369 S. Main St., 02632 (508–775–7223). *Expensive.* Heated pool, saunas, play area near Craigville Beach. Restaurant. Tennis near. Pets. Special packages in fall and spring, including golf weekends.

Chatham

Bradford Inn and Motel, 26 Cross St., 02633 (508–945–1030). *Deluxe.* Small motel with rooms decorated in Early American style.

Chatham Bars Inn and Cottages, Shore Rd., 02633 (508–945–0096). *Deluxe.* All resort pleasures: beach, boating, tennis, lawn games. Dining room, bar. Dancing, entertainment. Roomy cottages. No housekeeping. American Plan available.

Pleasant Bay Village, Rte. 28 in Chatham Port, 02633 (508–945–1133). *Deluxe.* Lovely grounds with play area, pool. Breakfast available. Open May–Oct. Weekly rates available.

Wequasset Inn, Pleasant Bay, 02633 (508–432–5400 or 800–225–7125). *Deluxe.* Rooms and suites in cottages overlooking water. Tennis, sailing, pool, nightclub. Golf nearby. Windsurfing instruction. Fine food served in 18th-century mansion. Open May–Oct.

Inn at the Dolphin, 352 Main St., 02633 (508–945–0070). *Deluxe–Expensive.* In Chatham's historic district. Spacious grounds. Heated pool, whirlpool bath.

Hawthorne Motel, 196 Shore Rd., 02633 (508–945–0372). *Expensive.* Private beach. Efficiencies available. Children over 8 welcome. Open June–Oct.

Seafarer, Rte. 28 and Ridgevale Rd., 02633 (508–432–1739). *Expensive.* Spacious rooms, quiet location ½ mile from beach. Two-room efficiencies. Off-season rates available.

Dennis

Edgewater Motor Lodge, Chase Ave., Dennis Port 02639 (508–398–6922). *Deluxe.* 72-unit motel on ocean. Pool, sauna, Jacuzzi. Near restaurants, shops. Spring and fall package deals.

Lighthouse Inn, Lighthouse Rd., W. Dennis 02670 (508–398–2244). *Deluxe.* Beachfront resort hotel, pool, tennis, play area, programs for children. Modified American Plan. Open mid-May–mid-Oct.

Soundings Resort Motel, 78 Chase Ave. Dennis Port 02639 (508–394–6561). *Deluxe.* Nicely decorated. Large private beach. Pools, putting green, sauna. Free coffee. Restaurant nearby. Open Apr.–Oct.; fall and spring packages available.

Corsair Resort Motel, 41 Chase Ave., Dennis Port 02639 (508–398–2279 or 800–332–2279). *Deluxe–Expensive.* Two-story motel with balconies on private beach. Pool. Free morning coffee. Refrigerators. Restaurant nearby. Children under 12 free.

Cross Rip, 33 Chase Ave., Dennis Port 02639 (508–398–6600 or 800–332–2279). *Deluxe–Expensive.* Two-story motel built around pool. Private beach. Sundecks overlook ocean. Nice view of Nantucket Sound. Near restaurants.

Sprouter Whale, 405 Old Wharf Rd., Dennis Port 02639 (508–398–8010). *Expensive.* On ocean with private beach. Some efficiencies. Patio, whirlpool. Children over five. Open April–mid-Oct.

Colonial Village, 426 Lower County Rd., Dennis Port 02639 (508–398–2071). *Moderate–Expensive.* Two-story motel with kitchen units and cottages with fireplaces. Pool, Jacuzzi. Open Apr.–Oct.

Cutty Sark, Old Wharf Rd., Dennis Port 02639 (508–398–9116). *Moderate.* Opposite town beach. Inn or motel rooms. Color cable TV. Pool. Restaurant nearby. Open late May–Oct.

Holiday Hill Motor Inn, 352 Main St, Dennis Port 02639 (508–394–5577) *Moderate.* Pool, game room. Two double beds in all rooms. Some efficiencies. Seasonal.

Huntsman Motor Lodge, 829 Main St., W. Dennis 02670 (508–394–5415). *Moderate.* Some efficiencies. Near beaches, fishing, tennis. Pool, grills. Excellent package plans. Open Apr.–Oct.

J.D. Star Inn, 177 Main St., Dennis 02638 (508–385–9770). *Moderate.* Modern motel. Pool. Continental breakfast. Restaurants and beach nearby.

Jonathan Edwards, Rte. 28, Dennis Port 02639 (508–398–2953). *Moderate.* Pool, play area, rec room. Coffee and rolls on the house. Some efficiencies. Weekly rates, seasonal.

Sea Lord, Chase Ave. and Inman Rd., Dennis Port 02639 (508–398–6900). *Moderate.* Beach across the street. Complimentary coffee. Pool. Restaurants nearby. Open mid-Apr.–late Oct.

Sea Shell Motel, 45 Chase Ave., Dennis Port 02639 (508–398–8965). *Moderate.* Private beach. Rooms in motel or main house. Kitchen units available; refrigerators in every room. Continental breakfast in season.

Sesuit Harbor, Rte. 6A, 02638 (508–385–3326). *Moderate.* Pool. Near shops and restaurants. Off-season rates.

William & Mary Motel, 433 Lower County Rd., Dennis Port 02639 (508–398–2931). *Moderate.* Pool. Five minutes from beach. Restaurant nearby. Kitchen units available. Open mid-Apr.–Oct.

Eastham

Sheraton Ocean Park Inn, Rte. 6, 02642 (508–255–5000). *Deluxe.* Attractive modern resort. Restaurant, lounge, entertainment. Health club, tennis, pools. Cafe. Off-season rates.

Captain's Quarters Motel, Rte. 6, N. Eastham 02651 (508–255–5686). *Expensive.* Clean, quiet, comfortable motel and conference center in the heart of the National Seashore.

Blue Dolphin, Rte. 6, N. Eastham 02651 (800–654–0504; 800–334–3251 in Mass.). *Moderate.* Comfortable quarters with refrigerator and private patio on wooded grounds. Pool, play area, tennis, bikes for rent. Restaurant and lounge. Near hiking and bicycle trails. Open Apr.–Nov.

Town Crier, Rte. 6, 02642 (508–255–4000 or 800–922–1434). *Moderate.* Enclosed heated pool, play area. Recreation room. Near National Seashore entrance. Pets.

Falmouth

Sea Crest Hotel, Old Silver Beach, 35 Quaker Rd., N. Falmouth 02556 (508–540–9400 or 800–225–3110). *Deluxe.* Large resort/conference center with restaurant, nightclub on private beach. Tennis, putting green, health club, pools. Modified American Plan available.

Sheraton Falmouth, 291 Jones Rd., 02540 (508–540–2000 or 800–325–3535). *Deluxe.* Large hotel. Indoor pool, sauna, sundeck. Near shopping, golf, beach shuttle. Restaurant, lounge, entertainment. Packages available.

Cape Codder, Cape Codder Rd., 02541 (508–540–1900). *Expensive.* Oceanside resort; ¼ mile of ocean front, pools, play area. Restaurant, bar. Dancing, entertainment. Modified American Plan. Open May–mid-Oct.

Cape Colony, Surf Dr., 02540 (508–548–3975). *Expensive.* Pool, play area. Directly on beach. Near harbor, shopping, restaurants. Free Continental breakfast. Open Memorial Day–Columbus Day.

Coonamesset Inn, Jones Rd. and Gifford St., 02541 (508–548–2300). *Expensive.* Beautiful gardens, Cape Cod-style buildings. Excellent restaurant, bar.

Falmouth Marina, Robbins Rd., 02541 (508–548–4300 or 800–835–0314). *Expensive.* In attractive grounds overlooking harbor. Pool. Weekend packages available. Open Apr.–Oct.

Falmouth Square Inn, 40 N. Main St., 02540 (508–457–0606 or 800–345–3080). *Expensive.* True New England–style hotel. In the village, near shops, restaurants, shuttle to ferries. Dining room, lounge, indoor pool.

Capewind, 34 Maravista Ave. Ext., E. Falmouth 02536 (508–548–3400). *Expensive.* Located on saltwater inlet. Heated pool, play area. Free in-room coffee. Boats available. Some kitchenettes.

Shoreway Acres, Shore St., 02541 (508–540–3000). *Expensive–Moderate.* Beautiful grounds, two pools, sauna. Some efficiencies. Off-season package rates. Complimentary full breakfast in season.

Falmouth Heights Motor Lodge, 146 Falmouth Heights Rd., 02540 (508–548–3623). *Moderate.* Heated pool. Play area. Free in-room coffee. Restaurant nearby. 5-min. walk to beach. Open mid-Apr.–Oct.

Green Harbor, Acapesket Rd., E. Falmouth 02536 (508–548–4747). *Moderate.* Pools. Private boating beach. Boats and package plans available. Some efficiencies.

Red Horse Inn Motel, 28 Falmouth Heights Rd., 02540 (508–548–0053). *Moderate.* Nicely kept. Within walking distance of summer boats to Martha's Vineyard. Near restaurants, stores.

Town and Beach Motel, 382 Main St., 02540 (508–548–1380). *Moderate.* In-town location near shops, restaurants, beaches. Well-kept.

Harwich

Wychmere Harbor Hotel and Beach Club, 23 Snow Inn Rd., Harwich Port 02646 (508–432–1000). *Deluxe.* Distinguished oceanfront resort. Private beach, dock, gourmet restaurant. Entertainment. Golf and health club privileges. Seasonal.

Commodore, 30 Earle Rd., W. Harwich 02671 (508–432–1180). *Expensive–Moderate.* Pool, play area. Putting green, shuffleboard. Beach nearby. Restaurant. Weekly rates.

Seadar Inn, Braddock La., Harwich Port, 02646 (508–432–0264). *Expensive–Moderate.* Opposite beach, walk to restaurants, shops. Includes buffet breakfast. Open mid-May–Oct.

Handkerchief Shoals, Rte. 28, S. Harwich 02661 (508–432–2200). *Moderate.* Off hwy. Play area. Near golf, tennis, fishing. Open May–Oct.

Moby Dick Motel, Main St., S. Harwich 02661 (508–432–1434). *Moderate.* Pool, play area, shuffleboard. Near golf courses, harbor, beaches. Open Apr.–Nov.

Wishing Well Motel, Rte. 28, W. Harwich 02671 (508–432–2150). *Moderate.* 20-unit motel near shopping, beach. Pool. Family entertainment. Efficiencies, continental breakfast.

Hyannis

Hyannis Regency, Rte. 132, 02601 (508–775–1153). *Deluxe.* Flexible rates for standard, king-size, or loft rooms. Restaurant, game room, indoor pool, Nautilus equipment. Near golf and tennis, Cape Cod Mall, airport.

Tara Hyannis, W. End Circle 02601 (508–775–7775). *Deluxe.* Resort hotel with golf, tennis, pools, play area. Restaurant, bar, dancing, entertainment. Modified American Plan available. Seasonal rates.

Hyannis Holiday Inn, Rte. 132, near airport, 02601 (508–775–6600). *Expensive.* Pool, tennis. Restaurant, bar, dancing, entertainment. Package plans available.

Courtyard, Main and Winter Sts., 02601 (508–775–8600). *Expensive.* Downtown location, near stores, entertainment, ferries. Enclosed pool, saunas. Restaurant. Package and family plans.

Hyannis Harborview, 213 Ocean St., 02601 (508–775–4420 or 800–537–0043). *Expensive.* Opposite pier. Pools. Indoor health center. Lounge. Weekend packages available.

Lewis Bay Motel and Marina, 53 South St., 02601 (508–775–6633). *Expensive.* Restaurants, cocktail lounges. Some efficiencies. Pets. Overlooks harbor, ferry, walk to town. Seasonal.

Days Inn, 867 Iyanough Rd., 02601 (508–771–6100 or 800–325–2525). *Moderate.* Indoor and outdoor pools. Game and fitness room. Near Cape Cod Mall and airport. Free coffee and rolls. Off-season package plans.

The Breakwaters, 432 Sea St., 02601 (508–775–6831). *Moderate.* Completely equipped cottage units on beach. Heated pool. Play area. Maid service. Weekly rates. Well located. Open May–mid-Oct.

Captain Gosnold Village, 230 Gosnold St., 02601 (508–775–9111). *Moderate.* Motel rooms or efficiency cottages. Pool, play area. Beach short walk away. Free in-room coffee. Maid service.

Country Lake Lodge, Rte. 132, 02601 (508–362–6455). *Moderate.* On lake, with fishing, boating available. Pool, play area. All activities, restaurants nearby. Free boats. Open Apr.–Nov.

Country Squire Motor Lodge, Main St., 02601 (508–775–5225) *Moderate.* Good location in town. 84 units. Both indoor and outdoor pools.

Sea Coast Resort, 33 Ocean St., 02601 (508–775–3828 or 800–332–2279). *Moderate.* All rooms have kitchen facilities, two double beds. Near Main St. shops and restaurants.

Hyannis Travel Inn, 16 North St., 02601 (508–775–8200). *Moderate.* Outdoor and heated indoor pools. Saunas, Jacuzzi. Free Continental breakfast. Near restaurants, stores, beaches. Open Feb.–Nov.

Park Square Village, 156 Main St., 02601 (508–771–0999). *Moderate.* Cottages, rooms, and efficiencies. Rooms in 1855 sea captain's house, modern motel. Good off-season rates. Close to Hyannis center. Low off-season rates. Pool. Tennis. Picnic area.

Presidential Motel, Iyanough Rd., 02601 (508–362–3957). *Moderate.* On pond with boats, fishing available. Play area. Opposite new 18-hole golf course. Open late May–Oct.

Rainbow Resort Motel, Iyanough Rd., 02601 (508–362–3217). *Moderate.* On pond, with boats, fishing available. Heated pool, play area, children's pool. Gift shop, breakfast shop, 18-hole golf course across street. Efficiencies available.

New Seabury

New Seabury Resort, Shore Dr. West, New Seabury 02649 (508–477–9111). *Deluxe.* Full-service resort village; tennis courts, 2 golf courses, pool, restaurants, shops, marina.

MASSACHUSETTS 291

Orleans

Nauset Knoll Motor Lodge, Beach Rd., E. Orleans 02643 (508–255–2364). *Expensive.* Oceanfront resort at Nauset Beach. Swimming, fishing, dune walks. Open Apr.–late Oct.

Skaket Beach Motel, Exit 12, Rte 6A, 02653 (508–255–1020 or 800–835–0298). *Expensive.* Heated pool, play area. Attractive rooms and Swiss-quality service. Quiet surroundings. Picnic area. Fresh muffins for breakfast.

Governor Prence Motor Inn, Jct. Rtes. 6A at 28, 02653 (508–255–1216). *Moderate.* Overlooking the cove. Package plans. Open Apr.–Nov.

Ridgewood Cottages and Motel, Jct. Rtes. 28 and 39, S. Orleans 02662 (508–255–0473). *Moderate.* Motel rooms and housekeeping cottages (seasonal); ideal for families. Pool. Play area. Near Pleasant Bay, tennis, golf, fishing. Picnic grounds with barbecues. Weekly rates.

Provincetown

Hargood House, 493 Commercial St., 02657 (508–487–1324). *Deluxe.* Pleasant, modern efficiency apartments near the harbor. Fine view from rear units. Private beach. One unit with fireplace. Two-day minimum off-season; weekly rentals or longer in summer.

Angel's Landing, 353 Commercial St., 02657 (508–487–1420). *Expensive.* Waterfront apartments, studios. Beach. Sundeck. Open mid-May–Nov.

Best Western Chateau, Bradford St., Rte. 6A, 02657 (508–487–1286). *Expensive.* Heated pool. Comfortable rooms overlook dunes. Open May–Oct.

Holiday Inn, Snail Rd., Rte. 6A, 02657 (508–487–1711). *Expensive.* Pool. Restaurant, bar. Near public beach. Entertainment, sitters available.

Provincetown Inn, 1 Commercial St., 02657 (508–487–9500 or 800–343–4444). *Expensive.* Fine location near tip of Cape. Restaurant. Heated indoor pool, private beach. Cocktail lounge, nightclub. Dune tours and bike rentals available.

Surfside Inn, 543 Commercial St., 02657 (508–487–1726). *Expensive.* Private beach, pool, convenient to town. Open Easter–Mid-Oct.

Bradford House and Motel, 41 Bradford St., 02657 (508–487–0173). *Expensive.* Pool. Pleasant, centrally located. Near restaurant. Open May–Oct.

Masthead, 31 Commercial St., 02657 (508–487–0523). *Expensive.* Motel, cottages and apartments facing ocean. Large sundeck, private beach. Near restaurant.

Ship's Bell Inn, 586 Commercial St., 02657 (508–487–1674). *Expensive.* Well-kept motel, studios, apartments, central location, private beach. Tennis, boating. Open Apr.–Nov.

Tides Motor Inn, Beach Point Rd., 02657 (508–487–1045). *Expensive.* Pool. Most rooms on private beach with patio or balcony overlooking harbor. Open mid-May–mid-Oct.

Meadows Motel and Cottages, Bradford St. Ext., 02657 (508–487–0880). *Moderate.* Motel and efficiency cottages, 3-min. to beach. Sightseeing and dune tours.

Sandwich

Daniel Webster Inn, 149 Main St., 02563 (508–888–3622). *Deluxe–Expensive.* Handsome inn with good restaurant, pool, in historic village. Modified American Plan available.

Shady Nook Inn, Rte. 6A, 02563 (508–888–0409, 800–338–5208). *Expensive.* Immaculate woodsy setting. Pool, coffee shop. Near marina, fishing. Suites, efficiencies.

Spring Hill Motor Lodge, Rte. 6A, E. Sandwich 02537 (508–888–1456). *Moderate.* Wooded setting. Color TV. Free morning coffee. Off-season rates.

Earl of Sandwich Motor Manor, Rte. 6A, E. Sandwich 02537 (508–888–1415). *Moderate.* Charming small motel with Tudor decor. Free coffee and rolls. Near restaurant, gift shops.

Truro

Cape View Motel, Rte. 6, N. Truro 02652 (508–487–0363). *Expensive.* View of Cape Cod Bay and dunes from 30 units, balconies. Some efficiencies. Complimentary coffee and doughnuts. Pool, play area. Near golf, bike trails.

Anchorage, Rte. 6A, N. Truro 02652 (508–487–0168). *Moderate.* Motel units or efficiencies. 300-ft. private beach on Cape Cod Bay, sundeck. Open Mar.–Oct.

Crow's Nest Motel, Rte. 6A, Beach Point, N. Truro 02652 (508–487–9031). *Moderate.* All efficiencies. Private beach. Scenic waterfront view. Near National Seashore, Provincetown, golf, fishing. Off-season rates. Open Apr.–Nov.

Outer Reach Resort, Rte. 6, N. Truro 02652 (508–487–9090 or 800–343–4444). *Moderate.* 70 rooms, panoramic view of Cape Cod Bay. Large acreage in the heart of National Seashore area. Access to beach; tennis and shuffleboard.

Wellfleet

Southfleet Motor Inn, Rte. 6, S. Wellfleet 02663 (508–349–3580). *Moderate.* Near National Seashore. Indoor and outdoor pools, saunas. Restaurant, bar. Entertainment in season.

Even' Tide, Rte. 6, S. Wellfleet 02663 (508–349–3410 or 800–368–0007). *Moderate.* Motel units and cottages. Color TV. Playground. Picnic area.

Wellfleet Motel, Rte. 6, S. Wellfleet 02663 (508–349–3535 or 800–852–2900). *Moderate.* Play area. Heated pool. Bar, coffee shop. In-room coffee and refrigerators. Some suites.

Woods Hole

Nautilus, Woods Hole Rd., 02543 (508–548–1525 or 800–654–2333). *Expensive.* Luxurious motor inn overlooking Vineyard Sound. Formal gardens, pool, bar, restaurant, tennis. Near island ferries. Open Apr.–Oct.

Sands of Time Motor Inn, Main Rd., 02543 (508–548–6300). *Expensive.* Overlooking harbor. Near island ferries. Pool, play area. Restaurant and bar. Open Apr.–Oct.

Yarmouth

All Seasons Motor Inn, Rte. 28, S. Yarmouth 02664 (508–394–7600). *Expensive.* Rooms have private balconies overlooking gardens and pool. Indoor pool.

Blue Rock Motor Inn, off High Bank Rd. S. Yarmouth 02664 (508–398–6962). *Expensive.* Private balconies. Pool, shuffleboard court, tennis. Restaurant. Near golf. Open Apr.–mid-Nov.

Green Harbor on the Ocean, 182 Baxter Ave., W. Yarmouth 02673 (508–771–1126). *Expensive.* Pool, private beach. Very attractive. Kitchen units and cottages with sundecks. Open May–Oct.

MARTHA'S VINEYARD

Accommodations on Martha's Vineyard can be booked through these reservation services: Dukes County Reservation Service, 1 Lake Ave., Box 2370, Oak Bluffs, MA 02577 (508–693–6505) and Martha's Vineyard Reservations, Box 1769, Vineyard Haven, MA 02568 (508–693–4111).

Edgartown

Governor Bradford Inn, 128 Main St. 02539 (508–627–9510). *Deluxe.* Gracefully restored inn. Continental breakfast. Lounge.

Harbor View Hotel, N. Water St. 02539 (508–627–4333). *Deluxe.* Turn-of-the-century grand hotel overlooking the harbor. First-class service. Restaurant, lounge, pool, tennis. Open May–Nov.

Harborside Inn, 3 S. Water St. 02539 (508–627–4321). *Deluxe.* Waterfront resort, boating. All 89 rooms have refrigerators. Outdoor heated pool. Restaurant and open-air bar. Open mid-Apr.–mid-Nov.

Edgartown Commons, Pease's Point Way, 02539 (508–627–4671). *Expensive.* Two blocks from Main St. 35 efficiency units surround pool and play area. Weekly rates. Open mid-May–Oct.

Oak Bluffs

Island Country Club, Beach Rd., 02557 (508–693–2002). *Deluxe.* Overlooking Farm Neck Golf Club and Nantucket Sound. Tennis, pool, golf. Dining room.

Wesley Hotel, 1 Lake Ave., 02557 (508–693–6611). *Moderate–Expensive.* Old-style Victorian hotel. Comfortable. Open May–Oct.

NANTUCKET

Accommodations on Nantucket can be booked by contacting Accommodations Inc. (508–228–7192 or 800–426–9257). For a complete listing of island accommodations, write the Chamber of Commerce (see *Tourist Information*) or Nantucket Lodging Association, Box 52, Nantucket, MA 02554.

The Harbor House, S. Beach St., 02554 (508–228–1500). *Deluxe.* Large village-like resort. Pool, restaurant, meeting rooms.

Nantucket Inn at Nobadeer, Macy's Lane, 02554 (508–228–6900 or 800–321–8484). *Deluxe.* Large hotel located near airport. Indoor, outdoor pools; health club, tennis courts, fine restaurant.

The Wauwinet, Box 2580, 02584 (508–228–0145 or 800–426–8718). *Deluxe.* Recently renovated 19th-century inn and cottages overlooking the water at Squam Head, 9 mi from town. Jitney service, tennis, water sports.

White Elephant, Easton St., 02554 (508–228–5500). *Deluxe.* Motel and cottages on Nantucket Harbor, walking distance to town. Putting green, tennis, sailing. Restaurant. Open mid-May–mid-Oct.

INNS, GUEST HOUSES, BED AND BREAKFASTS. An enjoyable lodging option for Cape vacationers is to stay at one of the many bed-and-breakfast homes in the area. For information, contact *Orleans Bed and Breakfast Associates,* Box 1312, Orleans 02653 (508–255–3824), private homes from Harwich to Truro; *Bed and Breakfast Cape Cod,* Box 341, W. Hyannis Port 02672 (508–775–2772), private homes and guest houses all over the Cape, doubles and singles; or *House Guests Cape Cod and the Islands,* Box 1881, Orleans, MA 02653 (508–896–7053 or 800–666–4678). Directory $3. A sample of inns and guest houses on the Cape follows. These usually fall into the *moderate to expensive* price ranges.

PLYMOUTH

Morton Park Place, 1 Morton Park Rd., 02360 (508–747–1730). New England colonial home turned B&B; easy walk to Plymouth Center and waterfront.

CAPE COD

Barnstable

Ashley Manor, 3660 Main St., 02630 (508–362–8044). A charming country inn, private baths, working fireplaces. Attractive grounds. Near shops, restaurants. Serves full breakfast.
Beechwood Inn, 2839 Main St., Rte. 6A, 02630 (508–362–6618). Romantic bed and breakfast with fireplaces in rooms, stunning views of beach and saltwater marshes. Afternoon tea served, four-course breakfast. Quiet surroundings. Walk to beach, harbor.

Brewster

Bramble Inn, 2019 Main St., 02631 (508–896–7644). A pleasant restored building in a quiet village setting. Restaurant and art gallery on premises. Free Continental breakfast. Near beach, shops, tennis, golf. No children under 8.
Captain Freeman Inn, 15 Breakwater Rd., 02631 (508–896–7481). Pleasant guest rooms in sea captain's mansion. Pool, walk to beach, bike trail. Continental breakfast, afternoon tea. No smoking.
Old Manse Inn, 186 Main St., Rte. 6A, 02631 (508–896–3149). Handsome 19th-century inn in former sea captain's home. Gardens, outdoor patio, restaurant; breakfast included. Central location. Off-season rates.

Centerville

The Inn at Fernbrook, 481 Main St., 02632 (508–775–4334). Victorian manse with rose garden; beautifully furnished. Delicious breakfast.

Chatham

Captain's House Inn, 371 Old Harbor Rd., 02633 (508–945–0127). A country inn of 1839 with 14 guest rooms. Fireplaces, canopy beds, antiques. Near beach and activities.

Chatham Town House Inn, 11 Library Lane 02642 (508–945–2180). Charming 19th-century sea captain's home with lodge, cottages, honeymoon suite, restaurant. Scandinavian breakfasts. No children under 8. Closed Jan.

Chatham Wayside Inn, 512 Main St., 02633 (508–945–1800 or 800–545–4667). Comfortable 19th-century inn close to town center. Restaurant lounge, entertainment. Outdoor pool. Year-round.

The Over Look Inn, County Rd., 02642 (508–255–1886). Victorian sea captain's home opposite National Seashore. Near trails, beaches, bike paths.

Eastham

The Penny House, Rte. 6, N. Eastham 02651 (508–255–6632). Restored bow-roof cape that belonged to a shipbuilder in the 1750s. Full country breakfast. No children under 13.

Whalewalk Inn, 169 Bridge Rd., 02642 (508–255–0617). Old whaling master's home. Antique furnishings. Rooms in inn or housekeeping cottages; some with fireplaces. Free breakfast for inn guests. Open Apr.–late Nov.

Falmouth

Elm Arch Inn, Elm Arch Way, 02540 (508–548–0133). Small historic inn, centrally located. Colonial furnishings, beamed ceilings. Pool.

Mostly Hall, 27 Main St., 02540 (508–548–3786). A cozy bed-and-breakfast inn serving copious breakfasts. In-town location, near ferries, museums, shops. Children over 16; no pets.

The Inn at One Main St., Woods Hole Rd., 02540 (508–540–7469). Charming old home just off the village green. Near shops, restaurants, churches.

Harwich

Country Inn, 86 Sisson Rd., Harwich Port 02646 (508–432–2769). Pool, tennis. Old Cape Cod house, taproom with fireplace. Meals available, prepared by owner-chef. Closed part of Jan.

Dunscroft Inn, 24 Pilgrim Rd., Harwich Port 02646 (508–432–0810). Large rooms in old home, antique furnishings, sunroom, brick terrace. Private baths. Full Continental breakfast. 300 ft. from water; picnic and play area.

Lion's Head Inn, 186 Belmont Rd., W. Harwich 02671 (508–432–7766). Handsome bed-and-breakfast inn. Near beach, golf, shops. Five rooms, two cottages can be rented on a weekly basis. Serves full breakfast.

Hyannis

Cranberry Cove, Rosetta St., 06601 (508–775–5049 or 800–992–0096). Charming B&B on 80-acre cranberry bog. Walk to beach and town.

The Homestead, Scudder Ave., Hyannis Port 02647 (508–778–4999). Year-round bed and breakfast. Well located near downtown Hyannis, beaches. Charming 1820 sea captain's home, porch, pretty grounds. Fireplaces, canopied beds. Full breakfast, afternoon tea.

Orleans

Cove House and Cottages, Rt. 6A, 02653 (508–255–1312). Inn rooms or one- or two-bedroom cottages with decks and fireplaces; on saltwater inlet.

The Farmhouse at Nauset Beach, 163 Beach Rd., E. Orleans 02653 (508–255–6654). 19th-century farmhouse, ocean views. Fresh muffins in the morning.

Hillbourne House, Rte. 28, S. Orleans 02662 (508–255–0780). Charming bed-and-breakfast guest house built in the 18th century. Accommodations also in small motel, four-room cottage, and carriage house. View of Pleasant Bay. Private beach, dock, boat moorings.

Ship's Knees Inn, Beach Rd., E. Orleans 02643 (508–255–1312). Small country inn. Private or semiprivate bath; ocean views. Pool, volleyball, tennis. Near Nauset Beach.

Provincetown

Watermark Inn, 603 Commercial St., 02657 (508–487–0165). Luxurious oceanfront suites; decks and patios, private beach.

White Wind Inn, 174 Commercial St., 02657 (508–487–1526). Victorian house across from the beach. Warm and hospitable. Cozy fireplace for off-season guests.

Wellfleet

Holden Inn, Commercial St., 02667 (508–349–3450). Cheerful rooms in restored home of Capt. Baker, one of Cape Cod's famous sea captains. Open June–Sept.

Inn at Duck Creek, E. Main St. 02667 (508–349–9333). Traditional inn decorated with antiques. Restaurants and lounge. Open May–Oct.

Yarmouth

Colonial House Inn, Rte. 6A, Yarmouth Port 02675 (508–362–4348). Vintage inn furnished with antiques. Quiet. Three dining rooms, lounge, reading room, Jacuzzi. Dinner and breakfast included.

Wedgewood Inn, 83 Main St., Rte. 6A, Yarmouth Port 02675 (508–362–5157). Small country inn. Antiques. Fireplaces. Full breakfast. Private bath in all rooms. Near shops, restaurants, beaches.

The Village Inn, 92 Main St., Yarmouth Port 02675 (508–362–3182). Built in 1795. Relaxed atmosphere, 10 rooms. Continental breakfast.

MARTHA'S VINEYARD

Edgartown

Charlotte Inn, S. Summer St., 02539 (508–627–4751). Antique filled, with superb restaurant. Some suites with fireplace. Art gallery.

Daggett House, N. Water St., 02539 (508–627–4600). Lovely traditional inn, gardens. Antique-furnished rooms.

Kelley House, Kelley St., 02539 (508–627–4394). One block from the waterfront. Good restaurant. Bar. Pool.

Colonial Inn, 38 N. Water St., 02539 (508–627–4711). Large inn in center of town; two restaurants, lounge. Continental breakfast. Open May–Oct.

Edgartown Inn, N. Water St., 02539 (508–627–4794). Historic old inn, near shops, restaurants, harbor. Open Apr.–Nov.

Menemsha

Beach Plum Inn, 02552 (508–645–9454). Overlooking the sea, with country-inn charm. Tennis courts. Rates include breakfast and dinner. Open mid-June–mid-Oct.

Vineyard Haven

Capt. Dexter House, 100 Main St., 02568 (508–693–6564). Handsome guest house, close to center of town. Antiques, fireplaces. Home-baked pastries for breakfast.

Lothrop Merry House, Owen Park, 02568 (508–693–1646). 18th-century guest house overlooking harbor. Rates include breakfast, served on patio. Private beach.

West Tisbury

Lambert's Cove Country Inn, Lambert's Cove Rd., 02575 (508–693–2298). Quiet, secluded inn in mid-island country setting. Near private beach. Beautiful gardens, beach, tennis.

NANTUCKET

Jared Coffin House, 29 Broad St., 02554 (508–228–2405). Charming restored mansion with many antiques, handwoven fabrics. Restaurant, bar, entertainment. Special Christmas celebration.

The Woodbox, 29 Fair St., 02554 (508–228–0587). Oldest inn on the island. Private bath with all rooms, some fireplaces. Restaurant. No credit cards. Open Jun.–Oct.

RESTAURANTS. Cape Cod is liberally dotted with interesting restaurants and inns. Although many restaurants are closed after the summer season, a growing number are open year-round for those interested in seeing the Cape after the sun worshippers have gone.

Our ratings are based on the price of an à la carte dinner. *Deluxe,* $35 and up; *Expensive,* $25–$35; *Moderate,* $15–$25; *Inexpensive,* under $15. Diners should keep in mind that lobster prices fluctuate considerably; when prices are up, expect to pay $15 or more for one of the creatures. The best bets for no-frills lobsters are often simple roadside establishments serving them boiled, on paper plates.

Note: Unless otherwise noted, the restaurants below are open year-round.

PLYMOUTH

Santé Restaurant Français, 320 Court St. (508–747–4226). *Expensive.* Fine French cuisine, both classic and nouvelle. Reservations advised.

Station One, 51 Main St. (508–746–6001). *Moderate.* Plymouth's first fire station, now an attractive contemporary restaurant. Diverse menu includes seafood, veal, duck. Lunch, dinner, Sun. brunch. Lounge, two bars.

The Inn For All Seasons, 97 Warren Ave. (508–746–8823). *Inexpensive.* Relaxed dining with crystal and candlelight. Continental cuisine. Sun. brunch, dinner starting at 5:00 P.M. Closed Monday.

The Original Lobster Hut, Town Wharf (508–746–2270). *Inexpensive.* Seafood at its best.

CAPE COD

Barnstable

Anthony's Cummaquid, Rte. 6A (508–362–4501). *Expensive.* One of the nicer restaurants; in colonial mansion. Lounge with fireplace. Dinners only.

The Dolphin, Rte. 6A (508–362–6610). *Moderate.* Local favorite, casual; fresh seafood. Closed Sun.

Mattakeese Wharf, Barnstable Harbor (508–362–4511). *Moderate.* Seafood: baked stuffed lobster, native fish. Outdoor dining overlooking harbor. Fish market on premises. Open May–early Oct.

Bourne

Bridge Restaurant, Rte. 6A, Sagamore (508–888–8144). *Moderate.* Fresh seafood, Italian specialties. Casual.

Chart Room, Shore Rd., Cataumet (508–563–5350). *Moderate.* Waterview. Fish and luncheon specialties. Piano bar. Open Memorial Day–Columbus Day.

The Dolphin Inn, Taylor's Point, Buzzards Bay (508–759–7522). *Moderate–Inexpensive.* Waterfront. Good seafood menu. Piano bar.

Lobster Trap, 290 Shore Rd., Bourne (508–759–3992). *Inexpensive.* Patio dining. Huge tasty portions of fried seafood; steamed clams; lobsters and lobster rolls. Open mid-June–mid-Sept.

Brewster

Bramble Inn, Rte. 6A (508–896–7644). *Deluxe.* Considered one of Cape's top restaurants. Four-course table d'hôte menu. Formal. Open Apr.–Dec.

Chillingsworth, Rte. 6A, E. Brewster (508–896–3640). *Expensive.* Award-winning restaurant in lovely colonial inn. Six- to-seven-course dinners based on superb fish, lamb, veal, duck, and beef tenderloin entrees. Own baking; fine wine list. Reservations suggested, two seatings nightly. Open late May–Dec. for dinner. Lunch on weekends year-round, daily in season, except Mon.

Old Manse Inn, 1861 Main St., Rte. 6A (508–896–3149). *Expensive.* Elegant four-course dinners. Specialties include filet mignon and grilled fish. Prix fixe. Open Wed.–Sat. Open May–Oct.

The Villages Restaurant, 1 Villages Dr., off Rte 6A. (508–896–6119). *Moderate.* Nice atmosphere, good food. Fireplace. Weekend entertainment. Excellent Sun. brunch.

Chatham

Queen Anne Inn, 70 Queen Anne Rd. (508–945–0394). *Expensive.* Contemporary cuisine in stately 19th-century inn. Traditional decor. Lounge area with outdoor patio. Extensive wine list. Open Apr.–Nov.

Captain's Table, 578 Main St. (508–945–1961). *Moderate.* Located in the town center. Yankee cooking: chicken pie, fresh fish, orange bread. Open Apr.–Nov.

Dennis

Captain Williams House, 106 Depot St., Dennis Port (508–398–3910). *Expensive.* American menu, Colonial decor. Prime rib and seafood specialties, impressive wine cellar. Open Apr.–Oct.

Captain's Clambake Emporium, 410 Lower County Rd., Dennis Port (508–398–0331). *Moderate.* Traditional New England clambake cooked on the spot. Casual. Children's menu. Make reservations.

Bob Brigg's Wee Packet, Lower County Rd., Dennis Port (508–398–2181). *Moderate.* Family-run restaurant with large selection of seafood dishes. Children's menu. "Home of the Cape Cod scallop" for four decades.

Swan River Seafood Restaurant, 5 Lower County Rd., Dennis Port (508–394–4466). *Inexpensive.* Good fresh fish; takeout available. Open late May–Sept.

Falmouth

Regatta, 217 Clinton Ave. (508–548–5400). *Expensive.* Creative cuisine with French and American inspiration. Romantic atmosphere. Fresh seafood, fine wines. Dinner only. Seasonal.

Coonamessett Inn, Jones Rd. and Gifford St. (508–548–2300). *Moderate.* Lovely traditional dining room serving seafood, steak. Open for breakfast, lunch, dinner. Bar with pianist, trio, dancing.

Lawrence's Restaurant, Nantucket Ave., Falmouth Heights (508–548–4441). *Moderate.* Very popular, steamed clams, homemade bread. Casual. Piano bar. Open May–Oct.

Harwich

Bishop's Terrace, Main St., W. Harwich (508–432–0253). *Moderate.* New England specialties; lobster, roast beef, steak. Terrace dining. Dinner nightly, lunch Mon.–Fri. Sun. Brunch. Closed Mon. year-round, Tues. off-season.

Brax Landing, Rte. 28 (508–432–5515). *Moderate.* Harbor views, outside dining. Full menu, raw seafood bar in summer. Lunch, dinner, and Sun. brunch.

Country Inn, Sisson Rd., Harwich Port (508–432–2769). *Moderate.* Cape Cod atmosphere in antique home. Desserts, breads a specialty. Dinners only. Closed Sun.

Thompson's Clam Bar, Snow Inn Wharf, Harwich Port (508–432–3595). *Moderate.* Outdoor patio overlooking Wychmere Harbor. Raw bar, lobsters, steamers; children's menu. Casual. June–Sept.

Hyannis

The Paddock, W. End Rotary (508–775–7677). *Expensive.* Victorian atmosphere, casual elegance. Duckling, beef, seafood specialties. Open Apr.–Nov.

Alberto's Ristorante, 337 Ocean St. (508–778–1770). *Expensive.* Northern Italian cuisine. Half orders; early-bird specials.

Asa Bearse House, 415 Main St. (508–771–4131). *Moderate.* Pleasant surroundings. Seafood. Jazz and piano; magnificent library room.

The Captain's Chair, 166 Bay View St. (508–775–5000). *Moderate.* Century-old home. Overlooks Lewis Bay. Pleasant atmosphere. Seafood specialties. Recommend reservations.
John's Loft, Barnstable Rd. (508–775–1111). *Inexpensive.* Comfortable, rustic atmosphere. Seafood and beef specialties. Salad bar; specials 4–6 P.M.

Mashpee

The Flume, Near Rte. 130 (508–477–1456). *Moderate.* Small country restaurant serving some of the best chowder and fish on the Cape. Informal.
Bobby Byrne's Pub, New Seabury Plaza (508–477–0600). *Inexpensive.* Pub atmosphere, sandwich and dinner menu. Open until 1 A.M., year-round.

Orleans

Captain Linnell House, Skaket Rd. (508–255–3400). *Expensive.* New American menu with an emphasis on seafood. Home-baked breads, desserts.
Lobster Claw, Rte. 6A (508–255–1800). *Inexpensive.* Casual family dining; seafood, lobster, steaks. Open Apr.–Nov.

Provincetown

Cafe at the Mews, 359 Commercial St. (508–487–1500). *Expensive.* Native seafood; duckling cassis; Chateaubriand. Bar with fireplace. Dinner nightly; Sun. brunch., June–early Sept.
Flagship, 463 Commercial St. (508–487–1200). *Expensive.* Elegant dining on the waterfront. Continental menu; lobster, seafood.
The Moors, Bradford St. Ext. (508–487–0840). *Moderate.* Portuguese cuisine: kale soup; pork tenderloin with ginger, cumin, coriander, and garlic. Open Apr.–Nov.
Napi's, 7 Freeman St. (508–487–9703). *Moderate.* Gallery. Popular with local artists, writers. Eclectic menu with nice suprises.
The Red Inn, Commercial St. (508–487–0050) *Moderate.* Waterview from nearly every seat. Local fresh fish. Large facility, tavern menu downstairs; lodging available. Serves breakfast, lunch, dinner.
Pucci's Harborside, 539 Commercial St. (508–487–1964). *Inexpensive.* Seafood and Italian specialties. Harbor view. Open May–Oct.

Truro

Whitman House, Great Hollow Rd. (508–487–1740). *Moderate.* Home baking. Lobster, roast beef. Entertainment. Open April–Nov.

Wellfleet

Aesop's Tables, Main St. (508–349–6450). *Expensive.* International cuisine in a restored sea captain's home. Open May–mid-Oct.
Sweet Seasons at the Inn at Duck Creek, E. Main St. (508–349–6535). *Expensive.* Chilled poached lobster, homemade caviar mayonnaise, steak au poivre au chemise. Excellent, leisurely Sun. brunch. Open mid-May–mid-Oct.
Serena's, Rte. 6 (508–349–9370). *Inexpensive.* Italian specialties and seafood. Informal family restaurant. Seasonal.

Woods Hole

Landfall, Woods Hole Rd. (508–548–1758). *Moderate.* Harbor front. Full meals, burgers, sandwiches, seafood. Lunch and dinner. Short walk to ferry slip. Seasonal.

Yarmouth

La Cipollina, 157 Main St., Rt. 6A, Yarmouth Port (508–362–4341). *Moderate.* Excellent Italian and country French cuisine. Open late Apr.–Oct.

Cranberry Moose, 43 Main St. (508–362–8153). *Moderate–Expensive.* International cuisine in 200-year-old inn. Paella, roasts, duckling a l'orange. Open May–Nov.

Old Yarmouth Inn, 223 Main St., Rte. 6A (508–362–3191). *Moderate.* In historic inn. Regional foods featured. Open Apr.–Nov.

MARTHA'S VINEYARD

Alcoholic beverages can be purchased only in Edgartown and Oak Bluffs; at restaurants in other towns on Martha's Vineyard you may bring your own beer, wine, or cocktails; set-ups are available.

Edgartown

L'Etoile, Charlotte Inn, S. Summer St. (508–627–4751). *Deluxe.* French cuisine in Victorian inn. First-class service, extensive wine list. Garden dining, weather permitting. Dinner and Sunday brunch only. Reservations.

Andrea's, Upper Main St. (508–627–5850). *Expensive.* A large home converted to a stylish restaurant specializing in northern Italian cuisine. Porch dining in summer. Reservations necessary. Open May–Dec.

The Seafood Shanty, Dock St. (508–627–8622). *Moderate.* Known for spectacular views of Edgartown Harbor, good seafood, and performing waiters and waitresses. Lunch and dinner, May–Nov.

Lawry's Seafood, Upper Main St. (508–627–8857). *Moderate.* Some of the freshest seafood on the island. No reservations. Take-out service. Open April–Oct.

Menemsha

Beach Plum Inn, North Rd. (508–645–9454). *Expensive.* Overlooks the water. Expertly prepared dinners, outstanding desserts; menu changes nightly. Limited seating, reservations necessary. Seasonal.

The Home Port, Basin Rd. (508–645–2679). *Moderate.* Stuffed lobster, broiled swordfish, and other simple, fresh seafood dishes. Lovely view, especially at sunset. Very popular; reservations. Open for dinner May–Oct.

Oak Bluffs

Giordano's, Circuit Ave. (508–693–0184). *Inexpensive.* Seafood, Italian dishes, pizza, burgers. Convenient to the ferry. Open May–Oct.

Vineyard Haven

LeGrenier, Main St. (508–693–4906). *Expensive.* Stylish French cuisine, salads, delicious desserts. No credit cards. Open Mar.–Dec.

Patisserie Francaise, Main St. (508–693–4906). *Moderate.* Sidewalk cafe below LeGrenier. Sandwiches, sweets, omelets. No credit cards.

NANTUCKET

Chanticleer, 9 New St., Siasconset (508–257–6231). *Deluxe.* Country French: foie gras; sea bass in sorrel, vermouth, and cream; raspberries grown on the premises. Lunch in rose garden. Open late May–Oct.

Jared's, at Jared Coffin House, 29 Broad St. (508–228–2400). *Expensive–Deluxe.* Attractive dining room, cozy tap room, patio in summer. Fresh seafood. Entertainment in season. Reservations.

Twenty-one Federal St., At 21 Federal St. (508–228–2121). *Expensive.* New American cuisine. Informal.

The Woodbox, 29 Fair St. (508–228–0587). *Expensive.* Nouvelle dining in charming inn, oldest (1709) on the island. Dinner seatings at 7 and 9:15 P.M. Open Jun.–Oct.

Obadiah's, 2 India St. (508–228–4430). *Moderate.* A fine-selection of fresh seafood like stuffed lobster. Clam bar in courtyard. Early Apr.–mid-Dec.

The Atlantic Cafe, 15 S. Water St. (508–228–0570). *Inexpensive.* Popular bar and grill just off Main St. Wide range of beers.

TOURIST INFORMATION. The best comprehensive source of information for tourists is the Cape Cod Chamber of Commerce in Hyannis 02601 (508–362–3225), located off Exit 6 southbound ramp of the Mid-Cape Highway, Rte. 6. It has racks of pamphlets on the area, including extensive directories for resorts, dining, and activities. Not every facility is listed, but it is a good start.

Individual towns, such as Falmouth (508–548–8500), Dennis (508–398–3568), Chatham (508–945–0342), and Yarmouth (508–775–4133), have Chambers of Commerce to provide detailed information about their communities. The Town of Provincetown (508–487–3424) will also provide visitor information. Both the Cape Cod Chamber of Commerce and the Bourne-Sandwich Chamber of Commerce (508–759–6202) maintain information booths at the Sagamore Bridge Rotary. The Mashpee Business Association (508–477–0792) staffs a booth at the New Seabury Rotary during the summer.

The Martha's Vineyard Chamber of Commerce, Box 1698, Vineyard Haven 02568 (508–693–0085), provides free information on island accommodations, events, and attractions and publishes an annual 100-page Visitor's Guide ($2).

The Nantucket Chamber of Commerce at the Pacific Club, Nantucket MA 02554 (508–228–1700), offers walk-in service and has island guidebooks. It also publishes an annual Visitor's Guide ($3).

The Plymouth Area Chamber of Commerce is located at 91 Samoset St., Plymouth, 02360 (508–746–3377). Reservations can be made at the Visitor Information Center on N. Park Ave. (508–746–4779).

A regional information center for southeastern Massachusetts is located in Plymouth at Exit 5 off Rte. 3. There are rest rooms, snacks, and picnic facilities.

SEASONAL EVENTS. April: Daffodil and antique car parade, Nantucket (late Apr.).

May: Pro-Am Boardsailing Race, Sea Crest Hotel, Old Silver Beach, N. Falmouth (mid-May); Harwich Chamber Golf Tournament, Cranberry Valley Golf Course (mid-May); Figawi Sailboat Race, from Hyannis Harbor to Nantucket (late May); Thornton Burgess Society Herb Festival, E. Sandwich (late May).

June: June Fair and Green Thumb Sale, First Congregational Church, Chatham (early June); Coors Sprint Triathalon, Craigville Beach, Craigville (early June); Bourne Farm Day, Rte. 28A, N. Falmouth (late June); Strawberry Festival, Falmouth Green, Falmouth (late June); Annual Chowder Festival, Cape Cod Melody Tent, Hyannis (late June); Annual Hyannis Harbor Festival, downtown Hyannis (late June); Strawberry Festival, Rider House, Wellfleet (late June); Annual Scottish Festival, Dennis-Yarmouth High School, S. Yarmouth (late June); Blessing of the Fleet, Provincetown (late June).

July: Fireworks and 4th celebrations, Falmouth, Hyannis, Yarmouth, Chatham, Provincetown, Plymouth (early July); House and Garden Tour, Nantucket (early July); Arts and Crafts Fair, Brooks Park, Harwich (early July); Wampanoag Indian Pow-Wow, Rte. 130, Mashpee (early July); Tisbury Street Fair, Main St., Martha's Vineyard (early July); Yacht Club Regatta, Hyannis Harbor (early July); Edgartown Regatta, Martha's Vineyard (mid-July); Wellfleet Library Book Sale (mid-July). Annual Barnstable County Fair, Rte. 151, E. Falmouth (late July); Falmouth Garden Club Tour, Falmouth area (late July).

August: Annual Hyannis Street Fair, downtown (early Aug.); Cape Cod Antiques Exposition, Orleans (early Aug.); Open House at Woods Hole Biological Laboratories, Woods Hole (early Aug.); Oriental Lotus Festival, Ashumet Holly Reservation, N. Falmouth (mid-Aug.); Annual Renaissance Arts and Crafts Fair, downtown Dennis, village green (mid-Aug.); Falmouth Road Race, Woods Hole (mid-Aug.); Dennis Festival Days, town wide (late Aug.). West Tisbury Agricultural Fair, Martha's Vineyard (late Aug.); Tuna Tournament, Provincetown (late Aug.); Chatham Festival of Arts, Chase Park, (late Aug.).

September: Bourne Scallop Festival, Main St., Buzzards Bay (early Sept.); Nantucket Seafest, Nantucket (early Sept.); Bud Light Triathalon, Hyannis (early Sept.); Wellfleet Days, town wide (early Sept.); Cranberry Harvest Festival, town wide, Harwich (mid-Sept.); Chatham Scallop Festival (mid-July). Franklinia Festival, Ashumet Holly Reservation, N. Falmouth (late Sept.); Harvest Festival, New Alchemy Institute, E. Falmouth (late Sept.); Annual antique auto show, Heritage Plantation, Sandwich (late Sept.); Striped Bass & Bluefish Derby, Martha's Vineyard (late Sept.–early Oct.).

October: Chatham Scallop Festival (early–mid-Oct.); Annual Columbus Discovery Yard Sale, First Congregational Church, Harwich (early–mid-Oct.); Annual Yarmouth Seaside Festival, townwide (mid-Oct.); annual Barnstable High School Halloween Haunted House (late Oct.).

November: Harvest Fair, Methodist Church, Chatham (early Nov.); Annual Thanksgiving celebration, Green Briar Nature Center, E. Sandwich (early Nov.); Festival of Lights, Village Marketplace, Hyannis (late Nov.); annual Holiday Antique Show, Church of the Holy Spirit, Orleans (late Nov.). Thanksgiving dinner and special activities, Plymouth (late Nov.).

December: Christmas in Sandwich Village, townwide (early Dec.); Christmas Shopper's Stroll, Hyannis (early Dec.); Annual Nantucket

Christmas Stroll, Nantucket (early Dec.); Christmas-by-the-Sea Weekend
and Parade, downtown Falmouth (early Dec.); Holly Days, Ashumet
Holly Reservation (mid-Dec.); Tisbury's Twelve Day's of Christmas (mid-
Dec.); Chatham Open House, Main St. (mid-Dec.).

TOURS. The Mass. Audubon Society sponsors weekly natural history
tours of Monomoy Island, Nauset Marsh and Pleasant Bay, as well as seal
cruises and excursions in Cape Cod Bay, guided field walks and class for
adults and children. For information, contact Massachusetts Audubon Society, Box 236, S. Wellfleet 02663, or call 508–349–2615. Mitch's Dune
Tours, which leave from the parking area of the Provincetown Inn, give
passengers a close-up look at the unusual flora and topography of the
Cape's tip. Call the inn for information (508–487–9500). For a different
perspective, sail out of Provincetown harbor on the schooner *Hindu* for
a two-hour, wind-powered circuit around Race Point. Call 508–487–0659
at MacMillan Wharf. One of the most fascinating cruises anywhere,
though, is a trip in search of migratory whales. Experienced crew members
help identify species; chances for sightings are excellent. Reservations are
necessary. For trips out of Provincetown Harbor: Capt. Al Avellar's
Whalewatch (508–255–3857 or 800–826–9300); Portuguese Princess
Whale Watch (508–487–2651 or 800–440–3188). Out of Barnstable Harbor: Hyannis Whale Watch Cruises (508–775–1622). Out of Plymouth
Harbor: Web of Life Science Center (508–866–5353).

Cars are best left behind on a day trip to Martha's Vineyard or any trip
to Nantucket. For a sightseeing bus tour of the Vineyard: Island Transport, Vineyard Haven (508–693–0058); Martha's Vineyard Sightseeing,
Oak Bluffs (508–693–4681); Gay Head Sightseeing, Oak Bluffs (508–
693–1555). On Nantucket: Barrett's Tours, 20 Federal St., and Island
Tours, Straight Wharf; taxi drivers will give personalized tours of historic
sights and outlying areas.

Winemaking has come to the Cape. For tours: Commonwealth Winery,
22 Lothrop St., Plymouth (508–746–4940); Plymouth Colony Winery,
Rte. 44, Plymouth (508–747–3334); Chicama Vineyard, Stoney Hill Rd.,
W. Tisbury, Martha's Vineyard (508–693–0309).

SPORTS. Bicycling: It is possible to bike from Boston to the Cape on
the state bike path, and numerous other trails are located around the Cape.
The 7-mile service road on either side of the Cape Cod Canal and the Shining Sea Bikeway in Falmouth are in the Upper Cape: The Cape Cod Rail
Trail for biking, jogging, and horseback riding is a 14-mile path from Dennis to Eastham. In the outer Cape, the Nauset Trail is in Eastham, the
Head of the Meadow Trail in North Truro, and the Province Lands Trail
in Provincetown; all these are within the National Seashore. Bicycles are
a way of life on the Islands, and rentals are readily available.

Boating and Fishing: A guide is available at the Cape Cod Chamber
of Commerce in Hyannis that lists all information pertaining to these activities, such as the location of boat launches, surf fishing access, shellfish-
ing regulations, location of freshwater ponds and streams, and herring
runs.

Golf: The Cape is well known for its golf courses, and relatively mild
climate, which makes golfing possible much of the year. Bass River Golf
Course, S. Yarmouth (508–398–9079); Blue Rock Par 3 Golf Course, S.
Yarmouth (508–398–9295); Cape Cod Country Club, N. Falmouth
(508–563–9842); Captains Golf Course, Brewster (508–896–5100); Chatham Bars Inn, Chatham (508–945–0096); Chequesset Country Club, Wellfleet (508–394–3704); Cotuit Highground Country Club, Cotuit

(508–428–9863); Cranberry Valley Golf Course, Harwich, (508–432–6300); Dennis Highlands Golf Course, S. Dennis (508–385–8347); Dennis Pines Golf Course, E. Dennis (508–385–8347); Tara Hyannis Golf Club, Hyannis (508–775–7775); Falmouth Country Club, E. Falmouth (508–548–3211); Paul Harney Golf Club, N. Falmouth (508–563–3454); Harwich Port Golf Club, Harwich Port (508–432–0250); Highland Golf Club, N. Truro (508–487–9201); Holly Ridge Golf Club, S. Sandwich (508–428–5577); New Seabury Country Club, New Seabury (508–477–9110); Ocean Edge Golf Club, E. Brewster (508–896–5911); Pocasset Golf Club, Bourne (508–563–7171); Quashnet Valley Country Club, Mashpee (508–477–4412); Round Hill Country Club, Sandwich (508–888–3384).

On Martha's Vineyard there's Mink Meadows (508–693–0600). On Nantucket, Miacomet Golf Club (508–693–2504) and Siasconset Golf Club (508–257–6596).

Horseback riding: Riding facilities are located in Bourne, Falmouth, Marstons Mills, Dennis, West Barnstable, Harwich, Provincetown, and in W. Tisbury on Martha's Vineyard. The extent of services ranges from boarding to lessons and shows as well as trail rides.

Racquetball: Enthusiasts will find courts in Falmouth at the Falmouth Sports Center and at Falmouth High School; in Dennis at the Dennis Racquet & Swim Club; in Hyannis at the Fitness Club; in N. Eastham at the Norseman Athletic Club; and in Yarmouth at the Mid-Cape Racquet Club.

Tennis: Most every town on the Cape has courts open to the public. Private facilities open to the public are located in Falmouth at the Sports Center and the Falmouth Tennis Club; Sandwich at the Holly Ridge Tennis Club; Mashpee at South Cape Resort; Cotuit at Kings Grant Racquet Club; Dennis at the Dennis Racquet and Swim Club, Marine Lodge, and Dennis Tennis Club; Hyannis at Tennis of Cape Cod; W. Barnstable at the Cape Cod Community College; Yarmouth at the Blue Rock Tennis Courts, and the Mid-Cape Racquet Club; Brewster at Bamburgh House Tennis Club and Four Havens; Chatham at the Chatham Bars Inn; Harwich at Mannings; Wellfleet at the Chequesset Yacht and Country Club; and Provincetown at Hawthorne Bissell's Tennis Courts and the Tennis Club.

HISTORIC SITES AND MUSEUMS. If you find that there's a rainy day while you're visiting Cape Cod or the Islands, don't worry that you may be wasting a day of your vacation. The area is full of wonderful museums and sites that chronicle the lives of the early settlers and the fishing, agriculture, and industry that became so much a part of the life and lore of Cape Cod. In addition to those listed, there are historical societies in Orleans, Truro, Wellfleet.

PLYMOUTH

Plymouth Rock, the Mayflower II, Cole's Hill, Burial Hill, and **Brewster Gardens,** all clustered in the same downtown area, at North Park Ave. and the waterfront. Burial Hill and Brewster Gardens, closer to the First Parish Church, at Town Sq. on Leyden St. No telephone numbers. With the exception of the ship, they may be visited at any time.

First Parish Church, Town Sq. (508–747–1606). Open Tues.–Fri. in summer; open for church services only the rest of the year. Building is the fourth successor to the original 1683 structure and home to a congregation begun by the Pilgrims.

Pilgrim Hall Museum, 75 Court St. (508–746–1620). Open daily year-round. Artwork and artifacts depicting the Pilgrim experience.

Plymouth National Wax Museum, 16 Carver St. (508–746–6468). Life-size scenes depict Pilgrim history.

Plimoth Plantation, Rte. 3A (508–746–1622). Open late Mar.–Nov. 30, daily. The crafts and daily living of the Pilgrims, circa 1627, practiced in authentic recreated Pilgrim Village by costumed men and women. Wampanoag Indian exhibits are also featured.

Cranberry World, Water St. (508–747–1000). Large cranberry trade exhibit. Free. Open Apr.–Nov.

CAPE COD

Barnstable

Donald G. Trayser Memorial Museum, Main St. (508–362–2092). Historical documents, Indian tools, marine exhibits and paintings. Open July–Sept.; Tues.–Sat.

Cape Cod Art Association Gallery and Studios, Rte. 6A (508–362–2909). Classes, exhibits. Apr.–Nov.

Olde Colonial Court House, Barnstable Village. Built 1772.

Sturgis Library, Rte. 6A (508–362–6636). Oldest public library building in the United States. Large genealogy and maritime history collection.

Bourne

Aptucxet Trading Post, 24 Aptucxet Rd., off Shore Rd. (508–759–5755). Replica of Pilgrim trading post. Native American artifacts. Open mid-Apr.–mid-Oct.

Brewster

Drummer Boy Museum, Rte. 6A, W. Brewster (508–896–3823). Scenes from American Revolution, with life-size figures. Guided tours. Late May–mid-Oct.

Cape Cod Museum of Natural History, Rte. 6A (508–896–3867). Animal and marine exhibits, nature trails. Daily May–Oct., Tues.–Sat. in winter.

New England Fire & History Museum, Rte. 6A (508–896–5711). Early fire engines and related memorabilia; Arthur Fiedler's Fire Collection. Daily mid-June–Labor Day.

Stoney Brook Mill, Stoney Brook Rd. Built in 1873; replica of one of the earliest gristmills in America. Grinds corn Wed., Fri., Sat. afternoons, July–Aug. Museum and herring run. See migrating fish in spring.

Centerville

Centerville Historical Society Museum, jct. of West Bay Rd. and Parker Rd. (508–775–0331). Early 19th-century captain's home. Doll collections, ship models. Tours Wed.–Sun, mid-June–mid-Sept.

Dennis

Cape Museum of Fine Arts, Theatre Marketplace, Rte. 6A (508–385–4477). Paintings, graphics, sculpture by Cape Cod artists; classes and lectures.

Jericho Historical Center, Old Main St., W. Dennis. Historic home and barn museum. Includes antique farm equipment and zoo. Open Wed.–Fri. afternoons in summer.

South Parish Congregational Church, S. Dennis. Oldest pipe organ (1762) in continuous use in the United States.

Eastham

Old Windmill (1793), Grist Mill Park opposite Town Hall, Rte. 6. Oldest windmill on Cape Cod. Open daily Memorial Day–Labor Day.

Schoolhouse Museum, Nauset Rd., off Rte. 6 (508–255–0788). 1869 one-room schoolhouse, Indian artifacts, farming tools. Open July–Aug.

Swift-Daley House, Rte. 6, (508–240–1247). Built 1741. Period furnishings, limited season and hours.

Capt. Edward Penniman House, Fort Hill Rd. Whaling captain's Victorian home (1867).

Falmouth

Ashumet Holly Reservation, north of Rte. 151 and Currier Rd., N. Falmouth (508–563–6390). Massachusetts Audubon Society. Self-guided nature walks, swallow colony, special events.

Falmouth Historical Society Museum, Village Green, Rte. 28 (508–548–4587). Two restored houses with period furniture, tools, costumes, whaling exhibits. Colonial garden. Open weekdays in summer.

New Alchemy Institute, 237 Hatchville Rd., E. Falmouth (508–564–6301). Solar greenhouses, aquaculture, organic gardens. Open year-round.

First Congregational Church, Falmouth Center. Built 1796. Steeple bell cast by Paul Revere.

Harwich

Harwich Historical Society, Main St. and Rte. 124, Harwich Center. Indian artifacts, toys, tools, documents.

Provincetown

Pilgrim Monument and Provincetown Museum, Town Hill (508–487–1310). Granite tower commemorates Pilgrims' first landing; museum of outer Cape Cod history. Open daily.

Provincetown Heritage Museum, 356 Commercial St. (508–487–0666). Local history, fishing, art, Victorian artifacts, scale model of fishing schooner.

Provincetown Art Association, 460 Commercial St. (508–487–1750). Regional art museum, classes. Open late May–Oct.

Seth Nickerson House, 72 Commercial St. Oldest house in Provincetown (1746). Daily, June–Oct.

Sandwich

Sandwich Glass Museum, Town Hall Sq. (508–888–0251). Display of renowned Sandwich glass of 1825–1888. Open Apr.–Nov.

Hoxie House & Dexter Grist Mill, Rte. 130, Sandwich Center. Restoration of 17th-century home and mill. Mid-June–early Oct. No phone.

Heritage Plantation, Grove and Pine Sts. (508–888–3300). Shaker round barn houses Barney Oldfield diorama, historic cars; Military Muse-

um contains Lilly collection of miniature soldiers, antique firearms; Arts
and Crafts Building exhibits colonial tools, paintings. Open May–Oct.

Thornton W. Burgess Museum, Water St. (508–888–6870). Children's
museum. Special activities. Operates Green Briar nature center and Jam
Kitchen in E. Sandwich, nature trails. Open year-round.

Yarmouth

Captain Bangs Hallet House, 8 Strawberry Lane, off Rte. 6A, Yarmouthport (508–362–3021). Home of Yarmouth Historical Association.
Early American exhibits. Garden, trails. June–mid-Oct.

Baxter Grist Mill, Rte 28, W. Yarmouth, Built in 1710, restored and
working.

Woods Hole

National Marine Fisheries Aquarium, Water St. waterfront
(508–548–7684). Cape Cod area sea life. Open mid-June–mid-Sept.

Bradley House, Woods Hole Rd. (508–548–7270). Woods Hole memorabilia.

MARTHA'S VINEYARD

Edgartown

Dukes County Historical Society, Cooke and School Sts.
(508–627–4441). Restored Thomas Cooke House (1765), with furnishings,
scrimshaw, whaling relics. Herb garden, library, genealogical records,
ships' logs, rare books. Tues.–Sat. in summer; Thurs.–Sat. rest of year.

Old Whaling Church, Main St. (508–627–4440). Greek Revival Church
(1843) now houses Performing Arts Center.

Windfarm Museum, Edgartown–Vineyard Haven Rd. (508–693–3658).
Solar- and wind-powered energy sources; organic farm; petting zoo.

Vineyard Haven

Tisbury Museum, Vineyard Haven. Open June–Oct. Exhibits in Federal-style Ritter House (1796) depict island life.

West Tisbury

Mayhew Chapel and Indian Burial Grounds, S. Indian Hill Rd. Site of
tiny chapel and burial grounds used by island Indians; wildflower sanctuary.

Gay Head

Gay Head Cliffs and Lighthouse. Glacially formed multicolored cliffs;
one of first electrified lighthouses nearby.

NANTUCKET

Jethro Coffin House (1686), Sunset Hill. Beautiful restoration of island's oldest house. No phone. June–Sept.

Whaling Museum, Broad St. (508–228–1736). 19th-century candle factory houses whaling relics. Late May–mid-Oct.

Peter Foulger Museum, Broad St. Early Nantucket history; reference library. For information, call Nantucket Historical Association, (508–228–1894).

Old Mill (1746), Prospect St. Windmill still grinds corn. June–early Sept.

Maria Mitchell Association (1790), 1 Vestal St. Birthplace of famous astronomer; observatory, library, natural science museum. Mid-June–mid-Sept. Library open all year, Mon.–Thurs. Observatory mid-June–mid-Sept., Wed. evenings only.

Hadwen House–Satler Memorial, Main and Pleasant Sts. 1844 Greek Revival mansion, period furnishings. June–late Oct. No phone.

MUSIC, DANCE, AND STAGE. Cape Cod offers excellent summer theater, usually Broadway favorites with professional casts. *Chatham:* **Monomoy Theatre,** Rte. 28 (508–945–1589), features student actors and young professionals, July–late Aug. *Dennis:* **Cape Playhouse,** Rte. 6A (508–385–3911), July and Aug. *Falmouth:* **Falmouth Playhouse,** off Rte. 151 (508–563–5922), May–Oct. *West Harwich:* **Harwich Junior Theatre,** Willow and Division Sts. (508–432–2002). Drama, musicals for children, July and Aug. *Hyannis:* **Cape Cod Melody Tent,** W. Main St. (508–775–9100), late June–Labor Day *Orleans:* **Academy Playhouse,** Main St. (508–255–9929), late June–late Aug. *Provincetown:* **Province-town Playhouse** (508–487–0955), repertory group specializing in O'Neill, July–Labor Day.

Year-round performances are offered by the **Cape Cod Symphony Orchestra,** the **Cape Cod Chamber Ensemble,** and the **Cape Cod Conservatory Wind Ensemble.** The **Plymouth Philharmonic Orchestra** gives five to six performances a year.

Outdoor summer concerts by local bands are quite popular in Chatham, Dennis, and Oak Bluffs on Martha's Vineyard.

Good folk music can be found at the **Woods Hole Community Theater** on Sunday Night and at the **First Encounter Coffee House** in Eastham.

Theater groups are numerous here. Look for shows by the **Cape Cod Repertory Theater,** the **Barnstable Comedy Club,** the **Provincetown Theater Company,** the **Academy of Performing Arts** in Orleans, the **Chatham Drama Guild,** the **Falmouth Theater Guild, Theater Workshop of Nantucket,** and **Theater on the Bay,** on the Massachusetts Military Reservation in Bourne.

SHOPPING. What you will find on Cape Cod are antiques, Americana, summer resort-geared gifts, and items that reflect conservative New England tastes. Don't miss shops that display the fine worksmanship of local artists and artisans. Quaint and unusual stores are everywhere.

The largest malls—**Cape Cod Mall, Capetown Mall,** and **Southwind Plaza**—are clustered together on Rte. 132 in Hyannis. There is a large mall on Rte. 28 in Falmouth; others are located in Orleans, Yarmouth, and Dennis. You can stop at **Cordage Park** in Plymouth.

In recent years, retail outlets have been cropping up everywhere: Hyannis—the **Sweater Bar,** Rte. 28; **Dansk,** Rte. 132; **Kitchen Inc.,** Main St. Falmouth—**Christmas Tree Shop,** Falmouth Plaza; **Van Heusen,** E. Falmouth. Bourne—**Christmas Tree Shop,** at the Sagamore Bridge; the **Cape Cod Factory Outlet,** which has Corning Ware and Carter Clothing shops. Yarmouth—**Quoddy,** S. Yarmouth, Rte. 28. In Plymouth you'll find several retail stores in a colonial setting at **Village Landing Marketplace,** Water St. The **Revere Copper and Brass Outlet** is also on Water St. in Plymouth; **Cordage Park,** Court St., has about 30 outlets in one location.

Auctions provide unique shopping entertainment. They are held at the **Sandwich Auction House** on Tupper Rd., **Richard Bourne's** in Hyannis, **Eldred's** in East Dennis, the Eastham **Auction House,** and **Merlyn Auctions** in North Harwich. Items range from fine art to estate jewelry to Sandwich glass to genuine junk.

NIGHTLIFE. When warmer weather rolls around, night spots that have been closed during the winter open their doors, and the Cape scene hits its stride. You can tap your toes to everything from reggae to Irish fiddle tunes to U2.

Barnstable (Hyannis)

The Dolphin, Main St., Barnstable Village (508–362–6610). Three-piece band, dancing. Popular spot, reservations necessary.

East Bay Lodge, E. Bay Rd., Osterville (508–428–6961). Piano weekly, quartet and dancing Fri. and Sat., year-round.

Gee Willikers, Rte. 132, Hyannis (508–775–6600). Night spot at the Holiday Inn. Nightly entertainment, DJ.

Guido Murphy's, W. End Market Place, Hyannis (508–775–7242). Memorable for one-man bands and oversized drinks.

Mitchell's Steak House, Rte. 28, Hyannis (508–775–6700). Across from airport. Wide-screen TV, live Irish music.

Pufferbellies, Ridgewood Ave., Hyannis. Popular rock-and-roll bands, live; younger crowd.

Tingles, West End Circle (508–775–7775). Popular disco bar at Tara Hyannis. All ages.

Wimpy's Friars Pub, Main St., Osterville (508–428–6300). Vocals, organ music Fri. and Sat.

Windjammer Lounge, Barnstable Rd., Hyannis (508–771–2020). Guitar and vocals, '50s music, open year-round.

Bourne

Casey's Pub, 618 MacArthur Blvd., Pocasset (508–564–4464). Open year-round. Low key, casual; dart tournament. $1 draft. Sing-alongs, Top 40s.

Dolphin Inn, Taylor's Point, Buzzards Bay (508–759–7522). Waterfront lounge, piano bar, singalongs. Thurs.–Sat. Open year-round.

Brewster

Longfellow's Pub, Rte. 6A (508–896–5413). Guitar soloist, pop and sing-along tunes on weekends.

Villages Restaurant, at Ocean Edge Resort (508–896–6119). Small, pleasant lounge at golf club.

Chatham

Chatham Bars Inn, Shore Rd. (508–945–0096). Live three-piece dance band. Coat and tie. Open summers.

Northport Seafood House, Orleans Rd. (508–945–9217) Lounge, vocalist on piano, dancing. Summers, five nights weekly; weekends in off-season.

Wequasset Inn, Rte. 28 (508–432–5400). Bayfront dining and dancing, easy-listening tunes.

Dennis

Christine's, Rte. 28, W. Dennis (508–394–7333). Comic acts, rock-and-roll bands.

Clancy's, Upper County Rd., Dennis Port (508–394–6661), traditional Irish music.

Sundancer's, Rte. 28, W. Dennis (508–394–1600). Live dance band, year-round.

Eastham

First Encounter Coffeehouse, Samoset Rd., off Rte. 6. Good folk music, local recording artists. (Located at Chapel in the Pines.)

Sheraton Ocean Park Inn, Rte. 6 (508–255–5000). Big-screen TV in lounge; live entertainment weekends in winter, five nights a week in summer; some rock, Top 40s, dancing.

Falmouth

Admiralty Inn, Teaticket Highway, E. Falmouth (508–548–4240). Popular lounge, live entertainment.

Brandy's at the Sheraton Falmouth, Jones Rd. (508–540–2000). DJ, Top 40s recording artists.

Casino-By-The-Sea, Grand Ave., Falmouth Heights (508–548–0777). Some big-name recording bands, live nightly in season. Three bars with outdoor porch. Popular with the college set. Dock boats at pier.

Century Irish Pub, 29 Locust St. (508–548–0196). Live Irish music nightly; happy hours, sing-alongs. Open May–Sept.

Flying Bridge, Scranton Ave. (508–548–2700). DJ, Top 40s, dancing. Dress code. Piano bar upstairs.

Irish Embassy Pub, Rte. 28, E. Falmouth (508–540–6656). Irish bands and European nightclub downstairs. Small, international flavor. Open Apr.–Nov.

Harwich

Bishop's Terrace, Rte. 28, W. Harwich (508–432–0253) Dine and dance, light piano music.

Spinnaker's, Rte. 28 (508–432–7677). Blues and popular music.

Mashpee

Bobby Byrne's Pub, New Seabury Rotary (508–477–0600). Sports bar, local hangout. Juke box. Year-round.

New Seabury Country Club, Shore Dr. West, New Seabury (508–477–9111). Lounge, live entertainment, dancing, mood music to light rock. Weekends year-round. Older crowd.

Orleans

Barley Neck Inn, Beach Rd. (508–255–6830). Contemporary music, acoustical jazz, rock, and folk. Local professionals, songwriters.

Captain Linnell House, Skaket Rd. (508–255–3400). Popular jazz pianist; also jazz trios and quartets, local and Boston talent. Dancing. Nightly performances during summer. Open year-round.

Orleans Inn, Rte. 6A (508–255–2222). Varied popular and show tunes.

Provincetown

Captain John's, Shankpainter Rd. (508–487–3899). DJs, rock, blues, and jazz.
Governor Bradford, 312 Commercial St. (508–487–9618). Reggae live and recorded, rock and pop in season.
Holiday Inn, Rte. 6A (508–487–1711). Live entertainment in season, popular dance tunes. Movies off-season.
The Surf Club, MacMillan Wharf (508–487–1367). In season features the well-known Provincetown Jug Band. Dancing, raw bar, full deck overlooking Cape Cod Bay.

Truro

The Outer Reach Resort, Rte. 6A (508–487–9090). Guitar and vocals, popular music. Seasonal.

Sandwich

Dan'l Webster Inn, Main St. (508–888–3622). Bar, piano, and occasional dinner theater. Dancing, sing-along. Year-round.
Horizons, Town Neck Rd. (508–888–6166). Outdoor deck with great view of the bay. Year-round.

Wellfleet

Aesop's Tables, Main St. (508–349–6450). Popular spot for enjoying jazz, piano and guitar, vocal entertainment. Seasonal.
Wellfleet Oyster House, E. Main St. (508–349–2134). Live entertainment summers only, varied schedule, guitar, rock. Year-round, weekends only off-season.

Yarmouth

Dorsie's Steak House, 325 Main St., Rte. 28, W. Yarmouth (508–771–5898). Live entertainment, dancing, year-round.
Mill Hill Club, 164 Main St., Rte. 28, W. Yarmouth. Big facility, popular, live bands, rock and roll.
Oliver's, Rte. 6A, Yarmouthport (508–362–6062). Lounge entertainment weekends; no dancing.

In **Plymouth** there's **Bert's,** Rte. 3A (508–746–3422). Live band, Top 40s, dancing; also country folk performers. Year-round. **The Inn For All Seasons,** Warren Ave. (508–746–8823). Live band, Top 40s. Dancing, some jazz. No cover. Good cross section of ages. Dress code. **Mermaid** at the Sheraton Inn, 180 Water St. (508–747–4900) Live bands, Top 40s, dancing. Year-round.

On **Martha's Vineyard** the well-known **Hot Tin Roof,** at the airport (508–693–1137), is the island's only bona fide nightclub, which books big-name entertainment. Started by singer Carly Simon. Tickets available at the club and island outlets. Edgartown and Oak Bluffs are the only towns on Martha's Vineyard where alcoholic beverages can be purchased; all other towns are "dry."

On **Nantucket** try **The Brotherhood,** Broad St. Nautical tavern setting, live folk music. **Harbor House.** S. Beach St. (508–228–1500). Piano bar, vocals, Year-round. **The Jared Coffin House Tap Room,** 29 Broad St. (508–228–2400). Easy-listening piano or guitar music, sometimes vocals. Year-round. **The Muse,** Atlantic Ave. (508–228–9716). Rock music and dancing, for the college crowd. Year-round. **Rose and Crown,** S. Water St. (508–228–2595). Rock, blues, jazz in season.

EAST CENTRAL MASSACHUSETTS

Like the spokes of a wheel, highways radiate from the "hub" of Boston toward a wide variety of attractions in Massachusetts's east-central interior. The places described below all make excellent day-trip destinations, if you plan to return to Boston, or convenient stopovers, if you're heading on to the Pioneer Valley or the Berkshires. From Lowell south to Sturbridge, this part of the commonwealth offers a broad sampling of history as well as a look at how everyday life has been lived here for centuries.

Lexington and Concord

A popular one-day trip out of Boston takes you to Lexington and Concord—where the American Revolution began in April 1775—with a return stop at Sudbury. Cross the Charles River at the Massachusetts Avenue bridge and proceed through Cambridge, bearing right for Arlington at Harvard Square. You will come to Arlington center in about 15 minutes. Drive straight ahead on Massachusetts Avenue to the first traffic light beyond the center, turn left into Jason Street, and stop at the Jason Russell House. As the Redcoats retreated from Concord on that April 19, they passed along Massachusetts Avenue and engaged a group of Colonists close by this house in the second major battle of that eventful day. A number of the Minutemen, nearly surrounded by the British, retreated to the Russell home. Russell and 11 others were killed on the first floor of the house, where bullet holes are still visible.

Continue west on Massachusetts Avenue, through Arlington Heights and East Lexington, where you will pass the Munroe Tavern, a colonial gathering place open to the public, and the entrance to the Museum of Our National Heritage, which houses exhibits illustrating American history since independence. Massachusetts Avenue soon reaches Lexington Green, where the Minutemen faced the line of British march. A statue and a large boulder mark the Colonists' line. On the stone is inscribed the command: "Stand your ground. Don't fire unless fired upon. But if they mean to have war, let it begin here."

On the right side of the green is Buckman Tavern, where the Minutemen gathered and waited for the British. The Hancock Clark house, a short way from the green on Hancock Street, is also open to the public. John Hancock was staying here when Paul Revere rode into Lexington warning that the British were coming from Boston. Samuel Adams, also in the house at the time, fled with Hancock to avoid capture. The house contains a notable collection of historical articles and is open the same days and hours as the Buckman Tavern.

This quiet suburban town comes alive each Patriots' Day (the Monday nearest April 19) with a celebration of these events, including a colorful battle reenactment at 6 A.M. and morning and afternoon parades. Volun-

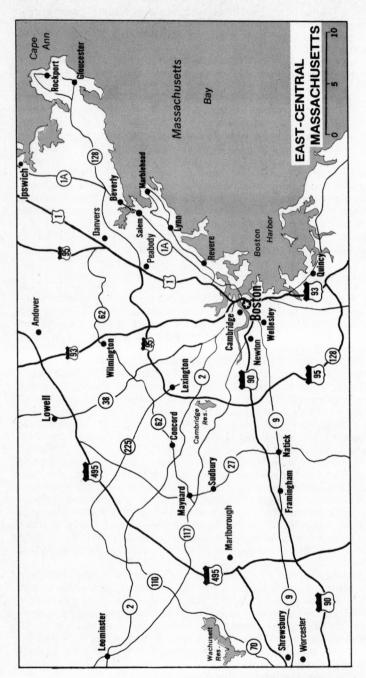

EAST-CENTRAL MASSACHUSETTS

teer regiments from area towns participate in these re-creations in authentic eighteenth-century dress and military equipage.

Leave Lexington on Massachusetts Avenue, which bears left from the green and connects with Route 2A to Concord (through Minuteman National Historical Park). Concord owes its distinguished place in American history not only to the events of April 19, 1775, but to the perseverance of the settlers who made it the first New England village to be situated away from the immediate seacoast and to the remarkable literary figures who made their homes here during the early nineteenth century. Many of their homes survive, in period style, and are open to the public.

As you approach Concord center from Lexington on Route 2A, you will pass Grapevine Cottage, where Ephriam Bull developed the Concord grape from local strains. Just beyond the cottage (now a private home) is The Wayside, a late seventeenth-century building once owned by Nathaniel Hawthorne. Among its occupants during Concord's literary heyday were Bronson Alcott and Margaret Sidney, author of *Five Little Peppers*. Nearby is the house where Bronson's famous daughter, Louisa May Alcott, lived when she wrote *Little Women*.

The Lexington Road next intersects with the Cambridge Turnpike, and at the fork stands the Concord Antiquarian Museum, which contains several fully furnished early New England rooms. The museum is richly endowed with personal possessions of Ralph Waldo Emerson and Henry David Thoreau, the two preeminent figures of Concord's Golden Age. Just around the corner from the museum is Emerson's house, in which the writer's study and other rooms look as they did when he lived there.

Pass through Monument Square, the town's center, and head out Monument Street toward the battlefield. Along the way you will pass the Old Manse, built by Emerson's grandfather and later lived in by Hawthorne. Take special notice of the faint inscriptions on one of the ancient windowpanes, made by Mrs. Hawthorne with her diamond ring.

Just beyond the manse is the North Bridge. Here stands the Minuteman statue commemorating the farmers who stood their ground against British troops in the opening engagement of the American Revolution. Here also are the graves of the British soldiers who fell that day. A brief walk up the hill from the bridge will bring you to the visitors' center, a mansion built by descendants of one of Concord's founders and later donated to the National Park Service. There is an informative slide show given every 15 minutes at the center, and the grounds are the site of frequent concerts and historical reenactments every summer. The acrid smell of black powder drifting over this field at Concord is the very stuff of history.

Leave Concord the way you came (Route 2A); turn right on a connecting road marked "Wayland" and left on Walden Street. Route 2A crosses Route 2 and becomes Highway 126. On the right lies Walden Pond, where Henry David Thoreau lived from 1845 to 1847 at an expense of about eight dollars a year. Thoreau's experiment in simple and natural living is described in the classic *Walden* (1854).

The site of Thoreau's cabin can be reached by walking to the right along a wooded path at the north end of the pond. Directly across the lake, in a lovely grove that is part of the 150-acre Walden Pond State Reservation, is a public picnic area. Another shore has a town bathing beach, and a large parking area is available.

Route 126 soon joins U.S. 20, where you should turn right and drive six miles to South Sudbury. A sign on the right points out the Wayside Inn. The inn, which has been providing food and lodging to travelers for almost 280 years, was originally known as Howe's Tavern and later Red Horse Tavern. It acquired its present name after Longfellow made it the scene of his *Tales of a Wayside Inn.* In 1923 it was bought by Henry Ford, who preserved it through a national trust. Burned in 1955, it has since been restored. The extensive gardens form a setting for the early nineteenth-century Old Redstone Hill School.

To return to Boston, turn around on U.S. 20 and head east. This road joins Commonwealth Avenue, which leads past the campus of Boston University and into Kenmore Square, after which it enters the Back Bay section of Boston.

Lowell

Everyone knows that the American Revolution started in Massachusetts. Until recently, however, little attention was paid to the fact that this state, in particular the Merrimack Valley, was the nurturing ground of another great change in our national life: the Industrial Revolution, which transformed a nation of farmers, merchants, and small tradesmen into the manufacturing colossus of the world. The story of America's industrialization is vividly recalled in the quintessential mill town of Lowell, site of both state and national historic parks dedicated to the memory of the days when the power loom was king along the Merrimack.

Approach Lowell from Boston either by Route 3 or by the less direct but probably quickest route of I–93 north, I–95 (Route 128) south, and 3 north. When you arrive, head for the National Park visitor center in the downtown Market Mills Complex for a thorough orientation and informative films. You can follow a walking itinerary along streets leading to the vast, largely restored mills where the modern American factory system was born, beginning in the 1820s; there are also barge rides along Lowell's historic canals and a trolley service, complete with replicas of turn-of-the-century cars.

Part of the fascination of Lowell is its amazing ethnic diversity, a legacy of the days when immigrants from throughout North America and Europe came here to work in the textile mills. (A major influx today is from Cambodia, and it was a Chinese immigrant, Dr. An Wang, who made Lowell into a center of computer manufacturing.) One of the major ethnic groups to migrate to Lowell in the heyday of the mills was the French-Canadians. The most famous son of French-Canadian Lowell was the poet and novelist Jack Kerouac, born here in 1922. Kerouac's memory is honored in the new Eastern Canal Plaza, where an array of plaques bear quotes from his "Lowell novels" and from *On The Road.*

Worcester

Worcester (pronounced "Wooster"), roughly 50 miles west of Boston via the Massachusetts Pike, is a major educational, industrial, and retail center with a history of uncommon achievements. Long ago, Isaiah Thomas worked here, printing chapbooks and starting, in 1770, a long-lived patriotic newspaper, *The Massachusetts Spy.* Destined to become the country's leading printer and the founder of the American Antiquarian Society (where his press can be viewed today), he gave the first reading of the Declaration of Independence in New England on July 4, 1776, in Worcester.

Worcester has been the birthplace of a number of ingenious inventions, ranging from the first calliope to the first liquid fuel rocket. It was also the site of the first women's suffrage national convention. Notable figures associated with Worcester include General Artemus Ward, first commander-in-chief of the American forces in the Revolution; Clara Barton;

Elias Howe; Eli Whitney; the horticulturist Luther Burbank; the baseball player and manager Connie Mack; and the humorist Robert Benchley.

Worcester's attractions range from water sports at nearby Lake Quinsigamond to the fascinating exhibits of the Worcester Science Museum to the Higgins Armory Museum displays of arms, armor, and art from the Middle Ages and Renaissance. The Worcester Art Museum houses one of the finest collections outside a major metropolitan area, and the American Antiquarian Society has amassed a priceless documentary record of American history and biography. Try to attend a concert at historic, restored Mechanics' Hall. Worcester's Centrum, at Foster and Commercial streets, is a new and successful civic center that programs top entertainers from around the country, sporting events, exhibitions, and conventions.

Old Sturbridge Village

New England has many villages that have been reconstructed to demonstrate the mode of life in the early days of the nation. Old Sturbridge Village, less than 20 miles southwest of Worcester, is among the most popular. A visit here—at any season—makes an interesting and pleasant side trip from Boston, about an hour away. (Write to the Tri-Community Chamber of Commerce, Southbridge MA 01550, for details about winter weekends and other attractions at Old Sturbridge.) It's just off the Massachusetts Turnpike (exit 9), an easy ride from Boston; from the south, take I–86 north from Hartford, Connecticut.

Visitors to Old Sturbridge meet history face to face. They can see a historic newspaper pulled from a 200-year-old printing press, a horseshoe shaped under a smith's hammer, or a traditional meeting house. Horses draw a carryall for the visitors to ride. An oxcart plies the village lanes and a flock of photogenic geese guard the millpond. You can sit in the shade of a maple tree on the village green and listen to a strolling minstrel sing his story-songs. In the village are found the homes, shops, general store, schoolhouse, tavern, and pillory of a typical New England village of the early 1800s. Craftsmen in period costumes re-create the life of the times, demonstrating spinning, weaving, printing, the making of pottery, and the skills of pewtersmith and tinsmith, as well as the domestic arts of fireplace cooking, herb gardening, and candle dipping. The farm work and cottage industries re-created at the village depend upon the same sources of energy tapped by early New Englanders—wood, water, and the muscle power of people and oxen. A visit to Old Sturbridge Village is an object lesson in the use of many "renewable" energy options that are being rediscovered today.

Many of the original buildings—there are nearly 40 in the village—were brought to Old Sturbridge from different parts of New England. Meals and lodging and a large parking lot are available. No cars are allowed within the village, but walking distances between the buildings are not great.

PRACTICAL INFORMATION FOR
EAST CENTRAL MASSACHUSETTS

HOW TO GET THERE AND AROUND. By plane: The nearest major airport to Worcester, Lowell, Sturbridge, and other points described in this section is Logan International. (See *Practical Information for Boston.*) Worcester Municipal Airport, Airport Dr. off Rte. 122, Worcester, is served by Eastern Express (flights to La Guardia, 508–756–1523 or 800–535–6660), Continental (flights to Newark), and Piedmont (flights to Baltimore with connections for points south; 508–795–7300).

By train: Amtrak's Boston-Chicago train, the *Lake Shore Limited,* stops at Worcester daily on both its eastbound and westbound runs. For information, call 800–USA–RAIL. Concord and Lowell may be reached from North Station, Boston, via Massachusetts Bay Transportation Authority (MBTA) trains operated by Amtrak (617–227–5070).

By bus: Service between Boston and Worcester is provided by Peter Pan Bus Lines (Boston terminal at ex-Trailways station, Atlantic Ave., 617–426–7838). MBTA bus service connects Boston with Lexington by way of Cambridge and Arlington.

By car: The main arteries in this part of the state are the Massachusetts Turnpike, running east–west through Worcester; I–190, a north–south route between the Connecticut border and Leominster, crossing the Massachusetts Pike at Worcester; and I–495, which circles the outer suburbs of Boston in a high arc between the North and South shores. Lowell lies at the intersection of rtes. 495 and 3. To reach Lexington and Concord from Boston, the most direct route is Rte. 2, which continues past Concord to cross I–495 and meets I–190 at Leominster.

HOTELS AND MOTELS. Lodgings in this part of Massachusetts are geared either to the transient trade, along the major highways, or to visitors to top attractions such as the Concord battlefield or Old Sturbridge Village. In the latter case, expect rates to increase during the peak summer season. The following price ranges are based on double occupancy: *Deluxe,* over $95; *Expensive,* $70–$95; *Moderate,* $45–$70; *Inexpensive,* under $45.

Concord

Colonial Inn, 48 Monument Sq., 01742 (508–369–9200). *Expensive* Traditional colonial inn on village green. Main rooms date to 1716. Restaurant, bar.

Concordian, Rte. 2, Acton, 01720 (508–263–7765). *Moderate.* Pool. Pets.

Howard Johnson, Rtes. 2 and 2A, 01742 (508–369–6100). *Expensive.* Restaurant, bar, pool.

Lexington

Sheraton-Lexington Motor Inn, Rte. 2A, 02173 (617–862–8700). *Deluxe.* Attractive rooms. Pool. Pets. Restaurant, bar.

Battle Green Motor Inn, 1720 Massachusetts Ave., 02173 (617–862–6100). *Moderate* Restaurant. Right in town near common.

Days Inn, 440 Bedford St., 02173 (617–861–0850). *Expensive.* Pool. Near restaurant.

Lowell

Lowell Hilton, 50 Warren St., 01852 (508–452–1200). *Deluxe.* Brand-new hotel in heart of historic district. Health club, indoor lap pool; two restaurants; airport limo; car rental.

Sturbridge

Sheraton Sturbridge Inn, Rte. 20, 01566 (508–347–7393). *Deluxe.* Pool. Restaurant, bar, entertainment. Health club, cross-country skiing. Near Old Sturbridge.

American Motor Lodge/Best Western, At jct. Rtes. 20, I–84, and I–86; Tpke. Exit 9, 01566 (508–347–9121). *Expensive.* Pool. Pets. Restaurant, bar. Sauna.

Days Inn/Carriage House, At jct. Rtes. 20 and 131, 01566 (508–347–9311). *Moderate.* Pool. Restaurant, bar nearby.

Publick House, Rte. 131, 2 mi. south of Tpke. Exit 9, 01566 (508–347–3313). *Expensive.* Charming late 18th-century inn. Restaurant, bar, entertainment.

Sturbridge Coach Motor Lodge, Rte. 20, 01566 (508–347–7327). *Moderate.* Pool. Near Old Sturbridge.

Quality Inn Colonial, Rte. 20, 01566 (508–347–3306). *Moderate.* Pool, play area, tennis. Restaurant adjacent. Cable TV.

Worcester

Worcester Marriott, 10 Lincoln Sq., 01608 (508–791–1600). *Deluxe.* Heated indoor-outdoor pool. Restaurant, lounge, entertainment. Weekend package plans.

Best Western Centrum Inn, 110 Summer St., 01608 (508–757–0400). *Moderate.* Downtown location. Suites and efficiencies available. Weekly and monthly rates. Restaurant adjacent.

Howard Johnson, 800 Southbridge St., 01610 (508–791–5501). *Moderate.* Pets. Restaurant, bar.

Pleasant View Motor Lodge. Rte. 146, Tpke. exits 10 and 11, 01527 (508–865–5222). *Inexpensive.* Pub-style restaurant.

INNS, GUEST HOUSES, BED AND BREAKFASTS. Although not exactly in the heart of the state's inn territory, east central Massachusetts does have a few pleasant small hostelries, with prices generally ranging from *moderate* to *expensive,* according to the hotel rate classifications given above. For a list of statewide bed-and-breakfast accommodations, write the Massachusetts Department of Commerce, Division of Tourism, 100 Cambridge St., Boston 02202. There is a *youth hostel* in Littleton, not far from Concord; for information, write Greater Boston Council, American Youth Hostels, 1020 Commonwealth Ave., Boston 02215 (617–731–5430).

The following is a sampling of the area's inns:

Concord

Hawthorne Inn, 462 Lexington Rd., 01742 (508–369–5610). A charming 19th-century home within a mile of Concord center. Antique-filled rooms, breakfast with fresh-baked breads and muffins.

Sturbridge

Colonel Ebenezer Crafts Inn, Fiske Hill, 01566 (508–347–3313). A small, cozy inn near Old Sturbridge Village. Meals served at the Publick House, of which the inn is a part (Continental breakfast at the inn). Swimming pool.

Sudbury

Wayside Inn, Wayside Inn Rd., off Rte. 20, South Sudbury, 01776 (508–443–8846). America's oldest continuously operating inn, made famous by Longfellow. Antiques everywhere; good restaurant.

Ware

Wildwood Inn, 121 Church St., 01082 (413–967–7798). A Victorian country inn, off Rte. 9, west of Worcester and not far from the Quabbin Reservoir. Delicious breakfasts keep guests coming back.

RESTAURANTS. Boston's cosmopolitan style of dining is spreading farther and farther west, although solid Yankee fare is still the order of the day in these parts. The cost of an à la carte dinner, without drinks and tip, is the basis of our price classifications: *Expensive,* $22 and up; *Moderate,* $12–$22; *Inexpensive,* under $12.

Acton

Chez Claude, 5 Strawberry Hill Rd. (508–263–3325). *Moderate.* Small, pleasant restaurant serving French cuisine.
Folsom's, 77 Great Rd. (508–263–3162). *Moderate.* Specializes in fresh seafood; fish market on premises.

Concord

Colonial Inn, 48 Monument Sq. (508–369–9200). *Expensive.* Traditional New England fare, taproom, antiques.
Different Drummer, 86 Thoreau St. (508–369–8700). *Moderate.* Fresh fish, low-cholesterol menu. Sun. brunch.

Lowell

The Himalaya, 45 Middle St. (508–937–9355). *Moderate.* A fine Indian restaurant with an extensive menu—lamb, chicken, and vegetable curries; Indian breads; chutneys; and tasty mango and yogurt drinks.
A.G. Pollard and Sons, Middle St. (508–459–4632). *Moderate.* Steaks, seafood, burgers, specials. Good soup and salad bar.

Sturbridge

Publick House, Rte. 131 (508–347–3313). *Moderate.* Colonial inn specializing in delicious lobster pie, baked shrimp. Bar. Bake shop on premises.
The Whistling Swan, 502 Main St. (508–347–2321). *Expensive.* Chef-owned, featuring American and Continental cuisine. Entertainment nightly. Closed Mon.
Rom's, Rte. 131 (508–347–3349). *Inexpensive.* A popular Italian spot. Smorgasboard served Wed. eve.

Worcester

Garden Court, Sheraton Lincoln Inn, 500 Lincoln St. (508–852–4000). *Moderate.* Lots of greenery, and not just in your salad. Prime rib, seafood, chateaubriand. Dancing in lounge Tues.–Sat.
Legal Seafoods, 1 Exchange Pl. (508–792–1600). *Moderate.* Boston's popular seafood spot moves west; this new branch keeps up the standards of fresh fish and shellfish in an astonishing variety.

TOURIST INFORMATION. Two major sources of information for visitors to east central Massachusetts are the headquarters of the Lowell

National Historical Park, 169 Merrimack St., Lowell 01852 (508–459–1000) and the Worcester County Convention and Visitors Bureau, 33 Waldo St., Worcester 01608 (508–753–2920). For information on sites and activities related to the Minuteman National Historical Park, contact the park at Box 160, Concord 01742 (508–369–6993 or 617–484–6156).

TOURS. Yankee Holidays, 20 Spring St., Saugus 01906 (617–231–2884) offers a four-day tour that includes Lexington and Concord as part of its itinerary. **Gray Line,** 275 Tremont St., Boston 02116 (617–426–8805) offers a three-hour tour of Lexington and Concord, leaving from Boston.

Special-Interest Tours. Lowell is the focus of some of the most interesting tours in Massachusetts. The main visitor center at **Lowell National Historical Park,** Market and Dutton Sts. downtown (508–459–1000) is the place to go for information on guided and self-guided tours of the city's restored mill buildings and canal structures. Also ask about canal boat tours and circa-1900 trolley rides, operating in downtown Lowell during the summer months.

SEASONAL EVENTS. April: Patriot's Day, reenactments of Revolutionary battles at Lexington and Concord.
June: Muster Day (re-creation of colonial militia gathering), Old Sturbridge Village. Beginning of summer cultural program and ethnic festivals in Lowell.
July: Acton-Boxborough Jamboree, Acton; Lily Show, Horticultural Society, Worcester.

PARKS AND FORESTS. Great Meadows National Wildlife Refuge takes in the land surrounding the tranquil Concord River just north of Concord (access off Rte. 225). See Canada geese, many other birds; a canoe is recommended. **Walden Pond State Reservation,** Rte. 126, Concord, preserves the site where Thoreau lived and wrote; there's a swimming beach, and a trail around the pond. **Wachusett Mountain State Reservation,** off Rte. 140, near Princeton, offers hikers scenic views from 2,006-ft. Mt. Wachusett. **Willard Brook State Forest,** Rte. 119, north of Fitchburg, is a good spot for a roadside picnic or day hike.

SUMMER SPORTS. Some of the state's best **canoeing** may be enjoyed on the same waters Thoreau wrote about in his book *A Week on the Concord and Merrimack Rivers.* The Merrimack is a bit fast for many canoeists, and there are dams, but the Concord and its tributary, the Sudbury, are fine for leisurely exploring—especially through the Great Meadows National Wildlife Refuge. For information on water conditions and put-in spots, contact Lincoln Guide Service in Lincoln (617–259–9204).

For a game of **golf,** try the Trull Brook Golf Club, Tewksbury (just south of Lowell at Rtes. 495 and 93; 508–851–6731).

There is a public **swimming beach** at Walden Pond, Rte. 126, Concord.

Boating and water skiing are popular on a lake in Webster, off Rte. 12, south of Worcester, that has the longest name you'll find this side of Wales: Lake Chargoggagaugmanchaugagoggchaubunagungamaaugg. The name is abbreviated on signs; it's also often called Lake Webster.

WINTER SPORTS. For a day of **downhill skiing,** try the slopes at Wachusett Mt. Ski Area, Mountain Rd., Princeton (508–464–5101).

Nashoba Valley, Power Rd., Westford (508–692–3033) also has some good Alpine runs. **Cross-country** skiers can find fine trails at the Harvard-owned Estabrook woods off Monument Street in Concord, contiguous with the lands of the Great Meadows National Wildlife Refuge. Also try the trails at Wachusett Mountain State Reservation, Princeton, and Great Brook Farm State Park, North St., Carlisle.

FISHING. Licensed anglers may try their luck in any number of rivers and ponds in east central Massachusetts, but the largest and most promising spot of all is the huge man-made Quabbin Reservoir, bounded by Rtes. 202, 9, 122, and 32, north of Ware and south of Athol. For regulations governing Quabbin, contact the Massachusetts Department of Fisheries and Wildlife, 100 Cambridge St., Boston, 02202 (617–727–3151).

HUNTING. Officials at the Department of Fisheries and Wildlife (details above) have information on hunting opportunities throughout the state.

CAMPING. Several of the state forests and parks in this part of the state maintain campsites. For information on permits, contact the Massachusetts Environmental Management Department, 100 Cambridge St., Boston, 02202 (617–727–3180).

HISTORIC SITES, HOMES, AND MUSEUMS. This is an important historic area. Call ahead to check days, hours, and admission charges for historic museums and homes.

Arlington/Lexington

Jason Russell House, Corner of Massachusetts Ave. and Jason St., Arlington (617–648–4300). Apr.–Oct., Tues.–Sat. Bullet holes mark the site of a revolutionary skirmish.

Buckman Tavern, 1 Bedford St., Lexington (617–862–5598). Open daily mid-Apr.–Oct. Minutemen gathered here April 19, 1775.

Hancock Clark House, 36 Hancock St., Lexington (617–861–0928). Open daily mid-Apr.–Oct. This is where Paul Revere warned John Hancock of the approach of the British before the Battle of Lexington.

Monroe Tavern, 1332 Massachusetts Ave., Lexington (617–862–1703). Used by the British as a hospital during the Battle of Lexington. George Washington was entertained here in 1789. Open daily mid-Apr.–Oct.

Museum of Our National Heritage, 33 Marrett Rd., Lexington (617–861–6559). Galleries of exhibits chronicle U.S. history and social development. Library; films and concerts.

De Cordova Museum, Sandy Pond Rd. (617–259–8355). Contemporary art; emphasis on New England artists. Music, theater, dance outdoors in summer.

Concord

The **Minuteman National Historical Park,** Liberty St. (508–369–6993). Commemorates the first skirmish of the Revolution. The Visitor Center, Monument St., is open daily. Audio-visual program. The exhibit room at Lincoln is open year-round. Fisk Hill Information Station and picnic area is on Rte 2A.

Emerson House, 28 Cambridge Tpke., Concord Museum (508–

369–2236). This was R. W. Emerson's house in his later years; his books, notes, and furnishings are here. Open mid-Apr.–Oct., Thurs.–Sun.

Old Manse, Monument St., (508–443–3270). (Minuteman National Historical Park.) Open daily mid-Apr.–Columbus Day. 18th-century house where Nathaniel Hawthorne lived.

Concord Museum, 200 Lexington Rd. (508–369–9609). Period rooms, Emerson and Thoreau artifacts.

Walden Pond, Rte. 126 near Rte. 2. State reservation offers swimming, fishing, picnicking; walk to site of Thoreau's cabin.

Lowell

The **Lowell National Historical Park** (508–459–1000). Includes mill buildings, old canals and locks; offers architectural and ethnic heritage tours. Trains from Boston; shuttle to Visitors' Center at corner of Market and Dutton streets. Call for reservations.

Sturbridge

Old Sturbridge Village (508–347–3362). More than 40 restored buildings re-create an early 19th-century community on a 200-acre site. Costumed guides explain exhibits. It is one of the best period restorations in the country and should not be missed. Working artisans demonstrate how crafts such as blacksmithing and weaving were practiced in preindustrial America. Adults, $12; children 6–15, $5. Open year-round.

Worcester

Worcester Art Museum, 55 Salisbury St. (508–799–4406). Closed Mon.; free Sat. A.M.

Worcester Historical Museum, 30 Elm St. (508–753–8278). Includes Salisbury Mansion, restored house of the 1830s. Open Tues.–Sun.

New England Science Center, Harrington Way (508–791–9211). Hands-on museum covers astronomy, ecology, and animal and earth sciences; small zoo features polar bears; Omnisphere planetarium. Great for kids. Open Mon.–Sat. 10 A.M.–5 P.M., Sun. 12–5 P.M.

American Antiquarian Society, 185 Salisbury St. (508–755–5221). Isaiah Thomas printing press, colonial history. Mon.–Fri.

THE PIONEER VALLEY

Springfield

Roughly two hours from Boston via the Massachusetts Turnpike, the 350-year-old city of Springfield stands at the southern gateway to the Pioneer Valley. Like the string of smaller but no less historic settlements that range from here north to the Vermont border, Springfield was built on the banks of the longest river in New England, called the Quinnitukqut ("long tidal river") by the Indians, the Connecticut by the English. The broad, generally navigable Connecticut River was a major avenue of trade and transportation during the days of colonial settlement (as the Vermont villages named after downstream towns will attest) and later figured in the valley's industrial development. After years of abuse, the Connecticut is responding to antipollution treatment, and shad and salmon can again be found in its waters.

Springfield, New England's fourth largest city and home of the Springfield and Garand rifles, has long been commercially important. The cycle of boom, bust, and renewal, common to the state's industrial areas, is in a new phase today; diversified tool, machine, and appliance enterprises are thriving along with a revival in retail trade.

Springfield's attractions reflect the city's past accomplishments, a healthy present-day cultural appetite, and its location at the geographic heart of New England. Undoubtedly this helps make the Eastern States Exposition, called the Big E and held here every September, one of the most popular fairs in the country. The exposition is a showcase of New England's industrial and agricultural accomplishments and a longed-for destination for thousands of young people involved in livestock and home-making projects with 4-H and other youth groups.

Not many cities can boast of giving birth to a major sport, but it was in a Springfield gymnasium in 1891 that Dr. James Naismith first organized teams to attempt stuffing a lively, unpredictable ball through hoops mounted tantalizingly out of reach. The Naismith Memorial Basketball Hall of Fame, located in downtown Springfield just off I–291, commemorates this fact and the great players of the past. The museum at the Springfield Armory recalls more serious business, with a collection representing every firearm manufactured at the old installation from 1795 to modern times.

Important Springfield cultural institutions located in the city's Museum Quadrangle include the Museum of Fine Arts, Science Museum, Connecticut Valley Historical Museum, and George Walter Vincent Smith Art Museum, housing an impressive collection of oriental rugs, armor, and decorative arts.

Holyoke, South Hadley, Northampton

Five miles north of Springfield, on U.S. 5, is Holyoke. The fine college of Mount Holyoke is just four miles from this busy industrial city on Highway 116. The grounds and buildings of the college are spacious and attractive, and the Dwight Memorial Art Museum, open weekdays, is worth visiting. Just north of the small town of South Hadley (the college's actual location) is Dinosaur Land, an interesting display of the fossil tracks of prehistoric animals who left imprints in the sandstone cliffs and riverbanks between Holyoke and Northampton.

Head from South Hadley on Highway 47 to the junction of the mountain road, about three miles from the village. The road leads through the Pass of Thermopylae, a narrow, winding road that goes under Titan's Piazza, an unusual trap rock formation on Mt. Holyoke that local people deem one of the seven wonders of the world. From the summit of the mountain road, return to Highway 47 and continue to Hadley. Turn left to Northampton, site of Smith College (where there is a fine collection of contemporary paintings and prints) and the Massachusetts home of Calvin Coolidge, our thirtieth president. (The Coolidge Room at the Forbes Library on West Street houses a collection of Coolidge papers and memorabilia.) There are many interesting, antique-filled houses, such as the Cornet Joseph Parsons House (1658), Northampton's oldest.

A fair is held here in September, and during the last weekend in July the nation's largest single-breed horse show, the Eastern National Morgan Horse Show, takes place at the fairgrounds. There are also a variety of outdoor activities, including boating, swimming, golf, and snowmobiling. Three miles south, off U.S. 5, is Mt. Tom, a major ski center.

Amherst to Deerfield

From Northampton, turn east on Route 9 to visit Amherst, site of the lifelong home of Emily Dickinson, the University of Massachusetts, and Amherst College. Returning to U.S. 5 and continuing north, drive 12 miles to the village of Old Deerfield, a National Historic District with 30 buildings more than a century and a half old. The village's history goes back much further. Today, Deerfield is not so much a town as the ghost of a town, one of the most fascinating of its kind in America. Other New England communities have been important, but Deerfield stands as a classic statement of the tragic and creative moment when one civilization destroys and displaces another. Little of consequence has happened there for nearly 300 years since the grim time from 1672 to 1704 when it was the northwest frontier of New England. Although it formed part of Dedham in 1663, no Dedhamite settled there until 1669, when Samuel Hindsdell, a squatter, began cultivation of the fertile soil where the Pocumtuck Indians had grown their corn, tobacco and pumpkins. By 1672, however, Samson Frary and others had joined Hinsdell; soon the population reached 125. This, according to the Pocumtucks, was carrying encroachment too far, and one dark night three years later, they struck in what is called the Bloody Brook Massacre. They either killed or drove off to hamlets farther south every single white person. It was a foretaste of the coming 200 years of struggle between the intruders and those whose lands were relentlessly usurped from Plymouth to Puget Sound.

For seven years Deerfield's houses were empty. Slowly the settlers returned, and in 1686 Deerfield held its first town meeting. The Indians attacked again in 1704, putting to the torch more than half the town's buildings; capturing more than 100 men, women and children for slaves; and killing 50 others who tried to resist. With this great raid, Deerfield's active life ended. But its memory lingers. The Deerfield Historical Society has restored many of the original buildings. Memorial Hall contains, along with many relics of early days, the front door of one of the Deerfield homes that survived the raid of 1704. The door bears the mark of a tomahawk. The Frary House is well worth a visit, as is the Indian House, with its second- and third-story overhangs, characteristic of the earliest colonial architecture. Many other fascinating early homes are open for inspection along Old Deerfield Street. Continue north from Old Deerfield on U.S. 5 to Greenfield and the start of the Mohawk Trail, going west into lovely Berkshire County. Drive through Greenfield for a preview of the gracious western New England town life you will find as you cross the Hoosac into Williamstown on the New York–Vermont border. Follow Maple Street to the top of Rocky Mountain for good views of the Berkshires to the west and the farmlands to the east. On Leyden Road is one of the last covered bridges to be found in Massachusetts. Because of its proximity to I–91, Greenfield has become a summer and winter sports center for the Pioneer Valley area.

PRACTICAL INFORMATION FOR THE PIONEER VALLEY

HOW TO GET THERE AND AROUND. By plane: Although many visitors to Springfield and the Pioneer Valley use Boston's Logan International Airport as their point of entry and departure, the area is also served by Bradley International Airport in Windsor Locks, Connecticut (just off I–91), approximately 18 mi. south of Springfield. Bradley is served by several major airlines, including US Air, American, Eastern, and Piedmont. Bus service from the airport to downtown Springfield is provided by Peter Pan Bus Lines (413–781–3320). Major car rental firms are also represented at Bradley.

By train: Amtrak provides service to Springfield from New York City by way of New Haven and Hartford, Connecticut. Amtrak's *Montrealer,* originating in Washington, D.C., stops at Springfield and Northampton on its north- and southbound runs. The *Lake Shore Limited,* a Boston–Chicago train, also makes a Springfield stop twice daily (once from either direction). (For information on all Amtrak service, call 800–USA–RAIL.)

By bus: Service between Springfield and Boston is provided by Peter Pan Bus Lines (413–781–3320).

By car: The main artery of the Pioneer Valley follows the Connecticut River along a north–south route. This is I–91, connecting New Haven and Hartford, Connecticut, with Springfield, Northampton, Greenfield, and other valley points, and continuing to Brattleboro, Vermont, and points north. From Boston and eastern Massachusetts, the main access roads are the Massachusetts Tpke. (a toll road), Rte. 20, and Rte. 2. The Pike connects with I–91 at Springfield; Rte. 2 crosses I–91 near Greenfield, near the Vermont border. Both roads continue west into the Berkshires before reaching the New York State border. Rte. 5 also parallels the Connecticut River, threading through most of the towns along the way.

HOTELS AND MOTELS. The major commercial center of Springfield and the college towns of the Pioneer Valley are well served by comfortable hostelries. The following price ranges are based upon double occupancy: *Deluxe,* over $95; *Expensive,* $70–$95; *Moderate,* $45–$70; *Inexpensive,* under $45.

Amherst

Lord Jeffrey Inn, 30 Boltwood Ave., 01002 (413–253–2576). *Deluxe.* Centrally located hotel, with colonial furnishings, charming gardens. Dining room, bar.

Howard Johnson, Rtes. 9 and 116, 01035 (413–586–0114). *Expensive.* Pool. Restaurant, bar.

University Motor Lodge, 345 N. Pleasant St., 01002 (413–256–8111). *Moderate.* Free in-room coffee. Golf nearby. Convenient to colleges. Family plan.

Deerfield

Deerfield Inn, Main St., 01342 (413–774–5587). *Deluxe.* Lovely old inn has undergone a complete restoration. Restaurant, bar.

Rainbow, 5 mi. south on Rtes. 5 and 10; I–91, exits 22 or 23, 01373 (413–665–8821). *Moderate.* Restaurant.

Hilltop, Rte. 2, Shelburne Falls 01320 (413–625–2587). *Inexpensive.* Some rooms with kitchens; also cottages.

Oxbow, Rte. 2, Charlemont 01339 (413–625–6011). *Inexpensive.* Restaurant, pub, game room. Theater, fishing, hunting, and ski packages available.

Greenfield

Candle Light, 208 Mohawk Trail, 01301 (413–772–0101). *Expensive.* At I–91, Exit 26. Pool; golf nearby.

Howard Johnson, 125 Mohawk Trail, 01301 (413–774–2211). *Moderate.* At I–91, Exit 26. Pool. Restaurant, bar.

Holyoke

Holiday Inn, 245 Whiting Farms Rd., 01040 (413–534–3311). *Expensive.* Restaurant, lounge. Indoor pool.

Northampton

Hotel Northampton, 36 King St. at jct. Rtes. 5 and 9, I–91, Exit 18, 01060 (413–584–3100). *Expensive.* Good restaurant, wine bar. Country shop in rear.
Northampton Hilton Inn, Rte. 5 at jct. I–91, Exit 18, 01060 (413–586–1211). *Expensive.* Pool, sauna, tennis. Restaurant, bar, dancing, entertainment.
Days Inn, Conz and Pleasant Sts., 01060 (413–586–1500). *Moderate.* Pool. Near restaurant.

Northfield

Bernardston Inn, Church & Brattleboro Sts., Bernardston 01337 (413–648–9282). *Moderate.* Comfortable. Cable TV. Restaurant. Near Greenfield and Rte. 91.

Springfield

Holiday Inn, 711 Dwight St. 01104 (413–781–0900). *Expensive.* Pool. Restaurant, bar, entertainment.
Sheraton West, 1080 Riverdale Rd., W. Springfield 01089 (413–781–8750). *Expensive.* Pool. Restaurant, lounge. Easy access to I–91.
Best Western Black Horse, 500 Riverdale St., W. Springfield 01089 (413–733–2161). *Moderate.* Pool. Picnic area. Near fairgrounds.
Howard Johnson, 1150 Riverdale St., W. Springfield 01089 (413–739–7261). *Moderate.* Restaurant, bar, pool. Convenient to exposition grounds.
Marriott, 1500 Main St. 01104 (413–781–7111). *Moderate.* Pool, saunas. Restaurant, bar, entertainment. Airport limo. Easy access to I–91, local attractions.
Ramada Inn, 357 Burnett Rd., Chicopee, just off I–291, 01020 (413–592–9101). *Moderate.* Pool, play area. Restaurant, bar, dancing, entertainment. Airport car available.
Arrowhead, 1573 Riverdale St., W. Springfield 01089 (413–788–9607). *Moderate.* Pool, play area. Near restaurant.
Best Western Chicopee Motor Lodge, 463 Memorial Dr., Chicopee 01020 (413–592–6171). *Moderate.* Pool. Restaurant adjacent. Near Massachusetts Tpke.
Capri, 1537 Riverdale St., W. Springfield 01089 (413–734–2176). *Inexpensive.* Pool. Near restaurant.
Lantern Lodge, 560 Riverdale St., W. Springfield 01089 (413–733–6678). *Inexpensive.* Pool. Near restaurant.
Seven Gables, 1356 Boston Rd. 01119 (413–783–2111). *Moderate.* Pool. Pets. Near restaurant. Bar. Swimming, fishing on lake.
Susse Chalet, Johnny Cake Hollow Rd., Chicopee 01020 (413–592–5141). *Inexpensive.* At Massachusetts Tpke. and I–291. Pool.

INNS, GUEST HOUSES, BED AND BREAKFASTS. The Pioneer Valley's smaller and more intimate hostelries offer a pleasant alternative to less personal accommodations. For bed-and-breakfast information, contact the Massachusetts Department of Commerce, Division of Tourism, 100 Cambridge St., Boston 02202. There are a number of youth hostels—in Springfield, Northfield, and Amherst. For details, write or call the Greater Boston Council, American Youth Hostels, 1020B Commonwealth Ave., Brookline 02146 (617–731–5430).

The following is a selection of Pioneer Valley inns:

Deerfield

Deerfield Inn, Main St., 01342 (413–774–5587). Plush accommodations near Deerfield Academy. Antiques, canopied beds, private baths—and a fine restaurant.

Holyoke

Yankee Pedlar Inn, 1866 Northampton St., 01040 (413–532–9494). A collection of Victorian structures with decor to match. The central building features a lounge (with entertainment), oyster bar, and fine dining room.

Northfield

Northfield Country House, School St., 01360 (413–498–2692). A big, handsome turn-of-the-century home with seven guest rooms, some with working fireplaces. Full breakfast, fresh baking.

RESTAURANTS. The flavors of the Pioneer Valley are traditional New England, along with the more sophisticated touches that go along with Springfield's increased prosperity and the influx of new ideas in the college towns. The cost of an à la carte dinner, without drinks and tip, is the basis of our price classifications: *Expensive,* $22 and up; *Moderate,* $12–$22; *Inexpensive,* under $12.

Amherst

Lord Jeffrey, On the common (413–253–2576). *Expensive.* Colonial atmosphere. Baked stuffed shrimp, variety of New England dishes.

Deerfield

Old Deerfield Gables Restaurant, Rtes. 5 and 10 (413–665–4643). *Inexpensive.* Steaks, seafood. Bar. Dancing Fri. and Sat.

Northampton

Beardsley's, 140 Main St. (413–586–2699). *Moderate.* Splendid service in an intimate French cafe setting. Steak, duckling, wonderful desserts. A fine spot for Sun. brunch.

Wiggins Tavern, 36 King St. (413–586–5000). *Moderate.* New England atmosphere prevails in century-old landmark. Candlelight dinner. Varied menu.

Sze's, 50 Main St. (413–586–5708). *Inexpensive.* Mandarin and Szechuan menu; also takeout. Sun. brunch buffet, 11:30 A.M.–3 P.M.

Springfield

The Student Prince and Fort, 8 Fort St. (413–734–7475). *Moderate.* Traditional American and German food; Oktoberfest and May Wine festivals. Seasonal menus; game festival in Feb.

TOURIST INFORMATION. The Pioneer Valley area has an umbrella organization for providing regional tourist information. It's the Greater Springfield Convention and Visitors Bureau, 56 Dwight St., Springfield, MA 01103 (413–787–1548).

TOURS. Peter Pan Bus Lines, 1776 Main St., Springfield 01103 (413–781–3320) offers one-day tours that leave from Springfield throughout the year and bus trips to the Eastern States Exposition, W. Springfield, departing from Boston during the "Big E" in Sept.

SEASONAL EVENTS. February: Winter Carnival, Northampton.
May: Antique Fair, Brimfield; Porter Memorial Horse Draw, Westfield.
June: Yankee Appaloosa Show, Coliseum, W. Springfield.
July: New England Morgan Horse Show, Northampton; Laurel Week, Westfield; Antique Fair, Brimfield.
August: Bridge of Flowers Art Festival, Shelburne Falls.
September: Eastern States Exposition, Springfield; Tri-County Fair, Northampton; Franklin County Fair, Greenfield; Foliage Festival, Greenfield; Antique Fair, Brimfield.

FORESTS AND PARKS. One of Massachusetts most beautiful urban parks is Springfield's **Forest Park,** near the city's southern border. Rent paddleboats on Porter Lake; visit the children's zoo. A string of state facilities extends throughout the Pioneer Valley. Outstanding spots are **Erving State Forest,** Erving, off Rte. 2; **Brimfield State Forest,** Rte. 20, between Springfield and Worcester, with hiking trails and a pond for swimming; and **Mt. Tom State Reservation,** just off Rte. 5 in Holyoke.

SUMMER SPORTS. In addition to **swimming** facilities at Brimfield and Erving State Forests (see *Forests and Parks*), nonresident swimmers paying a nominal fee can enjoy the 1,400-ft., municipally owned swimming pool in Greenfield.

Municipal facilities for **tennis** enthusiasts are scattered throughout the Pioneer Valley, most notably at Springfield's Forest Park, Greenfield's Veterans' Memorial Field, and Northampton's Look Memorial Park.

Public **golf** courses include the Agawam Country Club, Agawam (413–786–2194); Veterans Golf Club, Springfield (413–787–6449); Mohawk Meadows Golf Club, Deerfield (413–773–9047); and East Mountain Country Club, Westfield (413–568–1539).

WINTER SPORTS. The area's most popular **downhill ski** area is Mt. Tom, a privately managed facility about 2 mi. from the Mt. Tom State Reservation, Holyoke (413–527–4805). **Cross-country ski** trails are maintained at Erving State Forest, Erving; Warwick State Forest, Northfield; and Wendell State Forest, Wendell. Also, don't overlook larger urban parks and golf courses.

FISHING. Although numerous lakes and ponds throughout the Pioneer Valley area are stocked with trout by the state, the most interesting fishing possibilities hereabouts may lie in the Connecticut River, which has been the object of remarkably successful cleanup efforts in recent years. In addition to more common species, the Connecticut harbors shad, in season, and even an occasional salmon. Be sure to check Massachusetts fishing regulations, abstracts of which are available at town halls and sporting goods stores when you buy your license.

HUNTING. Although the southern Pioneer Valley is urbanized, at least near the Connecticut River, and all portions of the area have been subject to increasing suburban development, deer and upland game hunting are still popular, especially up near the Vermont border. Pheasant, grouse, and rabbit lead the upland list; for season dates and bag limits, pick up a copy of the fish and game law abstracts when you buy your hunting license.

CAMPING. State facilities with campsites in the Pioneer Valley area include Erving State Forest, Erving; Mohawk Trail State Forest, Charlemont; the farther western (almost in the Berkshires) Granville State Forest, Granville; and D.A.R. State Forest, Goshen. For information on permits and fees, contact the Massachusetts Environmental Management Department, 100 Cambridge St., Boston 02202 (617-727-3180).

HISTORIC SITES AND HOUSES. There are several interesting historic sites and restored homes in the Pioneer Valley. Call ahead to check days, hours, and admission charges.

Amherst

Emily Dickinson Homestead, 280 Main St. (413-542-8161). Birthplace and lifelong residence of the poet. Owned by Amherst College, which offers afternoon guided tours, Mar.–early Dec., by appointment ($3).

Deerfield

Site of the great Indian massacres of 1675, 1704. Twelve colonial homes are open, including **Frary House,** dating back to 1689, museums, and the old graveyard. For information, call 413-774-5581.
   Memorial Hall, Memorial St. (413-774-7476). Furniture and paintings from the 18th century. Open daily May–Oct.
   Indian House, Main St. (413-772-0845). Open May 1–Nov. 1. Closed Tues. Reproductions of building that survived the famous 1704 Indian raid.
   Historic Deerfield, Old Deerfield (413-774-5581). Restored 18th- and 19th-century houses with period furnishings.

Northampton

Calvin Coolidge House, 21 Massasoit St., Northampton. Not open to public.
   Forbes Library, 20 West St. (413-584-8399). Closed July 4, Christmas, Thanksgiving. Romanesque building houses Coolidge Room.
   Parsons House, 58 Bridge St., Northampton (413-584-6011). Open Wed., Sat., Sun. all year, 2–4:30 P.M. Built in 1712, one of the oldest houses in the city.

Shelburne Falls

Bridge of Flowers, 51 Bridge St. (413–625–9502). Open daily; floodlit until 10:30 P.M. in summer.

MUSEUMS. There are several fine museums in this area. Call ahead for days, hours, and fees. In addition to the listings below, some of the area colleges have fine collections.

Holyoke

Holyoke Museum, 335 Maple St. (413–534–2214). A small, regionally oriented art museum; changing cycle of exhibits spotlights local artists, past and present.
Wistariahurst Museum, 238 Cabot St. (413–534–2216). Period furniture; decorative arts; architectural detailing.

Springfield

George Walter Vincent Smith Museum, Museum Quadrangle (413–733–4214). Oriental rugs and decorative arts, 19th-century American art, period rooms. Closed Mon.
Springfield Science Museum, Museum Quadrangle (413–733–1194). Freshwater acquarium, ethnology, mounted animals, planetarium. Closed Mon.
Museum of Fine Arts, Museum Quadrangle (413–732–6092). European, Asian, American art. Closed Mon.
Springfield Armory Museum, 1 Armory Sq. (413–734–6477). Features examples of every weapon made at famous armory. Open daily; closed major holidays.
Connecticut Valley Historical Museum, 194 State St. (413–732–3080). Decorative arts; local business history and genealogical history. Open Mon.–Sun. afternoons; closed major holidays.
Indian Motorcycle Museum, 33 Hendee St. (413–737–2624). Collection of Indian motorcycles, in the city where they were built. Open daily.
Naismith Memorial Basketball Hall of Fame, W. Columbus Ave. (413–781–6500). Honors pro and amateur players throughout sport's history—it was invented in Springfield.

West Springfield

Storrowton Village, 1305 Memorial Ave. (413–787–0136). Authentic 200-year-old buildings in village setting.

MUSIC, DANCE, AND STAGE. StageWest, 1 Columbus Center, Springfield (413–781–2340), offer popular, classical, and newer dramatic and musical productions. And don't overlook the performing arts schedules offered by the region's many colleges, including the University of Massachusetts, Amherst; Mount Holyoke College, South Hadley; Amherst College, Amherst; Smith College, Northampton; and Holyoke Community College, Holyoke.

ART GALLERIES. Celebrations: An Artisans' Collective, Old School Commons, Northampton, exhibits the work of 40 member artisans; the **Springfield Art League,** composed of local painters, frequently exhibits at the Borgia Gallery at Elms College, 291 Springfield St., Chicopee (413–594–2761); the **Zone Center for the Arts,** 395 Dwight St., Springfield (413–732–1995) sponsors eclectic exhibits of modern art and photography. Most of the area's colleges have galleries exhibiting student work and permanent collections.

NIGHTLIFE. The Pioneer Valley consists of one college town after another, so the club scene is lively indeed. Some popular spots: **Iron Horse,** 20 Center St., Northampton (413–584–0610) books folk, blues, and jazz acts; **Jazzberries,** 406 Dwight St., Springfield (413–732–4606) specializes in jazz and comedy; **Katina's,** Route 9, Hadley (413–586–4463) is a rock and blues club; **Sheehan's Cafe,** 24 Pleasant St., Northampton (413–586–4258) is a hot rock 'n' roll spot; **Theodore's,** 201 Worthington St., Springfield (413–739–7637) features local rock bands, cover groups, and jazz. At most clubs, cover charges vary according to who's playing.

THE BERKSHIRES

The Berkshires can be approached from several directions: from Connecticut on U.S. 7 and Massachusetts 8; along feeder roads off New York's beautiful Taconic Parkway, through Columbia and Rensselaer counties; or from Vermont on Routes 7 and 8 and other smaller roads. But the most spectacular approach is via the Mohawk Trail, running alongside the Deerfield River through upland towns, farms, woods, and gorges that open up to beautiful mountain views.

Along the Mohawk Trail

The 67 miles of Route 2 between Greenfield and the New York boundary have been officially recognized by the Massachusetts legislature as the Mohawk Trail. A key link between the great Hudson and Connecticut River transport systems of New York and Massachusetts, the trail has been significant since it was first an Indian path stretching from New York's Finger Lakes to the villages of western and central Massachusetts. This was the route taken by colonial forces marching west to defend British outposts on the New York frontier during the French and Indian Wars. One of the recruits was a young silversmith named Paul Revere, traveling for the first time from his native Boston. Later, as settlers streamed west in their covered wagons, the Mohawk Trail became the prime road over the mountains and the lifeline for garrisons along the Hudson. In 1786, the trail became America's first toll-free road. Before then, most roads were privately owned and a toll was charged. During the nineteenth century the trail became a symbol of America's westward expansion and was the route followed by the stagecoaches. In 1913, it was engineered for auto travel, with many off-road parking areas for scenic vistas and historical markers.

The 4¾-mile Hoosac Railroad Tunnel, one of the engineering marvels of its time, crosses the trail north of the town of Florida. Completed in 1875—after 25 years, at a cost of 196 lives and 21.2 million dollars—the tunnel cuts the distance and the grades between Troy and Boston.

Leave Greenfield on Route 2 west and take alternate Route 2A into Shelburne Falls, an inadvertently but perfectly preserved "Main Street" town of the early twentieth century. Watch for the signs directing you to

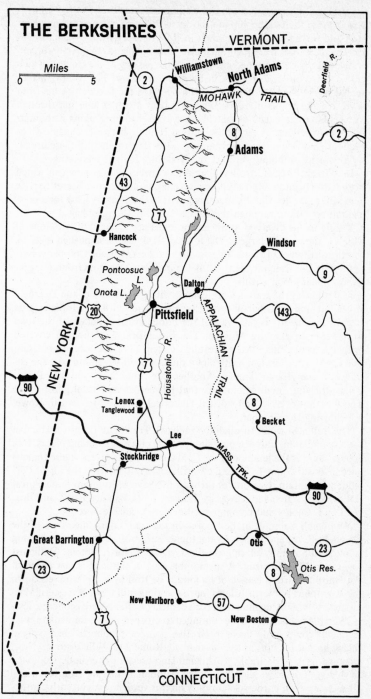

THE BERKSHIRES

VERMONT

Miles

0 ⸻ 5

Williamstown

North Adams

2

MOHAWK TRAIL

Deerfield R.

2

8

Adams

43

7

Hancock

Windsor

9

Pontoosuc L.

Onota L.

Dalton

143

20

Pittsfield

APPALACHIAN TRAIL

Housatonic R.

7

NEW YORK

90

8

Lenox

Tanglewood

Becket

Lee

MASS. TPK.

Stockbridge

90

Great Barrington

Otis

23

23

Otis Res.

8

New Marlboro

57

7

New Boston

CONNECTICUT

the Bridge of Flowers. Planted and maintained since 1929 by the Women's Association, the unique 400-foot bridge is a riot of color in spring, summer, and early fall. Originally built in 1908 to carry trolley tracks across the Deerfield River between Shelburne and Buckland, the five-arch concrete bridge was abandoned in 1927 with the passing of the trolleys, which hold a faded but special place in Berkshire memory: The trolley was invented by Stephen Dudley Field, who operated the first car on his front lawn in Stockbridge in 1880. Ten years later a trolley line ran through Pittsfield to Pontoosuc Lake. Soon other towns had lines, along with interurban connections. A parlor car started running between Canaan, Connecticut, and Bennington, Vermont, in 1903. The thought of these urban-style vehicles rumbling through the Berkshire Hills is intriguing.

In 1902, a Pittsfield trolley figured in a spectacular accident in which President Theodore Roosevelt was severely injured and a Secret Service man killed; Trolley Car 29, speeding guests to the Country Club for a presidential reception, rammed the landau carrying the president.

Visible in the riverbed at Shelburne Falls are glacial potholes, one of which is the world's largest. The town of Shelburne, established in 1756, was the birthplace of Linus Yale, founder of the Yale Lock Company. Farther along the trail, on the right, is the old Oak Meeting Ground, a pre-Revolutionary War shrine.

Midpoint on the trail is Charlemont, with good views of the Deerfield River and many unusual off-trail drives north and south. The Indian statue *Hail to the Sunrise* is just west of the bridge at the junction of the road to Monroe Bridge and Monroe. The Bissel Bridge, a modern covered bridge, is located here. An interesting side trip along the trail is a pleasant ride via Monroe Bridge, south along the Deerfield River and past the entrance to the Hoosac Tunnel. Another side route takes you into Rowe, a once-thriving small community that has become a virtual ghost town. There is, however, a well-stocked Historical Society Museum in Rowe, open during the summer.

The trail now winds through the Mohawk Trail State Forest. Attractive scenery and numerous camping sites provide pleasant stopping places. Boy Scouts camp at the junction of the Cold and Deerfield rivers where Indians once held war councils. Several off-trail drives radiate from the top of Forbidden Mountain. One circles through the Savoy Mountain State Forest (follow local signs) and travels by Tannery Falls, Balance Rock, and Beaver Pond. Cabins and camping facilities are available here.

Whitcomb Summit, highest point on the trail, offers fine views of the Deerfield River and overlooks the tunnel entrance. A short drive beyond is Western Summit, offering excellent views of North Adams, Williamstown, and Mt. Greylock. A memorable part of the trail is just ahead at the Hairpin Turn, a classic of its kind. The trail from here travels down the mountains to North Adams, once a leading mill town of western Massachusetts, now struggling to make a comeback after severe economic losses. North Adams might have continued to prosper, but its immediate environment could only have been the poorer if suburbs had spread throughout these hills as they have along Route 2 to Williamstown. Now, when patterns of desirable growth and land use are better understood, the town's revitalization should proceed without detracting from the rural landscape which borders so abruptly on this vestige of nineteenth-century industrialism.

Into the Heart of the Berkshires

North Adams is a gateway to the Berkshires, a region stretching from the Vermont line on the north to Connecticut on the south and bordering what the old-timers refer to as York State along the west. Here, on the outer edge of the Boston and New York megalopolis, is a region that treasures the values of slow growth even as pressures from outside for explosive change become increasingly difficult to withstand. It is a place of some of the most appealing landscapes on our continent, a place, like the Ile de France, whose beauty has been shaped by a long-standing, compatible relationship between man and nature. Here are the elm-shaded streets of gracious New England villages; meadows and wooded hills; winter and summer resorts; cultural riches and a long history of agriculture, diversified commerce, and industry.

An exploration of the Berkshires can begin with a short drive south to Mt. Greylock, which lies within an 8,660-acre state reservation with bridle paths, picnic facilities, hunting, and camping. A scenic road leading to the top can be reached from just west of North Adams, off Route 2 to the left. At 3,491 feet, Greylock is the state's highest peak, overlooking magnificent panoramas of western Massachusetts, the Hudson River Valley of New York, and the Green Mountains of southern Vermont. Many foot trails, including the Appalachian Trail, cross the summit. The more hardy tourists will find an hour's wandering on the trails close by the summit quite rewarding.

After driving down the mountain, return to State 2 and continue west to Williamstown. Although only five miles from North Adams—indeed, the two towns are connected, as most close settlements unfortunately are, by a stretch of burger stands, shopping centers, gas stations, trailer parks, and franchise operations—Williamstown is worlds removed. It grew up around a college rather than factories, and it has weathered like old brick into one of the loveliest towns in New England.

Williams was started here as a free school and became a college in 1793. The attractive campus is well worth a walking tour. The college's Thompson Memorial Chapel, a Gothic structure built in 1904, is on the north side of Main Street. Its stained glass windows are seen to best advantage from inside. Diagonally across the street is the Williams College Art Museum, in Lawrence Hall, identifiable by its octagonal form and Grecian rotunda; it houses fine collections of glass, pottery, bronzes and sculpture. On South Street, just west of the center of town, is the Sterling and Francine Clark Art Institute, one of the finest small art museums in America. It boasts great paintings (including a memorable collection of Renoirs), rare silver, furniture, and china, most of which was collected by the Clarks, who founded the art institute to share their loved possessions with others. Williamstown, with good restaurants, motels, and inns, is a delightful place to pause, and there is excellent skiing nearby. It has areas for hiking, riding, snowmobiling, and foliage watching. The Adams Memorial Theater is one of the leading summer theaters in the nation, and the Taconic and Waubeeka Springs golf courses are fine ones.

There are three ways south from Williamstown to Pittsfield—Route 43, Route 7, and Route 8—and all are pleasant. Route 43 lies to the west through North Hancock and Hancock Center, a delightful valley "discovered" by newcomers who are rapidly transforming its character from back-hills farming to residential and resort. The understandable temptation of farmers to sell their land to developers, however, has been mitigated by a new Massachusetts law which allows the state to purchase development rights from farmers, thus assuring continued agricultural use of the land and a fair deal for those who work it.

Here, too, is Jiminy Peak, a popular ski facility just three hours from Boston and New York and less than an hour from Albany. Turn left at N.Y. 22 in Stephentown and left onto U.S. 20 at Lebanon Springs.

Shaker Village

On the way into Pittsfield, as you come down the eastern slope of Lebanon Mountain, is the Hancock Shaker Village, open daily during the summer and early fall, weather permitting. This place has been fashioned into one of the nation's most popular and intriguing "living museums."

The Shakers first gathered at Hancock in the early 1780s when Mother Ann Lee, the English-born founder of the movement, an outgrowth of Quakerism, was still alive. They believed that religion should not be separated from the secular concerns which tend to dominate human life but should permeate all thought and action. They organized according to four principles: separation from the world; common property; confession of sin; and celibacy, with separation but equality of the sexes. During the 1830s there were six "families" at Hancock, each with elders, eldresses, and deacons. The total membership was about 300 men and women.

Each year, as more buildings are restored and opened to the public, more fascinating objects attesting to the genius of these spiritually motivated people for coping with the material world are revealed. The Round Stone Barn, scrupulously restored, is an architectural treasure. Those interested in Shaker architecture and design should take a short ride west on Route 20. Just beyond the New York State line, look for signs on the left pointing to the Darrow School, a private school housed in the fine old buildings of what once was the Mt. Lebanon Shaker community. About 20 miles farther west, in Old Chatham, New York, is a private Shaker museum (in non-Shaker structures) with an outstanding collection of Shaker objects. The legacy of the Shakers in design is one of an austere elegance proceeding from function. Their classic inventions include the wooden clothespin and the flat broom.

If you go south from Williamstown on Route 7, you will be taking the faster, more direct road to Pittsfield, passing through New Ashford (home of the popular Brodie Mountain ski area). The hills on your right are the eastern slopes of the mountains enfolding the Hancock settlements.

The easterly road south, Route 8, goes through Adams and Cheshire. Vistas in these towns sometimes resemble the English Lake District and sometimes are reminiscent of the factories and row houses of a Dickens setting. The environs are lovely to drive through at foliage time, and the side roads off the main routes are always worth exploring. From the home of suffragette Susan B. Anthony (private) at Bowen's Corners and East Road, for instance, drive to Highway 116 and bear left to the mountain village of Savoy. To the south of town, a well-marked road turns right, leading to the Jambs in Windsor State Forest, a deep flume or gorge cut through solid rock. This forest road joins Route 9. Turn left on Route 9 to reach the William Cullen Bryant homestead, open to the public for a small fee.

If you turn right (west) on Route 9, the ride down the hills toward the town of Dalton offers excellent views, particularly during foliage season. The Crane Museum of paper making, housed in the Old Stone Mill on the banks of the Housatonic, offers an interesting look at one of the area's oldest industries. At the foot of the hills, a well-marked road on the left leads to Wahconah Falls, a state park created around a waterfall in a clear, cold mountain stream. Continue west on Route 9, through Dalton to Pittsfield.

Pittsfield and the Berkshires Cultural Scene

Pittsfield, the Berkshire County seat, is at the geographic center of the county. It is a center of commerce and industry in a most inviting setting, surrounded by mountains, well watered and well forested. While Pittsfield has some of the problems of larger population centers, its saving grace is its reasonable size and attractive environs. The Berkshire Medical Center, superior to many hospitals serving much larger communities, meets the health needs not only of this large county but of neighboring areas in New York and Vermont. Pittsfield is a good stopping place for travelers who want to be in town and still be near the cultural and outdoor facilities for which the Berkshires are so noted. Pittsfield itself has two fine lakes (Onota and Pontoosuc) with public swimming. There are fishing, hiking, camping, hunting, snowmobiling, and other outdoor diversions in the Pittsfield State Forest. Bousquet's ski area, off U.S. 7 and 20, has excellent day and night facilities for novices and experts. At the southern edge of town, toward the great Berkshire cultural centers of Lenox, Lee, and Stockbridge, is South Mountain, with its fine vistas and the seasonal programs of the South Mountain Chamber Music Concerts. During the late nineteenth century William Stanley built a plant here utilizing work done in Great Barrington on alternating current for lighting. This was the genesis of General Electric, now the major employer in this city of 57,000.

Pittsfield's Berkshire Museum has an interesting collection of minerals and of Peary and Hawthorne memorabilia, as well as film programs. Students of New England history will find much of interest in a fine collection at the Berkshire Athenaeum, which houses, in its Melville Room, a matchless collection of papers and artifacts associated with the author. Melville's home, Arrowhead, is just outside Pittsfield on the Holmes Road. The old farmhouse has been restored and opened to visitors. Here is the room where, with a view of an undulating line of hills that reminded him of ocean waves, Melville wrote *Moby-Dick*. Many other literary and prominent figures of the mid-nineteenth century, including Hawthorne and Oliver Wendell Holmes, also lived or summered near here.

Lenox, Stockbridge, and the Southern Berkshires

If you're in a hurry to get down to Tanglewood in Lenox for the great summer festival of the Boston Symphony, just scoot south on U.S. 7. If you have a bit of time, take U.S. 20 west about five miles to State 41 and come in the back way through Richmond. Now a prosperous farming area and popular bedroom community for Pittsfield, it was once an important mining center—the iron used in the *Monitor's* cannon was produced here. The ruins of the early foundry are still visible. Off 41, turn left into Lenox Road for a short ride through the forest to Tanglewood. Here, every summer, on a 200-acre estate, students, world-renowned performers, the Boston Symphony, and just plain music lovers gather to learn, perform, and enjoy. The main shed seats 6,000 for the major concerts (July and August), but there's plenty of room for listening out on the great lawn; just bring a blanket or a folding chair—and a light sweater. The Theater Concert Hall is used for small orchestra and chamber concerts; the Chamber Music Hall seats 300 and accommodates chamber music groups, lectures, and large classes.

From Tanglewood, travel east on Highway 183 to Lenox. Nearby is the Pleasant Valley Wildlife Sanctuary, a Massachusetts Audubon Society facility sheltering many living specimens of regional plant and animal life. Other local attractions are the Avaloch ski area and the Eastover year-round resort.

Continue south on U.S. 20 to Lee, with its interesting Congregational church dating from 1857. Here, too, are the lime and marble quarries that yielded the stone for the capitol in Washington and the headstones for the soldiers' graves at Arlington National Cemetery.

To the south are the Oak 'n' Spruce Ski Area and, in West Becket, the great Jacob's Pillow Dance festival and school, founded by the late Ted Shawn. Top dancers from all over the world give regular performances to packed houses. Also in Lee is the 14,000-acre October Mountain State Forest. The Appalachian Trail runs through it, and there are facilities for hunting, fishing, camping, snowmobiling, and other outdoor activities. Return via U.S. 20 and State 102 to Stockbridge.

Stockbridge, to many the archetype of the New England small town, has a long history of attracting creative people. Here is where Jonathan Edwards spent the last eight years of his life writing theological treatises and serving as missionary to the Indians. In more recent times, the playwright Robert E. Sherwood summered here for many years. The playwright William Gibson and the novelist Norman Mailer also have made their homes in Stockbridge, and Norman Rockwell moved here after spending many years in Vermont. Arlo Guthrie immortalized Stockbridge for many as the scene of his comic protest song "Alice's Restaurant." Over 50 of Rockwell's paintings of the American scene are on exhibit in the Norman Rockwell Museum, a 1790 Federal mansion. There's an inviting inn here (the Red Lion) and one of the nation's top summer theaters, the Berkshire Playhouse. Other places worth visiting are the Mission House, Naumkeag Gardens, and Chesterwood, a 150-acre estate containing the studio of Daniel Chester French, sculptor of the famed Lincoln Memorial and of Concord's Minuteman. French said, "I live here six months of the year—in heaven. The other six months I live, well—in New York." Chesterwood, a National Trust property, is located off State 183, two miles west of Stockbridge.

A short, scenic drive south from Stockbridge on U.S. 7 takes you to Great Barrington, largest town and economic center of south Berkshire. The townspeople seized the courthouse from the British in August 1774; it has been claimed that this was the first act of open resistance to the crown in America. There are lovely views from atop Mt. Everett, a nice place to hike and picnic. Butternut Basin, two miles east on State 23, has fine skiing, as do Catamount and Jug End in nearby Egremont, just a couple of hours away from the New York and Boston metropolitan areas.

Take Route 23 a few miles southwest to South Egremont and then left onto Highway 41 to Bash Bish Falls Reservation. A large parking area is provided, and a short, pleasant footpath leads to the falls and a picnic area. Following a gorge cut deep into solid rock, the Bash Bish Brook plunges 50 feet into a deep, clear, rock-bottomed pool. According to the story, seemingly told at every waterfall in North America, an Indian maiden, unhappy in love, jumped to her death from the rocks above. Her tortured spirit, of course, haunts the falls. The spirit known as Jack Frost is also active here each fall: The Berkshires are known for Massachusetts's most vibrant display of autumn leaves.

Streams, falls, and historic houses are easy to find in this lovely south Berkshire farm country with its gentle mountains, inviting woods, and towns like Mount Washington, Sheffield, New Marlborough, Sandisfield,

Monterey, Otis, and Ashley Falls. Just to the west of Ashley Falls is nature's own rock garden, Bartholomew's Cobble, a protected public reservation noted for wildflowers and an extraordinary variety of ferns. Sheffield has the double falls of Sage's Ravine as well as Glen Falls, Bear Rock Falls, and Race Brook Falls. The first Berkshire town to be chartered, Sheffield is the only one left in the state with two covered bridges. From the flatlands of the Housatonic Valley in Sheffield to the uplands of Mount Washington, this corner of Berkshire County constitutes the essence of rural Massachusetts.

PRACTICAL INFORMATION FOR THE BERKSHIRES

HOW TO GET THERE AND AROUND. By plane: Although Berkshire Aviation Enterprises (413–528–1010) operates an air taxi and charter service out of Great Barrington Airport, Great Barrington, the nearest major commercial airports to the Berkshires are Logan International, in Boston, Albany Airport, in Albany, New York, and Bradley International Airport in Windsor Locks, Connecticut. Limousine and charter van service to major airports is provided by Abbott's Taxi, Greylock St., Lee (413–243–1645).

By train: Amtrak's *Lake Shore Limited* makes Pittsfield stops on its eastbound and westbound runs between Boston and Chicago. For information, call 800–USA–RAIL. New York City connections with the *Lake Shore* are by way of Albany, N.Y.

By bus: Peter Pan Bus Lines (413–442–4451) serves Lee and Pittsfield with buses from Boston and Albany; Bonanza Bus Lines (413–781–3220) connects points throughout the Berkshires with Albany, New York City, Springfield, and Providence, RI.

By car: The Massachusetts Turnpike continues past Springfield to reach the Berkshires towns of Lee and Stockbridge before ending at the New York State line; there it connects with the New York State Thruway's Berkshire section, which meets the thruway itself just south of Albany. If you are driving to the Berkshires from New York City, the most direct routes are the New York State Thruway or the more scenic Taconic State Parkway, with entry into Massachusetts at any of a number of points along the state's western border. The main north–south route through the Berkshires is Rte. 7, which runs through the towns of Sheffield (near the Connecticut border), Great Barrington, Stockbridge, Lenox, Pittsfield, and Williamstown (Vermont border). Rte. 2, the Mohawk Trail, enters Massachusetts from New York State at Williamstown and continues eastward to reach eastern Massachusetts points by way of Shelburne Falls and Greenfield.

HOTELS AND MOTELS. With the exception of Cape Cod, no part of Massachusetts is as well served by the hotel and motel industry as the Berkshires. Most places to stay are clustered along the corridors of Rtes. 7 and 2. The following price ranges are based on double occupancy: *Deluxe,* $100 and up; *Expensive,* $75–$100; *Moderate,* $50–$75; *Inexpensive,* under $50. Be forewarned, however, that the Tanglewood concert season, in summer, sends prices sky-high. Even 20 mi. from Tanglewood or more, $75 might buy you little more than a bare-bones room with a lumpy mattress and a black-and-white TV. Sad to say, but come Tanglewood time *everything* in these parts is expensive.

Great Barrington

Mountain View Motel, 304 State Rd., Rte. 23E., 01230 (413–528–0250). *Inexpensive.* Small, pleasant motel; cable TV, air-conditioning.

Lee

Oak n' Spruce Resort, Meadow St. S. Lee 01238 (413–243–3500). *Expensive.* Fully equipped resort. Golf, tennis. Pools. Nightclub. Skiing.
Gaslight Motor Lodge, Greenwater Pond, Rte. 20, E. Lee, 01238 (413–243–9701). *Moderate.* On lake near Appalachian Trail. Swimming, boats, fishing, hiking. All rooms have refrigerators.
Sunset, 114 Housatonic St., 01238 (413–243–0302). *Moderate.* Near restaurant. Pool. Seasonal rates.

Lenox

Eastover, East St., 01240 (413–637–0625). *Deluxe.* Year-round resort. Pools, riding, tennis, skiing, skating. Planned entertainment, dancing. Huge grounds. American Plan. Seasonal rates.
Lenox Motel, Pittsfield Rd., 01240 (413–499–0324). *Expensive.* 2 mi. from ski area. Pool. In-room coffee. Seasonal rates.
Quality Inn Lenox–Pittsfield Lodge, 390 Pittsfield Rd., 01240 (413–637–1100). *Expensive.* Outdoor and heated indoor pools; sauna; tennis; play area. Restaurant, lounge. Seasonal rates.
Tanglewood Motor Inn, Pittsfield-Lenox Rd., 01240 (413–442–4000). *Expensive.* Pool, play area. Efficiencies available. Near restaurant. Seasonal rates.

Pittsfield

Berkshire Hilton Inn, South St., 01201 (413–499–2000). *Expensive.* Pool. Restaurant, bar, entertainment, dancing. Family rates available.
Best Western Springs Motor Inn, Rte. 7, New Ashford 01237 (413–458–5945). *Expensive.* Pool. Tennis, near golf, skiing. Recreation room. Free in-room coffee. Restaurant, bar.
The Huntsman, 1350 W. Housatonic St., 01201 (413–442–8714). *Moderate.* Near lake. Restaurant.
Heart of the Berkshires, 970 W. Housatonic St., 01201 (413–443–1255). *Inexpensive.* Small motel on spacious grounds; pool, cable TV.

Williamstown

The Orchards, 222 Adams Rd., 01267 (413–458–9611). *Deluxe.* A lovely new 49-room inn filled with English antiques. Some rooms with refrigerators, some with fireplaces. Restaurant, lounge, pool, sauna, ice skating; golf and tennis nearby. Outdoor dining in season.
Williams Inn, on the green, 01267 (413–458–9371). *Expensive.* Traditional college town atmosphere. Pool. Saunas. Packages available.
Berkshire Hills, at jct. of Rtes. 7 and 2, 01267 (413–458–3950). *Moderate.* Pool. Complimentary Continental breakfast. Near restaurant.
Carriage House, Rte. 7, 01237 (413–458–5359). *Moderate.* Free in-room coffee. Restaurant. Pool, tennis.
1896 Motel, Cold Spring Rd., Rte. 7, 01267 (413–458–8125). *Moderate.* Quiet, secluded. Continental breakfast. Restaurant, bar.

INNS, GUEST HOUSES, BED AND BREAKFASTS. This is Massachusetts's real inn territory, from the plushest of antique-filled mansions to homey little three- or four-room hostelries. Bed-and-breakfast establishments are proliferating; for information on recommended places, contact *Berkshire Bed and Breakfast,* Box 211, Main St., Williamsburg 01096 (413–268–7244). With regard to price ranges for more formal inns, most will fall into the moderate and expensive categories, as listed above under *Hotels and Motels.* Keep in mind, though, that many offer a Modified American Plan. A selection follows:

Lenox

Gateways Inn, 71 Walker St., 01240 (413–637–2532). A large, elegantly restored mansion with many antiques. An enormous suite is available. Continental breakfast included. Restaurant.

Village Inn, 16 Church St., 01240 (413–637–0020). Cozy, cheerful inn. Restaurant, taproom with fireplace. One mi. from Tanglewood.

Great Barrington

Egremont Inn, Old Sheffield Road, S. Egremont (413–528–2111). Built as a country inn in 1780. Tennis, pool. Gracious tavern, dining, and common rooms. Modified American Plan.

Windflower, Rte. 23, 01230 (413–528–2720). A pleasant, rambling, antique-filled inn. Some rooms have fireplaces. Modified American Plan; excellent cuisine.

Sheffield

Ivanhoe Country House, Undermountain Rd., 01257 (413–229–2143). A secluded inn set amidst rolling hills. One room has a corner fireplace. Continental breakfast brought to your door. Rates quite reasonable.

Stockbridge

The Inn at Stockbridge, Rte. 7, 01262 (413–298–3337). A circa 1900 country inn, 1 mi. north of town. Outdoor pool.

Red Lion Inn, Rte. 7, 01262 (413–298–5545). Pool. Pets. Traditional colonial inn, beautifully restored with fine antique furniture, china, pewter collection. Excellent restaurant, bar. Exercise room.

Williamsville Inn, Rte. 41, W. Stockbridge 01266 (413–274–6118). 18th-century farmhouse. Quiet and secluded. Some rooms with fireplace. Restaurant features French country cuisine.

RESTAURANTS. From hot-dog stands to haute cuisine, you could very easily eat your way from Connecticut to the Vermont border. Some of the most ambitious culinary efforts are at the better inns; call ahead and make sure nonguests are served. During the Tanglewood season, call *any* restaurant you are considering to secure reservations in advance. The cost of an à la carte dinner, without drinks or tip, is the basis of our price classifications: *Expensive,* $22 and up; *Moderate,* $12–$22; *Inexpensive,* under $12.

Great Barrington

Egremont Inn, Old Sheffield Rd., S. Egremont (413–528–2111). *Moderate.* Supreme of salmon, chicken sautéed with tarragon, lemon sole, steak, veal, trout.

Windflower, Rte. 23 (413–528–2720). *Expensive.* Dinner by reservation only for nonguests. No printed menu; three selections per night, always changing. Veal and chicken dishes especially good. Prix fixe.

20 Railroad Street, (413–528–9345). *Inexpensive.* Good burgers, stew, quiche, daily specials in Victorian saloon atmosphere.

Lee

Cork 'n Hearth, Rte. 20 (413–243–0535). *Moderate.* Veal specialties, plus steak, seafood. Closed Mon. except in summer. Sun. brunch.

Morgan House, 33 Main St. (413–243–0181). *Moderate.* Lobster, lamb, homemade soups, breads and dessert. Cozy colonial atmosphere. Cocktails.

Lenox

Gateways Inn, 71 Walker St. (413–637–2532). *Expensive.* Continental specialties prepared by owner-chef. Shrimp stuffed with crabmeat, veal, and mushrooms; broiled scrod casino; beef Stroganoff.

Wheatleigh, W. Hawthorne Rd. (413–637–0610). *Expensive.* The dining room of the inn is open to the public for breakfast and dinner. A New York financier built Wheatleigh in 1893 and gave it to his daughter as a wedding gift. There are 17 opulent rooms behind the Mediterranean facade. Closed Mon.

Candlelight Inn, Walker St. (413–637–1555). *Moderate.* New American cuisine.

Lenox House, Pittsfield-Lenox Rd. (413–637–1341). *Moderate.* Scampi, roast beef. Homemade relishes, rolls, pies. Cocktails. Children's menu.

The Restaurant, 15 Franklin St. (413–637–9894). *Moderate.* Cantonese duckling, marinated beef, shrimp. Sat. and Sun. brunch.

The Seven Hills Inn, 100 Plunkett St. (413–637–0060). *Moderate.* Nouvelle cuisine. Open Thurs.–Sun.

Pittsfield

The Springs, Rte. 7, New Ashford (413–458–3465). *Expensive.* Veal Oscar, osso buco, tournedos Rossini, paella. Bar, dancing Sat.

Dakota, Pittsfield-Lenox Rd. (413–499–7900). *Moderate.* Steaks, seafood, and other standbys done nicely in a rustic Western atmosphere.

Stockbridge

Red Lion Inn, Main St. at Rte. 7 (413–298–5545). *Expensive.* Continental menu, elegant atmosphere. Outside dining overlooking flower-filled courtyard. Bar. Entertainment.

Williamsville Inn, Rte. 41, W. Stockbridge (413–274–6580). *Expensive.* 18th-century farmhouse. Good menu, including duck and salmon. Daily specials. Excellent desserts. Bar. Fine wine list. Breakfast served to house guests.

Williamstown

Le Jardin, 777 Cold Spring Rd. (413–458–8032). *Expensive.* Poached salmon hollandaise, duck with apple sauce. Pastries baked on premises. Breakfast in summer. Bar.

Country Restaurant, 52 North St. at Rte. 7 (413–458–4000). *Moderate.* Escalope de veau Oscar, clams à la marinara.

Mill on the Floss, at the Carriage House Motel, 9 mi. south on U.S. 7 (413–458–9123). *Moderate.* 18th-century house overlooking millpond. Patio dining. Suggestions: sweetbreads aux capres, tournedos. Bar. Open 5–10 P.M. Closed Tues.

TOURIST INFORMATION. The two most comprehensive sources of information for Berkshires visitors and travelers along the Mohawk Trail (Rte. 2 between Greenfield and Williamstown) are the Berkshire Visitors Bureau, Box SGB, The Common, Pittsfield 01201 (413–443–9186 or 800–237–5747), and the Mohawk Trail Association, Box J, Charlemont 01339 (413–664–6256).

TOURS. Berkshire Guided Tours, 30 Glenn Dr., Pittsfield 01201 (413–442–9366) offers small-group bus tours throughout the entire Berkshire County area, with emphasis on cultural and historical points of interest.

SEASONAL EVENTS. Major Berkshires cultural events are listed under *Music, Dance, and Stage.*

July: Fourth of July Parade, Pittsfield.

August: Shaker Kitchen Festival, Hancock Shaker Village, Hancock.

September: Barrington Fair, Great Barrington; Berkshire County Fair, Pittsfield; Foliage Festival, North Adams.

October: Lenox Apple Squeeze, Lenox; Festival in the Hills, Conway; Lenox Open House, Lenox.

PARKS AND FORESTS. Beartown State Forest, off Rte. 23 near Great Barrington, is an 10,879-acre tract including four major Berkshire peaks. **Mohawk Trail State Forest,** off Rte. 2 near Charlemont, is a scenic stopping point if you're driving the trail. **Mount Greylock State Reservation,** entrance near intersection of Rtes. 7 and 8, North Adams, covers 13,000 acres and features Massachusetts's highest mountain. **October Mountain State Forest,** Lee, is, at 15,000 acres, the largest state forest in Massachusetts. Schermerhorn Gorge is a favorite scenic spot here. **Pittsfield State Forest,** off Rte. 20 near the New York State border, has a ski area.

GARDENS. Two Berkshires spots attract thousands of garden lovers each year. **Naumkeag Gardens,** Prospect Hill Rd., Stockbridge (413–298–3239), are formal landscape gardens. The house was designed by Stanford White for the attorney Joseph Choate. Open Memorial Day–mid-Oct. The **Berkshire Garden Center,** Rtes. 102 and 183, Stockbridge (413–298–3926), covers 15 acres and includes a herb garden, wildflowers, lily pond, annuals and perennials, and a tropical greenhouse. Open daily, year-round.

SUMMER SPORTS. Lakes and ponds for **swimming** abound in the Berkshires. Popular spots are Clarksburg State Park, Rte. 8, Clarksburg;

Benedict Pond, in Beartown State Forest, Great Barrington; York Lake in Sandisfield State Forest, off Rte. 57, New Marlboro; and Prospect Lake Park, in N. Egremont. The YMCA Ponterril Outdoor Center, Rte. 7, Pittsfield, has three pools, swimming lessons. The same YMCA center also rents canoes and sailboats. Other popular **boating** spots featuring rentals are at Otis Reservoir, Reservoir Road, Otis; Hoosac Lake, Rte. 8, Cheshire; Greenwater Pond, Rte. 20, Becket; and Laurel Lake, Rte. 20, Lee.

Hiking trails are located in all the above-mentioned state parks and forests; the big attraction to hikers in this part of the state is the Appalachian Trail, which enters Massachusetts at Mt. Washington, on the Connecticut border, and reaches Vermont at Williamstown, Massachusetts. Along the way, the trail crosses Rtes. 41, 7, 23, 8, 9, and 2.

Golf courses open to the public include Bas Ridge Country Club, Hinsdale (413–655–2605), Pontoosuc Lake Country Club, Pittsfield (413–445–4217); Wahconah Country Club, Dalton (413–684–2864); and Taconic Golf Club, Williamstown (413–664–6265).

For **tennis,** try the Brodie Mt. Tennis and Racquetball Club, New Ashford (413–458–4677); Lakewood Park, Newell St., Pittsfield; Greylock Recreation Field, North Adams; and Greenock Country Club, Lee (413–243–9719).

WINTER SPORTS. The Berkshires are Massachusetts's prime **ski** territory. Even a partial list of downhill areas would have to include Bousquet, Pittsfield (413–442–8316), with two chairlifts and a 1.5 mi. run; Catamount, South Egremont (413–528–1262), four chairlifts, two T-bars, and a longest run of 2 mi.; and Jiminy Peak, Hancock (413–738–5500), with four chairlifts, one J-bar, and runs up to 2 mi. in length. Brodie, New Ashford (413–443–4752) has 24 trails, four chairlifts, and runs of up to 2.5 mi. Butternut Basin, Great Barrington (413–528–2000) has 21 trails, six chairlifts, and runs up to nearly 2 mi. in length.

Cross-country skiing is possible along the groomed snowmobile trails in the parks listed under *Parks and Forests* above and at the Oak 'n' Spruce Resort, S. Lee (413–243–3500); Stump Sprouts Ski Touring, W. Hawley (413–339–4265); and Otis Ridge Ski Area, Otis Ridge (413–269–4445).

FISHING. Berkshires rivers, lakes, and ponds offer bass, pike, and trout fishing. Stocked trout waters include the Hoosic River (S. Branch) near Cheshire; Green River, Great Barrington; Notch Brook and Windsor Lake, North Adams; Goose Pond and Beartown Brook, Lee; and Williams River, W. Stockbridge. Abstracts of fishing regulations are available at town halls and sporting goods stores where fishing licenses are sold.

HUNTING. The Berkshires offer the best deer hunting in Massachusetts, along with hunting for bear, wild turkey, and upland game species such as rabbit, quail, and pheasant. Fall and winter are the principal seasons; pick up a copy of game regulations, including season dates and bag limits, where you buy your hunting license.

CAMPING. State-operated campsites are available at all the state parks and forests listed above under *Forests and Parks,* as well as at smaller state facilities throughout the Berkshires. For information on permits and fees, contact the Massachusetts Environmental Management Department, 100 Cambridge St., Boston 02202 (617–727–3180). For a list of approved privately operated campgrounds, write the Berkshires Visitors Bureau, Box SGB, the Common, Pittsfield 01201 (413–443–9186 or 800–BERKSHR).

HISTORIC SITES AND HOUSES. In the *Savoy Area*—Susan B. Anthony House (private). East Rd., 1½ mi. off Hoosac St., Adams.

William Cullen Bryant Home, Rte. 112, Cummington (413–634–2244). Open mid-June–mid-Oct., Fri., Sat., Sun., holiday afternoons. Birthplace and longtime home of famous poet and editor.

In *Stockbridge*—Mission House, Sergeant St. (413–298–3383). Open Memorial Day–mid-Oct., Tues.–Sun.

In *Pittsfield*—**Arrowhead,** 780 Holmes Rd. (413–442–1793). This Berkshire farmhouse was the home of Herman Melville from 1850 to 1863; here he wrote part of *Moby-Dick.* Open daily June 1–Oct. 31; the rest of the year by appointment.

MUSEUMS AND GALLERIES. The museums and art galleries of the Berkshires are enriched by the many famous artists and writers who have summered here over the years. Call ahead to check days, hours, and admission charges.

Dalton

Crane Museum, Rte. 9, 5 mi. east of Pittsfield (413–684–2600). Evolution of American paper making. Open Memorial Day–mid-Oct, Mon.–Fri. afternoons.

Hancock

Hancock Shaker Village, Rtes. 20 and 41 (413–443–0188). Historic settlement of Shaker community, with restored buildings. Open daily June–Oct. 31.

Lenox

Pleasant Valley Wildlife Sanctuary, 472 W. Mountain Rd. (413–637–0320). Closed Mon.; museum open weekends only in the spring and fall and closed in the winter. 700-acre Massachusetts Audubon Society preserve; live exhibits in museum.

Pittsfield

Berkshire Athenaeum, 1 Wendell Ave. (413–499–9480). Open year-round, closed Sun. and holidays. Houses public library and Melville Memorial Room.

Berkshire Museum, 39 South St. (413–443–7171). Open daily July and Aug.; closed Mon. the rest of the year. Closed holidays. Excellent mineral collection; historical artifacts; Hudson River School and other paintings.

Rowe

Rowe Historical Society, Zoar Rd. (413–339–4238). July 4–Columbus Day, Sat.–Sun. afternoons. Revolutionary and Civil War artifacts.

Stockbridge

Chesterwood, Rte. 183 (413–298–3579). Studio of Daniel Chester French, sculptor of "The Minute Man of Concord," at Concord, and Lincoln Memorial, Washington, D.C. Plaster casts. Open May 31–Oct. 31.

Norman Rockwell Museum at Stockbridge, Main St. (413–298–3822). Extensive collection of Norman Rockwell paintings. Open daily, 10 A.M.–5 P.M.

Williamstown

Sterling and Francine Clark Art Institute, South St. (413–458–9545). Impressive marble building. Renoirs, Sargents, Corots, and many other masterpieces. Rare treasures exhibited also. Free. Closed Mon.; Feb.

Williams College Museum of Art, Williams Campus (413–597–2429). New gallery has 18th- to 20th-century American art and non-Western art. Open daily.

MUSIC, DANCE, AND STAGE. A list of all the Berkshires's cultural programs would fill a small guidebook in itself. For complete information, contact the Berkshires Visitors Bureau (see *Tourist Information*). Here are a few of the major performing arts series that come to life in the Berkshires each summer:

In Becket—**Jacob's Pillow Dance Festival,** Ted Shawn Theater (413–243–0745). Ballet, modern, ethnic dance (June–Aug.).

In Lenox—**Tanglewood Festival,** Tanglewood Music Center (617–266–1492): world-famous summer concert series of the Boston Symphony Orchestra with seating in the music shed or on the lawn; open rehearsals Sat. (late June–Aug.). **Shakespeare and Co.,** The Mount (413–637–3353): open-air amphitheater on grounds of Edith Wharton estate is site of Shakespeare performances (July and Aug.). **Berkshire Opera Company,** Cranwell Estate (413–243–1343): opera featuring international stars; picnicking on lawns during intermission (July and Aug.).

In Pittsfield—**Berkshire Public Theater,** 30 Union St. (413–445–4631): accomplished repertory performances (June–Aug.). South Mountain Concerts, Rtes. 7 and 20 (for information, write Box 23, Pittsfield 01202, or call 413–442–2106): chamber music on weekend afternoons (Aug.–Oct.).

In Williamstown—**Adams Memorial Theater,** Williams College Campus (413–597–3400). Williamstown Theater Festival presents world-class actors in impressive repertory lineup (July–Aug.).

ART GALLERIES. The hill towns of the Berkshires continue to attract artists and artisans, many of whom offer their work for sale in local galleries. A sampling:

In Lenox—**Towne Gallery,** 28 Walker St. (413–637–0053); paintings and prints by modern New England artists. **Clark Whitney Gallery,** 25 Church St. (413–637–2126); painting and sculpture by outstanding contemporary New England artists and nationally known names.

In Housatonic—**Great Barrington Pottery,** Rte. 41 (413–274–6259); Japanese-inspired pottery, handmade by Richard Bennett.

In Stockbridge—**Holsten Galleries,** Elm St. (413–298–3044); contemporary American painting, sculpture, jewelry, and art glass.

In Williamstown—**Beaverpond Gallery,** Hancock Rd. (413–738–5895). Berkshire landscape watercolors; local crafts.

SHOPPING. The sophisticated stream of summer visitors has made Berkshires shopping a different experience than in the days when the hill towns had general stores and not much else. A few possibilities:

In Great Barrington, **Jennifer House,** Rte. 7 (413–528–1500) features the J. Jill line of women's country clothing and household Americana.

In Lenox, there's **Lenox Kites,** 525 East St. (413–637–2115), with hand-made kites and windsocks in original designs—or you can design your own.

At the **Silver Sleigh Christmas Shop,** Brushwood Farm, Rtes. 7 and 20 (413–637–3522), it's Christmas all year round, in a big octagonal barn.

In Sheffield, try **Sheffield Pottery,** Rte. 7 (413–229–7700), for a complete line of locally made ceramic ware.

In Stockbridge, there's **Country Curtains,** at the Red Lion Inn, Main St. (413–298–5565), a famous nationwide mail order business offering the finest in curtains, spreads, and other textiles for the home.

NIGHTLIFE. In summer, nightlife in the Berkshires means a ticket to Tanglewood, Jacob's Pillow, or one of the theaters; in winter, the scene is likely to be après-ski. A few clubs stand out, however. In Lenox, try **The Night Spot** at Seven Hills Inn, Plunkett St. (413–637–0060); piano, jazz, and folk-rock. In West Stockbridge, the **Shaker Mill Tavern,** Rtes. 102 and 41 (413–232–8565), books acts from the Boston Comedy Connection in summer.

NEW HAMPSHIRE

By
STEPHEN BENNETT

Stephen Bennett, a resident of New Hampshire, has been founder and publisher of Publick Occurrences, *a New Hampshire seacoast weekly newspaper; editor of the* Irregular & Mt. Washington Valley News, *a North Conway, New Hampshire, weekly; editor of* New Hampshire Profiles, *the statewide magazine; and editor of* Business Digest *for central New Hampshire. He has written for the* Sun *of Baltimore, the* Boston Globe, Trial, Parade, *and* The Brief, *the magazine of the Boston University School of Law.*

New Hampshire is rocky, rushing, crystal-clear streams where a fisherman can walk for hours without encountering another human being. It is mountains, not lofty but sweeping and soul gripping. It is rocky shores and sandy beaches washed by the Atlantic Ocean. New Hampshire is steepled white churches in hamlets discovered after miles of driving the backways through thick forests, smoking chimneys atop houses built in clearings hacked from the wilderness two centuries ago, strips of farmland once carved by brute force out of soil embedded with granite rocks scattered by glaciers thousands of years ago.

New Hampshire is also ski slopes and fine inns, bargain factory outlets, arts festivals, and antique shops. It is old textile mills, many of which are now inhabited by modern high-tech tenants, and mini-skyscrapers filled with white-collar workers processing information. It is lobstermen rubbing shoulders with artists and plain-speaking farmers exchanging words at town meetings with urban executives turned country innkeepers.

> Just specimens is all New Hampshire has,
> One each of everything as in a showcase,
> Which naturally she doesn't care to sell.

So wrote Robert Frost, who lived here, in his poem "New Hampshire." New Hampshire is a small showcase, 180 miles from north to south, 100 miles at its widest point. The showcase holds quite a variety of specimens, and the best specimens, indeed, are not for sale. New Hampshire offers, free of charge, views of eight mountains reaching more than a mile high (and more than 150 rising a half mile) and the highest peak in the northeast, Mt. Washington, which ascends 6,200 feet to its snowcap. Forests cover 87 percent of the state. In autumn, visitors are treated to a grand spectacle: a riot of foliage colors.

More than 1,300 lakes and ponds grace the state, including the magnificent Lake Winnipesaukee, dotted with 274 habitable islands. Hundreds of streams and brooks beckon the traveler with rippling laughter. Sixteen rivers break the geography.

In the great 750,000-acre White Mountain National Forest, which dominates the north country and extends into Maine, 1,425 miles of hiking trails wind alongside white water rivers, descend into deep valleys, and rise through mountain passes. The seacoast, 18 miles of sandy beaches and rocky shoreline, is where the first white settlers landed more than 350 years ago.

In small towns secluded in forests or cradled in river-fed valleys and in mill towns along rivers, you still can find the natives of New Hampshire. Proportionally there are fewer and fewer natives in this state of a million inhabitants because out-of-staters have come in droves to join them. Taken as a whole, New Hampshire people are stubbornly independent, frugal, unpretentious, conservative, and plainspoken. They work hard; New Hampshire has the lowest unemployment rate in the nation. They are suspicious of government. The state motto is "Live Free or Die." In keeping with this independent character, New Hampshire is the only state in the nation with no personal income tax or general sales tax. New Hampshire's 425 citizen state legislators, who constitute the third largest legislative body in the world, are paid $200 each annually, plus expenses. The bulk of state income comes from "sin taxes"—lottery tickets, horse racing revenues, and liquor sold in state liquor stores—and from room, meal, and business profit taxes. In general, if you use it, you pay taxes on it.

Colonial Beginnings

The gateway to New Hampshire for the early white explorers was the Atlantic seacoast. The first recorded explorers were Captain Martin Pring and company, who sailed from the Atlantic up the Piscataqua River in June 1603 to observe "very goodly groves and woods replenished with tall Oakes, Beaches, Pine-trees, Firres-trees, Hasels, and Maples. We saw also sundry sorts of beasts, Deer, Bears, Wolves, Foxes, Lusernes, and Dogges with sharp noses."

The first settlers in what is now New Hampshire made the torturous journey from England for commercial, not religious, reasons. David Thomson and other fishermen sailed from Plymouth, England, landing at Odiorne's Point in what is now the town of Rye in April 1623. Their settlement, Pannaway Plantation, soon had a stone manor house, smithy, cooperage, fort, and facilities for drying fish. That same year, Edward and William Hilton, fishmongers from London, brought a small group to settle

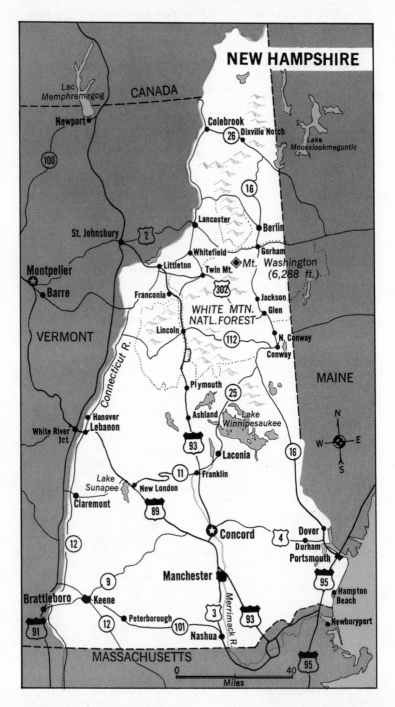

NEW HAMPSHIRE

Lac Memphremagog
CANADA
Newport
100
Colebrook
26 Dixville Notch
Lake Mooselookmeguntic
16
Lancaster
Berlin
St. Johnsbury
2
Whitefield
Gorham
Montpelier
Littleton
Twin Mt.
◆ Mt. Washington (6,288 ft.)
Barre
Franconia
302
Jackson
Glen
VERMONT
WHITE MTN. NATL. FOREST
Lincoln
112
N. Conway
Conway
MAINE
Plymouth
25
Ashland
Lake Winnipesaukee
Hanover
Lebanon
93
White River Jct
Laconia
16
11
Franklin
Lake Sunapee
New London
Claremont
89
Concord
4
Dover
12
Durham
Portsmouth
Manchester
95
Hampton Beach
9
Brattleboro
Keene
12
Peterborough
3
Merrimack R.
93
Newburyport
91
101
Nashua
95
MASSACHUSETTS
0   40
Miles

N
W   E
S

at Hilton's Point, the southernmost part of what is now Dover. They established the fishing industry.

In this new colony, four early towns were established: Strawbery Banke, now the city of Portsmouth; Dover; Exeter, founded in 1638; and later that year, Hampton, first named Winnacunnet. For 35 years this was civilized New Hampshire, and for nearly a century Portsmouth was the seat of government and the most influential of the towns. In 1732, more than a century after the first settlers arrived, the population of this struggling colony was only 12,500.

Feeling vulnerable, the four towns put themselves under the jurisdiction of Massachusetts in 1641, each town sending a representative to the Massachusetts General Court. New Hampshire remained a part of Massachusetts for 38 years until 1679, when it was made a royal province by King Charles II.

The king appointed a royal governor, John Cutt, and established a Governor's Council, whose members he appointed, and an assembly, to which the original four towns could send representatives. Cutt fell ill in 1681 and the council and assembly proclaimed a day of public fasting and prayer, "to be kept by all the inhabitants." Cutt died nonetheless. Today New Hampshire is still governed by a governor and executive council, and the legislature has taken the place of the assembly.

The interior of New Hampshire remained wilderness for a long period. Historians have estimated that when the white settlers came to the shores of New Hampshire, no more than 5,000 Indians, members of the Algonquin tribes, dwelled here. The Indians lived off the game and fruit of the forests and the fish of the rivers and lakes. They also cleared and cultivated forest lands, extracted maple syrup and sugar from the maple trees, and grew squash, pumpkins, many kinds of beans, and Indian corn. They had invented snowshoes and the swift, light birchbark canoe.

These were, for the most part, friendly people when the white settlers arrived, and it was only after the white settlers' encroachment—and encouragement by the French—that they became more warlike. The interior settlement by whites came slowly. From 1689 on, the French—less threatening to the Indians because they were mainly trappers and traders and thus less likely to settle and encroach on the Indian lands—gained most of the Indian tribes as allies and began to attack the English. Settlements were raided and settlers killed, their scalps taken. The settlers learned survival. One survivor was Hannah Dustin, mother of 12 children, who was captured by Indians in 1697 and taken to River Islet at Boscawen, near the present capital city of Concord. In the middle of the night she killed and scalped her 10 captors and escaped to freedom.

While Portsmouth had its old English elegance, those who ventured into the wilds of New Hampshire before the Revolution were not inclined to, or had no time for, frivolities. They dressed in homespun clothes and worked from dawn to dusk to scratch a living from the rocky soil or cut the timber for mercantilists, hunted and fished, trapped animals for fur to sell, and prayed for deliverance. It was hard living, yet settlers came nonetheless. By 1760, there were 61 towns chartered in New Hampshire, some of them settled by people from Massachusetts who moved up to the Connecticut Valley.

When new towns were settled, the first order of business was building a church, called the meeting house, and choosing a minister by majority vote of the townspeople, every taxpayer being assessed for the pastor's salary according to his ability to pay. The Congregationalist Church was the predominant church in the early years. In 1775, there were 84 Congregational churches, 15 Presbyterian, 11 Baptist, two Quaker, and two Episcopalian (one of them in Portsmouth, which had chosen the Church of England from the beginning).

The Revolution

New Hampshire exerted its independence early. In December 1774, New Hampshiremen captured a large store of munitions from the British at Fort William and Mary on the seacoast, distributing them to militia units in nine towns. Resentment toward the British brought a demand for the surrender of Governor John Wentworth, nephew of Benning Wentworth, in 1775, and he left Portsmouth. On January 5, 1776, the Provincial Congress of New Hampshire drew up a temporary constitution, thus becoming an independent colony seven months before the Declaration of Independence was signed.

More than 3,000 New Hampshiremen took part in privateering, aiding the American naval forces against the British. From 1776 to 1781, the *Raleigh, America,* and *Ranger* (made famous by John Paul Jones) were built at Portsmouth. Regiments of the state's militia fought in the Battle of Bunker Hill. In 1777, New Hampshire militiamen commanded by John Stark, who later became a general, defeated the British at the Battle of Bennington in Vermont. Famous today for his declaration, Live Free or Die, Stark also is known for his reputed admonition at the Battle of Bennington: "Now, my men, there are the Hessians: they were bought for seven pounds, ten pence a man. Are you worth more? Prove it. Tonight the American flag floats over yonder hill or Molly Stark sleeps a widow."

The 1800s saw a period of expansion for New Hampshire, which became a manufacturing state. In 1830, 83 percent of the workers still farmed; by 1850, there were 56 cotton manufacturing companies and 61 woolen mills, and before the end of the century manufacturing was the main livelihood for most New Hampshirites. In 1865, there were 700 miles of railroad tracks in New Hampshire.

While slavery existed during the colonial period of New Hampshire, sentiment opposed slavery by the time of the Civil War, when 33,000 New Hampshire soldiers fought for the Union. The antislavery party, called the Republican Party, had been founded here.

The Immigrant Wave

With more and more factories built, foreign workers were drawn to New Hampshire or were recruited by the industrialists. From the meager farms of Canada came French Canadians by the thousands. In 1870, there were 5,000 Franco-Americans in New Hampshire; by 1930, there were 122,000. The great Amoskeag Manufacturing Company, started in 1805, grew to one of the largest cotton and woolen mills in the country, by 1850 employing more than 15,000 workers and turning out cloth at the rate of a mile every minute of the working day. Irish, German, Slavic, and other foreign workers came, along with the French Canadians, to work 12-hour days. From the Amoskeag mills sprang the company town of Manchester, which today is the state's largest city.

Shoes and leathergoods, wood and forest products, and metal working, traditional manufactures in New Hampshire, grew during the 1900s. The Great Depression hit the New Hampshire industrial economy hard and labor strikes closed the great Amoskeag Mills in Manchester. Many city workers returned to the farmlands. But resourceful leaders revived many of the industries. By 1966, on the basis of percentage employed in manufacturing, New Hampshire ranked second as the most industrial in the United States.

Magnetic New Hampshire

In recent years, New Hampshire, once dominated by mammoth mills operated by unskilled labor, has moved increasingly to a skilled labor force and high-tech industry, along with a surge in the white-collar service industries. The favorable tax climate and laborers with a strong work ethic have attracted commerce and industry, and the relaxed style of living has attracted people in large numbers in recent years. The population increased 22 percent between 1960 and 1970 and 25 percent in the 1970s, and the tide of newcomers, mostly to the rapidly growing southern tier, continues today. Tourism, the state's second largest industry, booms in winter, when two dozen major ski areas open, and in spring, summer, and fall, when tens of thousands come to enjoy the natural wonders and play in this recreational wonderland.

Two main highways—Route 16 on the east and I–93 (with its scenic parallel Route 3)—span the state from the south to the north country. I–89 cuts northwest across the lower half of the state on the way to Vermont. An old Yankee joke has the tourist asking directions, to which the native replies, "You can't get there from here." You will recall this when you try to cross the state. Only a few main roads cross east to west, and sometimes you may take winding backroads that turn out to give you a better view of rural New Hampshire. The state is divided into six regions—Seacoast, White Mountains/Mt. Washington Valley, Lakes Region, Hanover/Lake Sunapee, Monadnock Region, and Merrimack Valley. Some, like the Lakes Region, are compact, with a lot packed into a relatively small area; others are spread out, like the vast White Mountains region. But the state map makes this state look deceptively spread out in distance; because it's such a small state, you can travel from the south to the top of the state in about four hours. There are plenty of roadside services, but keep this in mind: When driving in the evenings, make sure your gas tank is full because in many areas of the state you won't find a service station open after dark.

Exploring New Hampshire

THE SEACOAST REGION

Less than an hour from Boston, the seacoast of New Hampshire starts at Seabrook on the Massachusetts border and ends at Portsmouth, 18 miles north. The region takes in towns to the north and west of the seacoast proper. From I–95 or Route 1, take State Route 286 east into Seabrook. This is marsh country and you will soon smell the sea. It is a family vacation spot, complete with amusement rides and stretches of beach. The Seabrook Greyhound Park, offering dog racing, is located here.

Hampton Beach

Hampton Beach is the next population center, a playground for thousands of in-state and out-of-state tourists. The three-mile boardwalk is a seaside promenade of uninhibited strollers, a marvelous place to people-watch amid a swirl of neon lights and the carnival atmosphere of penny arcades, sketch artists, candy making, pizza booths, trinket vendors, palm readers, glass blowers and, in the evenings, music by big-name acts at the Hampton Beach Casino. The sandy beach is a sea of sunbathers, while hundreds swim in the chilly Atlantic Ocean.

For a nice autumn diversion, take Route 101E over to Route 1, then meander south a few miles to Hampton Falls where, if you turn west on Route 88, you'll come upon Applecrest Farm Orchards, the oldest and largest apple orchards in the seacoast region. Here you can pick your own apples or, if you time it right, enjoy a harvest festival.

On to Rye

Back on Route 1A heading north, you'll catch Great Boar's Head, a rock-lined spur jutting into the sea north of Hampton Beach and crowded with some handsome old and spacious houses. You will cross into North Hampton, where you may want to stop at Fuller Gardens, two acres of formal flower gardens. You will pass by what is called "millionaire's row," grand homes of diverse architectural styles sitting on a bluff overlooking the ocean. Past supervised beaches, the traveler will then enter the town of Rye, where the first settlers arrived more than 350 years ago. Petrified stumps of an ice-age forest may sometimes be seen when the tide is low; tangled in the stumps one may spot the remains of the first transatlantic cable, which was laid across the ocean floor in 1874.

From Rye, looking out to sea, you can see the Isles of Shoals, stony islands originally settled by early fishermen and visited by pirates. You can take a two-hour cruise to visit the isles. Driving onward, Route 1A becomes 1B and you will pass the castlelike Wentworth-by-the-Sea, now closed but once an elegant haunt for the rich and famous and the site of the signing of the Russo-Japanese treaty in 1905. You may want to stop at Odiorne State Park, a nice place to take a stroll on the spot where the first settlers landed in 1623. You will also discover World War II bunkers built for an eventuality that never occurred.

New Castle

The small, picturesque town of New Castle is next on the tour. Here is a marker for the six-man British garrison at Castle William and Mary, now named Fort Constitution, which was raided in December 1774 by several hundred New Hampshiremen who took military supplies and gunpowder and distributed them to nearby towns. Some of the powder was later used to fight the British at the Battle of Bunker Hill in Boston. This is a town to walk through and admire the eighteenth-century architecture.

Portsmouth's Strawbery Banke

Route 1B circles back into Portsmouth, which combines architecture reflecting its English heritage with a seafaring flavor. First tour Strawbery Banke—named for the profusion of wild berries found on the shores by the first English settlers in 1630—a collection of 37 historic structures standing on their original foundations and dating from 1695 to 1945. Saved from demolition and planned urban renewal in the late 1950s, some were once owned by wealthy residents, others by ordinary people who lived and worked in Strawbery Banke, which was renamed Portsmouth in 1653. Located on March Street near the waterfront, the historic neighborhood of relocated houses offers Historic Museum Neighborhood guided tours, workshops, and lectures. Here is the restored, elegantly furnished Goodwin Mansion, home of New Hampshire's Civil War governor, and the William Pitt Tavern of Revolutionary days. Potters, coopers, weavers, boat builders, and cabinetmakers carry on the old traditions of Portsmouth, demonstrating their crafts and selling their wares. There also are re-created historic landscapes, including the eighteenth-century vegetable and herb garden of Joseph Sherburne and the elaborate Victorian flower garden of Governor Goodwin's wife, Sarah.

This seacoast city, across the Piscataqua river from Kittery, Maine, was a prospering town by 1700, when 90 sawmills of the Piscataqua region were providing Britain's shipyards with the finest tall pine masts found anywhere in the world. Portsmouth was New Hampshire's city of culture. Walk from Strawbery Banke a few blocks to Market Square, the hub of this historic city, which transports the visitor's imagination to the age of a bustling seaport community.

Historic Houses

Visit the North Cemetery on Maplewood Avenue, which was purchased by the town in 1752. General William Whipple, signer of the Declaration of Independence; Governor John Langdon, signer of the United States Constitution; and Captain Thomas Thompson, of the Continental ship *Rawleigh* are among those buried here. You may want to get Portsmouth Trail tickets, available at the Chamber of Commerce or at the individual houses, which are good for visiting six historical houses ($7).

At the corner of Middle and State streets is the John Paul Jones house, a good place to start your house tour. It houses the Portsmouth Historical Society, formed more than 50 years ago in response to the threatened destruction of the house. The house was built in 1758 by Captain Gregory Purcell, who married the niece of royal governor, Benning Wentworth.

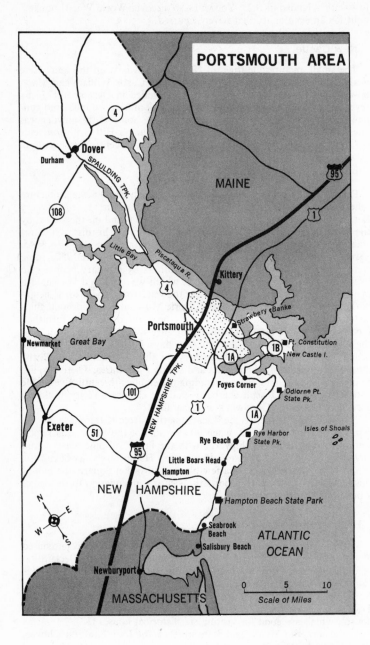

PORTSMOUTH AREA

After Purcell's death, his widow Sarah took in roomers, among whom was John Paul Jones, the early American naval commander. The Governor John Langdon House, built in 1784, is described by the Society for the Preservation of New England Antiquities as one of New England's finest eighteenth-century houses. Langdon was a prosperous merchant and ardent supporter of the American Revolution, personally financing General John Stark's expedition against Burgoyne in 1777. In 1785, Langdon became president of New Hampshire, as the governor's seat was then called out of antipathy to the former rule by royal governors, and was elected the first president of the United States Senate. The house was visited by George Washington, John Hancock, James Monroe, General Lafayette, and Louis Phillippe, later king of France.

The 1807 Rundlet-May House, with its original 1812 courtyard and garden layout, is a notable three-story Federal mansion built by Portsmouth merchant James Rundlet and is located at 364 Middle Street. A fine example of an early eighteenth-century brick house is the Warner House, 150 Daniel Street, which was built in 1716. The Moffatt-Ladd House, 154 Market Street, was built in 1763 and once belonged to General William Whipple; it contains eighteenth-century furniture and architecture and a broad staircase with a magnificent balustrade. An 1830 counting house overlooks the Piscataqua River where cargoes of the mercantilists Moffatt and Ladd were loaded. Take a drive on Little Harbor Road to visit the Wentworth Coolidge Mansion, which was the official royal governor's residence.

Portsmouth has many fine shops in restored old buildings. It is a place of fine restaurants and good theater. In summer there is the Prescott Park Arts Festival. Along the waterfront, you can see tugboats and fishing boats (and you may fish off the Prescott Park pier). The Piscataqua Gundalow Project at the Prescott Park Dock is a ship-museum, built by centuries-old techniques. The Port of Portsmouth Maritime Museum features a drydocked submarine, located on Market Street. In Portsmouth, the Isles of Shoals Steamship Co. offers boat tours of Portsmouth Harbor and the Isles of Shoals.

Dover

Twenty minutes north on Route 4-16 (the Spaulding Turnpike) brings you to Dover, the city first settled by the fishmongers Edward and William Hilton and their followers in 1623. Stop off at Hilton's Point, now a park, where they first settled. Dover, which grew as a mill town, has renewed itself in recent years. At the Woodman Institute, 182 Central Avenue, you can see stuffed animals representing many of the native species of New Hampshire, as well as early New Hampshire artifacts. There is an old Quaker Meeting House, a rarity in the early and late religious life of New Hampshire. (In 1661, Mayor Waldron of Dover ordered Anna Coleman, Mary Tompkins, and Alice Ambrose, who were Quakers, to be tied to a cart and drawn through the towns from Dover to Newburyport and publicly whipped upon their naked backs, all because of their different religious beliefs.)

The Garrison House is an example of the shuttered garrison houses from which early settlers defended themselves against attacking Indians. Dr. Jeremy Belknap, a 1762 graduate of Harvard College, was pastor of the First Congregational Church in Dover and publisher of the first history of New Hampshire; he founded the Massachusetts Historical Society in 1794.

Durham

You can head south from Dover on Route 108 and get to Durham in
15 minutes. Durham is the home of the University of New Hampshire,
which was founded in Hanover in 1868 and operated in conjunction with
Dartmouth College until it was moved to Durham in 1893. Paul Arts Center on campus has changing exhibitions, concerts, and theater. As you
drive into town on Route 108, instead of driving up Main Street, keep on
108 for a block and you will see the Oyster River and the area known as
Durham Landing. Here, in 1694, a force of about 250 Indians, under the
French soldier de Villies, killed or captured 100 settlers and destroyed five
garrison houses and numerous settlement houses on both sides of the river.
On the second floor of the Town Office Building is a historical museum.

Exeter

Follow Route 108 south to Exeter, home of Phillips Exeter Academy,
founded in 1783 and one of the most famous preparatory schools in the
country. The sprawling campus features ivy-covered brick buildings as
well as contemporary structures. Exeter's War Memorial is the work of
Daniel Chester French, a native of Exeter, best known for his statue of
Abraham Lincoln in the Lincoln Memorial in Washington, D.C. Founded
by the Reverend John Wheelwright in 1638, Exeter was one of the four
original towns in the colony. It served as the capital of the new state during
the American Revolution, and it was in Exeter that the Provincial Congress, in 1776, adopted the first state constitution that established the first
independent state government of the 13 colonies. There are many fine colo-
nial-period and nineteenth-century houses in Exeter; of special note is the
Gilman Garrison House, built about 1690. Located at 12 Water Street,
it was originally constructed as a fortified garrison, with massive hewn
logs forming the walls and a portcullis as the entry way.

PRACTICAL INFORMATION FOR THE SEACOAST REGION

Note: The area code for all New Hampshire is 603

HOW TO GET THERE AND AROUND. The Seacoast Region of New
Hampshire encompasses not only the 18-mi. seacoast but land-locked
towns off the coast, all within a 30-min. drive from Portsmouth. The heart
of the seacoast is about 45 min. by car from Boston, up I-95 or Rte. 1.
Logan International Airport in Boston is the closest airport, from which
you can take a Concord Trailways bus several times daily or a rental car.
To get around the seacoat requires a car, although there are some paid
tours.
   By air: Logan International in Boston is served by all major airlines.
It does have air service to Manchester, 55 min. from the seacoast, but to
get to the seacoast, it's quicker and easier to go by car from Logan.
   By bus: Concord Trailways offers daily bus service from Logan Airport
to the seacoast region, stopping in Portsmouth, Durham, Dover, and
Rochester. (Call Trailways toll free: 800-258-3722; in New Hampshire,
800-852-3317.)
   By car: Major car rental companies may be found at the airport. Drive
up I-95 north from Massachusetts to get to the New Hampshire seacoast,
45 min. or less away. An alternative, parallel route is Rte. 1, but I-95 is

the quickest. From Maine: I–95 south to Portsmouth. From Vermont: I–89 to I–93 south to Rte. 101 east to Portsmouth. From Connecticut: I–91 to Brattleboro, VT, east on Rte. 9 to Keene and Rte. 101 east to the coast. From Rhode Island: I–95 through Massachusetts to the New Hampshire seacoast.

HOTELS AND MOTELS. Accommodations in this region range from modern motels with swimming pools and cable TV to converted old summer houses. Some old and newer lodging places on the coast have kitchenettes. Rates are highest in the peak season, which runs June–Sept. The rates plummet in the remainder of the year, the off-season. Rates, based on double occupancy, in season: *Deluxe,* $90 and up; *Expensive,* $70–$90; *Moderate,* $50–$70; *Inexpensive,* $50 and under.

Dover

Friendship Inn, Silver St. and Spaulding Tpke., Exit 8E, 03820 (742–4100). *Expensive.* 80 rooms. Cable TV and pool. Bar with entertainment and dancing.

In-Towne Motel, 481 Central Ave., 03820 (742–0400). *Moderate.* 48 rooms and 10 suites. Pool and cable TV.

Durham

New England Center, Strafford Ave., 03824 (862–2810). *Expensive.* Gorgeous setting on campus. Restaurant, lounge, cable color TV.

Exeter

Best Western Hearthside Motor Inn, Portsmouth Ave. (772–3794). *Expensive.* 33 rooms, lounge, pool; free in-room movies; airport shuttle.

Exeter Inn, 90 Front St., 03833 (772–5901; reservations, 800–782–8444). *Expensive.* 50 rooms, Georgian setting, campus of Phillips Exeter Academy.

Hampton/Hampton Beach

Hampton House, 333 Ocean Blvd., Box 578, Hampton Beach 03842 (926–1033). *Deluxe.* Modern oceanfront hotel within walking distance of area attractions. Open year-round.

Hampton Beach Regal Inn, 162 Ashworth Ave., 03842 (926–7758). *Expensive.* Seasonal rates, package plans, group rates. One block from the beach.

Hampton Motor Inn, 815 Lafayette Rd., Hampton 03842 (926–6771). *Moderate–Expensive.* 3 mi. north on U.S. 1. Heated pool, whirlpool, 56 rooms, oversized beds. Kitchenettes, suites.

Seascape, 955 Ocean Blvd. at North Beach, 03842 (926–9153). *Moderate–Expensive.* Opposite the ocean, 19 rooms. Color TV.

Ashworth by the Sea, 295 Ocean Blvd., Rtes. 1-A and 51, 03842 (926–6762). *Moderate.* Oceanfront property with 107 rooms. Heated indoor-outdoor pools to go with the beach and ocean. Fine seafood restaurant, lounge.

Portsmouth

Anchorage Motor Inn, On the Portsmouth Traffic Circle, 03801 (431–8111). *Expensive.* Indoor pool, sauna. Pets. Color cable TV.

Howard Johnson, Interstate Highway, Exit 5 off I-95, 03801 (436-7600). *Moderate.* 135 rooms. Outdoor heated pool.

Rye/Rye Beach

Hoyt's Lodges, 891 Ocean Blvd., 03870 (436-5350). *Moderate-Expensive.* Oceanfront cottages with pine paneling, all with kitchenettes. Cable TV. Open Memorial Day to Columbus Day.

Rye Beach Motel and Cottages, Old Beach and Locke Rds., 03870 (964-5511). *Moderate-Expensive.* Housekeeping units and motel rooms. Beach. Color TV. Open May-Oct.

INNS, GUEST HOUSES, BED AND BREAKFASTS. On the seacoast there is a limited yet select offering of inns and bed and breakfasts in comparison with some other areas of the state. All listings below are *moderately* priced.

Dover

Silver St. Inn, 103 Silver St., 03820 (743-3000). *Expensive.* Bed and breakfast in a late 19th-century mansion. Full breakfast. Near University of New Hampshire, shopping, and Pease AFB.

Durham

Country House Bed & Breakfast, RR 2, Stagecoach Rd., 03824 (659-6565). *Moderate.* Near University of New Hampshire and beaches.

Dewey's Hannah House, Packers Falls Rd., 03824 (659-5500). *Inexpensive.* No credit cards, no smoking.

Hampton

Stone Gables Motor Inn, 869 Lafayette Rd., 03842 (926-6883). *Inexpensive.* Restaurants, beaches, and shopping nearby. Open year-round.

Sise Inn, 40 Court St., 03801 (433-1200). *Expensive.* Bed and breakfast in a late 19th-century home.

Portsmouth

Inn at Christian Shore, 335 Maplewood Ave., 03801 (431-6770). Federal-era home (1800) with period furnishings. Full-course breakfast included. Color cable TV.

Martin Hill Inn, 404 Islington St., 03801 (436-2287). Another 19th-century pearl with antiques in all six guest rooms; full-course breakfast included.

RESTAURANTS. Fine restaurants abound on the seacoast, from gourmet establishments to superb seafood places. There are plenty of family restaurants, clam shacks, and fast-food places. Price ranges for a meal for one person excluding beverage, tax, and tip; *Expensive,* $25 and up; *Moderate,* $10-$25; *Inexpensive,* $10 and under.

Dover

Firehouse One, 1 Orchard St. (749-3636). *Moderate.* Recycled fire station. Hearty American fare.

ASIA Chinese and Polynesian Restaurant, 42 Third St., 03820 (742–0040). *Moderate.* One of three ASIA restaurants in the Seacoast Region. Luncheon specials, function rooms, takeout.

Durham

New England Center Restaurant, Strafford Ave. (862–2815). *Moderate.* Award-winning cuisine, lovely natural setting.

Exeter

Exeter Inn, 90 Front St. (772–5901). *Moderate–Expensive.* Specialties are seafood and steak. Good luncheon stop.

Hampton/Hampton Beach

Ashworth's by the Sea, 295 Ocean Blvd. (926–6762). *Moderate–Expensive.* Plenty of seafood, especially lobster and clams. Light entertainment nightly. Three restaurants.
Galley Hatch, Rte. 1 (926–6152). *Moderate–Expensive.* Emphasis is on seafood, but they can rustle up a mean steak, too. Homemade soups and pastries.
Widow Fletchers Tavern, Rte. 1 (926–8800). *Moderate.* Prime ribs, seafood. Sun. brunch, 11 A.M.–3P.M.

Kingston

The Kingston 1686 House, Rte. 111 (Main St.) (642–3637). *Expensive.* Superb dinners prepared to order from fresh fish and seafood. Homemade desserts. Extensive wine list.

Portsmouth

Anthony's Al Dente Ristorante, 59 Penhallow St., Custom House Cellar (436–2527). *Expensive.* Traditional Italian cuisine.
Blue Strawbery, 29 Ceres St. (431–6420). *Expensive.* Gourmet fixed-price dining in the port city. Relax and enjoy. Small restaurant and popular, so be sure to make advance reservations.
Dinnerhorn Restaurant and Bratskeller, 980 Lafayette St. (436–0717). *Moderate.* International menu from sandwiches and pizza to seafood, beef, and poultry entrées. Beers and wines.
Pier II, State St. (436–0669). *Expensive.* Next to Memorial Bridge, overlooking the harbor. Seafood and steaks, chops, and chicken.
The Oar House, 55 Ceres St. (436–4025). *Moderate–Expensive.* Traditional fare in an 18th-century warehouse on the waterfront.
Tortilla Flat, Rte. 1 (431–6995). *Moderate.* Authentic Mexican food and a cozy, rustic atmosphere.

Rye

Pirate's Cove, Rte. 1-A (436–8733). *Moderate–Expensive.* Pirate decor. Fine seafood.

TOURIST INFORMATION. For information and literature on the Seacoast Region, contact the Seacoast Council on Tourism, Box 830, Durham 03824 (436–7678); Portsmouth Chamber of Commerce, Market St. Extension, Portsmouth 03801 (436–1118); Dover Chamber of Commerce, 299 Central Ave., Box 239, Dover 03820 (742–2218); Exeter Area Chamber of Commerce, 120 Water St., Exeter 03833 (772–2411); Hampton Beach Area Chamber of Commerce, 836 Lafayette Rd., Box 790, Hampton 03842 (926–8717). For general statewide information: New Hampshire Office of Vacation Travel, Box 856, Concord 03301 (271–2666).

TOURS. Bus tours: Insight Tours of Portsmouth, Box 61, New Castle 03854 (436–4223) offers group guided bus tours of the historic port city of Portsmouth.

On foot: Walking tour of Portsmouth Historical Trail; visit six furnished museum houses with guides. June to Mid-Oct. $2 per house, or ticket series for all houses, $6. Contact Portsmouth Historical Houses, Box 239, Portsmouth 03801 (436–1118). Or get tickets at Portsmouth Chamber of Commerce, Market St. Extension (436–1118).

By trolley: One-hour historical trolley tour of Portsmouth and New Castle, Harbor district, Strawbery Banke, etc. June 20–Labor Day, daily 11 A.M.–5 P.M. Adults, $3.25; children, $2. Or ride around at Hampton Beach: trolleys are the beach's public transportation—combined with a light narrative of local historical and current events. June 20–Labor Day. $1. Olde Port Trolley Co., Box 190, Dover 03820.

Boat tours and cruises: Isles of Shoals Steamship Co., (431–5500) takes you on a narrated tour to the Isles of Shoals. It also runs trips for whale-watching. Portsmouth Harbor Cruises (436–8084) gives harbor cruises, inland river cruises, Great Bay, narrated Isles of Shoals tours, etc. New Hampshire Seacoast Cruises (382–6743 or 964–5545) offers whale watches, May–Oct. narrated Isles of Shoals tours, Portsmouth Harbor cruise, trip to see lobster operation, whale watches off season.

SEASONAL EVENTS. May: Prescott Park Chowder Festival, Portsmouth (end of May).

June: Annual Blessing of the Fleet, State Fish Pier, Portsmouth (early June); annual Somersworth International Children's Festival, Somersworth (late June); Portsmouth Jazz Festival, Portsmouth (end of June); annual Strawberry Festival, Nottingham (end of June).

July: Annual Seacoast Muster and Cannon Shoot, mock battle, Greenland (mid–late July); Stratham Fair, Stratham (late July); Prescott Park Arts Festival, Portsmouth (July 4–early Aug.); Kingston Fair, Kingston (early July); fireworks, the night before the 4th, Hampton Beach; July 4th Celebration, Strawbery Banke, Portsmouth; Bow Street Fair, Portsmouth (early July).

August: Annual Children's Week Festival, Hampton Beach (late Aug.); Portsmouth Trail by Candlelight, Portsmouth (late Aug.).

September: Annual NEMA Midget Championships, Epping (early Sept.); 10-day Rochester Fair, Rochester (2nd week).

November: Annual Christmas Craft Fair, Portsmouth (early Nov.); annual Dover Christmas Parade, Dover (end of Nov.).

December: Annual Christmas Parade and Festival, Hampton (early Dec.); annual Rochester Christmas Parade, Rochester (early Dec.); Candlelight Stroll, Strawbery Banke, Portsmouth (early Dec.).

PARKS. Odiorne Point State Park, Rte. 1A, Rye. Site of landing of Scottish fishermen to create first permanent European settlement in New Hampshire. 137 acres of coastal park with unique and varied vegetation. Picnic sites, walkways for the handicapped. Open all year, free. Visitor Center open late June–late Aug. (436–7406).

Rye Harbor, Rye is a picnic area on a breezy, rocky promontory on the Atlantic. Saltwater fishing from a jetty, boat ramp, commercial wharf. Free.

GARDENS. Fuller Gardens, 10 Willow Ave., N. Hampton (964–5414). Two-acre formal flower gardens; roses, annuals, perennials, Japanese gardens. Adults $2.50; seniors $2.00; children under 18 free.
   The Greenery, 883 Lafayette Rd., Hampton (926–7540) Garden center with many in-ground "idea" planting gardens. Open all year, free.

BEACHES. Hampton Beach, Hampton. Two miles of sandy beach on the ocean. In summer, supervised, comfort station, first aid. Acres of metered parking.
   Jenness Beach, Rye. Ocean swimming, bathhouse, metered parking, lifeguards. Free.
   Fox Head Point, North Hampton. Ocean swimming, bathhouse, metered parking, lifeguards. Free.
   Wallis Sands, Rye. Ocean swimming on the open seacoast. The 700-ft.-long sandy beach is only 150 ft. wide at high tide. Ample parking near the beach. Free.

FALL FOLIAGE. While peak foliage, and most spectacular, is found north and west in the state, there are plenty of turning trees inland within the Seacoast Region. Try a tour through the Durham-Exeter area, taking side roads. Call 224–2525 or 2526 for taped foliage reports.

SUMMER SPORTS. Boating: There are plenty of boating opportunities in the Great Bay, inland rivers such as Cocecho and Lamphrey rivers, and the ocean. You can rent row boats in Hampton, but stay in the inlet; the outgoing tide is strong.
   Swimming: There's ample ocean beach, but some areas are rocky and slippery. Best stick to the four supervised beaches.
   Golf: Portsmouth Country Club, Greenland (436–9791). Sagamore-Hampton Golf Club, North Hampton (964–5341). Abenaqui Country Club, Rye Beach (964–5563). Exeter Country Club, Exeter (778–8080). Rockingham Country Club, Newmarket (659–6379).
   Hiking: In the town of New Castle, on an island next to Portsmouth, start at Fort Constitution where there's an asphalt hiking trail along a shaded route through the historic town. Nearby Odiorne Point State Park in Rye has hiking trails away from camping and picnic grounds leading to coastal rocks and sandy beaches.
   Horseback riding: Happy Hours Stables, Dover (749–4497) has trail rides on logging roads and in fields. Write to New Hampshire Office of Vacation Travel, Box 856, Concord 03301 (271–2343) for statewide list of horseback riding facilities.
   Bicycling. The New Hampshire section of the East Coast Bicycle Trail starts at Rte. 150 in South Hampton on the Massachusetts border and takes you through Exeter, Newmarket, Durham, and Barrington before heading up country. There's also a bicycle route with moderate-to-heavy traffic along the seacoast and a trail from Hampton Beach starting at Rte. 101D to Stratham and Greenland with low-to-moderate traffic. Write to Granite State Wheelmen, Inc., 16 Clinton St., Salem 03079, for detailed mappings of East Coast trail as well as other bicycling routes.

FISHING. For details on fishing, coastal or inland, contact the New Hampshire Fish and Game Dept., 34 Bridge St., Concord 03301

(322–5018 or 800–322–5018). Local chambers of commerce will have information concerning boat charters or guides in their areas.

CAMPING. A total of 15 camp grounds in the Seacoast Region are listed in the New Hampshire Camping Guide produced by the New Hampshire Division of Economic Development, Box 856, Concord 03301 (271–2666). All approved by the state.

SPECTATOR SPORTS. The University of New Hampshire at Durham has top-flight **hockey,** as well as **basketball** and **football,** during the school year.

Seabrook Greyhound Park, Rte. 107 (I–95, Exit 1) in Seabrook offers **greyhound dog racing** all year in the evenings, Mon.–Sat. Wagering. (474–3065).

Star Speedway, Rte. 27E, Epping 03042 (679–5306) has **stock car racing** Saturdays, 7:15 P.M., May–Sept.

HISTORIC SITES AND HOUSES. The seacoast, where the first white settlers arrived, is filled with history. Call ahead to check admission fees.

Dover

Dover Point, site of first Dover settlement, in 1623. Hilton State Park off Spaulding Tpke. and U.S. 4 in Dover. Open days year-round. Free.

Portsmouth

Strawbery Banke, Marcy St. near waterfront (433–1100). 37 original buildings, dated 1695–1820, all but five on original foundations. Recreated historic landscapes and flower gardens. Five authentically restored furnished houses of different time periods. Open daily, May 1–Oct. 31, 10 A.M.–5 P.M.

Governor John Langdon House (1784), 143 Pleasant St. (436–3205). Built for John Langdon, prosperous merchant and ardent supporter of Revolutionary War and later governor of the state. Interior has some of the finest carving in Portsmouth. Rooms furnished with family antiques and other pieces. Handsome landscaped grounds. Open June 1–Oct. 15, Wed.–Sun., 12–5 P.M.

Rundlett-May House (1807), 364 Middle St. (436–3205). Superb three-story federal mansion built by James Rundlet, Portsmouth merchant. Retains original 1812 courtyard and garden layout. Furnished entirely with family furniture and accessories, many pieces made by local craftsmen. June 1–Oct. 15, Wed.–Sun., 12–5 P.M.

John Paul Jones House, corner of Middle and State Sts. (436–8420). Built in 1758, the house became a boarding house in which John Paul Jones stayed for two periods while supervising the outfitting of the *Ranger* and the *America* for the Continental Navy. Open mid-May–mid-Oct., Mon.–Sat. and holidays.

Wentworth Gardner House (1760), 140 Mechanic St. (436–4406). A near-perfect example of Georgian architecture. Built for the younger brother of John Wentworth, last of the royal governors. It was once owned by the Metropolitan Museum of Art, which planned at one time to move it to Central Park. End of May to Columbus Day, 2–5 P.M. Tues.–Sun.

(There are a total of six houses on the Portsmouth Historic trail, including these. $6 for six-house tour. Portsmouth Chamber of Commerce, Market Street Extension, call 436–1118.)

Exeter

Gilman Garrison House, 12 Water St. (227–3956). 17th-century log construction with 18th-century wing and facade. Meeting place for Governor's Council during Revolutionary War. Originally a garrison house for protection against Indian attacks. Open June 1–Sept. 30, Tues., Thurs., Sat., Sun., 12–5 P.M.

War Memorial, Gale Park on Front St. Created in 1920 by sculptor Daniel Chester French, who sculpted the Lincoln figure in the Lincoln Memorial and the Minuteman statue at the Concord (Massachusetts) bridge.

New Castle

Fort Constitution, off Rte. 1B, on point overlooking Piscataqua River. Originally built in 1635; current structure built in 1808. Four months before Lexington and Concord, colonists took over the fort, taking gunpowder and cannon later used in the Battle of Bunker Hill. Open daily 9 A.M.–5 P.M., mid-June–Labor Day, weekends the rest of the year. Free.

Durham

Major General John Sullivan House, Rte. 108. Home of Revolutionary War general. Set back off the road. Private residence not open to the public.

Oyster River Massacre site, west, less than a quarter of a mile on Rte. 108 from Main St. Here, in 1694, about 250 Indians, under the French soldier de Villies, attacked settlements on both sides of the Oyster River, killing or capturing about 100 settlers and destroying five garrison houses and numerous dwellings. It was the most devastating French and Indian raid in New Hampshire during King Williams' War.

MUSEUMS. Museums in this area reflect the local maritime and colonial heritage. Call ahead to check admission fees.

Dover

Woodman Institute, 182 Central Ave. (742–1038). Natural history and military museum; bird, animal, and Indian exhibits showing the variety of wildlife that has existed in New Hampshire. Also, 17th-century Dame Garrison House.

Portsmouth

Piscataqua River Gundalow, Prescott Park Inlet (964–9079). Tour of reproduction of traditional river barge of Piscataqua Region. Donations $1, children under 12 free. Open May 1–Oct. 11 daily, 10 A.M.–4 P.M.

Port of Portsmouth Maritime Museum, Market St. (436–3680). Home of U.S.S. *Albacore,* submarine built at Portsmouth Naval Yard (across the river in Kittery) in 1952. Tour sub. Open late June–Labor Day.

Children's Museum of Portsmouth, March St. (436–3853). Open Tues.–Sat. 10 A.M.–5 P.M., Sun. 1–5 P.M., and Mon. 10 A.M.–5 P.M. during the summer and school vacations. 12 hands-on exhibits for children, workshops, performances.

Hampton

Tuck Memorial Museum, Meeting House Green, 40 Park Ave. Open July, Aug., Mon.–Fri., 10 A.M. to 4 P.M. One-room schoolhouse and a trolley collection. Free.

GALLERIES. In Durham—**University Art Galleries,** Paul Creative Arts Center, University of New Hampshire campus (862–3712). Fine arts, historical exhibits, contemporary crafts. Open Sept.–June, closed Fri.

In Exeter—**Lamont Gallery/Frederick R. Mayer Art Center,** Phillips Exeter Academy (772–4311, ext. 324). Exhibitions during school year.

In Portsmouth—**Vaughan Art Gallery,** 366 Islington St. (431–5373). Open Tues.–Sat., 12–4 P.M. Original paintings, prints, photos. Features Northeast artists. Free.

MUSIC, DANCE, AND STAGE. From big-name rock and popular music stars performing at the Hampton Beach Casino to excellent drama performed at Theatre by the Sea in Portsmouth, there is good-quality stage entertainment to choose from in the Seacoast Region, especially in summer. **Theatre by the Sea,** 125 Bow St., Portsmouth (431–6660) offers contemporary, traditional, and classical drama. The **Prescott Park Arts Festival** on the waterfront in Portsmouth (436–2848) offers a series of outdoor art, live music, and live theater productions throughout the summer. In Hampton, **Hampton Playhouse,** 357 Winnacunnet Rd. (926–3073) is open summers with musicals, comedies; children's plays on Sat. At the **Hampton Beach Sea Shell State Park,** a summer concert series on weekends offers free band concerts from a variety of artists, including jazz, popular, big-band sounds. **Hampton Beach Casino** (926–4541) offers top-name music on weekends. Also, free band concerts daily in summer. In Durham, the **University of New Hampshire Summer Concert Series,** Johnson Theatre (862–2404), offers big-band, jazz, and other musical concerts on Thurs. evenings.

SHOPPING. Fine shops abound in this area, especially in Portsmouth. **Salamandra Glass Studio and Gallery,** at 133 Market St., offers hand-blown treasures. **Bearly Kids,** at 7 Commercial Alley, has all the cuddly teddy bears you'll ever need. **Alie's Jewelry** has fine jewelry. The **Marcy Street Doll Company,** at 60 Marcy St., has an incredible doll collection, many for sale, and beautiful doll clothing. For a distinctive array of fabrics, visit the **Portsmouth Fabric Co.** at 112 Penhallow St. The **Red Sled,** at 36 State St., is a great Christmas shop. You'll also find a number of factory outlets in Portsmouth, including the **Artisan Outlet Village,** at 72 Mirona Rd., a complex of outlet shops featuring brand-name and designer apparel, footwear, housewares, and books. Two major shopping malls, located near each other, in next-door Newington, have both major department stores and fine shops: **Newington Mall,** with more than 70 stores and restaurants, at 45 Gosling Rd., and **Fox Runn Mall,** with more than 100 stores, at nearby Fox Run Rd. In Hampton Falls, on Drinkwater Rd., **Starvish Pewter** offers handcrafted early American reproductions and some contemporary pieces. A tip for Hampton Beach shoppers: about a week before Labor Day, you can find some super bargains in gold and silver jewelry.

NIGHTLIFE. The **Hampton Beach Club Casino** (926–4300) is a real nightclub, one of the few in New Hampshire in the traditional sense, with big-name musical entertainment. It's located right on the ocean in Hampton Beach. There's dancing at the **Ashworth by the Sea** on Ocean Blvd. on the beach (926–6762). Portsmouth is the major center of nightlife on the seacoast. For a distinctive atmosphere, go to the **Press Room Restaurant** at 77 Daniel St. (431–5186). It has jazz and other good music. The **Metro**, at 20 High St. (436–0521), offers jazz Fri. and Sat. There's good dancing music at **Luka's Another Restaurant** at 172 Hanover St. (431–5795). Other good night spots are the **Pelican Club** of Galley Hatch Restaurant (926–6152) on Rte. 1 (Lafayette Rd.) and **The Dolphin Striker** and **Spring Hill Tavern** at Ceres and Bow Sts. (431–5222).

THE WHITE MOUNTAINS—MT. WASHINGTON
VALLEY REGION

Departing the seacoast, you can head for the mountains straight up Route 16. In an hour and a half you will reach the beautiful Mt. Washington Valley and the town of Conway. The nineteenth-century artists of the White Mountains School of Art brought fame early to the region, their landscape paintings enticing tourists from all over the country. Travelers came by trains in the early days, and they keep coming by car today.

As you near the populated area of Conway, take a left on Route 112, the Kancamagus Highway, which people often wrongly pronounce Kang-ga-mang-us (it's Kan-ka-maw-gus). A quarter-mile down the road is the Kancamagus Snowshoe Center, where Treffle Bolduc, a violinist who once played with the Boston Pops Orchestra, turns out handmade white ash snowshoes, finely crafted using secrets he learned from Canadian Indians. Decide now whether to continue: Once you're on the highway, it takes an hour for a winding drive through an uninhabited national forest. Around hairpin curves, marvelous vistas will greet you. Alongside the highway runs the bolder-strewn Swift River, with scores of swimming holes, native trout, rushing falls, and Rocky Gorge, a thundering cascade. At the end is Lincoln, home of Loon Mountain, where you will find skiing in winter and New Hampshire's longest gondola aerial ride in summer.

For this tour we'll consider the Kancamagus Highway a side trip. Back on Route 16, drive north into Conway Village. Stop for a stroll through the old covered bridge, closed to vehicles. The bridge straddles the Saco River, with its crystal clear water gently flowing by sandy shores and its pebbled bottom through Conway and Maine. It's a perfect river for canoeing or floating along on an inner tube.

Continue through the village and make a dogleg left and continue on Route 16, viewing the dominating peak of Mt. Washington in the distance. Soon you will come to "the strip," that part of the artery crammed with restaurants, factory outlet stores, and tourist attractions. A few minutes later you'll be in North Conway Village. The village, with Mt. Washington serving as a backdrop, looks as if it came out of a Walt Disney set: The Conway Scenic Railroad huffs and puffs smoke as it slowly churns from the quaint, 1874 restored bright-yellow station; in front of the station is a vast village green across from charming old stores and the steepled white Congregational church.

You can take a one-hour, 11-mile round-trip ride on the railroad, shop in dozens of fine village shops, or drive or trek a short way to Mt. Cranmore, which offers skiing in winter and, in all seasons, skimobile rides with

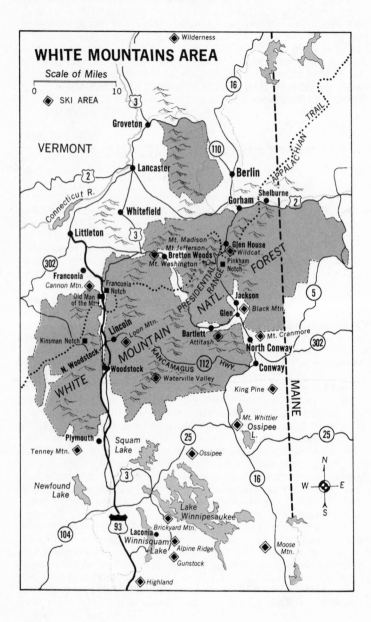

WHITE MOUNTAINS AREA

Scale of Miles

0   10

◆ SKI AREA

◆ Wilderness

⬣ 16

APPALACHIAN TRAIL

3

Groveton

VERMONT

110

2   Berlin

Lancaster

Connecticut R.   Shelburne

Whitefield   Gorham   2

3

Littleton

Mt. Madison   Glen House

Mt. Jefferson   Wildcat   NATL.   FOREST

302   Bretton Woods

Franconia   Mt. Washington   Pinkham
                                          Notch
Cannon Mtn.   Franconia
                   Notch

Old Man   Jackson   5
of the Mtn.   Black Mtn.

Lincoln   Loon Mtn.   Glen

Kinsman Notch   Mt. Cranmore

N. Woodstock   Bartlett   302
                     Attitash   North Conway

Woodstock   KANCAMAGUS 112 HWY.   Conway

WHITE MOUNTAIN   Waterville Valley   MAINE

                                   King Pine

                         Mt. Whittier
                             Ossipee
                               L.
Plymouth

Tenney Mtn.   Squam
                   Lake   25   25

Newfound   Ossipee
  Lake

                         16

                                    N
                                 W   E
                                    S

                   Lake
                 Winnipesaukee

            Brickyard Mtn.
93 Laconia   Moose
Winnisquam   Mtn.
104   Lake   Alpine Ridge

                 Gunstock

            Highland

high-altitude views of the entire valley. There's ample lodging all over the valley if it's crowded in North Conway: 8,000 beds in all kinds of lodging establishments.

Now continue north on Route 16 and straight on Route 302 to Attitash Mountain, where there's skiing in winter. In summer you can take a chairlift to the top and ski back down fast on dry or wet slopes. Head back down to the Route 16–302 intersection, turn onto Route 16 going north, and you will quickly come upon Storyland and Heritage New Hampshire, wholesome family entertainment. Storybook scenes, including Cinderella's Castle, greet you at Storyland; next door at Heritage New Hampshire you are introduced to Granite State history from a replica of a ship that brought early settlers from England to a typical New England town meeting scene. Farther on Route 16, turn right at the covered bridge that spans the sparkling Wildcat River and enter the small village of Jackson. You will find a reminder of that golden age of grand resort hotels in the restored Wentworth Resort Hotel, which had sat abandoned and dilapidated for years. Up the hill is Black Mountain, one of the five ski mountains in the Mt. Washington Valley. On the way down, stop at Jackson Falls for a relaxing pause.

Circle through the village to Route 16 and head north to Glen Ellis Falls Scenic Area. Now you're at Pinkham Notch, home of the Appalachian Mountain Club, and here is Wildcat Mountain, an excellent ski area. Head north to the Mt. Washington Auto Road, which will take you eight winding miles with truly breathtaking views to the summit of the highest mountain in the northeast. Carry warm clothing; temperatures drop dramatically at the top. A man named Darby Field journeyed by foot from the seacoast to climb this mountain in 1642. Today runners race up it, gasping and walking much of the way in an annual competition. You can travel the graveled road, built in 1861 as a carriage road, by car; there is some thrilling hairpin maneuvering. At the summit is a private research weather station operated by men who routinely experience frigid temperatures and 100-mile-an-hour winds. On April 12, 1934, the winds reached 231 miles per hour, the highest velocity ever recorded anywhere in the world. One tip: On the way down, pull over occasionally to rest your brakes. Many people prefer to take the paid chauffeured van tour.

Gorham and Berlin

On to Gorham. You now are in Coos County (pronounced Co-hos), which occupies about a million acres of alpine forested land. You may feel lonely or relish the isolation in this grand wilderness country. Turn right at Route 2 for a mile or so for the spectacular Shelburne birches, clustered on both sides of the road. Then continue on to Berlin (pronounced BER-lin in New Hampshire), the home of paper mills where lumberjacks once unclogged logjams on the Androscoggin River.

The True North Country

The country from here on up is wild and rugged and mostly uninhabited. Restaurants are scarce, so pack a lunch. Turn west at Route 26 off 16. When you reach Dixville Notch, you may recognize some of the people; this handful of voters casts the first presidential primary votes every four years, just after midnight, and gets prime-time TV coverage the next day. At the far end of Dixville Notch is the Wilderness Ski Area, where you will find The Balsams, the state's northernmost resort, which started as an inn on the stagecoach route. It is a spectacular setting, a Swiss-style

370 NEW ENGLAND

complex set upon a lake in a valley and in the middle of its own 15,000 acres.

Keep on Route 26 to Colebrook, across the Connecticut River from Vermont and eight miles from the Canadian border. This is a frontier town. North on Route 145 is the Colebrook Fish Hatchery. Continue up 145 to Pittsburg and the Connecticut Lakes, where the mighty Connecticut River begins. Pittsburg is the gateway to the former Indian Stream Territory, an independent nation established in 1832 during the border dispute between Canada and the United States. The largest township in the country, Pittsburg contains more than 300,000 acres of timberland, mountains, lakes, streams, and forest trails. This is prime hunting and fishing country, with large trout and an abundance of partridge, snowshoe rabbit, black bear, deer, and bobcat. You still can pan for gold at Indian Stream at Pittsburg.

Lancaster

From Pittsburg, take Route 3 south. Just south of Colebrook is the beautiful Shrine of Our Lady of Grace, 35 acres of landscaped grounds maintained by the Oblate Fathers and open to visitors. Down Route 3 about 30 miles you'll come to the town of Lancaster, county seat of Coos County and the first real settlement in this far-north country, founded in 1763. Charles Farrar Browne, whose famous pen name was Artemus Ward, spent his early writing years here. Jaunt southeast on Route 2 a few miles to see Santa's Village, with deer and ducks wandering the grounds and rides for children, and Six Gun City, a northeast version of the Wild West. A short way farther on Route 2 is Jefferson, home of the Waumbek Arts Center, which holds sculpture and crafts workshops and musical and dance performances in the summertime. Return northwest on Route 2 and turn south on Route 116, winding your way to the lovely little town of Whitefield. The Weathervane Theater here is the state's northernmost summer theater.

Crawford Notch

Take Route 3 south again, picking up Route 302 going south at Twin Mountain. You come to Crawford Notch State Park, where you can enjoy the Silver Cascade, and farther on a sign marks the spot where the entire Willey family was buried in 1816 by a great rock slide, recounted in Hawthorne's story *The Ambitious Guest.* Down the highway a few miles is the great Mt. Washington Hotel, built at the turn of the century and once a grand retreat of the wealthy, when up to 50 trains would arrive daily with guests. Here in 1944 was held the Bretton Woods Monetary Conference, which established the World Bank and chose the American dollar as the backbone of international exchange. The hotel, open in summers only, is in the heart of the Bretton Woods ski resort area.

Mt. Washington Cog Railway

A mile or so farther on Route 302 is the Mt. Washington Cog Railway, built in 1866 as the world's first mountain-climbing railway. A toothed wheel engages the center track to pull the powerful steam engines up the mountain. Since an accident in 1968 killed eight and injured more than 50 passengers, the state has tightened safety regulations.

Return on Route 302 past the Route 3 intersection to the unusual little town of Bethlehem. Its striking Victorian architecture once saw 10 trainloads a day of people arriving to stay the summer. Because it was virtually free of ragweed pollen, people with hay fever came first in trickles and then in droves. Presidents Grant, Taft, Cleveland, and Theodore Roosevelt vacationed here, as did Joseph Kennedy, Arturo Toscanini, the Rothschilds, and the S. S. Pierce family. Elvin Ivie, who was president of the Woolworth Corporation, had several homes and a church built in Bethlehem for his family.

Continue west on Route 302 to Littleton, where brothers Benjamin and Edward Kilburn produced and distributed thousands of stereoscopic views, the largest collection in the world. From Littleton, take I-93 south to the Franconia Notch exit. This is *the* Notch in New Hampshire. The house where Robert Frost lived for a few years is here. So is Cannon Mountain, the state-run ski area, where you can take an 80-passenger car to an observation platform at the summit. And here at the Notch is the famous Old Man of the Mountains, a stony profile formed more than 200 million years ago, towering high above Profile Lake. Along the notch is the Flume, a natural chasm in granite descending 700 feet deep. There are bus rides and many footpaths at the bottom. About 250,000 tourists visit the Flume each year.

Continuing down Route 3, you'll come to Lincoln, home of Loon Mountain described earlier, and about 10 miles south is Waterville Valley, another year-round resort noted for skiing. At North Woodstock, next to Lincoln, you can travel up Route 112 to Lost River, which disappears beneath ancient blocks of glacier-tumbled granite. Or head south from Lincoln on Route 118 to Warren, home of the Morse Museum. On entering town, you may be amused to see an early Army missile. The museum is a collection of mounted animals and memorabilia gathered in the African jungles and India by a retired shoe retailer and his family. Ask to see the trout pond in back; there are huge trout that nearly jump out of the water when fed special museum food.

Stay on Routes 25 and 118 (which join north of Warren) to the Polar Caves in Plymouth. These are a series of glacial caves that can be explored, and there's a Maple Sugar Museum where you can taste maple candy. Continue southeast on Route 25 to 3A, turning south to Bristol. Soon you will skirt Newfound Lake, the fourth largest lake in New Hampshire, with Mt. Cardigan as a backdrop. At Bristol take State 104 southwest to Danbury and turn right on Route 4, which leads to the Ruggles Mine, the oldest mica mine in the United States (1803). Here are mine tunnels, pits, and plenty of specimens to collect.

PRACTICAL INFORMATION FOR THE WHITE MOUNTAINS— MT. WASHINGTON VALLEY REGION

Note: The area code for all New Hampshire is 603

HOW TO GET THERE AND AROUND. This is far-flung country, and a car is necessary to get around.

By bus: Concord Trailways (800–258–3722; inside New Hampshire, 800–852–3317) offers bus service daily to the north country from Logan International Airport in Boston. Stops once a day in North Conway, Berlin, and Littleton. The trip is scenic, with a number of local stops as the bus snakes its way up the state. There is also a daily bus trip to North Conway from New York City (call Trailways).

By car: Major car rental companies are found at Logan Airport. From Massachusetts: Drive up I–95 and continue on the Spaulding Tpke. and

Rte. 16 all the way to Conway, a three-hour trip. From Maine: Rte. 2 from Bangor to Gorham. From Vermont: Rte. 2 from Montpelier to Lancaster and on to Gorham; Rte. 302 from Montpelier to Littleton; Rte. 91 north to Rtes. 302 or Rte. 2 farther north. From Connecticut: I–91 north to northern Vermont and cross over on 302 or 2. From Rhode Island: I–95 through Massachusetts into New Hampshire; continue north on Rte. 16 to Conway.

HOTELS AND MOTELS. Accommodations for every imaginable taste and budget are available in the White Mountains region. Full-service deluxe, modern hotels are found here. Comfortable, clean affordable rooms are also scattered throughout the region. Rates are highest in the peak seasons of summer, fall foliage, and skiing. Rates drop dramatically at some facilities during the remainder of the year. Rates, based on double occupancy, in season are *Deluxe,* $90 and up; *Expensive,* $70–$90; *Moderate,* $50–$70; *Inexpensive,* $50 and under.

Bartlett

Attitash Mountain Village, Rte. 302, 03812 (374–6501 or 800–862–1600). *Moderate–Deluxe.* Across from Attitash Ski Area. Condos and motel-style rooms. Kitchenettes and fireplaces. Beach and swimming. Alpine slide. Tennis, water slide, alpine and cross-country skiing in winter plus skating. Color cable TV.

Top Notch Management Co., Rte. 302, Box 429, 03812 (374–6633). *Expensive.* Motel suites and condo units. Ski to Attitash nearby.

North Colony Motel and Cottages, Rte. 302, 03812 (374–6679). *Moderate.* 14 modern rooms and 2 cottages. Mountain views, 1 mi. to Attitash. Large pool. Color cable TV.

Berlin

Traveler Motel, 25 Pleasant St., 03570 (752–2500). *Inexpensive.* 28 neat, clean rooms. Pets. Color cable TV.

Bethlehem

Wayside Inn and Motel, Rte. 302, 03574 (869–3364). *Moderate.* 19 historic inn rooms and 13 motel units overlooking the Ammonousuc River. Fireplace in common rooms. Private beach. Tennis. Pets. Snowmobile and cross-country ski trails. Downhill skiing nearby.

Bretton Woods

Mt. Washington Hotel, Rte. 302 (at the foot of the Presidential Range), 03575 (278–1000). *Expensive–Deluxe.* Spectacular setting. Grand Dame (1902) of New England's once-elegant summer hostelries. Open May to October. Tennis, golf, horses, fishing, indoor and outdoor pools. Fine food, lively entertainment nightly.

Bretton Arms, Rte. 302, 03575, (278–1000). *Expensive.* Small, elegant hotel built turn-of-century.

Lodge at Bretton Woods, Rte. 302 (across the street from the Mt. Washington Hotel), 03575 (278–1000). *Deluxe.* Weekly rates available. No pets. Indoor pool, good steaks in restaurant. Color TV.

Colebrook

Northern Comfort, 1 mi. south on U.S. 3, 03576 (237–4440). *Moderate.* 18 rooms; view of mountains. Cable TV. Open Apr.–early Jan. Closed early Jan.–March.

Sportsman's Lodge and Cottages, Big Diamond Lake, 03576 (237–5211). *Expensive.* Lodger rooms or stove-heated cottage units. Beach swimming, boating, fishing, hunting, cross-country skiing, snowmobiling. Pets. European or American Plan.

Conway

Tanglewood Motel and Cottages, Rte. 16, 03818 (447–5932). *Moderate.* Located 10 min. south of N. Conway. Set in a birch grove with a brook. Efficiency cottages (some with separate bedrooms) sleep two to six. Kitchens, screened porches. Motel units. Individual controlled heat. Two-day minimum in cottages.

Dixville Notch

The Balsams, Off Rte. 26, 03576 (255–3400; toll-free 800–255–0600, in New Hampshire 800–255–0800). *Deluxe* (Modified American Plan). 232 units. Spectacular, secluded setting in its own 15,000-acre site. Self-contained resort with alpine and cross-country skiing in winter. Sit-down dinners; superb cuisine. Golf, tennis, swimming, hiking, fishing. TV room.

Franconia

Gale River Motel, Rte. 18, 03580 (823–5655). *Moderate.* 13 rooms. Motel or housekeeping units. Spectacular mountain views. Heated pool, picnic area, grills. Pets. Color TV.

Raynor's Motor Lodge, jct. Rtes. 18 and 142, 03580 (823–9586). *Moderate.* 30 motel units and two kitchenettes. Heated pool. In-room coffee. Color TV.

Glen

Linderhof, Rte. 16, 03838 (383–4334, or toll-free 800–992–0074). *Moderate.* 33 rooms. Bavarian-style inn with modern facilities. Splendid mountain views. Lounge, dining room, pool.

Jackson

Christmas Farm Inn, Rte. 16B, 03846 (383–4313). *Deluxe* (Modified American Plan). 33 rooms. Yesterday setting (1778) with 20th-century services. True family feeling, full of charm. Excellent dining. Pool. Game room. On Jackson's cross-country ski trail network.

Eagle Mountain House, 2 Carter Notch Rd., 03846 (383–9111). *Deluxe.* Golf course, two restaurants, lounge, pool and sauna, tennis courts, and health club. An exquisite mountain view.

Wentworth Resort Hotel, Rte. 16A, 03846 (383–9700). *Deluxe.* 65 rooms. Overlooks Jackson Falls and views of the White Mountains. Cable TV. Golf course, tennis, country club, pool and river swimming, dining room, and lounge with entertainment.

Jefferson

Alpine Forest Motel, 2 mi. east of Rte. 115 on Rte. 2, near Six Gun City and Santa's Village, 03583 (586–4467). *Moderate.* 12 rooms. Hiking and snowmobiling, TV, pool, lawn games, gift shop.

Lancaster

Mary Elizabeth Motor Inn, Motel and Cottages, Rte. 3, 03584 (788–4621). *Inexpensive–Moderate.* Cottages and kitchenettes, pets, cable TV.

Morse Lodge and Motel, ½ mi. east on U.S. 2, 03584 (788–2096). *Inexpensive.* 1859 restored carriage house. Cable TV.

Lincoln/North Woodstock

Jack O'Lantern Resort, Box A, N. Woodstock 03262; Rte. 3 (745–8121). *Deluxe* (Modified American Plan). Restful site on 300 acres on Pemigewasset River, with golf, tennis, heated pool, recreation room. Restaurant. Bar. Color cable TV.

The Mountain Club on Loon, Kancamagus Hwy., Lincoln 03251 (745–8111). *Deluxe.* Right at Loon Mountain ski area. (Formerly Inn at Loon Mountain.) 105 rooms. Fine dining, lounge, nightly entertainment. Tennis, swimming in summer. Alpine and cross-country skiing in winter. Color cable TV.

The Mill House, Box 696, Lincoln 03251 (745–6261). *Expensive–Deluxe.* New full-service, 100-room luxury inn. Connected to the restored mill buildings of the Milford Marketplace. Indoor-outdoor pools, saunas, Jacuzzis. Luxury condo units available (800–654–6183).

Indian Head Motel Resort, Rte. 3, Lincoln 03251 (745–8181, toll-free 800–258–8912). *Expensive.* 100 motel units on 180 acres. Panoramic view of Indian Head profile. Fine restaurant, lounge, indoor and heated outdoor pools. Sauna, tennis, cross-country skiing. Color cable TV.

Beacon Motel, Rte. 3, Lincoln 03251 (745–8118, toll-free 800–258–8934). *Moderate–Expensive.* 100 units, motel rooms or cottages. Indoor and two outdoor heated pools, two restaurants, lounge, sauna, indoor tennis, color cable TV.

Drummer Boy Motor Inn, Rte. 3, Lincoln 03251; Exit 33 off I–93 (745–3661). *Moderate.* 53 motel units, four oversize rooms. Jacuzzi, indoor pool, sauna.

Kancamagus Motor Lodge, Rte. 112, Box 505, Lincoln. 03251 (745–3365). *Moderate.* Unheralded—clean, cozy, and in the right spot. In-room steam baths. Color cable TV. Heated outdoor pool. Breakfasts only.

Red Doors Motel, Rte. 3, Box 109A, Lincoln 03251 (745–2267). *Inexpensive–Moderate.* In-room coffee. Heated pool. Color cable TV. Game rooms.

North Conway

Fox Ridge Resort, South on Rte. 16, 03860 (356–3151). *Deluxe.* 136 rooms. Indoor and heated outdoor pools, whirlpool, sauna, tennis, cable color TV.

Stonehurst Manor, Rte. 16, 03860 (356–3271). *Expensive–Deluxe.* 27 rooms. Converted mansion, complete with fireplaces, oak decor. Outstanding food, lounge. Pool, tennis, shuffleboard, cable TV.

Red Jacket Motor Inn, Rte. 16, 03860 (356–5411). *Expensive–Deluxe.* 152 rooms. Fine restaurant, saloon, indoor and heated outdoor pools, whirlpool, sauna, tennis, game room. Townhouses.

Eastern Slope Inn, Rte. 16 at Rte. 302 03860 (356–6321). *Moderate–Expensive.* 109 rooms. Restaurant, bar. Heated pool, tennis, game room, sauna, Jacuzzi.

School House Motel, Rte. 16, 03860 (356–6829). *Moderate.* Cable color TV. Pool with mountain view.

Plymouth

Deep River Inn, Highland St. on the Baker River, 03264 (536–2155). *Moderate.* 21 rooms, six cottages. Fine views of mountains; pool and cable TV. Ski packages available.

King's Court Inn, RFD 1, 03264, Exit 27 off I–93 (536–3520). *Moderate.* 105 rooms. Lounge, pool, restaurant, sauna, game room, entertainment. Pets.

Pilgrim Motel, Rte. 3, 03264 (536–1319). *Moderate.* 10 rooms. Clean and cozy. Cable TV.

Thrifty Yankee Lodge, I–93 exit 26, on Rte. 3, 03264 (536–2330). *Moderate.* 33 rooms. Direct-dial telephones, color TV, 15 min. from Waterville Valley.

Shelbourne

Shelbourne Birches Motor Inn, Rte. 2, 03581 (466–3941). *Moderate.* 28 rooms. Magnificent view of White Mountains. Color TV–satellite movie channel. Swimming pool-spa, snowmobile trail.

Town and Country Motor Inn, Rte. 2, 03581 (466–3315). *Moderate.* 156 rooms. Restaurant, lounge. Indoor pool, pets, color TV.

Sugar Hill

Sunset Hill House, Off Rte. 117, 2 mi. west of Franconia, 03585 (823–5522). *Deluxe* (Modified American Plan). 35 rooms. Refurbished throwback to days of moneyed travelers. Superb meals, cozy lounge, golf, and tennis in summer, 75 miles of cross-country ski trails.

Twin Mountain

Four Seasons Motor Inn, Rte. 3, 03595 (846–5707). *Moderate.* A short distance from Bretton Woods. Ski areas and restaurants nearby.

Carroll Motel and Cottages, jct. Rtes. 302 and 3, 03595 (846–5553). *Inexpensive.* Cottages, kitchenettes, and motel rooms. Heated outdoor pool. Play area, picnic grills, free in-room coffee. Eight units accommodating up to 20.

Waterville Valley

Valley Inn and Tavern, Tecumseh Road, 03223 (236–8336). *Deluxe.* 50 rooms. Rustic, cozy, fireplace. Fine dining, lounge. Indoor-outdoor pool, sauna, exercise rooms, tanning beds, game room, and lounge.

Waterville Valley Condos, Village Rd., 03223 (236–8211). *Expensive-Deluxe.* 42 condos. Fireplaces, linens.

Whitefield

Spalding Inn & Club, Rte. 116, 03598 (837–2572). *Deluxe.* Known for splendid views. Golf, tennis, and bowling greens. Cottage suites available. Restaurant and bar.

Woodsville

All Seasons Motel, 36 Smith St., 03785 (747–2157). *Inexpensive.* A 13-room motel with outdoor pool and playground.

INNS, GUEST HOUSES, BED AND BREAKFASTS. The discriminating traveler will find a wealth of intimate settings from which to enjoy the beautiful White Mountains region, offered in a range of prices. Fireplaces, antiques, and old paneling lend a memorable atmosphere to many of the restored 18th-century buildings. Or a simple country farmhouse beckons you. Most of the following inns are *moderately* priced. Several with *deluxe* prices actually offer breakfast and dinner for two, the Modified American Plan (MAP).

Bethlehem

The Northern Star Inn, RFD 1, Box 5, 03574 (869–2215). Quaint country inn. 10 rooms, nestled in White Mountains. Country breakfast and dinner served daily. Cross-country trails begin at back door.

Chocorua

Stafford's in the Field, Rte. 113 off Rte. 16, 03817 (323–7766). 13 rooms. A 200-year-old inn with sensational dining (reservations a must). Tennis, hiking, skiing. (MAP).

Conway

Darby Field Inn, Bald Hill Rd. off Rte. 16, 03818 (447–2181). 13 rooms. Great view of the Mt. Washington Valley. Exquisite candlelight dining, bar, pool, cross-country skiing, TV room. (MAP).

Franconia

The Bungay Jar, Rte. 116, Box 15, 03580 (823–7775 or 444–2919). Quiet, private home in the woods under the Kinsman Range on the western edge of the White Mountains. Robert Frost's lovely Easton Valley.

Franconia Inn, Rte. 116, 03580 (823–5542). 33 rooms. Rustic inn with French cuisine. Mini resort, tennis, horses, hiking, fishing in summer (with golf nearby), Alpine (nearby) and cross-country skiing (on site) in winter. Bar. Open Memorial Day–Columbus Day, mid-Dec.–mid-Mar.

Hillwinds Inn, Rte. 18, 03580 (823–5533). Rooms in old inn and newer motel. Fine steak house, very active bar during ski season. Pool, sauna, TV.

Horse and Hound Inn, Off Rte. 18, 03580 (823–5501). 12 rooms with old pine paneling. This is a quiet spot with the emphasis on gentility, superb Continental cuisine.

Lovett's Inn, Rte. 18, 03580 (823–7761 or 800–356–3802). *Deluxe.* Built in 1784 and situated at the entrance to Franconia State Park. Near walking and hiking trails; scenic views; downhill and cross-country skiing. Highly rated dining room.

The Rivagale Inn, 195 Main St., Box 97, 03580 (823–9984). Conveniently located country inn with lodging, lounge, and dining room open to the public. Great apres-ski lounge, three fireplaces. 12 units; capacity: 24.

Sugar Hill Inn, Rte. 117, 03580 (823–5621). Built as a farmhouse in 1789 and converted to a 10-room inn plus six country cottages, each with private bath. Three-course breakfast, five-course dinner. (MAP).

Glen

Bernerhof Inn, Rte. 302, 03838 (383–4414). 10 rooms. European taproom, award-winning dining room. A Taste of the Mountains cooking school.

Intervale

The Forest-A Country Inn, Rte. 16A, 03845 (356–9772). 13 rooms in a 19th-century inn. Home-cooked meals. Peaceful setting. Pool.

The New England Inn, Box 428, North Conway 03860 (356–5541). 39 rooms, 9 cottages with fireplaces, Intervale Tavern, restaurants, three tennis courts, swimming pool, cross-country learning center, and touring trails. Package rates available.

Jackson

Whitney's Village Inn, Rte. 16B, 03846 (383–6886). 37 rooms at the base of Black Mt. Gourmet country dining. Features tennis, hiking, downhill and cross-country skiing.

Wildcat Inn and Tavern, Rte. 16A, Jackson Village, 03846 (383–4245). Charming colonial inn furnished with primitive antiques. Rustic tavern with entertainment. Dining room.

Littleton

Thayers Inn, 136 Main St., 03561 (444–6469). Listed in *National Register of Historic Places*. Classic, comfortable lodging in 40 rooms. Color cable TV.

North Conway

Cranmore Inn, Kearsage St., 03860 (356–5502). 23 rooms. Cable TV, pool, free breakfast, game room, lawn games, racquetball club.

The Scottish Lion, Rte. 16, 03860 (356–6381). Charming country inn of 7 rooms. Scottish tradition; bed and breakfast; private bath.

Wildflowers Guest House, Rte. 16. 03860 (356–2224). Six rooms in a century-old home. Private bath, fireplace, dining room. Breakfast available.

North Woodstock

The Woodstock Inn, Main Street, 03262 (745–3951). 100-year-old Victorian home restored to its authentic beauty. 15 antique-decorated rooms. Color cable TV. Riverfront swimming.

Snowville

Snowvillage Inn, 03849 (447–2818). Country inn with 14 rooms. Secluded with spectacular views. Tennis, swimming, hiking in summer. Cross-country touring center at the inn and King Pine ski area just around the corner in winter. Sauna. Pets. (MAP).

Sugar Hill

The Homestead, Main St., 03585 (823–5564). Historic inn built in 1802 by one of the town's first settlers. Ultrahomey, folksy atmosphere. Breakfast only. Some rooms with shared bath. Chalet available. Closed Nov. and Apr.–late May.

Ledgeland, Rte. 117, 03585 (823–5341). Charming country inn and cottages, all with private bath. Superb mountain view. Most cottage units have kitchen, fireplace, terrace, wood. Open year-round. Inn open July–mid-Oct. with free Continental breakfast.

Waterville Valley

Snowy Owl Inn, Village Center, 03223 (236–8366). 38 rooms. One of the nicest luxury lodges in ski country because of its tasteful decor. Heated outdoor pool, sauna, game room, huge stone fireplace; free cocoa, coffee, tea after skiing.

Whitefield

Spaulding Inn Club, Mountain View Rd. off Rte. 3, 03598 (837–2572). 70 rooms. Gracious 19th-century inn and deluxe cottages with golf, tennis, pool. Superb dining and wine cellar. Open June–mid-Oct.

The Weathervane Country Inn, Rte. 3, 03598 (837–2527). Casually elegant dining. Next to summer theater and cabaret. Heated outdoor pool.

RESTAURANTS. The sumptuous choices for dining in the White Mountains region are bound to please diners of every palate. The smorgasbord of restaurants, inns, and eateries offers everything from seafood and fresh brook trout to duckling and wild turkey. Per-person price ranges excluding beverage, tax, and tip are *Expensive,* $25 and up; *Moderate,* $10–$25; *Inexpensive,* $10 and under.

Bartlett

W.W. Doolittle's, Rte. 302, across from Attitash Ski Area (374–6055). *Moderate.* Upstairs lounge and downstairs dining. Lunch and dinner; good chicken cacciatore and seafood.

Bretton Woods

Darby's Tavern, Rte. 302 in Lodge at Bretton Woods (278–1500). *Moderate.* Steak house and seafood fare. Subdued decor.

Fabyan's Station, Rte. 302 (846–2222). *Moderate.* Renovated rail depot. Good range of seafood and meat dishes.

Conway

Darby Field Inn, Bald Hill Rd., off Rte. 16 (447–2181). *Moderate.* Valley views are mouth watering; the menu and cooking will finish you off. Candlelight dinner and daily specials. Recommended: lamb chops.

Dixville Notch

The Balsams Resort, off Rte. 26 (255–3400). *Deluxe* (Modified American Plan). Four-star resort. Facilities keep people busy, but the cooking keeps them coming back. Strong on beef and fresh fish.

Franconia

Franconia Inn, Rte. 116 (823–5542). *Expensive.* Rustic greenhouse gives appeal to the decor. Continental dining, excellent veal. Great desserts.
Lovett's Inn, Rte. 18 (823–7761). *Expensive.* Large American menu includes seafood, many desserts—and changes daily. Jacket and tie required. Breakfast and dinner only. Nonguests of the inn must make dinner reservations.
Horse and Hound Inn, off Rte. 18 (823–5501). *Moderate–Expensive.* A little off the beaten path but worth the background. Excellent meals heightened by wide selection of wine.
Hillwinds Sirloin Taverne, ¼ mi. south of the village of Franconia on Rte. 18 (823–5533). *Moderate.* Sumptuous dining, overlooking the picturesque Gale River.

Glen

Bernerhof Inn, Rte. 302 (383–4414). *Expensive.* Superb Continental dining and superior service in turn-of-century inn. Swiss bar and European feel to everything. Specialties: fondue, escargots, schnitzel. Children's portions.
Red Parka Pub, Rte. 302 (383–4344). *Moderate.* Great food, lively bar, good barbecued spare ribs.

Intervale

New England Inn, Rte. 16A (356–5541). *Moderate–Expensive.* Creative cuisine with popovers on the side. "Enjoyable" is an understatement. Try the Shaker cranberry pot roast: tender roast in a Shaker cranberry sauce.

Jackson

Wentworth Resort Hotel, Rte. 16B (383–9700). *Expensive.* Easy elegance in resurrected full-scale resort. Superb Continental dining. Scallops recommended.
Christmas Farm Inn, Rte. 16B (383–4413). *Moderate–Expensive.* Homemade soups, varied menu. Excellent prime ribs. Delightful desserts.
Wildcat Tavern, Rte. 16A in village (383–4245). *Moderate.* Colonial motif, homemade entrees, sinful desserts. Entertainment on weekends in ski season.

Lincoln–North Woodstock

Tavern at the Mill, Millfront and Market Pl. (745–2278). *Moderate–Expensive.* Multilevel dining room. Wide selection of entrees, but start with mussels or escargots. Homemade desserts.
Chalet Restaurant, Main St. (745–2256). *Moderate.* Known locally for lobsters. Daily specials.
Dad's Restaurant at Beacon Motel, Rte. 3 (745–8511). *Moderate.* Hearty fare. Lunches served only in summer.
Truants Taverne, jct. Rtes. 3 and 112 (745–2239). *Inexpensive.* Rustic schoolhouse decor; check out the old pull-down maps on the wall. Full dinners and sandwiches.

Littleton

Clam Shell, Dells Rd., Exit 42 off I–93 (444–6445). *Moderate.* Seafood, especially clams. Sunday brunch.
The Coffee Pot, Main St. (444–5722). *Inexpensive.* Basically breakfast and lunch spot. Good sandwiches.

North Conway

Stonehurst Manor, Rte. 16 (356–3113). *Expensive.* Superb dining in elegant setting; recycled mansion that oozes class. One suggestion: Beef Wellington.
The 1785 Inn, Rte. 16 (356–9025). *Moderate–Expensive.* At the Scenic Vista. Historic dining rooms with original fireplaces. Superior dining and an extraordinary wine list.
Merlino's Steak House, Rte. 16 (356–6006). *Moderate–Expensive.* Family dining with Italian and beef dishes front and center. Children's portions.
Snug Harbor, Rte. 16, "a few fathoms north" of village (356–3000). *Moderate–Expensive.* Fresh seafood specialties, fine chowder. Closed Tues.
Horsefeathers, Main St. in the village (356–2687). *Moderate.* Lively, fun place with cheap eats. Rowdy steak house atmosphere. Packed at lunch.
Scottish Lion, Rte. 16, just north of village (356–6381). *Moderate.* Traditional Scottish lineup—hearty soups and breads, beef and lamb, among others. Sun. brunch. Black Watch bar carries 30-plus brands of Scotch.

Plymouth

Suzanne's Kitchen, 56 S. Main St. (536–3304). *Inexpensive.* Fine soups, good spaghetti pie. Poetry Thurs. nights and live music Sun. nights.

Sugar Hill

Sunset Hill House, off Rte. 117 (823–5522). *Expensive.* Excellent dining, but it's the desserts that help set this inn apart.
Polly's Pancake Parlor, Rte. 117 (823–5575). *Inexpensive.* Great views and greater griddle cakes. French toast, too. Fine soups and muffins. Open summer and fall.

Waterville Valley

Valley Inn, Tecumseh Rd. (236–8336). *Expensive.* Quiet, rustic elegance. Excellent shrimp. Second pick: gingered beef tips.

Carnavale's Ristorante, Waterville Valley Rd. (726–3618). *Moderate–Expensive.* Northerm Italian foods.

Finish Line Restaurant, Rte. 49 (236–8800). *Moderate.* Selection of Italian specialties, appetizers and homemade soups.

The Yacht Club & Bar at Waterville, Town Sq. (236–8885). *Expensive.* A pleasant ambience; near Corcoran's Pond. Lunch and dinner daily.

TOURIST INFORMATION. For detailed information and literature on the White Mountains–Mt. Washington Valley Region: Mt. Washington Valley Chamber of Commerce, Box 385S, North Conway 03860 (356–3171). Farther north is the Area Chamber of Commerce, serving the Berlin-Gorham-Milan-Randolph-Shelburne-Jefferson region, 115 Main St., Box 298, Berlin, 03570 (752–6060). For information on White Mountain National Forest, contact the Regional Office, White Mountain National Forest, Box 638, Laconia 03247 (524–6450). Guidebooks to lodging, campgrounds, and skiing in the White Mountains is available from the White Mountains Visitors Center, Box 176, N. Woodstock 03262 (745–8720). For other regional and statewide information, contact New Hampshire Office of Vacation Travel, Box 856, Concord, 03301 (271–2666). For the far north country, Colebrook-Pittsburg Chamber of Commerce, Colebrook 03576 (237–8939).

TOURS. Conventional tours of the region are nonexistent. But there is the Mt. Washington Auto Road tour by chauffered van. Starts at Glen House, Rte. 16, Pinkham Notch. Open mid-May–mid-Oct, weather permitting. Roundtrip $12 per adult, $8 per child (466–3988).

By train: Conway Scenic Railroad, Main St., North Conway 03860 (846–5404 or 800–922–8825). One-hour, 11-mi. train ride on restored antique coaches pulled by a 66-year-old steam locomotive or an early-model diesel.

SEASONAL EVENTS. May: White Mountains Gateway Arts and Craft Festival (end of May).

June: Saco Bound Mass Start Canoe and Kayak Race (early June); Old-fashioned family sing-along, Schouler Park, North Conway (early June); Hot-air balloon rally (end of June); Mt. Washington Road Race (late June).

July: Waterville Valley Festival of the Arts, Waterville Valley (mid-July); Annual July 4th Cookout, Waterville Valley, field games, barbecue, fireworks (July 4); Gala July 4th Celebration, Mt. Washington Hotel, Rte. 302, Bretton Woods (evening, July 4); Fireworks on the 4th, North Conway; annual Mt. Washington Valley Craftsmen Fair (mid-July); Carroll County Kennel Club annual All Breed Dog Show and Obedience Trial (mid-July); Family Folk Festival, with country fiddling, Mime Rod Puppets, North Conway (late July); Concert-in-the-Park, pops with fireworks finale, North Conway (end of July).

August: Annual Arts and Crafts Fair, Loon Mountain Recreation Area, Lincoln (early Aug.); Mt. Washington Valley International Tennis Classic, Mt. Cranmore, North Conway (mid-Aug.); Mt. Washington Valley Equine Classic, Attitash Mountain area, a grand prix jumping event (mid-

Aug.); Annual Art Show, North Conway (mid-Aug.); Plymouth State Fair, Plymouth (late Aug.); Lancaster Fair, Lancaster (end of Aug.);

September: Labor Day Crafts Fair, Waterville Valley (early Sept.); World Championship Mud Bowl, Hog Coliseum, North Conway (early Sept.); Mt. Washington Hill Climb, a 7.6-mi. bicycle race to the summit (mid-Sept.).

October: Annual Bethlehem Craft Fair, Elementary School, Rte. 302, Bethlehem (2nd week of Oct.); Fall Foliage Festival, Loon Mountain, Lincoln (2nd week of Oct.); annual Fall Bazaar, Rte. 302, Glen (2nd week of Oct.).

PARKS. The **White Mountain National Forest** in this northern region of the state contains 724,000 acres, of which 678,000 are in New Hampshire, the remainder in Maine. It has more than 1,200 mi. of hiking trails; many miles of fishable streams (especially for trout), lakes and ponds; and 19 camping areas. The entire area is open for hunting and fishing, according to the seasons. Most areas are open year-round, but not maintained late Oct.–early May. Permits are required for all national park campfires in undeveloped sites, although not if you cook on a portable stove. No permit is required at improved roadside campgrounds and picnic areas where there are fireplaces. Permits may be obtained in person or by mail from the Forest Supervisor's Office, 719 North Main St., Laconia 03246 (524–6450), or from District Ranger offices: Trudeau Road, Bethlehem 03574 (869–2626); Kancamagus Highway, Conway 03818 (447–5448); 80 Glen Road, Gorham 03581 (466–2713); 127 Highland St., Plymouth 03264 (536–1310).

There are a dozen state parks in this northern region of the state. Many of the state parks charge admission during the main season on a per-person basis. Most state park recreation areas are open from Memorial Day weekend through mid-June on weekends only and daily from then to Labor Day. In winter, snowmobiles and all-terrain vehicles are allowed only on trails specifically designated for their use. For more park information, write or call the New Hampshire Division of Parks and Recreation, Box 856D, Concord 03301 (271–3254). Some selected state parks in this region:

Crawford Notch State Park, Rte. 302, Harts Location (846–5404). This is 6 mi. of unspoiled, rugged park in a scenic mountain pass. Hiking and fishing. Crossed by trails of Appalachian system. Campground with 30 tent sites. Scenic waterfall and Flume and Silver Cascades.

Franconia Notch State Park, Franconia and Lincoln (823–5563) is a deep valley of 6,440 acres between peaks of the Franconia and Kinsman mountain ranges. Swimming, camping, picknicking, hiking on Appalachian trails, alpine skiing in winter on a 27-mi. network of trails and slopes. (Adults, $3.50; children, $2.)

White Lake State Park, Rte. 16, Tamworth (323–7350). Fine sandy beach on tree-studded shore of White Lake. Shaded picnic grounds, swimming, boat rentals, trout fishing, hiking trails, snowmobiling in winter. A 72-acre stand of native pitch pine is a National Natural Landmark.

Other parks in the region include Echo Lake State Park, Conway; Lake Francis State Park, Pittsburg, and Coleman State Park, Stewartstown.

Private Parks: Bretzfelder Park, Prospect St., Bethlehem (444–6228). Open all year daily. 77-acre nature and wildlife park. Conducted tours summer and winter; walking trails, trout ponds. Summer nature programs for children. Free.

Loon Mountain Recreation Area, Lincoln (745–8111). Take gondola ride to summit where you will find hiking trails, picnic grounds, a playground, plus an inn and restaurant, tennis and a pool. Admission to gondola: adults, $5; children 6–12, $3.

Lost River Reservation, Rte. 112, N. Woodstock (745–8031). Tour river gorge on boardwalks as river appears and disappears. Paradise Falls, picnic area, nature garden, geological and ecological displays. Adults, $4.50; children 6–12, $2. Open May–Oct., 9 A.M.–5:30 P.M. daily.

FALL FOLIAGE. This is the region of the state with the grandest fall foliage. When the colors peak depends on the weather, but the first two weeks of Oct. are usually the prime viewing time. I–93 and Rtes. 3 and 16 provide great leaf peeking, but they're also very crowded. Hundreds of thousands of people head north for foliage watching in New Hampshire. Try some less-crowded backroads: Rte. 145, from Colebrook to Pittsburg and the beginning of the Connecticut Lakes Region, in the far north country; Rte. 115A, from Grange to Groveton; Rte. 110B, from Milan to West Milan; Rte. 110, from Berlin to Groveton; Rte. 153, from Effingham Falls to Conway; Rte. 142, from Franconia to Bethlehem; or Rte. 117, from Lisbon to Franconia Village. Contact New Hampshire Office of Vacation Travel, Box 856, Concord 03301 (271–2343) for additional foliage information. Call 224–2525 or 2526 for taped foliage conditions.

SUMMER SPORTS. Boating: In Conway, you can rent canoes at Saco Bound, Rte. 302 in Center Conway (447–2177) for canoeing down the Saco River. Rowboat rentals at White Lake State Park, Rte. 16, Tamworth (323–7350). There are other private canoe and boat rentals in the area. Most state parks with lakes have boat-launching areas.

Swimming: There are scores of swimming spots in the northern part of the state, from supervised sandy beaches at state parks to swimming holes in clean, clear rivers. There's swimming in Profile Lake, 1,200 ft. below the Old Man of the Mountains profile at Franconia Notch; Echo Lake in Conway; White Lake in Tamworth. Excellent swimming at various spots along the Swift River running alongside the Kancamagus Highway; the Saco River, with its sandy beaches, offers numerous spots to swim; the Wildcat River in Jackson is another lovely stream in which to take a dip. In the far north, such as at Lake Francis in Pittsburg, the water is ice cold; swimming is prohibited here.

Golf: Numerous golf courses dot the north country. Among them: North Conway Country Club, North Conway (356–9700); Colebrook Country Club, Colebrook (237–5566); Mojalaki Country Club, Franklin (934–3033); Androscoggin Valley Country Club, Gorham (466–9468); Eagle Mountain House, Jackson (383–4347); Sunset Hill House Golf Club, Sugar Hill (823–5522); Moosilauke Inn and Golf Club, Warren (764–5701); Waterville Valley Golf and Tennis, Waterville Valley (236–8666); Mountain View House Golf Club, Whitefield (837–2511); Jack O'Lantern Resort, Woodstock (745–8121). Other golf courses are found at places of lodging.

Bicycling: There are plenty of country roads for short bicycle jaunts, and this is breathtaking country—86 major mountains to view. Some sample routes: For the hardy, 34 mi. of mountain wilderness along the Kancamagus Highway (low-to-moderate traffic but steep); Rte. 113 through Chocorua and Madison to Conway, hilly, low-to-moderate traffic; Berlin to Errol, Rte. 16 and side road, flat to moderate, low-to-moderate traffic; Lancaster to Maine border on Rte. 2, moderate with hills, low-to-

NEW ENGLAND

moderate traffic. Write to Granite State Wheelmen Inc., 16 Clinton St., Salem 03079 for bicycling routes.

Hiking: This region is a hiker's paradise. More than 1,200 mi. of hiking trails are traversed in the White Mountains. *Caution:* Even in summer, violent storms and freezing temperatures occur, so unless you are an experienced, well-equipped hiker, keep your hikes short. A list of shorter hikes may be obtained from the White Mountain National Forest (Supervisor's Office, White Mountain National Forest, Box 638, Laconia 03247). Or stop by or call the Appalachian Mountain Club, Pinkham Notch (466–2727) for expert advice.

WINTER SPORTS. This is naturally the best ski country in the state, both downhill and cross-country. Take your pick of **downhill ski areas.** In the Mt. Washington Valley, you'll find Mt. Cranmore in North Conway (356–5543), Black Mountain in Jackson (383–4490); King Pine in Madison (367–8896); Attitash in Bartlett (374–2368); and Wildcat, Jackson (466–3326). There's Loon Mountain in Lincoln (745–8111); Mt. Tecumseh in Waterville Valley (236–8311); Cannon Mountain, the state-run ski mountain in Franconia (823–5563); Bretton Woods ski area in Bretton Woods (278–5000); Balsams/Wilderness ski area in Dixville Notch (255–3400).

Then there's unlimited **cross-country skiing.** You can head out on your own in the National Forest or in state forests. Or you may prefer an area with maintained trails. Jackson Ski Touring Foundation, Rte. 16A, Jackson (383–9355) has the largest cross-country touring complex in the east, 146 km of superbly maintained scenic trails. Lessons and equipment rental available. The Nestlenook Inn Ski Touring Center in Jackson (383–9443) has 35 km of groomed and tracked scenic wooded trails; rental equipment available. The Intervale Nordic Learning Center, Rte. 16A, Intervale (356–5541) has 40 km of well-groomed scenic trails for all ability levels, rental equipment, and instruction.

For more information on ski areas, contact the Mt. Washington Valley Chamber of Commerce, Box 385VG, North Conway 03860 (356–3171) or New Hampshire Office of Vacation Travel, Box 856E, Concord 03301 (271–2666). To learn New Hampshire downhill ski conditions when you're about to go skiing, call from outside New Hampshire 800–258–3608; in New Hampshire, 224–2525.

For **skimobilers,** there are designated trails in various state parks. For information, write or call the New Hampshire Division of Parks and Recreation, Box 856D, Concord 03301 (271–3254). New Hampshire leases thousands of acres of land with groomed trails for free snowmobiling. A map is available. Contact the Bureau of Off-Highway Vehicles, Box 856, Concord 03301. Vehicles are required to be registered; the fee is $17 for nonresidents; reciprocity is granted with the states of Vermont and Maine and the province of Quebec.

FISHING. This region offers some of the best trout fishing streams and lakes in the state. For serious trout fishermen, the Connecticut Lakes region and the Connecticut River that begins there offer the best opportunity for large trout in the state. There's also salmon to be caught in the First and Second Connecticut Lakes. Trout is stocked in many streams in the White Mountains region. You can pick almost any clear stream and find trout. On lakes in the region, there are trout, too, as well as bass and other varieties in southern lakes. There are 45 lakes and ponds and 650 mi. of fishable streams in the National Forest. Licenses are required for freshwater fishing. Write to New Hampshire Fish and Game Department, 34 Bridge St., Concord 03301.

HUNTING. The White Mountain National Forest is open to hunting. Deer, bear, bobcat, and other game are available. You must have a valid New Hampshire hunting license. For information, write to New Hampshire Fish and Game Department, 34 Bridge St., Concord 03301.

CAMPING. Camping facilities are plentiful in this region. The White Mountain National Forest has 20 roadside campgrounds. Facilities consist of family units composed of an individual parking spur, tent pad, table and fire grate. Drinking water and sanitary facilities are available. No special hookup facilities are provided for trailers but they may be used at most areas. Sites are available on a first-come, first-served basis. Length of stay is limited to 14 days. Dogs are permitted only on a leash. Campgrounds normally open about May 15 and close about Oct. 15, depending on weather and maintenance situations. Fees are charged on a site-per-night basis. For detailed information, write or call the White Mountain National Forest, Box 638, Lanconia 03247 (524–6450).

A few state parks in the region also offer camping facilities. Sites available on first-come, first-served basis and reservations are not accepted. Length of stay is limited to 14 days. Fees are charged on a site-per-night basis. Trailers are welcome, but there are no hookups. Campgrounds are normally open mid-May–mid-Oct. Lafayette in Franconia Notch and White Lake remain open for winter camping, but there is no water available. For further information, write or call the New Hampshire Division of Parks and Recreation, Box 856D, Concord 03301 (271–3254).

In addition, there are numerous private campgrounds in the region. For information, write to White Mountains Attractions, Box 51786L, North Woodstock 03262.

SPECTATOR SPORTS. Annual Saco Bound Mass Start Canoe and Kayak Race, Conway, is held in early June (447–2177). Mt. Washington Valley Equine Classic, North Conway, a jumping event of top horsemen, is held in July.

HISTORIC SITES AND HOUSES. This area was settled much later than the Seacoast Region, of course, but settlers were in various towns in the 1700s. Call ahead to check admission fees.

Bethlehem

The Rocks Estate, Rtes. 302 and I–93 (444–6228). Turn-of-century farm estate with operating dairy farm; self-guided trail. Barn open at milking time 4:30–6 P.M. Listed in *National Register of Historic Places.* Open year-round, Sat.–Wed., 1–5 P.M.

Franconia

The Robert Frost Place, Ridge Rd. (823–8038). Open Memorial Day–Columbus Day, daily 1–5 P.M. Weekends only, June and after Labor Day.

Lancaster

Wilder-Holton House, north jct. of U.S. 2 and U.S. 3 in Lancaster. Open daily by appointment (788–2328). Erected by Major Jonas Wilder beginning in 1780 from boards planed and nails wrought on the site. Coos County's first two-story dwelling. Now a museum.

Littleton

Site of Kilburn Brothers' Stereoscopic View Factory. Here, from 1867 to 1909, Benjamin and Edward Kilburn produced and distributed thousands of stereoscopic views. Their collection was the largest in the world. Contact Littleton Historical Society (444–5741).

MUSEUMS. Museums in this region are diverse, ranging from skiing to classic autos. Call ahead for admission fees.

Bethlehem

Crossroads of America Museum, Rte. 302 and Trudeau Rd. (869–3919). Largest 3/16 scale model railroad in the world open to the public. Smaller model railroads, exhibit of cars, trucks. Open June 1st–mid–Oct., Tues.–Sun., 9 A.M.–6 P.M.

Franconia

New England Ski Museum, Cannon Mountain (823–7177). Artifacts and audiovisual slide show. Open May 30–mid-Oct., daily 10 A.M.–4 P.M.

Glen

The Grand Manor, Rte. 16 (356–9366). Weekends only in May. 40 mint-condition antique and classic autos, vintage 1908–57. Open weekends Spring and Fall, daily Summer. 9:30 A.M.–5 P.M.

Plymouth/Ashland

Doll-Fan Attic Museum, Rte. 175 between Plymouth and Ashland (536–4416). 3,000 dolls and memorabilia. Open May–Oct., usually daily, 10 A.M.–5 P.M.

Sugar Hill

Sugar Hill Historical Museum, 03585. Rare photographic collection, complete genealogy of early town settlers. Open July 1–late Oct., Thurs. and Sat., 1–4 P.M., Sun., 2–5 P.M.

MUSIC, DANCE, AND STAGE. There are numerous concerts, theater productions, and festivals in this region, especially in the summertime. In North Conway on the green, there are regular old-fashioned band concerts where spectators sit on the grass. The **Mt. Washington Valley Theatre Co.** (356–5776) presents fine musicals, with excellent professional young talent. The annual Mt. Washington Valley Arts Jubilee presents events throughout the summer, including symphony concerts, strings, choirs, folk festivals, ballet, jazz, barbershop and banjo music. At the beautiful **Mt. Washington Hotel** in BrettonWoods (278–1000), there is big-band music and dancing to the sounds of the 40s. Loon Mountain in Lincoln (745–8111) has a **Summer Music Festival,** from classical music to Gershwin, Foster, and Porter. The **North Country Chamber Players** (823–5392) present concerts at various places in the north country during the summer.

In Whitefield, the **Weathervane Theatre Players** (837–9010) present both musicals and drama.

GALLERIES. R.G. Packer Art Gallery and Studio, S. Main St., North Conway (356–2834) has oil paintings, landscapes, seascapes, still lifes. New England and European. Open year-round. The **Art Gallery of Plymouth State College,** Hyde Hall, Plymouth (536–5000, ext. 2201) is open Tues.-Sat. when school is in session. Tues., Thurs., Fri., 10 A.M.–5 P.M.; Wed., 10 A.M.–8 P.M.; Sat., 12–5 P.M.

SHOPPING. From North Conway, which has become the outlet store capital of New Hampshire, to small gift shops and craft stores in small towns in the Mt. Washington Valley and beyond, the region offers plenty of shopping. In North Conway you can pick up bargains in these outlet stores: **Clothesworks/Jack Winter Outlet,** Rtes. 16 and 302, women's sportswear; **Banister—The 40 Brand Store Outlet,** Rtes. 16 and 302, for shoes; the **Down Outlet,** Rte. 16; **Anne Klein Outlet,** Rtes. 16 and 302; **CFO Men's and Boys' Sportswear; Corning Factory Store,** Rtes. 16 and 302; **Dansk Factory Outlet,** Rtes. 16 and 302; **Designer's Outlet,** Rtes. 16 and 302; Frye Boot Factory Outlet, rtes. 16 and 302; **Barbizon Lingerie Factory Outlet,** rtes. 16 and 302; Aileen Factory Outlet, rtes. 16 and 302. In Conway Village, **Crystal Works,** Rte. 16, offers first-quality European lead crystal. For a full list of outlets, contact the Mt. Washington Chamber of Commerce, Box 385, North Conway 03061 (356–3171). The **North Conway League of New Hampshire Craftsmen,** South Main St., North Conway, offers juried crafts. There's also a League of New Hampshire Craftsmen store in the Glaessel Building, Franconia. In the village of North Conway, stroll around and wander into some of the small shops. **North Country Fair,** on North Main St., offers fine-crafted jewelry. In Bethlehem, the **Broken Tree Woodworking Studio,** on Main St., sells exotic and native hardwood jewelry boxes and chests, from ring boxes to sewing chests. In Intervale, 400 ft. east of the rest area, you'll find the **Abenaki Indian Shop,** which sells Indian handicrafts.

NIGHTLIFE. There are plenty of "watering holes" in the Mt. Washington Valley area; just about all accommodations offer some form of evening entertainment. In ski season, the lounges are full, the places are hopping. There's plenty of music in the clubs year-round. In North Conway, there are favorite pubs like **Horsefeathers** on North Main St. (356–2687). Out in Glen on Rte. 302, you'll find an active crowd at the **Red Parka Pub** (383–4344). In Jackson, there's the rustic tavern at the **Wildcat Inn and Tavern** (383–4245) and a fun pub, **The Shannon Door** (383–4211), both in the village.

THE LAKES REGION

Many New Hampshire lakes bear the names given to them by Indians, for example, Squam (the setting for the movie *On Golden Pond*), Waukewan, Winnisquam, Ossipee, and Winnipesaukee, which means "the smile of the great spirit." Winnipesaukee covers 72 square miles, with 274 habitable islands and a shoreline 283 miles long that dips in and out of countless coves. Eight towns stand along its shores.

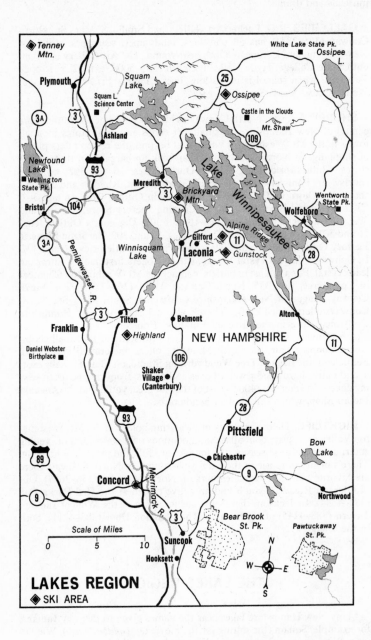

Tenney Mtn.

White Lake State Pk.

Ossipee L.

Plymouth

Squam Lake

25

Ossipee

Squam L. Science Center

Castle in the Clouds

Ashland

Mt. Shaw

109

Newfound Lake

93

Meredith

Lake Winnipesaukee

Wellington State Pk.

Brickyard Mtn.

Bristol

104

Wentworth State Pk.

Wolfeboro

3A

Pemigewasset R.

Winnisquam Lake

Gilford

Alpine Ridge

11

Laconia

28

Gunstock

Tilton

Belmont

Alton

Franklin

Highland

NEW HAMPSHIRE

11

Daniel Webster Birthplace

106

Shaker Village (Canterbury)

93

28

89

Pittsfield

Bow Lake

9

Chichester

Concord

9

Merrimack R.

Northwood

3

Bear Brook St. Pk.

Pawtuckaway St. Pk.

Scale of Miles

0   5   10

Suncook

N

Hooksett

W   E

S

LAKES REGION

◆ SKI AREA

From Ruggles Mine turn east on Route 4 until you come to the intersection of Route 104, then take 104 northeast to Meredith, one of the towns that borders Lake Winnipesaukee as well as the lakes Waukewan, Pemigewasset, Wicwas, and Winnisquam. Daytime cruises of Meredith Bay and the islands are available aboard the *Dorris E,* which you can board at the town docks. Meredith is the home of the famous Annalee Dolls, on Route 104, which includes a doll museum and gift shop open seven days a week. Heading clockwise around Winnipesaukee, take Route 25 from Meredith to Center Harbor for a nice view of Winnipesaukee and Squam Lake, then take Route 25B back west, picking up Route 3 north to Holderness. Here is the Squam Lake Science Center, offering live animal lectures and field trips. Take Route 113 from here and pass through the village of Center Sandwich, then head southeast on Route 109 to Moultonborough. Five miles from Moultonborough Center on Route 171 is Castle in the Clouds, built as a private estate by Thomas Gustave Plant, a shoe manufacturer and inventor who was born poor and died poor. In his heyday he built a magnificent mansion at a cost of $7 million, including the 6,000 acres on which it was built during the 1910–20 period. Plant hired a thousand Italian stonemasons from Boston to do the work, which involved blasting and carving granite into five-sided blocks. Plant furnished the estate lavishly, including memorabilia of Napoleon, his idol.

On to Wolfeboro

Continue south on Route 109 to Wolfeboro. From here the spacious excursion ship *Mount Washington* leaves for a 50-mile cruise of Lake Winnipesaukee. The evening cruises offer dinner and dancing. (The ship also departs Weirs Beach, Center Harbor, and Alton Bay.) You may want to stop at Hampshire Pewter, which regularly supplies original pewter decorations for the New Hampshire Christmas tree in Washington, D.C. Here craftsmen use the techniques and pewter alloy formula which date back to the original master pewterers. It was in Wolfeboro in 1763 that Governor John Wentworth, who governed both New Hampshire and Massachusetts from Boston, built the first summer home in the country—and Wolfeboro therefore calls itself the oldest summer resort in America.

Turn south on Route 28 and drive to Alton Bay; on your way around the lake, head northeast on Route 11. At West Alton, 11A takes you to another of the New Hampshire ski areas, Gunstock. On Gilford East Drive near Laconia you will find the Pepi Herrmann Crystal factory, where custom crystal work is handcrafted. If you continue northeast on 11, you'll want to veer off on 11B for Weirs Beach, a family amusement area with a water slide, giant wave pool, surf coaster, arcades, and fireworks displays. Then take Route 3 south into Laconia, a revitalized city with charm. Here is the 1823 Belknap Mill, the oldest unaltered brick textile mill in the country, which has been turned into a cultural center. Continue south on Route 3 to Franklin, which still has the cabin where U.S. Senator Daniel Webster, the great orator, was born and the Village Congregational Church where he worshiped.

PRACTICAL INFORMATION FOR THE LAKES REGION

Note: The area code for all New Hampshire is 603

HOW TO GET THERE AND AROUND. You will need a car to get around. There are more than two dozen auto rental firms in the Lakes Region.

By bus: Concord Trailways has daily bus service to Laconia from Logan Airport in Boston via Manchester and Concord. (Call Trailways toll-free at 800–258–3722; inside New Hampshire, 800–852–3317.)

By car: From Massachusetts, take I–93 through Concord to the Tilton exit, No. 20, and Rte. 3 north into Laconia. From Maine, take I–95 south to Portsmouth, then up Rte. 16 to 109 and west to Wolfeboro; or Rte. 302 in Maine to Rte. 16 south to Rte. 25 to Meredith and Laconia. From Vermont, take I–89 to New London, then Rte. 11 to Tilton. From Connecticut, take I–91 to Rte. 4 east at Lebanon to 104 northeast to Meredith. From Rhode Island, take I–95 to Boston, then I–93 to Tilton exit (20) to Laconia.

HOTELS AND MOTELS. The Lakes Region of New Hampshire offers a gold mine of lodging from which any traveler may chose with assurance. Large, small, lakeside, wooded, cabins, resorts, motels, cottages, and accommodations of every kind abound in this magnificently beautiful region. Rates are highest in the peak season, which runs June–Sept. Rates, based on double occupancy, in season: *Deluxe,* $90 and up; *Expensive,* $70–$90; *Moderate,* $50–$70; *Inexpensive,* $50 and less.

Alton

Bay-Side Motel, on Alton Bay, 03809 (875–5005). *Moderate.* Some kitchenettes and family units. Beach, boating, fishing.

Riverview Motel, Rtes. 11 and 28, 03809 (875–5001). *Inexpensive.* Picturesque setting on small river, five kitchenettes. Color TV.

Ashland

Blackhorse Motor Court, RFD 1, Box 46, 03217 (968–7116). *Moderate.* 17 housekeeping cabins and motel units (two-room suites). Excellent beach, lawn games, fishing, boats, dock, horseback riding, golf, tennis nearby. Near skiing and major attractions.

Little Holland Court, Rtes. 3 and 175, 03217 (968–4434). *Moderate.* Cottages on Little Squam Lake, 15 units; private beach, fishing, boating, canoeing. Play area includes horseshoes, volleyball, table tennis.

East Madison

Purity Spring Resort, Rte. 153, 03849 (367–8897). *Expensive.* On private lake. Beach, boating, canoeing. Tennis, shuffleboard, lawn games. King Pine ski area next door and snowmobile trails. Closed Apr.–May, late Oct.–late Nov.

Gilford

B. Mae's Resort Inn and Conference Center, Rte. 11, 03246 (293–7526). *Expensive–Deluxe.* 60 rooms. Indoor pool, Jacuzzi, cable TV, room phones, game room, patios. Fine dining at B. Mae Denny's.

Gunstock Inn, Rte. 11A, 03246 (293–2021). *Expensive.* Four-diamond rating, 27 rooms, New England antiques. Overlooking lake and mountains. Fine dining, olympic-size pool, whirlpool, saunas, steam room, fitness room, massage therapy. One minute to Gunstock Recreation Area.

Silver Sands, Rte. 11B on Lake Winnipesaukee, 03246 (293–4481). *Moderate.* Lakefront site, private beach, boating, kitchenettes. Heated pool. Open Apr.–mid-Oct.

Holderness

The Manor, Rte. 3, 03245 (968–3348). *Deluxe* (Modified American Plan). Comfortable and attractive, excellent food. Tennis, pool, putting green, lake swimming and boating.
Boulders, Rte. 3, 03245 (968–3600). *Moderate.* Overlooking Little Squam Lake. Beach, swimming, TV.

Laconia

The Margate Resort, Rte. 3 on Lake Winnisquam, 03246 (524–5210). *Expensive–Deluxe.* 154 rooms. 400-ft. sandy beach, newly remodeled restaurant, lounge, courtyard; indoor pool with nautilus health club.
Lord Hampshire Resort, Rte. 3 on Lake Winnisquam, 03246 (524–4331). *Moderate–Expensive.* 20 rooms. Stables, lawn games, 500-ft. beach.
The Anchorage, Rte. 3 on Lake Winnisquam, 03246 (524–3248). *Moderate.* 30 cottages and two big houses. Housekeeping on wooded 32-acre estate. Three beaches, play area, boating, canoeing, board sailing. Open mid-May–mid-Oct.

Meredith

Olmec Motor Lodge, Pleasant St., off Rte. 25, 03253 (279–8584). *Moderate.* Nine units, tucked away on Meredith Bay. Swimming, boating, TV.

Moultonborough

Kona Mansion Inn, Moultonborough Neck Rd., 03254 (253–4900). *Deluxe.* Par-3 golf and tennis to go with swimming. Restaurant and lounge. TV.
Red Hill Motel and Cottages, Rte. 25, 03254 (253–6712). *Moderate–Expensive.* Heated pool, badminton, Ping-Pong. 10-plus acres for hiking, cross-country skiing in winter.

Silverlake

Silver Lake Motor Lodge, Rtes. 41 and 113S, 03875 (367–4786). *Inexpensive–Moderate.* 16 rooms. Private beach, free boats, fishing, game room.

Tilton

Wayland Motel, Rte. 3 at exit 20, off I–93, 03276 (286–4430). *Moderate.* 11 motel rooms and five cottages, outdoor pool, cable color TV.

Weirs Beach

Brickyard Cedar Lodge, Rte. 3, 03246 (366–4316). *Expensive–Deluxe.* Hotel-motel plus time-sharing condos. Indoor and outdoor pools, tennis, and beach. Color cable TV.
Grand View Motel, Rte. 3, 03246 (366–4973). *Expensive.* Panoramic view of Lake Winnipesaukee and mountains. Pool, recreation area. Open Apr. 1–Nov. 1.

Wolfeboro

Pick Point Lodge and Cottages, Tuftonboro Neck on Lake Winnipesauke, 03894 (569–1338). *Deluxe.* Lodge and 10 efficiencies. Half-mile beach and shoreline, boats, fishing, tennis, putting green. Game room, TV. Open late May–late Oct.

The Lake Motel, Rte. 28, S. Main St., 03894 (569–1100). *Expensive.* Five efficiency units on lake, private sandy beach, tennis, boats, docks. Open mid-May–mid-Oct.

Museum Lodges, Star Rte. 1 on Lake Winnipesauke, 03894 (569–1551). *Moderate–Expensive.* Tall pines, quiet and private. Fireplaces, boats, docks, beach, fish.

INNS, GUEST HOUSES, BED AND BREAKFASTS. There is a variety of settings from which to choose, and memorable and distinctive lodging in the Lakes Region. You can choose from rooms with fireplaces in 18th-century restored homes and other possibilities. Some offer country charm and a return to a quieter time, others the range of modern amenities. The following inns have *moderate–expensive* prices.

For a full listing of bed and breakfasts in the state, write to Traditional Bed and Breakfast Association of New Hampshire, Box 6104, Lakeport 03246.

Center Harbor

Dearborn Place, Rte. 25, 03226 (253–6711). Restored Victorian home with private baths; five rooms, sitting rooms. Overlooking Lake Winnipesaukee.

Center Sandwich

Corner House Inn, Main St., 03327 (284–6219). 19th-century village is the setting. The inn, in constant operation for the past 100 years, offers cozy rooms upstairs. Dining rooms serving guests in candlelight atmosphere.

Henniker

Colby Hill Inn, Box 778, 03242 (428–3281). *Moderate.* Early 19th-century farmhouse. No children under six, no pets. Dining room. Pool.

Holderness

The Inn on Golden Pond, Rte. 3, 03245 (968–7269). An 1879 traditional colonial home located on 55 wooded acres. Walking trails and ski trails. Eight guest rooms, six with private bath. Breakfast and game rooms. Across the road is Squam Lake, setting for the film *On Golden Pond.*

Meredith

Inn at Mill Falls, Rtes. 3 and 25, 03253 (279–7006). 54 rooms. Elegant country inn at Lake Winnipesaukee. Indoor pool, whirlpool, spa and sauna. Beaches, marinas, golf and tennis. 20 distinctive shops and art gallery.

RESTAURANTS. The culinary offerings of the lakes region are nearly as numerous as the lakes. Per-person price ranges used excluding beverage, tax, and tip: *Expensive,* $25 and up; *Moderate,* $10–$25; *Inexpensive,* $10 and under.

Alton/Alton Bay

Sandy Point Restaurant, Rte. 11 on Lake Winnipesaukee (875–6001). *Moderate.* Double lobster special. Dock space available for boating diners.

Ashland

The Common Man, Main St. (968–7030). *Moderate.* Good enough for the locals to stop in. Hearty portions of seafood, veal.

Gilford

(See also Laconia, Weirs Beach)

B. Mae Denny's, jct. Rtes. 11 and 11B (293–4351). *Moderate–Expensive.* Superb steak house (owned by the same folks who run Red Parka Pub in Glen). Fresh fish and homemade soups, breads, desserts. Victorian decor.

Mountain Air Resort, Rte. 11A (293–2021). *Moderate.* Mountains at your back, lake in front of you. Excellent Continental dining.

Holderness

Café Normandie (Normandie Farms Inn), Rte. 3 (968–7940). *Moderate–Expensive.* French cuisine.

The Manor on Golden Pond, Rte. 3 (968–3348). *Moderate–Expensive.* Fireplaces and lake view. Exquisite gourmet cuisine.

Laconia

(See also Gilford, Weirs Beach)

St. Pierre's, Church St. (524–3275). *Moderate–Expensive.* Seafood is the specialty, from breaded haddock to shrimp scampi, seafood Rockefeller to a surf 'n' turf.

Summerfield's, 1106 Union Ave. (524–3111). *Moderate–Expensive.* Recycled 1870 barn with Tiffany lamps, superb food. Baby back ribs or prime rib are recommended.

Hickory Stick Farm, 2 mi. off jct. Rtes. 3 and 11 (524–3333). *Moderate.* Country-style roast duckling right from this converted farm. Children's portions. Open Memorial Day–Columbus Day.

Windmill, 155 Lake St. (524–1023). *Inexpensive.* Specializes in prime ribs, surf 'n' turf, fisherman's platter. Salad bar.

Meredith

Hart's Turkey Farm, jct. Rtes. 3 and 104 (279–6212). *Moderate–Expensive.* Family-style dinners; varied menu, from turkey to beef to seafood. Children's portions. Weekends only in winter.

Meredith Station, Rte. 3 (279–7777). *Moderate.* Specializes in veal Oscar, baked stuffed shrimp. Renovated railroad station.

Mill Works, Rte. 3 (279–4116). *Moderate.* Recycled mill building. Go for the prime ribs.

Jade Island, Rte. 3 (279–8184). *Inexpensive–Moderate.* A change of pace from steak and seafood; offerings include Chinese (Cantonese) and Polynesian dishes. Takeout.

North Barnstead

Crystal Quail, Sullivan Rd. Center Barnstead (269–4151). *Deluxe.* Magnificent dining in 18th-century home. 12 patrons per sitting. Specializes in game. Highly recommended. Reservations required.

Ossipee

Sunny Villa, Rte. 16 (539–2252). *Moderate–Expensive.* Typical northeast fare for over 50 years. Excellent homemade soups, desserts. Kids' portions.

Whittier House, Rte. 16 (539–4513). *Moderate–Expensive.* Family dining. Bake shop.

Weirs Beach

(See also Gilford, Laconia)

Nothin' Fancy, Weirs Beach Village, 03246. Mexican food, Margaritaville lounge, family dining. Near the public docks.

Wolfeboro

Wolfeboro Inn, Rte. 109 (569–3016). *Expensive.* Colonial atmosphere, regional menu. Home-baked treats.

Lake View Inn, 120 N. Main St. (569–1335). *Moderate.* Specializes in prime rib, seafood, boneless breast of chicken.

TOURIST INFORMATION. For more information and literature on the Lakes Region, write or call the Lakes Region Association, Box 33, Wolfeboro 03894 (569–1117). For other information on the region or the state, write or call the New Hampshire Office of Vacation Travel, Box 856, Concord 03301 (271–2666).

TOURS. By boat: The M/S *Mt. Washington,* Lake Winnipesaukee, Weirs Beach 03246 (366–5531). Open May 24–Oct. 19. A 3¼-hr., 50-mi. cruise on 230-ft. excursion ship from Weirs Beach (daily 9 A.M., 12:15 P.M.); Wolfeboro (daily, 11 A.M.); Center Harbor (Mon., Wed., Fri., 9:45 A.M.); Alton Bay (Tues., Thurs., Sat., Sun., 10:15 A.M.). Departures scheduled from all ports, June 15–Labor Day. Breakfast and luncheon buffet daily, Sunday champagne brunch. Also dinner-dance moonlight cruises. Adults, $11; children 5–12, $5; under 5, free.

M/V *Sophie C.* (U.S. Mail Boat), Weirs Beach, Lake Winnipesaukee (366–5531 or 366–4837). Open June 15–Sept. 13, daily. 1¾-hr. cruise departs Weirs Beach at 1 P.M. Added cruises July 1–Labor Day, 11 A.M. and 3 P.M. Adults, $7; children $3.50.

M/V *Doris E.,* Lake Winnipesaukee, Weirs Beach 03246 (366–5531 or 366–4837). July 1–Labor Day, daily. Departs Weirs Beach 10 A.M., 12 P.M., 2 P.M., and 4 P.M. Departs Meredith at 10:30 A.M., 12:30 P.M., 2:30 P.M. A 1¾-hr. cruise. Twilight cruise daily at 6:30 P.M. Adults, $6.50; children 5–12, $3.25.

By train: Winnipesaukee Railroad, Weirs Beach and Meredith (528–2330). Open May 24–Oct. 13, daily 10 A.M.–4 P.M.; weekends only from May 24–June 23 and Sept. 6–Oct. 13. Scenic ride along shores of Lake Winnipesaukee. Sunset special departs Meredith 6:45 P.M. for 2½-hr. trip Thurs.–Sat. Adults, $6; children, $4.

Special-Interest Tours: New Hampshire Winery, RFD 6, Box 218, Laconia 03857 (524–0174). Located 2½ mi. south of Laconia at intersection of Rte. 107 and Durrell Mountain Rd., Belmont 03220. Open June–Sept., daily, 11 A.M. to 4 P.M. Site of New England's first winery founded in 1969. Operated by Howard Cellars. Also a distillery for New England Spirits, Inc. Bus tours and special events scheduled by phone in advance.

Hampshire Pewter, 9 Mill St., Wolfeboro 03894 (569–4944). Handcast and hand-finished pewter. Free factory tours, Mon.–Fri., 9 A.M.–3 P.M. on the hour.

SEASONAL EVENTS. May: Marjorie Field Lilac Festival, Central Square, Bristol (late May).

June: Summertime Doll Show and Sale, Alton, Memorial School, Alton (late June).

July: July 4th Parade, 1st Newmarket Militia Co., Wolfeboro; Annual Antique and Classic Boat Show, Weirs Beach, Laconia (late July).

August: Annual Old Time Farm Day, New Hampshire Farm Museum, Milton (early Aug.); Belknap County 4-H Fair, Laconia (mid-Aug.); Art Show on the Green, Center Sandwich (late Aug.); Annual Model Railroad Show, Kingswood Regional High School, Wolfeboro (late Aug.).

October: Sandwich Fair, Sandwich (mid-Oct.).

PARKS. Parks are scarcer in this region. For information on state parks, write or call the New Hampshire Division of Parks and Recreation, Box 856D, Concord 03301 (271–3254).

Wentworth State Park, Wolfeboro, is a small park on the shore of scenic Lake Wentworth. Swimming, picnicking. Bathhouse.

Gunstock Recreation Area, Rte. 11A, Gilford 03246 (293–4341) is a 2,000-acre ski resort and 300-site campground owned by Belknap County. Olympic-size swimming pool, fishing, paddleboats, playground.

BEACHES. There are plenty of beaches along Lake Winnipesaukee and other lakes in the region, of course, but most are privately owned, either by individuals or lodging establishments. Stay the night and get a beach. Ellacoya State Beach in Gilford is a 600-ft.-long beach on the southwest shore of Lake Winnipesaukee. Swimming, picnicking.

FALL FOLIAGE. Get on the backroads of New Hampshire, away from the heavy traffic, and explore some of the small towns as you view the foliage. One suggested route: 113A from Center Harbor to Center Sandwich and back down Rte. 109 to Moultonborough. Or take 25 northeast to Rte. 25, then north on 113 to Tamworth. For foliage conditions, call 800–258–3608; from New Hampshire, 224–2525 or 2526.

OTHER ATTRACTIONS. In Laconia at **Weirs Beach,** there's a carnival-atmosphere amusement park area with rides, including a Giant Wave Pool and water slide. (Weirs Beach Chamber of Commerce, Box 336, Weirs Beach 03246; 366–4770.)

In Moultonboro, **Castle in the Clouds,** Rte. 171, 03254 (476–2352) is open May 3–mid-Oct. daily, 9 A.M.–6 P.M.; weekends only, early May–June

14, 9 A.M.–5 P.M. Tour of this famous country estate built by an eccentric millionaire for $7 million. 75-mile views. Adults, $6; children 6–12, $4.

Libby Museum, Box 09, Wolfeboro 03894 (569–1035). Seasonal. Natural history museum; Indian relics.

SUMMER SPORTS. Boating: This is boating country, for sure, and boats from cabin cruisers to sailboats dot the lake. All motor boats must be registered with the State Department of Safety, Division of Motor Vehicles. There are a number of boat liveries where you may register your boat or motor, or you may apply directly to the motor vehicle department in Concord. There are plenty of rental boats on most of the lakes in the region, already registered—from small motor boats to large boats to pull water skiers. You may reserve boats in advance before leaving on your vacation at various boat agencies. Check with the Lakes Region Association, Wolfeboro 03894 (569–1117) for information on rental places.

Horseback riding: There are a number of riding stables in the area. White Oak Farm, Ltd., Laconia 03246 (366–5814), has an indoor arena and lessons. Brookfield Farm, Ltd., Alton 03809 (569–3252), offers riding lessons; call for appointment. Castle in the Clouds, Rte. 171, Moultonboro 03254 (476–2352), has riding trails and horses for rent (call for rates).

Golf: Golf courses in this region include Kingswood Golf Club, Wolfeboro (569–3569); Indian Mound Golf Club, Center Ossipee (539–7733); Mojalaki Country Club, Franklin (934–3033). Pheasant Ridge Country Club, Laconia (524–7808); Oak Hill Golf Club, Meredith (279–4438); Waukewan Golf Club, Meredith (279–6661); Den Brae Golf Club, Sanbornton (934–9818).

Hiking: As elsewhere in New Hampshire, there is plenty of room to hike in this region, but you may want to get away from the heavy traffic of the main roads, especially around Lake Winnipesaukee. In Gilford, there's Mt. Major at Gunstock, or take most any of the backroads in Meredith, Moultonborough, Sandwich, Center Sandwich, or East Sandwich. The Squam Mountains on the northern end of Squam Lake offer mountain as well as lake views.

Bicycling: You can bicycle around Lake Winnipesaukee starting on the southwest end on Rte. 11, pick up 11B, then Rte. 25B to Center Sandwich, then Rte. 109 south. This is a low-to-medium traffic route. Rte. 104 from Danbury, through Bristol, along the Pemigewasset River, has better biking conditions, still low-to-medium traffic. The New Hampshire section of the East Coast Bicycle Trail takes you up Rte. 109 through Center Tuftonboro along the lower end of Winnipesaukee.

WINTER SPORTS. Not as mountainous as the northern and southwestern regions of New Hampshire, this area still affords **downhill skiing** as well as **Alpine.** At Gunstock ski area (293–4341) there are 25 ski trails. Farther up in Moultonboro, Ossipee Mountain (476–9491) has five ski trails. And there are plenty of **cross-country ski trails** in the area. The Nordic Skier Touring Center, Wolfeboro (569–3151) has 19 trails, 20 km of ski tracks and large expanses of ungroomed backcountry trails. Deer Cap Ski Touring Center, Center Ossipee (539–6030) has 12 groomed trails totaling 20 km. Gunstock in Laconia (293–4341) has 25 km and 11 ski trails.

This is also an increasingly popular **skimobiling** area, with skimobilers often touring in groups, crossing the icy lakes in wintertime.

FISHING. This is great lake fishing country, especially for lake trout and salmon in Lake Winnipesaukee. You need a boat to get away from the crowded docks and to the best fishing. At ice-out in late Apr.–early May, Alton Bay and Merrymeeting River at Winnipesaukee are hot spots for salmon. The smaller lakes, too, have lake trout and bass; some of them have salmon. Fishing licenses are, of course, required. Write or call the New Hampshire Fish and Game Department, 34 Bridge St., Concord 03301 (271–3421).

CAMPING. There are 41 campgrounds listed in the New Hampshire Camping Guide put out by the New Hampshire Campground Owners' Association, which lists both members and nonmembers. For information, write New Hampshire Campground Owners' Association, Box 141, Twin Mountain 03595. The six state parks in this area are all listed in the New Hampshire Campground Owners' Association Camping Guide.

HISTORIC SITES AND HOUSES. The Lakes region, while a modern tourist recreation area, has a long history as both a tourist resort and a place of industry.

Effingham

Squire Lord's Great House, Rte. 153, S. Lords Hill (539–4803). Open all year by appointment only. 19th-century Federal-style mansion with many authentic features.

Laconia

Belknap Mill (524–8813), the oldest brick textile mill in America, has been restored and made into a center for the arts.

Wolfeboro

A marker spots the area on Rte. 109 at Wentworth State Park Wayside Area in Wolfeboro where John Wentworth, last of the royal governors (1767–75) had his 4,000-acre summer estate. The manor house, erected in 1769, was the earliest summer home in the Lakes Region. It was destroyed by fire in 1820. Archeological digs have been going on at the site.

MUSEUMS. There are a few specialized museums in the area. Call ahead for admission fees.

Alton

The Gilman Museum, Main St. Collection of antique furniture, large collection of china. Open May 30, then July 1–Sept. 30, Wed. and Sat., 2–5 P.M., 1st Sun. of month 2–5 P.M. and by appointment.

Laconia

Carpenter Museum of Antique Outboard Motors, Rte. 107, Belmont (524–7611). Over 300 antique outboard motors, from the late 1800s through the 1960s, on premises. Open all year by appointment, 9 A.M.–9 P.M.

Meredith

Annalee Doll Museum (279–6543). Open year-round. Daily, 10 A.M.–4 P.M. winter; 9 A.M.–5 P.M. summer. More than 1,000 dolls.

Milton

New Hampshire Farm Museum, Rte. 16, Plummer's Ridge (652–7840). Here you explore New Hampshire's agricultural heritage. Open July–mid-Oct., Fri., Sat., Sun., 10 A.M.–4 P.M.

Wolfeboro

Clark House Historical Exhibit and Museum, South Main St. (569–4997). 1778 Cape Cod house authentically furnished; one-room schoolhouse, c. 1820; fire museum with old, restored equipment. Open July 1–Sept. 1, Mon.–Sat., 10 A.M.–4:30 P.M.

MUSIC, DANCE, AND STAGE. In Tamworth, you'll find New Hampshire's oldest professional theater and one of the oldest continuing summer theaters in America. **The Barnstormers** begins its 60th year in 1990. It puts on eight weeks of plays, each running one week, July–Aug. All performances are Tues.–Sat., 8:30 P.M. Write or call The Barnstormers, Tamworth 03886 (323–8500; off-season, 323–7733). There's an annual **Barbershop Jamboree** each year in early Aug. at Alton Bay, and in Wolfeboro, **Friends of Music** put on a series of six concerts—chorale, piano, brass quintet, traditional folk music, etc.—at the public library. The **Kingwood Summer Theatre for Children** in Wolfeboro puts on plays during the summer (569–3593).

SHOPPING. In this region, there are numerous shops offering hand-crafted and unique gifts. For a full current listing, contact the Chamber of Commerce in each town.

For fine arts and crafts: **The Meredith-Laconia League of New Hampshire Craftsmen,** Rte. 3, Meredith (279–7920), retail shop featuring juried crafts; **Pepi Herrmann Crystal,** Gilford East Dr., Gilford, tours through crystal-cutting studio—fine crystal for sale. Also in Meredith is the **Annalee Doll Museum and Gift Shop,** with 1,000 Annalee dolls to view (enter via Hemlock Dr. or Reservoir Rd.).

NIGHTLIFE. This is family vacation country, so Wiers Beach, with its carnival atmosphere and rides, is a big nighttime attraction. But there are some nice adult clubs in the area. Try **B. Mae Denny's Eating and Drinking Establishment,** Rte. 11, Gilford (293–4351), where you'll find good top-40s band music. **Meredith Station Restaurant,** Rte. 3, Meredith (279–7777), is a hot spot for music and commingling. **Margate Resort,** 76 Lake St., Lakeport (524–5210) has good top-40s band music. In Belmont, there's **Zachary's Club** on Rte. 106 (528–4399), a popular spot. The **Inn of All Seasons,** 480 Main St., Laconia (524–8000) has a good lounge.

THE DARTMOUTH–LAKE SUNAPEE REGION

The Dartmouth–Lake Sunapee area is part of the rich Connecticut Valley, a region of immaculate colonial villages set on the lush banks of the Connecticut River, an area of culture and rural serenity. A hundred lakes, rolling hills, and gentle mountains make exploring it a joy. From Franklin, take Route 11 west to I–89 and zip up to Hanover, home of Dartmouth

College (or get off Route 11 onto Route 4 and wind your way to Hanover, stopping at Enfield to visit the La Salette Shrine and Center, a place of prayer and meditation near Lake Mascoma). On I–89 on the way to Hanover, stop at New London, the home of Colby Sawyer College and a lovely town with many shops. In Hanover, Dartmouth College, with its college green and Federal and Georgian buildings, dates to 1761 when it was started as a school for Indians. In 1769, King George III chartered it as Dartmouth College, making it the oldest educational institution in New Hampshire.

On campus, visit the Baker Library, which displays Orozco's famous murals and has a rare books division, and the Hood Museum of Art, which is connected to the Hopkins Center for the Creative and Performing Arts—a must. The Hopkins Center offers concerts, plays, films, and art galleries as well as free tours that look in on student sculptors at work. Main Street has fashionable shops, a large bookstore, fine restaurants, and street vendors.

Along the Connecticut River

The next-door town of Lebanon, chartered on July 4, 1761, by King George III, is a mill city worth a view for the contrasts between it and the Ivy League college town of Hanover. If you're an antiques buff, the Colonial Shopping Center has an enormous conglomeration of booths with fine antiques and collectibles. From Lebanon, head north on Route 10 along the Connecticut River to the little town of Orford. Here you will find stately homes and manicured lawns behind fences and, in an area called The Ridge, seven homes built between 1773 and 1839, designed by an associate of Charles Bulfinch. You can drive all over the area without finding a restaurant, but country stores have plenty of furnishings for a picnic.

Cornish

Retrace your path, taking Route 10 back to Lebanon, then 120 south to Cornish, home of the Cornish Colony (1885–1935). The colony was a group of artists, sculptors, writers, journalists, poets, and musicians who joined the sculptor Augustus Saint-Gaudens in Cornish to live and work. Among them were the sculptor Herbert Adams, the architect Charles A. Platt, the artist Stephen Parrish, and his son, Maxfield Parrish, whose paintings adorned the covers of *Collier's* and *Ladies' Home Journal* for years. J. D. Salinger, author of *Catcher in the Rye*, lives here, secluded from the press and public. The highlight of the cultural tour is the Saint-Gaudens National Historic Site, which consists of the home, gardens, and studios of Saint-Gaudens (1848–1907), one of America's great sculptors. Saint-Gaudens's work included the statue of Lincoln now found in Chicago's Lincoln Park, the Adams Memorial in Washington, D.C., and the statue of Admiral David Farragut in New York's Madison Square. Sculpture and copies of sculpture by Saint-Gaudens are everywhere, and the grounds and buildings provide a soothing, relaxing walk. The longest covered bridge in the United States, built in 1866, crosses the Connecticut River in Cornish.

This also was the home of the American writer Winston Churchill, author of *The Crisis* and *Richard Carvel*, and the home of Salmon P. Chase, for a time Lincoln's secretary of the treasury and a founder of the Republican party (Chase's picture appears on the $10,000 bill). Near the Saint-

Gaudens site in nearby Plainfield is the Maxfield Parrish Museum, once his studio.

Claremont

Continue south on 120 to Claremont, an old mill city. Here you will find Old St. Mary's, which resembles a townhouse but is the oldest Catholic church in the state, erected in 1823. Also in town is Union Church, a wood-frame structure that is the oldest standing Episcopal church in the state, having been built in 1771–73. Take Route 11-103 out of Claremont to Newport, which was the birthplace and home of Sarah Josepha Buell Hale, who edited *Godey's Lady Book,* a popular magazine, from 1837 to 1877. Hale moved successfully for a presidential proclamation of Thanksgiving Day, was an advocate of higher education for women, and wrote *Mary Had a Little Lamb.* She taught school here before launching her journalistic career.

Route 103 will take you southeast to Sunapee State Park on Lake Sunapee, where you can ride four-passenger gondolas 2,700 feet to the summit of Mount Sunapee. Head back to Claremont on 103, turning south on Route 11-12 to Charlestown, where you'll find a re-creation of the original Fort at No. 4, used for colonial defense during the French and Indian War. It contains a re-creation of a pre-Revolutionary village as it was when it was built in 1746. Interpreters in period dress guide you through the stockade, where there are crafts demonstrations of the period and exhibits of tools, furnishings, and costumes of an eighteenth-century community.

PRACTICAL INFORMATION FOR THE DARTMOUTH–LAKE SUNAPEE REGION

Note: The area code for all New Hampshire is 603

HOW TO GET THERE AND AROUND. As in most regions of New Hampshire, public transportation is limited and you need a car to get around. Auto rentals are available in the Hanover–Lebanon area.

By plane: Information on schedules and airports may be obtained from United (800–241–6522) or Eastern Express (800–327–8376).

By bus: Concord Trailways has daily bus service to Hanover and nearby White River Junction, Vermont. (Call toll-free 800–258–3722; inside New Hampshire, 800–852–3317.)

By car: From Massachusetts, Take I–93 to I–89 to Hanover–Lebanon. If you're approaching the state from Boston on I–95, take State 101 west at Hampton to Manchester, where you'll pick up I–93 north. From Maine, Rte. 2 to I–91 in Vermont, down to Lebanon junction; from Kittery area, Rte. 4 to Concord, then I–89 to Hanover–Lebanon. From Vermont, I–91 to Lebanon; I–89 south to Lebanon; Rte. 4 to Lebanon. From Connecticut, I–91 north to Lebanon–Hanover exits. From Rhode Island, I–95 to Boston, then I–93 to Concord, picking up I–89 to Hanover–Lebanon.

HOTELS AND MOTELS. A variety of establishments stand ready to serve you when you visit the historic Dartmouth–Lake Sunapee Region. The range of accommodations in both size and type will afford you comfortable lodging no matter what your taste or budget. Price ranges based on double occupancy: *Deluxe,* $90 and up; *Expensive,* $70–$90; *Moderate,* $50–70; *Inexpensive,* $50 and under.

Claremont

Stone Eagle Motel, Rtes. 11 and 103, 03743 (542–2511). *Inexpensive–Moderate.* Nice hilltop site, handy to attractions, shopping, but away from main traffic. 16 rooms. Coffee shop.

Hanover

Hanover Inn. Main and Wheelock Sts., 03755 (643–4300). *Deluxe.* Dartmouth-run, two-centuries-old inn on The Green, next to Hopkins Center, at head of Main St. First-rate meals, comfortable rooms, colonial-decor lounge. Pets. Color cable TV.

Lyme

Loch Lyme Lodge and Cottages, on Post Pond, 03768 (795–2141). *Inexpensive.* Main lodge is a farmhouse built in 1784, and there are 26 cottages (including 13 housekeeping units) sprinkled around the grounds. Bed and breakfast available. Pond swimming, canoeing, boating, fishing. Tennis, badminton, croquet, hiking. In winter, cross-country skiing, skating, ice fishing. European Plan or Modified American Plan.

New London

Hide-Away Lodge, Twin Lake Villa Rd., off Rte. 11, 03257 (526–4861). *Moderate–Expensive.* (Modified American Plan) Rooms in cottage and lodge. Woodland setting. Gracious dining, lounge. Open year-round except Apr.

Newport

Hilltop Motel, Rtes. 11 and 103, 03733 (863–3456). *Moderate.* Italian restaurant. Pool. Color TV.
Newport Motel, Rtes. 11 and 103, 03773 (863–1440). *Moderate.* Play area, pool, recreation room, 18 rooms. Color cable TV.

West Lebanon

Sheraton North Country Inn, Airport Rd., just off Rte. 12A, 03784 (298–5906). *Expensive–Deluxe.* Restaurant and lounge well-known for nightly live entertainment. 126 rooms. Color TV (cable). Indoor pool.
Airport Econo Inn, Exit 105, I–91, 03784 (298–8888). *Inexpensive.* Near shopping mall, ski areas; short distance from Dartmouth College. Continental breakfast.

INNS, GUEST HOUSES, BED AND BREAKFASTS. The Hanover–Lake Sunapee Region will give travelers an adequate range of choices in selecting fine lodging accommodations throughout the area. Country inns, some nestled in seclusion and others right on the "beaten path," enable you to plan according to your taste and schedule. Most of the following have *moderate–expensive* price ranges.

Andover

Andover Meadow Inn, Rte. 11, 03216 (735–5224). Nothing pretentious, just comfortable. Outdoor pool. TV. Serves breakfast and dinner.

Canaan

The Inn on Canaan Street, Exit 17, off I-89, go east on Rte. 4, 10 mi. to Canaan, 03741 (523-7310/9011). *Deluxe.* A year-round small inn, airy rooms, fireplaces, wide porches, situated on 14 acres of gardens and woodlands. Canoeing, fishing, swimming, skiing, picnic-basket luncheons, dinners by reservation.

Cornish

Chase House Bed & Breakfast, I-91 north, Exit 8 to Rte. 131 east, Cornish 03745 (675-5391). Historic surroundings on 45 acres.

Hanover

Chieftain Motor Inn, Rte. 10, 03755 (643-2550). Small (22 rooms), overlooks Connecticut River. Continental breakfast. Pool, boating, fishing. Color cable TV.

Lyme

Lyme Inn, On the Village Common, 03768 (795-2222). Ex-stagecoach stop (1809) between Montreal and Boston. Each room drips with atmosphere and antiques (many for sale). Every room has canopy beds, private bath. Fine, relaxed dining; dining room closed Tues. Inn closes for three weeks in Apr., Dec.

New London

New London Inn, Main St., 03257 (526-2791). Medium-sized, 30-room, attractive inn that goes back to 1792. One formal dining room.

Pleasant Lake Inn, Pleasant St., 03257 (526-6271). A four-season, 1790 country inn off the shore of Pleasant Lake. Swim, fish, hike, golf. Dinner and breakfast.

North Charlestown

Indian Shutters Inn, Rte. 12, 03603 (826-4445). View of Connecticut River and Mt. Ascutney. Charming, authentic 1791 stagecoach inn. All meals homemade.

Plainfield

Home Hill Country Inn, River Rd. (off Rte. 12A), 03745 (675-6165). *Deluxe.* Restored mansion with only six rooms. Superb French restaurant. Delicious desserts. Closed Sun. and Mon.

Sunapee

The Backside Inn, RFD 2, Box 213, 03773 (863-5161). *Deluxe.* 10-room country inn with shared or private baths, full breakfast. Mt. Sunapee State Park and Lake just 4 mi. away. Dinner served nightly.

Sutton Mills

The Village House at Sutton Mills, RFD 1, Box 151, 03221 (927–4765). *Deluxe.* A Victorian country house nestled in the heart of the Lake Sunapee region, 2.5 mi. from I–89 exit. Charming rooms furnished with antiques and country quilts. Continental breakfast included. Antique shop on premise.

RESTAURANTS. Dining in the Hanover–Lake Sunapee area offers some genuine culinary delights. Fine steak, soups, seafood, oriental food, stews, and quiches are only a random sampling of the fare available. Per-person price ranges excluding beverage, tax, and tip: *Expensive,* $25 and up; *Moderate,* $10–$25, *Inexpensive,* $10 and under.

Charlestown

Indian Shutter's Inn, Rte. 12 (826–4445). *Moderate.* Lovely old (1791) country inn. Varied menu. Homemade soups.

Claremont

Martin Croix, Pleasant St. (542–9289). *Moderate–Expensive.* Green-house setting. Good steaks, even better veal.
Royal Dragon, Rte. 11 (543–1211). *Inexpensive–Moderate.* Everything your Far-Eastern appetite could want. Go for the barbecued spareribs and chicken with cashews.

Hanover

Jesse's, Rte. 120 (643–4111). *Expensive.* Steak and seafood in an over-sized log cabin. Steak teriyaki is recommended.
Bentley's, 11 S. Main St. (643–4075). *Moderate–Expensive.* Sister to the Bentley's in Woodstock, Vermont, and just as pleasing. Good lunches, great dinners.
Molly's Balloon, 43 S. Main St. (643–2570). *Moderate–Expensive.* Hanging plants. Good quiches.
5 Olde Nugget Alley, 5 Olde Nugget Alley (643–5081). *Moderate.* Soups, salads, and sandwiches for lunch or late in the day. Immense burgers.
Peter Christian's, 39 S. Main St. (643–2345). *Moderate.* Rustic atmosphere, stoneware, bowls, mugs, etc.; cheese and meat boards, stews, soups, desserts.

Lebanon

Owl's Nest, 213 Mechanic St. (448–2074). *Moderate.* Wooden decor with Tiffany lamps. Large salad bar. Good prime ribs.
Lander's Restaurant, Rte. 120 (448–1243). *Moderate.* Heavy local favorite. Nice job with fish.
Riverside Grill Restaurant, Exit 17 off I–89, Rte. 4 (448–2571). *Inexpensive–Moderate.* A full menu with daily specials and homemade breads.

Lyme

D'Artagnan's, 13 Dartmouth College Hwy. (795–2137). *Expensive.* "Rural French" cuisine with the emphasis on lightness. Reservations recommended. Prix fixe, five-course meal or à la carte selections. Closed Mon. and Tues.

New London

Hide-Away Lodge (526–4861). *Expensive.* A restaurant with national acclaim. Gourmet food featuring seasonal specialties and one of the best wine selections in the state.

Millstone Restaurant, Newport Rd. (526–4201). *Moderate–Expensive.* Casually elegant. Sun. brunch.

The Gray House Restaurant, Rte. 11 (526–6603). *Moderate.* Fine seafood in midst of mountains.

Peter Christian's Tavern, Main St. (526–4042). *Moderate.* Rustic atmosphere; stews, soups, quiches, complete dinner menu, and full bar service.

West Lebanon

Mascoma River Waterworks at the Powerhouse, Rte. 12A (298–8813). *Expensive.* Unusually fine menu, with dinner specials on Sunday.

China Lite, Rte. 12A (298–8222). *Moderate–Expensive.* Polynesian and Cantonese menu. Mounds of food. Excellent big ribs.

TOURIST INFORMATION. For detailed information and literature on the Dartmouth–Lake Sunapee region, contact the Hanover Chamber of Commerce, Box 930, Hanover 03755 (643–3115). Other information on this region and the state may be obtained from the New Hampshire Office of Vacation Travel, Box 856, Concord 03301 (271–2666).

TOURS. By boat: Two boats cruise Lake Sunapee—the M.V. *Mt. Sunapee II* (763–4030) and the M.V. *Kearsarge* (763–5477). Each leaves daily from Sunapee Harbor, off Rte. 11, from late May to early Sept. M.V. *Mt. Sunapee II* offers twice-daily cruises of the lake during the day and the Kearsarge has two dinner cruises (buffet style) daily.

SEASONAL EVENTS. In Andover, visit the Farmers' Market, mid-July–mid-Sept., Sat., 9 A.M.–noon: vegetables, baked goods, crafts. Bradford has various community events during the summer, on Fri. and Sat. evenings, including fairs, pig roasts, dinners, fishing tournaments (938–5309). Pick your own apples, Sept. 15–Oct. 15, at LaValley Orchard, Page Hill Road, Newport (863–2230). Cider, maple syrup, and apples available at Walhowdon Farm Orchard, off Laplante Rd., Lebanon (448–4500).

February: Dartmouth College Winter Festival, Hanover.

June: Annual Old Timers Fair, on the Green, Hanover Center (late June); Strawberry Festival, Baptist Church Yard, Main St., Bradford (late June).

July: Crafts Fair at Fort No. 4, Charlestown (early July); Family Fair, Rte. 4A, Enfield (mid-July); New London Garden Club Antiques Show and Sale, New London (late July); North Haverhill Fair, North Haverhill (late July, early Aug.); Annual Old Home Day Arts and Crafts Festival, School Gym, Rte. 11, Sunapee (3rd week of July); Sunapee Old Homeday Festival and Antique Collectible Show and Sale (3rd week of July).

August: Annual Old Home Days, Canaan, (1st week of Aug.); Annual Craftsmen's Fair of the League of New Hampshire Craftsmen Foundation, Mt. Sunapee State Park, Newbury (1st week of Aug.); Sunday in the Park (old-fashioned ice cream social, antique cars, etc.), Claremont (mid-

Aug.); Old Home Day, South Sutton (mid-Aug.); Annual Old Home Day and Antiques Fair, Salisbury Green, Rte. 4, Salisbury (mid-Aug.); Annual Lions Club Soap Box Derby, Canaan (early Aug.); Andover Historical Society Antique Auction, Andover (early Aug.); Annual Shrine Maple Sugar Bowl Game, Dartmouth College Memorial Field (all-star high school football), Hanover (early Aug.); Cornish Fair, Cornish (mid-Aug.); Battle Weekend of the Revolutionary War at Fort No. 4, Charlestown (mid-Aug.); 6th Annual Muster Day, Muster Field Farm, North Sutton (late Aug.).

September: Harvest Festival at Fort No. 4, Charlestown (late Sept.).

October: 40th Annual Warner Fall Foliage Festival, Warner (early Oct.).

November: Thanksgiving at Fort No. 4, Charlestown (late Nov.).

PARKS. Mount Sunapee State Park, Newbury (763–2356), offers hiking, swimming, picnicking, skiing on a network of 130 acres of slopes and trails. 2,700-ft. summit of Sunapee Mountain.

Cardigan State Park, Orange. A mountain road leads to a pleasant picnic spot on the west slope of Mt. Cardigan. Hiking trails lead to 3,100-ft. summit.

Pillsbury State Park, Washington. A wooded area with hiking trails to nearby mountains. Campground with 20 primitive sites on the shores of a pond. Stream and pond fishing, picnicking.

FALL FOLIAGE. A good backroad foliage route is to take I–89 to New London and take Rte. 11 west to Claremont, then north on Rte. 12A, along the Connecticut River to the Hanover–West Lebanon area. For foliage conditions, call from New England, 800–258–3608 or 3609; from New Hampshire, 224–2525 or 2526. This area is the last in which foliage colors turn.

SUMMER SPORTS. Boating: Lake Sunapee has motor and boat rentals, including sailboats, and piers and public launch sites. The Connecticut River has boat launches.

Swimming: There's swimming at Mt. Sunapee State Park, Newbury (763–2356) and in numerous streams in the region.

Golf: A number of golf courses can be found in this region, including Eastman Golf Links, Grantham (863–4500); Hanover Country Club, Hanover (646–2000); Carter Country Club, Lebanon (448–9832); John H. Cain Golf Club, Newport (863–9818); Country Club of New Hampshire, North Sutton (927–4246); Claremont Country Club, Claremont (542–9551).

Bicycling: There are several good routes, low-to-medium traffic, in this region: along Rte. 12A from North Charleston to Cornish; Rte. 120 from Cornish to Lebanon; along Rte. 4 from Danbury to Enfield; and, a particularly good stretch, along 4A from West Andover to Enfield. For further information on routes, write Granite State Wheelmen Inc., 16 Clinton St., Salem 03079.

WINTER SPORTS. There are several **downhill ski slopes** in the Hanover–Lake Sunapee region and plenty of **cross-country skiing** territory. Ski mountains include Dartmouth Skiway, Lyme Center (795–2143); Eastman Pond, Grantham (863–4241); King Ridge, New London (526–6966); Mt. Sunapee, Sunapee (763–2356); Tenney Mountain, Plymouth (536–1717; out of state, 800–222–2SKI); and Whaleback, Lebanon (448–2607).

Mt. Sunapee State Park, Newbury (763–2356) has plenty of **cross-country trails.**

There are a number of ski touring areas, including Eastman Ski Touring Center, Grantham (863–4500); Mt. Cube Ski Touring, Orford (353–4709); Norsk Touring Center, New London (526–4685).

Hiking. Walking and hiking trails lead to the 2,700-ft. Mt. Sunapee summit. At Cardigan State Park in Orange, hiking trails lead to the 3,100-ft. summit. There are hiking trails from Pillsbury State Park in Washington to nearby mountains. The Applachian Trail winds through the middle of Hanover. The Dartmouth Outing Club at Dartmouth College, Hanover, offers area trail information. Or contact the Appalachian Mt. Club, Box 298, Pinkham Notch 03581 (466–2725).

FISHING. There is excellent fishing for bass, and above the Wilder Dam in Lebanon, for walleye pike, on the Connecticut River. Lake Sunapee, a deep cold-water lake, has a reputation for exceptional lake trout and salmon fishing. There are eight commercial and municipal launch sites, two state-owned ramps. You can rent boats at state park.

CAMPING. Of the state park campgrounds, only one is located in this area: 20 elementary tent sites at Pillsbury State Park in Washington (863–2860). There are 9 private campgrounds listed for this region in the New Hampshire Camping Guide, all members of the New Hampshire Campground Owners' Association, which inspects each site. For further information, contact New Hampshire Campground Owners' Association, Box 320, Twin Mountain 03595.

SPECTATOR SPORTS. Football at Dartmouth College in Hanover is the spectator sport in this region.

HISTORIC SITES AND HOMES. This region was settled by people who came north from Massachusetts the colonial period to this rich valley along the Connecticut River. Some, like the sculptor Augustus Saint-Gaudens, came much later to serve as the spur for a late 19th-century artist colony in Cornish. Check ahead for admission fees.

Canaan

Canaan Historic District, Canaan St. Late 18th-century, early 19th-century rural community, including Old Meeting House (1793), North Church (1828).

Charlestown

Old Fort No. 4, Rte. 12 (826–5700). Reconstruction of French and Indian War stockade built on site in 1744. Costumed guides and 25-min. audiovisual program. Open 7 days mid-June–Labor day, weekends to Columbus Day, 10 A.M.–5 P.M. daily in summer, 11 A.M.–5 P.M. on autumn weekends.

Claremont

Historic Mill District, walking tour of 37 historic sites. Map and guide available from Claremont Chamber of Commerce, Tremont Sq. (543–1296).

Claremont Opera House and Atrium. Authentically restored 1897 opera house, listed in *National Register of Historic Places.* Write Chamber of Commerce for schedule of events. Open Mon.–Fri., 9 A.M.–5 P.M.

Little Red Schoolhouse, Rte. 10, 2½ mi. south of Newport (863–2079). One-room school from around 1835; original interior maintained by New Hampshire Daughters of the American Revolution. Open July 4–Labor Day, Wed. only, 1–4 P.M.

Cornish

Saint-Gaudens National Historic Site, Saint-Gaudens Rd., Cornish (675–2175). Guided tours of the home, gardens, and studios of Saint-Gaudens (1848–1907), one of America's foremost sculptors. Open mid-May–Oct. 31, 8:30 A.M.–4:30 P.M.; grounds open till dusk.

Windsor-Cornish Covered Bridge crosses the Connecticut River at Cornish. At 460 ft., the longest covered bridge in the United States, built in 1866.

Newport

Newport Opera House, Main St. On National Register of Historic Places. Once considered the largest stage north of Boston. Revere bell in front of building, now in multiple use.

MUSEUMS. You will discover a good deal of local history in the museums of this area.

Andover

Andover Historical Society Museum, Rte. 4 at Rte. 11, Potter Place. Classical 1874 Victorian railroad station with authentically furnished station master's office. Homesite and grave of noted early 19th-century black magician Richard Potter. Open June 1–Oct. 13, weekends only, Sat. 10 A.M.–3 P.M., Sun. 1–3 P.M.

Enfield

Lockehaven Schoolhouse Museum, Village of Lockhaven on Crystal Lake (632–7740). 1864 one-room schoolhouse, restored. Open June 5–Oct. 2, Sun. only, 2–5 P.M.

Hanover

Montshire Museum of Science, 45 Lyme Rd. (643–5672). Numerous exhibits on various aspects of science; special emphasis on natural history of northern New England. Open all year, Tues.–Sat., 10 A.M.–5 P.M., Sun. 1–5 P.M.

Sunapee

Lake Sunapee Historical Society Museum, Sunapee Harbor. Extensive collection of photographs, memorabilia and artifacts from Lake Sunapee's steamboat era. Open July 2–Aug. 27, Wed. eves., 7:30–9:30 P.M. Weekend schedule.

Sutton

Buildings on Meeting House Hill Rd., S. Sutton (927–4183). 1863 one-room schoolhouse with furnishings, c. 1800 typical church, and old school museum.

Washington

Washington Museum. Exhibits of American transportation from colonial times to early auto age. Inquire at Post Office. Open all year by appointment; closed Sun.

MUSIC, DANCE, AND STAGE. At Dartmouth College, Hanover, the region's center of culture, the **Hopkins Center for Creative and Performing Arts** offers first-rate concerts, plays, films, art galleries (646–2422). Open all year, daily, 7:30 A.M.–11 P.M. Two theaters. Write or call for free calendar and schedule.

In New London—**Barn Playhouse,** Main St. (Box 285), New London 03257 (526–4631/6710). Open June 24–Aug. 31. Curtain 8:30 P.M., Tues.–Fri. Established in 1933, 1820s refurbished barn. For information about square dance clubs throughout New Hampshire, contact Square Dance Foundation of N.E., c/o Severance, 105 Oak Hill Ave., Manchester 03104 (623–2692).

ART GALLERIES. In Hanover—**Hood Museum of Art,** Dartmouth College (646–2348). Open during school year. **2 AVA Art Gallery,** 5 Allen St. (643–2841). Open year-round. Collective art gallery featuring work by New Hampshire and Vermont artists.

In Newport—**Newport Library Arts Center,** 58 N. Main St. (863–3040). Open Apr. 1–Dec. 10.

In Claremont—**Claremont Opera House and Atrium Gallery,** City Hall Complex (542–2458). Open May–Oct. Work of area artists in all art forms.

SHOPPING. Fine shops abound in this region, especially stores with handcrafted wares. In Hanover, try **Designer Gold,** Paul Gross, Goldsmith, 68 S. Main St., for one-of-a-kind and limited-edition gold jewelry, or **Hanover League of New Hampshire Craftsmen,** 13 Lebanon St., local and regional New Hampshire crafts; On Depot St. in Potter Pl., there's **Wild Pottery** by Sam Wild, hand-painted stoneware pottery with nature motifs; New London has **The Crafty Goose,** Main St., handcrafted items, and **Artisans Workshop,** Main St., jewelry, pottery, weavings.

NIGHTLIFE. In West Lebanon, a favorite lounge is **Sheraton North Country Inn,** Airport Rd., off Rte. 12A (298–5906). In Hanover, try **Peter Christian's Tavern,** 39 S. Main St. (526–4042), a nice classy pub. There are some fine restaurants in the region, but most places in small towns close down after dark.

THE MONADNOCK REGION

Continue from Charlestown down Route 12 and into Keene, the largest city and hub of the Monadnock Region. The home of Keene State College, this small city has one of the widest main streets in the world, with stately homes and oak trees lining much of it. But you have to get away from the hub to see this Currier and Ives country, with its dominant Mt. Monadnock, covered bridges, and eighteenth-century small towns. Head down Route 10 to West Swanzey; there are six covered bridges within a five-mile area, one in West Swanzey, a couple in nearby Swanzey Village. Joyce Kilmer wrote his famous poem "Trees" here. Continue down 10, where if you head northwest you can take in the Hinsdale Raceway, which features greyhound racing. Just before the 119–10 intersection, try Route 119 to Fitzwilliam, a beautiful old American village, where some 16 acres of rhododendron burst into bloom at the Rhododendron State Park around mid-July.

Cathedral of the Pines

Continue on Route 119 to Rindge, where you'll find Cathedral of the Pines, a memorial to a son lost during World War II, built on the site he had selected for his future home. The Altar of the Nation within the cathedral was recognized by Congress and dedicated as a memorial to all American war dead. Open every day from May through September, it offers services daily. More than seven million people have visited the cathedral, which is actually the pine forest. From Rindge, go north on Route 202 to Jaffrey, founded in 1773. Behind the colonial Meeting House is buried Amos Fortune, an African-born slave who purchased his freedom, established a tannery, and left funds for the Jaffrey church and schools. Replicas of his gravestone and that of his wife, Violate, are in the Smithsonian Institution in Washington, D.C. The distinguished American writer Willa Cather is also buried in Jaffrey.

Up Mt. Monadnock

Take 124 east from Jaffrey and turn right on the road that leads to Monadnock State Park. The Monadnock Ecocenter sponsors guided walks and lectures on the region's natural bounty. Then climb Mt. Monadnock, centerpiece of the region and one of the most-climbed mountains in the world. You can start here, but there are 30 miles of trails approaching the summit; check at the park for a suitable trail for you. The round-trip hike to the top will take about three hours. Henry David Thoreau and Ralph Waldo Emerson both climbed to the top, which is rocky and barren because farmers in 1820 set fire to the trees to drive out the wolves that were killing their sheep. Now continue north on that park road to Dublin, the highest town in New England at 1,439 feet. This is the home of *Yankee* magazine and *Old Farmer's Almanac,* and the town was once the nucleus of a larger summer colony that attracted such figures as Mark Twain and Amy Lowell. Continue north to Harrisville, a mill town that offers a lake for boating and the Gallery of Monadnock Artists. Drive up through Nelson to Route 9, take a right on Route 9 going east to 202, then head south to Peterborough.

Peterborough: "Our Town"

Peterborough, believed to be the model for Thornton Wilder's *Our Town,* is the home of the MacDowell Colony. After the death of composer Edward MacDowell, his wife and friends established this composers' and writers' refuge in his memory. Among other artists who came through the years were Edwin Arlington Robinson, Stephen Vincent Benet, Willa Cather, and Elinor Wylie. The colony still brings creative artists to live and work. Today Peterborough is known also as a major publishing center, particularly for high-tech and computer magazines and magazine publishers, including *Cobblestone,* CW Communications, McGraw-Hill, and Wayne Green Enterprises. From here, take 123 south to New Ipswich, which was the site of the first New Hampshire textile mill. Stop at the

Barrett House, an exceptional three-story Federal residence built in 1800; it is in the house guide of the Society for the Preservation of New England Antiquities.

Continue on to Greenville, which boasts the highest railroad bridge in New Hampshire, and to Mason, a picturesque village that was the boyhood home of Samuel Wilson (1766–1854), who was generally known as "Uncle Sam." Wilson supplied beef to the army in 1812; the brand on his barrel was "U.S." The transition from U.S. to Uncle Sam followed, and he became the popular symbol for the United States. Now return to Greenville and head north on Route 31 through Wilton to Bennington, home of Crotched Mountain West Ski Area. From there, take 202 to Hillsborough. Here is the homestead of Franklin Pierce, the fourteenth president. Built in 1804 by his father, it is a mansion of elegance uncommon to rural New Hampshire of the 1800s.

PRACTICAL INFORMATION FOR THE MONADNOCK REGION

NOTE: The area code for all New Hampshire is 603

HOW TO GET THERE AND AROUND. You'll need a car to get around here. Auto rentals are available in Keene.

By plane: Manchester Airport has daily flight service by United Airlines (800–241–6522); USAIR (800–428–4322); Eastern Express, (800–327–8376). Auto rentals available from airport. Take 101 west to Keene.

By bus: Vermont Transit (800–451–3292) serves cities in this area and throughout central and northern New Hampshire.

By car: From Manchester, take Rte. 101 west to Keene. From Massachusetts, take Rte. 3 to Nashua and from there, 101A to 101 to Keene. From Connecticut, I–91 to Springfield, Maine, then U.S. 202 to Keene. From Vermont, I–89 to I–93 at Concord, south to Manchester and 101 West to Keene. From Maine, I–95 south to Portsmouth, then 101 west through Manchester to Keene. From Rhode Island, I–95 to Boston, then I–93 north to Manchester, then Rte. 101 west to Keene.

HOTELS AND MOTELS. The Monadnock Region, a historic and beautifully scenic area of New Hampshire, offers the traveler variety in its hotels and motels, as well as its in vacation activities. While choices are not as extensive as in some other areas of the state, the visitor will not be disappointed with the available lodgings. Per-person price ranges are *Deluxe,* $90 and up; *Expensive,* $70–90; *Moderate,* $50–$70; *Inexpensive,* $50 and under.

Francestown

Tory Pines Resort, Rte. 47, 03043 (588–2000). *Moderate–Expensive.* Converted barn. Golf, tennis, pool. Skating and 25 mi. of cross-country ski trails. Good lunch spot, fine dinners, lounge.

Jaffrey

Woodbound Inn, Woodbound Rd., 03452 (532–8341). *Deluxe* (American Plan). 55 rooms and lakeside cottages with fireplaces. Pets in cottages only. Restaurant.

Keene

Valley Green Motel, 379 West St., 03431 (352–7350). *Moderate.* 58 units. Heated outdoor pool. Color cable TV. Restaurant.

Yankee Traveler Motel, Rte. 12 Westmoreland 03467 (357–0044). *Inexpensive.* 12 units. Nice rooms in country setting.

Ramada Inn, 401 Winchester St., Exit 3, I–91, 03431 (357–3038). *Moderate.* Indoor pool. Restaurant and lounge entertainment.

Peterborough

Salzburg Inn, Steele Rd., 03458 (924–3808). *Moderate.* 26 rooms. Old New England inn on 146 acres. Motel or inn rooms. pool, pets, TV.

Troy

Inn at East Hill Farm, Mountain Rd., 03465 (242–6495). *Moderate.* 50 rooms. Farm setting for modest resort that includes hefty family-style meals, beach with swimming, hiking, water skiing, horseback riding, kids' programs. In winter, sleigh rides and 300 acres of cross-country skiing.

INNS, GUEST HOUSES, BED AND BREAKFASTS. The Monadnock Region offers a particularly rich array of historic, intimate settings where you can get the real flavor of this area named for Mt. Monadnock, which means "one that stands alone." The following inns fall into the *moderate* price category. For bed and breakfast listings, contact Monadnock Bed and Breakfast Association, Box 236, Jaffrey 03452 (585–6540).

Fitzwilliam

Amos A. Parker House, Rte. 119 west, 03447 (585–6540). Elegant Federal home in Historic District. Private baths/shared bath, one spacious suite. Panoramic mountain, garden views. Full breakfast.

Francestown

The Francestown Bed and Breakfast, Main St., Box 236, 03043 (547–6635). In the heart of a picturesque rural village. Nearby skiing, golf, scenic roads, antique shops. Fireside breakfasts in the historic 1814 Timothy Gay Store. Weekends only.

Hancock

John Hancock Inn, Main St., 03449 (525–3318). Closing out 2nd century of hospitality (since 1789); the state's oldest operating inn. Fine dining by candlelight; lounge, 10 rooms.

Jaffrey

Monadnock Inn, Rte. 124, 03452 (532–7001). 14 rooms in this 1860 Victorian Inn in the Jaffrey Center Historic District in the shadows of Mt. Monadnock. Dining rooms, sitting room, tavern, and screened porch for summer dining.

Keene

Carriage Barn Guest House, 358 Main St., 03431 (357–3812). Four quiet charming rooms, each with bath, in remodeled barn. Beautiful country setting in the heart of downtown Keene. Homemade Continental breakfast.

Marlborough

Thatcher Hill Inn, Thatcher Hill Rd., 03455 (876–3361). Revitalized 1790s farmhouse. Tastefully furnished, spacious rooms, all baths private. Wheelchair access. Splendid Monadnock views.

Temple

Birchwood Inn, Rte. 45, 03084 (878–3285). Original New England inn. Seven cozy guest rooms; listed in *National Register of Historic Places.*

RESTAURANTS. The Monadnock area offers fine dining. While there are fewer restaurants than in some other areas of the state, variety and quality are easily found. Per-person price ranges excluding beverage, tax, and tip are *Expensive,* $25 and up; *Moderate:* $10–$25; *Inexpensive,* $10 and under.

Brookline

Riverside, Rte. 13 (673–4698). *Moderate.* Fresh fish and seafood are the specialties.

Francestown

Maitre Jacq, Mountain Rd. and Rte. 47 (588–6655). *Moderate–Expensive.* Seafood stands out on a large seasonal menu. The chef, from Brittany, bakes his own bread. Closed Sun.

Hancock

John Hancock Inn, Main St. (525–3318). *Moderate–Expensive.* Wide variety of fish and meat entrees. Prime ribs are locals' choice.

Keene

Christmas Inn, Rte. 12, south of city (357–1064). *Moderate.* Large menu features prime rib; one of the best values.
Henry David's, 81 Main St. (352–0608). *Moderate.* Taking Thoreau's name, this restaurant has a greenhouse design and skylights. Fine soups.

Marlborough

Marlborough Meeting House, Rte. 101 *Moderate.* Fine seafood in a streamside setting. Fantastic breads and soups. Open Tues.–Sat.

Peterborough

Salzburg Inn, Steel Rd. (924–3808). *Moderate.* Traditional New England and Austrian cuisine. Schnitzel is noteworthy.

TOURIST INFORMATION. For information on the Monadnock Region, write or call the Greater Keene Chamber of Commerce, 8 Central Sq., Keene 03431 (352–1303). For general state information, contact the New Hampshire Office of Vacation Travel, Box 856, Concord 03301 (271–2666).

TOURS. You're on your own in touring this region, but there are plenty of self-guided tours. Walk the grounds of the Cathedral of the Pines, off Rte. 119 in Rindge, or walk through 16 acres of wild rhododendron that bloom in mid-July at Rhododendron State Park on Rte. 119 in Fitzwilliam. You can take guided tours of the Peterborough Historical Society Museum of Americana, 19 Grove St., Peterborough, 03458 (924–3235). Silver Ranch, Inc., Rte. 124, Jaffrey 03452 (532–8870), offers scenic area airplane rides.

SEASONAL EVENTS. June: Strawberry Festival, Fitzwilliam (early June); Annual Rotary Fourth Celebration, Alumni Field, Keene (July 4); Giant Rhododendron Walk, Rhododendron State Park, Fitzwilliam (early July); Annual Oak Park Festival, with parade and flea market, Greenfield (early July); Cheshire Fair, N. Swanzey (late July, early Aug.).
August: Old Home Day, Town Square, Hancock (mid-Aug.); Annual Monadnock Antique Show & Sale, Peterborough (late Aug.).
October: Octoberfest, with games food and music, Crotched Mountain Ski Area, Francestown (early Oct.).

PARKS. A number of state parks are located in the Monadnock Region. For detailed information on state parks, write or call the New Hampshire Division of Parks and Recreation, Box 856D, Concord 03301 (271–3254).
Monadnock State Park, off State Rte. 124, Jaffrey 03452 (532–8862). Here is Mt. Monadnock, the centerpiece of the region and a hiker's and climber's mecca. A 30-mi. network of well-maintained trails to the 3,165-ft. summit. Picnic grounds. Visitors' center.
Greenfield State Park, off Rte. 136, Greenfield 03047 (547–3497). 351 acres on Otter Lake. Swimming, large picnic grounds, nature trails. Recreation area open May 14–Columbus Day.
Rhododendron State Park, Rte. 119, Fitzwilliam 03447 (532–8862). More than 16 acres of wild rhododendron which burst into blossom around mid-July. One of the largest tracts of the hardy shrubs north of the Allegheny Mountains. Walking path around the entire glen. Picnic grounds in shaded pine groves.
Miller State Park, Rte. 101, Peterborough 03458. Scenic auto road to summit of Pack Monadnock Mountain, elevation 2,280 ft. Picnic sites, walking trails around the summit.
Bear Den Geological Park, Gilsum 03448. A thriving mining town in the 19th century. More than 50 abandoned mines. 1½ miles from the center of town are mountainside "potholes" said once to have been dens for a large number of bears.
Pisgah State Park, off Rtes. 63 or 119, Chesterfield, Hinsdale, and Winchester. A 13,000-acre wilderness area, with parking area, hiking, hunting, fishing, and, in winter, ski touring and snowmobiling.

WILDLIFE PRESERVES. Drummer Hill Preserve, off Elm St., Keene. A series of unmarked logging roads that wind through 140 acres of public and private conservation land. Good pond in area.

Horatio Colony Trust, off Daniels Hill Rd., Keene. A bird and animal preserve of about 450 acres of unspoiled woods.

Depierrefeu–Willard Pond Sanctuary, off Rte. 123, Antrim (524–4428 or 9909). More than 800 acres. Bobcat, beaver, otter, and fisher country; home to nesting loons. Nature programs by appointment. Open all year.

FALL FOLIAGE. Strike out on any route through these small towns to get a taste of New England in the fall. Some recommended foliage routes: From Peterborough, Rte. 101 west to Rte. 137, then south to Jaffrey. Then go west on Rte. 124 for 12 mi. of scenic splendor to Marlborough. Next head east on Rte. 101, skirting Dublin Lake. Or start at Keene on the old Walpole Road about 12 mi. to Walpole. Take Rte. 12 to Rte. 63, bear right for about 1½ mi. until you reach River Rd. Take this road about 7 mi., meandering along the Connecticut River.

SUMMER SPORTS. Boating: You can boat on many of the lakes in the region. State park boat rentals are available at Greenfield State Park, off State Rte. 136, Greenfield 03047 (547–3497). Many campgrounds in the region also offer boat rentals. If you bring your own boat, you must have it registered with the State Department of Safety, Division of Motor Vehicles.

Horseback riding: The Silver Ranch, Rte. 124, Jaffrey 03452 (532–7363 or 7354, 7621, 8870): Horseback riding lessons and carriage drives, English style riding, $15, Honey Lane Stables, RFD 2, Box 127, Peterborough 03458 (563–8078), located in Dublin: miles of trails, riding lessons.

Hiking: This is picturesque hiking country, with choices everywhere. In the parks already mentioned, there are hiking and walking trails.

The Wapack Trail is a 21-mi. ridge-line trail that stretches from Mt. Watatic in Massachusetts to North Pack Monadnock in Greenfield. The trail, offering spectacular views, is marked by yellow paint marks on trees and is easily followed.

Metacomet Trail: Designed for backpackers, it's good for day hikers since it crosses many roads. Trail marked with white rectangles, usually on the right side.

Crotched Mountain: Three trails to the summit of this 2,055-ft. mountain. One trail starts 3 mi. north of Greenfield on Rte. 31. One starts at Crotched Mountain Rehabilitation Center buildings. Francestown Trail starts at base area of Crotched Mountain ski area.

Fox State Forest, Center Rd. in Hillsboro, offers more than 20 mi. of trails for the day hiker and over 1,432 acres of woodland.

Bicycling: With Keene as the center, more than a half-dozen spokes in all directions offer scenic bicycling. Rte. 9 northeast of Keene offers good bicycling with low-to-moderate traffic. A picturesque route takes you along the Ashuelot River, which is crossed by a half dozen or so covered bridges. The Greater Keene Chamber of Commerce, 8 Central Square, Keene 03431 (352–1303) has maps of planned bicycling routes in the region.

Swimming: There are plenty of streams and lakes in which to swim in the area. There is swimming at Wadleigh State Park in Sutton, on the shores of Kezar Lake, as well as at Greenfield State Park, Greenfield, and Surrey Mountain Dam on Rte. 12A.

WINTER SPORTS. Skiing: In the Monadnock Region, Crotched Mountain ski area in Francestown (588–6345) has a 1,000-ft. vertical drop and 28 trails.

Cross-country skiing: There are a number of ski touring centers in the region, including B.U. Sargent Camp, Peterborough (525–3311), 25 trails, 40 km; Hollis Hof Ski Touring, Hollis (465–2633), eight trails, 15 km; Temple Mountain Touring, Peterborough (924–6949), 20 trails; Tory Pines Resort, Francestown (588–2000), 55 km of trails; Windblown Ski Touring, New Ipswich (878–2869), 15 trails of 30 km. There's also ski touring and snowmobiling at Greenfield State Park, Greenfield, and at Pisgah State Park, the 13,000-acre wilderness area off rtes. 63 or 119 (Chesterfield, Hinsdale, Winchester).

FISHING. More than 200 bodies of water in the region offer plenty of good fishing. The Ashuelot River has good rainbow and brown trout fishing, especially between Marlow and Gilsum, with access from Rte. 10, which winds alongside it. The lower part of the Connecticut River is good for warm weather bass fishing. A popular trout pond is Dublin Lake on Rte. 101 between Peterborough and Keene. Smallmouth bass and white perch come in big sizes in Goose Pond near West Canaan. There's good bass fishing in the 711-acre Highland Lake off Rte. 123. Fishing licenses are required: New Hampshire Fish and Game Department, 34 Bridge St., Concord 03301 (271–3211; out of state, 800–322–5018). Some stores also distribute fishing licenses.

HUNTING. There's good hunting here, as in many rural areas of New Hampshire, especially for deer in season, as well as for such birds as pheasant and grouse. License required. New Hampshire law requires all first-time hunters in the state to be certified graduates of a hunter-education course. Contact New Hampshire Fish and Game Department, 34 Bridge St., Concord 03301 (271–3421; out of state, 800–322–5018).

CAMPING. There's camping at Monadnock State Park, off State Rte. 124, Jaffrey 03452 (271–3254). 21 family tent sites. No swimming. Open Apr. 11–Nov. 11 $8 per site per night.

Greenfield State Park, 1 mi. west of Greenfield via Rte. 136 (547–3497). 252 campsites. Swimming, pond fishing, small boats, restricted speed. Flush toilets, showers. Open May 14–Columbus Day. $10 per site per night.

There are also at least 10 private campgrounds in the region, many offering swimming, boating, and boat rentals, fishing. Write New Hampshire Campground Owners' Association, Box 141, Twin Mountain 03595, for a complete list of campgrounds.

SPECTATOR SPORTS. Dog racing: Hinsdale Race Track, Rte. 119, Hinsdale 03451 (336–5382). Greyhound racing, Tues.–Sat. at 8 P.M.; Fri., Sat., Sun. at 1:30 P.M. Open all year.

Auto racing: Monadnock Speedway, Rte. 10, Winchester 03470 (239–4067). Stock car racing. Special thrill shows. Open weekends only, May 4–early Oct., Fri. 5–10:30 P.M., Sun. 2–6 P.M. Adults, $6; children under 12, $1.

HISTORIC SITES AND HOUSES. This area has its share of historic houses dating to the time when people from Massachusetts migrated north. Check ahead for admission fees.

Hillsboro

Franklin Pierce Homestead, Rte. 31 (478–3165). Boyhood home of the 14th president. Built in 1804 by Benjamin Pierce, a general in the American Revolution, twice governor of New Hampshire, and father of President Franklin Pierce. Open Memorial Day–Labor Day, Fri.–Sun. or by appointment.

Keene

Wyman Tavern, 339 Main St. (352–1895). This was site of the Dartmouth College trustees' first meeting, in 1770. 29 Minutemen gathered here to start their march to Lexington, Massachusetts, in 1775. Open June–Oct., Fri. and Sat., 1–4 P.M. Tours.

Horatio Colony House, 199 Main St. (352–0460). Built in 1806, it houses a collection of furniture, art, and knickknacks from around the world. May–Oct, Tues.–Sat., 11 A.M.–4 P.M. or by appointment.

New Ipswich

The Barrett Mansion, Main St. (227–3956). Late 18th-century architecture and furnishings in the grand manner. June–Oct., Tues., Thurs., Sat., and Sun., noon–5 P.M.

MUSEUMS. There are museums in the area to appeal to a variety of interests. Call ahead to check days, hours, and admission fees.

Charlestown

Foundation for Biblical Research and Preservation of Primitive Christianity, Main and Parris Sts. Early Bibles and historical material on Christian Science. Open Tues.–Sat., 10 A.M.–4 P.M., closed holidays.

Hillsboro

Kemp's Antique Truck Collection, off Rte. 149. Extensive antique truck collection of Ford, Mack, International, and more.

Jaffrey

Jaffrey-Gilmore Foundation Museum, Rte. 124 (532–6527). Early American tools and utensils. Open July–Labor Day, daily 1:30–5:30 P.M.

Keene

Colony House Museum, 104 West St. (357–0889). Home of Keene's first mayor, built in 1819. Early glass, pottery, dolls, toys, Staffordshire pewter, historical documents.

Archive Center of the Historical Society of Cheshire County, 246 Main St., (352–1895). Has collection of books, maps, manuscripts, photographs. Tues. and Thurs., 9 A.M.–noon and 1–4 P.M.

Peterborough

The Game Preserve, 110 Spring Rd. (924–6710). More than 800 early American card and board games, antiques, period costumes, books, collectibles. Open year-round by chance or appointment.

Peterborough Historical Society Museum of Americana, 19 Grove St. (924–3235). Historical and genealogical library. Special exhibits sometimes: ceramics, early toys, dolls, china, pewter. Open 10 A.M.–4 P.M. and by appointment. Tours, 2–4 P.M., July–Aug.

MUSIC, DANCE, AND STAGE. The **Peterborough Players,** Box 1, Peterborough 03458 (924–7585), has been turning out excellent plays since the 1930s. The theater group performs in a converted barn on the Sterns Farm on Middle Hancock Rd. in Peterborough. In Swanzey, native Denman Thompson's classic play about local characters has been performed for 46 years. The play is performed in the **Potash Bowl,** a natural amphitheater in Swanzey Center, under the full moon. For music lovers, a series of free concerts—orchestral, chamber, and opera—are performed in July and Aug. by **Monadnock Music,** an orchestra of fine quality. Performances are held throughout the region. For a schedule, write Box 255, Peterborough 03458 (924–7610). The **Apple Hill Chamber Players,** a group with national recognition, performs in the Louise Skonk Kelly barn in Nelson during the summer (847–3371). The **New Hampshire Symphony Orchestra** performs in Keene regularly.

ART GALLERIES. Keene—**Thorne-Sagendorph Art Gallery,** Appian Way, Keene State College (352–1909). Open during school sessions, Mon.–Fri., 12–5 P.M.; Sat.–Sun., 1–4 P.M. Wed. 6–8 P.M. Open Mon.–Thurs. during summer session. Paintings, drawings, sculpture, craft, photography. Free.

In Sharon—**Sharon Arts Center,** Rte. 123 (924–7256). School of arts and crafts, with courses open all year. Gallery with changing exhibits. Open Sat., 10 A.M.–5 P.M.; Sun., 1–4 P.M.

SHOPPING. For a full current list of shops and factory outlets in the Monadnock area, contact Keene Chamber of Commerce, 8 Central Sq., Keene 03431 (352–1303). **Clayfire Crockery,** Rte. 101, 7 mi. east of Keene, is a pottery studio and craft loft, with hand-thrown stoneware items. **Country Artisans Crafts Gallery,** Colony Mill Marketplace, Keene, is a gallery and sales outlet for more than 300 artisans. Pottery, weaving, stained glass, quilts, jewelry.

Factory outlets include **Cuddle Toys** by Douglas at 391 West St., Keene; **Dexter Shoe Factory Outlet,** Rte. 12, Swanzey; and **Dunham Footwear Factory Outlet,** Rte. 12, Swanzey. For a modern shopping mall in an old setting, visit the **Colony Mill Marketplace,** West St., Keene. It's a beautifully renovated 150-year-old woolen mill which houses 40 shops offering clothing, handcrafts, homemade candies, and the like. **Hidden Spring Mall,** Rte. 12 south, North Swanzey, offers **Family Boot and Shoe Outlet** and the **Hill Top Crafters Ceramic Studio.** Keene's largest shopping center is **Riverside Plaza** on Winchester St., with nationally known stores. Between Brattleboro and Keene on Rte. 9 in Spofford is **World Famous Howard's Leather Store.** Two fine gift shops in Keene are the **Eagle's Loft Ltd.,** 391 West St. and **Springhouse & Springhouse Elegant,** 222 West St. There are a number of sugar maple houses in the area, including **Bacon's Sugar House** on Dublin Rd. in Jaffrey Center and the **Old Brick Sugar**

House, Summit Rd., Keene. In Peterborough, try the **Peterborough Basket Co.** At **The Artistry,** on Rte. 123 in Alstead, a mother and daughter offer original designs in handweaving and sewing. **Donald A. Dunlap,** cabinetmaker, produces custom furniture from his house on Goodell Rd. in Antrim.

NIGHTLIFE. The Monadnock Region is not noted for its hot nightlife, but a must spot is **The Folkway,** 85 Grove St., Peterborough (924–7484), which features top folk artists and some jazz. **The Colonial Theatre,** 95 Main St., Keene (352–2033) books live acts.

THE MERRIMACK VALLEY REGION

More than half the population of New Hampshire lives in this region, yet a drive of 15 to 20 minutes from any large city will take you to tranquil forests and clear streams. From Hillsborough, take Route 9-202 through Henniker and on to Hopkinton, where you'll view impressive, well-kept colonial houses, and into Concord, the state capital. The city was founded as a trading post in 1659. A royal land grant was made in 1725, when it was called Plantation of Penacock. In 1733 it became Rumford, then in 1765 it was named Concord by Governor Wentworth. Concord was made the state capital in 1808. The granite State House, completed in 1819, displays New Hampshire battle flags from the eighteenth century on and more than 150 portraits of major political figures. The visitor's center is just inside the front door.

Concord, the State Capital

Concord was the home of the famous Concord Coach. For a century beginning in 1827, 40 styles of commercial and pleasure vehicles and 14 styles of Concord Coaches were manufactured here and sent all over the United States. The coaches, used by Wells Fargo, helped open the American West; you can see one of them in the New Hampshire Historical Society, 30 Park Street, which was founded in 1823. The society maintains a library of 50,000 volumes and presents exhibits of New Hampshire historical memorabilia and decorative arts.

On the site of the First Church of Christ Scientist, at North State and School streets, the first Concord service of Christian Scientists was held in 1897. Mary Baker Eddy, the church founder, who was born in nearby Bow, built this Neo-Gothic and Romanesque granite church in 1901. The church features photographic memorabilia of Mrs. Eddy. Concord was also the home of Christa McAuliffe, who was to have been the first teacher in space when the Challenger exploded in 1986.

From Concord, take I–93 to the Canterbury cutoff and drive east to a sign directing you to Canterbury Center and the Shaker Settlement. Here the last of the Shaker sect still guard their heritage and make their home. Examples of Shaker handicrafts and inventions, including fine Shaker chairs, are displayed at the museum, open mid-May through mid-October. The first of the buildings in the settlement was built in 1722.

You may want to see the town in which Grace Metalious wrote *Peyton Place,* a risqué novel of the 1950s about private lives in a New England town. Take the Canterbury Road to Route 106, turn north to Route 140, then east. If you saw the movie *Peyton Place,* you won't recognize the town of Gilmanton Ironworks. Natives may be reluctant to point you in the direction of Grace Metalious's house. Now take Route 129 south to Route 107 and turn southeast on 107 at Route 28, where you'll turn south. At this juncture is the town of Pittsfield, set in a valley and worth the view.

Continue on Route 28 to the Epsom Circle, where you may want to stop at Billy's restaurant for a huge breakfast or a hearty steak-and-potato meal. Billy's is filled with native New Hampshirites and often with legislators, many of whom stop here on their way to Concord from their hometowns across the state.

Unvarnished New Hampshire

The traveler who wants to discover the rural New Hampshire of the past should drive a couple of miles east on Route 4 from Epsom Circle and look to the left for a faded old colonial house. This was the Knowles Store, identified by a well-worn sign, where the Knowles brothers tended the dusty shelves and the wood stove around which visitors sat and chatted in winter. Here you might have bought a few groceries, maybe some fishhooks from faded boxes, or penny candy. Drive back to Epsom Circle and around it to Route 28 south and on to Manchester, the state's largest city with about 100,000 population.

The cultural gem of the city is the Currier Gallery of Art, 192 Orange Street, one of the finest small museums in America. There are plenty of paintings by the masters as well as an outstanding collection of New England furniture, sculpture, silver, and glassware. The Manchester Historic Association, 129 Amherst Street, has displays of early documents, Indian relics, period dress, and old tools. Be sure to drive by the Amoskeag Millyard, once the largest textile manufacturer in the world, a conglomeration of brick mill buildings stretching along the Merrimack River. Many of the buildings have been converted for high-tech and office use.

From Manchester, take Route 101 east to Route 43 and turn left into Candia, where Sam Walter Foss began a well-known poem, "Let me live in my house by the side of the road." Route 43 merges with Route 107 and takes you to Deerfield, where John Simpson, who fired the first shot at the battle of Bunker Hill, lived. Simpson went back to farming after the war and never applied for a pension. "My country is too poor to pay for pensions," he said. This is backwoods country, 30 minutes from Manchester, where roads lead to old colonial houses and farms tucked away in hidden places.

Horace Greeley's Birthplace

Return to Route 101 and head west, circling Manchester, and continue on 101 to Amherst, birthplace of Horace Greeley, founder of the *New York Tribune*. George W. Kendall, who founded the *New Orleans Picayune,* was also born here. President Pierce married Jane Appleton here in 1834. From Amherst, continue south to 101A to Nashua, known as the Gateway City. An industrial city, Nashua was originally a trading post to which Indians brought fur pelts from the north. Take Route 102 from Nashua to Derry, where you will find the Robert Frost House. Frost lived here several years and farmed (unsuccessfully) and wrote poetry (successfully). This is also the home of America's first astronaut, Alan Shepard, Jr. From Derry, take State 28 to the intersection of State 111, where you turn east toward Salem to Mystery Hill. Mystery Hill bills itself as America's Stonehenge because of the strange stone structures bearing similarities to early stonework found in Western Europe. How they came to be is the mystery.

From here State 111 will take you southwest to Benson's Wild Animal Farm, where you can see trained bears and lions perform.

PRACTICAL INFORMATION FOR
THE MERRIMACK VALLEY REGION

Note: The area code for all New Hampshire is 603

HOW TO GET THERE AND AROUND. Your best bet is to drive, for there's little between-town public transportation. Other means of arriving in the area include the following.

By plane: Manchester Airport has daily flight service with three scheduled airlines: United Airlines (800–241–6522); USAir (800–428–4322); Eastern Express, (800–327–8376). Auto rentals by Avis, Hertz, National, and Budget are available at the airport. Taxi service from the airport to downtown is about $9.

By bus: Concord Trailways has daily service from Logan Airport and Boston to Manchester and Concord. (Call 800–258–3722; inside New Hampshire, 800–852–3317.) Some trips from New York City to Manchester via Peter Pan Bus Lines (call Trailways).

Concord Trailways has daily bus service between Manchester and Concord. In Manchester, the Manchester Transit Authority (623–8801) has regular service on bus lines all over the city. The best bet for covering the region, though, is by car. There are plenty of auto rentals offered in the Manchester-Concord area.

By car: From Massachusetts, take I–93 into Manchester or I–95 to Rte. 101 at Hampton and go west to Manchester. From Maine, take I–95 south to Portsmouth, then Rte. 101 west to Manchester. From Vermont, take I–89 south to Concord. From Connecticut, take I–95 to Springfield, Massachusetts, then U.S. 202 to Keene, and Rte. 101 east to Manchester. From Rhode Island, take I–95 to Boston, then I–93 to Manchester.

HOTELS AND MOTELS. The Merrimack Valley Region is rich in lodging accommodations, with offerings to suit a variety of desires. Whether it's a stunningly elegant mix of old with new in a restored colonial building with Italian marble baths, Scottish flavor, or basic simplicity, you will find it all in the Merrimack Valley Region. Prices, based on double occupancy, are *Deluxe,* $90 and up; *Expensive,* $70–$90; *Moderate,* $50–$70; *Inexpensive,* $50 and under.

Bedford

Bedford Village Inn, 2 Old Bedford Rd., 03102 (472–2001). *Deluxe.* 12 suites, 2 apartments. Elegant authenticity. Italian marble baths, collector's oriental rugs, Kohler whirlpools. Cable TV.

Sheraton Tara Wayfarer Inn, jct. Rtes. 3 and 101, 03102 (622–3766). *Expensive–Deluxe.* Excellent dining room, lively bar. Landscaped grounds, including small covered bridge. 196 rooms. Indoor and outdoor pools, sauna, and a waterfall. Pets. Color cable TV.

Boscawen

Daniel Webster Motor Lodge, Rtes. 3 and 4, 03303 (796–2136). *Moderate.* Daniel Webster Homestead. Peaceful setting. Motel and eight efficiencies. Coffeemaker in each room. Pool. Pets. Color cable TV.

Concord

Ramada Inn, 172 N. Main St., 03301 (224–9534 or 800–2–RAMADA). *Expensive.* 95 rooms. Excellent dining facilities, live entertainment in lounge; pool, sauna, and guest box office video rental.

Brick Tower Motor Inn, 414 S. Main St., 03301 (224–9565). *Moderate.* 51 rooms, outdoor pool.

Concord Coach Motor Inn, 406 S. Main St. 03301 (224–2511). *Moderate.* Kids' area, heated pool, color TV.

Henniker

Henniker Motel, at Pat's Peak, off Rte. 114, 03242 (428–3536). *Moderate.* Heated indoor pool, whirlpool. Color cable TV.

Manchester

Center of New Hampshire–Holiday Inn, 700 Elm St., 03102 (625–1000). *Expensive.* 251 rooms. Two restaurants, two lounges. Health club, sauna, pool, Jacuzzi.

Budget Traveler Motor Lodge, 75 W. Hancock St. (624–0111). *Inexpensive.* Color TV, in-room movies.

The Inn at Highlander Village, Brown Ave., 03103 (625–6426). *Expensive.* 70 rooms, pool, tennis, cross-country skiing.

Koala Inn, 55 John E. Devine Dr., 03103 (668–6610). *Moderate.* 125 rooms. Swimming pool. Pets allowed.

Merrimack

Hilton of Merrimack, Exit 11 off Rte. 3 (Everett Tpk.), 03054 (424–6181). *Expensive.* 200 rooms, convention facilities; indoor pool, sauna, Jacuzzi. Restaurant, piano bar. Tranquil, wooded site.

Nashua

Best Western Hallmark Motor Inn, 220 Daniel Webster Hwy., 03060 (888–1200). *Moderate.* 81 rooms. Valet service, airport transportation.

Salem

Fireside Inn Motel, Rte. 28, 03079 (893–3584). *Moderate.* Cable TV, outdoor pool. Across from Rockingham Race Track.

INNS, GUEST HOUSES, BED AND BREAKFASTS. A limited number of inns and bed and breakfast facilities are available in the Merrimack Valley Region. The following are *moderate–expensive.*

Chichester

The Hitching Post, U.S. 4 and 202, Dover Rd., 03263 (798–4951). 1787 cozy colonial with a touch of Scandinavian charm. Four rooms with shared baths. Easy driving distance to ocean, lakes, and mountains.

Henniker

Colby Hill Inn, W. Main St., 03242 (428–3281). Comfortable old-fashioned inn (1800). Fine dining Tues.–Sun. Bar, pool, TV.

Merrimack

Appleton Inn, Everett Tpke., 03054 (424–7500). Early colonial furnishings. Complimentary Continental breakfast.

RESTAURANTS. Restaurants of the Merrimack Valley Region offer a variety of ethnic foods, atmosphere, and budgetary needs. Manchester, the state's largest city, offers the most abundant variety, but fine restaurants are scattered throughout the region. Per-person price ranges excluding beverage, tax, and tip: *Expensive,* $25 and up; *Moderate,* $10–$25; *Inexpensive,* $10 and under.

Bedford

Four Seasons Restaurant, jct. Rtes. 3 and 101 (622–3766). *Expensive.* At the Sheraton-Wayfarer. Relaxing intimate setting. Excellent lobster, steak. Outdoor dining in season.

Drygala Haus, Rte. 3 (623–3611). *Moderate.* All-smorgasbord dining all the time. Live entertainment Fri. and Sat. Sun. brunch. Closed Tues.

Concord

Millstone Restaurant II, 1 Eagle Sq. (across from State House) (228–1982). *Moderate–Expensive.* Classic dining in elegant surroundings. Entrees include veal, quail, seafood. Superb appetizers.

Thursdays Restaurant, 6–8 Pleasant St. (224–2626). *Moderate.* Homemade crepes, quiches, and desserts.

Manchester

The Vault, 874 Elm St. (next to City Hall) (627–2900). *Moderate–Expensive.* Frequented by presidential primary politicos. Fine fare. Barbecued lamb from an open flame. Steaks, seafood. Near Eastern and Italian foods.

Hennessey House, Exit 1 off I–293, left 500 yards (623–2324). *Moderate–Expensive.* Excellent French country-style dining.

The Millyard, 333 Turner St. (668–5584). *Moderate.* Good steak, prime ribs, seafood, surf 'n' turf. Recycled factory building. Nicely done.

The Hunan Restaurant, 1017 Second St. (622–3419). *Inexpensive–Moderate.* Superb Chinese food, with Hunan and Szechuan specialties.

Merrimack

Country Gourmet at Riddle's Tavern, Rte. 3 (424–2755). *Moderate–Expensive.* International menu with French cuisine as well as dishes from the Orient and Mediterranean.

Levi Lowell's, Daniel Webster Hwy. (429–0885). *Moderate–Expensive.* International cuisine and gracious dining.

Nashua

River Club Restaurant, Nashua Dr. (882–4433). *Moderate-Expensive.*
Housed in 1919 hydroelectric plant overlooking a waterfall on Nashua
River. Seafood and prime ribs are specialties. Children's menu.

New Boston

Molly Stark Tavern, Rte. 13S (487–2733). *Moderate.* Restored colonial-
period building named after wife of New Hampshire's famous Revolutionary War general, John Stark. Hospitality and fine dining.

TOURIST INFORMATION. For information about the Merrimack
Valley Region, you must contact individual city Chambers of Commerce.
Write or call the Concord Chamber of Commerce, 244 N. Main St., Concord 03301 (224–2508); the Greater Manchester Chamber of Commerce,
889 Elm St., Manchester 03101 (625–5753); the Nashua Chamber of Commerce, 4 Manchester Dr., Nashua 03060 (891–2471). For other information on the region and general information on the state, write or call the
New Hampshire Office of Vacation Travel, Box 856, Concord 03301
(271–2666).

TOURS. In Concord, the state capital of New Hampshire, you can walk
what is called the Coach and Eagle Trail, a self-guided tour. You can get
a pamphlet with description and a map from the Greater Concord Chamber of Commerce at Carrigain Commons at 244 N. Main St. (224–2508).
The tour includes the State House and various historical houses in the
area. Guided group tours are given at the State House (go to the Visitor's
Center, located in the main lobby). At Shaker Village in Canterbury
(783–9511). Tours are conducted hourly, mid-May–mid-Oct., adults, $6;
children 6–12, $2.50. In Merrimack (exit 8 from the Everett Tpke.), An-
heuser-Busch, Inc. offers tours of the brewery free of charge. You can sample the company's products in the Hospitality Room. Tours conducted
Memorial Day–Oct. 31, Mon.–Sun., 9:30 A.M.-3:30 P.M.; Nov. 1–Memorial
Day, Wed.–Sun., 9:30 A.M.–3:30 P.M.

SEASONAL EVENTS. May: Annual New Hampshire Sheep and Wool
Festival, Hillsborough County 4-H Youth Center, Rte. 13, New Boston
(early May); Shaker Village Herb Fair, Canterbury (mid-May); Shaker
Village by Candlelight, Canterbury, Fri. (mid-May–mid-Oct.).
June: Annual Coach and Carriage Festival, New Hampshire Technical
Institute, Concord (early June); annual Concord Aviation Day, with aero-
batics shows (late June).
July: July 4th Fireworks, Manchester's Arms Park on the Merrimack
River (usually held July 3); Annual Registered ATA Trap Shoots, Fish
and Game Club, Pelham (mid-July); Annual Antique Fire Truck Meet
and Muster, Memorial Park, Pembroke (mid-July); Auburn Olde Home
Days, parade, woodsmen contest, fireworks, Auburn (late July); Canter-
bury Fair, Annual Canterbury Fair, Canterbury Center (late July).
August: Annual Official New Hampshire Antique Dealers Show, Center
of New Hampshire Holiday Inn, Manchester (early Aug.); Londonderry
Old Home Days, Londonderry Town Common (mid-Aug.): Pembroke
Old Home Day, Pembroke (late Aug.); Hopkinton Fair, Contoocook, real
old-fashioned country fair (late-Aug., early Sept.).

September: Annual Scira Sailboat Races, Island Pond, Derry (early–mid-Sept.); Annual Antique Show and Sale, First Congregational Church Parrish House, Union St., Milford (early Sept.); Riverfest, annual celebration at Arms Park on the river, Manchester (early Sept.); Hillsboro County Agricultural Fair, New Boston (early Sept.); Deerfield Fair, one of oldest and largest in the state, Deerfield (late Sept.).

October: Annual Oktoberfest Arts and Crafts Festival, Capital Shopping Center, Storrs St., Concord (early Oct.); Annual Tri-State Collector's Exhibition (coins, stamps, postcards, other collectibles), Community Center, 39 Green St., Concord (late Oct.).

November: Merrimack County artisan Fall Craft Fair, Concord (early Nov.).

PARKS. Three major state parks are located in this region. Despite the build-up in population in the region, there also are quite a number of private campgrounds from which to choose.

Bear Brook State Park, Rte. 28, Allentown (485–9874). This 9,600-acre park is heavily forested, but there is a superb recreational area with supervised beach, picnic areas (with grills for cooking), rental boats. Open May 14–Columbus Day. Adults, $3; children over 6, $1.

Clough State Park, off Rte. 114, Weare. Swimming in a 150-acre river pool with a 900-ft. beach. Bathhouse and boat rentals, large picnic areas.

Pawtuckaway State Park, Nottingham, 3½ miles north of jct. of Rtes. 101 and 156 in Raymond (895–3031). Large forested park, with 700-ft. swimming beach, bathhouse. Large family picnic area. Hiking, ski touring, snowmobiling in winter. Open May 14–Columbus Day.

BEACHES. Kingston State Park, off Rte. 125, Kingston. The southernmost freshwater park, 44 acres on the northeast shore of Great Pond. Swimming, picnicking.

Silver Lake State Park, Rte. 122, Hollis. Sandy 1,000-ft. beach curves along the 34-acre lake. Swimming, bathhouse, picnic grounds in a picturesque pine grove.

FALL FOLIAGE. While it's not as dramatic as up north or down in the Monadnock Region, the foliage in the small towns of the Merrimack Valley Region is nevertheless bright with color. Drive from Manchester out to Weare on Rte. 114, take Rte. 101 east to Rte. 43 into Deerfield, or head out of Concord on Rte. 4 and take a left going north on Rte. 28 to Barnstead. Or head down to New Boston by taking Rte. 114 out of Manchester, then the winding Rte. 13. Call 224–2525 or 2526 for foliage condition reports; out of state, from New England and New York and New Jersey, dial 800–258–3608 or 3609.

SUMMER SPORTS. Boating: You can rent boats at Bear Brook State Park, Rte. 28, Allentown (485–9874). or at Clough State Park, off Rte. 114, Weare. You can boat on Manchester's huge reservoir, Massabesic Lake (fishing, but no swimming). There's boating in Pawtuckaway State Park's lake. If you bring your own boat, you will need a license from the New Hampshire Motor Vehicle Department, Concord.

Swimming: Bear Brook State Park, Clough State Park, and Pawtuckaway State Park all have beaches for swimming. Don't swim in the Merrimack River in the Manchester area, but you can go farther north and swim the river. Manchester has a public pool and a public beach (call the Parks and Recreation Department, 624–6565). There also are some streams in the area where you can find a place to swim.

Horseback riding: Dawn Mar Riding Academy, Rte. 1, Concord 03301 (746–3884) offers $15-an-hour horseback riding on miles of scenic dirt roads, sleigh rides for $10 and $15 trail rides.

Golf: There are plenty of golf courses in this populated region. A sampler: Derryfield Country Club, Manchester (669–0235); Intervale Country Club, Manchester (623–9180); Duston Country Club, Hopkinton (746–4234); Hoodkroft Country Club, Derry (434–0651); Angus Lea Golf Course, Hillsboro (464–5404); Whip-Poor-Will Golf Club, Hudson (889–9706); Londonderry Country Club, Londonderry (432–9789); Pine Valley Golf Links, Pelham (635–8305); Plausawa Valley Country Club, Pembroke (224–6267).

Hiking: There's plenty of space to hike in the region, especially at Bear Brook and Pawtuckaway state parks (see "Parks," above). In most of the small towns in the region, there are little-traveled roads on which to hike.

Bicycling: Out of the urban centers, there are a number of trails outlined on the biking map published by the New Hampshire Department of Public Works and Highways. There are routes through Goffstown, Bedford, Hooksett, Candia, Deerfield, leaving the outskirts of Manchester; routes such as State Rte. 13 from Concord to Weare or Rte. 106 to 202 into Chichester; along Rte. 102, Rte. 111, and Rte. 130 out of Nashua, all described as having low-to-moderate traffic, with fair pedaling conditions. Out in the smaller towns, 5 mi. or so out of the cities, it's scenic and strictly rural, especially west of Manchester and around Concord. For detailed information, write to the Granite State Wheelmen, Inc., 16 Clinton St., Salem 03079.

WINTER SPORTS. The Merrimack Valley Region's biggest **ski** slope is Pat's Peak (800–258–3218) with 14 trails in Henniker, west of Concord. Manchester is one of the few cities anywhere with its own ski slope: McIntyre Ski Area on Smith Rd. in the city (622–6571), primarily a beginner's slope but with night as well as day skiing to give advanced skiers a workout. At the edge of the region north, there's Highlands Mountain, Exit 19, I–93 in Northfield (286–4334), with 10 trails.

Cross-country skiing: Many people drive to area farms and ask permission of landowners to ski through the woods. There are some touring centers: Plausawa Valley Touring Center, Pembroke 03275 (224–6267), 5 trails for a total of 15 km; Quaker Hollow Farm Ski Touring, Henniker 03242 (428–7639), 10 trails totaling 12 km; and Valley View Country Club Ski Touring, Dunbarton 03045 (774–5031), 11 trails totaling 22 km; Charming Fare Ski Touring Center, Candia (483–2307) has lovely ski touring fields just 15 min. from Manchester.

Sleigh rides: At Charming Fare in Candia (483–2307), you can get horse-drawn sleigh rides through snowy fields and woods. Dawn Mark Riding Academy, Hopkinton (746–3884), also gives ski rides, as does the James Anthony Farm on Dudley Brook Road, Weare (529–1123). The Anthony Farm is 175 years old in a beautiful country setting.

FISHING. The Merrimack River, above Manchester at the dam in Hooksett Village, is a much-fished river, excellent for bass. Manchester's Massabesic Lake is also a good bass-fishing lake, but you will need your own boat. At Bear Brook State Park in Allentown, there is a stocked trout pond and trout fishing on the river. There's also good fishing at Pawtuckaway State Park in Nottingham, a large lake with plenty of bass. Or drive out to almost any of the small towns in the region and find a nice stream that likely will have some stocked trout. You need a fishing license, which many stores in the region sell.

HUNTING. Although it's populated, there still is hunting in this region, around the small towns where deer thrive in the woods. But be careful, especially in deer season, because many hunters are out. You must have a hunting license (and a certificate from a hunting education course is required); contact New Hampshire Fish and Game Department, 34 Bridge St., Concord 03301 (271–3421; out of state, toll-free 800–322–5018).

CAMPING. State park campgrounds include Bear Brook State Park, Rte. 28, Allentown (485–9874). 81 tent sites, flush toilets, $10 per site per night, open May 14–Columbus Day; Pawtuckaway State Park, Nottingham (895–3031), 170 tent sites, flush toilets, showers, $10 per night, open May 14–Columbus Day. A number of private campgrounds are located in the region. Contact the New Hampshire Campground Owners' Association, Twin Mountain 03595, for a complete list of campgrounds and amenities.

SPECTATOR SPORTS. Horse racing: Rockingham Park, Rte. 28 and I-93, Salem 03079 (898–2311), offers thoroughbred racing Apr. 18–Nov. 30. Big-purse sweepstakes, day and evening sessions. Admission: grandstand, $2.50; under 12 free with adult. Wagering.
Auto races: Sugar Hill Speedway, S. Sugarhill Rd. just off Rte. 77, Weare 03281 (529–2479). Open May 11–Oct. 12, 6–11 P.M. weekends—most races Sat. nights. Adults, $5 and up, depending upon event; under 13 free. Bryar Motorsport Park, Rte. 106, Loudon 03301 (783–4744). Open Apr. 12–Oct. 19. Sports car, motorcycle, karting. Most activities on weekends. Sat. night stock cars, May–Aug. Admission varies with event.

HISTORIC SITES AND HOUSES. In this heavily populated area, industry came early, and there are plenty of historic sites.

Canterbury

Shaker Village, off Rte. 106 (783–9511). Walking tours of five historic Shaker buildings by guides who interpret 200 years of Canterbury Shaker history. Open May 15–Oct. 18, daily Tues.–Sat., 10 A.M.–4 P.M.

Concord

The State House, 107 N. Main St. (271–2154). Completed in 1819 of granite quarried in the Concord area. Visitor's Center open all year, Mon.–Fri., 8 A.M.–4:30 P.M.
The Pierce Manse, 14 Penacook St., (224–9620). Only home owned by Franklin Pierce, 14th U.S. president, in Concord. Pierce memorabilia. Open June 2–Aug. 29, Mon.–Fri., 11–3 P.M.
First Church of Christ Scientist, North State St. (224–0818).

Derry

Robert Frost Farm, Rte. 28 (432–3091). Home of the poet Robert Frost from 1901 to 1909. Simple, two-story, white clapboard house built in 1880s. Period furnishings, Frost exhibits. Open May 24–Sept. 1, Wed.–Sun., 10 A.M.–6 P.M.

Manchester

Amoskeag Millyard, which stretches along the Merrimack River in the city, once housed the largest textile mills in the country. Now most house other industries and offices, although the textile industry is still present.
Gen. John Stark House, 2000 Elm St. Built in 1736. The hero of the Battle of Bennington grew up in this house, which was moved to this site. Period furnishings. Open mid-May–mid-Oct., Wed. and Sun. only.

Salem

America's Stonehenge (Mystery Hill), off Rte. 111 in North Salem (893–8300). Controversial site which claims to be a 4,000-year-old astronomical complex built by Celts who came here from Europe's Iberian Peninsula. Unusual rock formations. Open May 1–Oct. 31, 9:30 A.M.–5 P.M. in summer, 10 A.M.–4 P.M. off season.

MUSEUMS. Take some time to explore this region's museums, which take you back to the age of tight-fisted industrialists and beyond to the precolonial days of the Indians.

Concord

New Hampshire Historical Society Museum and Library, Park St. (225–3381). Displays of New Hampshire history, including Concord Coach. Fine and decorative arts, furniture. Open Mon.–Sat., 9 A.M.–4:30 P.M.; Wed. til 8 P.M.

Manchester

Manchester Historic Association, 120 Amherst St. (622–7531). Local history, Indian artifacts, fire-fighting equipment, period costumes, furniture, library. Open all year, daily, Tues.–Fri., 9 A.M.–4 P.M.; Sat., 10 A.M.–4 P.M.
Scouting Museum and Library, Camp Carpenter, Bodwell Rd. (627–1492). Scouting artifacts and memorabilia. Extensive library. Open daily, July and Aug., 10 A.M.–4 P.M.; Sept.–June, Sat. only, 10 A.M.–4 P.M.

Nashua

Nashua Historical Society, 5 Abbot St. (883–0015). Information regarding Nashua's origin as part of Massachusetts, evolution of mill town in 1800s, Indian artifacts. Open March–early Dec., Sat. 12–4 P.M., or by appointment.
Nashua Center for the Arts, 14 Court St., 03060 (883–1506). Cultural displays, courses in the arts, and concerts. Open year-round.

Sandown

Old Sandown Depot Railroad Museum, Rte. 121A (887–4621). Railroad memorabilia, telegraph equipment, two flanger cars, motorized handcar and velocipede. Open May 30–Oct., Sun. 2–4 P.M.

MUSIC, DANCE, AND STAGE. There is plenty of fine symphony music, opera, and drama in this area. The **Palace Theater** (668–5588;

669–8021 business office) is home to the New Hampshire Symphony Orchestra, opera performances by the New England Opera Co., and drama and musicals, as well as special entertainment events. In Milford, the **American Stage Festival, Mt.** Vernon St., Rte. 13N (673–7515), presents performances June–early Sept. In Salem, the **Town and Country Playhouse,** Geremonty St. (893–8301) is open late June–late Aug. **Notre Dame College** (669–4298) hosts band concerts in July and Aug., as does the **Nevers' 2nd Regiment Band of Concord** (225–3684), from June into Aug.

ART GALLERIES. The gem of Manchester and New Hampshire is the **Currier Gallery of Art,** recognized as one of the finest small art museums in the country. Located at 192 Orange St., Manchester, the gallery features paintings by the masters, exquisite glassware, fine furniture, and exhibits of well-known modern artists. The **Manchester Institute of Arts and Sciences,** 148 Concord St., has changing gallery exhibitions. The **Chapel Art Center** of St. Anselm College, Goffstown, has changing monthly exhibitions.

In Milford, there is **The Golden Toad Gallery,** 65 Elm St., showcasing a blend of country and contemporary styles in pottery, wood, glass, leather, and jewelry. The **River College Art Gallery,** S. Main St., Nashua, offers exhibitions during school sessions. **The New Hampshire Art Association,** 26 Hanover St., Manchester, has continuous exhibitions featuring sculpture, watercolors, oils, acrylics, etc. **The League of New Hampshire Craftsmen** gallery at 36 N. Main St., Concord, has rotating exhibits of the work of nationally known craftsmen.

SHOPPING. This highly populated region of New Hampshire is rife with shopping centers. The largest shopping center in New Hampshire is the **Pheasant Tree Lane Mall** on Daniel Webster Hwy., Nashua, with scores of shops of every description in a well-designed, aesthetic shopping mall. The **Mall of New Hampshire,** Rte. 101, Manchester, is another large mall, with many small shops as well as department stores. In Manchester, there are a number of factory outlets, such as the **Burlington Coat Factory** and **Pandora Factory Store** (this is a Manchester industry) on Canal St. Many new fine shops are located in the restored Machinists' Building on Hanover Street in Manchester. At the Millyard Mall at 88 Pine St. Ext. in Nashua, there are numerous specialty stores, including **Baskets & Blades, Linens 'n Things** and **Clothesworks.** In Concord, **The Suitcase** on N. Main St. offers fine luxury gift items. **Concord Arts & Crafts,** 36 N. Main St., Concord, offers fine handcrafted items in all price ranges. At Shaker Village in Canterbury, cabinetmaker David W. Lamb creates custom furniture in Shaker, contemporary, and traditional styles. Also in Canterbury, on Hannah Dustin Rd., is **Heritage Herbs & Baskets.**

NIGHTLIFE. In the Merrimack Valley Region, especially in the Manchester and Nashua areas, there is ample nighttime entertainment. In Manchester, a hot spot for top 40s music and dancing is **Kristopher's,** 1050 Bicentennial Dr. (644–5700). **Crystal's,** at the Center of New Hampshire-Holiday Inn, 700 Elm St. (625–1000), features a disc jockey spinning top 40s hits. For jazz and folk music, try **The Millyard,** 333 N. Turner St. (668–5584). In Bedford, **The Laurels Lounge** at the Sheraton Tara Wayfarer Inn, Rte. 3 at Bedford Interchange 622–3766), offers lively music and dancing. In Nashua, the **Bounty Lounge** at the Holiday Inn, 9 Northeastern Blvd. (888–1551), is a popular spot.

RHODE ISLAND

By
BOB MURPHY and **HELEN DALZELL**

Bob Murphy and Helen Dalzell, two Rhode Island residents, are a hus-
band-and-wife team of free-lance travel writers. The two have led coastal
tours for the Boston Center for Adult Education, the Providence Learning
Connection, and the Sierra Club's New England chapter.

Rhode Island is a bright sliver of a state divided by Narragansett Bay.
It is small; generations of travel writers have reminded their readers that
Rhode Island is the tiniest state in the Union. What matters for places,
as well as for people, however, is character, and in this department Rhode
Island is always a winner. Along Rhode Island's saltwater shores are some
of the finest beaches in the Northeast. With almost 400 miles of coastline,
Rhode Island is clearly the Ocean State. And Providence and Newport,
two of America's early seaports, are coastal cities with cultural and historic attractions that can be enjoyed in every season.

Rhode Island is particularly popular with travelers on their way to Boston, Cape Cod, or northern New England. And it's easy to understand
why. Many of Rhode Island's best-known sites can be quickly reached
from I–95 or from I–195, the interstate highway that connects Providence
with Cape Cod. For travelers using Amtrak, it's possible to stop in Providence for a few hours to sample the city's attractions before continuing
on to other destinations. The new Providence railroad depot is close to
Rhode Island's handsome state capitol building and within easy walking
distance of the Roger Williams National Memorial.

The Lively Experiment

Colonial Rhode Island was established during the 1600s as a haven for assorted idealists, freethinkers, and individualists who had fled from Puritan persecution in Massachusetts in order to find refuge among the Narragansett Indians. For over a century, wits in Massachusetts called their small neighbor Rogues Island.

On a June day in 1636, Roger Williams and a handful of followers paddled around Fox Point and up what is now the Providence River, landing on the river's east side, where they established a new settlement. Williams named the village Providence "in commemoration of God's providence." Providence soon attracted a fiery mix of refugees and rebels who somehow managed to form one community. The settlement's center is marked today by the Roger Williams National Memorial.

Anne Hutchinson arrived in Rhode Island in 1638. Hutchinson is still celebrated for having been, in the words of the historian Samuel Eliot Morison, "the first woman to play a leading role in American history." She had clashed repeatedly with Boston's Puritan authorities and was finally excommunicated and banished to the wilderness. Williams invited Hutchinson to Rhode Island, and she and her party soon settled on the island of Aquidneck, which was later divided into the Rhode Island towns of Portsmouth, Middletown, and Newport. Fearing further harassment from Massachusetts officials, Anne Hutchinson moved to the Dutch colony of New Amsterdam in 1642. But her influence survived in Rhode Island long after her departure. Many of Anne Hutchinson's early associates had become Rhode Island Quakers by the 1660s.

The combination of religious freedom, rich agricultural lands, and sheltered harbors made Rhode Island a colonial success story. As early as the 1640s, Rhode Island businessmen were shipping farm products to Boston, to New York, to the southern colonies, and to the West Indies. Newport had become one of the principal ports in North America by the 1690s. The young colony accepted Quakers and Jews, other minorities, and individuals who lacked religious commitments. In 1663, Rhode Island received a charter from England's King Charles II establishing "the Colony of Rhode Island and Providence Plantations." The 1663 charter affirmed that Rhode Island was to be "a lively experiment," a self-governing colony in which all individuals were to be free from religious persecution. At the time, the Rhode Island experiment seemed to be almost revolutionary.

The good relations between colonists and Native Americans in Rhode Island came to an end during the 1670s. In 1675, fighting broke out between the Wampanoags and the Plymouth Colony militia near the Wampanoag village at Mount Hope, in what is now the town of Bristol. For months the fighting swirled around and through Rhode Island, pulling other colonies and tribes into the vicious struggle that became known as King Philip's War. When the war ended in 1676, many of Rhode Island's settlements had been burned, and the powerful Narragansett tribe had been devastated.

Rhode Island rose to commercial prominence during the 1700s. This was the period when Newport rivaled Boston, New York, and Philadelphia as a major trade and cultural center. It was the period when Rhode Island merchants moved from simple tax evasion to open acts of rebellion and to advocating complete political separation from Great Britain. Often Rhode Island seemed to be ahead of the other American colonies in pressing toward revolution and the Declaration of Independence.

For a suggestion of what made Rhode Island prosper during the eighteenth century, look at the ornaments in colonial homes in Newport. The West Indian pineapple was the symbol of Rhode Island's prosperity and hospitality. And, for much of the eighteenth century, the West Indian trade was booming. Specializing in tropical crops, the West Indian planters needed corn, beef, mutton, fish, and horses, items that Rhode Islanders produced or could easily obtain. In exchange, Rhode Island merchants took pineapples and molasses—lots of molasses—for distilling into Rhode Island rum.

The West Indian trade gradually evolved into the infamous "triangle trade." Rhode Island traders sent rum to Africa, traded the drink for slaves, then carried the unfortunate captives across the Atlantic to the West Indies, where slaves could be traded for molasses and sugar. The molasses was sent to Rhode Island "rummeries," more rum was produced, and the sad trade continued. By the 1760s, Newport was the major slave-trading port in the British empire. Most slaves were sold in the West Indies or in the South, but a few were imported into colonial Rhode Island, and the prosperous farmers of the southwestern corner of the colony—South County—developed a small plantation economy of their own.

Rebels and Patriots

For years Rhode Island had been notorious as a smugglers' haven. After 1763, when British naval vessels were sent to police Narragansett Bay, Rhode Islanders became increasingly defiant. In 1764, two members of the governor's council ordered the colony's gunner on Newport's Goat Island to open fire on the patrol ship *St. John.* The gunner fired, the *St. John* escaped, and the council members promptly sent a note to Goat Island, criticizing the gunner for failing to sink his target! Other skirmishes with the Royal Navy soon followed. In 1772, when His Majesty's ship *Gaspee* ran aground off Warwick, a Providence crowd descended on the vessel, removed the crew, and set the *Gaspee* on fire. When the American Revolution officially began in 1775, Rhode Island regiments fought in a long series of campaigns from the seige of Boston to the final victory at Yorktown in 1781.

The British Navy struck back at Rhode Islanders during the Revolution. Newport's excellent harbor and its strategic position between Boston and New York had long been appreciated by British admirals. In December 1776, Newport was seized by a British naval expedition and, although the Americans tried various plans in order to win the town back, Newport remained in enemy hands for almost three years.

Newport's maritime trade collapsed during the British occupation, and Newport never regained the commercial power that it had known before the war. Trade and industry shifted to Providence and to other ports. A visitor standing today in Fort Adams State Park in Newport and looking across the harbor at Newport's downtown sees a skyline that seems little changed since the night in 1781 when every house, large and small, burned candles in its windows to welcome General Washington to Newport.

The Gilded Age

The key event in Rhode Island's modern history occurred in 1790, when Samuel Slater—financed by Moses Brown, a well-to-do Providence merchant—launched America's Industrial Revolution by building in Pawtucket the nation's first successful cotton mill, powered by the Blackstone River. Slater's mills were the high-tech marvels of their time. One of Sla-

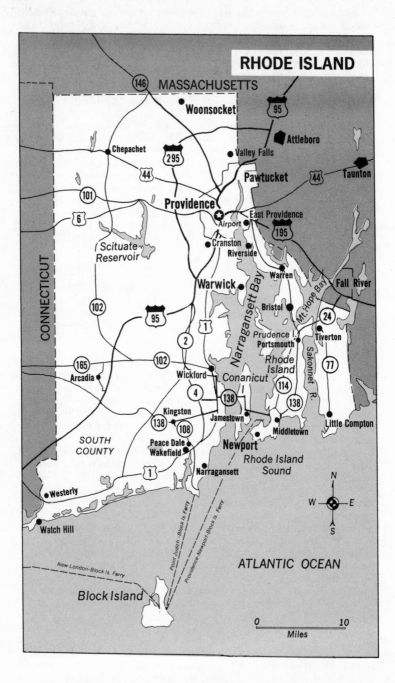

RHODE ISLAND

MASSACHUSETTS

Woonsocket

Attleboro

Chepachet

Valley Falls

Taunton

Pawtucket

Providence

Airport

East Providence

CONNECTICUT

Scituate Reservoir

Cranston

Riverside

Warren

Warwick

Bristol

Fall River

Narragansett Bay

Mt. Hope Bay

Tiverton

Prudence I.

Portsmouth

Arcadia

Wickford

Conanicut

Rhode Island

Sakonnet R.

Kingston

Jamestown

Middletown

Little Compton

SOUTH COUNTY

Peace Dale

Wakefield

Newport

Rhode Island Sound

Narragansett

N

Westerly

W   E

Watch Hill

S

ATLANTIC OCEAN

New London-Block Is. Ferry

Point Judith-Block Is. Ferry

Providence-Newport-Block Is. Ferry

Block Island

0   10

Miles

ter's creations has been preserved at the Slater Mill National Historic Site in Pawtucket, a spot worth visiting.

In the years between the Revolution and the American Civil War, Rhode Island transformed itself from a maritime to an industrial society. By 1831, Rhode Island was producing one-fifth of America's yarn and one-sixth of its cloth. As Rhode Island's textile mills expanded, thousands of immigrants arrived in the state, eager to work the looms. The immigrants came at first from England, Ireland, and English-speaking Canada, and later from Quebec, Italy, Germany, Eastern Europe, the Azores, the Cape Verde Islands, and other lands. By 1910, census figures showed that 69 percent of Rhode Island's people were either foreign born or the children of immigrants.

During the 1800s, industrial Rhode Island was an arena for hard-fought political and social battles. Rhode Island had the distinction of having been the first colony to renounce its loyalty to King George III—May 4, 1776, is still remembered as Rhode Island Independence Day—and Rhode Island also had the distinction of having been the last of the 13 original states to ratify the Constitution. In the 1840s, Rhode Island endured a civil war of sorts—the Dorr War—as landless men fought to win the right to vote. At one point in 1842 the state had two constitutions and two elected governors, each with his own band of armed supporters.

The 1850s saw Newport transformed from a sleepy seaport into a fashionable resort. Before the Civil War, Newport was popular with Southern planters eager to escape the summer heat of Georgia and the Carolinas. After the Civil War, Newport became the summer playground of New York's superrich. This was the period that Mark Twain called the Gilded Age, a time when income tax was unheard of and conspicuous consumption was very much in style. The moneyed families who came to summer in Newport—Astors, Morgans, Vanderbilts, Belmonts, and others—entertained each other in grand châteaus and villas with, as one observer said, "a measure of luxury not witnessed since the fall of Rome." America had never seen anything like it, and nothing on that scale has been seen since. Several of Newport's "summer cottages" are now open to the public. There is still wealth and style in Newport, but Newport society is now more discreet than it was in the 1890s.

Rhode Island's industrial economy began to falter in the early 1900s. Textile mills moved South, leaving behind half-abandoned mill villages. Gradually Rhode Island, like the rest of New England, has had to adjust to a new period of "deindustrialization." New businesses are now being attracted to the state. And, fortunately, as Rhode Islanders have reassessed their state's resources, many have gained a new respect for Rhode Island's natural beauty and history. The Rhode Islanders of colonial days looked to Narragansett Bay for their livelihood, and today visitors to Rhode Island still enjoy the opportunities for fishing, boating, and relaxing that the bay generously provides. The Ocean State's future, like its past, is tied to the sea.

Such cities as Newport and Providence are now experiencing the same kind of revival that can be seen elsewhere on New England's coast. In New Bedford and Newburyport in Massachusetts; in Portsmouth, New Hampshire; and in Portland, Maine, old seaports are becoming attractive commericial and cultural centers with their own distinctive little-city style. Most Rhode Islanders merely nod and accept the new trend without comment, for in Rhode Island everyone knows that small can be beautiful.

Exploring Rhode Island

NEWPORT

A tour of Rhode Island should begin with Newport, still a New England seaport. Newport is known first for its high-society splendor: Million-dollar yachts can still be seen skimming across Narragansett Bay waters, with or without the America's Cup in sight. Along Bellevue Avenue and Ocean Drive you can see the summer mansions that go with yachts and society balls. Newport is famous also as a navy town, and a visit to the Naval War College Museum will help to explain Rhode Island's historic involvement with naval strategists and fighting ships. Then there is Newport's colonial waterfront, with more restored eighteenth-century homes than in Williamsburg or Boston, first-rate restaurants, jazz and folk festivals, a lively nightlife, and special events throughout the year.

Newport first came to life in 1639. Among the people who followed Anne Hutchinson to Rhode Island were merchants who took advantage of the fine harbor at the southern tip of Aquidneck Island. The names of the Quaker traders who shaped early Newport—Coddington, Easton, and Clarke, among others—are preserved in the names of Newport's streets. The Newport that they built grew until it became one of America's major colonial cities. The Point section of Newport, extending north along the waterfront from Marsh Street to Battery Street and back as far as Farewell Street, contains fine homes from the colonial era, many of them carefully restored since 1968 by the Newport Restoration Foundation. The Washington Square area and the Historic Hill section, between Touro Street and Memorial Boulevard, also contain many attractive colonial structures. It is a pleasant and rewarding stroll from Newport's old Colony House to Trinity Church and Queen Anne Square via Touro Street and part of Bellevue Avenue.

Washington Square

Begin your tour of colonial Newport at Washington Square. Parking is available nearby. At the head of Washington Square stands the Colony House, built in 1739 at the crossroads of old Newport. This is where the Newport settlement began. Until 1900, the Colony House in Newport alternated with the Old State House in Providence as the seat of the Rhode Island state government until, finally, Rhode Islanders decided that one state capital was all that Rhode Island needed. From the central balcony of Newport's Colony House, Rhode Island received the news of George III's coronation in 1760; 16 years later, the Declaration of Independence was proclaimed from the same balcony. During the Revolution, the Colony House was used as a British barracks and later as a hospital for America's French allies. George Washington met the French commander, Count Rochambeau, at the Colony House in 1781 to plan the campaign that led to the British defeat at Yorktown. Within the Colony House, you'll find a portrait of Washington by Gilbert Stuart, one of Rhode Island's best-known colonial artists.

At the foot of Washington Square is the Brick Market, built in 1760–72 to serve as a market house and a storage place. The arches at street level, now windows, were open in colonial times so that market carts could be taken inside. Adjacent to the Brick Market building, along Thames Street (pronounced Thaymz), is an assortment of shops and moderately priced restaurants. Keep these attractions in mind for a later visit. For the moment, proceed from the Colony House, up Broadway, to the Wanton-Lyman-Hazard House, the oldest restored house in Newport and one of the few buildings in the city that survives from the late 1600s. Richard Ward owned the house in 1724, but a subsequent owner, Martin Howard, nearly lost the structure when he accepted the position of stamp master in order to enforce Great Britain's Stamp Act in 1765. After hanging Howard in effigy, angry Sons of Liberty broke into his home, where they smashed windows and tore paneling off the walls. Howard found protection on a British warship in the harbor and never returned to Newport. Quaker John Wanton bought the house in 1772. The Wanton-Lyman-Hazard House, owned by the Newport Historical Society, is open to the public during the summer.

From Broadway, follow Spring Street to Touro Street. Turn left. At 72 Touro Street is the Touro Synagogue, the oldest Jewish house of worship in North America. Like the Quakers and other religious minorities, Jewish merchants were attracted to colonial Rhode Island because of the colony's reputation for religious tolerance. Jewish families arrived in Newport from Portugal and the Netherlands during the 1650s. By the 1770s, between 25 and 30 Jewish families were living in Newport. Under the guidance of Isaac de Touro, the construction of Newport's first synagogue began in 1759. It was to this congregation that President Washington responded in 1790, assuring the members that the government of the United States "gives bigotry no sanction, to persecution no assistance." Founded by Spanish-Portugese Jews, the Touro Synagogue still follows the Sephardic Orthodox ritual. Worshippers stand in prayer before the Holy Ark, facing eastward toward Jerusalem. Guided tours of the synagogue are conducted during visiting hours.

Colonial Newport

Beyond the Touro Synagogue on Touro Street is the group of buildings that constitutes the Newport Historical Society. One of these buildings is a colonial meeting house built in 1729, the oldest Seventh Day Baptist meeting house in America. The Newport Historical Society maintains an excellent collection of early American furniture, silver, china, and paintings on display for the public. After visiting the society, continue up Touro Street, turning right on Bellevue Avenue.

At 50 Bellevue Avenue stands the Redwood Library, the oldest library building in the United States in continuous use. The Redwood Library was designed by architect Peter Harrison, who also designed the Touro Synagogue and Newport's Brick Market. Named for its benefactor Abraham Redwood, the library was built as a private library in 1748; it is a wood structure that appears to be made of stone. Inside the library are paintings by early Newport artists. The building is open to the public during library hours.

Newport's Mystery Tower

Strolling along Bellevue Avenue, visitors soon arrive at Mill Street and Touro Park. In the midst of Touro Park stands—well, there are several different stories about Touro Park's "mystery tower." Some say that the Old Stone Mill was built by the Vikings, and Henry Wadsworth Longfellow wrote an epic poem in support of this theory. Others have argued for the ancient Celts or early Portuguese mariners. Contemporary archaeologists and historians, however, have argued more often than not that the "mystery tower" is all that remains of a colonial windmill built on the site during the 1600s. Whatever it may have been in the past, the Old Stone Mill today is popular with photographers and painters. The Newport Art Museum, on Bellevue Avenue opposite Touro Park, contains the work of Newport artists.

Trinity Church

Walk down Mill Street toward the waterfront. Turn right on Spring Street in order to see Trinity Church and the Queen Anne Square area. If you stand in Queen Anne Square for a moment, you can see what Newport was like in the 1770s. Built in 1725, Trinity Church was an Anglican Church, attended by many of Newport's prosperous merchants and government officials. The Anglican philosopher George Berkeley, dean of Derry in Ireland and later bishop of Cloyne, arrived in Newport in 1729 while awaiting support for a university proposed for Bermuda. Berkeley often preached at Trinity Church, and he established a lively circle of artists and intellectuals in Newport. Although Berkeley's plans for Bermuda never materialized, he left behind a cultural legacy that inspired the formation of the Literary and Philosophical Society, which inspired the construction of the Redwood Library. Berkeley's Whitehall estate, on Berkeley Avenue in the town of Middletown, has been preserved, and visitors may tour George Berkeley's home during the summer. Berkeley's wit, his gentility, his learning, and his sharp intellect made him a popular figure during his three years in the Newport area. It's easy to imagine the sound of harpsichords and the clink of wineglasses that were heard when Berkeley and his admirers met for an evening's entertainment. Eighteenth-century Newport was a spirited place.

Walk north on Spring Street as you return to Washington Square. Turn left on Mary Street, then right on Clarke Street. At the corner of Mary and Clarke streets is the Vernon house, built in 1756. In 1780–81 this elegant home was the headquarters of Jean Baptist Donatien de Vimeur, Comte de Rochambeau, the commander of America's French allies in North America, known simply in Rhode Island history as Count Rochambeau. When French naval forces came to America's aid in 1778–79, Newport became a difficult base for the British to maintain. Newport's British garrison was quietly withdrawn in 1779. The French entered Newport in 1780 and, despite some initial wariness, the new arrivals soon won the hearts of war-weary Newporters, who had been much abused by the British. Count Rochambeau paid in gold for all supplies, and French soldiers and sailors were courteous when dealing with civilians. When the French departed for Yorktown in 1781, much of Newport was on the waterfront to bid them a fond farewell.

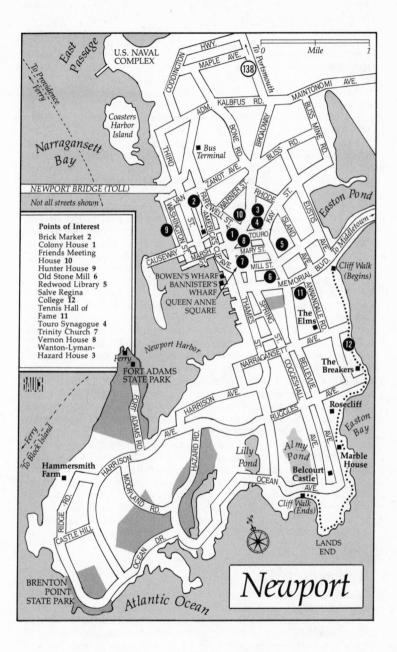

East Passage

U.S. NAVAL COMPLEX

To Providence Ferry

Coasters Harbor Island

Narragansett Bay

NEWPORT BRIDGE (TOLL)

Not all streets shown

HWY.

CODDINGTON

MAPLE AVE.

To Portsmouth

138

Mile

0   1

ADM.

KALBFUS RD.

MAINTONOMI AVE.

BROADWAY

BLISS MINE RD.

BONE RD.

BLISS RD.

Easton Pond

THIRD

VAN ZANDT AVE.

Bus Terminal

WARNER ST.

RHODE ST.

EUSTIS AVE.

To Middletown

WASHINGTON ST.

FAREWELL ST.

AMERICAS CUP AVE.

KAY ST.

ISLAND AVE.

2

9

10

3

4

1

8

TOURO

5

MARSH ST.

MARY ST.

CAUSEWAY

7

MILL ST.

Cliff Walk (Begins)

BOWEN'S WHARF

BANNISTER'S WHARF

6

MEMORIAL BLVD.

ANNANDALE RD.

11

Points of Interest

Brick Market 2
Colony House 1
Friends Meeting House 10
Hunter House 9
Old Stone Mill 6
Redwood Library 5
Salve Regina College 12
Tennis Hall of Fame 11
Touro Synagogue 4
Trinity Church 7
Vernon House 8
Wanton-Lyman-Hazard House 3

QUEEN ANNE SQUARE

THAMES

SPRING ST.

The Elms

AVE.

12

The Breakers

Newport Harbor

Ferry

FORT ADAMS STATE PARK

NARRAGANSETT

COGGESHALL

BELLEVUE

Rosecliff

BAUER

Ferry To Block Island

FORT ADAMS RD.

HARRISON AVE.

HAZARD RD.

RUGGLES

AVE.

Easton Bay

Marble House

Hammersmith Farm

HARRISON

MOORLAND RD.

Lilly Pond

Almy Pond

Belcourt Castle

AVE.

RIDGE RD.

OCEAN

AVE.

CASTLE HILL

OCEAN DR.

Cliff Walk (Ends)

BRENTON POINT STATE PARK

LANDS END

Atlantic Ocean

Newport

Mansions and Museums

The Newport Artillery Company Armory, at 23 Clarke Street, houses a small military museum filled with relics from America's military past. Clarke Street is bordered on both sides by attractive restored homes from the 1700s and early 1800s. Continue on Clarke Street until you reach Touro Street, where you'll be in sight of Washington Square, where your brief tour of Newport began. At this point you may wish to walk downhill to explore the shops and attractions of Thames Street and Newport's Brick Market area.

There is more, always more, to see in old Newport. Principal attractions include the Friends Meeting House, at Marlborough and Farewell Streets, and the White Horse Tavern, built during the 1670s and still functioning near the Friends Meeting House. Certainly no trip to Newport is complete without a visit to Bowen's Wharf and Bannister's Wharf, where old sail lofts and sheds have been converted into fashionable shops, restaurants, and cafes. For a final glimpse of colonial Newport, stop by the Hunter House, at 54 Washington Street, in the Point section on the waterfront. Maintained by the Preservation Society of Newport, the Hunter House is furnished with outstanding examples of colonial Newport furniture by period cabinetmakers such as the Townsends and the Goddards. This is the kind of home that a merchant prince would have appreciated during the 1700s. Built in 1748, close to the wharves, the Hunter House had a splendid view of a bustling harbor. In 1780–81, the Hunter House was the headquarters of Admiral Charles de Ternay, commander of the French fleet in North America. The restored Hunter House is one of the finest examples of colonial architecture and design in the United States.

Beyond Newport's colonial waterfront are other Newport attractions. Nine magnificent mansions from the late 1800s are now open to the public on or near Bellevue Avenue, and readers eager to pay a call on the summer homes of the Vanderbilts and the Astors may wish to skip ahead to the Newport mansions listing. Beyond the mansions, Newport has a Museum of Yachting, at Fort Adams State Park on Ocean Drive, and the Newport Casino, at 194 Bellevue Avenue, offers the International Tennis Hall of Fame, at the site where the first National Championships were held in 1881. The Navy has an interesting museum at the Naval War College. Outside Newport, travelers can drive north on Route 114 or Route 138 through the towns of Middletown and Portsmouth, which share Aquidneck Island with Newport. Although much of the island has been covered over with homes and shopping centers, you can still see here and there the lush fields that caused early visitors to call Aquidneck the Eden of America. North of Aquidneck is Bristol, an interesting and attractive town on the way to I–195.

Outside Newport

Route 114 leads from Newport to the Prescott Farm complex, close to the town line between Middletown and Portsmouth. This small park is owned and maintained by the Newport Restoration Foundation. There's a large windmill, a country store, and various farm buildings to see, all dating from the eighteenth or early nineteenth century, with flocks of ducks and a gaggle of geese outside, all quacking and honking. On a nearby rise—but not open to the public—is the famous Prescott (Nichols-Overing) House, in which occurred the sensational capture of General Richard Prescott, the commander of Newport's British garrison, in 1777.

General Prescott was detested by many Aquidneck islanders during the British occupation, although he did find favor with the wife of Henry Overing. On the night of July 9, 1777, while visiting the Overing home, General Prescott was surprised and pulled out of bed by a team of American raiders who had slipped behind enemy lines. Barefoot and in his night-clothes, Prescott was hustled off the island and held as a prisoner of war, later to be exchanged for an American general who had been captured by the British. The leader of the American raiders was Lieutenant Colonel William Barton, a Rhode Island hatter transformed by the Revolution into a soldier.

In the year following General Prescott's capture, the Americans were back on Aquidneck Island, this time in large numbers, supported by their recently acquired French allies. What resulted, in August 1778, was the Battle of Rhode Island, part of a mismanaged campaign that we will note when we reach the Sakonnet lands. For the moment, drive on to Portsmouth and Bristol. You'll see a memorial to some of the Americans who fought at the Battle of Rhode Island near the junction of Route 114 and Route 24.

Beyond the Prescott farm, on Cory's Lane off Route 114 in Portsmouth, is Green Animals, an impressive collection of sculptured trees and shrubs shaped to resemble animals and other figures that children may enjoy. Green Animals is one of the finest examples of topiary gardening in the United States. Also on Cory's Lane is the Portsmouth Priory and the Chapel of St. Gregory, a contemporary chapel that has won international recognition for its design.

Bristol

Portsmouth was the town that Anne Hutchinson and her associates established in 1638; unfortunately, very little remains in Portsmouth to remind visitors of Hutchinson and her times. Across the Mount Hope Bridge on Route 114 is Bristol, an attractive peninsula town famous for its all-out Fourth of July celebrations. Among Bristol's attractions is the Haffenreffer Museum of Anthropology, off Route 136. The museum displays items from Native American, African, and Oceanic cultures. King Philip's War began near Bristol in 1675; it was the last war between the colonists and the Indians in southern New England. Not far from the Haffenreffer, the Wampanoag leader Metacom—who was known to the English as King Philip—was killed in a surprise attack in 1676. The museum staff can provide you with additional information on King Philip's War. From Bristol, you can drive on Route 136 to I–195 in Massachusetts, the interstate highway that connects Providence to New Bedford and Cape Cod. Or double back, cross the Mount Hope Bridge again, and explore Aquidneck along the Route 138 side on your way back to Newport. At Route 138 and Hedley Avenue is the modest Friends' Meeting House, erected in 1702, when most of Portsmouth's residents were Quakers. In Middletown, on Berkeley Avenue, is Whitehall, the home of George Berkeley. On the eastern side of Middletown is the Norman Bird Sanctuary, with 15 miles of easy hiking trails for bird watchers and shore lovers. Purgatory Chasm nearby is a dramatic 160-foot break in the earth, the inspiration for tales told and retold by Indians and colonists.

Jamestown

Across from Newport, on Conanicut Island, is Jamestown. Easily reached from Newport via the Newport Bridge, Jamestown rests at the mouth of Narragansett Bay. From Beavertail Lighthouse, at the southern-most tip of Conanicut, you can enjoy a spectacular view of the Atlantic. The view from Beavertail, in any season, is one of the finest ocean views in Rhode Island. Mackerel Cove, on the road to Beavertail, is an attractive place to swim and picnic. If you follow Route 138 from Jamestown west, you'll drive across the Jamestown Bridge into South County on your way to I–95 and Providence.

PRACTICAL INFORMATION FOR NEWPORT

Note: The area code for all Rhode Island is 401

HOW TO GET THERE. By plane: The Theodore Francis Green State Airport, in Warwick, south of Providence, is Rhode Island's major airport. Charter companies provide connecting flights from Green State Airport to the Newport State Airport. (Call 846–2200.) The Airport Shuttle Service provides year-round shuttle service connecting Newport hotels and naval facilities to Green State Airport. (In Newport, call 846–2500.)

By train: Amtrak provides service to Providence and Boston. For information, call 800–USA–RAIL.

By bus: Bonanza Bus Lines (846–1820) provides service to Newport from Providence, Boston, and New York City. The Rhode Island Public Transit Authority (RIPTA) provides Newport area bus service. (In Newport, call 847–0209).

By car: From I–95: Follow Rte. 138 over the Jamestown and Newport bridges into Newport. From I–195: In Fall River, Mass., take Rte. 24 south to Rte. 138 in Rhode Island.

HOW TO GET AROUND. Car rentals: Automobile rental agencies with offices in Newport and at Green State Airport include Avis (846–1843 or 800–331–1212); Hertz (846–6540); and Pontiac (847–5600).

On foot: The Newport County Convention and Visitors' Bureau provides free maps and brochures for Newport visitors. Write the Newport County Convention and Visitors' Bureau, 23 America's Cup Ave., Newport 02840 (849–8048). The Newport Historical Society, 82 Touro St., has walking tours of Newport on Fri. and Sat., June–Sept. (846–0813).

HOTELS AND MOTELS. Newport provides comfortable accommodations throughout the year. Price ranges are based on double occupancy during the summer season: *Deluxe,* $100 and up; *Expensive,* $60–$100; *Moderate,* $45–$60. All listings include the European Plan, except where indicated.

Middletown

Greenhouse Inn & Restaurant, 30 Wave Ave., Newport 02840 (846–0310). *Moderate.* A mid-sized beach hotel in Middletown, despite its Newport address. Open year-round. Continental breakfast served during off-season only. Off-season package rates.

Howard Johnson Lodge, 349 W. Main Rd., Middletown 02840 (849–4306 or 800–654–2000). *Moderate.* Two miles from historic Newport. Indoor pool. Tennis courts. 24-hour restaurant.

West Main Lodge, 1359 W. Main Rd., Middletown 02840 (849–2718). *Moderate.* Near the naval base. Open year-round.

Newport

The Inn at Castle Hill, Ocean Dr., 02840 (849–3800). *Deluxe.* A Newport mansion converted into a fine hotel. Ocean view. Tennis. Excellent restaurant. Continental breakfast included with cost.

The Marriott, 25 America's Cup Ave., 02840 (849–1000 or 800–228–9290). *Expensive.* Luxury hotel at Long Wharf. Suites. Conference facilities. Health club. Restaurant.

Newport Harbor Treadway Inn. 49 America's Cup Ave., 02840 (847–9000 or 800–631–0182). *Expensive.* Resort facility in the heart of Newport's historic wharf district. Indoor pool. Sauna. Restaurant. Marina.

Sheraton Islander Inn, Goat Island, 02840 (849–2600 or 800–325–3535). *Expensive.* Access to Goat Island by causeway from Washington St. A resort hotel with an impressive view of the harbor and colonial Newport. Indoor and outdoor pools. Tennis courts. Marina. Restaurant. Conference facilities.

Viking Hotel and Motor Inn. 1 Bellevue Ave., 02840 (847–3300 or 800–556–7126). *Expensive.* Large hotel and conference center. Indoor pool. Sauna. Restaurant.

INNS, GUEST HOUSES, BED AND BREAKFASTS. Newport has a variety of inns, small hotels, and bed-and-breakfast accommodations. The inns that follow fall in the *moderate* price category. For additional information on bed-and-breakfast arrangements in Rhode Island, contact Bed and Breakfast of Rhode Island, Inc., Box 3291, Newport 02840 (849–1298).

The Brinley Victorian Inn, 23 Brinley St., Newport 02840 (849–7645). 17 rooms, 12 with private bath. Two parlors, a library, and a Victorian courtyard.

Cliffside Inn, 2 Seaview Ave., Newport 02840 (847–1811). Victorian home, built in 1880. Near Newport's Cliff Walk. 10 rooms, all with baths. Open May–Oct. Does not accept children under 10.

The Melville House, 39 Clarke St., Newport 02840 (847–0640). Seven rooms furnished in colonial style. House built in 1750. Historic neighborhood.

Mill Street Inn, 75 Mill St., Newport 02840 (849–9500). Small all-suite hotel on the waterfront. Complimentary Continental breakfast.

The Pilgrim House, 123 Spring St., Newport 02840 (846–0040). Victorian house, built in 1809.

Queen Anne Inn, 16 Clarke St., Newport 02840 (846–5676). Near Washington Sq. Nine rooms, 5 with shared baths.

Sanford-Covell House, 72 Washington St., Newport 02840 (847–0206). Victorian summer home, built in 1869–70. Private pier. In Point area, where many of Newport's restored colonial homes are located.

Thames Street Inn, 398 Thames St., Newport 02840 (847–4559). Victorian building, recently restored. Close to waterfront.

Yankee Peddler Inn, 113 Touro St., Newport 02840 (846–1323). 20 rooms, most with private baths. Open Feb.–Dec. Reduced rates during off-season.

RESTAURANTS. Newport is a gourmet's town. Price ranges for local restaurants are as follows: *Deluxe,* $25 and up; *Expensive,* $18 to $25; *Moderate,* $10–$18; and *Inexpensive,* $10 or under. These prices are per person excluding beverage, tax, and tip.

The Black Pearl, Bannister's Wharf (864–5264). *Deluxe.* An elegant French restaurant in the midst of the Newport waterfront district. The tavern section is a bit less expensive.

Clarke Cooke House, Bannister's Wharf (849–2900). *Deluxe.* Upstairs, fine French cuisine. Downstairs, the **Candy Store Cafe,** a popular, more informal restaurant.

Inn at Castle Hill, Ocean Dr. (849–3800). *Deluxe.* Continental cuisine with a glorious view of Narragansett Bay. A popular place for Sun. brunch.

Le Petite Auberge, 19 Charles St. (846–6669). *Deluxe.* Small, romantic French restaurant. One of New England's best. Reservations encouraged.

The Star Clipper Dinner Train, Visitors' Center, 23 America's Cup Ave. (849–8098). *Deluxe.* Departs twice a day in season, weekends during the off-season, for a two-hour, four-course dinner in restored old-fashioned dining cars.

Le Bistro, Bowen's Wharf (849–7778). *Expensive.* Attractive French restaurant, not too formal.

White Horse Tavern, Corner of Marlborough and Farewell Sts. (849–3600). *Expensive.* The oldest tavern in America. The White Horse offers a Continental menu in an elegant, colonial Newport setting.

Brick Alley Pub, 140 Thames St. (849–6334). *Moderate.* Sandwiches, fresh fish, chowder.

Newport Creamery, 49 Long Wharf Mall (849–8469). *Inexpensive.* When the kids want hamburgers, try the Creamery. Relaxed; close to the waterfront.

Salas', 341 Thames St. (846–8772). *Moderate.* Seafood and Italian specialties. A lively, good-natured waterfront restaurant, with lobsters, clams, and corn on the cob. No reservations.

TOURIST INFORMATION. For information on Newport attractions and special events, contact the Newport County Convention and Visitors' Bureau, 23 America's Cup Ave., 02840 (849–8048). The Bureau's offices, next to The Marriott, are open year-round during the day. For Bristol County information, contact the Bristol County Chamber of Commerce, 654 Metacom Ave., Warren 02885 (245–0750).

TOURS. *The Spirit of Newport* (849–3575) gives one-hour minicruises of Newport Harbor and Narragansett Bay. Departs from Treadway Inn, America's Cup Ave., every 90 minutes in season.

Viking Bus Tours of Newport, Brick Marketplace (847–6921), provides a variety of Newport tours on board air-conditioned buses. Buses leave from the Newport County Convention and Visitors' Bureau.

The Newport County Convention and Visitors' Bureau rents several auto cassette tapes, providing motorists with easy-to-use guided tours of Newport.

The Old Colony & Newport Railway, with offices at 1 America's Cup Ave., follows an 8-mile scenic route along Narragansett Bay, from Newport to Green Animals in Portsmouth. Leaves Newport at 1:30 P.M., Sun., May–Dec.; also, 1:30 P.M. departures daily in July and Aug. and 6:30 P.M. on Weds. Round trip takes a bit over 2 hours. Call 624–6951 or write Old Colony & Newport Railway, Box 343, Newport 02840.

The Newport Freedom Trail (351–8700) winds through the downtown area. It makes almost a complete loop around the city, beginning at the Historical Society on Touro Street and ending at the Automobile Museum.

SEASONAL EVENTS. There is a great deal going on in the Newport area in every season. Check local newspapers for details.

July: Independence Day celebrations in Bristol are among the most spirited in New England. For information: 253–8397. The Tennis Hall of Fame, in Newport, hosts a Grand Prix tennis tournament in mid-July. For information: 849–3990. The Newport Music Festival, in mid-July, offers a popular series of concerts in Newport mansions. For information: Newport Music Festival (849–0700 for tickets).

August: The Newport Folk Festival, held at Fort Adams State Park, is usually scheduled for early Aug. For information: Box 605, Newport 02840. The Kool Jazz Festival in Newport, also held at Fort Adams State Park, is usually scheduled for mid-Aug. For information: Box 605, Newport 02840 (847–3700).

December: The Christmas season in Newport starts in late Nov. and lasts until Jan. Several of the Bellevue Ave. mansions are open for the holidays, and there are crafts fairs, holiday concerts, and candlelight tours of colonial homes, all through Dec. For information: Christmas in Newport, Box 716, Newport 02840 (849–6454).

BEACHES. Sandy beaches have been attracting visitors to Newport since the 1840s. In Newport—**Fort Adams State Park,** Ocean Dr. Small beach, picnic area. Lifeguards during summer. Parking fee. **Easton's Beach,** Memorial Blvd., extends from the Cliff Walk to Middletown. Also known as First Beach. One of the area's most popular beaches. Bathhouses. Parking fee. **King Park,** Wellington Ave. Lifeguards during summer. Parking on Wellington Ave.

In Middletown—**Sachuest Beach,** Sachuest Point area. Also known as Second Beach. Three miles of shore. Sand dunes. Beach campground. Parking fee. **Third Beach,** Sachuest Point area, on Sakonnet River. Boat ramp.

In Portsmouth—**Sandy Point Beach,** off Sandy Point Ave. Picnic area. Lifeguards during summer. Parking fee.

In Jamestown—**Mackerel Cove,** Beaver Tail Rd. Rocky beach.

In Bristol—**Bristol Town Beach,** Colt Dr. Parking fee.

GARDENS AND NATURE CENTERS. Visitors in the 1600s called Aquidneck Island "the Eden of America." North of Aquidneck, the Mount Hope area, in Bristol, is still an attractive region with an interesting history.

Green Animals, Cory's Lane, off Rte. 114 in Portsmouth (847–1000). The Green Animals gardens are, perhaps, the most extensive topiary gardens in the United States, with almost a hundred sculptured trees and shrubs, representing birds, animals, boats, and even a policeman. Maintained by the Preservation Society of Newport County. Open daily, May–Sept., 10 A.M.–5 P.M.; also, weekends in Oct. Admission fee.

Norman Bird Sanctuary, Third Beach Rd. in Middletown (846–2577). A 450-acre sanctuary with nature trails, guided tours, and a small natural history museum. Open daily all year, 9 A.M.–5 P.M.

Blithewold Gardens and Arboretum, Ferry Rd. in Bristol (253–2707). A grand Victorian-era mansion set in 33 acres of landscaped grounds, with a rock garden, a water garden, a bamboo grove, and even a West Coast redwood tree. Guided tours of mansion; grounds are open year-round, 10 A.M.–4 P.M., except Mon. and holidays.

INDIANS. The Mount Hope area, north of Aquidneck, was the home of the Wampanoag Indians, who also dominated the Sakonnet lands and much of southeastern Massachusetts during the 1600s. The Wampanoags were the Indians who feasted with the Pilgrims during the first Thanksgiving Day celebration in Plymouth, Massachusetts. The Plimoth Plantation restoration in modern Plymouth includes a replica of a Wampanoag summer camp. King Philip's War, 1675–76, led to the defeat of the early Wampanoags, but many of their descendants still live in New England.

The **Haffenreffer Museum of Anthropology,** Tower St., off Rte. 136 in Bristol (253–8388) is maintained by Brown University. Exhibits focus on the native peoples of Africa, Asia, Oceania, and the Americas. Museum staff can provide information on New England Indians and King Philip's War. Open Tues.–Sun., June–Aug., 1–5 P.M.; also, weekends, spring and fall, 1–5 P.M. Admission fee.

SUMMER SPORTS. Boating: Oldport Marine Services, Sayer's Wharf, Newport, has boat rentals (847–9109).

Tennis: The Tennis Hall of Fame, 194 Bellevue Ave., has a dozen grass courts—open to the public—and a court tennis court, where tennis is played as it was in 13th-century Europe (849–3990).

Golf: In Jamestown, try the Jamestown Golf and Country Club, E. Shore Rd. (423–9930). In Portsmouth, 3 courses are open to the public: The Montaup Country Club, Anthony Rd. (683–0955); The Pocasset Country Club, 807 Bristol Ferry Rd. (683–2266); The Green Valley Country Club, 371 Union St. (847–9543).

Bikes and Mopeds: Try Ten Speed Spokes, 79 Thames St. (847–5609), for bikes, and Newport Rent-a-Ped, 2 Washington St. (846–7788), for mopeds.

FISHING. No license is required for saltwater fishing, although anglers should check with local bait shops for information on minimum size limits. Charter boats depart daily from Newport, from the spring through the fall, for offshore and inshore fishing. For bait and tackle, visit Newport Bait and Tackle, 462 Thames St., Newport (849–4987); also, Zeek's Creek Bait and Tackle, 194 North Rd., Jamestown (423–1170). For charter boats, contact Black Horse Fishing Charters, Long Wharf Moorings, Newport (846–0540).

Spectator Sports. Newport Jai Alai, 150 Admiral Kalbfus Rd, Newport (849–5000). "The fastest game on two feet." Professional jai alai and pari-mutuel betting.

HISTORIC SITES AND HOUSES. Much of colonial Newport has been preserved through the efforts of private organizations such as the Newport Restoration Foundation and the Preservation Society of Newport. Call ahead for admission fees.

Middletown

Whitehall, off Berkeley Ave. (846–3790). The home of George Berkeley, the Anglican philosopher. Built in 1729. Berkeley lived here, 1729–31. Open daily July–Labor Day, 10 A.M. to 5 P.M.; in June and Sept. by appointment.

Prescott Farm, off Rte. 114 (847–6230 or 849–7300). A collection of restored buildings from the 1700s and early 1800s, including a windmill, a country store, and a British guard house. The Overing House—where American raiders surprised and captured a British general in 1777—is nearby but is not open to the public. The Prescott Farm is open daily, Apr.–Nov., 10 A.M.–4 P.M.

Newport

Hunter House, 54 Washington St., in the Point section of Newport (847–1000). Fine example of a colonial merchant's mansion, close to the waterfront. Furnished with Newport china, silver, and furniture by the Goddard and Townsend families. Open May–Oct. 10 A.M.–5 P.M.

Touro Synagogue, 72 Touro St. (847–4791). Oldest Jewish house of worship in North America. Built 1759–63. A masterpiece of colonial architecture. The synagogue continues as the place of worship for Congregation Jeshuat Israel. Open to visitors Sun.–Fri., 10 A.M.–5 P.M. Guided tours during visiting hours. Also open during the remainder of the year by appointment.

Trinity Church, Spring and Church Sts. is an Anglican (Episcopal) church built in 1725–26. George Washington worshiped here. George Berkeley, the Anglican philosopher, preached here during his three-year stay in the Newport area, 1729–31.

Old Colony House, Washington Sq. (846–2980). Built in 1739, still in use as one of the Rhode Island state capitol buildings until 1900. Open Mon.–Fri., 9:30 A.M.–noon and 1–4 P.M.; also weekend mornings July–Labor Day.

Friends Meeting House, Farewell and Marlboro Sts. (846–0813). Quaker meeting house, built in 1700. Quaker families were prominent in Newport's commercial and civic life during the 1600s and early 1700s.

Brick Market, Washington Sq., on Thames St. (849–3441). Colonial market building, built in 1762. Now used as a gift shop. Upstairs gallery displays original art and Newport prints. Open all week. Summer hours: 10 A.M.–9 P.M.; Sun., 12–9 P.M. Winter hours: 10 A.M.–5 P.M.; Sun., 12–5 P.M.

Wanton-Lyman-Hazard House, 17 Broadway (846–0813). Oldest restored house in Newport, built in 1675. Owned by the Newport Historical Society. Open mid-June–Aug., Tues.–Sat., 10 A.M.–5 P.M.

Redwood Library, 50 Bellevue Ave. (847–0292). The oldest library building in continuous use in the United States. The library contains a large collection of American paintings. Open to the public Mon.–Sat., 9:30 A.M.–5 P.M.

Old Stone Mill, Touro Park at Bellevue Ave. and Mill St. Newport's "mystery tower." Some say that it was built by the Vikings. Some say that it was built as a colonial windmill. The ancient Celts and early Portugese explorers are also in the running.

NEWPORT MANSIONS. The adjectives spill onto the page: *gaudy, magnificent, excessive, wonderful.* Newport's 19th-century mansions inspire adjectives, and, still, there's no easy way to explain Newport's grand style. Other towns may have their big houses and large estates; Newport has its mansions—lots of mansions. Six Newport mansions are maintained by the Preservation Society of Newport County, and mansion-minded visitors may wish to purchase a combination ticket—available at any of the society's properties—in order to enjoy a discount on admission prices at Newport's "summer cottages." Guided tours are provided at all the society's mansions. Each tour lasts for approximately 1 hour. For information on any of the mansions, call the society at 847–1000.

The Breakers, Ochre Point Ave. The grandest of Newport's summer palaces, and the one most popular with visitors. Built in 1893–95 for Cornelius Vanderbilt II and his family. The Breakers—like most of Newport's mansions—was used only for the summer months. It contains 70 rooms (40 servants were needed to keep everything in order). This 4-story limestone villa, with its tall rose alabaster pillars in the dining room, its blue marble fireplace in the music room, and its massive wrought iron gates, may seem like an Italian nobleman's palazzo. For the Vanderbilts, it was just "a cottage by the sea."

The Elms, Bellevue Ave. Built for Edward Julius Berwind, completed in 1901. Berwind and his brothers had made their fortune in the bituminous coal business as the largest supplier of coal to the American merchant marine. The Elms was modeled after the Château d'Asnieres near Paris. With its classical design and its broad lawn, fountains, and formal gardens, many visitors regard the Berwind home as being the most graceful of Newport's mansions. The Elms cost the Berwinds $1.4 million—at a time when many Americans were working for a dollar a day.

Marble House, Bellevue Ave. The Marble House was where Alva Belmont spent her summers when she was Mrs. Vanderbilt. Born Alva Erskine Smith, the daughter of an Alabama cotton planter, she was married first to William Vanderbilt of New York. Marble House—its dazzling gold ballroom would have made Louis XIV blush with envy—was Mr. Vanderbilt's gift to his wife in 1892. In 1895 Alva divorced William and the following year she married Oliver Perry Belmont. Alva became the lady of Belcourt Castle, but, following Oliver's death in 1908, she was back at Marble House. As a dedicated suffragist, Mrs. Belmont devoted much of her time and talent to campaigning for women's rights, and in the great kitchen at Marble House can be seen plates marked "Votes for Women." A Chinese teahouse at the back of the estate, built in 1913 by Mrs. Belmont, is open to visitors during the summer.

Chateau Sur Mer, Bellevue Ave. This was the first of Bellevue Avenue's stone mansions, built in 1851–52. Compared to some of its opulent neighbors built during the 1890s, the Castle on the Sea seems rather modest. The house was enlarged and transformed by the architect Richard Morris Hunt during the 1870s. There is a toy collection here that may delight children, and the mansion is a popular place to visit in Dec., when the house is decorated for a Victorian Christmas.

Rosecliff, Bellevue Ave. An Irish immigrant, James Graham Fair, was one of four partners who discovered Nevada's fabulous Comstock Lode. Fair became a multimillionaire and a United States senator from Nevada, and his daughter Theresa married Hermann Oelrichs, a man prominent in New York society. Construction on Rosecliffe began in 1898 and was completed in 1902. The 40-room home includes the Court of Love, inspired by a similar court at Versailles. Rosecliffe is a mansion for romantics; not surprisingly, it has been featured in several movies, including *The Great Gatsby* in 1974.

Kingscote, Bowery St., off Bellevue Ave. Built in 1839–41, Kingscote is a remainder that Newport was a popular resort for wealthy Southerners before the Civil War. Kingscote was built for George Noble Jones, a plantation owner from Savannah. The Jones family, and other Southern families, enjoyed Newport's congenial summer climate during the 1840s and '50s, until the outbreak of the Civil War in 1861. In 1863, the house was sold to the King family of Rhode Island. Kingscote today is furnished with antique furniture, glass, and oriental art collected by four generations of Kings.

In addition to its six Victorian-era mansions in Newport, the Preservation Society of Newport County maintains the colonial **Hunter House,** at 54 Washington St., and the **Green Animals** gardens, in Portsmouth.

These sites can be visited by purchasing one of the society's combination tickets.

In addition to the mansions preserved by the Preservation Society, there are other 19th-century homes that are open to the public. Each one differs a bit from its neighbors.

Beechwood, 580 Bellevue Ave. (846–3772). The summer home of Mrs. Astor, the grande dame of New York and Newport society. Actors and actresses portray life in the Gilded Age. Open daily, 10 A.M.–5 P.M.

Belcourt Castle, Bellevue Ave. (846–0669 or 849–1566). Alva Belmont lived here. Today the castle contains an impressive collection of European and oriental treasures. Complimentary tea is served to visitors. Open daily, Apr.–Jan., 10 A.M.–5 P.M.

Hammersmith Farm, Ocean Dr., near Fort Adams (846–7346). The site of the wedding reception of Jacqueline Bouvier and John F. Kennedy in 1953. Used as a summer White House by President Kennedy. An attractive estate, now functioning as Newport's only working farm. Open daily, Apr.–mid-Nov., 10 A.M.–5 P.M. Summer hours until 7 P.M.

Ochre Court, Salve Regina College. One of Newport's early "summer cottages," now serving as the administration building for Salve Regina College. Open to visitors, 9 A.M.–4 P.M.

MUSEUMS AND GALLERIES. Museum of Yachting, at Fort Adams, on Ocean Dr. (847–1018). Exhibits depict the fabulous yachts owned by the Astors, the Vanderbilts, and the Belmonts. Open mid-May–Oct., Tues.–Sun., 10 A.M.–5 P.M.

International Tennis Hall of Fame and **The Tennis Museum,** at the Casino, 194 Bellevue Ave. (849–3990). The first National Championships were held at the Casino in 1881. The museum contains photographs, memorabilia, and displays honoring more than a century of tennis history. Open daily, May–Oct., 11 A.M.–5 P.M.; Nov.–Apr., 11 A.M.–4 P.M.

Naval War College Museum, Coasters Harbor Island. Enter at Gate One of the Naval Education and Training Center (no phone). Newport is known as "The Campus of the Navy" because of the Naval War College and other Navy schools. The Naval War College tells the story of the Navy in Narragansett Bay. Open to the public, weekdays, June–Sept., 10 A.M.–4 P.M.; also, Sat. and Sun., 12–4 P.M.

Newport Artillery Company Armory and Museum, 23 Clarke St. (847–2648). Military history museum. Open Apr.–Oct. by appointment.

Newport Art Museum and Art Association, 76 Bellevue Ave. (847–0179). Changing exhibits. Open Tues.–Sat., 10 A.M.–5 P.M.; Sun., 1–5 P.M.

Newport Historical Society, 82 Touro St. (846–0813). Displays early American paintings, furniture, silver, and china, together with pictures and maps of old Newport. Interesting marine museum. Open Tues.–Fri., 9:30 A.M.–4:30 P.M. (also Sat., mid-June–Labor Day).

MUSIC, DANCE, AND STAGE. The Newport County Convention and Visitors' Bureau, 23 America's Cup Ave. (849–8048), can provide visitors with information on concerts, shows, and special events. Or check the entertainment listings in Newport and Providence newspapers.

The **Rhode Island Shakespeare Theatre,** Webster St. (849–7892), has excellent theater in all seasons.

The **Blau Haus Theatre,** at the Blue Pelican on West Broadway (847–5675). Performances Wed.–Sun.

For contemporary drama, the **Kinderhook Theatre,** 102 Connell Hwy. (847–9910).

The Children's Theatre, at Astor's Beechwood, Bellevue Ave. (848–0266 or 846–5526), has 3 or 4 major productions for children each year.

SHOPPING. Many of Newport's arts and antiques shops can be found on Thames St. or close to the waterfront. The Brick Market area—between Thames St. and America's Cup Ave.—has more than 50 shops, all of them open year-round. Try Spring and Franklin Sts. for antiques. Also try the Wharfs: Bowen's and Bannisters.

On *Thames St.*—**Black Duck Gallery,** 543 Thames St., has decoys and carvings. **Lamp Works,** at 626 Thames St., has restored antique lighting and lampshades. **Atelier 629,** 629 Thames St., has jewelry, ceramics, prints. **Thames Street Glass,** 688 Thames St., has handblown glass.

On the *Waterfront*—**Spring Pottery,** 4 Bowens Wharf, is a gallery and retail shop. **The Spectrum,** Bannisters Wharf, has paintings and prints.

NIGHTLIFE. At night, Newport may be the liveliest town between New York and Boston. While Cape Cod slumbers through the winter, Newport sizzles.

The Ark, 348 Thames St. (849–3808). Piano bar on weekends; jazz Sun.

Blue Pelican, 40 W. Broadway (846–5675). Jazz. One of Rhode Island's most popular clubs.

Clarke Cooke House, Bannisters Wharf (849–2900). Piano bar upstairs, disco and swing downstairs. Always popular.

Viking Hotel, 1 Bellevue Ave. (847–3300). Mainstream jazz on Sun. afternoon.

PROVIDENCE

Fine restaurants, historic homes, a nationally renowned theater company, specialty shops, the Rhode Island School of Design and its excellent art museum—all of this and more may encourage the New England traveler to exit from I–95 or I–195 in order to take a closer look at Providence. Prices in Providence, for excellent meals, lodging, and entertainment, tend to be a bit more modest than they are in Boston, which is good news for many travelers. The Great Woods Center for the Performing Arts in Mansfield, Massachusetts, is within 20 minutes of Providence eating establishments and hotels.

A tour of Providence should begin at the State House on Smith Hill, overlooking the downtown area. Parking is available nearby. This impressive turn-of-the-century structure—Rhode Island's capitol building since 1900—holds the state legislature and the governor's office. Along the corridors are flags, cannon, and statues memorializing the wars in which Rhode Islanders fought. Atop the State House dome is a statute of the Independent Man, an allegorical figure representing Rhode Island's independent spirit.

Roger Williams Memorial

Walk down Smith Street to the Roger Williams National Memorial. It was on this site in 1636 that the Providence settlement began. Roger Williams's home was across the street from a natural source of fresh water known as the Roger Williams Spring. The spring is now dry, but Williams's legacy keeps bubbling forth. Out of early Providence came the concern with individual rights and the uneasiness with centralized authority that now seem very American.

By all accounts, Roger Williams was a remarkable man. At a time when Puritan authorities had tied church and state together, Williams called for the strict separation of church and state powers. For this act of rebellion he was banished from Massachusetts. Williams had strong opinions of his own, but he tolerated dissenters and welcomed many of them to Rhode Island. Williams also insisted on fair trading with the Indians, and he learned several Indian languages. For 40 years Williams acted as a peacekeeper between his Puritan and Indian neighbors, although in the end he was unable to prevent the collision of cultures—known as King Philip's War—that shook the New England frontier during the 1670s.

Continue on North Main Street, going south. South of the Roger Williams Spring, up toward Benefit Street, is the Old State House. Erected in 1762, this brick building was one of Rhode Island's capitol buildings at the time of the Revolution. For many years the seat of Rhode Island government moved back and forth between here and Newport's Old Colony House. Not until 1900 did Rhode Island settle on one permanent state capital. The Old State House now houses the offices of the State Historical Preservation Commission.

Go under the old railroad bridge to Thomas Street. At the foot of the hill is the First Baptist Meeting House. Other cities may have first Baptist churches of their own, but this structure is unique because it shelters the congregation of the First Baptist Church in America, the church that Roger Williams founded in 1638. The present church building was completed in 1775. Inside you'll see a large gallery, on three sides of the church, supported by Ionic columns. A great Waterford glass chandelier shines overhead. In addition to being the site of regular religious services, the Meeting House is the site of Brown University's graduation exercises. Brown, an Ivy League school, is up the hill on the East Side of Providence.

Benefit Street

Climb Thomas Street and turn right on Benefit Street. At 224 Benefit Street is the Rhode Island School of Design's Museum of Art, one of the best of America's mid-sized art museums and one of Providence's leading cultural attractions. Inside the museum are collections of art from Europe, Asia, Africa, and the Americas. To be enjoyed properly, the Museum of Art requires an hour or more of time. If you're in a hurry, come back another day, when you can fully enjoy all that the museum has to offer.

The templelike building at 251 Benefit Street is the Providence Athenaeum, a private library. In the quiet library corners, Edgar Allan Poe courted Sarah Helen Whitman. Sarah didn't marry Edgar—which, considering Poe's frailties, may have been for the best—but she never quite dismissed him, and long after Poe's death in 1849, Sarah Whitman was still one of Poe's active literary defenders. Whitman helped to make certain that Edgar Allan Poe would be remembered and appreciated by later generations.

Benefit Street is known today as the Mile of History. All along Benefit Street and throughout much of Providence's East Side—not to be confused with East Providence, which is a separate city—are restored homes from the 1700s and the 1800s, many of them preserved since the 1950s through the work of the Providence Preservation Society. The society's headquarters, at 24 Meeting Street, provides information on historic pres-

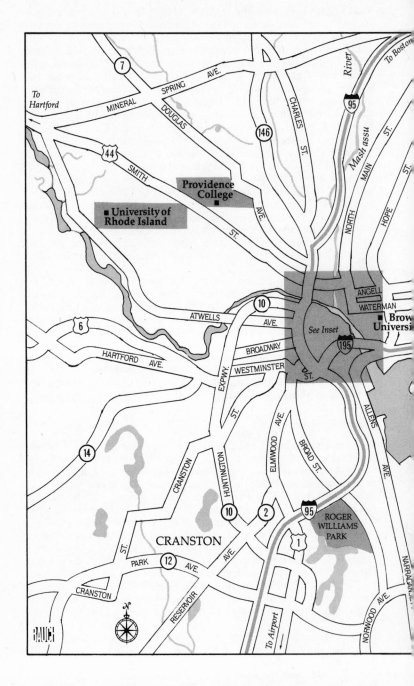

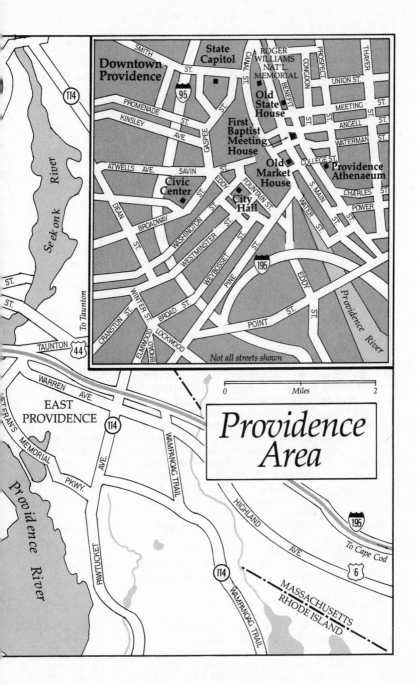

Providence Area

ervation and on Providence history. The society also sponsors walking tours and house tours.

At the corner of Benefit and Hopkins streets is the home of Stephen Hopkins, one of the Rhode Islanders who signed the Declaration of Independence. Theatergoers who have seen the musical *1776* may remember Hopkins as the salty, rum-drinking delegate to the Continental Congress—one of the oldest men present—who helped to nudge other delegates into supporting the idea of independence. History suggests that Hopkins had a fondness for rum, but it records, too, that Hopkins was a shrewd statesman who ably served his state in several positions of public trust, including 10 terms as Rhode Island's governor. Stephen Hopkins was allied politically with the powerful Brown brothers, who will be mentioned again in a moment. The restored Hopkins home is open to the public from April through December; it's a simple home, reflecting the modest Quaker style of the 1700s.

The Brown Brothers

At 285 Benefit Street stands the First Unitarian Church, built in 1815–16. At the corner of Benefit and Power streets, above a wide lawn, is the John Brown mansion, described by John Quincy Adams as "the most magnificent and elegant mansion" that he had seen in North America. Enter on the Power Street side. If you have the time to tour only one historic home in Providence, this is the one to see.

There have been Browns in Providence since 1638. It was at the time of the Revolution and in the years that followed, however, that the Browns had their greatest impact on Providence. Four Brown brothers shaped the city's future. John, who became the wealthiest, sent the first Rhode Island ship to China in 1787, while completing the mansion that now stands at 52 Power Street. He was a shrewd, aggressive merchant who made his first fortune through slave trading and privateering. John's brother Joseph was an engineer, an amateur astronomer, and an architect who designed several of the city's best-known buildings, including the First Baptist Meeting House, the Market House, and John Brown's mansion. Nicholas Brown, the oldest of the four brothers, guided the family businesses and was influential in establishing Rhode Island College, later known as Brown University. Moses Brown, the youngest brother, became a Quaker; he was a pacifist during the Revolution, and he actively opposed the slave trade. Moses did something else worth noting: With his son-in-law, William Almy, and Samuel Slater, Moses Brown established America's first successful cotton textile mill, in Pawtucket in 1790.

A visit to the John Brown mansion introduces the four remarkable Brown brothers—"Nick, Joe, John, and Moe"—and the remarkable times in which they lived. Inside the John Brown mansion is a collection of Brown family furniture, Chinese export ware, fine glass, and silver. The mansion is maintained by the Rhode Island Historical Society.

The Waterfront

Follow Power Street downhill to South Main Street. During the 1700s and early 1800s, this section of the waterfront was one of the busiest places in Rhode Island. Today old warehouses have been transformed into attractive shops and restaurants. Turn right on South Main Street and walk back toward the center of Providence. Pause for a moment at Old Stone Square. The recently restored Old Stone Bank building, at 86 South Main Street, was built in 1898. Architect Joseph Brown lived at 50 South Main Street.

Ahead, near the county courthouse, is the old Market House, another building designed by Joseph Brown. This was the marketplace where Providence people gathered during colonial times in order to buy country produce and to hear the latest news and gossip. A visitor to Market Square during the 1770s might have seen John Brown's sloop, the *Katy,* at anchor in the Providence River. When the Continental Congress, pressured by Stephen Hopkins, moved to establish an American navy, the *Katy,* renamed the *Providence,* became the navy's first ship. Stephen's brother Esek became the navy's first commander. A modern replica of the *Providence* still sails on Narragansett Bay, often appearing at Providence and Newport for waterfront festivals.

From Market Square you may wish to cross the Providence River in order to explore part of downtown Providence. Follow Westminster Street past the Hospital Trust Building, through the Providence financial district, to the Providence Arcade, at 130 Westminster Street.

Built in 1828, the Arcade is America's first indoor shopping mall. Shoppers still walk along the Arcade's different levels, admiring shop displays and pausing to make purchases. If you want to know where Americans first discovered mall shopping, this is the place to be. Beyond the Arcade there's very little to see in what was once a vibrant downtown shopping area. The new, easy-to-reach malls in Warwick and Cranston have taken merchants and customers out of the city and into the suburbs.

Returning to the Market House on the East Side, follow South Main Street until it becomes North Main Street. You'll recognize the First Baptist Meeting House and other sites that you saw earlier in the day. An easy climb up Smith Hill will take you back to the State House.

Theater and Shopping

Several other attractions in the Providence area may interest visitors. A large arched gateway over Atwells Avenue, with a bronze Italian *pigna* (pine cone) at its apex, marks the beginning of Providence's Little Italy, a friendly neighborhood with Italian restaurants, shops, and sidewalk cafes. At the corner of Point Street and Eddy Street in Providence, the old Davol Rubber Company factory has been restored as Davol Square, a marketplace with shops, kiosks, and eateries.

Driving north from Providence on I–95, look for Exit 28 and the signs that point the way to the Slater Mill Historic Site on Pawtucket's Roosevelt Avenue. The old Slater Mill was one of America's first textile mills. Visit the mill and you'll learn about the Industrial Revolution of the early 1800s and what it meant to New England families. The Children's Museum of Rhode Island, at 58 Walcott Street in Pawtucket, not far from the Slater Mill area, may also fascinate young travelers, and the Pitcher-Goff mansion, which houses the museum, may interest their parents and grandparents. The mansion was built in 1840 for Ellis B. Pitcher, a wealthy textile manufacturer. This portion of Pawtucket, where the mill owners lived, was known as Quality Hill. Quality Hill and the Slater Mill complex together help to tell the story of life in nineteenth-century Rhode Island.

Back in Providence, there are cultural delights for all tastes. The nationally known Trinity Square Repertory Company, at the restored Lederer Theatre, 201 Washington Street in Providence, draws theatergoers from all of southern New England. The Providence Performing Arts Center, at 220 Weybosset Street, offers Broadway shows, classical music, and dance. At the Providence Civic Center, 1 LaSalle Square, the aisles shake with the excitement of rock concerts, ice shows, professional sports, and other popular attractions. Check the *Providence Journal* for information on what's currently in town.

The College Hill area is an East Side neighborhood dominated by Brown University and the Rhode Island School of Design, and a stroll along Thayer Street will acquaint you with what's current in clothing, music, and literature on campus. The Wickendon and Thayer streets bookstores are a source of the writings of Howard Philips Lovecraft, the fantasy writer of the 1920s and 1930s, who lived nearby.

At the moment, Providence is going through an urban rebirth. The downtown parking lots that span the Providence River—once described as the widest bridge in the world—are being removed in order to provide Providence with an attractive waterfront. The new Capitol Center development, near the State House, will help to extend the downtown area beyond Kennedy Plaza. Commuter rail service has been restored between Providence and Boston and is appreciated by both commuters and daytrippers. Providence may never be one of America's largest cities, but, for quality of life, Rhode Island's state capital stands among the best.

PRACTICAL INFORMATION FOR PROVIDENCE

Note: The area code for all Rhode Island is 401

HOW TO GET THERE. By plane: The Theodore Francis Green State Airport, in Warwick, is 9 mi. south of Providence by I-95. This is the second largest commercial airport in New England. Served by American Airlines, Eastern Airlines, Piedmont, Ransome, United, and several small local airlines. Flight time from New York City is about 45 min. Limousine and Bonanza Bus Lines service available to downtown Providence.

By train: Providence is served by Amtrak. From New York City, the train trip is about 4 hours; 1 hour from Boston. Commuter rail service from Providence to Boston, less expensive than regular Amtrak service, is available weekdays from Union Station, 100 Gaspee St. (751–5416).

By bus: Greyhound (751–8800); and Bonanza (751–8800, also.) The Rhode Island Public Transit Authority (781–9400 in Providence or 800–662–5088) provides service to many points, including Newport.

By car: From New York or Boston, the quickest way to Providence is via the New England Thruway (I-95). Rte. I-195 connects Providence to New Bedford and Cape Cod.

HOW TO GET AROUND. From the airport: The Theodore Francis Green State Airport, 9 mi. from downtown Providence, has Bonanza Bus Lines, taxi, and airport limousine service to provide visitors with easy access to the city. The Providence bus depot is at 1 Sabin St.

By car: Overnight parking is not allowed on Providence streets. Use your motel parking lot or a public garage for overnight parking.

Car rentals: Automobile rental agencies with airport and downtown offices include Avis (738–5800 or 800–331–1212); Budget (751–5400 or 739–8908); Hertz (738–7500 or 274–9600); National (861–6500 or 737–4800); and Sears (739–0487).

Public transportation: The Rhode Island Public Transit Authority provides bus service in the Providence area (781–9400).

On foot: The East Side of Providence, although hilly, is popular with walkers. Information on walking tours, usually scheduled for the warm-weather months, is available from the Providence Preservation Society, 24 Meeting St. (831–7440).

HOTELS AND MOTELS. Accommodations in the Providence area include airport motels, in Warwick, and representatives of well-known chains, close to Rte. I-95. The Omni Biltmore Hotel, near Kennedy Plaza, is the last of the city's "grand hotels," in the downtown area. Price ranges are based on double occupancy: *Deluxe,* $100 and up; *Expensive,* $60-$100; *Moderate,* $45-$60. All listings include the European Plan.

Pawtucket

Howard Johnson Motor Lodge, 2 George St., 02860 (723-6700 or 800-654-2000). *Moderate.* Large, comfortable motel, close to Exit 27 on I-95. Near Slater's Mill National Historic Site. Restaurant. Pool. Sauna. No pets.

Providence

Omni Biltmore Hotel, Kennedy Plaza, 02903 (421-0700 or 800-843-6664). *Deluxe.* Large, nicely renovated hotel in downtown area, one of the major hotels in southern New England. Take Exit 21 from I-95. Free garage parking. Suites. Convention facilities. Restaurant and cafe. Health club. Weekend packages available.

Holiday Inn, 21 Atwells Ave., 02903 (831-3900 or 800-465-4329). *Moderate.* High-rise motel, close to Exit 21 on I-95. Near Providence Civic Center. Free garage parking. Meeting rooms. Restaurant. Free airport limousine.

Marriott Inn, Charles and Orms Sts., 02904 (272-2400 or 800-228-9290). *Moderate.* In-town resort motel, near Exit 23 on I-95. Near State House and state government offices. Indoor and outdoor pools. Saunas. Suites. Convention facilities. Restaurant. Weekend packages available.

Seekonk

Johnson and Wales Inn, 217 Taunton Ave., 02771 (508-336-8700). *Moderate.* Resort motel, near jct. of Rtes. 114A and 44 in Massachusetts. Service provided by students from Johnson and Wales College. A nice discovery, moderately priced. Near Providence in suburban area. Suites. Convention facilities. Resort facilities include golf, tennis, jogging trail, pools, and indoor fitness center. Restaurant. Complimentary breakfasts for guests.

Warwick

Howard Johnson Motor Lodge, 20 Jefferson Blvd., 02886 (467-9800 or 800-654-2000). *Moderate.* Large motel close to airport and highway, near Exit 15 on I-95. Pool. 24-hour restaurant. No pets.

Sheraton Airport Inn, 1850 Post Rd., 02886 (738-4000 or 800-325-3535). *Moderate.* Airport motel. Take Exit 13 off I-95. Indoor pool. Saunas. Meeting rooms. Free airport transportation.

Susse Chalet Inn, 36 Jefferson Blvd., 02886 (941-6600 or 800-258-1980). *Moderate.* Near airport. Take Exit 15 off I-95. Less elaborate, less expensive than other airport motels. Near restaurants. No pets.

INNS, GUEST HOUSES, BED AND BREAKFASTS. The Providence area, surprisingly, offers comparatively little in the way of bed-and-breakfast accommodations. Doubtless, the situation will improve. For information on what is currently available, contact Bed and Breakfast of Rhode Island, Inc., Box 3291, Newport 02840 (849–1298). The following inns are *moderately priced.*

Attleboro

Colonel Blackington Inn, 203 N. Main St., Attleboro, MA 02703 (508–222–6022). 16 rooms in Victorian home, most with private baths. Full breakfast. Afternoon tea. No smoking in dining room.

Providence

The Old Court, 144 Benefit St., 02903 (751–2002). Episcopal Church rectory, built in 1863, converted into luxury bed and breakfast. 10 rooms, each with private bath and telephone. Nice location on historic East Side, close to the Rhode Island School of Design's art museum and Brown University.

RESTAURANTS. Providence has a fine mix of ethnic traditions—Italian, Portugese, Chinese, Greek, and more—and some of the city's finest restaurants were established by immigrant families. Atwells Ave., on Federal Hill, has a good selection of Italian restaurants. Davol Sq. and the Arcade both offer a nice mix of cafes, snack bars, and more formal eating establishments. Along N. Main St. and S. Main St. and up on the East Side near Brown University are places that are popular with students and young professionals. Price ranges for local restaurants are as follows: *Deluxe,* $25 and up; *Expensive,* $18–$25; *Moderate,* $10–$18; and *Inexpensive,* $10 or under. These prices are per person, excluding beverage, tax, and tip.

American

Beau James, 1075 N. Main St. (751–8220). *Expensive.* Soft candlelight and freshly cut flowers. Nice but not too formal. Steaks, lobsters. Deli-style sandwiches. Lunches and dinners.

Chef & Apprentices, 1150 Narragansett Blvd., in Cranston (467–8025). *Moderate.* Fine dining.

Shepards, 80 Washington St. (351–7770). *Moderate.* Elegant restaurant in the downtown area. Fresh pasta, charcoal-grilled steaks, sauteed veal. Lunches and dinners.

Winkler's Steak House, 63 Washington St. (521–4626). *Moderate.* Steaks and chops. Candlelight dining. Always courteous.

Haven Brothers Diner, corner of Fulton and Dorrance Sts. near Kennedy Plaza (861–7777). *Inexpensive.* This venerable diner—known to some as "the aluminium room"—has been serving late-night chow to Rhode Islanders for decades. Don't look for the diner during the day, since it's not pulled into its parking spot until suppertime.

Chinese

Bean Sprouts Oriental Cafe, 11 S. Angell St., Wayland Sq. (861–0097). *Moderate.* Popular Chinese dishes and specialties from Thailand and the Phillipines. Attractive restaurant near East Side shopping area. Lunches and dinners.

The China Inn, 65 Weybosset St. (331–1717). *Inexpensive.* Chinese fast food. One of several small restaurants at the Arcade; close to the business district.

Continental

La France, 960 Hope St. (331–9233). *Expensive.* Small, elegant French restaurant on the East Side. Reservations recommended.

Pot au Feu, 44 Custom House St. (273–8953). *Expensive.* One of Rhode Island's best. Sophisticated excellent cuisine. Attractive decor. Close to the Providence financial district. Worth a special trip into Providence.

Italian

Al Forno, 7 Steeple St. (273–9760). *Expensive.* Stylish, intimate. One of the city's best.

Camille's Roman Garden, 71 Bradford St. (751–4812). *Expensive.* The Atwells Ave. area has many fine Italian restaurants, but Camille's is among the very best. A bit formal. Reservations encouraged.

Angelo's Civita Farnese, 141 Atwells Ave. (621–8171). *Moderate.* Family-style Italian dining, with generous servings. Informal.

Seafood

Bluepoint Oyster Bar, 99 N. Main St. (272–6145). *Expensive.* Popular gathering place after business hours. Good drinks and an impressive menu.

Rusty Scupper, 530 N. Main St. (831–5120). *Moderate.* Seafood and steaks. Reservations encouraged.

Hemenway's Seafood Grill, 1 Old Stone Sq. (351–8570). *Moderate.* Grilled and broiled seafood—everything from cod and halibut to Norwegian salmon and Mako shark. Semiformal. Located off S. Main St.

Specialty

Amara's, 63 Warren Ave., East Providence (434–9506). *Moderate.* Natural foods restaurant, across the Seekonk River in East Providence. Vegetarian specialties, chicken and fish. Informal.

The Cafe at Brooke's, 244 Wickenden St. (521–6445). *Moderate.* An attractive East Side cafe, with a full luncheon and dinner menu.

New Japan, 145 Washington St. (351–0300). *Moderate.* Located near the Trinity Sq. Repertory Company and the downtown area. A small, very popular Japanese restaurant. Informal. Reservations a must.

La Serre, 182 Angell St. (331–3312). *Moderate.* Prize-winning pasta and other pleasures.

Shalimar, 303 S. Main St. (274–1703). *Moderate.* Indian and Pakistani specialties.

Murphy's Delicatessen, 55 Union St. (621–8467). *Inexpensive.* A delicatessen named Murphy's? This one offers hefty sandwiches, coffee, pie. Near the Biltmore Plaza Hotel.

TOURIST INFORMATION. If you're planning a trip to Providence, contact the Greater Providence Convention and Visitors Bureau, 30 Exchange Terrace, Providence 02903 (274–1636), or the Rhode Island Department of Economic Development, 7 Jackson Walkway, 02903 (277–2601). For the Pawtucket and Woonsocket areas, contact the Blackstone Valley Tourism Council, Box 7663, Cumberland 02864 (722–1839). For Warwick, the Warwick Chamber of Commerce, 3280 Post Rd., Warwick 02886 (732–1100). Once you've arrived in the area, stop by the Convention and Visitors Bureau offices, off Kennedy Plaza, or the Roger Williams National Memorial, at the corner of N. Main and Smith Sts., for more information on what's happening in the Providence area. The *Providence Journal* and the *Evening Bulletin*—Rhode Island's largest daily newspapers—provide up-to-date information on local sports, movies, and cultural events. The Friday paper has a weekend calendar of events.

TOURS. For a do-it-yourself orientation of the city, hop on and off the local trolleys, which loop around central Providence on weekdays, 11 A.M.–2 P.M. (467–8844).

From May until Oct., the **Providence Preservation Society** offers free tours of the historic East Side. The self-guided cassette walking tours last 90 minutes. Groups should make advance reservations. The society's offices are located at 24 Meeting St. (831–7440).

Scenic rail excursions in southern New England are provided by the Providence and Worcester Railroad. Write Box 1188, Worcester, MA 01601.

Intrepid travelers may wish to go aloft with **Stumf Balloons.** Special champagne and fall-foliage flights can be arranged. Write Box 1143, Providence 02901. In Bristol call 253–0111.

Netop Tours in Cranston (781–9370) offers morning and afternoon tours of Providence, Mon., Wed., and Fri. year-round; pickup from major hotels.

SEASONAL EVENTS. For detailed information on seasonal events in Rhode Island, contact Tourist Promotion Division, Rhode Island Department of Economic Development, 7 Jackson Walkway, Providence 02903 (277–2601). For the Providence area, there are several annual events worth noting.

March: Ireland's St. Patrick's Day is celebrated on Mar. 17. A St. Patrick's Day parade is usually scheduled for the Smith Hill area, in Providence, for the preceding weekend. Italy's St. Joseph's Day takes place on Mar. 19. Festivities along Atwells Ave. on Federal Hill.

May: Rhode Island Independence Day—the day when Rhode Island disavowed its allegiance to King George III—is celebrated on May 4. All May is Rhode Island Heritage Month. The Providence Preservation Society sponsors an annual Festival of Historic Homes early in May. May breakfasts, scheduled throughout the month, are held by churches, yacht clubs, and social organizations. Check local newspapers for schedules.

June: Gaspee Days in Warwick commemorate the burning of HMS *Gaspee* in 1772. Parades, feasts, entertainment, with celebrations spread over several weekends.

July: Providence Fourth of July celebration in Roger Williams Park. Fireworks and holiday attractions at Rocky Point Amusement Park, off Rte. 117, Warwick Neck.

September: Annual Heritage Festival, late in Sept., on State House lawn, presents ethnic music, dance, food, art, and crafts. Many nations represented.

October: Columbus Day is a major holiday in Providence. The Scituate Art Festival in N. Scituate, in mid-Oct., is one of the state's largest and best antiques and crafts exhibits.

December: Special holiday activities in Providence and at the Slater Mill Historic Site in Pawtucket. First Night Providence, Dec. 31, is a family-oriented, citywide celebration of New Year's Eve. Music, art, dance, parades, and fireworks.

PARKS AND FORESTS. Visitors can depart from downtown Providence and be in a pleasant wooded area—north, south, or west of the city—in about 20 minutes. Several of the Providence-area parks deserve special mention.

Lincoln Woods State Park, in Lincoln, is one of Rhode Island's most popular state parks. Excellent freshwater swimming. Miles of hiking trails wind through the oak woods bordering Olney Pond. Take exit 9 from I–95 and follow Rte. 146 south to Cobble Hill Road.

Pulaski Memorial State Park, in Glocester, also offers hiking and fresh-water swimming. Take Rte. 44 (Putnam Pike) to within half a mile of the Connecticut border.

Diamond Hill State Park, in Cumberland, on Rte. 114, is one of the few ski areas in Rhode Island. The long hill that forms the park includes a mile-long vein of quartz.

Goddard Park, about a mile from East Greenwich, on Ives Rd., off Forge Rd., is a 470-acre state park with saltwater swimming, stables, and a public golf course.

Blackstone Valley State Park encompasses a corridor of land from Worcester, Mass., to Providence that is brand new and great for biking. Contact the Blackstone Valley Tourism Council, Box 7663, Cumberland 02864 (722–1839).

MUNICIPAL PARKS. Roger Williams Park, the major city park for Providence, is located on Elmwood Ave. This is a nice destination for an afternoon's expedition. Within the park are the **Betsy Williams Cottage,** built in 1773; the **Temple of Music,** famous for summer concerts; the **Park Museum of Natural History** and its planetarium; and the **Roger Williams Park Zoo,** one of the largest zoos in New England. There's plenty of room for children to run and play. Bring a picnic lunch and have a family cele-bration.

SUMMER SPORTS. Swimming: For saltwater swimming and clean beaches, head for South County, the Newport area, or the Sakonnet lands. All are easily accessible from the Providence area. For freshwater swim-ming, try Olney Pond, in Lincoln Woods State Park, in Lincoln; Gorton's Pond, in Warwick; or Twin Rivers Beach, in North Providence.

Golf: Public golf courses near Providence include the Cranston Country Club, 69 Burlingame Rd., Cranston; the East Greenwich Golf Course, 1646 Division Rd., East Greenwich; the Foster Country Club, Foster Rd., Foster; and the Midville Country Club, Lombardi Lane, in West Warwick.

Tennis: Tennis clubs in the Providence area include the Centre Court Tennis Club, 55 Hospital Rd., East Providence; the Fore Court Tennis Club, with indoor courts at 4 Court Dr., Lincoln, and at 44 Cray St., Cum-berland; and Tennis Rhode Island, Inc., with courts at 70 Boyd Ave., East Providence, and at 636 Centervale Rd., Warwick. All these privately man-aged clubs are open to the public.

SPECTATOR SPORTS. Brown University, Providence College, and the University of Rhode Island actively compete in intercollegiate football, basketball, and hockey. Check the Providence dailies for details.

The New England Patriots football team uses Bryant College, Smith-field, for summer practice (232–6070).

The Pawtucket Red Sox—the farm team for the Boston Red Sox—play AAA International League baseball at McCoy Stadium, Pawtucket, from mid-Apr.–early Sept. (724–7303).

The pups run at the Lincoln Downs Greyhound Park, Rte. 246, Lincoln (723–3200).

HISTORIC SITES AND HOMES. Throughout this part of Rhode Is-land, you'll be able to see historic buildings that have been carefully preserved. Many of these buildings are open to the public, and several charge admission.

Coventry

General Nathanael Greene Homestead, 50 Taft St., off Rte. 117 (821–8630). Nathanel Greene was Washington's second-in-command during the American Revolution. He was a capable strategist who helped guide American forces to victory in the South, 1780–81. Built by General Greene in 1774, this simple farmhouse has been preserved as a memorial honoring Rhode Island's best-known military hero. The Greene house is open Wed., Sat., and Sun., Mar.–Nov.

Cranston

Governor Sprague Mansion, 1353 Cranston St. (944–9226). Built in 1790 and enlarged in 1864, this splendid mansion was the home of the Sprague family, one of the wealthiest of Rhode Island's industrial families during the 1800s. Governor William Sprague is portrayed in Gore Vidal's novel *Lincoln*. The mansion is open Sun. 2–4 P.M., July–Labor Day, and by appointment.

East Greenwich

General James Mitchell Varnum House, 57 Peirce St. (884–4110). East Greenwich is an old seaport with many interesting homes from the 1700s and early 1800s. The Varnum house, built in 1773, was the home of James Mitchell Varnum, a brigadier general in the American army during the American Revolution. The house is open afternoons, Mon.–Sat., in July and Aug.

Providence

First Baptist Meeting House, 75 N. Main St. (751–2266). The First Baptist Church in America, founded by Roger Williams in 1638. The present church structure was built in 1774–75. Free guided tours are provided by volunteers, Mon.–Fri., 10 A.M.–3 P.M., Sat., 10 A.M.–noon., Apr.–Oct. Sun. tours are offered at 10:30 A.M. in summer, at noon in winter.

Roger Williams Memorial, Prospect Terrace, off Congdon St. Small East Side park with panoramic view of Providence. Roger Williams is buried here.

Roger Williams National Memorial Park, N. Main St. (528–5385). Small park and visitors' reception area, maintained by the National Park Service. Site of the first Providence settlement, in 1636. Open Mon.–Fri., Nov.–Apr. Open weekdays and summer weekends. Parking. Visitor information. Rest rooms. A nice place to begin your tour of Providence.

Governor Stephen Hopkins House, 10 Hopkins St., off Benefit St. (421–0694). Modest home of Stephen Hopkins, a prominent Rhode Island statesman of the colonial era who signed the Declaration of Independence. Open Wed. and Sat., 1–4 P.M., Apr.–Dec.

John Brown House, 52 Power St., off Benefit St. (331–8575). Built in 1785–86; restored and maintained by the Rhode Island Historical Society. One of the most impressive of America's 18th-century mansions. John Brown was a wealthy China trade merchant, slave trader, and privateer. Open Tues.–Sat., 11 A.M.–4 P.M.; Sun., 1–4 P.M. Closed weekdays during Jan. and Feb. Guided tour takes approximately one hour and includes a slide presentation on life in Providence during the 1700s.

The Old State House, 150 Benefit St. (277–2678). Built in 1762. Open weekdays. It was here that the General Assembly of Rhode Island renounced its allegiance to King George III of Great Britain on May 4, 1776, 2 months prior to the Declaration of Independence. The Old State House now houses the offices of the Rhode Island Historic Preservation Commission. Open weekdays.

The State House, Smith St. (277–2311). Rhode Island's "new" state capitol—first occupied in 1900—is a handsome building that overlooks Providence and I–95. Built of white Georgia marble, the State House was designed by the New York firm of McKim, Mead, and White. Visitors welcome. Tours are conducted Mon.–Fri., 9:30 A.M.–3:30 P.M.

Providence City Hall, Kennedy Plaza (421–7740). Completed in 1878. Designed in the manner of the Louvre and Tuileries in Paris. Tours 8:30 A.M.–4:30 P.M.

Sullivan Dorr House, 109 Benefit St. An elegant Federal mansion, built in 1809, that was the boyhood home of Thomas Wilson Dorr, the populist leader of the 1840s. Dorr and his associates fought to expand suffrage in Rhode Island so that landless men could enjoy the right to vote. Private home.

Old Market House, Market Sq. The center of commercial and civic life in Providence during the late 1700s. Designed by Joseph Brown, with assistance from Stephen Hopkins. Opened in 1775. Owned by the Rhode Island School of Design.

The Arcade, 133 Westminster St. (456–5403). Connects Westminster St. to Weybosset St. America's first indoor shopping mall. Built in 1828. A nice place for shopping or lunch.

MUSEUMS AND GALLERIES. Most of the major museums in the Providence area are open throughout the year. The *Providence Journal* and the *Evening Bulletin* can provide you with information on current exhibits and special programs. Call ahead for admission fees.

Pawtucket

Children's Museum of Rhode Island, 58 Walcott St. (726–2591). Hands-on museum with exhibits that encourage curiosity, imagination, and discovery. From Sept. to June, the museum is open on Sun., Wed., and Thurs., 1–5 P.M.; and on Fri. and Sat., 10 A.M.–5 P.M. In July and Aug., the museum is open to the public Tues.–Sat., 10 A.M.–5 P.M.; and Sun., 1–5 P.M.

Providence

Museum of Art of the Rhode Island School of Design, 224 Benefit St. (331–3511). One of the finest of America's mid-sized art museums. A permanent collection of 60,000 works in 45 galleries. Highlights include treasures from ancient Egypt, Greece, and Rome; oriental art; and a collection of French art, with works by Picasso, Degas, Manet, Matisse, and Cézanne. American furniture and decorative arts are on display in the Pendleton House, the museum's "American Wing." Winter hours: Tues., Wed., Fri., and Sat., 10:30 A.M.–5 P.M.; Thurs., 1–9 P.M.; Sun. and holidays, 2–5 P.M. Summer hours: Wed.–Sat., 11 A.M.–4 P.M.

Woods-Gerry Gallery, 62 Prospect St. (331–3511). Small gallery featuring new works by students and faculty of the Rhode Island School of Design. Exhibits change weekly. Open Mon., Tues., Thurs., Fri., and Sat., 11 A.M.–4 P.M.; and Sun., 2–5 P.M.

Bell Gallery, 64 College St. (863–2421). Part of Brown University's List Art Center. Exhibits vary, but Brown faculty and students are often featured. Open during the school year. Weekdays, 11 A.M.–4 P.M.; weekends, 1–4 P.M.

Providence Art Club, 11 Thomas St. (334–1114). Specializes in Rhode Island artists. Exhibits change every 2 weeks. Open Mon.–Sat., 10 A.M.–4 P.M.; Sun., 3–5 P.M.

Rhode Island Historical Society, 110 Benevolent St. (331–8575). Exhibits and educational programs on Rhode Island history. The Rhode Island Historical Society is one of the nation's oldest historical societies. Open Mon.–Sat., 11 A.M.–4 P.M.; Sun., 1–4 P.M.

Museum of Natural History, Roger Williams Park, Elmwood Ave. (785–9450). Small Victorian-era museum with exhibits on natural and social history. Planetarium. Open Sat., 8:30 A.M.–4:30 P.M.; Sun., 2–5 P.M.

MUSIC, DANCE, AND STAGE. Providence is a lively city throughout the year. On most weekends, the city offers concerts and shows to satisfy a variety of tastes.

The **Trinity Square Repertory Company,** 201 Washington St. (351–4242), offers an impressive mix of classic and contemporary plays at affordable ticket prices. A fine dinner in Providence and tickets for two at the Trinity Rep cost less than you would expect to pay for an evening's entertainment in Boston or New York.

The **Providence Performing Arts Center,** 220 Weybosset St. (421–2787), is one of New England's great movie palaces that has kept all its rococo splendor. The arts center offers Broadway shows, concerts, comedy, and dance. The Festival Ballet of Rhode Island and the Rhode Island Philharmonic are often featured.

The **Providence Civic Center,** 1 LaSalle Sq. (331–6700), is for rock concerts, exhibitions, and ice shows. When circus wagons come to Providence, they usually head for the Civic Center. Easy access from Exit 21 on I–95.

Good theater on a small scale can be found at several places in Providence. Consider **The Players,** Barker Playhouse, 400 Benefit St. (421–2855); **Brown University Theater,** at three stages (863–2838); **Rhode Island College Theatre,** Roberts Hall, 600 Pleasant Ave. (456–8144).

The **Great Woods Center for the Performing Arts,** in Mansfield, Mass., is only a 20-minute drive from Providence, traveling north on Rte. I–95. The Great Woods Center offers summer programs ranging from classical music to jazz, folk, rock, and dance. For information write Great Woods Center, Box 810, Mansfield, MA 02048 or call 508–339–2333.

SHOPPING. The department stores that once dominated downtown Providence trade have either closed or moved to the large malls in Warwick. A few areas in Providence, however, are still worth exploring if you're in search of specialty items.

On Atwells Ave., Federal Hill, Italian grocers can provide you with fresh pasta, crusty bread, spices, and virgin olive oil.

The Arcade, 130 Westminster St. is a three-tiered indoor shopping mall, beautifully restored, where shoppers have been making history since 1828.

Davol Sq. Marketplace, at Point and Eddy Sts., is a 19th-century factory converted into a new home for stores, offices, and pushcarts. Shops include Talbots and Laura Ashley.

Wickenden St. on the East Side has antique shops, art galleries, and second-hand book dealers. Part of the East Side's Fox Point district. Thayer St. on the East Side is a six-block retail area, serving students of Brown University and the Rhode Island School of Design with bookstores and clothing and record shops. And Wayland Sq. is a fashionable shopping district on the East Side's eastern side.

Factory outlet stores in the Pawtucket area offer good buys on items such as coats, curtains, braided rugs, and sweaters. For further information, contact Blackstone Valley Factory Outlet Association, Box 1627, Pawtucket 02862.

NIGHTLIFE. Providence is a college town, a white-collar town, and a town where different ethnic groups come together, so it has a bit of everything.

Nightclubs—**Sh-Booms,** 108 N. Main St. (751–1200). '50s and '60s rock 'n' roll dance club.

Muldoon's Saloon, 250 S. Water St. (331–7523). Irish bar with Irish music.

Bars— **L'Elizabeth's,** 285 S. Main St. (621–9113). Elegant, romantic bar. Relaxed.

Custom House Tavern, 36 Weybosset St. (751–3630). Candlelight, white tablecloths. Located in the financial district.

Players Corner Pub, 194 Washington St. (621–8738). Near the Trinity Rep. A friendly English pub that offers sing-along entertainment.

König-City Pub, 2 Davol Sq. (351–2040). German pub and restaurant at the Davol Sq. Marketplace.

SOUTH COUNTY

The salt water attracts most visitors to South County. From Watch Hill to Narragansett Pier, Rhode Island's southwestern shore is nearly one continuous beach, much of it open to the public. The settlement at Galilee, a commercial fishermen's place where the smell of nets and fuel hangs in the air, offers excellent seafood and opportunities to charter a boat to the Atlantic fishing grounds. At Point Judith you can admire an octagon-shaped lighthouse. A few miles north, the old port of Wickford, filled with quaint shops and seafarers' homes, is the town that inspired John Updike's novel *The Witches of Eastwick.*

South County—officially it's Washington County, but local people call it South County—is the most rural county in Rhode Island. Travelers who know that Rhode Island is one of the most urbanized states in the union are sometimes puzzled as they cross the Rhode Island state line on I–95 and drive north past rock ledges and trees. Venture into Hope Valley or Wood River Junction and you may think that you're in Maine or central New Hampshire.

Native Rhode Islanders may tell you that South County is "the real Rhode Island." This is the home of the Narragansett Indians, people whose families have been here for centuries. Inland, the South County region is covered with fields and forests, dotted with ponds and parks, crossed by hiking trails and rivers easy for canoeists. There are places in South County for freshwater and saltwater fishing and for shellfish gathering. Narragansett names like Quonochontaug and Pettaquamscutt may seem like tongue twisters, but they fit nicely the South County places that you may want to explore.

Along the Coast

Coastal South County can be seen along old Route 1 and along scenic Route 1A. Start at Watch Hill, a quiet Victorian resort, part of the town of Westerly. Watch Hill has been a seaside haven since 1840, when the local lighthouse keeper built the area's first beach hotel. The Watch Hill beach is still small, nicely managed, and popular with families. Near the beach, children can ride on the famous Flying Horse Carousel. No one knows for certain the age of the carousel—it may be the nation's oldest—but it was assembled in Watch Hill during the 1870s and it has delighted generations of young Americans.

From Watch Hill you may want to drive to Misquamicut State Beach. In contrast to the quiet Victorian streets of Watch Hill, Misquamicut in the summer may seem a bit boisterous. There's a fine state beach here, although the undertow is strong. Misquamicut also offers a small amusement park. If Misquamicut seems crowded, drive north along the coast. Route 1A merges with Route 1; continue on Route 1 as you enter Charlestown. Burlingame State Park, which is off Kings Factory Road, on your left, has excellent freshwater swimming at Watchaug Pond. When ocean beaches become crowded, Rhode Island families often retreat to Burlingame. On the coast, you may want to see the remains of old Fort Ninigret, south of Route 1, on Fort Neck Road. During the early 1600s, this was a Dutch outpost where New Amsterdam traders met with local Indians. The Dutch were in and out of Rhode Island during the 1630s, but the English won the territory.

The town of South Kingstown offers a series of excellent public beaches, not far from Route 1. From south to north, the major South Kingstown beaches are Green Hill Beach, Moonstone Beach, Roy Carpenter's Beach, A. B. Carpenter's Beach, Matunuck Beach, and East Matunuck State Beach. On a hot day in July or August, all these beaches are likely to be packed, so plan to arrive early if you want a parking spot and a place on the sand.

South County Plantations

Beyond South Kingstown is the town of Narragansett. If you want to visit the Galilee fishing village, exit from Route 1 and drive down Route 109 to Galilee Road. Turn right. If you continue on Route 108, the highway will merge into Ocean Road, which ends at the lighthouse at Point Judith. In fair weather you'll have a fine view of the sea. If you follow Ocean Road back along the shore, you'll pass through the Victorian resort of Narragansett Pier. At this point you've rejoined Route 1A. The twin arches spanning the highway, connected to curved stone towers, are all that remains of a large casino that burned in 1900. Along Narragansett's shores are several public beaches, notably Scarborough State Beach and Narragansett Beach.

Route 1A stays close to the shore as you cross from Narragansett into North Kingstown. The Silas Casey farm, north of Ferry Road, is a partially restored South County plantation with cattle, horses, sheep, and goats. The farm is maintained by the Society for the Preservation of New England Antiquities, one of the major historic preservation groups in New England. First developed between 1725 and 1750, the farm was typical of the Northern plantations that produced farm products for Newport merchants, who sold Rhode Island horses, meat, and corn to West Indian planters. Silas Casey, the farm's owner at the time of the Revolution, was a wealthy shipowner and coastal squire who followed Newport trade and fashions. Newport-made Queen Anne chairs and other colonial pieces have been preserved at the Casey home. The estate is open to the public from mid-June until mid-October.

Between Route 1A and Route 1, on Gilbert Stuart Road, is the birthplace of the artist. You already know Stuart's most famous work; think of George Washington and you'll probably imagine him as he appears in one of Gilbert Stuart's portraits. Born in 1755, Stuart began life as the son of a Scottish millwright who produced snuff from Rhode Island tobacco. The family business became unsuccessful, and in 1761 the Stuarts moved to Newport. What remains today of Stuart's birthplace is a lovely barn-red colonial home, furnished with antiques, that contains a restored snuff mill powered by a large waterwheel. The Stuart home is open to the public throughout most of the year.

Wickford and Cocumscussoc

Routes 1A and 1 both lead to Wickford, John Updike's Eastwick. Appropriately enough, the settlement was known as Updike's Newtown during the early 1700s, named for the landowner Lodowick Updike. There's a John Updike house in Wickford (not open to the public) that was built in 1745 by Lodowick's grandson. Modern Wickford has 20 or more homes dating back to colonial times, most of them on Main, West Main, and Pleasant streets. During the 1700s, the products of South County plantations were shipped from Wickford's small harbor to Newport's merchants. Today most of the boats in Wickford's harbor are pleasure craft, and shoppers stroll along Brown and Main streets, visiting small shops and galleries.

The U.S. Navy still has a base at Davisville at Quonset Point (yes, this is where the Quonset hut was developed), and further along on Route 1 you'll reach East Greenwich, another historic seaport on Narragansett Bay. But at East Greenwich you'll be out of South County, so we'll turn back at Quonset in order to note other South County sites.

A bit north of Wickford, off Route 1, is Smith's Castle at Cocumscussoc. The large garrison home on the property is as solid as a colonial fortress. In December 1675, this site was the meeting place for colonial troops sent against the Narragansett Indians. At the time, the Puritan colonies were locked in a bloody struggle with the Wampanoags, the Indians who dominated the eastern side of Narragansett Bay. Unable to defeat each other militarily, the two sides raided villages, burned crops, and harried noncombatants. The Narragansetts tried to remain outside the war but provided shelter to their Indian neighbors, and there were rumors that the Narragansetts might ally with the Wampanoags during the spring. In a surprise attack, troops from Massachusetts landed at the Smith plantation, then pressed inland through the snows in order to assault the Narragansetts in the principal Indian village. The battle that followed in the Great Swamp may have been the most brutal in New England history. Dozens of Narragansett women and children perished in the flames when their huts caught fire. The colonists, too, took severe losses, and their retreat back to Smith's plantation, after winning the battle, was a nightmare. Forty men were later buried in the "great grave" on the plantation's north lawn. The Smith home was burned by the Indians when the garrison withdrew, but the castle was rebuilt when King Philip's War ended. Today the home is open to the public for much of the year.

South Kingstown

Inland, off Route 2 in South Kingstown, the site of the Narragansetts' defeat is marked by a simple memorial. Modern Narragansetts live in nearby towns. In 1983, the Narragansetts became a federally recognized tribe. The tribe holds an August meeting each year in Charlestown, which the public may attend; the small Tomaquag Museum in Exeter, in the midst of the Arcadia Management Area, helps to interpret the Narragansett past to visitors.

Kingston village, at the junction of Route 138 and Route 108, is a quiet, rural settlement that preserves many fine homes from the eighteenth and nineteenth centuries. The main campus of the University of Rhode Island is here. In colonial times Kingston village was an inland trade center where South County plantation owners gathered. Rhode Island's plantations were modest by Southern standards, but a slave-owning aristocracy developed during the 1700s, and some planters became quite prosperous. Most Rhode Islanders, however, were uneasy with slavery in the years following the Revolution. Moses Brown of Providence joined with others in 1789 to establish the Providence Society for Abolishing the Slave Trade. By the early 1800s, slavery in Rhode Island had nearly ended. What remained were the great homes of the plantation era—Smith's Castle near Wickford, the Silas Casey estate, and others—together with tales of a rural way of life that seem to belong more to the South than to New England.

PRACTICAL INFORMATION FOR THE SOUTH COUNTY

Note: The area code for all Rhode Island is 401

HOW TO GET THERE AND AROUND. By plane: The Theodore Francis Green Airport, in Warwick, is Rhode Island's major airport and is served by American, Eastern, Piedmont, United, and several small local airlines.

By train: Amtrak provides rail service for Kingston, Westerly, and East Greenwich (751–5416 or 800–872–7245).

By bus: The Rhode Island Public Transit Authority provides limited commuter service between Westerly and Kingston and Providence (781–9400).

By car: South County is easily accessible from I-95. Exit 1 and Rte. 3 lead to Westerly. Exit 3A leads to Rte. 138, the principle route to Kingston, North Kingstown, and Newport. Rte. 1 and Rte. 1A follow the coast, close to South County beaches. The coastal routes are the scenic routes, poking around and through old South County towns.

It's easy to become disoriented on South County's rural roads, so ask for a Rhode Island map at one of the regional information centers before exploring unfamiliar areas. Maps and travel literature can also be obtained from Tourism Division, Rhode Island Department of Economic Development, 7 Jackson Walkway, Providence 02903 (277–2601 or 800–556–2484). South County is divided by I-95, with most of the larger towns south and east of the highway. The village of Kingston—part of South Kingstown—and the village of Wickford—part of North Kingstown—are two of South County's early settlements. Galilee is an active fishing port, part of the town of Narragansett. Wakefield is the commercial center for South Kingstown and for much of South County. Saunderstown is the coastal settlement in the southern portion of North Kingstown, along Rte. 1A.

HOTELS AND MOTELS. Motels in southwestern Rhode Island are usually located near the major centers of population: Westerly, Wakefield, Narragansett, and the Wickford area. Price ranges are based on double occupancy and European plan arrangements, except as noted: *Deluxe*, $100 and up; *Expensive*, $60–$100; *Moderate*, $45–$60; *Inexpensive*, under $45.

Charlestown

The Willows Lodge, Box 1260, Charlestown 02813 (364–7727). *Moderate*. On Rte. 1. Pool. Rental boats. Boat ramp and dock. Tennis. Shuttle service to beaches. Open mid-May–Oct.

Kingstown Area

Admiral Dewey Inn, 668 Matunuck Beach Rd., South Kingstown 02874 (783–2090). *Expensive*. Victorian decor. All rooms with private bath. Continental breakfast.

Cove Motel, 7835 Post Rd., North Kingstown 02852 (294–4888). *Moderate*. On Rte. 1. A small resort. Pool. Restaurant. Open year-round.

Quality Inn, Tower Hill Rd., South Kingstown 02874 (789–1051). *Moderate*. Near jct. of Rte. 1 and Rte. 138. Near beaches, fishing. Convenient to University of Rhode Island. Restaurant. Open year-round.

Kingstown Motel, 6530 Post Rd., North Kingstown 02852 (884–1160). *Moderate*. On Rte. 1. Near Wickford village. Open year-round.

Larchwood Inn, 521 Main St., South Kingstown 02879 (783–5454). *Moderate*. A comfortable and attractive inn that was once a country mansion. Restaurant. Open year-round.

Bob Bean Motel, 600 Boston Neck Rd., North Kingstown 02852 (294–2411). *Inexpensive*. On Rte. 1A. Comfortable motel near beaches, scenic attractions. Open year-round.

Narragansett

Dutch Inn Motel, Great Island Rd., 02882 (789–9341). *Expensive*. In Galilee. Convenient to Block Island ferry, beaches, charter boats. Indoor pool. Tennis courts. Restaurant. Open year-round.

Stone Lea, Newton Ave., 02882 (783–9546). *Expensive*. Bed and breakfast with 9 rooms, a mile from the pier. The front lawn reaches to the water.

Atlantic Motor Inn, 85 Ocean Rd., Narragansett Pier 02882 (783–5534). *Moderate*. Modern motel. Open year-round.

Watch Hill

Ocean House, 2 Bluff Ave., 02891 (348–8161). *Expensive*. One of the grand hotels that made Watch Hill famous as a resort. Built in the 1860s. 59 rooms. Private ocean beach. Open July 1–Labor Day.

Watch Hill Inn, 50 Bay St., 02891 (348–8912). *Expensive*. 16-room inn overlooking Little Narragansett Bay. Near shops, beaches. Year-round.

Westerly

Breezeway, 70 Winnapaug Rd., 02891 (348–8953). *Moderate*. In Misquamicut. Near beach. Open mid-Apr.–Nov.

Pine Lodge, Rural Rte. 3, Box 562, Westerly 02891 (322–0333). *Moderate*. On Rte. 1. Weekly rates available. Open mid-June–mid-Sept.

Pony Barn Motel, Shore Rd., Westerly 02891 (348–8216). *Moderate.* Small motel. Pool. Pets. Open year-round.

INNS, GUEST HOUSES, BED AND BREAKFASTS. For information on bed-and-breakfast accommodations in Rhode Island, contact Bed and Breakfast of Rhode Island, Inc., Box 3291, Newport 02840 (849–1298). The following are *moderately* priced.

Narragansett

The Phoenix, 29 Gibson Ave., 02882 (783–1918). Five rooms, one with private bath, in attractive Victorian home.
Starr Cottage, 68 Caswell St., 02882 (783–2411). Four rooms with shared baths in large Victorian home.
The Summer House Inn, 87 Narragansett Ave., 02882 (783–0123). 24 rooms in large Victorian inn, most with private baths. Near beaches.

North Kingstown

The John Updike House, 19 Pleasant St., Wickford 02852 (294–4905). Two rooms with shared bath in restored colonial home. Located in historic area.

Wakefield

Highland Farm, Tower Hill Rd., 02879 (783–2408). Three rooms with shared baths in South County farmhouse.

Westerly

Inn on the Hill, 29 Summer St., 02891 (596–3791). Seven rooms with shared baths in restored Victorian home.
Sunny Rest Lodge, Shore Rd., 02891 (348–8637). 12 rooms, most with shared baths. Near beaches.
Woody Hill, RFD 3, Box 676E 02891 (322–0452). Four rooms with shared baths.

RESTAURANTS. Clambakes are to Rhode Island what barbecues are to Texas: hearty summertime feasts, prepared and eaten outdoors. Instead of chili, Rhode Islanders eat clam chowder—clams are known as "quahogs" in this part of the world—and, if you're fortunate, you'll be able to sample the different entries at a chowder contest. And, possibly, too, you'll be able to try Rhode Island's traditional johnny cakes. Johnny cakes are corn cakes prepared on a griddle. Eat them like pancakes with bacon or sausage and butter and syrup, or try them unadorned with meat or fish.

The price ranges for South County restaurants are as follows: *Deluxe,* $25 and up; *Expensive,* $18–$25; *Moderate,* $10–$18; and *Inexpensive,* $10 or under. These prices are based on cost per person, excluding beverage, tax, and tip.

Exeter

Dovecrest Restaurant, Summit Rd., in Arcadia (539–7795). *Inexpensive.* A Native American restaurant—with fresh fish, chowders, and johnny cakes—in the midst of Rhode Island's major wilderness area. Popular with hikers and canoeists.

Galilee

George's of Galilee, Great Island Rd. (783–2306). *Moderate.* Seafood restaurant in a working port. Open year-round.

Kenyon

Nordic Lodge, Off Rte. 2 (783–4515). *Expensive.* The lodge offers a bountiful smorgasbord, with lobsters, scallops, stuffed shrimp, prime ribs, and a good deal more. Closed Jan.–Mar.

Narragansett

Casa Rossi, 90 Point Judith Rd. (789–6385). *Moderate.* Italian dishes from the north and south.
Coast Guard House, 40 Ocean Blvd. (789–0700). *Moderate.* Ocean view. Continental menu. Reservations encouraged.
Spain Restaurant, 1 Beach St. at the Village Inn (783–9770). *Moderate.* Strictly Spanish cuisine.

North Kingstown

Red Rooster Tavern, 7385 Post Rd. (884–1987 or 295–8804). *Expensive.* Good country dinners, with fresh meat and fish. Excellent wine list.
The Canterbury Inn, 7511 Post Rd. (295–2707). *Moderate.* Prime ribs and lobsters. Sunday brunch.

Wakefield

Larchwood Inn, 521 Main St. (783–5454). *Moderate.* American cuisine in a country-inn setting.

Warwick

Rocky Point Park, Warwick Neck (737–8000). *Moderate.* The Rocky Point Amusement Park is outside South County—the park is 10 mi. south of Providence—but Rocky Point claims to have the world's largest shore dinner hall and it shouldn't be missed. Up to 3,000 eaters, at a sitting, feast on clams, lobsters, clam cakes, corn on the cob, and all the other ingredients that go into a true Rhode Island shore dinner. Open during the summer.

Watch Hill

Olympia Tea Room, 30 Bay St. (348–8211). *Moderate.* Charbroiled seafood lunches and dinners. Small and informal.
Watch Hill Inn, 50 Bay St. (348–8912). *Moderate.* Italian cuisine. Dancing Sat. nights.

Westerly

Shelter Harbor Inn, Post Rd., east of Westerly (322–8883). *Moderate.* New England fare. Open year-round.
Villa Trombino Restaurant, Route 3 (596–3444). *Moderate.* Italian specialties.

TOURIST INFORMATION. During the summer months, the state of Rhode Island maintains a visitor information service, off I-95, just beyond the Connecticut state line. Year-round visitor information services are available in Westerly, at 159 Main St. (596–7761), and in North Kingstown, at 55 Brown St., in Wickford Village (295–5566). The Towers, the stone arches that span Rte. 1A (Ocean Rd.) in Narragansett, mark the site of a local Chamber of Commerce information office (783–7121).

PARKS AND FORESTS. All Rhode Island's public parks are open, without charge, throughout the year, although parking fees are required at popular sites during the summer.
  Burlingame State Park, off Rte. 1, in Charlestown (322–7337 or 322–7994). 2,100 acres. Freshwater swimming, camping, picnic areas. Boating and fishing on Watchaug Pond. Near ocean beaches.
  Great Swamp Management Area, access from Rte. 138, South Kingstown (789–0281). 3,000 acres. Undeveloped area. Access to the Great Swamp Fight historic site is from Rte. 2.

WILDLIFE REFUGES. The Rhode Island Audubon Society owns 39 wildlife refuges in Rhode Island and one in Massachusetts. Several are open to hikers and naturalists. For information: Rhode Island Audubon Society, 40 Bowen St., Providence 02903 (521–1670).
  Kimball Wildlife Refuge, off Rte. 1, in Charlestown, near Burlingame State Park (521–1670). 30 acres with trails. Nature programs. Open 8 A.M.–6 P.M.
  Ninigret National Wildlife Refuge, off Rte. 1, in Charlestown (364–3106). Wildlife refuge maintained by the U.S. Fish and Wildlife Service. The Ninigret Conservation Area, a 2-mi. barrier beach, is a protected area managed by the state. **Ninigret Park,** on the site of the old Naval Air Field, is a recreational and cultural area that includes the Frosty Drew Nature Center.
  Trustom Pond National Wildlife Refuge, on Matunuck School Rd., in Charlestown (364–3106). Nature center. Trails. Swimming not permitted in Trustom Pond.

BEACHES. From Watch Hill in Westerly to Narragansett Pier, the South County coast seems like one long, beautiful beach. Most beaches are open to the public. During the summer, parking fees are charged at major beaches.
  In Westerly—**Misquamicut State Beach,** Rte. 1A. One of Rhode Island's most popular beaches. Large parking area. Picnic tables, concessions, amusements.
  In Charlestown—**Ninigret Beach,** off Rte. 1, access from E. Beach Rd. Two miles of dunes, backed by Ninigret Pond.
  In South Kingstown—**Moonstone Beach,** off Rte. 1, access from Moonstone Beach Rd. Part of the Trustom Pond National Wildlife Refuge. Much of Moonstone Beach is a "clothes optional" beach, one of the few on the East Coast.
  Roy Carpenter's Beach, off Rte. 1, access from Matunuck Beach Rd. A private beach, open to the public. Snack bar, bathhouse.
  East Matunuck State Beach, off Rte. 1, access from Succotash Rd. High surf, picnic areas, bathhouse.
  In Narragansett—**Roger Wheeler State Beach,** Sand Hill Rd., Point Judith. Excellent family beach. Picnic areas, playground. Near Galilee.
  Scarborough State Beach, Rte. 1A. High surf. Very popular on weekends. Bathhouse, concessions.

Narragansett Town Beach, Rte. 1A, close to Narragansett Pier. Pavilion has changing rooms, showers, and concessions. Parking and entrance fees.

SUMMER SPORTS. Golf: South County courses include The Winnapaug Golf and Country Club, Shore Rd., Westerly (596–9164); The Woodland Greens Golf Club, 655 Old Baptist Rd., North Kingstown (294–2872); The Meadow Brook Golf Course, Rte. 138, Wyoming (539–8491); The North Kingstown Municipal Golf Course, Quonset Point, North Kingstown (294–4051).

Tennis: Pond View Racquet Club, Shore Rd., Westerly (322–1100).

Horseback riding: Stepping Stone Ranch, Escoheag Hill Rd., West Greenwich (397–3725).

Canoe rentals: South County's small rivers and easy-flowing streams make it an attractive area for novice canoeists. For information and canoe rentals: Quaker Lane Bait Shop, 4019 Quaker La., North Kingstown (294–9642).

Hiking: South County is an excellent area for hikers. One of the best trail guides for the region—and for the rest of Rhode Island and Massachusetts, too—is *The AMC Massachusetts and Rhode Island Trail Guide.* The book can be purchased at local outdoors shops or from the Appalachian Mountain Club. The Rhode Island Audubon Society offers interesting hikes and field expeditions for members and nonmembers. For information: Rhode Island Audubon Society, 40 Bowen St., Providence 02903 (521–1670). The Sierra Club and the Appalachian Mountain Club both have active groups in Rhode Island. Sierra Club: 3 Joy St., Rm. 12, Boston, MA 02114 (617–227–5339). Appalachian Mountain Club: 5 Joy St., Boston, MA 02114 (617–523–0636).

FISHING. For freshwater fishing, a Rhode Island fishing license is required. Licenses can be obtained from town clerks' offices and at most bait and tackle shops. Information on fishing and boating laws: Business Affairs, Department of Environmental Management, 22 Hayes St., Providence 02903 (277–6647).

No license is required for surf casting. Block Island Sound is famous for striped bass, bluefish, weakfish, mackerel, and bluefin tuna, all migrating species that first appear in Rhode Island waters during the spring or early summer. Cod, pollock, and flounder are caught throughout the year.

Bait and Tackle Shops: Ocean House Marina, 12 Town Dock Rd., Charlestown (364–6040); Quaker Lane Bait, 4019 Quaker La., North Kingstown (294–9642); Wickford Bait and Tackle, 1 Phillips St., Wickford (295–8845).

Charters, a central booking agent at Snug Harbor on Gooseneck Rd. in S. Kingstown, can tell you of captains who skipper charters (783–7766).

HUNTING. The State of Rhode Island manages over 32,000 acres of woodlands, fields, and marsh for anglers and hunters. State hunting licenses are required. For information on licenses and permits: Rhode Island Department of Environmental Management, 9 Hayes St., Providence 02903 (277–2771).

CAMPING. For information on private and state-owned camping areas in Rhode Island, contact Tourism Division, Rhode Island Department of Economic Development, 7 Jackson Walkway, Providence 02903 (277–2601 or 800–556–2484).

Whispering Pines Campground, Saw Mill Rd., Hope Valley 02832 (539–7011). Near Rte. 138. 130 trailer sites, 20 tent sites. Privately owned. Open Feb.–Dec. 31.

In *Charlestown*—**Burlingame State Park.** Write Division of Parks and Recreation, 83 Park St., Providence 02903 (322–7994). Off Rte. 1. 755 tent sites. A major state park with freshwater swimming, boating, fishing. Open mid-Apr.–Dec. 31.

In *Narragansett*—**Fishermen's Memorial State Park.** Write Division of Parks and Recreation, 83 Park St., Providence 02908 (789–8374). Off Rte. 108. 140 tent sites, 40 trailer sites. State park near saltwater beaches. Open mid-Apr.–Oct. 31. Reservations (beginning Jan. 15) encouraged.

HISTORIC SITES AND HOMES. South County has an unusual history that sets the region apart from the rest of New England.

Charlestown

Narragansett Indian Church, Narrow La., off Rte. 2-112. Built in 1859 by Narragansett Indian stone masons. Used for weekly church services, Apr.–Nov.
Fort Ninigret, Fort Neck Rd., off Rte. 1. The remains of an earthwork fort, built by Dutch traders during the early 1600s.

Exeter

Tomaquag Indian Museum, Summit Rd., off Arcadia Rd. (539–7795). Small Narragansett Indian museum. Craft classes. Closed Feb.

Narragansett

South County Museum, off Rte. 1A (783–5400). Farm museum and local history. Open June–Oct.

North Kingstown

Silas Casey Farm, Rte. 1A (227–3956). A working colonial farm, one of the South County plantations. Open June–Oct., Tues., Thurs., and Sat., 1–5 P.M.
Gilbert Stuart Birthplace, Rte. 1A, in Saunderstown (294–3001). Built in 1751. Birthplace of Gilbert Stuart, early American artist. Large waterwheel powers colonial snuff mill. Open Mar.–Dec., daily except Fri., 11 A.M.–5 P.M.
Smith's Castle, off Rte. 1, north of Wickford in Cocumscussoc (294–3521). Early trading post, later one of the South County plantations. The present structure was built in 1678. Open mid-Apr.–Nov., 10 A.M.–5 P.M., on Thurs., Fri., and Sat.; also, Sun., 1–5 P.M.

South Kingstown

Old Washington County Jail, 1348 Kingstown Rd. (783–1328). Built in 1792, the old jail now houses the Pettaquamscutt Historical Society. Interesting exhibits on Kingston village life. Open Tues., Thurs., and Sat., 1–4 P.M.
Helme House, 1319 Kingstown Rd. (783–9072). Headquarters for the South County Art Association. Open during exhibitions.
Fayerweather Craft Center, Moorsfield Rd., Rte. 138 (789–9072). Built in 1820, this was the home of George Fayerweather, a son of slaves who

had worked on South County plantations. George Fayerweather was the Kingston village blacksmith. His home is now a crafts center, offering crafts classes and exhibits. Open May–Dec., Tues.–Sat., 11 A.M.–4 P.M.

Great Swamp Fight Monument, off Rte. 2, in West Kingston. A rough obelisk marks the site of one of the bloodiest battles—December 19, 1675—in New England history. Puritan troops overwhelmed a Narragansett Indian village on this site.

Usquepaugh

Kenyon Grist Mill, off Rte. 138, near the Richmond–South Kingstown town line (783–4054). Old Rhode Island gristmill that still produces stoneground corn meal. Visitors welcome.

Westerly

Babcock-Smith House, 124 Granite St. (596–4424). Colonial home, built c. 1750. Open July and Aug. weekends, 1–4 P.M.

THE SAKONNET LANDS

The gentle Sakonnet lands in Rhode Island's southeastern corner are part of a coastal area that most tourists never see. Fishermen may have heard about the saltwater fishing at Little Compton. Bicyclists may have heard about the excellent cycling roads close to Adamsville. And wine tasters may know about Rhode Island's Sakonnet Vineyards. Yet most visitors to southeastern New England bypass the Sakonnet area, pressing on to Cape Cod and other destinations. The Sakonnet people sit back, relax, and listen to radio reports about summertime traffic jams in Bourne and Sandwich.

What's true for the Rhode Island towns of Little Compton and Tiverton is also true for the nearby Massachusetts towns of Westport and Dartmouth. You won't find many places to stay in this area once you get close to the salt water. Nor will you find any seaside shopping malls or fast food restaurants. What you will find are beautiful beaches, nice parks, and some interesting places off the beaten path. Horseneck Beach in Westport—it's across the state line in Massachusetts but it's still worth mentioning—is one of New England's largest and best. In Rhode Island, Goosewing Beach in Little Compton is a favorite with beachcombers in all seasons.

Fort Barton

In Tiverton, at Lawton and Highland avenues, are the ruins of Fort Barton, built during the American Revolution. Named for Lieutenant Colonel William Barton, who captured Newport's British commander, the fort's modern observation tower offers a fine view of Aquidneck. Fort Barton was one of several points from which American soldiers watched Aquidneck after the British captured the island in 1776. William Barton and other raiders kept the British on their toes.

In August 1778, the Americans and their newly acquired French allies were ready to launch a major attack on Aquidneck. The French fleet had arrived in Narragansett Bay, throwing the British in Newport into a panic, and 10,000 American soldiers were assembled at Fort Barton, ready for an amphibious assault. Unfortunately for the Americans, a series of mishaps and errors soon followed. The Americans reached Aquidneck without opposition, but the French fleet was lured into an inconclusive engagement with a British fleet that had arrived from New York. The two fleets were scattered in a storm, and the French retreated to Boston to refit. Without French support, the American siege of Newport soon collapsed. The Americans withdrew to the northern end of Aquidneck, with the British in pursuit. The two sides clashed in some sharp fighting during the Battle of Rhode Island. Again the results were inconclusive, but the Americans quietly withdrew from the island, and Newport and the rest of Aquidneck remained in British hands. Fort Barton again became a lonely outpost, where the Americans watched and waited until the British withdrew from Newport in 1779.

Behind the remains of Fort Barton is a network of trails leading into a partially developed park known as the Glen of Sin and Flesh. This is an attractive area for hikers, but caution is advised since there are few trail signs and no uniformity of paint blazing. Easier paths can be found at the Emilie Ruecker Wildlife Refuge, maintained by the Rhode Island Audubon Society, on the coast off Sapowet Road.

Rejoin Route 77 and drive south. The village of Tiverton is located at the junction of Routes 77 and 179. In this area you'll find interesting shopping, a gourmet shop (The Provender) that will pack a picnic lunch for you, and other attractions. The Soule-Seabury house, at the junction's northeast corner, was the home of a seafaring family during the late 1700s and early 1800s. The house is open to the public during the summer. The Chace-Cory House, south of the junction, is another eighteenth-century home, also open to visitors during the warm-weather months.

Little Compton

South of Tiverton is Little Compton. All along Route 77—known as West Main Road—you'll see farmhouses from the 1700s near stately Victorian summer homes. The Wilbour House, on West Main Road, maintained by the Little Compton Historical Society, was built in 1680 and occupied by the same family until the 1920s. Inside you can see how family tastes changed from generation to generation. The adjacent Wilbour House barn is a museum containing antique farming tools, carriages, and the farm wagons that were once part of everyday life in rural Little Compton.

The Sakonnet Vineyards (635–8486), off the West Main Road, have been a part of Little Compton since 1975. Traveling south on Route 77, you'll find the vineyard entrance on your left, about three miles from Tiverton Four Corners. Tours of the vineyard are given on Wednesdays, Saturdays, and Sundays from the end of May until the end of October. The vineyard is open for tasting and retail sales daily, 10 A.M. to 6 P.M., May 31–Oct. 31, and 11 A.M. to 5 P.M. in winter. This is a wonderful place for a summer picnic, with cheeses, fresh-baked bread, and fruit available at nearby shops and roadside stands.

At the southernmost tip of Little Compton are Sakonnet Point and Sakonnet Harbor. The Indian name Sakonnet means "place of the wild black goose." On crisp autumn and spring days you can see flocks of wild geese flying along the coast, making their seasonal migrations. Sakonnet Harbor follows the seasons closely, for it is still a small fishing village dependent on the Atlantic.

Follow Route 77 back into the center of Little Compton, turning right on Swamp Road. Soon you'll see the dirt road that leads into Wilbour's

Woods. This is a 40-acre park that hikers and bird watchers may enjoy. The park has a monument to Awashonks, the Indian woman who was the chief of the Sakonnet Indians at the time of King Philip's War. It was not unusual in the 1600s for a woman to be a village chief; Awashonks was one of several. What mattered, notes one historian, was that the villagers had "a sachem whom they could respect and follow."

Goosewing Beach

Continue on Swamp Road until you reach South Commons Road. Turn left and follow South Commons Road into the Commons area. Here you'll find the kind of idyllic town center that has nearly vanished from much of New England. There's a traditional white-spired Congregational church looking over the town hall, the firehouse, the village school, and the general store. At the Commons Lunch you can dine on quahog pie and johnny cakes and other Rhode Island specialties while you chat with townspeople and anyone else who may have stopped by for a cup of coffee.

Goosewing Beach in Little Compton extends for a mile or so along the ocean, close to Massachusetts. It's one of the most attractive beaches in Rhode Island. Goosewing Beach is at the end of Long Highway. Also close to Massachusetts, at the junction of Routes 179 and 81, is Adamsville. This is an active crossroads settlement, part of Little Compton, that supports antique shops, country stores, and Abraham Manchester's Restaurant and Tavern. Across the road from Manchester's is a monument to the Rhode Island Red—a famous breed of chicken that was developed in the area, not far from where the chicken memorial now stands. Local people say that this is the only monument to a chicken in the world and, indeed, it's difficult to think of any others.

Venture across the state line into Massachusetts and you'll find some pleasant places along the coast. Horseneck State Beach is at the end of Route 88 in Westport. The state park at Horseneck has picnic facilities and campsites. To the north and east of Westport is Dartmouth. It, too, has a popular family beach, at Demarest Lloyd State Park. Pandaram Village, in Dartmouth, is a fashionable coastal resort. By now, you've almost reached New Bedford, Massachusetts.

PRACTICAL INFORMATION FOR THE SAKONNET LANDS

Note: The area code for all Rhode Island is 401

HOW TO GET THERE AND AROUND. By car: From the Newport area, take Rte. 138 north to Portsmouth, cross the Sakonnet River Bridge into Tiverton. From Fall River, exit from Rte. I–195 onto Rte. 24, drive south toward Newport. In Tiverton, follow Rte. 77 south, along the Sakonnet River to Little Compton. The Massachusetts towns of Westport and Dartmouth can be reached from exits on Rte. I–195. Look for exit signs between Fall River and New Bedford.

By bus: The Rhode Island Public Transit Authority (RIPTA) provides bus service from Providence to Tiverton and Little Compton. Service is limited to commuter hours. For information, telephone the RIPTA office in Providence: 781–9400.

HOTELS AND MOTELS. Unless you've rented a summer cottage in the area, you'll find it difficult to find overnight accommodations in Tiverton or Little Compton. Price ranges are based on double occupancy at summer rates and all listings are for European plan arrangements, except as noted: *Deluxe,* $100 and up; *Expensive,* $60–$100; *Moderate,* $45–$60.

Portsmouth

Ramada Inn, 144 Anthony Rd., 02871 (683–3600). *Expensive.* Large motel, close to Rte. 138. Indoor pool. Restaurant. Open year-round.
Founder's Brook Motel, 314 Boyd's La., 02871 (683–1244). *Moderate.* Small motel, across from Founder's Brook Park.

Westport

The Hampton Inn, 66 State St., Westport, MA 02790 (508–675–7185). *Moderate.* 134 rooms. Continental breakfast included. Jacuzzi, TV. Adjacent to White's Restaurant.

RESTAURANTS. Price ranges for Sakonnet area restaurants for a meal for one person excluding beverage, tax, and tip: *Deluxe,* $25 and up; *Expensive,* $18–$25; *Moderate,* $10–$18; and *Inexpensive,* $10 and under.

Little Compton

Abraham Manchester's Restaurant, At the jct. of Rtes. 179 and 81, in Adamsville (625–2700). *Moderate.* An old-time country restaurant and tavern. Italian and American specialties. Turkey cooked daily.
Country Harvest, Maine Rd. (635–4579). *Moderate.* Sea, shore, and pasta dishes. Overlooks water. Sun. brunch.
Crowther's Restaurant, Pottersville Rd. (635–8367). *Moderate.* Between John Dyer Rd. and Long Hwy. American cuisine. Seafood. Very good.
Fo'c's'le Restaurant, Sakonnet Point (635–9508). *Moderate.* Seafood restaurant. An informal setting, overlooking Sakonnet harbor. Open during the summer.
Common's Restaurant, Little Compton Commons (635–4388). *Inexpensive.* Johnny cakes for breakfast. Quahog pie. A village cafe where local people meet for coffee and news.

Tiverton

The Coachmen, 1215 Main Rd. (624–8423). *Moderate.* American and Continental food. Seafood. Bar. Reservations encouraged. Open year-round.
Jade Garden, 221 Main Rd. (624–9800). *Moderate.* Chinese food. Open year-round.
Sunderland's, 2753 Main Rd. (624–3991). *Moderate.* Country-style dining in a rambling farmhouse. Bar. Closed Jan. and Feb.

Westport

Cate Corey's at Bittersweet Farm, 438 Main Rd., Westport, MA (508–636–5559). *Moderate.* Continental dishes in renovated barn atmosphere. Lunch, dinner.
Moby Dick Wharf Restaurant, 1 Bridge Rd., Westport Point, MA (508–636–4465). *Moderate.* Overlooking Westport Harbor. Seafood. Open Apr.–Nov.

TOURIST INFORMATION. Surprisingly little has been written about the Sakonnet lands. For maps and general information on the Tiverton and Little Compton area, write the Tourism Division, Department of Economic Development, 7 Jackson Walkway, Providence 02903 (277-2601). In Massachusetts, information on **Bristol County** attractions is available from the Bristol County Development Council, 70 N. Second St., New Bedford, MA 02740 (508-997-1250).

SPORTS. For information on bicycle rentals and golf courses, see *Practical Information for Newport.*

Horseback riding: Roseland Acres Equestrian Center, 594 East Rd., Tiverton (624-8866), gives riding instruction, boards horses.

FISHING. Bait and tackle shops in the Sakonnet area include Westport Marine Specialists, 1111 Main Rd., Westport, MA (508-636-8100), and Riverside Marine, 211 Riverside Dr., Tiverton (625-5231).

For fishing parties, contact Captain Bud Phillips, Snell Rd., Little Compton (635-4592).

No license is required for saltwater fishing.

CAMPING. There are several campgrounds in the Sakonnet area. Reservations are encouraged during the summer.

In *Westport*—**Westport Camping Grounds,** 346 Old County Rd., Westport, MA 02790 (508-636-2555). Tent sites, close to the saltwater. Open Apr.–Oct.

Horseneck Beach State Park. 100 tent sites. Massachusetts state park. For information: Massachusetts Department of Environmental Management, 100 Cambridge St., Boston, MA 02114 (617-727-3180).

HISTORIC SITES AND HOMES. The Sakonnet lands have much to offer in beautiful scenery and attractive homes. It's a pleasant area to explore by bicycle or automobile.

Little Compton

Wilbour House, W. Main Rd. (635-4559). Occupied by the Wilbour family from 1680 until the 1920s. Open mid-June–mid-Sept., Tues.–Sun., 2–5 P.M.

Little Compton Commons, Meeting House La. One of the most attractive villages in Rhode Island. The large United Congregational Church, which dominates the area, was built in 1832 to replace an earlier structure. The church burial ground, nearby, was laid out in 1675–77, at the time of King Philip's War.

Tiverton

Fort Barton, Lawton and Highland Aves. The remains of a fort built during the American Revolution. A modern observation tower provides a fine view of Aquidneck Island.

Tiverton Four Corners, jct. West Main Rd. (Rte. 77) and East Rd. (Rte. 179). Historic homes in this area include the Soule-Seabury House, built in 1760, at the northeast corner of the jct., and the Chace-Cory House, built in 1730 and modernized in 1816, south of the jct. Both homes are open to the public during the summer.

BLOCK ISLAND

Block Island is where you go when you want to relax on a hotel veranda, admire the ocean view, and perhaps do a bit of bicycling or beachcombing late in the afternoon. Less pretentious and less expensive than some of New England's other offshore resorts, Block Island is still an easygoing isle somewhat removed from the fast-changing fashions of Boston and New York.

The Narragansett Indians called Block Island Manisses, meaning "Island of the Little God." Adrian Block, a Dutch explorer, visited the island in 1614 and decided to name the spot for himself. Modern seafarers know Block Island as a small dewdrop-shaped piece of land rising 12 miles south of Rhode Island's mainland. Nowadays visitors often reach Block Island by ferry from Galilee, Rhode Island. During the summer, ferry service is also available from Providence and Newport; from New London, Connecticut; and from Montauk Point, at the end of Long Island. You probably won't need an automobile on Block Island—bicycles can be rented, and taxi service is available—but if you decide to bring your car, be sure to make your ferry reservations well in advance.

Old Harbor and New Harbor

Block Island has two harbors: Old Harbor and New Harbor. The Old Harbor commercial district extends along Water, Dodge, and Main streets. From the sea, this section of the waterfront seems to be dominated by old Victorian hotels, with Block Island easily resembling a resort town from the late 1800s. Once ashore, you can rent a bicycle during the warm-weather months or you can walk along Water Street. The Block Island Historical Society, on Main Street at Harbor Road, is open on weekdays from July until September.

Corn Neck Road takes you north from the Old Harbor area toward New Harbor and the Block Island National Wildlife Refuge, at Sandy Point. There are restaurants and places to stay at New Harbor, and this is where the ferry from New London arrives during the summer. At Sandy Point you'll see the Old North Light, a lighthouse built in 1867 after three previous lighthouses had collapsed because of shifting sands and ocean storms. The Old North Light is no longer in operation. Nearby is Settlers' Rock, where Block Island's colonial settlers landed in 1662, and Cow Cove, named for a colonial cow who swam ashore from a wrecked vessel. The cow was fortunate that she wasn't ground into hamburger by Block Island's pounding surf.

Alone on the Atlantic, Block Island has had a difficult history. The Narragansett Indians who first inhabited the island were defeated and removed during the 1600s. Lacking an adequate natural harbor, the island's colonial settlers struggled to survive by farming and by fishing. At times the ocean storms that struck Block Island were devastating. In 1938, a hurricane nearly tore the island in half, destroying most of the island's fishing fleet.

Pirate Treasure

As mainland Rhode Island began to prosper during the late 1600s and early 1700s, pirates and enemy privateers swarmed into the area to plunder where they could. Block Island was an open outpost on a saltwater frontier. Between 1698 and 1706, the island was captured and sacked by French privateers on three occasions. A fourth attack was made by an unidentified enemy, driven away by armed fishermen and farmers. Black Sam Bellamy, in the pirate ship *Whidah,* captured ships not far from Block Island in 1717, finally capturing one ship laden with sweet Madeira wine. After a night of carousing, the *Whidah* smashed into the beaches of Cape Cod, drowning Black Sam and most of his crew in the ocean. Captain William Kidd of New York and Thomas Tew, a gentleman pirate from Newport, also visited the Block Island area, but these rovers confined their attacks to other seas and they remained on good terms with Rhode Island merchants. Some say that there's still pirate gold buried on Block Island and on the islands of Narragansett Bay, but most of the loot was probably spent long ago in local rum shops. Most pirates died in poverty.

Block Island's early settlers learned to watch the horizon for enemy sails, and they learned, too, to watch for ships in distress. Half the 2,000 reported shipwrecks on the southern New England coast occurred near Block Island. Island salvage crews—"wreckers"—knew how to pick a broken ship apart quickly, saving everything of value that could be taken ashore. There are stories that tell of islanders luring ships into destruction by using false signals, but at this late date it's hard to separate fact from fiction. So many ships came to grief on Block Island for natural reasons that it seems somehow unlikely that the islanders would have resorted to trickery.

The 200-foot-high Mohegan Bluffs and Southeast Point Light are at the southeastern end of Block Island. Follow Spring Street to Southeast Road in order to see these attractions. Near the lighthouse there's a long wooden stairway that can take you down to the Mohegan Bluffs beach. This is a rugged beach, and while it's fun for hikers and hardy swimmers, families may prefer Crescent Beach and some of the other beaches along the island's eastern shore.

People come to Block Island in order to relax. The island is a popular place to visit during the spring and fall, and in a good year swimming can be enjoyed as late as October. Block Island summers are delightful; the winters can be brutal. This is an island where everyone feels comfortable three seasons out of four, and visitors have rejoiced in this fact for generations.

PRACTICAL INFORMATION FOR BLOCK ISLAND

Note: The area code for all Rhode Island is 401

HOW TO GET THERE. By plane: *New England Airlines* provides air service from Westerly State Airport, in Westerly, to Block Island (596–2460 or 800–243–2460; on Block Island, 5959). Year-round service. Reservations required. *Action Air* has scheduled flights from Groton, Connecticut, to Block Island from June–Oct. (800–243–8623).

By ferry: Scheduled ferry service is available, year-round, from Galilee. Automobiles are carried but reservations are required. Write Interstate Navigation Co., Galilee State Pier, Point Judith 02882 (783–4613 or

789–3502). Summer service to Block Island is available from New London and from Long Island. For information on New London service, write Nelseco Navigation Co., Box 482, New London, CT 06320 (203–442–7891). For information on Montauk service, call Viking Fishing Fleet (516–668–2214). The Montauk ferries carry passengers only. During the summer, passenger boats travel from Providence via Newport to Block Island. For information, contact the Interstate Navigation Co. at the company's Point Judith address.

HOW TO GET AROUND. Block Island is only 7 mi. long and less than 4 mi. wide, so it's easy to move about the island on foot or on a rented bicycle or moped. Several of the island hotels provide courtesy vans to assist guests with their luggage. Taxis are also available.

Car rentals: Block Island Car Rental (466–2297) and Block Island Boat Basin (466–2631).

Bicycle and moped rentals: Esta's at Old Harbor (466–2651), Old Harbor Bike Shop (466–2029), and Block Island Boat Basin (466–2631).

HOTELS AND MOTELS. The listings that follow are for European Plan arrangements, except as noted: *Deluxe,* $100 and up; *Expensive,* $60–$100; *Moderate,* $45–$60; *Inexpensive,* under $45.

Island Manor Resort, Chapel St., 02807 (466–5567). *Expensive.* The island's first motel, now converted to time-sharing units. Rentals available.

1661 Inn and **Manisses Hotel,** Box 367A, 02807 (466–2421 or 466–2063). *Expensive.* Near Old Harbor. Two of Block Island's grand Victorian hotels, both under the same management. The 1661 Inn is open year-round.

Ballard's Inn, Water St., 02807 (466–5095). *Moderate.* Seaview rooms have fine view of harbor. Restaurant.

Narragansett Inn, Ocean Rd, 02807 (466–2626). *Moderate.* In New Harbor. One of the best bargains on the island. Rates include breakfast and dinner. Open May–mid-Sept.

The New National Hotel, Box 64, 02807 (466–2901 or 800–225–2449). *Moderate.* Overlooking Old Harbor. Open year-round.

Seacrest Inn, High St., 02807 (466–2882). *Moderate.* A restored inn with 19th-century charm.

Spring House, Box 206, 02807 (466–2633). *Moderate.* On Spring St. Long porch, rocking-chair hotel with ocean vista. Restaurant. Room rate includes breakfast and dinner.

Surf Hotel, 02807 (466–2241 or 466–2147). *Moderate.* Near Old Harbor. A fine Victorian hotel. Central location.

INNS, GUEST HOUSES, BED AND BREAKFASTS. For additional information on Block Island bed-and-breakfast accommodations, contact the Block Island Chamber of Commerce, Drawer D, Block Island 02807. The following inns are *moderately* priced:

Atlantic Inn, Box 188, 02807 (466–2005). 354 High St. 22 rooms with private baths.

The Barrington, Box 90, 02807 (466–5510). Eight rooms. Open mid-Feb.–mid-Dec.

Blue Dory Inn, Box 488, 02807 (466–2254). On Dodge St. All rooms have private baths, ocean or harbor views. Open year-round.

Hardy Smith House, High St., 02807 (466–2466). Eight rooms with shared bath. Continental breakfast, wine and cheese in the afternoon. Antique furnishings.

New Shoreham House Inn, Box 356, 02807 (466–2651). Victorian inn. Ocean view. Full breakfast. Room prices—in spring, fall, and winter—include use of bicycles. Open year-round.

Old Town Inn, Box 351, 02807 (466–5958). 12 rooms in an 1832 home. Full breakfast.

RESTAURANTS. Price ranges for Block Island restaurants for one person excluding beverage, tax, and tip: *Deluxe,* $25 and up; *Expensive,* $18–$25; *Moderate,* $10–$18; and *Inexpensive,* $10 and under.

Ballard's Inn, Old Harbor (466–5095). *Moderate.* Large dining area and terrace overlooking beach. Italian and American specialties. Seafood. Entertainment. Open May–Oct.

Harborside Inn, Old Harbor (466–5504). *Moderate.* Seafood, steaks, and a fine ocean view.

Samuel Peckham Tavern, New Harbor (466–2439). *Moderate.* Country breakfasts, lobster dinners. Open year-round.

Smugglers Cove, New Harbor (466–2828). *Moderate.* Seafood restaurant. Close to docks.

Finn's Seafood Bar, Old Harbor (466–2473). *Inexpensive.* Snacks and take-out items.

TOURIST INFORMATION. For visitor information on Block Island, contact the Block Island Chamber of Commerce, Drawer D, Block Island 02807 (466–2982).

BEACHES. Block Island State Beach—on the island's eastern side—is the most popular family beach. It's close to the Old Harbor and New Harbor settlements, and the long, wide strip of white sand makes it an ideal place for building sand castles.

Block Island State Beach, off Corn Neck Rd. Picnic tables, bathhouse. Lifeguards on duty during the summer.

Scotch Beach, north of State Beach. Less crowded than its neighbor.

Mohegan Bluffs, which rise 200 ft. from the sea, wrap around the island's southeastern shore. Islanders say that the bluffs were named for a Mohegan war party, cornered by the island's Narragansett Indians and driven over the cliffs in 1590. A long stairway at the Mohegan Bluffs Overlook, near the Southeast Lighthouse, takes visitors down to the shore. State rangers conduct summer programs at the overlook on the history and geology of Block Island.

Rodman's Hollow, off Cooneymus Rd. A quiet, rugged area, where hikers are welcome. No access to the shore.

CAMPING. *Camping is not permitted on Block Island.*

SHOPPING. Block Island prices are a bit higher than back home and visitors may want to purchase necessities such as toothpaste and suntan lotion on the mainland before heading out to sea.

The **Star Department Store,** Water St., really a general store, has a bit of everything. For arts and crafts, there's **Pottery by the Sea,** Dodge St. Gift shops include **The Sandpiper** *Moderate* and **Distant Shores** on Water St.

VERMONT

By
MARILYN STOUT

Marilyn Stout, a resident of Vermont, is a free-lance writer who has published travel articles in a variety of national newspapers and magazines. She also coauthored a book about Vermont.

It has been said that all people feel as though they are coming home when they visit Vermont, even when they have never been there before. In Vermont there is often a sense that the old values still hold and that the commercialism that is rampant elsewhere has been held at bay. Some of this is true, but the picture is much more complicated. Billboards are not permitted anywhere in the state, but there are still factories and businesses. People need to work. Is Vermont the most conservative state? Some commentators now say it may be the most liberal. It has a broad streak of tolerance and fair play that leads it to send members of both parties to Congress to support strong aid to education and restraint in involvement in foreign wars. The late Senator George Aiken is remembered fondly for articulating a commonsense notion: Say we won in Vietnam and get out. Making sense is a virtue here. And if one person's sense is another's folly, it's talked about and voted on at the annual Town Meeting.

A Look Back

A consideration of the dynamic and colorful history of the region may help to explain the sense of tradition and solidity that prevails in this small state. In 1973, the remains of a 3,000-year-old Indian culture were un-earthed in Swanton, in the northwestern corner of the state not far from Canada, an area inhabited by Indian descendants to this day.

Digs along the shores of Lake Champlain and Otter Creek have turned up Indian fishing and hunting tools, artifacts, and pottery dating as far back as 2000 B.C. Scholars have connected these things with the Old Algon-kians (2000 B.C. to A.D. 1300). The Swanton findings turned up evidence of a prewoodland people called the Adenas, and some assert that Paleo-Indian hunters may have roamed the forest of the Champlain valley 4,000 years ago.

When Samuel de Champlain first saw in 1609 the magnificent lake that would bear his name, he was accompanied by Algonkians who had prom-ised to show him the great lake of the Iroquois. When the party sighted the Iroquois, a battle ensued, with the reluctant aid of Champlain's armed party. The Iroquois' hatred of the French began with that battle. The first white settlement in what is now Vermont was a French military outpost, Fort St. Anne, built in 1666 on Isle La Motte in the Champlain Islands. From there, raids against the Iroquois were launched. The first English settlement was at Fort Dummer near Brattleboro in 1724.

Vermont's was a tug-of-war history in which tracts of land were granted in moments of caprice by kings, governors, and land speculators. Natural-ly, land bestowed at a distance became subject to controversy on the spot. All the area that is now Vermont was once part of the British province of New York. New Hampshire's governor, however, began taking land as far west as Bennington. By 1764, these New Hampshire grants com-prised 131 townships.

That same year, George III ruled that the disputed territory belonged to New York. With their lands threatened, the settlers rallied in a loose-knit military group called the Green Mountain Boys. In 1770–71, the band began to drive the New Yorkers off the disputed lands. Soon the territorial rivalry was eclipsed by the outbreak of the colonies' struggle for indepen-dence from the British. The Green Mountain Boys played a vital role in the Revolution by capturing Fort Ticonderoga and Crown Point and sup-plying Washington with a hundred British cannons.

Vermont on Its Own

After the signing of the Declaration of Independence, Vermont declared itself an independent republic in 1777. Its constitution adopted at Windsor was the first in the nation to permit voting by all men without property qualifications. Vermonters fought the British during the Revolution as a "people's militia," defeating General John Burgoyne and his troops at the Battle of Bennington (actually fought just across the border near Hoosick, New York). In a letter to England after the battle, Burgoyne wrote, "The Hampshire Grants in particular . . . now abounds with the most active and rebellious race on the continent." Vermonters take pride in this.

In 1791, Vermont joined the Union. The original 13 colonies had de-layed the admission partly out of antagonism over Vermont's revolt from New York's authority. George Washington believed Vermont might have to be subdued by arms. As late as 1782, Vermont arrested and ejected a New York sheriff's posse for violating the state's border. Congress protest-ed and Vermont refused to back down. Eventually, Congress ceased to question Vermont's state sovereignty and approved it. Vermont became the fourteenth state.

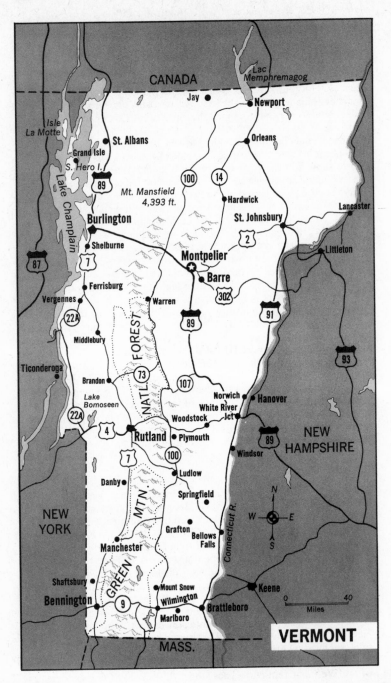

CANADA

Lac
Memphremagog

Isle
La Motte

Jay

Newport

St. Albans

Orleans

Grand Isle
S. Hero I.

89

100   14

Mt. Mansfield
4,393 ft.

Hardwick

Lancaster

St. Johnsbury

Burlington

Lake Champlain

Shelburne

Montpelier

Littleton

87

7

Barre

2

Ferrisburg

302

Warren

Vergennes

89   91

22A

Middlebury

Brandon

73

107

93

Ticonderoga

Lake
Bomoseen

Norwich   Hanover

22A

White River
Jct.

NEW
HAMPSHIRE

4

Woodstock

Rutland

Plymouth

89

7

100

Ludlow

Windsor

Danby

Springfield

NEW
YORK

Grafton

Bellows
Falls

N
W   E
S

Manchester

Connecticut R.

Shaftsbury

Keene

Bennington

9

Mount Snow
Wilmington

Brattleboro

0   40
Miles

Marlboro

MASS.

VERMONT

As It Is Today

Vermont has been a leader in environmental protection. It has a lovely environment to protect. Responding to the voracious appetite of developers and land speculators, it passed Act 250, a set of strict land-use laws, in 1970. When he was inaugurated in 1973, Governor Thomas P. Salmon spoke for the majority in saying, "Vermont is *not* for sale." In the mid-1960s, the state passed the nation's first law banning billboards on all roads. Vermont was second only to Oregon in banning nonreturnable bottles and cans.

In the 1960s and 1970s, many young people came to Vermont looking for an alternative to the acquisitive, mass-produced way of life. (Vermonters do not interfere with independent ways of living.) Many stayed on and are now credited with helping to revitalize such places as Brattleboro and Burlington. One is Bernard Sanders, who classifies himself a socialist and was elected mayor of Burlington in 1981. Ben Cohen and Jerry Greenfield started Ben & Jerry's Ice Cream in 1978 in a former Burlington gas station, scooping cones at a counter in the repair bay. The Common Ground Community Restaurant in Brattleboro, still owned and run by a workers' cooperative, is now the oldest natural food restaurant in New England.

Visiting Vermont

Vermont is a small state that can be crossed at its widest point in about a two-hour drive. It is somewhat wedge shaped, 151.6 miles from north to south and 40 to 90 miles wide. Its total area ranks forty-third among the 50 states. Montpelier is the capital, and Burlington, with about 40,000 people, is the largest city. About a fourth of the state's population lives in the northwest section around Burlington in Chittenden County.

The only New England state without an ocean coastline, Vermont has the freshwater Lake Champlain for about half of its western border. Champlain ranks just after the Great Lakes in size. The Green Mountains run north and south through Vermont like a spine and are a great source of recreation opportunities.

Vermont is an agricultural state that has been marked as the country's most rural. Residents, even in populous Chittenden County, often live in towns of under 2,000 people. A traveler in the state reaps the benefit of the lands left open by the hardworking farmers who clear and maintain the fields. These lands contribute to the green vistas spreading from hill to hill that delight the eye. A hundred years ago, Vermont was mostly forest; it takes hard work to keep the forest from taking over again.

The Northeast Kingdom, so called in the 1940s by Senator Aiken, is indeed a bit apart. It is less settled, more rural, and it has dense forests in the northeast section. It is also less visited by tourists. Some might say it is Vermont distilled to its essence.

Those of us who live here would find it hard to choose a favorite section. We like them all for different reasons. Your pleasure and opportunity are to discover them for yourself.

Exploring Vermont

SOUTHERN VERMONT

Around Bennington

At the junction of U.S. 7 and Route 9, Bennington is the southwestern gateway to Vermont. If you approach Bennington from U.S. 7, you will first drive through the southernmost town in this part of the state, Pownal. The Pownal Valley is a handsome area. Vermont's only pari-mutuel race track, Green Mountain Race Track, where greyhounds race between March and November, is in Pownal.

In the apple orchards scattered throughout the area, scenic rides are offered in the fall as well as in spring when the trees are in blossom. During the harvest, orchards are open for you to pick your own apples.

Northeast of the junction of Route 346 and U.S. 7 is Barber Pond Road. This is a typical Vermont dirt road that takes you up into the hills, past farms, fields, and streams. The road eventually leads to Route 9, just east of the center of Bennington. Turn left on Route 9 (Main Street) and continue west approximately five miles to the Bennington Museum in Old Bennington.

Here is one of the country's finest regional museums. It has a large collection of Bennington pottery, a rare collection of American blown and pressed glass, the oldest Stars and Stripes in existence, rare documents, costumes, uniforms, and furnishings. It also houses the largest collection of Grandma Moses paintings, and her furniture and memorabilia. The Grandma Moses Schoolhouse, moved from Eagle Bridge, New York, where she lived, is on the grounds.

Just up the hill and to your right in historic Old Bennington is a 306-foot obelisk, the Bennington Battle Monument, commemorating the victory of the American forces. Visitors can take an elevator to the top.

South from the green where the monument stands is the lovely Old First Church, built in 1805 and designed by Lavius Fillmore, the architect of the Middlebury Congregational Church. The churchyard has a number of interesting monuments, not the least of which is that of the poet Robert Frost.

Bennington College is nearby. It is a small, coeducational college that pioneered many progressive teaching methods. The college is a year-round center for music, art, dance, lectures, and movies, most of which are open to the public. Famous sculptors, painters, and writers are often in residence. Three covered bridges give additional character to the college area.

North Bennington, once called Sage City, is the home of the Sage City Symphony, under the direction of composer-musician Louis Calabro. The symphony performs an ambitious schedule of new works. Here also is the Park-McCullough House, a national historic site and now a center of cultural and community events. Tours are given through this elaborate Victorian mansion.

Moving north on Route 7A, you'll pass Harwood Hill Orchards as you drive into Shaftsbury. The state's first Baptist Church was built in Shaftsbury in 1768; it is now the Shaftsbury Historical Society. It is adjoined by an historic graveyard. The distinctive home of nine-term governor James Galusha was designed by Lavius Fillmore, and architects consider its Palladian window to be one of the most beautiful in a private home. On a back road is the Peter Matteson Tavern, an authentic eighteenth-century tavern with outbuildings.

Manchester and the Mountains

On to Arlington on Route 7A. The late Dorothy Canfield Fisher, author of many novels and histories, lived here, as did Norman Rockwell. During the 1940s and early 1950s, Rockwell painted many of his neighbors onto the covers of the *Saturday Evening Post* and the famous *Four Freedoms* series. Some of them are still residents of Arlington.

Continue north on Route 7A to Sunderland. Here is the entrance to the Skyline Drive, a steep narrow toll road (closed in winter) that winds its way to the summit of Mt. Equinox. You can see, nestled below, the Carthusian Monastery, built of Vermont granite and closed to the public. The views from here are magnificent; for a closer look at the wildlife, follow one of the hiking trails that begin at the summit.

After your journey up the 3,816-foot mountain, continue north to Manchester, a famous nineteenth-century summer resort town. U.S. 7 is lined with stately old trees and equally stately homes. The enormous historic Equinox Hotel, just up the street, reopened in 1985. Abraham Lincoln had reservations to stay there when he was assassinated; his son, Robert, owned an estate, Hildene, at the other end of the street, which is now open to the public.

A notable place to visit is the Orvis Company, one of America's largest and oldest producers of fishing equipment. The Fly Fishing Museum is near the Equinox.

Just north of the Equinox, West Road branches off and parallels U.S. 7. From West Road you can reach the Southern Vermont Art Center, formerly an estate. The center has fine views, a sculpture garden, art exhibits, and a tearoom. There are concerts and films.

Back on Route 7A you will come to a shopping area called Factory Point Square, where Manchester bustles with commerce. In Manchester, U.S. 7 meets Route 30, which goes northwest–southeast. If you bear left onto Route 30, you will head toward Dorset, where Vermont marble was first quarried. Dorset's elegance is simpler and quieter than Manchester's. The Dorset Inn is at the town's center on a handsome green. Dorset Playhouse, one of the oldest summer theaters in New England, is quartered here.

Northwest on Route 315 is Rupert, where the Merck Forest Foundation, a private preserve for environmental study, is open most of the year for hiking, cross-country skiing, or simply enjoying nature. After going back to Manchester on Route 30 and heading north on U.S. 7, you'll find peaceful Emerald Lake State Park, surrounded by mountains and marble quarries used many years ago. The lake has a strikingly vivid green hue.

Backtracking to the south at the junction of U.S. 7 with Routes 11 and 30, go east on 11-30 to Bromley Ski Area, home of the world's longest Alpine slide (open Memorial Day through October).

Proceeding east on 11 you will come to Peru, a lovely mountaintop village. North of Peru on a partially paved road is North Landgrove, another picturesque tiny community.

Circle Landgrove and head south to Route 100 toward Londonderry, which is on Route 11, and South Londonderry, on Route 100. Magic Mountain Ski Area is in Londonderry, as are the scenic Lowell Lakes and mountains.

Route 100 runs into Route 30; go west just over two miles to the entry to Stratton Mountain, one of the first four-season resorts in the east. In winter, its trails host World Cup and pro races; in summer, the activities continue with a golf academy, tennis school, and the Volvo International Tennis Tournament in early August. In fall, it presents a month-long Stratton Arts Festival with dance and concerts, crafts, and the visual arts.

From Stratton, wind northeast on a partially paved road or go back to Route 30 and head east to Jamaica, where white-water slaloms are held in spring. South on Route 100 lies West Dover, home of Mount Snow, a large four-season resort now run by the same owners as Killington. Two smaller areas nearby are Carinthia and Haystack.

Coming down about a thousand feet, you reach Wilmington, now a center for tourists and skiers in southern Vermont. Shops abound. Turning west on Route 9, you head toward the mountain town of Searsburg. At Searsburg and the junction with Route 8, turn south on Route 8 and travel until Routes 8 and 100 meet, taking the latter to Readsboro, Whitingham, and Jacksonville. Then turn back north to Route 9. This is truly one of the most scenic Vermont rides; here the mountain roads seem to carry you to the top of the world. A monument to Brigham Young stands in Whitingham, his birthplace.

On to Brattleboro

Continue east on Route 9 to Hogback Mountain, with its renowned 100-mile view of mountain ranges in New Hampshire and Massachusetts as well as the Green Mountains. Perched atop a ridge is a restaurant; you can enjoy the panorama and lunch at the same time. Further on, at Marlboro, the famous Marlboro Music Festival presents summer weekend concerts during July and August under the direction of Rudolf Serkin. The Brattleboro Music Center offers further concerts on the Marlboro College campus.

Continuing east, you reach Brattleboro, a lively town with many shops and restaurants. It is also headquarters of the dairy farmers' Holstein-Friesan Association. A collection of old Estey and Minshall organs, made here in the nineteenth century, is on display at the Brattleboro Museum and Art Center in the old train depot.

North on Route 30 in Dummerston, Rudyard Kipling built his home, Naulahka, for his local bride. Here he wrote *Captains Courageous, Just So Stories,* and the two *Jungle Books.* The house is now sadly deteriorating. In West Dummerston is a long, latticed, covered bridge.

Continue north on Route 30 to Newfane. A Greek Revival courthouse stands at the center of the village. Around the green are white houses and two impressive inns. Teddy Roosevelt was once a visitor; now the economist John Kenneth Galbraith is its most prominent summer resident. Take Route 30 north to Townshend, then Route 35 to Grafton, one of Vermont's prettiest villages. Grafton has been restored; one of its finest buildings is the Old Tavern, an inn visited by figures as diverse as Henry David Thoreau, Daniel Webster, and Paul Newman and Joanne Woodward. West of Grafton lies untouched forest land.

From Grafton, follow Route 121 east to Saxtons River, then north on a paved secondary road to Rockingham to see one of the state's oldest meeting houses. The churchyard is notable for its very old gravestones.

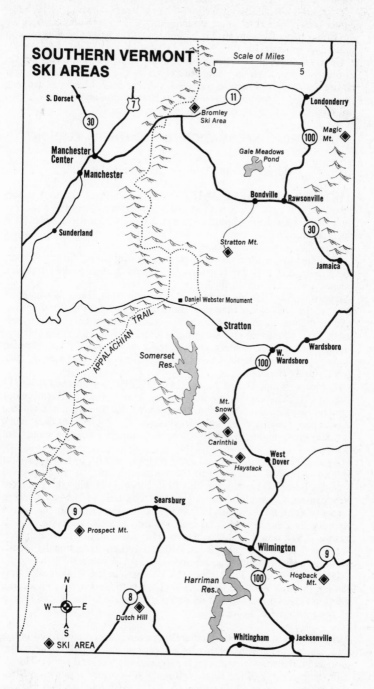

SOUTHERN VERMONT SKI AREAS

Scale of Miles
0   5

S. Dorset

(7)

(11)

Londonderry

Bromley
Ski Area

(30)

(100)

Magic
Mt.

Manchester
Center

Gale Meadows
Pond

Manchester

Bondville

Rawsonville

Sunderland

(30)

Stratton Mt.

Jamaica

Daniel Webster Monument

APPALACHIAN TRAIL

Stratton

Somerset
Res.

(100)

W.
Wardsboro

Wardsboro

Mt.
Snow

Carinthia

West
Dover

Haystack

Searsburg

(9)

Prospect Mt.

Wilmington

(9)

Harriman
Res.

(100)

Hogback
Mt.

N

W   E

S

(8)

Dutch Hill

Whitingham

Jacksonville

◆ SKI AREA

Go south on Route 103 to Bellows Falls where, in the mid-1980s, a fish ladder was designed to entice the Atlantic salmon into coming back up the Connecticut River to spawn farther north; the first fish returning was spotted in summer 1985.

Continue south on U.S. 5 to Putney, home of the internationally known Putney School. There is a fine old country store here. Harlow's Sugar House has maple products as well as strawberry fields where you can pick your own. U.S. 5 will bring you back to Brattleboro, and you have come full circle on a tour of the two southern counties.

PRACTICAL INFORMATION FOR SOUTHERN VERMONT

Note: The area code for all Vermont is 802

HOW TO GET THERE AND AROUND. Southern Vermont is bordered by New York on the west and Massachusetts on the south and separated from New Hampshire on the east by the Connecticut River. It is easily approached by highway from any direction, and its compact size (only about 50 mi. wide) makes easy touring.

By plane: Major air access is from neighboring states: Albany Airport and Bradley Field serving Hartford–Springfield. Keene, New Hampshire, is served by Precision Airlines.

By train: Amtrak's Montrealer, an overnight train, leaves Washington, D.C., in the evening and arrives in Brattleboro, Bellows Falls, and Springfield in the middle of the night. At the same time, its sister train travels south from Montreal, also stopping at those towns after midnight. For further information, contact any Amtrak office. Another line between New York and Montreal passes through Albany and Glens Falls, New York, during the day.

By bus: Vermont Transit Lines, 135 St. Paul St., Burlington (864–6811 or 800–451–3292) and its connecting lines serve Vermont from all major points in New England and from New York City, Montreal, and Quebec City. Connections are through Greyhound. The route from New York City stops in Bennington and Brattleboro. Connections can be made from Boston.

By car: From New York, take the thruway to exit 24 to Rte. 7. Out of Troy, Rte. 7 will take you to the Vermont border, at which point it becomes Rte. 9 to Bennington and Brattleboro. I–91 will take you from New Haven, Connecticut, through Massachusetts, to the southeastern corner of Vermont. I–91 then follows the Connecticut River up the eastern boundry, as does the scenic and more leisurely U.S. 5. The major western route is U.S. 7, now a limited-access road from Bennington to Manchester. Use Rte. 7A as a shunpike. Routes 30 and 100 are exceptionally scenic, winding through mountains, ski areas, and small villages.

On foot: The Long Trail, called "A Footpath in the Wilderness," runs 264 mi. through Vermont from Massachusetts to Quebec. In this section, it follows the Appalachian Trail, entering the state at the Massachusetts border southeast of Pownal.

HOTELS AND MOTELS. Generally speaking, accommodations in this area are excellent with a range of establishments geared to the winter sportsman, the summer vacation family, and the weekend visitor. Hotels, with the exception of the newly restored 19th-century Equinox in Manchester and the Latchis in Brattleboro, do not exist in this section. However, resort lodges, often large with luxurious touches, may be found around the ski areas of Stratton, Manchester, and Mt. Snow. Rates may be lower in the off-season, summer and fall, although not necessarily in foliage season. Inquire when making reservations. Motels, some older but with all the amenities such as color TV, convey the essence of small-town life. Unless otherwise indicated, properties are open year-round. Prices are based on double occupancy, European Plan (room only) unless indicated: *Deluxe*, $75 and up, *Expensive*, $50–$75, *Moderate*, $30–$50, *Inexpensive*, $30 and under.

Arlington

Candlelight Motel, Rte. 7A, 05250 (375–6647). *Moderate–Expensive.* 17 units on 3½ acres of grounds. Fishing, pool, mountain views.
Cutleaf Maples Motel & Inn, Rte. 7A, 05250 (375–2725). *Moderate.* Home-cooked breakfast available, lounge with fireplace. Pets, free crib.

Bellows Falls

Highlands Motel, jct. U.S. 5 and Rte. 103, 05101 (463–9840). *Moderate.* Restaurant and lounge.

Bennington

Best Western New Englander Motor Inn, 220 Northside Dr., 05201 (442–6311). *Expensive.* Some moderate rooms, children under 12 free. In-room coffee, HBO, a few steam baths-whirlpool, refrigerators, heated pool, restaurant.
Ramada Inn, U.S. 7 at Kocher Dr., 05201 (442–8145). *Expensive.* Children under 18 free. Four-story contemporary building, indoor pool and whirlpool, game room, outdoor tennis. Restaurant, lounge, dancing.
Bennington Motor Inn, 143 W. Main St., 05201 (442–5479). *Moderate–Expensive.* Quiet in-town setting, restaurant adjacent.
Fife 'n Drum Motel, U.S. 7, 05201 (442–4074). *Moderate–Expensive.* Panoramic view, refrigerators, in-room coffee. Heated pool, playground.
Catamount Motel, 500 South St., 05201 (442–5977). *Moderate.* Lower rates Nov.–Apr. 16 pleasant units, one efficiency unit. In-room coffee, pool.
Darling Kelly's Motel, U.S. 7, 05201 (442–2322). *Moderate.* 24 units on five landscaped acres, mountain view, pool.
Harwood Hill Motel, Rte. 7A, 05201 (442–6278). *Moderate.* Sweeping grounds with fine view.
Kirkside Motor Lodge, 250 W. Main St., 05201 (447–7596). *Moderate.* Each room individually decorated, some antiques. In-room coffee.
Knotty Pine Motel, 130 Northside Dr., 05201 (442–5487). *Moderate.* Lower rates Nov.–Apr., In-room coffee, some efficiencies and refrigerators, pool.

Brattleboro

Quality Inn, U.S. 5, 05301 (254–8701). *Expensive.* Italian restaurant, lounge, pool, pets.
Colonial Motel & Tavern, U.S. 5, 05301 (257–7733). *Moderate.* Restaurant, lounge, patio dining in warm weather. Pool.
Dalem's Chalet, 16 South St., West Brattleboro 05301 (254–4323). *Moderate–Expensive.* Back from the highway, balconies, winter and summer pools, restaurant with Swiss-German specialties.

The Latchis Hotel, 50 Main St., 05301 (254–6300). *Moderate–Expensive.* Restored 1930s art deco hotel.

Red Coach Motor Inn, U.S. 5, 05301 (254–6007, 800–258–1980). *Moderate.* Large motel with restaurant, bar. Pool, laundry.

Londonderry

Blue Gentian Lodge, Rte. 11, 05148 (824–5908). *Moderate–Expensive.* Ponds, secluded pool, lounge with fireplace (bring your own liquor), two game rooms. Ample country meals. American Plan available.

Dostal's Motor Lodge, Magic Mt. Ski Area, 05148 (824–6700). *Moderate–Expensive.* Indoor and outdoor pools, whirlpools, game room.

Magic View Motel, Rte. 11, 05148 (824–3793). *Moderate–Expensive.* 18 rooms, game room, pets.

Swiss Inn, Rte. 11, 05148 (824–3442). *Moderate–Expensive.* Includes a hearty breakfast, dining on premises. Tennis court, swimming pool.

Manchester

The Equinox, Rte. 7A, Manchester Village 05254 (362–4700 or 362–4747). *Deluxe.* Vermont's most historic resort hotel, now with 174 newly restored guest rooms. The 19th-century ambience blends with very modern amenities, golf, tennis, heated pool, cross-country skiing, conference rooms. Dining rooms.

Wilburton Inn, River Rd., 05254 (362–2500). *Deluxe.* Luxurious former estate with 30 guest rooms in Georgian mansion, 5 housekeeping units. Dining room, bar, putting green. The inn also serves tea in the afternoon.

Four Winds Inn and Motel, U.S. 7, 05255 (362–1105). *Expensive.* Rooms in 1854 inn and motel addition. Fireside breakfast available, dining room; golf and tennis privileges at adjacent Manchester Country Club.

Kandahar Lodge, jct. Rtes. 11 and 30, 05255 (824–5531). *Expensive.* Reduced rates in spring. Free sauna, 2-acre trout pond, canoes, heated pool, lounge, restaurants. Golf and tennis privileges available; near hiking trails.

Chalet Motel, Rte. 11, 05255 (362–1622 or 343–9900). *Expensive–Deluxe.* Oversize beds, refrigerator, in-room coffee, free Continental breakfast. Game room, heated pool, hot tubs, golf and tennis privileges.

Palmer House Resort, Rte. 7A, Box 657, 05255 (362–3600). *Expensive–Deluxe.* 22 landscaped acres within walking distance of town. In-room coffee and Continental breakfast, refrigerators. Heated pool, indoor Jacuzzi, sauna.

Aspen Motel, U.S. 7, 05255 (362–2450). *Moderate–Expensive.* Spacious grounds, pool; golf and tennis at adjacent country club.

Barnstead Innstead, Bonnet St., Box 88, 05255 (362–1619). *Moderate–Expensive.* Interesting architect's conversion of a c. 1830 barn with appropriate furnishings. Heated pool and golf and tennis at adjacent country club.

Red Sled Motel, Rte. 11, 05255 (362–2161). *Moderate–Expensive.* In-room refrigerators, AM/FM clock radios, HBO, coffee. Stocked trout pond, picnic area with grills.

Toll Road Motor Inn, Rtes. 11 and 30, Box 813, 05255 (362–1711). *Moderate–Expensive.* Glass-enclosed lobby with fireplace, in-room coffee, refrigerators, pool.

Weathervane Motel, U.S. 7, 05255 (362–2444). *Moderate–Expensive.* Oil paintings in large rooms, in-room coffee, Continental breakfast. Pool and golf privileges.

Mount Snow Region

Mount Snow Resort Center, Mount Snow, 05356 (464–3333). *Deluxe.* 100-room hotel and 250-unit condominium complex at the base of Mount Snow. All have sports center with indoor pools, fitness centers, saunas, and Jacuzzis. Restaurants, nightclub within walking distance.

Waldwinkel Inn, Rte. 100, Mount Snow 05356 (464–5281). *Expensive.* Pool, two recreation rooms, full breakfast included.

Alp-Hof Lodge, Handle Rd., West Dover 05356 (464–3344). *Moderate–Expensive.* Tyrolean lodge, 400 yards from base area. Heated pool, whirlpool, sauna, game rooms.

Andirons Motor Lodge, Rte. 100, West Dover 05356 (464–2114). *Moderate–Expensive.* Three fireplaces and two lounges, dining room. Indoor pool, sauna, whirlpool, game room.

Tamarack Inn at Mount Snow, Upper Handle Rd., Mount Snow 05356 (464–8850). *Moderate–Expensive.* Balcony rooms, 5-minute walk to slopes. Fireplace. Restaurant.

Weathervane Lodge, Dorr Fitch Rd., Mount Snow 05356 (464–5426). *Moderate–Expensive.* Tyrolean-style lodge, large lounge (bring your own liquor), fireplaces.

Putney

Putney Motor Inn, Depot Rd. 05346 (387–5517). *Moderate.* Old house with motel addition, comfortable public rooms and popular dining room, friendly bar. Adjacent to I–91.

Stratton Mountain

Liftline Lodge, Base Area, 05155 (297–2600). *Deluxe.* Close to ski lifts, some apartment units. Dining, lounge, fireplaces. Pool, tennis, sauna, whirlpool, massage.

Stratton Mountain Inn, Base Area, 05155 (297–2500). *Deluxe.* Dining room, lounge, weekend entertainment. Pool, tennis, golf, riding. Next to ski lifts.

Stratton Mountain Resort, 05155 (297–2200). *Deluxe.* Mountain condominiums, 27-hole golf course, tennis, sports center.

Birkenhaus, Base Area 05155 (297–2000). *Moderate–Expensive.* Small lodge in birch grove. Double and bunk rooms, private baths. Continental cuisine.

INNS, GUEST HOUSES, BED AND BREAKFASTS. Many come to Vermont for just such places, which usually provide the one-of-a-kind atmosphere so rare in our increasingly homogenized lodging picture. Happily, the small inn and bed-and-breakfast business is perhaps the most expansive now. Nearly every village in this section will have such a spot. Ask at the general store, consult listings at tourist-information stands, or contact such groups as American Bed and Breakfast, Box 983, St. Albans 05478; Bed and Breakfast Network of New England, Box 815, Brattleboro 05301 (257–5252); or Vermont Bed and Breakfast, Box 139, Browns Trace, Jericho 05465 (899–2354, 800–442–1404). Rates at inns generally fall in the *moderate–expensive* categories, ranging from about $35 per room to $90 double occupancy without meals and upwards to $200 with breakfast and dinner for two (Modified American Plan[MAP]) and can vary a good deal by season. Bed-and-breakfast accommodations are usually in the *moderate* price range for a double room, sometimes with shared bath. A sampling of inns follows:

Arlington

Arlington Inn, Rte. 7A, 05250 (375–6532). 1848 Greek Revival inn with Victorian furniture, French-Italian dinners.

Hill Farm Inn, Sunderland Rd., 05250 (375–2269). The last of the area's farm inns. Rural friendliness; seven rooms and summer cabins.

West Mountain Inn, Rte 313, 05250 (375–6516). Seven-gabled, hilltop inn surrounded by 150 acres of trails, pastures, and ponds. Cross-country skiing, breakfast, dinner, Sun. brunch.

Bennington

Four Chimneys, 21 West Rd., 05201 (442–3500). Inn and restaurant at former estate, three rooms, Continental breakfast.

Walloomsac Inn, Monument Ave., 05201 (442–4865). The oldest inn (c. 1766) in Vermont, definitely not restored, still provides simple rooms inexpensively. Closed Nov. 1–May 30.

Chester

The Inn at Long Last, Main St., 05143 (875–2444). Cheery updating of an old village inn. Outdoor pool, tennis, game rooms. MAP, public dining.

Dorset

Barrows House, 05251 (867–4455) A miniresort with nicely decorated inn rooms, seven cottages, swimming pool, two tennis courts, bike and cross-country ski rentals. Fine dining room, MAP. Closed Nov.

Dorset Inn, 05251 (867–5500). Attractive newly decorated rooms in 200-year-old inn with fine dining for guests and public. MAP.

Grafton

The Old Tavern, 05146 (843–2231). An 1801 inn, lavishly restored in mid-1960s with many antiques, pleasant dining rooms (jackets please), a natural pond swimming pool, tennis, and lawn games. Gracious; not geared to children.

Londonderry—South Londonderry

Highland House, Rte. 100, Londonderry 05148 (824–3019). Quiet, comfortable inn in 1842 structure and carriage house. Fine dining, pool.

Londonderry Inn, Box 301, South Londonderry 05148 (824–5226). Another old homestead (1826), with welcoming public rooms, charming hillside view over West River, buffet breakfast.

Manchester

The Inn at Manchester, Box 452, 05254 (362–1793). Mansion with big porch restored imaginatively. 22 rooms, game room, pool. Good breakfast; dinner on weekends in winter.

Reluctant Panther Inn, West Rd., Box 678, 05254 (362–2568). Small inn, almost equally notable for delicious Continental cuisine and purple decor. Four of seven guest rooms have fireplaces. Public dining, bar. Closed Nov. and Apr.

Skylight Lodge, Rte. 11, 05255 (362–2566). Last of the original lodge owners from "back when." Family atmosphere, dormitory rooms or modest, cozy doubles. Family-style meals. Cellar with piano and stone fireplace (bring your own liquor).

The Village Country Inn, Rte. 7A, 05254 (362–1792). Completely renovated old Worthy Inn, now with French atmosphere, Breakfast, dinner. Pool.

Marlboro

Longwood Inn, Rte. 9, 05344 (257–1545). An inn set in a 200-year-old farmhouse, attractive rooms, popular dining room, pond for swimming and skating.

Mount Snow

The Hermitage, Coldbrook Rd., Wilmington 05363 (464–3511). 16 guest rooms, excellent dining, wide selection of wines. Cross-country ski center, game-bird farm, sauna.

Inn at Sawmill Farm, Rte. 100, West Dover 05356 (464–8131) Elegant is the word. Superb meals, fine wine selection. Restored group of farm buildings. Trout pond, swimming, tennis.

Nutmeg Inn, Rte. 9, Wilmington 05363 (464–3351). Early American farmhouse at village edge converted to nine-room inn. Informal, cozy, bar (bring your own liquor). MAP in winter.

Snow Den Inn, West Dover 05356 (464–9355). Small, warm atmosphere, in village. MAP in winter.

The White House, Rte. 9, Wilmington 05363 (464–2135). Marvelous knolltop site for this handsome former mansion. Elegance and fine dining. Sauna, whirlpool, steam room, cross-country skiing.

Newfane

The Four Columns Inn, 230 West St., 05345 (365–7713). Greek Revival mansion, now with 12 guest rooms and renowned restaurant in adjoining barn. Pond skating, pool. On green.

Old Newfane Inn, 05345 (365–4427). The other "book end" in this town of two notable inns on the green. Antiques-drenched rooms, beamed dining room, Swiss-French cuisine. Closed Nov. and Apr.

Peru

Johnny Seesaw's, Rte. 11, 05152 (824–5533). Rustic, comfortable, informal early ski inn. 24 rooms ranging from dormitories to bedrooms with fireplaces; four cottages.

The Wiley Inn, Rte. 11, 05152 (824–6600). Meandering 200-year-old inn with 13 guest rooms, library, home cooking.

Putney

Hickory Ridge House, Hickory Ridge Rd., 05346 (387–5709). Former 1808 estate house with 7 rooms. 23 acres for hiking, cross-country skiing. Home-cooked breakfast.

Saxtons River

Saxtons River Inn, Main St., 05154 (869–2110). Turn-of-the century decor, each room individually decorated. Public dining, popular pub.

Weston

Colonial House Inn and Motel, Box 138, 05161 (824–6286). Fine combination of six inn rooms and nine motel units with a dining room between; homemade breads and pies. Breakfast included.
The Inn at Weston, Rte. 100, 05161 (824–5804). Delightful dining with daily menu changes. Pub with fireplace, game rooms for adults and children.

RESTAURANTS. The range of good eating is enormous in the area, from down-home diners to very sophisticated resort fare. The following price ranges are based on a complete dinner for one person, excluding beverage, tax, and tip: *Deluxe,* $30 and up, *Expensive,* $20–$30, *Moderate,* $10–$20, *Inexpensive,* under $10.

Bennington

Four Chimneys, Rte. 9 (442–5257). *Expensive.* Converted mansion, French and Continental cuisine. Lounge, wine cellar.
Bennington Station, Depot St. (447–1080). *Moderate–Expensive.* Choose Iron Horse chili for lunch, prime rib for dinner, in a wonderful converted railroad station.
The Brasserie, 324 County St. (447–7922). *Moderate–Expensive.* French tavern-style restaurant with varied daily menu plus salads, pâtés.
Publyk House, Rte. 7A (442–8301). *Inexpensive–Moderate.* Remodeled barn, sensational view of Mt. Anthony and battle monument. Steak and seafood. Own baking, children's portions.
Blue Benn Diner, U.S. 7 (442–8977). *Inexpensive.* This is a find: traditional meat-and-potatoes diner food with vegetarian specials like tabouli, falafel, and eggplant parmigiana. From 5 A.M. through late afternoon.

Brattleboro

The Country Kitchen, Rte. 9 (257–0338). *Moderate–Expensive.* Large, many rooms, New England beef and seafood dishes, daily specials.
Dalem's Chalet, South St. (254–4323). *Moderate–Expensive.* Dinner only by reservation at this motel restaurant with Swiss-German menu.
Jolly Butcher, Rte. 9 (254–6043). *Moderate–Expensive.* Wide range of beef and seafood, from burgers on up.
The Common Ground, 25 Elliot St. (257–0855). *Inexpensive–Moderate.* Cooperatively owned and operated with a natural foods choice of high-quality ethnic dishes, including Mexican and Greek. Fish and chicken served, also wine and beer. No smoking.
Jade Wah, 40 Main St. (254–2392). *Inexpensive–Moderate.* Simple family place with Szechuan-Mandarin dishes, some American food.

Dorset

Barrows House, Rte. 30 (867–4455). *Expensive.* Built in 1776, now an inn specializing in good food. Varied menu of veal, beef, and seafood.

Chanticleer, U.S. 7, East Dorset (362–1616). *Moderate–Expensive.* One-time dairy farm, now has candlelight dining in French country mood. Beef, seafood, duckling, homemade pastries.

Village Auberge, Rte. 30 (867–5715). *Moderate–Expensive.* Restored inn. Quiet luxury, sheer heaven at the dinner table with excellent French cuisine.

Grafton

The Old Tavern, Rte. 121 (842–2231). *Expensive.* Delightful restored 1801 inn. New England beef and chicken specialties. Reservations required for dinner; jackets preferred for men.

Londonderry–South Londonderry

Three Clock Inn, off Rte. 100, S. Londonderry (824–6327). *Expensive–Deluxe.* Two cozy dining rooms serving delicious veal dishes and other delights for many years. Desserts are special. Porch dining.

Londonderry Inn, Rte. 100, S. Londonderry (824–5226). *Moderate–Expensive.* Breakfast and dinner in old-fashioned dining room with new innovative menu including unusual soups.

Nordic Inn, Rte. 11 (824–6444). *Moderate–Expensive.* Solarium dining area, informal lunch, ambitious dinner menu.

Garden Restaurant, Rte. 11 (824–9574). *Inexpensive–Moderate.* Informal riverside place with brickwork, intimate bar. Lunch all day, with additional chicken, seafood, and vegetarian offerings at night.

Manchester

Reluctant Panther, West Rd. (362–2568). *Expensive.* Imaginative five-course dinners in elegant setting. Selections might include brace of quail or trout. Reservations advised.

Sirloin Saloon, Rte. 11 (362–3600). *Moderate–Expensive.* More than a steak house; they also do a fine job with chicken, lobster, crab. Victorian decor, children's portions.

Toll Gate Lodge, off Rtes. 11 and 30 (362–1779). *Moderate–Expensive.* The rushing brook sets off a special Continental dining experience.

Harvest Inn, Manchester Village (362–2125). *Moderate.* Everyone eats hearty American dinners here, popular for years.

The Buttery, U.S. 7, in the Jelly Mill (362–3544). *Inexpensive.* Often-crowded luncheon spot, excellent sandwiches, soups, desserts.

Double Hex, Rtes. 11 and 30 (362–1270). *Inexpensive.* The real stuff: all varieties of burger, franks, chicken, shakes.

Quality Restaurant, U.S. 7 (362–9839). *Inexpensive.* A vintage downtown breakfast, lunch, and dinner spot that was the setting for Norman Rockwell's "War News," a print of which is on view.

Marlboro

Skyline Restaurant, Rte. 9 (464–5535). *Moderate.* Sensational view, and real maple syrup on your pancakes and waffles, country fare for lunch and dinner. Nothing fancy.

Mount Snow Area

The Hermitage, Coldbrook Rd., Wilmington (464–3759). *Expensive.* Four dining rooms with an intimate feel. Splendid meals and a 30,000-bottle wine cellar. Lunch and dinner; no credit cards.

Inn at Sawmill Farm, Rte. 100, West Dover (464–8131). *Expensive.* Elegance in a rustic setting, superior roast duck, wide choice of unusual appetizers, and super desserts. Reservations.

The White House, Rte. 9, Wilmington (464–2135). *Expensive.* Wood paneled, fireplace, and well-regarded Continental dinners.

Costello's, Rte. 9, Wilmington (464–2812). *Moderate.* Northern Italian food, but separate pizza and sandwich menu for addicts; a family place.

Poncho's Wreck, Main St., Wilmington (464–9320). *Moderate.* Casual and good, the place for Mexican food, seafood, smoked meats, and fish.

Newfane

Four Columns Inn, 230 West St. (365–7713). *Deluxe.* Restored 1830 inn. French cuisine using local products when possible. Dinner only, jackets for men, reservations recommended.

Old Newfane Inn, on the green (365–4427). *Expensive.* Distinguished 1787 inn with fireside dining; superb Continental cusine, with unusual soups, veal, and frogs legs.

Stratton Mountain

Birkenhaus, Base Area (297–2000). *Moderate–Expensive.* Make reservations for an Austrian dinner here in the appropriate setting.

Liftline Lodge, Base Area (297–2600). *Moderate–Expensive.* Wild game specialties are part of the Austrian offerings here. Nice for lunch also.

Three Mountain Inn, Rtes. 30 and 100, Jamaica (874–4140). *Moderate.* Plank floors and candlelight, smoked trout and pampered veal.

Weston

The Inn at Weston, Rte. 100 (824–5804). *Moderate–Expensive.* Small inn with big visions of how to prepare good food. Everything homemade. Reservations recommended.

Weston Playhouse Dinner Theater, the Common (824–5288). *Moderate.* Dining downstairs July–Sept., Thurs.–Mon.; lunch Sat.

The Bryant House, Main St. (824–6287). *Inexpensive.* Owned by Vermont Country Store, this is the place for lunch and tea, featuring old-time Vermont cheddar and common crackers, sandwiches, chicken pie. Open 11:30 A.M.–2:30 P.M.

TOURIST INFORMATION. For the most complete information, stop at the Vermont Welcome Center at Guilford on I–91 at the Massachusetts border, which offers maps and brochures of all kinds. Also Greater Bennington Chamber of Commerce, U.S. 7, Bennington (442–5900); Brattleboro Area Chamber of Commerce, 180 Main St., Brattleboro (254–4565); Manchester and the Mountains Chamber of Commerce, Manchester Center (362–2100); Mt. Snow Region Chamber of Commerce, Wilmington (474–8092).

VERMONT

TOURS. *Belle of Brattleboro* (254–8080) offers Connecticut River tours in 49-passenger boat from Brattleboro. Daily, except Mon., Memorial Day–Oct. 15.

SEASONAL EVENTS. January: Week-long winter carnival at Okemo Ski Area.

February: Brattleboro Winter Carnival, a week ending with big Washington's Birthday cross-country ski race around Brattleboro area's extensive trail system. Winter carnivals in Manchester, Springfield, and Chester.

March: The first Tues. is Town Meeting Day; visitors welcome.

April: Mud season; many inns close. Easter sunrise service on top of Mt. Snow.

May: Outing and canoe clubs sponsor white water slalom championships on West River, Jamaica. Memorial Day, state parks open.

June: Mid-June, Annual garden party at Hildene, Manchester (reservations 362–1788). Late June, strawberry supper at Dummerston Center grange.

July: Fourth of July parades in Bennington and Brattleboro. Bennington Museum Antique Show weekend, mid-July. Marlboro Music Festival, mid-July–mid-Aug. Month-long Yellow Barn Music Festival in Putney.

August: Bennington Battle Day Weekend in Bennington, mid-Aug., with parade, barbecue, entertainment. Volvo International Tennis Tournament, Stratton Mt. Resort.

September: Newfane Heritage Festival. Month-long Stratton Arts Festival.

October: Apple Pie Festival, Dummerston Center. Fall foliage at peak by second week.

November: Deer season opens 12 days before Thanksgiving.

December: Candlelight tours of Hildene in Manchester.

PARKS AND FORESTS. Living Memorial Park, Rte. 9, west of Brattleboro, is an unusually expansive and well-equipped municipal park, with a swimming pool (June–Labor Day, fee), ice-skating rink (Dec.–Mar., fee), lawn games, 9-hole golf course, ski hill with T-bar lift.

Dutton Pines State Park, 5 mi. north of Brattleboro on U.S.5 (254–2277), picnicking.

Fort Dummer State Park, 2 mi. south of Brattleboro (254–2610), camping, hiking.

Jamaica State Park, Town Rd., Jamaica (874–4600), camping, hiking, nature trail, naturalist, West River fishing, canoeing.

Molly Stark State Park, Rte. 9, Wilmington (464–5460), camping, hiking to Mt. Olga fire tower, picnicking.

Lake Shaftsbury State Park, Rte. 7A, Shaftsbury (375–9978), group camping area, swimming, picnics, trails, rental boats and canoes, fishing.

Townshend State Park, Town Rd., Newfane (365–7500), camping, Townshend Dam fishing, hiking.

Note: State parks open the Fri. before Memorial Day and close the day after Labor Day. They charge fees; camping reservations recommended.

FALL FOLIAGE. Vermont's patchwork-quilt countryside, picturesque villages, and forests are ideal for self-conducted tours during foliage season when the hills are afire with color. This is Vermont's busiest tourist season, so advance overnight reservations are a must.

From Brattleboro: Follow Rte. 30 to Rawsonville, Rte. 100 to Londonderry, Rte. 11 to Chester, Rte. 103 to Rockingham, U.S. 5 back to Brattleboro (approximately 90 mi.).

From Manchester Center: Take Rte. 7A to South Shaftsbury, Rte. 67 to North Bennington, Prospect St. and Silk Rd. to Old Bennington, U.S. 7 to Pownal and Williamstown, Massachusetts, north via Rtes. 2, 100, and 8 to Searsburg (side trip to Somerset Reservoir on unmarked road), Rte. 9 to Bennington, north to Manchester Depot via unmarked road through East Arlington, Chiselville, and Sunderland (approximately 104 mi.).

SUMMER SPORTS. Bicycling: Backroads here are great for biking. The West Hill Shop, Putney, at I–91 exit (387–5718), is a center for cycling information, tour suggestions, and rentals. In Wilmington, it's Valley Cyclery (464–2728) and in Grafton, Gretchen's Bicycle Rentals (843–2234). Bike Vermont (457–3553) has weekend and five-day trips, May–Oct.

Boating and Canoeing: Good flat-water canoeing on the Connecticut River between Bellows Falls and the Vernon Dam; white-water boating in Apr. on the West River near East Jamaica. Boat rental at Harriman Reservoir, Wilmington. For *Boating and Water Sports* booklet, write Vermont Travel Division, 134 State St., Montpelier 05602.

Golf: Courses in the area: Mt. Snow Country Club, West Dover (464–3333), rolling course at 2,000 ft.; Haystack, Wilmington (464–5321), spectacular mountain scenery; Equinox Country Club, Manchester (362–3223), well-groomed, rolling; Stratton Mt. Country Club (297–1880), Geoffrey Cornish design, also used by Stratton Golf School (297–2200).

Swimming: Two beaches at Harriman Reservoir, Wilmington; Living Memorial Park pool, Brattleboro; Townshend Dam, West Townshend.

Tennis: Public courts at Manchester by the hour or weekly membership; Stratton Mt. (297–2200) has 15 outdoor and four indoor courts, major Volvo tournament, early Aug.

Horseback riding: West River Lodge and Stable (365–7745), Brookline (2 mi. to Newfane), has inn, stable, riding school. Homestead Farm and Riding Stables, Newfane (348–7834), and Windhill Farm Stable, Manchester (362–2604), trail rides, instruction.

WINTER SPORTS. Downhill skiing: Stratton Mt., Stratton (297–2200) with 1,900-ft. drop, highly ranked for facilities; Mt. Snow, West Dover (464–3333), 1,700-ft. drop, all-around resort; Magic Mountain, Londonderry (824–5567), 1,600-ft. drop, Swiss atmosphere; Haystack, Wilmington (464–5321), 1,400-ft. drop, family area; Bromley, Peru (824–5522), 1,334-ft. drop, founded 1937, friendly; Okemo, Ludlow (228–4041), 2,150-ft. drop, recent expansion of trails, lifts. See state ski brochure for small areas.

Cross-country skiing: Touring centers include Hermitage, Wilmington (464–3511); Dutch Hill, Heartwellville (694–1202); White House, Wilmington (464–2136); Viking (824–6444) and Nordic Inn (824–3933), Londonderry; Hildene, Manchester (362–1788).

Snowmobiling is forbidden on public highways, except to cross, and on private land or water without owner's written consent. See Agency of Environmental Conservation map for six areas in state on public land.

Ice skating: Living Memorial Park, Brattleboro; Dana L. Thompson Recreation Area, Manchester.

FISHING. State's most famous trout stream is the Battenkill in Manchester; Orvis Fly Fishing School (362–3434) nearby. Nearly every river or lake has a fishing access; see pamphlet, *Vermont Guide to Fishing,* for a map detailing species and location. License available from town clerk, some sports shops.

HUNTING. Hunting season is Oct.–Nov., with weeks for deer, hare, and rabbit, grey squirrel, partridge. See pamphlet, *Vermont Guide to Hunting,* for details; license from town clerk or game warden.

CAMPING. The Department of Forests, Parks, and Recreation (828–3375) operates 35 state campgrounds. See *Parks and Forests,* above for locations in southern Vermont. For reservations, call the department before May or specific parks after that date. Private campgrounds information may be obtained where tourist information is available.

SPECTATOR SPORTS. Volvo International Tennis Tournament, Stratton (297–2900), the first week of Aug., is a major tennis event. Pari-mutuel Greyhound racing at Green Mt. Racetrack, U.S. 7, Pownal (823–7311), Feb.–Oct.

HISTORIC SITES AND HOUSES. The following provide the visitor with a "low-key" link with history. Call ahead to check hours and admission fees.

Bennington

Historic Bennington Walking Tours, with self-guided map from Chamber of Commerce, includes 306-ft. limestone shaft of Bennington Battle Monument, Old First Church, and Burying Ground (Robert Frost's epitaph is, "He had a lover's quarrel with the world.")

Park-McCullough House, Rte. 67A, N. Bennington (442–2747). Splendid 35-room Victorian mansion with period furniture and delightful children's playhouse in the same style. Tours May–Oct. Closed Sat.

Manchester

Hildene (362–1768), Robert Todd Lincoln's 24-room Georgian Revival mansion on 412 acres, has formal gardens, paths, picnic tables. Daily tours late May–late Oct.

Rockingham

Old Rockingham Meeting House, Vermont's oldest (1787) unchanged public building; a simple and serene country church with box pews, old burial ground.

Whitingham

Brigham Young, the Morman prophet, was born here and is commemorated by a monument on Town Hill and at the site of his birthplace on Stimpson Hill.

MUSEUMS. There are a few museums of note in the area. Keep in mind that many close for part of the year. Check ahead for admission fees.

Bennington

Bennington Museum, Rte. 9 (447–1571), houses one of the best collections of early American glass and Bennington Pottery and the largest collection of Grandma Moses paintings. Daily Mar. 1–Dec. 22; weekends Jan. and Feb.

Brattleboro

Brattleboro Museum and Art Center, old railroad station (257–0124). Interesting historical exhibits and creative changing art exhibits. Apr.–Dec. 15, Tues.–Sun. 1–4 P.M.

Manchester

Southern Vermont Art Center, off West Rd. (362–1405). Paintings, sculpture, prints, photographs, lovely grounds, tearoom. June–mid-Oct. Closed Mon., Sun. morning.
Museum of American Fly Fishing, Rte. 7A. Over 1,000 rods and reels made by famous rod builders or owned by famous anglers. Handsome 19th-century hand-tied flys. Daily 10 A.M.–4 P.M.

Marlboro

Luman Nelson Museum of New England Wildlife, Rte. 9 (464–5494). Its name says it all: stuffed exhibits of animals and birds. Open daily.

MUSIC, DANCE, AND STAGE. Southern Vermont is alive with fine music. The most famous event, the **Marlboro Music Festival** (254–8163) is held on the Marlboro College campus in July and Aug. Chamber concerts range from baroque to contemporary. Concerts are Sat. evenings, Sun. afternoons, some Fri. evenings. Tickets: Marlboro Music Festival, 135 S. 18th St., Philadelphia, PA 19103; after June 10, Marlboro Festival, Marlboro, VT 05344. More good chamber music at **Yellow Barn Music Festival,** Putney (387–6637), with three concerts a week, July and Aug., and **Kinhaven Music Center,** Weston (824–9592). **Brattleboro Music Center** (257–4523) gives a Bach Festival every fall, other programs, winter and spring. **Bennington Choral Society and Orchestra** (442–8772) performs major works year-round; **Sage City Symphony** (Bennington College Music Department, 442–5401) gives five concerts a year featuring new works commissioned by the orchestra. **Bennington College** also presents dance concerts. Summer theaters: **Dorset Playhouse** (867–5777), **Weston Playhouse** (824–5288), professional companies.
Oldcastle Theater Company, Bennington (474–0564), offers a wide range of drama Apr.–Oct., and the **River Valley Playhouse and Arts Center,** Putney (387–4355), has plays, music, and dance in its own 450-seat theater.

ART GALLERIES. The Peel Gallery, U.S. 7, Danby (293–5230), for contemporary art.
Gallery North Star, Grafton (843–2465), has a second gallery at Stratton Mountain. Both feature works by regional artists.

SHOPPING. Vermont is blessed with unique, interesting shops in unexpected places. Among them in Putney are **Carol Brown,** for natural fiber fabrics, especially Irish wool; and **Green Mt. Spinnery** for heathery and natural yarns spun from local sheep. In Bennington, **Potter's Yard,** County St., for contemporary, well-styled Bennington Pottery, Catamount Glass, and ovenproof cookware. **Candle Mill Village,** Arlington, is a collection of shops featuring candles, cookware, music boxes, and toys. The **Newfane Country Store,** Newfane, is stuffed with quilts, herbs, Christmas ornaments, cheese, and maple syrup. Fine crafts and Scottish woolens star at **Quaigh Design Center,** Wilmington. The granddaddy of mail-order country stores is the **Vermont Country Store,** Weston, and its branch in Rockingham. Stop in. For the best in woodenware, try **J.K. Adams Co.,** Rte. 30, Dorset, or **Weston Bowl Mill,** Weston. The **Jelly Mill,** Manchester Center, is three floors of crafts, gifts, cards, and interesting et ceteras. **Weston Toy Works** makes toys, games, and puzzles in the center of town.

NIGHTLIFE. In Brattleboro, the **Mole's Eye Cafe** (257–0771) is a live music club and **Flat Street** (254–8257) has rock. Among the après ski spots on Rte. 100 between Wilmington and Mt. Snow look for **Sitzmark Lodge** (464–3384), **Snow Barn Entertainment Center** (464–3333), and **Andirons** (464–2114).

CENTRAL VERMONT

Rutland and Marble Country

North of Manchester on U.S. 7 and of Pawlet on Route 30 is Rutland County. Rutland is the largest city in the county and the second largest city in Vermont at about 19,000 population. This is marble country. The John F. Kennedy Center in Washington, D.C., the U.S. Supreme Court Building, and the New York Public Library are constructed of marble quarried in this section.

A scenic entry to Rutland County is from Route 30. On your way through the village of Pawlet, you might stop at the Old Station Restaurant and Ice Cream Parlor, in a building that was once a railroad station. North of Pawlet is Poultney, with the pleasant campus of Green Mountain College, a two-year women's college. East Poultney has a distinctive triangular green, faced by buildings approaching their second century. While it may seem an unlikely place for two distinguished journalistic careers to have begun, Horace Greeley worked four years here as a typesetter, and George Jones, who later helped found the *New York Times,* was a co-worker. The East Poultney Historical Society Museum, built in the eighteenth century, was once a blacksmith shop and melodeon factory.

From Poultney, take Route 140 east to the old spa town of Middletown Springs, which has enjoyed periodic prosperity. A century ago, elegant people came to take the "healing waters." The mineral springs have once again been uncovered, and a replica of a Victorian springhouse sits over the bubbling waters. The Community Church dates from 1796, making it one of the state's oldest. Backtrack to Route 30, then head northwest on Route 22A to Fair Haven. This town was the center of Vermont's slate industry. Note two marble-faced houses on the green. Traveling east on Route 4A, then north on Route 30 brings you to Lake Bomoseen, the largest lake wholly within Vermont. In the 1930s, the writer Alexander Woollcott had a summer house on Neshobe Island and entertained friends whose pranks spawned tales that are still told.

Farther north on Route 30 is Hubbardton, the site of the only Revolutionary battle fought on Vermont soil, July 7, 1777. There is disagreement as to whether the American side suffered a defeat, fought to a standstill, or achieved a moral victory, but General Burgoyne's forces turned back to Fort Ticonderoga before they headed south to battles at Bennington and Saratoga. The Hubbardton Battlefield Museum has an audiovisual display reenacting the battle, as well as a visitor's center.

Head south, again to Route 4A and the town of Castleton, to see an outstanding group of buildings designed by early nineteenth-century architect Thomas Royal Dake. Many are styled in Greek Revival with Ionic columns, Corinthian porticoes, and Palladian motifs blended in his frequently photographed houses that are open when the town celebrates Colonial Day in midsummer. This is also the home of Castleton State College. The Green Mountain Boys planned the attack on Fort Ticonderoga in Castleton.

Now head east on 4A, then north on Route 3 to the marble quarrying town of Proctor. The Vermont Marble Company is a major world producer of marble, and the town reflects this heritage. Walk on marble sidewalks and over a graceful marble bridge; if you live here, you can even go to a marble high school. From Memorial Day to mid-October, you may visit the interesting marble exhibit that includes a movie, viewing of carving, and a gift shop. The quarries are underground and cannot be seen.

Return south on Route 3 to Route 4A and continue to Rutland. This small industrial city is lined with trees and bounded by the Taconic Mountains on the west and the higher Green Mountains to the east. In early September crowds attend the State Fair, and in summer there are band concerts on the green on Sunday evenings. On U.S. 7 you can visit the Chaffee Art Center in one of Rutland's many old mansions, as well as the Tuttle Publishing Company of Rutland and Tokyo. For 40 years Tuttle has published books about the Far East as well as Americana and related subjects. On the lowest level of its offices is a used-book store, and next door is a showroom of its current books.

Travel north on U.S. 7 to Brandon, hometown of Stephen A. Douglas, who campaigned against Abraham Lincoln in a series of historic debates. Douglas was one of many Vermonters who gained fame elsewhere. The trend of more people leaving the state than moving to it has finally reversed; now more people move in. Brandon is worth exploring for the fine collection of old houses, including one of marble and a number of robust Victorians.

Traveling east on Route 73 through Brandon Gap, a dramatic mountain pass, you descend into Rochester, a snug town between the mountains. A hostel welcomes the many bicyclists along Route 100. Continue south on Route 100 to Sherburne Center and the Killington Ski Area, the state's largest and one that extends its skiing season into June (with the help of snowmaking). Summer and fall, it offers a seven-mile round-trip gondola ski-lift ride and many other activities. It is thought that in 1763 the Reverend Samuel Peters ascended Killington Peak on horseback and christened the land Verd Mont. Now Long Trail and Appalachian hikers make the same ascent on foot. The Appalachian Trail turns east toward New Hampshire and the White Mountains at Sherburne Pass. Pico Ski Area is on the western slope of the pass.

Woodstock, Plymouth, and Weston

Driving south on Route 100, you enter Windsor County. At West Bridgewater, take U.S. 4 east to Woodstock, passing through Bridgewater

Corners, which has a shopping mall converted from an old woolen mill that is worth a stop.

Graceful Woodstock with its rare oval green is a year-round attraction for tourists, especially at foliage time. It has been the "shire town" or county seat for 200 years and has thrived as a legal and commercial center, attracting a large number of wealthy people who have appreciated its beauty and helped protect it from too rapid and unwanted change. Stroll about and enjoy the well-kept houses that radiate a nineteenth-century calm. Power lines are buried out of sight, courtesy of a generous grant from summer resident Laurance Rockefeller, who lives with his wife in her grandfather's brick mansion at the edge of town. Mrs. Rockefeller's grandfather was Frederick Billings, who grew up poor in Woodstock but returned much later after he became a California lawyer during the gold rush and saved the Northern Pacific Railroad.

The green has impressive buildings on both sides: the Woodstock Inn, the Norman Williams Public Library in Romanesque style, and a classic courthouse. There are four Paul Revere bells in town, and one can be seen, slightly cracked, on display on the porch of the Congregational Church. Pick up a map showing a walking tour of the town; in summer, there is a tourist information booth on the green.

East of Woodstock is Quechee Gorge, 163 feet deep, formed by the Ottauquechee River. The village of Quechee has a well-known glassblowing shop, Simon Pearce, in the old mill.

North of Woodstock on a back road is scenic Pomfret, with the Skyline Trail for hikers, ski tourists, and horseback riders. Nearby Barnard has a small ski area, Sonnenberg. Suicide Six is the major ski area in Woodstock.

From Woodstock, drive west on U.S. 4 to Route 100A, then continue south to Plymouth to visit Calvin Coolidge's birthplace in Plymouth Notch, open May to October. Here at his father's small house, Coolidge took the oath of office of president, given by his father, a justice of the peace, on the death of President Warren Harding. At the little crossroads settlement are his mother's house, the Wilder House (now a coffee shop), a barn housing an agricultural museum, and a cheese factory. Coolidge is buried in the cemetery here.

South of Plymouth on Route 100, three public fishing areas—Echo and Amherst Lakes and Lake Rescue—lead into Ludlow. North of town on Route 103 in Healdville, you may watch cheese being made at Crowley's, Vermont's oldest cheese factory.

Ludlow is a fairly typical old mill town now making the change to tourism. Okemo Mountain Ski Area was a local ski hill that has now become a growing four-season operation. Heading south out of town on Route 100, you go over Terrible Mountain, a seven-mile humpback in the road that leads to Weston, a village founded in 1799 that retains some early charm. Here are the well-known Vermont Country Store and restaurant, where you can buy all kinds of old-time things, including the common crackers the store makes itself. Across the street is a *real* general store. The Farrar-Mansur house on the green is an early tavern that is now a memorial to the town's earliest settlers and a house museum. Also on the green, the Weston Playhouse is Vermont's oldest professional summer theater. North of town is the beautifully situated Weston Priory, a Benedictine abbey open to visitors. The monks sell eggs, honey, cider, crafts, and records of the music for which they are famous.

NEW ENGLAND

506

Windsor

From Weston, a secondary road will take you to Route 11, which leads to Chester, a pleasant town with an inn right in the center and an impressive double row of stone buildings on North Street. Continuing on Route 11, you reach Springfield, a center of the machine tool industry now undergoing hard times. Just north is Ascutney State Park.

From Springfield, take either I–91 or U.S. 5 to Windsor. Here, in 1777, delegates adopted the constitution of the "free and independent State of Vermont." The republic lasted until 1791; the Old Constitution House, originally a 1772 tavern, is open to visitors. Windsor has many fine old houses, principally along Main Street. Walk along Main Street past the Windsor House, a fine building containing the state craft center and Vermont Public Radio, on to the American Precision Museum, which displays inventions and hand and machine tools from the Industrial Revolution to the present. Built in 1846 as an armory, it made 50,000 rifles during the Civil War. Vermont gave generously of men in that war, and nearly every village has a memorial to them. There is a notable example of religious art—a seven-panel painting, "Seven Sacraments"—by artist and member, George Tooker, in St. Francis of Assisi Roman Catholic Church. Tooker's work hangs in major museums. The longest U.S. covered bridge crosses from Windsor to Cornish, New Hampshire.

PRACTICAL INFORMATION FOR CENTRAL VERMONT

Note: The area code for all Vermont is 802

HOW TO GET THERE AND AROUND. Central Vermont is easily reached by highway from New Hampshire, Massachusetts, and New York and its compact size makes touring a pleasure.

By plane: The Lebanon, New Hampshire, airport, just across the Connecticut River from White River Junction, is served by Precision Airlines. Rutland Airport is also served by Precision Airlines.

By train: Amtrak's Montrealer stops at White River Junction and Springfield on its Washington-Montreal route.

By car: I–91 follows the Connecticut River north from Massachusetts to White River Junction where it meets I–89 to Burlington. I–91 continues to the Canadian border. U.S. 7 is the main north–south route on the western side. U.S. 4 crosses Central Vermont east to west, passing through the large Killington ski area and picturesque Woodstock. Route 100 is scenic and leisurely.

On foot: The Appalachian Trail branches off from the Long Trail east of Mendon; the Long Trail continues north.

HOTELS AND MOTELS. Resort lodging flourishes around Killington and, on a quieter scale, in Woodstock. Large motels and Vermont's last railroad hotel cluster at White River Junction at the confluence of two interstate highways and an Amtrak station. Prices are based on double occupancy, European Plan (room only) unless otherwise indicated: *Deluxe,* $75 and up; *Expensive,* $50–$75; *Moderate,* $30–$50; *Inexpensive,* $30 and under.

Brownsville

Ascutney Mountain Resort Hotel, Rte. 44 at Ascutney Mt. Resort, 05037 (484–7711). *Deluxe.* Tastefully designed in keeping with village style. Restaurant, bar, with health club nearby. Ski in, ski out.

Chittenden

Mountain Top Inn, 6 mi. off U.S. 4, 05737 (483–2311). *Expensive.* Lovely miniresort on 500 mountain-top acres overlooking Chittenden Reservoir and across gorgeous long-range vistas. Notable dining, heated pool, sauna, tennis, riding, fishing, hiking, cross-country ski trails. (Modified American Plan)

Killington-Pico Area

Note: Killington Lodging Bureau (422–3711) or Pico Holidays (775–1927) will make reservations.

Cascades Lodge, Killington Rd., Killington, 05751 (422–3731). *Deluxe.* Candlelight dining, lounge with fireplace, indoor pool, sauna, whirlpool, exercise room. Much cheaper in summer.

Cortina Inn, U.S. 4, Killington 05751 (773–3331). *Deluxe.* Vestpocket resort, a little of everything. Indoor and outdoor pools, sauna, exercise room, tennis. Candlelight dining.

The Mountain Inn, Killington Rd., Killington 05751 (422–3595). *Deluxe.* A luxury lodge within walking distance of the lifts. Sauna, game room, entertainment in lounge.

Summit Lodge, Killington Rd., Killington 05751 (422–3535). *Deluxe.* Great hilltop site, excellent facilities, five fireplaces, heated pool, sauna, raquetball, tennis.

Edelweiss Motel and Chalets, U.S. 4, Rutland 05751 (775–5577). *Moderate.* Apartments, chalets, and motel rooms. Heated pool, game room, picnic area.

Grey Bonnet Inn, Rte. 100, Killington 05751 (775–2537). *Moderate.* Modern inn with game room, pool, sauna, tennis. Modified American Plan in winter.

Mountain Meadows Lodge, 20 Thundering Brook Rd., Killington 05751 (775–1010). *Moderate.* Family-style lodge with dormitory or inn rooms. Pool, hiking.

Sherburne-Killington Motel, U.S. 4, Box HC-34, Killington 05751 (733–9535). *Moderate.* Large rooms, Continental breakfast.

Turn of River Lodge, U.S. 4, Killington 05751 (422–3766). *Moderate.* Rustic, several dormitory-style rooms. Big stone fireplace and setup bar. Continental breakfast.

Val Roc Motel, U.S. 4, Killington 05751 (422–3881). *Moderate.* Some kitchenettes, in-room coffee. Pool, tennis.

Lake Bomoseen

Prospect House, Rte. 30, Bomoseen 05732 (468–5581). *Moderate.* Lakefront motel and nine-hole golf course. Restaurant, beach, boating, fishing, May–Oct.

Ludlow

Note: Okemo Lodging Bureau (228–4041), can help make reservations for slopeside condominiums or surrounding lodging facilities.

Inn Towne Motel, Rte. 103, 05149 (228–8884). *Moderate.* In the middle of town; kitchenettes. Pool.

Plymouth

Farmbrook Motel, Rte. 100A, 05056 (672–3621). *Moderate.* Small motel near brook, picnic tables with outdoor fireplaces, in-room coffee.

Rutland

Best Western Hogge Penny Motor Inn, U.S. 4, 05701 (773–3200). *Expensive–Deluxe.* Condomotel with luxury suites or motel rooms. Two tennis courts, heated pool, restaurant, lounge.

Holiday Inn, U.S. 7, 05701 (775–1911). *Expensive.* Basic Holiday Inn with expanded facilities, new health club and restaurant, indoor pool.

Royal Motel, U.S. 4, 05701 (775–9176). *Moderate.* In-room steam bath, heated pool. Winter weekend rates are more expensive.

Rutland Motel, U.S. 4, 05701 (775–4348). *Moderate.* Modern facility with kitchenettes, heated pool, coffee shop.

Country Squire, U.S. 7B and Rte. 103, N. Clarendon 05759 (773–3805). *Inexpensive.* Small, quiet; free Continental breakfast. Play area. Pets.

Springfield

Howard Johnson Motor Lodge, Exit 7 at I–91, 05156 (885–4516). *Expensive.*

Abby Lynn Motel, Rtes. 106 and 10, 05156 (886–2223). *Moderate.* Attractive, lawn games, grill and picnic area, heated pool, Continental breakfast.

Pa-Lo-Mar Motel, Rte. 11, 05156 (885–4142). *Moderate.* Small, some kitchenettes, heated pool, picnic area.

Quechee

Quechee Gorge Motor Inn, U.S. 4, 05059 (295–7600). *Moderate.* Set among the tall pines, some suites and efficiency units. Restaurant.

White River Junction

Holiday Inn, off U.S. 5, 05001 (295–7537). *Expensive.* Indoor and outdoor pools, sauna, whirlpool, two restaurants.

Howard Johnson Motor Lodge, jct. I–89 and I–91, 05001 (295–3015). *Expensive.* Indoor pool, sauna, game room, coin laundry.

Hotel Coolidge, 118 Main St., 05001 (295–3118). *Moderate.* A real find. One of the last railroad hotels, now spruced up with a comfortable lobby and informal pub and restaurant.

Susse Chalet Motor Lodge, U.S. 5, 05001 (295–3051). *Moderate.* Budget motel with 85 units, pool.

Woodstock

Woodstock Inn and Resort, U.S. 4 on the green, 05091 (457–1100). *Deluxe.* Luxurious modern inn with old-time touches, enormous lobby fireplace, quilts on beds, a Rockresort with adjacent pool, tennis, paddleball, new health club, Robert Trent Jones golf course, nature walks. Stanley Steamer rides in summer, sleigh rides in winter. Downhill and cross-country skiing nearby.

Braeside Motel, U.S. 4, 05091 (457–1366). *Moderate.* Overlooking valley, free Continental breakfast.

Pond Ridge Motel, U.S. 4, 05091 (457–1667). *Moderate.* Roadside motel with river swimming, tennis, picnic area, lawn games.

INNS, GUEST HOUSES, BED AND BREAKFASTS. This is heaven for country inn lovers and bed-and-breakfast enthusiasts. There are many choices. Some include meals, some do not; some have seasonal rates. It is best to check rates individually. Rates at inns generally fall in the *moderate–expensive* categories, ranging from about $35 to $90 per room double occupancy without meals, and upwards to $200 with breakfast and dinner for two (Modified American Plan). Bed-and-breakfast accommodations are usually in the *moderate* price range for a double, sometimes with shared bath. For listings of bed-and-breakfast homes, contact American Bed and Breakfast, Box 983, St. Albans 05478; Bed and Breakfast Network of New England, Box 815, Brattleboro 05301 (257–5252); or Vermont Bed and Breakfast, Box 139, Browns Trace, Jericho 05465 (899–2354, 800–442–1404).

Bethel

Greenhurst Inn, River St., 05032 (234–9474). Turreted Victorian inn with tennis, gazebo, croquet.

Brandon

The Churchill House Inn, Rte. 73, 05733 (247–3300). Center of cross-country ski inn-to-inn tours, century-old farmhouse, ski trails, and hearty breakfasts and dinners.

Chittenden

Tulip Tree Inn, Chittenden Dam Rd., 05737 (483–6213). Former inventor's home, now a small inn beside trout stream, near Chittenden Reservoir. Candlelit fine dining.

Fair Haven

Vermont Marble Inn, 12 W. Park Place, 05743 (265–8383). Splendid Victorian decor and memorable dining.

Goshen

Blueberry Hill Inn, off Rte. 73, 05733 (247–6735). A popular cozy inn with antiques in rooms, good food on the stove. Cross-country ski center, inn-to-inn tours.

Gassets

Old Town Farm Lodge, Rte. 13, RD 1, Chester Depot 05143 (878–2346). Family-style lodge. Functional, not fancy; pond for swimming or skating.

Killington-Pico Area

Inn at Long Trail, U.S. 4 at Sherburne Pass, Killington 05751 (775–7181). The first inn built for skiers in the state (1938); rustic, trees for interior supports, large boulder in dining room. Lively bar, Guinness on tap.

The Vermont Inn, U.S. 4, Killington 05751 (773–9847). 19th-century farmhouse with 16 rooms; candlelit dining, sauna, tennis, swimming. Rustic bar.

Lake St. Catherine

Lake St. Catherine Inn, Rte. 30, Poultney 05764 (287–9347). Rustic inn on small lake; dining room. Open May–Oct.

Ludlow

Combles Family Inn, off Rte. 100, 05149 (228–8799). Secluded farmhouse inn with small motel addition, family-style meals.

Country Peasant Inn, 82 Andover St., 05149 (228–8926). Village home; tavern and dining room. Spring-fed pond.

Governor's Inn, Rte. 103 on the green, 05149 (228–8830). Splendid Victorian decoration, gracious service, 8 guest rooms, elegant dining room with excellent food.

The Okemo Inn, Rte. 100, 05149 (228–2031). 1810 home with 12 guest rooms, family-style meals, reading room, sauna, pool.

Plymouth

Echo Lake Inn, Rte. 100, Tyson 05149 (228–8602). A Victorian summer hotel survivor, with long, white porch, some shared baths. Informal, dining room, tennis, pool, beach, canoes. Condominium units in carriage house.

Norwich

The Inn at Norwich, 225 Main St., 05055 (649–1143). Early inn, now much modernized, Victorian lounge, popular dining room, motel addition.

Proctorsville

Golden Stage Inn, off Rte. 103, 05153 (226–7744). A 1796 white clapboard coach stop, now with 10 comfortable rooms, good dining.

Okemo Lantern House, Rte. 131 near 103, 05153 (226–7770). A pearl among country inns, seven rooms in a former mansion with convivial family dining table.

Quechee

Inn at Marshland Farm, River Rd., 05059 (295–3133). Farm-style luxury, 22 guest rooms, spacious lounge, good meals, guest privileges at the Quechee Club.

Shrewsbury

Shrewsbury Inn, Rte. 103, Cuttingsville 05738 (492–3355). 1830s mansion with six rooms in small town. Dining room.

Springfield

Hartness House, 30 Orchard St., 05156 (885–2115). Former mansion of a governor-inventor on a bluff, 45 guest rooms, gracious dining room, lively bar-game room.

Weathersfield

The Inn at Weathersfield, Rte. 106, 05151 (263–9217). This is a delight. 18th-century country home, now with nicely decorated public and guest rooms, elegant dining.

Windsor

Juniper Hill Inn, Juniper Hill Rd., 05089 (674–5273). 15 rooms with private bath; library and 3 parlors in a mansion built in 1901 and listed on the National Register of Historic Places.

Woodstock

The Kedron Valley Inn, Rte. 106, S. Woodstock 05071 (457–1473). Antique quilts in rooms dispersed among 1828 inn, 1824 tavern, and log cabin motel annex. "Nouvelle Vermont" menu, riding stable, pond. Quiet village.

Lincoln Covered Bridge Inn, U.S. 4, 05091 (457–3312). Country inn with six rooms, restaurant.

The Village Inn of Woodstock, Pleasant St., 05091 (457–1255). Old-fashioned comfort, in-town location, informal, nine rooms, varied menu, bar.

RESTAURANTS. Don't overlook the inns for dining around here; many serve dinner to the public. Call ahead. There is no atmosphere quite like a *real* country inn. Restaurant designers can't match it. The price ranges given are based on a complete dinner for one person, excluding beverage, tax, and tip: *Deluxe,* $30 and up; *Expensive,* $20–$30; *Moderate,* $10–$20; *Inexpensive,* under $10.

Barnard

Barnard Inn, Rte. 12 (234–9961). *Deluxe.* Swiss-born-and-trained owner-chef produces wonderful roast duck with seasonal sauces, fresh vegetables creatively cooked, gorgeous desserts from a trolley, and excellent service. Elegantly rustic atmosphere; jackets for men. Worth every penny. Reservations.

Brandon

The Adams, U.S. 7 (247–6644). *Moderate.* This restaurant in the pictur-esque Otter Valley serves a varied menu with its own pastries. Bar.

Chittenden

Mountain Top Inn, 6 mi. off U.S. 4 (483–2311). *Expensive.* Charming dining area with colonial decor. Prime ribs are featured. Bar.

Killington-Pico Area

Cortina Inn, U.S. 4 (773–3331). *Expensive–Deluxe.* Fine dining in quiet comfort. Lively bar.

Hemingway's, U.S. 4 (422–3886). *Expensive–Deluxe.* A special experi-ence; everything is fresh, beautifully cooked and served. "Regional, classic cuisine" includes pheasant, rabbit, fine wine.

Grist Mill, Killington Rd. (422–3970). *Moderate–Expensive.* Big stone hearth in a pondside restaurant. Fish, beef, pasta, vegetable stir-fry.

Back Behind Saloon, jct. U.S. 4 and 100, W. Bridgewater (422–9907). *Moderate.* Burgers, steaks, seafood, and lots of it. Grab a beer in the ca-boose wing.

Charity's 1887 Saloon Restaurant, Killington Rd. (422–3800). *Moder-ate.* Good for burgers, onion soup, Reuben sandwich, or steak. Victorian decor.

Ludlow

Nikki's, Rte. 100 (228–7797). *Expensive–Deluxe.* Stained glass and ex-posed wood ambience, with good homemade soups and varied dinner spe-cials, including medallions of pork, sinful desserts.

Clock Works, Okemo Mountain (228–2800). *Moderate–Expensive.* Waffles for breakfast, scallops for dinner; the variety is extensive.

Michael's Seafood and Steak House, Main St. (228–5622). *Moderate.* A venerable dinner spot for hearty eaters. Popular pub, Sun. buffet.

The Hatchery, Rte. 103 (228–8654). *Inexpensive–Moderate.* Perfect spot to plan the day over a king-size omelet.

Pot Belly Pub, Rte. 103 (228–9813). *Inexpensive–Moderate.* Excellent lunch spot for soup and large sandwiches, or go for imaginative dinner menu.

Norwich

Carpenter Street, Carpenter St. (649–2922). *Moderate–Expensive.* Fine cuisine, locally popular, make reservations.

Plymouth

Echo Lake Inn, Rte. 100 (228–8602). *Moderate–Expensive.* Winterized old summer hotel with inviting, cozy dining, enjoyable Sun. brunch.

Quechee

Inn at Marshland Farm, River Rd. (296–3133). *Deluxe.* Fine candlelit dinners in country formality. Jackets for men. Reservations a must.

Parker House Inn & French Restaurant, Main St. (295–6077). *Expensive.* Wonderful site by the Ottauquechee River and creative menu well prepared. Four guest rooms in Victorian house.

Simon Pearce, Main St. (295–4070). *Moderate.* Fine country cooking (American, English, Irish) in handsome mill owned by Irish glassblower.

The Red Pines Restaurant, U.S. 4 (295–1302). *Inexpensive–Moderate.* Unusually tasty roadside food next to Quechee Gorge Motel.

Rutland

Countryman's Pleasure, Mendon (773–7141). *Moderate–Expensive.* Chef-owned. European touch with snails in mushroom caps, mussels, sauerbraten.

Governor Williams House, 49 N. Main St. (775–7277). *Moderate–Expensive.* Fireplaces, mellow atmosphere, in 1787 exgovernor's house; varied menu includes veal, beef, seafood. Sun. brunch.

Ernie's Hearthside Grill and Bar, U.S. 7 (775–0856). *Moderate–Expensive.* A longtime favorite, with New England menu in comfortably simple surroundings. Gourmet shop next door.

Sirloin Saloon, U.S. 7 (773–9847). *Moderate.* Just as much emphasis on "sirloin" as on "saloon." Also good for seafood. Victorian decor, of course.

Vermont Inn, U.S. 4, Mendon (775–9847). *Moderate.* Charming farmhouse, fireplaces, homemade New England and Continental food. Children's portions.

Sharon

Brooksie's Family Restaurant, at Exit 2 of I–89 (763–8407). *Inexpensive–Moderate.* One side is a diner, the other a restaurant, and you can eat just like home at either. All three meals.

Springfield

The Paddock, Rte. 11 (885–2720). *Moderate.* Oversized, family-style servings of American and Continental food in nice converted barn.

Penelope's/McKinley's, on the square (885–9186). *Moderate.* Penelope's upstairs, McKinley's (limited menu, entertainment) downstairs. Homemade breads, soups; specials include vegetarian dishes.

Shanghai Gardens, 129 Clinton St. (885–5555). *Inexpensive.* This converted diner has mild and spicy Chinese food, well cooked and delivered fast.

Windsor

Windsor Station Restaurant, off Main St. (674–9907). *Moderate–Expensive.* Renovated train depot. Menu leans toward steaks and seafood.

Woodstock

Prince and the Pauper, 24 Elm St. (457–1818). *Expensive–Deluxe.* Rustic elegance, candlelight, French-influenced menu, very good. Expensive and worth it. Cozy bar.

Woodstock Inn, on the green (457–1100). *Expensive–Deluxe.* Less expensive menu in coffee shop, but the dining room is the main attraction, with Continental fare using fresh local ingredients when possible. Reservations, jackets for men.

Bentley's, 7 Elm St. (457–3232). *Moderate–Expensive.* Hanging plants; a bentwood sort of place that does pasta, salads, veal in interesting ways. Popular, live entertainment weekends.

Kedron Valley Inn, Rte. 106, S. Woodstock (457–1473). *Moderate–Expensive.* New owners and new "nouvelle Vermont" menu in old inn. Local vegetables in season.

Rumble Seat Rathskeller, Woodstock East mall (457–3609). *Moderate–Expensive.* Stone basement setting, excellent luncheon sandwiches, Italian specialties.

Spooner's, U.S. 4 (457–4022). *Moderate–Expensive.* Fresh seafood, prime rib, chicken, salad bar in a greenhouse setting.

Enes' Table, 5 mi. north on Rte. 12 (457–2512). *Moderate.* Italian cuisine with *prima clasa* lasagne, next to Valley View Motel.

TOURIST INFORMATION SERVICES. Killington-Pico Area Association, Box 14, Killington 05751 (775–7070); Ludlow Area Chamber of Commerce, Ludlow (228–5318); Springfield Chamber of Commerce, on the square, Springfield (885–2779); Windsor Area Chamber of Commerce, 54 Main St., Windsor (674–5910); Woodstock Area Chamber of Commerce, 4 Central St., Woodstock (457–3555).

SEASONAL EVENTS. January: Okemo Winter Carnival (mid-Jan.). **February:** Woodstock Winter Carnival Week, Washington's Birthday. **March:** Maple sugaring begins; some sugar houses open to visitors. **June:** Windsor's Annual House Tour. **July:** Woodstock July 4–6 Summer Festival. **August:** From July to mid-Aug., Sat. night baked-bean and salad suppers at Brownsville Grange Hall for over 50 years. Vermont State Craft Fairs, Killington (late Aug.). **September:** Vermont State Fair, Rutland (after Labor Day). **October:** Peak foliage (2nd week in Oct.). **December:** Woodstock Christmas Wassail Weekend (early Dec.).

PARKS AND FORESTS. Ascutney State Park, Windsor (674–2060), camping, hiking scenic mountain toll road, snowmobile trails.

Bomoseen State Park, W. Shore Rd., Fair Haven, (265–4242), camping, swimming, fishing, boat rentals, picnicking, nature guide.

Half Moon State Park, Town Rd., Fair Haven (273–2848), camping, boating, boat and canoe rentals, fishing, nature trails, nature guide.

Brandbury State Park, Rte. 53, Brandon (247–5925), camping, swimming, boating, fishing, hiking, nature museum, nature trails, a nature guide.

Camp Plymouth State Park, east side of Echo Lake, Ludlow (228–2025), swimming beach, picnic area, trails, group camping area, rental boats, fishing.

Coolidge State Park, Rte. 100, Plymouth (672–3612), camping, fishing, hiking trails, snowmobile trails, Coolidge Museum village.

Gifford Woods State Park, Rte. 100, Killington (775–5354), camping, fishing, hiking, picnicking.

Quechee Gorge State Park, U.S. 4, White River Junction (295–2990), camping, river fishing, hiking trails, scenic gorge.

Silver Lake State Park, Town Rd., Barnard (234–9451), camping, swimming, boating, canoe and boat rentals, fishing, picnicking.

Lake St. Catherine State Park, Rte. 30, Poultney (287–9158), camping, swimming, boating, rental boats, fishing, nature museum, nature trail.

Wilgus State Park, U.S. 5, Ascutney (674–5422), camping, Connecticut River fishing, canoeing, boating, trails, picnicking.

FALL FOLIAGE. This area abounds in good foliage routes through mountains along Rte. 100 and modest hills and picturesque villages just about everywhere else.

From Woodstock: take Rte. 106 to Felchville, west to Tyson, north on Rte. 100 to Rochester, east to Bethel, north on Rte. 12 to Randolph, east on Rte. 66 to E. Randolph, then Tunbridge to Strafford and S. Strafford, south on Rte. 132 to Sharon, south to S. Pomfert, and back to Woodstock (130 mi., very scenic).

SUMMER SPORTS. Bicycling: Bike path from W. Woodstock to Taftsville with its covered bridge.

Boating and canoeing: Favorite spots are Lake Bomoseen, Lake St. Catherine, Lake Dunmore, and White River and Connecticut River for canoeing. The Norwich-Hanover, New Hampshire, area is a canoeing, sculling, and kyaking center. Canoe and kyak rentals at Ledyard Canoe Club, Hanover (603–646–2753).

Golf: Fox Run Resort, Ludlow (228–8871), 9 holes; Crown Point Country Club, Springfield (885–2703), rolling terrain; Windsor Country Club, Windsor (674–6491); Woodstock Country Club, Woodstock (457–2112), 18-holes by Robert Trent Jones.

Hiking: Long Trail and Appalachian Trail split off near Mendon; Woodstock's Faulkner Park in town has gentle, switchback trail to top of Mt. Tom.

Horseback riding: Woodstock is an equestrian center. Green Mt. Horse Association, S. Woodstock (457–1509), sponsors 100-mi. Labor Day ride, shows, trials. Boarding, rentals, lessons at Kedron Valley Inn Stables (457–1480).

Swimming: See *Parks and Forests,* above.

Tennis: Courts at Woodstock Country Club; see town recreations areas for other public courts. Killington School for Tennis, Killington (422–3613), 9 courts, summer.

WINTER SPORTS. Downhill skiing: Major areas are Okemo, Ludlow (228–4041), 2,150-ft. drop, expanded lifts and trails; Suicide Six, Woodstock (457–1666), 625-ft. drop, part of Woodstock Inn and Resort complex with updated base lodge and facilities, complimentary beginners' J-bar; Killington, Sherburne (422–3333), the *big* one, six parking lots, base lodges, and interconnected mountains, 3½-mile gondola; Ascutney Mt. Resort, Brownsville (484–7711), 1,500-ft. drop, newly expanded with condo-hotel.

Cross-country skiing: Fox Run Ski Touring, Ludlow (228–8871); Churchill House, Brandon (247–3300), 40 km, lodging, inn-to-inn skiing; Mountain Meadows, Killington (775–7077), gentle wooded hills; Mountain Top Ski Touring Center, Chittenden (483–6089), endless high meadows and wooded trails; Woodstock Ski Touring Center (457–2114), golf course and two trail networks. Downhill areas also have cross-country centers.

FISHING. Popular spots include the string of lakes near Ludlow, trout fishing on White River near Bethel and S. Royalton, Connecticut River.

HUNTING. Hunting season is Oct. and Nov., with weeks for deer, hare and rabbit, grey squirrel, partridge. See pamphlet *Vermont Guide to Hunting* for details; license from town clerk or game warden.

CAMPING. See *Parks and Forests* for locations. For reservations, call the Department of Forests, Parks, and Recreation (828–3375) before May or specific parks after that date. Information on private campgrounds may be obtained where tourist information is available.

SPECTATOR SPORTS. Check the ski areas for races and schools for athletic events.

HISTORIC SITES AND HOUSES. Most properties are open summer and fall. Call ahead to check hours and admission fees.

Hubbardton

Hubbardton Battlefield and Museum, 7 mi. off Rte. 4 (273–2282). Site of a brief Revolutionary battle on July 7, 1777, the lone Revolutionary skirmish in Vermont. Visitor's reception center and museum. Open late May–mid-Oct., daily except Mon. and Tues.

Plymouth

Calvin Coolidge Homestead, Rte. 100A (672–3773). Birthplace of the former president; seven restored buildings, including the home where he took the oath of office, his birthplace, a church, and a store. Coolidge is buried nearby in family plot. Visitors center with museum. Open May 16–Oct. 17.

Proctor

Vermont Marble Company exhibit hall, off Rte. 3 (459–3311). Production center for marble company (quarrying is underground, however); 20-minute movie of the story of marble, usually artisans at work. Daily mid-May–late Oct., 9 A.M.–5:30 P.M.

Sharon

Joseph Smith Memorial, off Rte. 14. A 38-ft. granite obelisk marks the birthplace of the founder of the Mormons; landscaped site on 360-acre tract, reflecting pool.

Springfield

Eureka Schoolhouse and covered bridge, on Rte. 11 between Springfield and Exit 7 of I–91. Oldest (1785) schoolhouse in Vermont. Open late May–mid-Oct.

Strafford

Justin Smith Morrill Homestead, south of village common. One-time home of the man who authored the Land Grants Act that paved the way for many colleges to be opened. Interesting Gothic Revival house, maintained by the state. Daily except Mon., mid-May–Columbus Day.

Windsor

Old Constitution House, U.S. 5 (674–6628). Former tavern where the Republic of Vermont was declared in July 1777. Daily except Mon., late May–mid-Oct.

Windsor House, Main St. (674–6729). Greek Revival brick building, once the largest hotel between Boston and Montreal, now the home to the state craft center shop and Vermont Public Radio.

Windsor-Cornish Covered Bridge, Union St. off U.S. 5. Built in 1866 and, at 460 ft., the nation's longest covered bridge. Under repair.

Woodstock

Dana House, 26 Elm St. (457–1822). A chance to enter a graceful 1807 house furnished with period portraits, historical documents, and antiques. Headquarters for Woodstock Historical Society, has yard sweeping to river. Open late May–Oct. 31.

DAR House and Museum, on the green. Revolutionary-era furnishings, memorabilia of Woodstock railroad. Mon.–Sat. 2–4 P.M. July–Sept.

Billings Farm and Museum, Rte. 12 and River Rd. (457–2355). Well worth a visit, excellent displays of Vermont farm life in the 1890s with daily activities and special events, plus an operating farm with Belgian workhorses. Open May 15–Oct. 31.

MUSEUMS. Small museums offer a closer look at the area. Call ahead to check hours and admission fees.

Ludlow

Black River Academy Museum, High St. Calvin Coolidge was an 1890 graduate, Vermont and other local artifacts. Open May 26–Oct. 13.

Plymouth

Vermont Agricultural Museum, Coolidge Homestead (672–3773). Modest museum in a century-old barn. More an oversized collection of tools, buggies, and other farm gear than a conventional museum.

Springfield

Springfield Art and Historical Society, 9 Elm Hill (885–2415). Features Bennington Pottery, pewter, primitive portraits, dolls, carriages, and changing art exhibits. Open May–Dec., Mon.–Fri., noon–4:30 P.M.

Windsor

American Precision Museum, 196 Main St. (674–5781). Pieces of the Industrial Revolution, from hand and machine tools to precision machinery. May 26–Nov. 1.

Old Constitution House, N. Main St. (674–6628). Former tavern where delegates adopted Vermont's constitution. Prints, documents, tools, cookware, fabrics. Open daily late May–mid-Oct.

MUSIC, DANCE, AND STAGE. Summer theater centers on the **Green Mt. Guild** (295–6228), which plays from the Junction Playhouse at White

River Junction and the Killington Playhouse at Snowshed Base Lodge. The **Hopkins Center for the Arts,** Hanover, New Hampshire (603–646–2422), is a magnet for the eastern part of Vermont with a packed year-round schedule of plays, concerts, films. Interesting amateur theater in **Woodstock** and college-sponsored performances at **Castleton State College,** Castleton.

ART GALLERIES. In Rutland, the **Chaffee Art Gallery,** U.S. 7 (775–0356), is an active site with permanent and changing exhibits, and **Moon Brook Gallery,** 21 Center St. (775–9548), features local artists, readings, and films. In Woodstock, **Gallery 2** is the place to see work by established and new artists.

SHOPPING. Strolling Elm and Central Sts. in Woodstock takes you to many one-of-a-kind shops, including **F. H. Gillingham & Sons,** for old-time grocery store atmosphere and unusual food from the past and present. The **Silk Purse & Sows Ear,** Rte. 107, Bethel, is an excellent outlet for New England crafts. **Rathdowney,** 3 River St., Bethel, has a large selection of herbs for the kitchen. **Simon Pearce Glass,** the Mill, Quechee Village, sells fine but practical glassware blown on the premises. In Norwich, the **Toybrary** on Main St. circulates a library of games and toys for all ages on an annual basis, while **Stave Puzzles** makes fiendishly difficult adult puzzles. Cheesemakers (and sellers) are **Crowley,** Rte. 103, Healdville, and **Plymouth Cheese Corp.,** at Calvin Coolidge's home in Plymouth. Don't miss the **Vermont State Craft Center** at Windsor House, Main St., Windsor, both for its high-quality items and setting in a fine old building preserved from the wrecker's ball.

NIGHTLIFE. Clubs and bars come and go around the ski areas; check locally. **Chuckles** (228–5530), in an old barn on Rte. 103, Ludlow, has good food and live entertainment on weekends. On Killington Rd., there is late-night entertainment, food, and drink at **The Wobbly Barn** (422–3392), **King's Four** (422–3549), **The Night Spot** (422–9885), and **Pickle Barrel** (422–3035).

THE NORTHERN MOUNTAIN AREA

The Capital and the Granite City

Barre, at the junction of Route 14 and U.S. 302, is the granite center not only of Vermont but possibly of the world. Here you can visit the world's largest granite quarry, Rock of Ages. Unlike Proctor, where marble cannot be seen, here you can view the whole quarry several hundred feet deep. These quarries have been worked since the Civil War. There are free guided tours, a tourist center, a craftsmen's center, and a picnic area. The tourist center is open May to October, the craftsmen's center, year-round, Monday through Friday; from June through September, a small open train departs every half hour for the quarries farther uphill. These quarries are actually a few miles southeast of Barre at Graniteville. Many Barre residents came from the quarrying regions of Italy, or their ancestors did, and the skill of the carvers can be seen in profusion in the many elaborate memorials in Hope Cemetery. That the Scots were among other early settlers may account for the excellent golf course.

Montpelier, the capital, with its 8,500 residents, is set in a valley of the Winooski River, four miles west of Barre on Route 302. It is dominated by the green hills on each side, against which the gold dome of the State House stands out in sharp and elegant relief. There is something very appropriate to Vermont in this simple structure, modeled after the Temple of Theseus; the style is conservative and understated, yet dignified and grand, while the scale is modest and eminently human. The interior decor is Victorian, with a number of interesting details such as the chandelier in the House of Representatives. The governor's ceremonial office was recently restored to full Victorian accuracy. The State House, built in 1857, cost less than $160,000.

Next to the State House stands the Pavilion Office Building, originally built in 1876 as a hotel for the legislators. It was bought in 1965 by the state and, after a four-year battle between conservationists and demolitionists, was rebuilt in its present hybrid form. It looks like the old hotel from the front, and indeed the old marble lobby is just inside the front door; however, the building was completely demolished and rebuilt. The State Historical Society now occupies the front rooms, and the rest of the building is occupied by state offices. The Historical Society Museum, with its changing shows of considerable interest, is well worth a visit.

Many of the city's fine old houses are along State, Elm, and Main streets, and some contain state offices. Other points of interest are the Wood Art Gallery at Vermont College and Athenwood, a splendid example of wooden Gothic Revival architecture, just outside town on Route 12.

Montpelier is alive with activities most of the year, and the State House can be visited anytime. The legislature meets January to April.

North of Montpelier on Route 14 is the scenic Worcester Range area. You can take backroads (if you have a road map) west through Maple Corner to Route 12. Take Route 12 north to Morrisville for more scenery and then follow Route 100 back south to Stowe, or take Route 100 north to the Jay Peak area south of Canada. An alternate, and highly recommended, summer and fall scenic route is to head west from Morrisville on Route 15 to Jeffersonville. Then take Route 108 through Smuggler's Notch to Stowe.

Stowe and the Mad River Valley

Smugglers' Notch is a dramatic cut in the towering mountain cliffs. The notch was used as a passage between Canada and the United States during the War of 1812. Always slightly mysterious, usually shaded and cool in summer, it is usually fairly well populated with others as impressed as yourself. The road is closed by late fall until May.

Stowe calls itself the ski capital of the East; however, it was a popular summer resort long before skiing took over in the 1930s. There are now six skiing mountains in the area: two at Stowe, three at Smugglers' Notch, and one at Bolton Valley. Of some 60 lodges at Stowe, most are open in summer also, and Stowe is becoming very much a year-round resort. There is a summer alpine slide and a Mt. Mansfield gondola ride, as well as an auto toll road to the mountain's summit.

By going south on Route 100 you reach several hiking trails that lead to the Long Trail on Camel's Hump, another of the state's tall peaks. Camel's Hump has been declared a natural area, never to be developed. Trails lead to the summit, which has rare alpine flora.

Further south on Route 100 is the Waitsfield-Warren-Fayston area, alternately known as either Mad River Valley (for the fast-flowing river) or Sugarbush Valley because of the fast-growing resort. Sugarbush bought

Glen Ellen in 1978 and renamed it Sugarbush North. It has high-elevation snow-making equipment to provide snow cover for skiing from October to mid-May. Way down below is Lincoln Gap, or Pass, considered by some to be the most scenic spot in the state. Here is the grandeur of Vermont with dense green mountains towering to the sky. Hiking trails cover this area.

Warren is a pretty little off-the-highway spot with a country store that has branched out into clothes and baked goods. Waitsfield is a bit larger, with a fine covered bridge right in the center of town, several shops, and places to settle down for a bite to eat.

There are weekend polo matches in Waitsfield, and the Sugarbush-Warren Airport is the site of glider soaring in summer; it is closed in winter. Also in summer, there is the John Gardner Tennis Camp at Sugarbush Inn and a Robert Trent Jones golf course, as well as an indoor sports center, tennis courts, and hiking.

PRACTICAL INFORMATION FOR NORTHERN MOUNTAIN AREA

Note: The area code for all Vermont is 802

HOW TO GET THERE AND AROUND. The major air gateway of Burlington is within a 45-min.–1-hr. drive of most of this area. The ski areas of Stowe, Smuggler's Notch, Bolton Valley, Jay Peak, and Sugarbush provide van service. Scenic Rte. 100 runs north–south through many of these resorts, and I–89 is a quick approach from east or west. Montpelier, the capital, and Barre, the granite center, have I–89 exits, as does Rte. 100. The smaller roads are well cared for and always worth exploring for country villages and breathtaking views you feel only you have discovered.

By plane: The airport serving Montpelier-Barre has Precision Airlines. Burlington has Continental, Eastern Express, US Air, United, and Delta Express. Rental cars: Hertz, Avis, Budget.

By train: Amtrak's *Montrealer* stops at Montpelier and Waterbury.

By bus: Vermont Transit serves the area from New York and Boston, and by connections from south and west.

By car: I–89 in this section has won awards for beauty and offers some of the best views of the mountains.

On foot: The Long Trail continues north to the Canadian border over the highest section of the Green Mountains.

HOTELS AND MOTELS. Resort lodges and motels are readily available here in winter and summer; be sure to book ahead, especially in foliage season when the bus tours come, too. Prices are based on double occupancy, European Plan (room only) unless Modified American Plan (MAP) is indicated: *Deluxe,* $75 and up; *Expensive,* $50–$75; *Moderate,* $30–$50; *Inexpensive,* $30 and under.

Barre

Hollow Motel, 278 S. Main on U.S. 302, 05641 (479–9313). *Moderate–Expensive.* Big rooms, Continental breakfast, fitness center, lounge (bring your own liquor).

Arnholm's Motel, U.S. 302, 05641 (476–5921). *Moderate.* Small but neat rooms, antique furnishings. Play area. Open May–Oct.

Heiress Motel, 573 Main, 05641 (476–4109). *Moderate.* In-room coffee, heated pool. Pets.

Bolton (Bolton Valley)

Bolton Valley Resort, off U.S. 2 and I–89, 05477 (434–2131). *Expensive–Deluxe.* Complete four-season resort on 6,000-acre mountaintop setting. Condominiums or hotel rooms. Choice of dining rooms, bar, Italian cafe. New sports center with indoor and outdoor pools and tennis. Night skiing, cross-country center, children's program, game room; good for families.

Black Bear Lodge, Bolton Valley Rd., 05477 (434–2126). *Expensive.* Next to the ski slopes, guests use sports center. Modern inn with magnificent view, flower-filled balconies in summer. Homecooked meals, bar, recreation room, heated pool.

Jay Peak Area

Hotel Jay, at the lifts, Jay 05859 (988–2611). *Expensive.* A modern 48-room lodge with nice dining room, game room, pool, tennis.

Jay Village Inn, Jay 05859 (988–2634). *Moderate.* 16 rooms with large dining room, pleasant lounge. MAP in ski season.

Jeffersonville (Smugglers' Notch Area)

Village at Smugglers' Notch, Rte. 108, 05464 (644–8851). *Deluxe.* Self-contained resort village with lodging and nice restaurants, indoor pool, supervised kids' summer activities. Downhill, cross-country skiing, tennis, hiking.

Best Western Deerun Motel, Rte. 15, 05464 (800–528–1234, 644–8866). *Moderate.* 25 units with an outdoor pool, sauna, and summer restaurant.

Montpelier

Brown Derby Motel, 101 Northfield St., 05602 (223–5258). *Moderate.* 54 rooms, half-mile from State House, restaurant, lounge.

LaGue Inns, Exit 7 off I–89, opposite hospital, 05602 (229–5766). *Moderate.* 80 units, basic motel, restaurant.

Montpelier Tavern Hotel, 100 State St., 05602 (223–5252). *Moderate.* Right in town opposite the State House, shopping adjacent, restaurant, lounge, 114 rooms.

Stowe

The Inn at the Mountain, Rte. 108, 05672 (253–7311). *Deluxe.* Condo-hotel a mile from the slopes, cross-country ski center nearby, pool, tennis, cozy dining room.

Stowhof, Edson Hill Rd. off Rte. 108, 05672 (253–9722). *Deluxe.* Built like a ship's prow, with windows spanning a breathtaking view; no two rooms alike. European cuisine, lounge, library, game room, sauna.

Topnotch at Stowe, Rte. 108, 05672 (253–8585). *Deluxe.* Not many places as nice as this, each room individually decorated, hushed elegance throughout. Fine dining. Heated pool, sauna, whirlpool, 10 outdoor and four indoor tennis courts, health spa, stables.

Trapp Family Lodge, Luce Hill Rd. off Rte. 108, 05672 (253–8511). *Deluxe.* A special place with splendid views of the valley, trails for hiking and cross-country skiing, tasteful new lodge with Austrian atmosphere, fine food, heated pool. Cross-country center, Austrian tea room with the right tortes.

Alpine Motor Lodge, Rte. 108, 05672 (253–7700). *Moderate–Expensive.* Small lodge, breakfast only, setup bar. Heated pool, putting green, golf privileges, game room.

Andersen's Lodge, Rte. 108, 05672 (253–7336). *Moderate–Expensive.* Authentic Austrian atmosphere and Austrian dining. Comfortable sitting room with fireplace, game room, heated pool.

Buccaneer Motel and Lodge, Rte. 108, 05672 (253–4772). *Moderate–Expensive.* Full breakfast, pine-paneled rooms, some dormitory rooms, fireside lounge, pool. Childhood home of Olympic skier Billy Kidd.

Country Squire Motor Lodge, Rte. 100 south, 05672 (253–4207). *Moderate–Expensive.* Alpine architecture, view of Mt. Mansfield, Continental breakfast, steam baths, in-room coffee.

Golden Eagle Motor Inn, Rte. 108, 05672 (253–4811). *Moderate–Expensive.* Large, on landscaped grounds, many rooms with fireplace and balcony, kitchenettes available. Coffee shop, heated pool, tennis, sauna, whirlpool, exercise room.

Grey Fox Inn, Rte. 108, 05672 (253–8921). *Moderate–Expensive.* Informal, pool, sauna, home-baked bread and desserts, fine dining.

Innsbruck Motor Inn, Rte. 108, 05672 (253–8582). *Moderate–Expensive.* Crêpes for breakfast, dining room, bar, sauna, cross-country skiing.

Salzburg Motor Inn, Rte. 108, 05672 (253–8541). *Moderate–Expensive.* Right next door to Innsbruck, a motel with resort extras, sauna, massage, indoor and outdoor pools, restaurant.

Scandinavia Inn and Chalets, Rte. 108, 05672 (253–8555). *Moderate–Expensive.* Swedish pancakes with lingonberries to start the day, motel-style rooms, 3 chalets. Whirlpool, sauna, game room, pool.

Yodler Motor Inn, Rte. 108, 05672 (253–4836). *Moderate–Expensive.* One of the oldies, with inn rooms, most rooms in motel annex; close to town, good buffets in dining room.

Waitsfield-Warren (Mad River Valley Area)

The Bridges Resort and Racquet Club, Sugarbush Valley, Warren 05674 (583–2922). *Deluxe.* Luxurious condominiums by night or longer, with fireplaces, sundecks. Indoor pool, tennis, squash, saunas.

Sugarbush Hotel and Sugarbush Village Condominiums, Warren 05674, at base of lifts (583–3000, 451–4326). *Deluxe.* Ski home, adjacent indoor sports center, restaurants, ski and summer rates.

Sugarbush Inn, Mountain Rd. off Rte. 100, Warren 05674 (583–2301). *Deluxe.* Colonial-style decor with chalets for families, 14 kitchenettes. Lush condominiums. Sports center, indoor pool, tennis, golf.

Tucker Hill Lodge, Rte. 17, Waitsfield 05673 (496–3983). *Deluxe.* Comfortable rooms with quilts, hearth in inviting living room. Fine dining, pool, cross-country ski trails in woods, tennis. MAP.

Christmas Tree Inn, Mountain Rd. off Rte. 100, Warren 05674 (583–4800). *Moderate–Expensive.* Inn and condominiums. Dining room, small bar.

Madbush Resort, Rte. 100, Waitsfield 05673 (496–3966). *Moderate–Expensive.* Nice dining room, comfortable sitting room, game room, bar (bring your own liquor), hot tub, sauna, pond swimming or skating.

Mad River Barn, Rte. 17, Waitsfield 05673 (496–3310). *Moderate–Expensive.* Very old-time, with comfortable lounge, game room. Pine-paneled rooms, large cross-country ski trail network, own touring center. MAP.

White Horse Inn, German Flats Rd., Waitsfield, 05673 (496–3450). *Moderate–Expensive.* Between Sugarbush and Sugarbush North, three dormitory rooms. Fireplace in lounge, dining room. MAP.

Waterbury Center

Holiday Inn, Rte. 100, 05677 (244–7822). *Expensive.* Exceptional view, motel with resort facilities of sauna, steambaths, tennis, heated pool, nature trail, restaurant, lounge.

INNS, GUEST HOUSES, BED AND BREAKFASTS. As in other sections of the state, the small, older inns and bed-and-breakfast facilities offer a homelike ambience and sense of the past. Rates vary from season to season; some are MAP, others offer only a room or a room with breakfast. It is best to check rates. Rates at inns generally fall in the *moderate–expensive* categories, ranging from about $35 to $90 per room, double occupancy, without meals and upwards to $200 with breakfast and dinner for two (MAP). Bed-and-breakfast accommodations are usually in the *moderate* price range for a double, sometimes with shared bath. For listings of bed-and-breakfast homes, contact American Bed and Breakfast, Box 983, St. Albans 05478; Bed and Breakfast Network of New England, Box 815, Brattleboro 05301 (257–5252); or Vermont Bed and Breakfast, Box 139, Browns Trace, Jericho 05465 (899–2354, 800–442–1404).

Jay Peak Area

Black Lantern Inn, Montgomery 05470 (326–4507). Very pleasant way to unwind in 1803 brick inn, 11 rooms, cozy public rooms, nice dining.
The Inn on Trout River, Montgomery Center 05471 (326–4391). Lumber baron's home with 12 rooms, elegant little game and dining rooms. MAP.

Jeffersonville (Smugglers' Notch Area)

Three Mountain Lodge, Rte. 108, 05464 (644–8851). A log-built lodge with dormitory-style rooms, fieldstone fireplace, family-style meals.
Windridge Inn, in town, Jeffersonville 05464 (644–8281). A personal kind of inn, from quilts to hand-braided rugs. Tennis inside and out on clay courts. Four rooms. Excellent dining.

Stowe

Butternut Inn at Stowe, Rte. 108, 05672 (253–4277). Three chalets and 18 rooms, pine-paneled living room, dining room, spacious grounds, pool, afternoon tea.
Charda, Rte. 100 north, 05672 (253–4598). Brick farmhouse with an admired Hungarian restaurant, six rooms, five more in new wing.
Edson Hill Manor, Edson Hill Rd. off Rte. 108, 05672 (253–7371). A special one, brick manor with beamed ceilings, 27 rooms. 300 acres on hill with stable and ski touring center.
Foxfire Inn, Rte. 100 north, 05672 (253–4887). A tidy farmhouse inn with five rooms, cabin, and chalet. The dining room offers excellent Italian cooking.

The Gables Inn, Rte. 108, 05672 (253–7730). Wide plank floors and antiques, 24 rooms including bunk space and motel addition. Winter candlelit family-style dinners, summer breakfast on lawn.

Green Mountain Inn, Main St., 05672 (253–7301). In the center of downtown but with pool and new health spa. 61 rooms in 150-year-old inn, all newly refurbished and decorated. Dining room, The Whip taproom.

Logwood Inn, Edson Hill Rd. off Rte. 108, 05672 (253–7354). First lodge built for skiers, stone and log construction, wooded site. Fieldstone hearth, 18 rooms, pool, buffet meals.

Ski Inn, Rte. 108, 05672 (253–4050). Way up near the lifts, a gracious 10-room spot with paneled bar (bring your own liquor), pleasant dining room.

Spruce Pond Inn, Rte. 100 south, 05672 (253–4825). Four inn rooms with motel addition, pond swimming and skating. Popular dining room.

Ten Acres Lodge, Barrows Rd. off Rte. 108, 05672 (253–7638). Despite the name, there are 40 acres at this very attractive 17-room inn with esteemed dining room.

Waitsfield-Warren (Mad River Valley Area)

Carpenter Farm, Meadow Rd., Moretown 05602 (496–3433). Family rooms, family meals. Working farm for 20 years. Good home-style cooking.

Knoll Farm Country Inn, Bragg Hill Rd., Waitsfield 05673 (496–3939). A unique inn on a high-hill farm with spectacular views. Highland cattle, pond, hiking.

Mountain View Inn, Rte. 17, Waitsfield 05673 (496–2646). Farmhouse turned inn holds 14 guests, lots of antiques and quilts, hearty family-style meals.

Sugartree Inn, Sugarbush Access Rd., Warren 05674 (583–3211). Up near the slopes and sports center, friendly inn with early American quilts and antiques, breakfast included.

Waitsfield Inn, Rte. 100, Waitsfield 05673 (496–3979). Old country inn (1825) given new life with renovation. Good meals and atmosphere.

Waterbury Center

The Inn at Thatcher Brook Falls, Rte. 100, 05677 (244–5911). Restored Victorian with turrets, 6 inn rooms plus modern addition. Elegant dining room.

RESTAURANTS. Vermont may be out of the way geographically, but it is definitely in the mainstream of the new appreciation for creative cooking with fresh ingredients. Chef's skills are on display all over this region. Price ranges are based on a complete dinner for one person, excluding beverage, tax, and tip: *Deluxe,* $30 and up; *Expensive,* $20–$30; *Moderate,* $10–$20; *Inexpensive,* under $10.

Barre

Country House Restaurant, 276 Main St. (476–4282). *Moderate.* Italian fare plus Maine lobster, prime ribs. Closed Sun.

Jack's Back Yard, 9 Maple Ave. (479–9134). *Moderate.* A little different, such as alternating Italian and Chinese luncheon specials. Quiches, chili, soups, sandwiches.

Green Mountain Diner, 240 N. Main (476–6292). *Inexpensive.* Opens at 6 A.M. for all three meals; blackboard specials daily.

Berlin

Philuria's, Rte. 302 (479–0892). *Moderate.* Victorian motif, good fish, extensive wine list.

Wayside Restaurant, Barre-Montpelier Rd. (223–6611). *Inexpensive.* Loyal patrons here for three meals of home cooking; bakery, too.

Bolton

Fireside Restaurant, Bolton Valley Resort off U.S. 2 (434–2131). *Moderate–Expensive.* Top restaurant at the resort; fireside meals. Continental cuisine, large breakfasts. Kids' dining, entertainment program. Italian cafe; pizza spot in basement.

Calais

The White House, Kent's Corner, (229–9847). *Expensive.* Country house restaurant. Dinners, Wed.–Sat., Fri., lunch, Sun., brunch.

Jay Peak Area

Zack's on the Rocks, Rte. 58, Montgomery Center (326–4500). *Deluxe.* Highly admired for food and view and the benevolent eccentricities of the owner. Very much out of the way in location as well as in culinary experience. Reservations. Closed Mon.

The Belfry, Rte. 242, Montgomery Center (326–4400). *Moderate.* Informal restaurant-pub in former schoolhouse; prime ribs, seafood, steaks, burgers.

Jeffersonville (Smugglers' Notch Area)

Chez Moustach, Rte. 108 (644–5567). *Moderate–Expensive.* Dinner only in a one-of-a-kind place; convivial, eclectic menu that pleases.

Crown and Anchor, Smugglers' Village (644–5567). *Moderate–Expensive.* An English pub decor in the only old building in the ski village; well regarded for lunch and dinner.

Windridge Inn, in town, Jeffersonville (644–8281). *Moderate–Expensive.* Continental cuisine, home-baked breads, glass-walled dining room in old inn.

Jana's Cupboard, Rte. 15, Jeffersonville (644–5454). *Inexpensive.* Roadside food that is well above the usual. Have the hearty breakfast they serve all day Sat. and Sun.

Windridge Dairy Kitchen, in town, Jeffersonville (644–8207). *Inexpensive.* A wonderful bakery and coffee shop with take-out breads, rolls, and pies.

Montpelier

Tubbs, 22 Elm St. at Jailhouse Common (229–9202). *Moderate–Expensive.* Part of New England Culinary Institute system; nouvelle cuisine with master chef supervising student apprentices. Usually high marks. Closed Sun. Also, try **Elm Street Cafe,** 38 Elm St. (223–3188), another institute project but more informal.

The Brown Derby, 101 Northfield St. (223–5258). *Moderate.* Beef, seafood, children's portions.

Lobster Pot, 118 Main St. (223–3961). *Moderate.* Seafood and Italian dishes every day except Sun. Children's portions.

The Stockyard, 3 Bailey Ave. Ext. (223–7811). *Moderate.* As the name implies, go for the beef.

Horn of the Moon, 8 Langdon St. (223–2895). *Inexpensive.* You can settle down here at this vegetarian retreat; homey, well-prepared soups and salads, imaginative ethnic specialties.

The Thrush, 107 State St. (223–2030). *Inexpensive.* Just a step up from a political hangout; luncheons fast and hefty, dinners about the same.

Stowe

Isle de France, Rte. 108 (253–7751). *Deluxe.* Very French in atmosphere and menu with frogs legs and veal entrecote as possibilities.

Ten Acres Lodge, Barrows Rd. (253–7638). *Deluxe.* Venison steak or rainbow trout, or maybe pheasant? For dessert, apple spice cake with maple frosting. All very good.

Topnotch at Stowe, Rte. 108 (253–8585). *Deluxe.* Quality and professionalism are the watchwords with fine food well prepared. Variety of French-influenced fish and veal.

Foxfire Inn, Rte. 100 north (253–4887). *Expensive.* Dinner only for Northern Italian menu.

Trapp Family Lodge, Luce Hill Rd. (253–8511). *Expensive.* You have a choice of 10 entrees in a prix fixe dinner, and you won't go wrong with any of them. Austrian specialties. Try the Austrian tearoom on the premises for lunch or tea; marvelous view and sturdy soups, specials, and tortes.

Hapleton's West Branch Cafe, Main St. (253–4653). *Moderate.* A dressed-up pub with trendy, tasty lunches and dinners.

The Shed, Rte. 108 (253–4364). *Moderate.* It started with the Shedburger and went on to packed popularity with prime ribs, tacos, baked onion soup, and a bar. Outdoor terrace.

Stowe-Away Lodge and Restaurant, Rte. 108 (253–8972). *Moderate.* Good Mexican dishes in a traditional New England farmhouse.

Three Green Doors, Rte. 108 (253–8979). *Moderate.* Another venerable place with a wide assortment, from burgers and seafood to pizza.

The Village Kitchen, Stowe Village (253–9381). *Inexpensive.* Yes, there is a simple place for breakfast and lunch, and the food is homemade, too.

Waitsfield-Warren (Mad River Valley Area)

Chez Henri, Sugarbush Village (583–2600). *Moderate–Expensive.* A real bistro by the slopes. Have onion soup or mussels in the cafe or a candlelight dinner in the dining room.

Phoenix, Sugarbush Village (583–2777). *Moderate–Expensive.* Excellent international cuisine, antique decor, plants. Wonderful desserts.

Sam Rupert's, Access Rd. off Rte. 100 (583–2421). *Moderate–Expensive.* A respected restaurant with greenery all around and a menu featuring seafood, lamb, veal, and vegetarian specials. Dinner.

Tucker Hill Lodge, Rte. 17, Waitsfield (496–3983). *Moderate–Expensive.* An imaginative menu featuring Vermont lamb, duckling, and veal. Dinner only, lunch in ski season.

Waitsfield Inn, Rte. 100 (496–3979). *Moderate–Expensive.* Continental dining in 1820s atmosphere.

Mooselips, Rte. 100 and 107 (496–3937). *Inexpensive.* A landmark for "hanging loose," major pizza, subs, and sandwich eating. Game room.

Odyssey, Sugarbush Village (583–2001). *Inexpensive.* Italian menu, beer and wine, pleasant and unpretentious. Takeouts.

Waterbury–Waterbury Center

Golden Horn East, Kneeland Flat Rd. (244–7855). *Moderate–Expensive.* Continental dining in a converted barn. Pastries from their own bakery up the road.

The Inn at Thatcher Brook Falls, Rte. 100 north (244–5911). *Moderate–Expensive.* A recent addition in a roadside Victorian house with a menu specializing in rack of lamb, duckling, and fresh fish.

Villa Tragara, Rte. 100, Waterbury Center (244–5288). *Moderate–Expensive.* An 1820 farmhouse, now housing an exceptionally nice Northern Italian restaurant. Serene atmosphere, attentive service.

TOURIST INFORMATION. The most important source of information in Vermont is in Montpelier at the Vermont Travel Division, 134 State St., Montpelier 05602 (828–3236). Write or stop by. Also contact Stowe Area Association, Box 1230, Main St., Stowe 05672 (253–7321), for lodging, dining, and activities. In the Mad River Valley, the Valley Area Association, Box 173, Waitsfield 05673 (496–3409). For Jay Peak, it's Jay Area Association, Jay 05859 (988–4363). For Smugglers' Notch, it's Smugglers' Notch Area Chamber of Commerce, Box 3264, Jeffersonville 05464 (644–5440). Central Vermont Chamber of Commerce, Barre (229–5711) covers the Montpelier-Barre area.

SEASONAL EVENTS. January: Stowe Winter Carnival (mid-Jan.); Jay Winter Festival (mid-Jan.).

March: Tucker Hill Triathlon, Warren (canoe, bicycle, cross-country ski) (late Mar.).

July: Third of July Air Show, Warren; Fool's Fest (clowning, mime, vaudeville), Montpelier (on a weekend in mid-July).

August: Grand Prix Tennis Tournament, Stowe (early Aug.).

September: Vermont Quilt Festival, Northfield (Labor Day weekend).

October: Fall Festival of Vermont Crafts, Montpelier (mid-Oct.); Stowe Octoberfest (3 weekends in Oct.).

December: Christmas bazaar season, local churches. Most popular ski week is Christmas–New Year's.

PARKS AND FORESTS. The **Green Mountain National Forest** covers much of this area and includes the state's highest mountain, Mansfield, (4,343 ft.), and the one with the most distinctive profile (Camel's Hump). Mt. Mansfield has toll road to summit (Stowe) and numerous hiking trails including the Long Trail; view from the top is worth the climb. Camel's Hump (Huntington) has side trails to Long Trail, open summit with 360° view.

Elmore State Park, Rte. 12, Lake Elmore (888–2982). camping, swimming, fishing, boating, canoeing, hiking.

Little River State Park, from U.S. 2 north, 3½ mi. on Little River Rd., Waterbury (244–7103), camping, marked nature trails.

Smugglers' Notch State Park, Rte. 108, Stowe (253–4014), camping, hiking, picnicking.

Underhill State Park, 4 mi. east on gravel road off paved Town Rd., Underhill Center (899–3022), camping, hiking trails on Mt. Mansfield.

Groton State Forest, State recreation areas in Marshfield: Big Deer Campground (584–3822), Boulder Beach Day Use Area (584–3824), New Discovery Campground (584–3820), Kettle Pond Group Camping Area (584–3820), Osmore Pond Picnic Area (584–3820), Owl's Head Mt. (584–3820), Ricker Campground (584–3821), Stillwater Campground (584–3821); in Groton: Seyon Fly Fishing Area (584–3829).

FALL FOLIAGE. On a clear day, the view from the top of Mt. Mansfield (toll road or hike) extends to Lake Champlain, but the earthbound view from I–89 is one of the best for seeing the red and gold hillsides because the highway slices through the mountains and the vistas are wide. Backroads offer the close-up experience of course.

From Stowe: north on Rte. 100 2 mi. to left fork going to Morristown Corners, left to Johnson; right on Rte. 100 to Morrisville, Rte. 12 to Lake Elmore, left to Rte. 15, left to turnoff to North Wolcott, left in Craftsbury to Eden Mills, left on Rte. 100, right on Rte. 118 to Rte. 109 to Waterville, first left in Waterville to Johnson, right on Rte. 15 to Underhill, left in Underhill to Pleasant Valley, right in Pleasant Valley to Jeffersonville, right in Jeffersonville on Rte. 108 to Stowe (approximately 100 mi.).

SUMMER SPORTS. Bicycling: Shaw's General Store, Stowe, rents bicycles. This is hill country, but the scenic rewards are great.

Boating and Canoeing: Pick up the guide to boating, canoeing, and fishing by the Lamoille County Development Council at the Stowe Area Association. Canoe Vermont! of Waitsfield (496–2409) sponsors canoe trips, and Clearwater Canoe, Waitsfield (496–2708), has lessons and children's programs.

Golf: Sugarbush Golf Club, Warren (583–2722), 18-hole Robert Trent Jones course; Montpelier Country Club (223–2600), nine holes; Barre Country Club (476–7658), a well-rated 18 holes; Northfield Country Club, nine holes; Stowe Country Club (253–4269), 18 holes, practice range.

Hiking: The Long Trail covers the highest peaks here and is heavily traveled; trail wet before Memorial Day. See *Guide Book of the Long Trail* ($7 at bookshops) for details. Side trails for shorter hikes. Worcester Range, north of Montpelier, offers splendid scenery, good hiking, and fewer hikers.

Horseback riding: Knoll Farm Inn, Waitsfield (496–3939); Applewood Riding Center, Warren (496–8896); East Hill Farm, Plainfield (479–9258); Edson Hill Manor, Stowe (253–8954).

Swimming: The Sugarbush Sports Center, Warren; Wrightsville Dam Recreation Area, Rte. 12 north of Montpelier.

Tennis: Sugarbush Sports Center and the Alpine Inn, Warren; public courts on upper Elm St., Montpelier; The Racquet Club at Topnotch, Stowe (253–9308), for indoor and outdoor courts; Mt. Mansfield Tennis Courts at Inn at the Mountain, Stowe (253–7311).

WINTER SPORTS. Downhill Skiing: Stowe (253–7311), 2,350-ft. drop, three base lodges, 43 trails; Smugglers' Notch, Jeffersonville (644–8851), 2,610-ft. drop spread over 3 peaks, condo-hotel village; Jay Peak, Jay (988–2611), 2,100-ft. drop, tramway; Mad River Glen, Waitsfield (496–3551), 2,000-ft. drop, challenging, small, friendly; Sugarbush Valley, Warren (583–2381), 2,400-ft. drop and Sugarbush North, Fayston, big area, new indoor sports facility, trailside condominiums; Bolton Valley, Bolton (434–2131), 1,100-ft. drop, lodging, food, entertainment on the mountain beside the lifts.

Cross-country skiing: Camel's Hump Nordic Ski Center, Huntington (434–2704); Sherman Hollow, Huntington (434–2057); Hazen's Notch Cross-Country Ski Area, Montgomery Center (326–4708); Blueberry Lake Cross-Country Center, Warren (496–6687); Mad River Glen Nordic Center, Waitsfield (496–5851); Ole's Cross-Country Center, Warren (296–3430); Sugarbush Inn–Rossignol Ski Touring Center, Warren (583–2301; Tucker Hill Ski Touring Center, Waitsfield (496–3203); Edson Hill Ski Touring, Stowe (253–8954); Topnotch Ski Touring, Stowe (253–8585); Trapp Family Lodge Ski Touring Center, Stowe (253–8511); Montpelier Ski Touring Center, Montpelier (223–7457). All downhill ski areas have cross-country centers.

FISHING. Try the Lamoille River between Cambridge and Johnson for brown trout, the Missisquoi near Enosburg Falls and the Trout River at Montgomery Center for brook trout.

HUNTING. Hunting season is Oct. and Nov., with weeks for deer, hare and rabbit, grey squirrel, partridge. See pamphlet *Vermont Guide to Hunting* for details, license from town clerk or game warden.

CAMPING. See *Parks and Forests* for locations. For reservations call the Department of Forests, Parks, and Recreation (828–3375) before May or specific parks after that date. Information on private campgrounds may be obtained where tourist information is available.

SPECTATOR SPORTS. High-ranked tennis players battle at the Grand Prix Tennis Tournament at Topnotch, Stowe, in early Aug.

HISTORIC SITES, HOUSES, AND MUSEUMS. Children's interests may be caught by the granite quarries and the Vermont Museum's exhibits. Call ahead to check admission fees.

Barre

Barre Historical Society Museum, Washington St., 2nd floor of Aldrich Public Library (479–0450). Focus on the granite industry and ethnic heritage of the city. Hours vary.

Rock of Ages Quarry and Craftsmen Center in nearby Graniteville (476–3115). Quarry open June–Sept. for tours of Craftsmen Center to view stone being sculpted into memorials. Open year-round.

Calais

Kent Tavern Museum at the crossroads in Kents Corners (828–2291). 1837 coach stop attached to country store. Miniature rooms, spinning and weaving rooms, herb garden. Tues.–Sun. noon–5 P.M., July–Labor Day, foliage season.

Montpelier

The Vermont Museum, Pavilion Bldg., 109 State St. (828–2291). Interesting changing exhibits by Vermont Historical Society, original lobby from old Pavilion Hotel, Vermont in a nutshell. Mon–Fri., weekends July, Aug., foliage season.

Vermont State House, State St. (828–2228). A very well-kept 1857 granite, gold-domed state house, small enough to enjoy. July–Oct.; tours Mon.–Fri. at 10 A.M. and 3 P.M.

Wood Art Gallery, College Hall of Vermont College (229–0522, ext. 301). 19th- and 20th-century collection displayed in imaginative shows; also contemporary exhibits. Tues.–Sun., noon–4 P.M.

MUSIC, THEATER, AND DANCE. The Vermont Council on the Arts, at 136 State St., Montpelier 05602 (828–3291), is the source of information on the arts in this area, as well as in all Vermont. The restored **Barre Opera House,** Prospect and Main Sts., Barre (476–8188), hosts the Vermont Opera Co. productions as well as other events. At the tiny **Hyde Park Opera House,** Hyde Park, north of Stowe, the amateur and very spirited Lamoille County Players present *The Sound of Music* every foliage season and two other productions annually. **Stowe Summer Stage** (253–4325) presents a summer of Broadway musicals at The Playhouse.

SHOPPING. In the village of Waitsfield, **Tul:p Tree Crafts** is a good place to choose work by many Vermont craftspeople or one of the owner's quilted pictures. Then stop by **Green Mt. Coffee Roasters** for a pound of the state's premier coffee, 30 varieties roasted and sold here, some available at other gourmet food shops. **The Artisan's Hand,** 7 Langdon St., Montpelier, is another quality craft shop, cooperatively run by 90 artists. On the corner of Langdon and Main, **Bear Pond Books** is an especially welcoming bookstore with a good selection of New England titles. Everyone browses at **Shaw's General Store** in Stowe; it's crammed with sports clothes and equipment. Nearby, the **Wool and Feather** shop sells yarn spun from the owners' own sheep; **Exclusively Vermont** showcases the state's crafts and food; and **Stowe Pottery** by the bridge is the studio and shop of long-time potter Jean Paul Patnode. At **Cold Hollow Cider Mill** in Waterbury Center, you can buy excellent cider as well as all manner of country items, honey, jellies, and maple syrup. The **Johnson Woolen Mill,** Rte. 15 in Johnson, has been making its own woolen clothes and blankets for 80 years and also sells other selected labels. Everything in this crowded salesroom is made to last. Runners and cross-country skiiers should check out **Vermont Voyageur Equipment,** Montgomery Center, which makes a fine line of Gortex parkas, pants, and overmitts sold by mail order or at the shop.

NIGHTLIFE. Gallaghers Pub and Steak House, Waitsfield, has been a rock and dance spot for years, and near the Sugarbush slopes, **The Blue Tooth,** open ski season, is the place for drinks, snacks, and entertainment. In Stowe, there are close to 60 bars, with **Rusty Nail** and **Baggy Knees,** popular music and dance spots on the Mountain Rd. At Smugglers' Notch, the **Salty Dog** on Rte. 108 has live bands on weekends.

THE CHAMPLAIN VALLEY

The Champlain Valley is a very fortunate place: it has mountains on both sides and a large, sparkling lake in the middle. Of course, nothing in Vermont is very long—the distance between Middlebury and Burlington is only 30 miles. From Burlington to the Champlain Islands is a half-hour drive. Nevertheless, it is pretty much a north–south sort of journey in this area.

Middlebury, on U.S. 7, is a very agreeable college town centered on a green flanked by the Middlebury Inn and two churches. The white-spired

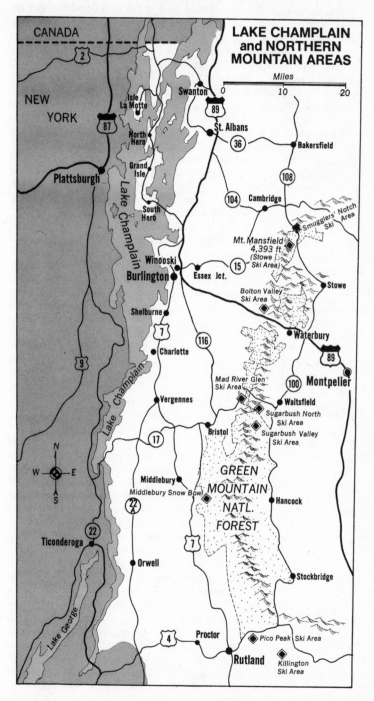

LAKE CHAMPLAIN
and NORTHERN
MOUNTAIN AREAS

Miles

0   10   20

CANADA

NEW
YORK

Plattsburgh

Isle
La Motte

North
Hero

Grand
Isle

South
Hero

Lake Champlain

Swanton

St. Albans

Bakersfield

Cambridge

Smugglers' Notch
Ski Area

Mt. Mansfield
4,393 ft.
(Stowe
Ski Area)

Stowe

Winooski

Burlington

Essex Jct.

Bolton Valley
Ski Area

Waterbury

Shelburne

Charlotte

Montpelier

Mad River Glen
Ski Area

Waitsfield

Sugarbush North
Ski Area

Sugarbush Valley
Ski Area

Vergennes

Bristol

GREEN
MOUNTAIN
NATL.
FOREST

Middlebury

Middlebury Snow Bowl

Hancock

N
W   E
S

Ticonderoga

Orwell

Stockbridge

Lake George

Proctor

Pico Peak Ski Area

Rutland

Killington
Ski Area

Congregational Church was built in 1806 and is considered an excellent example of the classic New England church. The gray stone Middlebury College is a short walk away, in summer augmented by a cosmopolitan group at the Summer Language Schools speaking everything from German to Arabic to Japanese. The Bread Loaf School of English and Writers Conference is held in summer at the old Bread Loaf Inn in Ripton on Route 125. Walk around Middlebury, poke into the shops; don't miss the Frog Hollow Mill down by the river and the Frog Hollow State Craft Center. You can also dine quite well here.

Ripton was Robert Frost's last permanent residence. His farm has been registered as a National Historic Landmark, but the cabin where he wrote is open only by appointment through the college or on Labor Day. The Bread Loaf campus, with a wide view over the mountains, was once owned by the eccentric, dictatorial, but generous Joseph Battell. Battell left thousands of acres to Middlebury College. His farm in nearby Waybridge was one of the first centers for the development of the purebred Morgan horse. It is now operated by the University of Vermont, and visitors are welcome to see the descendents of the bay stallion, Justin Morgan, the first breed of horse developed in America.

Continue north to Vergennes, which lays claim to the dubious title of Smallest City in the U.S.A. It has been nicely spruced up and has an attractive group of nineteenth-century buildings complete with enormous Queen Anne houses. The Bixby Library has a small museum with Indian artifacts.

Take U.S. 7 north. At Charlotte, you can drive up to the top of Mt. Philo, in a small state park, for a spectacular view of Lake Champlain. Mt. Philo is only 980 feet, modest as a mountain but special as a wide-angle vista. From Charlotte, you can take a ferry across the lake (20 minutes) to Essex, New York, a nineteenth-century village that retains all its charm. North on U.S. 7 brings you to Shelburne, with two unusual places to visit: the Shelburne Museum and Shelburne Farms.

Shelburne Museum (open May to October) was established in 1947 by Electra Havemeyer Webb and J. Watson Webb. It is a vast collection of collections, all housed in original buildings moved to the site. Covering 45 acres, and with 35 buildings, it requires that the visitor allow it plenty of time. While it can be enjoyed in half a day, you will want to stay longer once you discover the fascination of the things gathered together here. Most of the buildings, including a round barn, covered bridge, schoolhouse, country store, jail, lighthouse, and even a sidewheeler steamboat and a private railroad car, came from elsewhere in Vermont. Inside these buildings are doll and quilt collections, decoys, wagons and sleighs, tools, a country store, and uncounted treasures of our heritage. Except for their own collection of European paintings (including Degas and Monet) in one building, the museum is devoted to Americana.

Just down the road is Shelburne Farms, the century-old lakeside estate of the Webb family, now open to the public in the summer and fall for tours, concerts, and environmental programs. A gatehouse shop is open year-round for the sale of the farmhouse cheese made from the herd of Brown Swiss on the farm, as well as other Vermont products. The 1,000-acre estate, beautifully landscaped and with enormous barns and manor house (turned into an inn in 1987), provides a glimpse of a bygone way of life.

Burlington, St. Albans, and the Islands

Continue north on U.S. 7 to Burlington, a vital hub of commercial, financial, and academic activity. It grew from the lakefront, once crowded with sailing ships and lumbering firms, up a steep hill on which the lumber barons built mansions, to the University of Vermont at the top of the hill. Today a visitor can enjoy restaurants on the still largely undeveloped harbor, sidewalk cafes and shops along the downtown pedestrian mall, the fine variety of nineteenth-century architecture, and the rich artistic schedule of events. These include the Vermont Mozart Festival (summer and winter), Champlain Shakespeare Festival (summer), and the events at the Flynn Theater for the Performing Arts. The Robert Hull Fleming Museum at the university is the state's major art museum, and Billings Center on the green was the last work of architect H. H. Richardson (1885). There is ferry service from Port Kent, New York, to Burlington (spring through fall), and swimming at the city parks of Oakledge, North, and Leddy. A 10-mile bike and jogging path follows the lake north from Oakledge. Mallets Bay at Colchester, north of Burlington, is a boating center.

Follow U.S. 7 or I-89 north to St. Albans, an old railroad town with an impressive large park in the center and a number of graceful houses to remind you of its once affluent past. The St. Albans Raid, the northernmost skirmish of the Civil War, took place here. Canada is less than a half-hour drive away.

An alternate route north from Burlington is to the Champlain Islands via either U.S. 7 or I-89 and then Route 2. Interconnected by bridges, the islands include Grand Isle, North Hero, and Isle La Motte. With part of the peninsula north of them, they form one county 30 miles long and eight miles wide. They are quiet, low, peaceful lands, ringed by water and caught between the Adirondacks to the west and the Green Mountains to the east.

The Shrine of St. Anne on Isle La Motte is on the site of Fort St. Anne, Vermont's oldest settlement (1666) and where the first mass was said in the state. Northward is Alburg, a promontory linking Vermont to Canada. It was once a home of the Abnaki Indians and is a good place for fishing. Route 78 crosses back to the mainland, running through the Missisquoi National Wildlife Refuge, which is alive with waterfowl. Return to Burlington via U.S. 7 or I-89.

PRACTICAL INFORMATION FOR THE CHAMPLAIN VALLEY

Note: The area code for all Vermont is 802

HOW TO GET THERE AND AROUND. Burlington is the air hub of the state, and the Amtrak station for the area is at Essex Junction, 7 mi. away. Bus transportation flows into the Valley up U.S. 7 and from I-89. The most enjoyable approach is by ferry from New York State. Visitors will find Rte. 22A along the wide, fertile farmland bordering Lake Champlain and U.S. 2 through the Champlain Islands particularly scenic. Route 15 from Burlington leads to the mountains a mere 45 min. away.

By plane: Burlington International Airport served by Continental, US Air, United, Eastern Express, Delta Express.

By train: Amtrak's Montrealer to Essex Junction arrives around 8:45 A.M. northbound and 10 P.M. southbound.

By bus: Vermont Transit to Middlebury, Burlington, and St. Albans.

By ferry: Lake Champlain Transportation Co., King St. Dock, Burlington (864–9804) for information. Crossings year-round at Grand Isle, Vermont–Plattsburgh, New York; spring, summer, and fall at Burlington, Vermont–Port Kent, New York; May–early Jan. at Charlotte, Vermont–Essex, New York.

By car: Major routes are I–89, U.S. 7, Rte. 116, and U.S. 2 east–west.

Car rentals: Hertz, Avis, Budget, Dollar, National.

HOTELS AND MOTELS. Other than the Radisson Hotel in Burlington, motels are in order. Numerous choices cluster around the edges of towns and intersections of major routes. Prices are based on double rooms, European Plan (room only) unless indicated: *Deluxe,* $75 and up; *Expensive,* $50–$75; *Moderate,* $30–$50; *Inexpensive,* $30 and under.

Bristol

Bristol Commons Inn, Rtes. 116 and 17, 05443 (453–2326). *Moderate–Expensive.* Back from the road on 23 acres with a view of the mountains. Italian restaurant.

Burlington

Holiday Inn, U.S. 2, S. Burlington 05403 (863–6363). *Deluxe.* Four-story, elevator, pool, at I–89 exit. Restaurant, lounge with entertainment.

Radisson Burlington Hotel, 60 Battery St., 05401 (658–6500). *Deluxe.* Near the lake, 257-room hotel with city amenities, luxurious penthouse suites, restaurants, bar, indoor pool.

Sheraton-Burlington Inn, U.S. 2 at I–89, S. Burlington 05403 (862–6576). *Deluxe.* Pool, health club, play area, mountain views.

Howard Johnson, 1720 Shelburne Rd., S. Burlington (865–2174). *Expensive.* Big and new. Exercise room, sauna, whirlpool, indoor pool.

Ramada Inn, U.S. 2, S. Burlington 05403 (658–0250). *Expensive.* Restaurant, lounge, coffee shop, pool.

Anchorage Motor Inn, 198 Dorset St., S. Burlington 05403 (658–3351). *Moderate.* Heated pool, whirlpool, near shopping centers.

Econo Lodge, 1076 Williston Rd., S. Burlington 05403 (863–1125). *Moderate.* 177 rooms with outdoor pool, sauna, exercise room, adjacent good restaurant (The Windjammer).

Redwood Best Western, U.S. 7 near I–89, S. Burlington 05403 (862–6421). *Moderate.* Newly redecorated, New England dining, big breakfasts.

Town and Country Motel, 490 Shelburne Rd. (U.S. 7), S. Burlington 05403 (862–5754). *Moderate.* Coffee shop, pool, small, in town.

Middlebury

Greystone Motel, U.S. 7 south, 05753 (388–4935). *Moderate.* Nice, small place, homelike. Pets allowed.

Maple Manor Motel, U.S. 7 south, 05753 (388–2193). *Moderate.* 12 motel units, 8 chalets, including housekeeping units.

Sugarhouse Motor Inn, U.S. 7 north, 05753 (388–7773). *Moderate.* 14 rooms with mountain views, maple sugaring artifacts here and in restaurant next door.

Blue Spruce Motel, U.S. 7 south, 05753 (388–7512). *Inexpensive–Moderate.* Small homey motel, nice furnishings.

North Hero–South Hero

Sandbar Motel Inn & Restaurant, U.S. 2, South Hero 05486 (372–6911). *Moderate.* On the lake across from marina and boat rental, open year-round.
Shore Acres Resort Motel and Lodge, U.S. 2, North Hero 05474 (372–8722, winter 372–5545). *Moderate.* Half-mile shoreline, 18 rooms facing lake, boating, fishing, restaurant, lounge. Open May–late Oct., but reserve early for summer.

St. Albans

Cadillac Motel, U.S. 7, 05478 (524–2191). *Moderate.* Small motel with coffee shop for breakfast in summer.
Champlain Inn and Motel. U.S. 7, 05478 (524–5956). *Moderate.* Restaurant, lounge, in-room coffee. Pool.

Shelburne

Red Carpet Inn, 3000 Shelburne Rd. (985–3377). *Expensive.* Some suites with kitchens, handicapped suites, pool. Continental breakfast.
Driftwood Motel, U.S. 7, 05482 (985–3334). *Moderate–Expensive.* Modern motel with pool, picnic area. Lower rates in winter.
Yankee Doodle Motel, U.S. 7, 05482 (985–8004). *Moderate–Expensive.* Antiques, free Continental breakfast.
Dutch Mill Motel, U.S. 7, 05482 (985–3568). *Moderate.* One of the oldies, with a windmill office. Modernized, two pools, spacious lawns.

Swanton

Royale Swans Country Inn and Motel, U.S. 7 north, 05488 (868–2010). *Moderate.* 18 rooms, some in renovated 200-year-old farmhouse, spacious grounds. Breakfast and dinner in restaurant.

INNS, GUEST HOUSES, BED AND BREAKFASTS. Long gone are any verandah-encircled summer hotels on the lake, but the century-old Basin Harbor Club still thrives as a lakeside resort. The Middlebury area has some country inns, and the bed-and-breakfast movement is alive and well all over the Champlain Valley. The rates vary, sometimes seasonally, and some are Modified American Plan (MAP), so check each individually. Rates at inns generally fall in the *moderate–expensive* categories, ranging from about $35 to $90 per room double occupancy without meals and upwards to $200 with breakfast and dinner for two (MAP). Bed-and-breakfast accommodations are usually in the *moderate* price range for a double, sometimes with shared bath. For listings of bed-and-breakfast homes, contact American Bed and Breakfast, Box 983, St. Albans 05478; Bed and Breakfast Network of New England, Box 815, Brattleboro 05301 (257–5252); or Vermont Bed and Breakfast, Box 139, Browns Trace, Jericho 05465 (899–2354, 800–442–1404).

Highgate Springs

The Tyler Place, U.S. 7, 05460 (868–3301). Potpourri of buildings and a favorite of families for generations. Inn, apartments, cottages in 165 wooden acres on Lake Champlain. Water sports, tennis, riding, golf privileges, complete supervised program for children.

Middlebury Area

Chipman Inn, Rte. 125, Ripton 05766 (388–2390). Near Bread Loaf, 10 rooms in restored 1828 farmhouse; large dinner served family style.

The Long Run Inn, Lincoln, 4 mi. east of Bristol on road to Lincoln Gap, RD 1, Box 114, Bristol 05443 (453–3233). Very much a country inn, hiking on Mt. Abraham, trail lunch provided. On small river.

Middlebury Inn, U.S. 7 on the green, 05753 (388–4961). Rooms in 1827 inn, motel annex. Relaxing parlor, dining, buffets in summer.

Swift House Inn, U.S. 7, 05753 (388–2766). In-town 1815 estate converted to elegant little nine-room inn. Fireplaces, breakfast included, dining in candlelit dining room.

Waybury Inn, Rte. 125, East Middlebury 05740 (388–4015). 12 rooms, all different; hearty breakfast and fine dinner, country setting.

North Hero

North Hero House, U.S. 2, 05474 (372–8237). 22-room inn with annexes on a quiet cove of Lake Champlain. Easygoing, water sports, tennis, biking. Good dining room. Open mid-June–Labor Day.

Orwell

Brookside Farms, Rte. 22A, 05760 (948–2727). A stunning 1843 Greek Revival mansion on a country road, rooms in main house or guest annex. Breakfast; tea, lunch, and dinner by request.

Shelburne

Shelburne House, Shelburne Farms, 05482 (985–8498, June–mid-Oct.; 985–8686, mid-Oct.–May). The 1899 brick manor house on the 1,000-acre lakeside estate opened for guests in 1987. Unique, beautifully restored. Open June 1–mid-Oct.

Shelburne Inn, U.S. 7 (near Shelburne Museum), 05482 (985–3305). Old inn, much modernized, with motel units. Fine dining with special desserts.

Vergennes

Basin Harbor Club, off Rte. 22A, 05491 (475–2311). Distinguished resort on 700 lakefront acres. Inn, cottages scattered on cove, 18-hole golf course, five tennis courts, pool, airstrip, summer children's program. Open June–Oct.

RESTAURANTS. Eating as entertainment has really taken off here. A restaurant renaissance has brought new places springing up like mushrooms—shiitake mushrooms at that. You can dine very well here. This list is a sampling; ask locally for other suggestions. Price ranges are based on a complete dinner for one person, excluding beverage, tax, and tip: *Deluxe,* $30 and up; *Expensive,* $20–$30; *Moderate,* $10–$20; *Inexpensive,* under $10.

Mary's, 11 Main St. (453–2432). *Moderate–Expensive.* Casual atmosphere, excellent food with seasonal ingredients. Sun. brunch. Chefowned. Reservations. Closed Mon.

Rosemarie's at Bristol Commons Inn, Rtes. 116 and 17 (453–2326). *Moderate–Expensive.* Calamari and all sorts of unusual and fine Italian dishes. Closed Tues.

Burlington–South Burlington

Deja-Vu Cafe, 185 Pearl St. (864–7917). *Expensive.* Decor is wonderfully dim, woody, and accented with brass. Popular for lunch and dinner with a French-inspired menu.

Ice House Restaurant, 171 Battery St. (863–9330). *Expensive.* Recycled harborside building, now pleasant stone-and-glass dining room with fine meals, seafood a specialty. Oyster bar.

Pauline's, U.S. 7, 1834 Shelburne Rd. (862–1081). *Expensive.* One of the best. Innovative menu carefully prepared with attention to fresh local ingredients.

Perry's Fish House, U.S. 7, 1080 Shelburne Rd. (862–1300). *Expensive.* All kinds of good fish here in a shore-shanty atmosphere. Dinner only.

Sweetwater's, 118 Church St. (964–9800). *Expensive.* Trendy dishes and a summer sidewalk cafe for people watching.

Dockside Cafe, 209 Battery St. (864–5266). *Moderate–Expensive.* On the harbor, seafood of all kinds in casual century-old stone building.

Five-Spice Restaurant, 175 Church St. (864–4045). *Moderate–Expensive.* Cozy, new-style Asian cafe. Hot and mild stir-frys.

Francesca's, U.S. 7 at Jelly Mill Common (985–3373). *Moderate–Expensive.* All fresh pasta and Northern Italian cuisine. Lunch, dinner, Sun. brunch.

Sakura, 2 Church St. (863–1988). *Moderate–Expensive.* Sushi, tempura, soba, and other Japanese dishes.

What's Your Beef, 152 St. Paul St. (862–0326), and 1710 Shelburne Rd., S. Burlington (865–3700). *Moderate–Expensive.* Prime ribs, steaks, and seafood, too, in a casual sugarshack atmosphere. Dinner, closed Sun.

Cork and Board, 100 Dorset St. (864–5656). *Moderate.* All three meals well prepared in a warm, woody room. Fresh berry pancakes for breakfast.

The Daily Planet, 15 Center St. (862–9647). *Moderate.* Bistro-type place with excellent worldwide menu, informal. Bar.

Windjammer, U.S. 2, 1076 Williston Rd. (862–6585). *Moderate.* Popular seafood and beef, hanging-plant sort of place. Salad bar.

Bove's, 68 Pearl St. (985–3279). *Inexpensive–Moderate.* A down-home Italian restaurant; small, family run.

Carbur's, 119 St. Paul St. (862–4106). *Inexpensive–Moderate.* Victorian decor, dazzling array of sandwiches and other goodies.

Rusty Scuffer, 148 Church St. (864–9451). *Inexpensive–Moderate.* Lobster and steak at reasonable prices. Lunch and dinner, bar.

Tortilla Flat, 317 Riverside Ave. (864–4874). *Inexpensive–Moderate.* Tacos, enchiladas, and other Mexican dishes in casual informality.

Middlebury

Middlebury Inn, on the green (388–4961). *Expensive.* Outdoor screened-porch dining in summer; comfortable old-inn dining room. New England menu.

Woody's Restaurant, Bakery La. (388–3385). *Expensive.* Eye-catching Art Deco oceanliner design and fine food made on the premises.

Dog Team Tavern, off U.S. 7 north (388–7651). *Moderate–Expensive.* A popular spot for New England meals in warm, innlike dining room. Lunch late spring–foliage season, dinner year-round. Closed Mon.

Fire and Ice, 26 Seymour St. (388–4961). *Moderate–Expensive.* Informal, stained glass, innovative sandwiches and specials. Convivial bar. Lunch, dinner, Sun. brunch.

Mr. Up's, Bakery Lane (388–6724). *Moderate–Expensive.* Summer dining on the terrace by the river; Italian and Cajun specials.

Otter Creek Cafe, Mill St. (388–7342). *Moderate.* Garden vegetables, subtle sauces, perfect pastries. In the old riverside mill building.

Rosie's, U.S. 7 south (388–7052). *Inexpensive–Moderate.* A real find for family meals. Good food at very modest prices.

St. Albans

The Blue Lion, 71 N. Main St. (524–3060). *Moderate.* A venerable restaurant with rathskeller decor serving beef, seafood, and Italian dishes. Open 9 A.M.–9 P.M. daily.

Vergennes

Basin Harbor Club, off Rte. 22A (475–2311). *Expensive–Deluxe.* Wide range of dishes in resort's spacious dining room and cocktail area. Popular, lavish outdoor buffet lunch. Jackets and ties required in dining room. Open June–mid-Oct.

Painter's Tavern Restaurant, on the green (877–3413). *Expensive.* Interesting American menu featuring Cajun, Southern, and New England specialties. Nicely renovated old inn.

TOURIST INFORMATION. The Lake Champlain Regional Chamber of Commerce, 209 Battery St., Burlington 045401 (863–3489), can tell you all about this area. Write or drop by the office by the harbor for pamphlets on everything. Also contact Addison County Chamber of Commerce, 35 Court St. Middlebury (388–7579), and St. Albans Chamber of Commerce (524–2444).

SEASONAL EVENTS. January: Ice fishing for lake perch and smelt. **February:** Middlebury Winter Carnival (mid-Feb.). **April:** Maple Sugar Festival, a week long (early to mid-Apr.). **June:** Lake Champlain Discovery Festival, events all around lake (June 4–July 4); Jazz Festival, Burlington (mid-June). Annual Fishing Derby, many prizes (mid-June). **September:** Weekend with Robert Frost, cabin open, Ripton (Labor Day weekend); Champlain Valley Fair, big regional fair with midway, agricultural exhibits, entertainment (1st week in Sept.). **November:** Vermont Handcrafters Fair, many sellers, Burlington (3rd week in Nov.). **December:** Christmas weekend at Shelburne Museum, Shelburne (early Dec.). First Night, New Year's Eve gala for the arts, over 100 performances, downtown Burlington.

PARKS AND FORESTS. The Burlington parks system has a 10-mi. bike path along the lake from the mouth of the Winooski River. Access is from Perkins Pier, Leddy Park, Oakledge Park, North Beach; swimming at all but Perkins Pier.

Burton Island State Park, island off St. Albans Bay (524–6353), accessible by launch, no cars; boating, camping, fishing, trails, nature center.

Lake Carmi State Park, Rte. 236 Enosburgh Falls (933–8383), camping, swimming, boat rentals, fishing, nature trails, a nature guide, playground.

Grand Isle State Park, U.S. 2, Grand Isle (372–4300). Camping, Lake Champlain, boating, rentals, fishing, nature guide.

Kamp Kill Kare State Park, Town Rd. off Rte. 36 (524–6021), Lake Champlain, picnic area, access to Burton Island.

Knight Point State Park, U.S. 2, North Hero (372–8389). Lake Champlain, picnic area, swimming, boating.

North Hero State Park, off U.S. 2, North Hero (372–8727), Lake Champlain, camping, boating, fishing, hiking, trails.

St. Albans Bay State Park, Rte. 36, St. Albans, Lake Champlain, beach, picnicking, fishing.

Sand Bar State Park, U.S. 2 at causeway, Milton (372–8240), swimming, picnicking, boating, beach.

Button Bay State Park, off Rte. 22A, Vergennes (475–2377), Lake Champlain, camping, boat rentals, dock, fishing, nature museum, nature trails (also for blind), swimming, naturalist.

DAR State Park, Rte. 17, Vergennes (759–2354), camping, Lake Champlain, boating, fishing, playground, naturalist.

FALL FOLIAGE. Many foliage viewers make the valley their headquarters; reserve a room well in advance. The 1st and 2nd weekends in Oct. are booked up well in advance. The 1st week is considered to be the usual prime time for color.

From Middlebury: to Ripton via Rte. 125, Ripton to Jerusalem via unmarked road through Lincoln and Downingville; Jerusalem to Irasville via unmarked road and Rte. 17; Irasville to Hancock via Rte. 100; Hancock to Bread Loaf via Rte. 125; continue and take left to Goshen on unmarked road 1 mi. before Ripton; Goshen to Goshen Corners via unmarked road; Goshen Corners to Brandon via Rte. 73; Brandon to Leicester via U.S. 7; circle Fern Lake and Lake Dunmore via unmarked road through Fernville, Lake Dunmore, and Salisbury; Salisbury to Middlebury via unmarked road and U.S. 7 (approximately 116 mi.).

SUMMER SPORTS. Bicycling: Several bike touring specialists have appeared; ask at sports shops for details. Vermont Bicycle Touring, Monkton Rd., Bristol (453–4811), is the oldest. It organizes weekend or longer trips inn to inn. Headquarters for biking information in Burlington: Ski Rack, 81 Main St. (858–3313). The Champlain Islands is good biking territory, especially on the backroads.

Boating and canoeing: Lake Champlain is a major sailing lake with yachts as well as day sailers. Marinas at Grand Isle, Colchester, Burlington, Shelburne, Charlotte. Canoeing is popular on the Winooski and Lamoille rivers. Smaller rivers: Otter Creek (still wide and fast in sections) and Lemon Fair in Middlebury area. Always check map for canoeable sections.

Golf: Alburg Country Club, Alburg (796–3586), 18 holes; Burlington Country Club, Burlington (864–9532), 18 holes; Rocky Ridge Golf Club, St. George (482–2191), 18 holes; Kwiniaska, Shelburne (985–3672), 18 holes. Ralph Myhre Golf Course, owned by Middlebury College (388–3711), 18 holes.

Hiking: Trails on Mt. Moosalamoo on east side of Lake Dunmore; Long Trail runs through eastern edge of this area. Inn-to-inn hiking tours (brochure from Churchill House, Brandon (247–3300).

Horseback riding: Firefly Ranch, Bristol (453–2223), has lodging, meals, horses, guides; Happy Hollow Riding Stable, Hinesburg (482–2729), trail rides, lessons; Contentment Farm Riding Stable, South Hero (372–4087), trail riding, lessons, pony rides, tack shop, boarding.

Swimming: See *Parks and Forests.*

Tennis: Public courts in parks in Middlebury, Burlington. Indoor courts at Twin Oaks Tennis Center, Burlington (658–0001).

WINTER SPORTS. Downhill skiing: Middlebury College Snow Bowl, Rte. 125 at Bread Loaf (388–4356), 1,100-ft. drop, lessons, rentals, restaurant.

Cross-country skiing: Bread Loaf Touring Center, Rte. 125, Ripton (388–7946); Catamount Family Center, Williston (879–6001); Wolf Run Ski Touring Center, Bakersfield (933–4007).

FISHING. See state *Guide to Fishing* brochure for detailed information about Lake Champlain fishing. Salmon, lake trout and steelhead rainbow are restocked annually. Fishing licenses: $8 for three days, $14 for 14 days from town clerks or some sports shops. Big Fishing Derby, in mid-June, covers entire lake, Derby headquarters Perkins Pier, Burlington.

HUNTING. Hunting season is Oct. and Nov., with weeks for deer, hare and rabbit, grey squirrel, partridge. See pamphlet *Vermont Guide to Hunting* for details; license from town clerk or game warden.

CAMPING. See *Parks and Forests* for locations. For reservations, call the Department of Forests, Parks, and Recreation (828–3375) before May or specific parks after that date. Information on private campgrounds may be obtained where tourist information is available.

SPECTATOR SPORTS. University of Vermont hockey is popular; university doesn't play football but has soccer, basketball, baseball, track. Middlebury College plays full schedule of football, etc.

HISTORIC HOUSES AND MUSEUMS. Some sites are open seasonally. Call ahead to check details.

Addison

General John Strong Mansion, Rte. 17. A 1795 house built of stone from ruins of Ft. Crown Pt. across the lake. Period rooms, collections of china and glass. Open May 15–Oct. 15; closed Tues.

Burlington

Robert Hull Fleming Museum, Colchester Ave. (656–2090). Series of permanent and changing art exhibits from pre-Columbian to 20th century in graceful colonial Revival building newly expanded. Open Tues.–Fri. 10 A.M.–5 P.M., Sat. and Sun. noon–5 P.M.

Ferrisburg

Rokeby, U.S. 7 (877–3406). An interesting 1784 homestead of Rowland E. Robinson, 19th-century writer. Antiques and decorative arts. Open late May–Oct., Thurs.–Sun. Tours at 11, 12:30, 2.

Grand Isle

Hyde Log Cabin, U.S. 2. Built in 1783, probably the oldest log cabin in the United States. Open July 4–Labor Day, closed Tues. and Wed.

Middlebury

The Sheldon Museum, Park St. (388–2117). A window on life in the 19th century; very interesting collection of rooms with tools, clothes, books, period furnishings. Open June–Oct., 10 A.M.–4:30 P.M.; Nov.–May, Wed.–Fri. 1–4 P.M.

The Johnson Gallery, Middlebury College, has a permanent collection of paintings and sculpture with changing exhibits. Open daily noon–5 P.M.

Morgan Horse Farm, Waybridge. Breeding and training center for the Vermont-bred Morgan horse; farm operated by University of Vermont. Tours May–Oct. by reservation (388–2011); farm open rest of year, Tues.–Fri.

Richmond

Old Round Church, off I–89. A 16-sided white church built in 1812–13; unique in the state. Handsome belfry.

Ripton

Robert Frost's Cabin, off Rte. 125. Home to the late poet in the last summers of his life. Open Labor Day weekend and by appointment through Middlebury College (388–3711).

St. Albans

Franklin County Museum, on Taylor Park, is housed in 1861 school. Unusually interesting historical society museum with old-time doctor's office (furniture from Rockwell's picture), railroad memorabilia, and historical items from Civil War raid. Open July and Aug., Tues.–Sat. 2–5 P.M.

Shelburne

Shelburne Museum, U.S. 7 (985–3344). 100 acres of Americana and folk art; original buildings moved to site include sidewheeler steamer, railroad cars, lighthouse; also American art and gallery of European art, including Impressionists. Shop, cafeteria, picnic area. Open mid-May–mid.-Oct.

Shelburne Farms, Harbor Rd. (985–8686). Grand century-old estate on Lake Champlain, now an operating farm and environmental and cultural center. Beautiful 1,000-acre setting, manor house, enormous barns. Gift shop for farmhouse cheese, Vermont products. Tours summer and fall.

MUSIC, DANCE, AND STAGE. The **Flynn Theater for the Performing Arts,** 153 Main St., Burlington (863–5966), a restored Art Deco movie palace, is a center for information on what is happening in the arts in this area. Tickets to most events can also be ordered there. The lively arts scene includes The **George Bishop Lane Series** (656–3085), sponsor of major artists; **Vermont Symphony Orchestra** (864–5741); **Vermont Mozart Festival** (862–7352); summer **Champlain Shakespeare Festival** (656–7352); professional **St. Michael's Summer Playhouse** (655–2000); and **Vermont Repertory Theater** (655–9620). **Middlebury College** sponsors a concert series, **St. Michael's College** (Winnoski) has a distinguished theater department with frequent plays, **University of Vermont** students perform an ambitious season, and **Trinity College** sponsors events as well.

ART GALLERIES. Galleries include **Brady Galleries Inc.,** 88 Main St., Middlebury (388–3350) for 19th- and early 20th-century American paintings; **Collectors Gallery,** Jelly Mill Common, Shelburne (985–2141) for local artists as well as antique and wildlife prints; **Pennino's,** 100 Dorset St., S. Burlington (862–6100); **Frame of Mind,** Champlain Mill, Winooski (655–1221); **Passepartout,** 13 E. Allen, Winooski (655–3710), for contemporary artists. **Lapham & Dibble Gallery,** Shoreham (897–5531), has 19th- and 20th-century paintings.

SHOPPING. In Middlebury, **Skihaus** is the U.S. importer for Geiger of Austria boiled wool clothing; check the bargains on the lower floor. **Store Two** nearby is full of Vermont products, toys, and unusual gifts. **Frog Hollow Mill** houses a state crafts center of high-quality items, from note cards to quilts. The **Vermont Bookshop** on Main St. is excellent; it has a music section as well as books. **Kennedy Brothers** in Vergennes has woodworkers turning out household products you can buy in the shop, and there are two floors of crafts and antiques.

On Burlington's four-block **Marketplace,** the downtown pedestrian mall, are departments stores, **Designers' Circle** for Vermont crafts, four bookstores (**Chassman & Bem** is most comprehensive with a children's shop also), **Laura Ashley,** yarn shops, numerous small emporiums, and vendor's carts selling silk-screened T-shirts by Vermont artists, handmade jewelry, and hot pretzels. The Burlington Sq. entrance leads to an underground shopping mall. **Bennington Potters North,** 127 College St., is a three-floor bazaar of Bennington Pottery seconds, kitchenware, and home furnishings. Pine St., a former industrial area by the lake, has spawned an eclectic group of entrepreneurs. Stop at **The Cheese Outlet** (400) for bargains in wine, too; at Champlain Chocolate (431) for handmade truffles and solid chocolate cows and watch them made through the big window.

In Winooski, the old **Champlain Mill** is now a stylish shopping emporium of carefully selected shops, including those selling Vermont crafts, Scandinavian designs, ethnic clothes, and off-beat paper products. Restaurants too. **Dakin Farm,** on the lower level, is good for maple products and Vermont gourmet foods. Their main shop on U.S. 7 at Ferrisburg is worth a visit for many country items.

NIGHTLIFE. In Burlington, **Nectar's,** 188 Main St. (658–4771), can be counted on for the best of the bands, local and imported, with dancing here and upstairs at **Border,** 188 Main St., (864–0107). **Sneakers,** 36 Main St., Winooski (655–9081), jumps to live jazz Tues. nights. **Baxters Lounge** (862–6576) at the Sheraton-Burlington and **Patches Pub** (856–6363) at the Holiday Inn books combos regularly.

THE NORTHEAST KINGDOM

The Northeast Kingdom does seem a little like a world apart, as Senator George Aiken implied when he used the term for the first time in the 1940s. It is the most remote and least populated area of Vermont. A vestige of wilderness clings to the dense forested area in the northeast, and the tiny villages and lakes that are scattered throughout speak of a quieter life. That it is hard to make a living in the Northeast Kingdom has perhaps preserved its scenery for visitors, but it is a problem for residents. They have a fierce pride in their land even in its harsh winters and semi-isolation. It is, in any case, a beautiful place to live.

Derby Line, Newport, and the Lake District

Derby Line is on the Canadian border. Its library and opera house (on the second floor) are divided internationally so that the books and stage are in one country and the check-out desk and audience are in another. Walking through town and periodically entering Canada is a unique experience. I–91 goes south through the Northeast Kingdom from Derby Line, but the smaller roads offer the true experience of the area. Newport, a few miles southwest of Derby Line, is a pleasant town on the large international Lake Memphremagog. Shops and restaurants on the main street make a nice stop.

You may travel south on U.S. 5 to Barton on Crystal Lake with its state park or on U.S. 5, then Route 14 to the Craftsbury area. Leave Route 14, map in hand, and go to Craftsbury, Craftsbury Common, and East Craftsbury. Craftsbury Common is a picturebook village on a high plateau and with a noble green larger than those in many much bigger towns. The green is ringed with white houses, and the town has a fine inn, a year-round sports center, and a two-year college (Sterling) specializing in farming and the environment. Craftsbury has another good inn and general store, and East Craftsbury has a little library in a former country store. The sense of serenity and natural beauty is pervasive.

From East Craftsbury, continue south on the paved unmarked road to another special place, Caspian Lake and the village of Greensboro. Drive (or run or bike) the seven miles around the clear, cool lake, which is a haven for sailing and for the large, loyal summer colony that gathers here, sometimes into the fourth generation. Willeys Store is the general store to end all general stores. It seemingly goes on forever and is well worth exploring.

St. Johnsbury and Beyond

From Greensboro, travel south on the unmarked road to Hardwick and from there on Route 15 east to Danville, well known as the headquarters of the American Society of Dowsers (water searchers), which holds its annual convention in mid-September. The convention brings hundreds of believers to town just before foliage season to dowse on the green and hold lectures, contests, and suppers that are open to the public. Its small Caledonia National Bank is unusual for its strict security, fortified after a bank robbery years ago.

Continue east to St. Johnsbury, located at the intersection of U.S. 2, U.S. 5, and I–91. Three rivers meet here also: the Passumpsic, Moose, and Sleeper's. Like many river valley towns, it is terraced, and several fine Victorian houses, as well as the Fairbanks Museum and Planetarium and the Athenaeum, are located on its highest streets. Here Thaddeus Fairbanks invented the platform scale in 1830; the family fortune is largely responsible for the exceptional cultural facilities in the town. Today the Catamount Arts Center brings nationally ranked performers to the town and to smaller towns in the area.

The Fairbanks Museum of Natural History, housed in a splendid Romanesque Revival fortress, is as active as it was a century ago with exhibits inside and outside and a 50-seat planetarium. The Athenaeum is a handsome library of the same vintage, but its pearl is the rear gallery, considered the oldest unaltered art gallery in the United States; it breathes the atmosphere of a wealthy nineteenth-century collector's special enthusiasms. Most outstanding is the huge "Domes of Yosemite" by Albert Bierstadt. Other Hudson River School paintings are also notable.

The Maple Grove Museum and Sugar House, east of town on U.S. 2, the largest maple sugar plant in the United States, offers tours year-round. North of St. Johnsbury on U.S. 5 lies Lyndonville, a pleasant town that is home to Lyndon State College. A few miles northeast on Route 114 is East Burke and the Burke Mountain Ski Area, which is medium-sized and popular with people in the area as well as with Canadians. Burke Mt. Academy, a prep school for ski racers, has produced many of the country's finest young skiers.

Returning to St. Johnsbury, head south on U.S. 5 to Barnet, then west on the unmarked road to West Barnet and the lovely little Harvey's Lake and on to Peacham. This is one of the most photographed villages in the state, particularly the scene of the barn next to the church. With six other villages it participates in the Northeast Kingdom Fall Foliage Festival in early October; each town hosts a day of activities. At Victory and Granby, hamlets east of St. Johnsbury, thousands come to a Fall Festival the last weekend of September. All these villages are set off vividly during the red-orange-yellow fall season.

Returning to Route 5, you can enjoy the journey along the Connecticut River through such towns as Fairlee with Lake Morey and the picturesque Thetfords. Thetford Hill is a tiny jewel of a village.

Your trip could end at Norwich, which is several miles from Hanover, New Hampshire; both towns have good collections of inns, shops, and restaurants.

PRACTICAL INFORMATION FOR THE NORTHEAST KINGDOM

Note: The area code for all Vermont is 802

HOW TO GET THERE AND AROUND. The arrival of I–91 in recent years makes this area accessible, but it retains the network of small backroads that give meaning to "you can't get there from here." Actually, you can and should.

By plane: The closest airports are in Burlington, Montpelier, and Lebanon, New Hampshire.

By train: Amtrak's Montrealer to White River Junction.

By bus: Vermont Transit via White River Junction from New York and Boston and from Burlington to Newport and St. Johnsbury.

By car: I–91 to St. Johnsbury and Canada, Rte. 100 to Jay Peak area, U.S. 5 to Newport, east–west Rte. 105, and U.S. 2.

HOTELS AND MOTELS. There are motels in all sections and inns in small villages. Prices are based on double rooms, European Plan (room only) unless indicated: *Deluxe,* $75 and up; *Expensive,* $50–$75; *Moderate,* $30–$50; *Inexpensive,* $30 and under.

Hardwick

Village Motel, Rte. 15 east, 05843 (472–5211). *Moderate.* Pine-paneled rooms, trout stream in rear.

Lyndonville

Colonnade Motor Inn and Tavern, off I–91, 05851 (626–9316). *Moderate.* 40 rooms in modern motel, cafe, laundry, bar.
Lynburke Motel, U.S. 5 and Rte. 114, 05851 (626–3346). *Moderate.* Comfortable, pool, restaurant, wax room, 6 miles to Burke Mt.

Newport

Border Motel, U.S. 5 and Rte. 105, 05855 (766–2213). *Moderate.* 40 rooms with breakfast and dinner; cafe, bar.
Newport City Motel, 974 Main St., 05855 (334–6558). *Moderate.* 65 rooms near Lake Memphremagog, restaurants.

St. Johnsbury

Aime's Motel, U.S. 2 and Rte. 18, 05819 (748–3194). *Moderate.* Family owned for decades, dining room with on-premises baking, lounge.
Maple Center Motel, 20 Hastings St., 05819 (U.S. 5) (748–2393). *Moderate.* Restaurant next door, lounge.
Yankee Traveler Motel, 65 Portland St., 05819 (U.S. 2) (748–3156). *Moderate.* Early American decor.

INNS, GUEST HOUSES, BED AND BREAKFASTS. Here in Vermont's lake district you can *really* get away from it all at lakeside inns and tiny bed and breakfasts, all relatively informal and geared to enjoying the outdoors even if from fireside or front porch. As elsewhere in the state, rates vary seasonally or do or don't include meals, so check them individually. Rates at inns generally fall in the *moderate–expensive* categories, ranging from about $35 to $90 per room double occupancy without meals to $200 with breakfast and dinner for two (Modified American Plan). Bed-and-breakfast accommodations are usually in the *moderate* price range for a double, sometimes with shared bath. For listings of bed-and-breakfast homes, contact American Bed and Breakfast, Box 983, St. Albans 05478; Bed and Breakfast Network of New England, Box 815, Brattleboro 05301 (257–5252); or Vermont Bed and Breakfast, Box 139, Browns Trace, Jericho 05465 (899–2354, 800–442–1404).

Averill

Quimby Country, Forest Lake, 05901 (822–5533). 19th-century lodge, 20 cabins with devoted family clientele. Rustic, meals in dining room or housekeeping, supervised children's activities. Open May–Sept.

Craftsbury Common

Craftsbury Inn, Craftsbury 05826 (586–2848). A comfortably restored 1850 hostelry; dining room open to the public.

The Inn on the Common, Main St., 05827 (586–9619). The most elegant inn in this area, with 18 rooms; a delightful gracious oasis retaining pleasant informality, wonderful dinners.

East Burke

Old Cutter Inn, Burke Mt. Access Rd., 05832 (626–5152). A farmhouse inn with nine cozy rooms and a good dining room.

Fairlee

Lake Morey Inn and Country Club, on Lake Morey, 05045 (333–4311). A four-season resort, private beach, pool, boating, tennis, golf course, sauna, health club.

Rutledge Inn and Cottages, Lake Morey Dr., 05045 (333–9722). Lakeside, boating, tennis, family oriented. Open June–Labor Day.

Greensboro

Highland Lodge, Caspian Lake, 05841 (533–2647). Family-owned inn for 30 years. Beautiful lake, private beach, boating, canoeing, fishing, tennis; in winter, extensive cross-country trails with rentals and instruction. 65 lodge guests plus 10 cottages.

Morgan

Seymour Lake Lodge, Rte. 111, 05853 (895–2752). Rustic, casual for fishermen, hunters, and outdoors lovers in general. 15 guests, family-style meals.

Lower Waterford

Rabbit Hill Motor Inn, 05848 (748–5168). An 1840 inn with motel wing, extensive lawn with lawn games, cross-country ski trails, in picturesque village. Good dining.

RESTAURANTS. While eating out is not the sport here that it is in the other areas of Vermont, you can have very good meals. Price ranges are based on a complete dinner for one person excluding beverage, tax, and tip: *Deluxe,* $30 and up; *Expensive,* $20–$30; *Moderate,* $10–$20; *Inexpensive,* under $10.

Bradford

Colatina Exit, Main St. (222–9008). *Inexpensive–Moderate.* Italy on the Connecticut River. All the favorites, from pizza to lasagna to veal scallopine and clam soup.

Coventry

Heermansmith Farm Inn (754–8866). *Moderate–Expensive.* This small farmhouse with three inn rooms has earned a reputation for fine meals. Dinner only, reservations suggested. Closed Tues.

Danville

Creamery Restaurant (648–3616). *Moderate.* A neat little restaurant in a former creamery; blackboard menu, all foods homemade.

East Burke

Old Cutter Inn, Burke Mt. Access Rd. (626–5152). *Moderate–Expensive.* Some well-cooked dinners here in an inviting dining room, closed Wed. Light meals in lounge.

Fairlee

Lake Morey Inn, off U.S. 5 (333–4211). *Moderate–Expensive.* New England fare with Continental flourishes. Sun. night buffet.
Rutledge Inn, Lake Morey Dr. (333–9722). *Moderate.* Homemade baking in a summer hotel, three meals, open June–Labor Day.
Fairlee Diner, U.S. 5. *Inexpensive.* Road food praised widely. Simple surroundings, friendly atmosphere; homemade rolls, daily specials, apple crisp.

Greensboro

Highland Lodge (533–2647). *Moderate.* All three meals served to public, homemade pancakes, muffins, soups, and bountiful dinners.

Hardwick

Alpha Warner's, Main St. (472–5470). *Moderate–Expensive.* Experienced chefs work magic with fresh seafood and soups.

Island Pond

Buck and Doe, 135 Main St. (723–4712). *Moderate.* A real surprise in an out-of-the-way place. Huge menu and huge portions. "Mile-high" pie a specialty.

Lyndonville

Town and Country Restaurant, U.S. 5 and 114 (626–9713). *Moderate.* A family kind of place with the usual favorites.
Luigi's Restaurant and Cellar Lounge, 33 Depot St. (626–9209). *Moderate.* Pizza is just a starter, also subs, sandwiches, shrimp, chicken, pasta.

Newport

The Landing, by the lake (334–2777). *Moderate.* A rare chance to dine on Lake Memphremagog. Well-rated, interesting specials.

St. Johnsbury

Aime's, U.S. 2 and Rte. 18 (748–3553). *Moderate.* A dependable motel restaurant with something for the whole family.

Catamount Arts Center, 60 Eastern Ave. (748–2600). *Inexpensive–Moderate.* A small cafe for midmorning coffee or lunch. Open 9:30 A.M.–2 P.M.

Wells River

The Happy Hour Restaurant, Main St. (757–3466). *Moderate.* An established small-town spot for old-fashioned square meals, salad bar.

TOURIST INFORMATION. St. Johnsbury Chamber of Commerce, 30 Western Ave. (748–3678) will assist in answering questions on the entire area. Also Newport Chamber of Commerce, Newport (334–7782) will assist you with the lake area.

SEASONAL EVENTS. January: Craftsbury Winter Weekend, Sports Center, cross-country ski races, winter activities (mid-Jan.).

February: Winterfest, Newport, skating races, cross-country ski races, curling, hockey, activities (dates vary).

May: White Water Canoe Race, E. Burke (May 1). Sheep and Wool Festival, Burklyn Barn, E. Burke (mid-July).

July: Memphremagog International Aquafest, Newport, swimming races, many activities (mid-July). Uniques and Antiques Festival, Craftsbury Common.

August: Barton Fair, old-fashioned county fair (mid-Aug.). Old Stone House Day, Brownington Center, crafts demonstrations, picnicking, historical buildings (mid-Aug.). Domestic Resurrection Circus, Glover, Bread and Puppet Theater, pageant-performance, thousands come (early weekend).

September: Dowsers National Convention, Danville, 2nd week in Sept. Holiday in the Hills, Victory and Granby, backcountry fall festival (last weekend in Sept.).

September–October: Northeast Kingdom Fall Foliage Festival, hosted by six towns (ask St. Johnsbury Chamber of Commerce for details) (last week in Sept.–1st week in Oct.).

December: Christmas Fair (crafts), St. Johnsbury (1st weekend in Dec.).

PARKS AND FORESTS. Brighton State Park, off Rte. 105, Island Pond (723–4360), camping, swimming, fishing, boat rentals, nature trails, natural guide.

Crystal Lake State Park, off Rte. 16, Barton (525–6205), swimming, picnics, fishing.

Maidstone State Park, from Rte. 102 southwest 5 mi. on state forest road, Guildhall (676–3930), camping, swimming, trout and salmon fishing, canoe rentals, hiking, picnics, natural guide.

Willoughby State Forest, Rte. 5A, 7,000 acres of forest with hiking trails, views of spectacular lake.

FALL FOLIAGE. Prime time here is the last week in Sept. and the 1st week in Oct. The rolling hills are ablaze and the foliage festivals are a treat. It is a festive time in the small villages (see *Seasonal Events*).

From St. Johnsbury: to Danville via U.S. 2, Rte. 15 to Hardwick, Rte. 14 to Irasburg, to Lowell via Rtes. 14 and 58, Rte. 100 to Troy, Rte. 101 to N. Troy with side trip to Jay Peak via Rte. 242, N. Troy to W. Charleston via Rte. 105, to Lyndonville via Rte. 5A and U.S. 5, to Island Pond via Rte. 114, then to Bloomfield via Rte. 105, back to St. Johnsbury by Rte. 102 and U.S. 2 (approximately 208 mi.).

SUMMER SPORTS. Bicycling: The Craftsbury area is a favorite for biking. It's a 7-mi. trip around Caspian Lake.

Boating and canoeing: All the Northeast Kingdom lakes are ideal for boating and canoeing. Canoes may be rented from the Craftsbury Sports Center. See the *Vermont Guide to Fishing* pamphlet for access points on rivers.

Golf: Newport Country Club, Newport (334–7715), 18 holes overlooking Lake Memphremagog; Orleans Country Club (754–9392), 18 holes; Mountain View Country Club, Greensboro (533–9294), nine holes; St. Johnsbury Country Club (748–9894), nine holes.

Hiking: Mt. Pisgah and Mt. Hor have trails in the Willoughby Forest with spectacular views of the White Mountains; on Wheeler Mt. in Barton, trails lead to a summit view of Crystal Lake and Lake Willoughby.

Horseback riding: Sunny Brook Farm, West Burke (467–3380), instruction, summer girls' camp; Still Hill Acres, Glover (525–6623), summer trail rides, lessons.

Swimming: Harvey's Lake, West Barnet; Crystal Lake State Beach, Barton; Pageant Park, Crystal Lake, Barton; Shadow Lake Beach, Glover; Lake Willoughby beaches at northern and southern ends; Lake Seymour at Morgan Center; Caspian Lake at Greensboro.

WINTER SPORTS. Downhill skiing: Burke Mountain, East Burke (626–3305), 2,000-ft. drop, upper and lower base lodges, children's programs, Burke Mt. Academy prep school for ski racers. (For Jay Peak, see *Northern Mountain Area* section.)

Cross-country skiing: Craftsbury Nordic Ski Center, Craftsbury (586–2514), lodging, day care, dining hall, lessons, guided tours; Highland Lodge, Greensboro (533–2647), cross-country center at an inn; Hilltop Cross-Country Center, Wolcott (888–3710); Rabbit Hill Inn Cross-Country Ski Center, Lower Waterford (748–5168); also cross-country ski centers at Burke Mt. Ski Area and Jay Peak.

FISHING. This is fishing country, with salmon, brook, and rainbow trout to be caught in the many lakes and ponds. The *Vermont Guide to Fishing* pamphlet is indispensable; get it from tourist information spots.

HUNTING. Hunting season is Oct. and Nov., with weeks for deer, hare and rabbit, grey squirrel, partridge. See pamphlet *Vermont Guide to Hunting* for details; license from town clerk or game warden.

CAMPING. See *Parks and Forests,* for locations. For reservations call the Department of Forests, Parks, and Recreation (828–3375) before May or specific parks after that date. Information on private campgrounds may be obtained where tourist information is available.

MUSEUMS. The following museums are truly unique and well worth a visit. Call ahead for hours and admission fees.

Brownington Center

The Old Stone House (754–2022), a noble, four-story stone building built largely by hand in 1836. Now a very well-maintained museum of the Orlean Country Historical Society with 18th- and 19th-century exhibits. Open daily July–Aug.; Fri–Tues., May 15–June 30, Sept–Oct. 15.

Glover

Bread and Puppet Theater Museum, Rte. 122 (525–3031). The home of the giant puppets and other fantastic creatures who appear in the company's productions here and abroad. Open Mar.–Nov.

St. Johnsbury

Fairbanks Museum and Planetarium, 83 Main St. (748–2372). Remarkable small-town science museum in fine 19th-century Romanesque Revival building, some hands-on exhibits. 50-seat planetarium, outdoor exhibits. Open daily year-round.
   St. Johnsbury Athenaeum Art Gallery, 30 Main St. (748–8291). In rear of century-old library, oldest unaltered art gallery in United States, Hudson River School paintings.

MUSIC, THEATER, AND DANCE. Catamount Film and Art Center, 60 Eastern Ave., St. Johnsbury (748–2600), sponsors an ambitious schedule of nationally known performers throughout the area. **Craftsbury Chamber Players,** a professional group, performs at Hardwick Thurs. evenings in July and Aug.

SHOPPING. Willey's Store in Greensboro is a world-class general store with seemingly every need satisfied from its rambling shelves. Across the street, stop at **The Miller's Thumb,** open summer, for an interesting selection of worldwide handmade items. **Cabot Farmers' Co-op Creamery** in Cabot produces widely admired sharp or mild cheddar and sweet butter as well as other products. You can buy them at the Creamery or in Vermont grocery stores. One of the oldest craft's shops is **The Craft Shop at Molly's Pond** in Marshfield specializing in the owner's own silver jewelry, but also stocking the nice work of others. At **American Maple Products,** Bluff Rd., Newport, the maple syrup is discounted 10%.

Index

Marlborough (NH), 412
Marshfield (MA), 267
Martha's Vineyard (MA), 37, 280–282
  accommodations on, 293, 296–297
  historic sites and museums on, 308
  map of, 279
  nightlilfe on, 312
  restaurants on, 301–302
  seasonal events on, 303–304
Mashpee (MA), 275, 300, 311
Mason (NH), 410
Massachusetts, 212–343. *See also*
  Boston
  accommodations in, 258–260,
    268–269, 285–297, 318–320,
    326–328, 339–341
  art galleries in, 265–266, 331–332,
    345–346
  beaches of, 257, 263, 270,
    273–275, 279, 280, 281
  camping in, 24, 264, 271, 318, 330,
    344
  character of, 5–6, 214–215
  colleges of, 216, 232–233, 320–321,
    331
  dance festival in, 331, 339
  drinking laws in, 20
  geology of, 219–220
  historic sites and houses in, 264–265,
    268, 277, 279–281, 305–309,
    322–323, 330–331, 345
  history of, 215, 217–219, 272–273,
    277, 280, 283
  how to get there and around in, 258,
    268, 284–285, 317–318, 325–326,
    339
  maps of, 216, 222, 229, 232–233,
    254–255, 272, 276, 314, 333
  museums in, 265–266, 271–272,
    305–309, 322–323, 331, 345–346
  music in, 266, 272, 309, 331, 346
  nightlife, 266, 310–313, 332, 347
  parks and gardens in, 262, 270, 321,
    329, 343
  restaurants in, 260–262, 269–270,
    297–302, 320, 328–329, 341–343
  seasonal events in, 21, 262, 270,
    303–304, 321, 329, 343
  shopping in, 266, 309–310, 346–347
  sports in, 21–25, 263–264, 271,
    304–305, 321–322, 329–330,
    343–344
  telephones in, 25
  theater in, 266, 272, 309, 328, 331,
    346

tourist information for, 12, 262, 270,
  302, 320–321, 329, 343
tours of, 262, 270, 304, 321, 329,
  343
Massachusetts, USS, 268
Massachusetts Institute of Technology,
  235
Mayflower II (ship replica), 273, 302
Menemsha (MA), 282, 297, 301
Meredith (NH), 389, 391, 392,
  393–394, 397
Merrimack (NH), 421, 422
Mexican restaurants, 55, 112, 244, 267,
  357, 391, 493, 494, 522, 533
Mica mine, 371
Middleboro (MA), 269
Middlebury (CT), 111
Middlebury (VT), 33, 530, 532, 534,
  536, 537–538, 541
Middletown (CT), 98, 100, 101, 103,
  104
Middletown (RI), 439, 440, 444–445
Middletown Springs (VT), 503
Milbridge (ME), 179
Milford (CT), 48, 52, 57
Milford (NH), 421, 424
Millinocket (ME), 201, 203
Milton (MA), 269
Milton (NH), 356, 394
Mineral store, 183, 193
Misquamicut State Beach (RI), 464
Mohawk Trail (MA), 35, 332, 334
Monadnock Mountain (NH), 409
Monhegan Island (ME), 144, 148, 150,
  157
Monmouth (ME), 197
Montpelier (VT), 519, 521, 525–526,
  529–530
Moodus (CT), 98, 100, 103
Moosehead Lake (ME), 30, 200, 204
Morgan (VT), 596
Moultonborough (NH), 389, 391
Mount Desert Island (ME), 30, 117,
  161–162, 165, 169
  map of, 163
Mount Equinox (VT), 487
Mount Greylock (MA), 35, 335
Mount Katahdin (ME), 117, 201
Mount Kineo (ME), 200
Mount Mansfield (VT), 515
Mount Monadnock (NH), 31, 409
Mount Philo (VT), 532
Mount Snow (VT), 488, 493, 495,
  498
Mount Sunapee (NH), 400

Fodor's Travel Guides

U.S. Guides

Alaska
Arizona
Atlantic City & the
  New Jersey Shore
Boston
California
Cape Cod
Carolinas & the
  Georgia Coast
The Chesapeake Region
Chicago
Colorado
Dallas & Fort
  Worth

Disney World & the
  Orlando Area
Florida
Hawaii
Houston &
  Galveston
Las Vegas
Los Angeles, Orange
  County, Palm Springs
Maui
Miami, Fort Lauderdale,
  Palm Beach
Michigan, Wisconsin,
  Minnesota

New England
New Mexico
New Orleans
New Orleans *(Pocket
  Guide)*
New York City
New York City *(Pocket
  Guide)*
New York State
Pacific North Coast
Philadelphia
The Rockies
San Diego
San Francisco

San Francisco *(Pocket
  Guide)*
The South
Texas
USA
Virgin Islands
Virginia
Waikiki
Washington, DC
Williamsburg

Foreign Guides

Acapulco
Amsterdam
Australia, New Zealand,
  The South Pacific
Austria
Bahamas
Bahamas *(Pocket
  Guide)*
Baja & the Pacific
  Coast Resorts
Barbados
Belgium & Luxembourg
Bermuda
Brazil
Britain *(Great Travel
  Values)*
Budget Europe
Canada
Canada *(Great Travel
  Values)*
Canada's Atlantic
  Provinces
Cancún, Cozumel,
  Mérida, the
  Yucatán
Caribbean

Caribbean *(Great
  Travel Values)*
Central America
China
China's Great Cities
Eastern Europe
Egypt
Europe
Europe's Great Cities
Florence & Venice
France
France *(Great Travel
  Values)*
Germany
Germany *(Great Travel
  Values)*
Great Britain
Greece
The Himalayan
  Countries
Holland
Hong Kong
Hungary
India, including Nepal
Ireland
Israel

Italy
Italy *(Great Travel
  Values)*
Jamaica
Japan
Japan *(Great Travel
  Values)*
Jordan & the Holy Land
Kenya, Tanzania,
  the Seychelles
Korea
Lisbon
Loire Valley
London
London *(Great Travel
  Values)*
London *(Pocket Guide)*
Madrid & Barcelona
Mexico
Mexico City
Montreal &
  Quebec City
Munich
New Zealand
North Africa
Paris

Paris *(Pocket Guide)*
Portugal
Rio de Janeiro
The Riviera *(Fun on)*
Rome
Saint Martin &
  Sint Maarten
Scandinavia
Scandinavian Cities
Scotland
Singapore
South America
South Pacific
Southeast Asia
Soviet Union
Spain
Spain *(Great Travel
  Values)*
Sweden
Switzerland
Sydney
Tokyo
Toronto
Turkey
Vienna
Yugoslavia

Special-Interest Guides

Bed & Breakfast
  Guide: North America
Health & Fitness
  Vacations

Royalty Watching
Selected Hotels of
  Europe

Selected Resorts
  and Hotels of the U.S.
Shopping in Europe

Skiing in North
  America
Sunday in New York